An Introduction
to Computational
Risk Management
of Equity-Linked
Insurance

CHAPMAN & HALL/CRC
Financial Mathematics Series

Aims and scope:
The field of financial mathematics forms an ever-expanding slice of the financial sector. This series aims to capture new developments and summarize what is known over the whole spectrum of this field. It will include a broad range of textbooks, reference works and handbooks that are meant to appeal to both academics and practitioners. The inclusion of numerical code and concrete real-world examples is highly encouraged.

Series Editors
M. A. H. Dempster
Centre for Financial Research
Department of Pure Mathematics and Statistics
University of Cambridge

Dilip B. Madan
Robert H. Smith School of Business
University of Maryland

Rama Cont
Department of Mathematics
Imperial College

Stochastic Volatility Modeling
Lorenzo Bergomi

The Financial Mathematics of Market Liquidity
From Optimal Execution to Market Making
Olivier Gueant

C++ for Financial Mathematics
John Armstrong

Model-free Hedging
A Martingale Optimal Transport Viewpoint
Pierre Henry-Labordere

Stochastic Finance
A Numeraire Approach
Jan Vecer

Equity-Linked Life Insurance
Partial Hedging Methods
Alexander Melnikov, Amir Nosrati

High-Performance Computing in Finance
Problems, Methods, and Solutions
M. A. H. Dempster, Juho Kanniainen, John Keane, Erik Vynckier

For more information about this series please visit: *https://www.crcpress.com/ Chapman-and-HallCRC-Financial-Mathematics-Series/book-series/CHFINANCMTH*

An Introduction to Computational Risk Management of Equity-Linked Insurance

Runhuan Feng

CRC Press

Taylor & Francis Group

Boca Raton London New York

CRC Press is an imprint of the
Taylor & Francis Group, an **informa** business

A CHAPMAN & HALL BOOK

CRC Press
Taylor & Francis Group
6000 Broken Sound Parkway NW, Suite 300
Boca Raton, FL 33487-2742

First issued in paperback 2020

© 2018 by Taylor & Francis Group, LLC
CRC Press is an imprint of Taylor & Francis Group, an Informa business

No claim to original U.S. Government works

ISBN-13: 978-1-4987-4216-0 (hbk)
ISBN-13: 978-0-367-73431-2 (pbk)

Visit the Taylor & Francis Web site at
http://www.taylorandfrancis.com

and the CRC Press Web site at
http://www.crcpress.com

To my beloved Ge, Kelsey and Kyler.

Contents

List of Figures

List of Tables

Symbols

$\overline{A}_x$	expected present value of a life insurance that pays 1 immediately upon the death of a life-age x
$\overline{a}_x$	expected present value of an annuity continuously payable at the rate of 1 per period for life time of a life-age x
$\overline{a}_{x:\overline{t}|m}$	expected present value of an annuity continuously payable at the rate of 1 per period lasting for t periods computed with the force of interest m per period
$_tp_x$	probability that a life-age x survives t years
$_tq_x$	probability that a life-age x dies within t years
μ_{x+t}	force of mortality, intensity with which death occurs at age $x + t$, $\mu_{x+t} = -(\mathrm{d}\,_tp_x/\,\mathrm{d}t)/\,_tp_x$
T_x	future lifetime of a life-age x
K_x	curtate future lifetime of a life-age x, $K_x = \lfloor T_x \rfloor$
$\mathbb{E}$	expectation
$\mathbb{V}, \sigma^2$	variance
$\mathbb{C}$	covariance
F_X	cumulative distribution function of random variable X
$\overline{F}_X$	survival function of random variable X
ϕ	standard normal density function
Φ	standard normal cumulative distribution function
$[\cdot, \cdot]$	cross/quadratic variation
$\langle \cdot \rangle$	total variation
$\lfloor x \rfloor$	largest integer smaller than or equal to x
$\lceil x \rceil$	smallest integer larger than or equal to x
x_+	maximum of x and 0
$\mapsto$	maps to
$x \vee y$	maximum of x and y
$x \wedge y$	minimum of x and y
$:=$	is defined as

Preface

While the concept of risk management may be as old as our civilization, the quantitative modeling of complex systems of interacting risks is a fairly recent development in financial and insurance industries.

Most traditional insurance products were developed to protect against particular types of risks. For example, life insurance and annuities provide coverages for mortality and longevity risks, whereas property and casualty insurance compensates for losses from human hazards and natural disasters. However, over the past decades, there have been tremendous innovation and development in the insurance industry with increasingly sophisticated coverages. As the particular focus of this book, the introduction of equity-linked insurance brings revolutionary changes to the market, exposing life insurers not only to traditional mortality and longevity risks but also to unprecedented financial risks. As the industry moves into a new territory of managing many intertwined financial and insurance risks, non-traditional problems and challenges arise, presenting great opportunities for technology development.

Today's computational power and technology make it possible for the life insurance industry to develop highly sophisticated models, which were impossible just a decade ago. Nonetheless, as more industrial practices and regulations move towards dependence on stochastic models, the demand for computational power continues to grow. While the industry continues to rely heavily on hardware innovations, trying to make brute force methods faster and more palatable, we are approaching a crossroads about how to proceed. There are many practitioners' publications on such issues, most of which, however, lack fine-level technical details due to the protection of their proprietary interests. This book is intended not only to provide a resource for students and entry-level professionals to understand the fundamentals of industrial modeling practice, but also to give a glimpse of academic research on "software" methodologies for modeling and computational efficiency.

Computational risk management in the title of this book refers to a collection of computational models and techniques drawn from various fields for the purpose of quantifying and managing risks emerging from equity-linked insurance. The book contains a fair amount of computational techniques well adopted in the insurance industry and their underpinning theoretical foundations. However, this book is by no means a comprehensive review of literature on the subject matter. Readers are encouraged to explore the topics further with references in the bibliographical notes at the end of each chapter.

As a guiding principle of presentation in this introductory book, we only intend to illustrate fundamental structure of practical models without regressing to accounting details. For example, we would only touch on reserves at a high level with a brief discussion of distinctions between statutory reserve, generally accepted accounting principle (GAAP) reserve, or tax reserve, etc. None of the examples or models in the book would require any accounting experience.

The idea of writing a book on this subject matter was inspired by my coauthor Dr. Jan Vecer, who have always multitasked many creative projects of his own. Part of this book has grown out of lecture notes for a one-semester topics course the author taught a few times at the University of Illinois at Urbana-Champaign. It is not assumed that the reader has any substantial knowledge of life insurance or advanced mathematics beyond the level of calculus sequence and a first course in probability and statistics. The book aims to be self-contained and should be accessible to most of upper level undergraduate students from a quantitative background. However, as a reviewer of this book wittily quoted the Greek mathematician Euclid, "there is no royal road to geometry". It is difficult to cover theoretical underpinnings of some sophisticated modeling without advanced machinery. Therefore, the book is written with the aim to strike a delicate balance between theory and practice. The author is receptive to hearing of any criticism and suggestion.

Many students helped through the production of this book by pointing out typos and errors in the earlier versions of the lecture notes and demanding more examples. Special thanks should go to Haoen Cui, Longhao Jin, Fan Yang, who helped create many graphs and examples in the book, and Justin Ho, Chongda Liu, Saumil Padhya for correcting typos and valuable suggestions which improved the presentation of the book.

During the development of this text, the author received an endowed professorship from the State Farm Companies Foundation and research grants from the Society of Actuaries and the Actuarial Foundation. Any opinions expressed in this material are those of the author and do not reflect the views of the State Farm Companies, the Society of Actuaries or the Actuarial Foundation. The author is very grateful for their generous support.

The author would also like to thank the Society of Actuaries for permission to adapt materials in Chapter 7 from the research report *Nested Stochastic Modeling for Insurance Companies* (copyright © 2016 by Society of Actuaries).

Runhuan Feng, PhD, FSA, CERA
Urbana and Champaign, Illinois
rfeng@illinois.edu

1

Modeling of Equity-linked Insurance

1.1 Fundamental principles of traditional insurance

Life insurance and annuities are contracts of financial arrangement under which an insurer agrees to provide policyholders or their beneficiaries at times of adversity with benefits in exchange for premiums. For examples, a life insurance can make a much needed lump sum benefit payment to a family to cover their sudden loss of income due to the death of a family member. An annuity can provide living expenses for an insured retiree who outlasts his or her lifetime savings. Given that the industry is in the business of long-term financial services, the design, production and management of insurance are as much an art as a science. However, as the intent of this book is to provide a thorough introduction and overview of fundamentals of equity-linked insurance, we tend to focus on the scientific and theoretical underpinning of computational models and techniques used in the literature and in practice.

While there is probably no "theory of everything" in insurance mathematics, there are certainly fundamental principles that form the bases of computational models used in this field, which shall be reviewed in this chapter.

1.1.1 Time value of money

One dollar today is not the same as one dollar in the future. The entire State of Alaska was purchased by the United States from Russia in 1827 at the price of 7.2 million dollars. In today's dollars, the same amount is probably only enough to buy a penthouse in downtown Chicago. The sharp contrast of purchasing power is best explained by the concept of *time value of money* in the classical theory of interest.

An elementary tool to quantify the time value of money is the accumulation function, usually denoted by $a(t)$, as a function of time t. It describes the accumulated value at time t of an original investment of one dollar at time 0. By definition, $a(0) = 1$. The one dollar is called *principal*. An investor makes the investment of principal in expectation of financial returns. The amount by which the accumulated value of the investment exceeds the principal is called *interest*. Here we assume that the term of investment has no bearing on the underlying interest rate. Under this assumption, for any long-term risk-free investment, it is sensible in the market to develop an investment growth mechanism so that the accumulation satisfies the following equality at all times

$$a(t + s) = a(t)a(s), \qquad t, s \geq 0, \tag{1.1}$$

which means the amount of interest earned by an initial deposit of one dollar over $t + s$ periods is equal to the amount of interest earned if the deposit of one dollar is withdrawn at time t and then immediately deposited back for an additional s periods. The violation of such a simple property creates problems for both the lender and the borrower. On one hand, if a bank provides a savings account that offers interest rates such that $a(t + s) < a(t)a(s)$, then it is to the advantage of investors to withdraw money and re-deposit instantly since it accrues more interest in such a way. The faster one can withdraw and re-deposit, the more gains. Hence in theory any rational investor would want to maximize the proceeds by continuously opening and closing accounts, which induces infinite amount of transaction costs for the bank. On the other hand, if the bank provides a savings account where interests are calculated in such a way that $a(t + s) > a(t)a(s)$, then a new investor who brings in the money in amount of $a(t)$ at time t would never earn at any time in the future as much as an old investor whose account equally values at $a(t)$ at time t. Knowing it is to the disadvantage of new investors to invest any time after the account is offered, no rational new investor would open a new account and the bank would soon run out of the business due to the inability to attract new clients.

It can be shown mathematically[*] that the only continuous solution to (1.1) with the condition $a(0) = 1$ must be

$$a(t) = e^{rt}, \qquad t > 0,$$

for some constant r, known as the force of interest, which is the intensity with which interest is operating on each one dollar invested at t. In theory of interest, this type of accumulation is known as the investment with *compound interest*.

The force of interest is sometimes referred as continuously compounding interest rate. For example, the accumulated value at time t of one dollar invested at time 0 with a fixed annual interest rate of r payable once per year is given by $(1 + r)^t$. If the interest is compounded n times per year, i.e. the interest payment is divided n times and payable every $1/n$-th of a year, then the accumulated value at time t is

$$a(t) = \left(1 + \frac{r}{n}\right)^{nt}.$$

If the interest is continuously compounded, then the accumulated value at time t is given by

$$a(t) = \lim_{n \to \infty} \left(1 + \frac{r}{n}\right)^{nt} = e^{rt}. \tag{1.2}$$

Hence the name for r continuously compounding interest rate.

---

[*]For example, a proof can be derived from a result on D'Angelo and West [22, p. 163].

1.1.2 Law of large numbers

The quintessence of an insurance business is the pooling of funds from a large number of policyholders to pay for losses incurred by a few policyholders. It is difficult for individuals to absorb their own risks because potential losses can be too large or too unpredictable. However, an insurance company can manage the collective risk because the aggregated nature makes it more predictable. The mathematical principle behind the predictability of the collective risk is the *law of large numbers* (LLN).

Theorem 1.1 (Law of large numbers). *Let $X_1, X_2, \cdots$, be an infinite sequence of i.i.d. random variables with $E(X_1) = E(X_2) = \cdots = \mu$. Then*

$$\overline{X}_n := \frac{1}{n}(X_1 + \cdots + X_n) \to \mu, \qquad n \to \infty. \tag{1.3}$$

We can think of random variables $\{X_1, X_2, \cdots\}$ as individual claims from an insurance coverage on any insurable risk, whether short-term insurance, such as fire, automobile, homeowner insurances, or long-term insurance, such as life and annuities. Despite the uncertainty as to the timing and size of any individual claim, the LLN dictates that the average claim size $\overline{X}_n$, representing the collective risk, is roughly the theoretical mean of any individual claim, which is a fixed amount. This is precisely why the collective risk is much more manageable, as the insurer is expected to pay a fixed amount for each contract on average.

Example 1.2 (Pure endowment). Let us consider a simple example of insurable risk – mortality risk, which is a risk of potential losses to a life insurer resulting from the uncertainty with the timing of policyholders' deaths. Suppose that an insurer sells to n policyholders of the same age x a pure endowment life insurance, which pays a lump sum of B dollars upon the survival of the policyholder at the end of T years. We denote the future lifetime of the i-th policyholder at age x by $T_x^{(i)}$. and the survival probability by $_T p_x := \mathbb{P}(T_x^{(i)} > T)$. Following actuarial convention, we write the probability that the i-th policyholder survives k years,

$$_k p_x := \mathbb{P}(T_x^{(i)} > k).$$

Then the insurance claim from the i-th policyholder can be represented by $BI(T_x^{(i)} \geq T)$ where the indicator $I(A) = 1$ if the event A is true or 0 otherwise. Even though there is uncertainty as to whether each contract incurs a claim, the LLN says that the percentage of survivors is almost certain and so is the average claim (survival benefit) from each contract, i.e.

$$\frac{1}{n} \sum_{i=1}^{n} BI(T_x^{(i)} \geq T) \longrightarrow \mathbb{E}[BI(T_x^{(1)} \geq T)] = B \,_T p_x, \qquad n \to \infty.$$

In other words, on average, the cost of each contract, which is the amount to cover a claim, would be fixed. Therefore, mortality risk is considered a *diversifiable* risk, meaning the uncertainty can be eliminated through the diversification of underwriting a large portfolio of homogeneous contracts.

Example 1.3 (Whole life insurance). Suppose that an insurer sells to n policyholders all at age x the same life insurance, which pays a lump sum of B dollars at the end of year of a policyholder's death. Earlier death benefit payments represent higher costs to insurers due to the *time value of money*. Assume that the overall continuously compounding yield rate on an insurer's assets backing up its liabilities is r per year. Then the accumulated value of one dollar investment after T years would be e^{rT}. Assuming that the growth of an investment is proportional to its principal, in order to pay one dollar at time T, the insurer should invest with compound interest e^{-rT} dollars, which is called the *present value* of one dollar to be paid at time T. Therefore, the present value of death benefit to be paid at the end of the year of death is given by

$$X_i := Be^{-r\lceil T_x^{(i)} \rceil},$$

where $\lceil y \rceil$ is the smallest integer greater than y. Or equivalently, we can rewrite it as

$$X_i := \sum_{k=1}^{\infty} Be^{-rk} I\big(k-1 < T_x^{(i)} \le k\big).$$

Following actuarial convention, we write the probability that the i-th policyholder survives k years and dies within n years thereafter,

$${}_n q_{x+k} := \mathbb{P}(T_{x+k}^{(i)} < n) = \mathbb{P}(T_x^{(i)} < k+n | T_x^{(i)} > k).$$

We often suppress the subscript on the lower left corner if $n = 1$. Therefore,

$$\mathbb{P}(k-1 < T_x^{(i)} \le k) = \mathbb{P}(T_x^{(i)} < k | T_x^{(i)} > k-1)\mathbb{P}(T_x^{(i)} > k-1) = {}_{k-1}p_x\, q_{x+k-1}.$$

While the actual present value of death benefit is uncertain for each contract, the average cost of the life insurance is fixed with a sufficiently large pool of policies.

$$\frac{1}{n}\sum_{i=1}^{\infty} X_i \longrightarrow \mathbb{E}[X_i] = \sum_{k=1}^{\infty} Be^{-rk}\mathbb{P}\big(k-1 < T_x^{(i)} \le k\big) = \sum_{k=1}^{\infty} Be^{-rk}\, {}_{k-1}p_x\, q_{x+k-1}.$$

Therefore, mortality risk is considered a *diversifiable* risk, meaning the uncertainty can be eliminated through the diversification of underwriting a large portfolio of homogeneous contracts. □

Example 1.4 (Immediate life annuity). Another example of insurable risk is longevity risk, which is a risk of potential losses to an annuity writer resulting from the uncertainty with the amount of annuity payments. Since annuity payments are guaranteed for lifetime, typically higher life expectancy of a policyholder translates to a larger loss for an annuity writer. Consider a life annuity under which the first payment occurs one year from now and all payments of level amount C are made on an annual basis. In any given year $[k, k+1]$, a payment is made as long as the policyholder is still alive. Hence its present value is given by $e^{-r(k+1)}CI(T_x^{(i)} \geq k)$. Adding present values of all future annuity payments yields the present value of the life annuity,

$$X_i := \sum_{k=0}^{\infty} Ce^{-r(k+1)}I(T_x^{(i)} \geq k).$$

Although there is uncertainty about how long the annuity payments last, the average cost of the life annuity is known to be fixed according to the LLN,

$$\frac{1}{n}\sum_{i=1}^{n} X_i \to \mathbb{E}[X_i] = C\sum_{k=0}^{\infty} e^{-r(k+1)}\mathbb{P}(T_x^{(i)} \geq k) = C\sum_{k=0}^{\infty} e^{-r(k+1)}\,_kp_x,$$

as $n \to \infty$, provided that the infinite summation is finite.

1.1.3 Equivalence premium principle

A remarkable consequence of the LLN is that an insurer can charge a fixed premium to cover random claims. A very common form of the payment for short term insurance is a single premium to be paid at the inception of the contract. To consider the net cost of an insurance liability, we often do not take into account expenses and taxes and the single premium to be determined, denoted by P, is called a *net premium*. From the viewpoint of an insurance company, the *individual net liability* of the i-th contract is the net present value of future liability less future income, denoted by L_i.

$$L_i = X_i - P. \tag{1.4}$$

Whenever there is no ambiguity, we shall suppress the subscript i for brevity. As common in the literature, we often refer to a positive net liability as a *loss* and the negative net liability as a *profit*.

Justified by the LLN, we can set the premium such that the average claims outgo matches the average premium income, i.e. the average individual net liability would be zero

$$\mathbb{E}(L) = 0, \tag{1.5}$$

which implies, in the case of a single premium, that

$$P = \mathbb{E}(X), \tag{1.6}$$

where we use X as the generic random variable for i.i.d. $\{X_1, \cdots, X_n\}$. This approach is known as the *equivalence principle*.

Example 1.5 (Pure endowment). The net premium for the pure endowment contract is the expected present value of future survival benefit.

$$P = e^{-rT} B \, _Tp_x,$$

where the factor e^{-rT} represents the present value of asset investment in order to accumulate to 1 at time T.   □

Example 1.6 (Pure endowment (continued)). Consider the survival benefit to be $B = 100$, the probability of survival $_Tp_x = 0.1$, the T-year discount factor $e^{-rT} = 0.9$. Then the net premium is given by 9. Therefore, the net liability from a single pure endowment insurance contract is given by

$$L_i = \begin{cases} 81, & \text{with probability } 0.1; \\ -9, & \text{with probability } 0.9. \end{cases}$$

Note that $\mathbb{E}(L_i) = 0$ and $\mathbb{V}(L_i) = 729$. For each individual contract, there is a 10% chance of the insurer suffering a loss as big as 81, which is more than nine times the premium collected. However, if the insurer sells to 1000 policyholders, it is easy to see that the average loss for each contract, i.e. $\overline{L} := (1/1000) \sum_{i=1}^{1000} L_i$ has mean 0 and variance $\mathbb{V}(L_i)/1000 = 0.729$. The variation of profit/loss is so small that even the probability of having a loss bigger than 2 is nearly zero. To be exact, $\mathbb{P}(\overline{L} > 2) = 0.0030395484$. This is an example of the dramatic effect of the diversification of mortality risk.

In the early days of life insurance, most contracts are issued on an annual basis. As explained by the LLN and the equivalence principle, the annual premium would be set at the average cost of annual insurance claims. As a policyholder ages, an insurer would charge a higher premium every year in order to cover rising average cost of claims. Life insurance would become unaffordable at advanced ages when the coverage is needed the most. Therefore, the funding mechanism of merely matching incoming and outgoing cash flows on an annual basis became an impediment to the development of long term insurance. A radical development came about in the late eighteenth century, when life actuaries developed the concept of level premium. The new funding mechanism allows policyholders to lock in a level premium rate for a number of years or life time. These policies quickly gained popularity and became a standard practice as level premiums were much cheaper than annual premiums for the elder, thereby insurers can retain policies for longer periods.

The innovation with level premium relies not only on the diversification effect among a large portfolio of policyholders, but also on the redistribution of insurance costs across different ages. In other words, the sustainability of level premium is the result of young and mid-age policyholders contributing more than their actual average costs to compensate for the elderly paying less than their actual average costs.

Example 1.7 (Whole life insurance). Consider a whole life insurance that pays a lump sum B immediately upon a policyholder's death. Level premiums are payable continuously at the rate of P per year until the policyholder's death. Note that in this case, both the insurance liability and premium income are life contingent, that is, the income and outgo cash flows depend on the time of the policyholder's death. Suppose that the overall yield rate on the insurer's assets backing up the liability is given by r per year. The present value of the insurer's net liability for the i-th contract is given by

$$L_i = Be^{-rT_x^{(i)}} - P \int_0^{T_x^{(i)}} e^{-rt} \, \mathrm{d}t. \tag{1.7}$$

According to the LLN, the per unit average cost of the death benefit is given by

$$\overline{A}_x := \mathbb{E}(e^{-rT_x}).$$

Similarly, the average of a policyholder's regular payments of 1 per time unit, known as a life annuity, is given by

$$\overline{a}_x := \mathbb{E} \left(\int_0^{T_x} e^{-rt} \, \mathrm{d}t \right).$$

There is a well-known relation between life insurance and annuity,

$$1 = \overline{A}_x + r\overline{a}_x.$$

This is in fact an application of the simple calculus rule - integration by parts,

$$1 - e^{-rt} = r \int_0^t e^{-rs} \, \mathrm{d}s.$$

Therefore, the equivalence principle in (1.5) implies that

$$B\overline{A}_x - P\overline{a}_x = 0,$$

from which we obtain the net premium $P := B\overline{A}_x/\overline{a}_x$. While the insurer may make a profit or loss on an individual contract, the product breaks even when the life insurance is sold at the net premium.

Example 1.8. (Deferred life annuity) In contrast with Example 1.4, the stream of payments under a deferred life annuity starts after a deferred period. This is often offered as an employee benefit to current employees, for which annuity incomes are paid after their retirement. Consider a whole life annuity payable continuously at the rate of C per year and deferred for n years. Suppose that the deferred annuity is purchased with a single premium P. Then the present value of the net liability for the i-th contract is given by

$$L_i = C \int_n^{T_x^{(i)} \vee n} e^{-rt} \, \mathrm{d}t - P.$$

According to the LLN, the average cost of the deferred annuity per dollar annuity payment is given by

$$\mathbb{E}\left(\int_n^{T_x^{(i)} \vee n} e^{-rt}\, dt\right) = \mathbb{E}\left(I(T_x^{(i)} > n)e^{-rn}\int_0^{T_x^{(i)}-n} e^{-rt}\, dt\right)$$

$$= e^{-rn} {}_n p_x \bar{a}_{x+n}.$$

Therefore, the equivalent principle in (1.5) implies that the net premium for the deferred annuity is given by

$$P := e^{-rn} {}_n p_x \bar{a}_{x+n}.$$

1.1.4   Central limit theorem

A second mathematical principle of great significance in insurance modeling is the central limit theorem (CLT). While there are many variations of the CLT, we present a version most commonly used in actuarial practice.

Theorem 1.9 (Lindeberg-Lévy central limit theorem). *Let $X_1, X_2, \cdots$, be an infinite sequence of i.i.d. random variables with finite mean and variance. Then*

$$Z_n := \frac{\overline{X}_n - \mathbb{E}(\overline{X}_n)}{\sqrt{\mathbb{V}(\overline{X}_n)}} \to Z, \qquad n \to \infty, \tag{1.8}$$

where Z is a standard normal random variable.

The type of limits used in both (1.3) and (1.8) is known as *convergence in distribution*. It means that for any given $z \in (-\infty, \infty)$, the sequence of distribution functions $\{\mathbb{P}(Z_n \leq z), n = 1, 2, \cdots\}$ converges to $\mathbb{P}(Z \leq z)$ as n goes to infinity.

1.1.5   Portfolio percentile premium principle

While net premiums determined by the equivalence principle are used for many purposes in the insurance industry, a more common approach of setting premiums is based on profitability tests at the level of a business line. The *aggregate net liability*, denoted by $\mathfrak{L}$, is the sum of individual net liabilities in the whole portfolio of policies.

$$\mathfrak{L} = \sum_{i=1}^n L_i. \tag{1.9}$$

The most important objective for insurance risk management is to ensure that there is enough fund for the insurer to cover its liabilities. An alternative premium principle sets a premium P so that there is a specified probability, say $\alpha \in (0,1)$, that the aggregate net liability is negative (or the product is profitable). If $\mathcal{L}$ is a continuous random variable[*], then

$$\mathbb{P}(\mathcal{L} < 0) = \alpha. \tag{1.10}$$

This is often called the *portfolio percentile premium principle*. Of course, applying such a principle requires one's knowledge of the aggregate net liability, the exact distribution of which can be difficult to obtain. However, central limit theorem (CLT) tells us that $\mathcal{L}$ is approximately normally distributed with $\mathbb{E}(\mathcal{L}) = n\mathbb{E}(L_i)$ and $\mathbb{V}(\mathcal{L}) = n\mathbb{V}(L_i)$. Therefore, the premium P can be determined by

$$\mathbb{P}(\mathcal{L} < 0) = \mathbb{P}\left(\frac{\mathcal{L} - \mathbb{E}(\mathcal{L})}{\sqrt{\mathbb{V}(\mathcal{L})}} < \frac{-\mathbb{E}(\mathcal{L})}{\sqrt{\mathbb{V}(\mathcal{L})}}\right) \approx \Phi\left(\frac{-\mathbb{E}(\mathcal{L})}{\sqrt{\mathbb{V}(\mathcal{L})}}\right) = \alpha. \tag{1.11}$$

Here we denote the distribution of a standard normal random variable by Φ and its inverse by Φ^{-1}. In view of (1.4) and (1.9), it follows immediately from (1.11) that the approximate portfolio percentile premium is given by

$$P = \frac{\sqrt{\mathbb{V}(X)}\Phi^{-1}(\alpha)}{\sqrt{n}} + \mathbb{E}(X). \tag{1.12}$$

It is clear that, as the size of portfolio increases to infinity, the limit of portfolio percentile premium is the premium determined by the equivalence principle in (1.6).

Example 1.10 (Pure endowment). The individual claim from the i-th contract is given by
$$X_i = e^{-rT}BI(T_x^{(i)} \geq T).$$

Then it is easy to see that

$$\mathbb{E}(X) = e^{-rT}B\,_Tp_x, \qquad \mathbb{V}(X) = e^{-rT}B\,_Tp_x\,_Tq_x,$$

where $_Tq_x$ is the probability of death, i.e. $_Tq_x = 1 - \,_Tp_x$. Substitution of mean and variance in (1.12) yields the premium under which the insurer's income exceeds its liability with the probability of p.

1.2 Variable annuities

Variable annuities are modern long-term life insurance products that offer policyholders participation in the profit sharing of equity investment.

---

[*]Otherwise, we find P to be the smallest premium such that $\mathbb{P}(\mathcal{L} < 0) > \alpha$.

Policyholders contribute premiums, also known as purchase payments, into investment accounts at the policy issue and expect to reap financial gain on the investment of their payments. Typically policyholders are offered a variety of investment "sub-accounts", each of which is invested in a particular equity (stock) fund with a distinct investment objective. Although subject to different regulations, these "sub-accounts" are analogues of publicly available mutual funds. Here is an example of various investment options:

- Aggressive Allocation Portfolio (80% stocks/20% bonds)

- Balanced Portfolio (60% stocks/40% bonds)

- Conservative Allocation Portfolio (40% bonds/60% stocks)

Once selected, the performance of a sub-account is linked in proportion to the fluctuation of equity index or equity fund in which it invests. This is known as the *equity-linking mechanism*. For this reason, variable annuities are often known as *unit-linked products* in Europe. These sub-accounts may include domestic and international common stock funds, bond funds, money market funds, and specialty funds (e.g. real estate investment trusts, etc.).

All of policyholders' premiums in subaccounts are typically invested and managed by third party professional vendors. From an accounting point of view, these assets are owned by policyholders and considered to be in *separate accounts*, apart from an insurer's own investment assets, which are in *general accounts*. Hence variable annuities are often referred to as *segregated funds products* in Canada.

Immediate variable annuities are those for which periodic payments to policyholders commence on the purchase of the annuity, whereas *deferred variable annuities* are those for which benefit payments to policyholders are deferred to some future date, for example, a retirement age. Note, however, policyholders may elect to take their money at the future date in a lump sum, in which case the variable annuity is not an annuity in the strict sense. Or they may elect to annuitize their money, in which case a series of benefit payments occur afterwards.

1.2.1 Mechanics of deferred variable annuity

Sources of investment

There are two sources of variable annuity sales in the US market. The majority of annuity sales come from *qualified assets*, which are funds that comply with federal tax code retirement plans such as traditional individual retirement accounts (IRA), etc. and therefore are eligible for certain tax advantages, whereas other retail sales are referred to *non-qualified assets* which come from an after-tax source such as a savings account, the sale of real estate, etc. Sometimes variable annuity designs specify different investment guarantees for qualified and non-qualified assets.

Investment guarantees

In the early days, variable annuity writers merely act as the steward of policyholders' investments and the financial risks of subaccounts are entirely transferred to policyholders. In the early 2000s, there have been some changes to the US tax code with a result that many tax advantages of variable annuity start to diminish. In order to compete with mutual funds, nearly all major variable annuity writers introduced various types of investment guarantees, such as guaranteed minimum maturity benefit (GMMB), guaranteed minimum death benefit (GMDB), guaranteed minimum accumulation benefit (GMAB), guaranteed minimum withdrawal benefit (GMWB), etc. These investment guarantees are considered riders to base contracts and in essence transfer the downside risk of financial investment from policyholders to back insurers. We shall explore the details of these riders in the next few subsections.

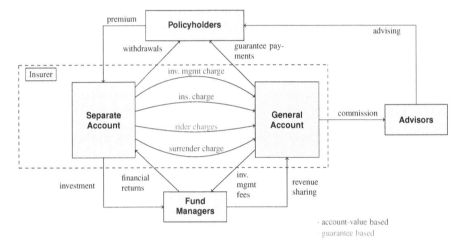

FIGURE 1.1: Diagram of cash flows for variable annuity contracts

Sources of revenue

In order to compensate for all necessary business costs and to maintain healthy and profitable operations, insurers levy on policyholders a range of fees and charges, which are typically unbundled and disclosed in a transparent manner on product prospectus. While there are one-time or annual fixed fees by policy, most fees and charges are assessed and deducted from policyholders' subaccounts on a daily basis as percentages of account values or guarantee values. While terminology varies greatly in the market, the common fees and charges are usually in the following categories.

- Rider charge: These charges compensate insurers for the costs of various investment guarantees and usually split by benefits. These are often stated as percentages of guaranteed values.

- Insurance charge: This charge is used to compensate insurers for providing a base GMDB and also quoted as a percentage of the account value.

- Administrative expense charge: this charge covers the costs associated with serving and distributing the products. It can be an annual per policy fixed rate or a percentage of the account value. Expense charge is often combined with insurance charge and known as mortality and expenses fee (M&E fee).

- Investment management fee: This fee is paid to professional fund managers for their services. It is typically stated as a percentage of the account value.

- Surrender charge: This is also known as contingent deferred sales charge (CDSC). These charges are imposed in the event of policy lapse and intended to offset upfront costs associated with policy issue. The charges are typically set high on the first year and gradually decline to zero. The ramp structure is used to discourage early lapsation. They are often a percentage of the account value. This may also include withdrawal charge, which apply to a policyholder who makes a partial withdrawal in excess of a maximal penalty-free amount.

Sources of expenses

Many expenses are implicitly funded by various fees and charges. For example, there are several types of expenses that affect products' profitability.

- Acquisition costs: These include agent sales commissions, marketing costs, underwriting costs, etc.

- Hedging costs: Market risks associated with investment guarantees are often mitigated by acquiring and managing hedging portfolios.

Modeling

While there is a great variety of product development in the industry, the focus of this book is to provide an understanding of the modeling and risk management of common product features. Therefore, we shall always take a minimalist approach to consider simplified models in order to bring out the essential elements and general ideas.

To facilitate the discussion of stochastic models for variable annuities, we introduce the alphabet soup of notation to be used throughout the notes. Details will be provided as they appear in the following sections.

- S_t, the market value of the underlying equity index or fund at t. If more than one fund is involved, this is considered to be the portfolio value of all funds.

- F_t, the market value of the policyholder's subaccounts at $t \geq 0$. F_0 is considered to be the initial premium invested at the start of the contract.

- G_t, the guaranteed base used to determine the amount of payment to the policyholder from various riders at time $t \geq 0$. Examples will follow in the next section.

- n, the number of valuations per year.

- m, the nominal annualized rate at which asset-value-based fees are deducted from subaccounts. Although we do not explicitly indicate the frequency of fee payments, we typically assume that the payment period matches the valuation period.

The portion available for funding the guarantee cost is called margin offset or rider charge and is usually split by benefit. In the notes, we denote the annualized rate of charges allocated to the GMMB by m_e and that of the charges allocated to the GMDB by m_d. Note that in general $m > m_e + m_d$ to allow for overheads, commissions and other expenses.

- h, the annualized rate at which guarantee-based fees are deducted from subaccounts.

- r, the continuously compounding annual risk-free rate. This typically reflects the overall yield rate of assets in the insurer's general account backing up guaranteed benefits.

- T, the target value date (or called maturity date), typically a rider anniversary on which the insurer is liable for guarantee payments.

- T_x is the future lifetime of the policyholder of age x at inception.

- L, the net present value of future liabilities at the start of the contract. The techniques to be introduced in the notes can be used to analyze liabilities at any other valuation date. We shall focus on the start of the contract for simplicity.

Let us first consider the cash flows of a stand-alone variable annuity contract. The life cycle of a variable annuity contract can be broken down into two phases.

Accumulation phase

Policyholders' investment accounts grow in proportion to certain equity-indices in which policyholders choose to invest at the inception. In practice, a policyholder' account value is often calculated by two measurements.

- (Accumulation unit) The policyholder's account is credited with a number of accumulation units based on the policyholder's net asset value. The number of accumulation units is equal to the initial purchase payment divided by the accumulation unit value. Additional purchase payments and transfers into the subaccount increase the number of accumulation units, while withdrawals, transfers out of the sub-account and deduction of certain contract charges often decrease the number of accumulation units.

- (Accumulation unit value) The initial accumulation unit value for each subaccount is often set arbitrarily. Each sub-account's accumulation unit value is then adjusted each business day to reflect income and capital gains of underlying equity index/fund, and the deduction of M&E fees, etc.

For example, if you make an initial purchase payment of $1,000$ on Monday and the accumulation unit value at the end of day is 10, then your account is credited with 100 units. If you take a withdrawal of 100 before the end of Tuesday, then the number of accumulation units reduces to 90 units. After the stock exchange closes on Tuesday, it is determined that each unit value increases from \$10 to \$10.25 for your selection of investment fund. Then your account is worth $\$10.25 \times 90 = \$922.5$ on Tuesday night. In other words, the policyholder's total value for each sub-account is the product of the number of accumulation units and accumulation unit value, each of which fluctuates for various reasons. These measurements are intuitive and necessary for practical purposes, such as easy-to-explain for policyholders and transparency of fees and charges, etc. However, they unnecessarily produce lengthy notation for the mathematical model to be introduced. Therefore, in order to bring out a concise model, we ignore the nuances of changes to accumulation unit versus those to unit value and only consider the evolution of total values of a sub-account throughout the book, rather than the breakdown of accumulation unit and unit value.

First consider the discrete time model with a valuation period of $1/n$ of a time unit, i.e. $t = 1/n, 2/n, \cdots, k/n, \cdots, T$. The fees and charges by annuity writers are typically taken as a fixed percentage of the-then-current account values for each period. The equity-linked mechanism for variable annuity dictates that at the end of each trading day, the account value fluctuates in proportion to the value of equity fund in which it invests and deducted by account-value-based fees.

$$F_{k/n} = F_0 \frac{S_{k/n}}{S_0} \left(1 - \frac{m}{n}\right)^k, \qquad k = 1, 2, \cdots, nT, \tag{1.13}$$

where m is the annual rate of total charge compounded n times per year, and all charges are made at the beginning of each valuation period.

Observe that the income from the insurer's perspective is generated by a stream of account-value-based payments. The present value of fee incomes, also called margin offset, up to the k-th valuation period is given by

$$M_{k/n} = \sum_{j=1}^{k} e^{-r(j-1)/n} \left(\frac{m_e}{n}\right) F_{(j-1)/n}. \tag{1.14}$$

Income phase

The second phase typically starts when variable annuity becomes a source of income for a policyholder. For example, the policyholder may receive a lump sum payment, annuitize accumulated asset base or begin taking regular withdrawals from subaccounts. Since incomes from variable annuities are largely proceeds from subaccounts, policyholders bear certain investment risk. However, depending on the generosity of riders, insurers also assume some degree of investment risk by providing minimum guarantees. Product designs vary greatly at the income phase. We shall devote the rest of this section on common types of investment guarantees.

Before diving into details of various riders, we take a moment to discuss the common types of guarantee base, from which all benefits are determined. Guarantee base is the notional amount used solely for the purpose of determining guarantee benefits. Variable annuities generally provide guaranteed appreciation of the guarantee base regardless of the performance of the policyholder's account value.

1.2.2 Resets, roll-ups and ratchets

Reset option is typically associated with the automatic renewal of variable annuity contracts with fixed terms. It is intended to allow a policyholder to lock in investment returns. When the contract is renewed, the new guarantee base is reset at the level which is the greater of the guarantee base from the previous term and the account value at the renewal date. Let $\{T_1, T_2, \cdots, \}$ be a sequence of renewal dates with the understanding that $T_0 = 0$. With a reset option, the guarantee base at time T_k is given by

$$G_{T_k} = \max\{G_{T_{k-1}}, F_{T_k}\}, \qquad k = 1, 2, \cdots$$

Roll-up option allows the guarantee base to accrue interest throughout the term of the policy. For example, if the roll-up rate ρ is a nominal rate payable n times per year, then the guarantee base is determined by

$$G_{(k+1)/n} = G_{k/n}\left(1 + \frac{\rho}{n}\right), \qquad \text{for } k = 0, 1, \cdots.$$

Note that this recursive relation implies that

$$G_{k/n} = G_0\left(1 + \frac{\rho}{n}\right)^k.$$

Step-up option, which is also known as ratchet option, is in essence a form of reset option. The guarantee base can increase with the policyholder's investment account at the end of each period. However, the guarantee base would never decrease, even if the investment account loses value. There are two common types of methods to step-up the guarantee base.

- *Lifetime high step-up*: This first type of step-up is based on lifetime high. If the current account value exceeds the guarantee base from the previous period, then the guarantee is reset to the current account value. Otherwise, the guarantee base remains the same.

$$G_{(k+1)/n} = \max\left\{G_{k/n}, F_{(k+1)/n}\right\}, \qquad \text{for } k = 0, 1, \cdots. \qquad (1.15)$$

Observe that this recursive relation leads to the representation

$$G_{k/n} = \max_{j=0,1,\cdots,k}\left\{F_{j/n}\right\}.$$

- *Annual high step-up*: With the second type of step-up, the current account value is compared to its value at the previous policy anniversary. If the current account value exceeds its previous value, then the guarantee base is increased by the same percentage as the account value since the last anniversary.

$$G_{(k+1)/n} = \frac{G_{k/n}}{F_{k/n}} \max\left\{F_{k/n}, F_{(k+1)/n}\right\}, \qquad \text{for } k = 0, 1, \cdots.$$

By rearrangement, the recursive relation can also be written as

$$\frac{G_{(k+1)/n} - G_{k/n}}{G_{k/n}} = \frac{(F_{(k+1)/n} - F_{k/n})_+}{F_{k/n}}, \tag{1.16}$$

where $(x)_+ = \max\{x, 0\}$. Note that this recursive relation yields the following representation

$$G_{k/n} = G_0 \prod_{j=0}^{k-1} \max\left\{1, \frac{F_{(j+1)/n}}{F_{j/n}}\right\}.$$

Sometimes these options are combined to offer guaranteed compound growth on the guarantee base and to allow the guarantee base to "lock in" gains from the policyholder's designated investment:

$$G_{(k+1)/n} = \max\left\{G_{k/n}\left(1 + \frac{\rho}{n}\right), F_{(k+1)/n}\right\}, \qquad \text{for } k = 0, \cdots. \tag{1.17}$$

Observe that this option also has a representation

$$G_{k/n} = \left(1 + \frac{\rho}{n}\right)^k \max_{j=0,\cdots,k}\left\{\left(1 + \frac{\rho}{n}\right)^{-j} F_{j/n}\right\}, \tag{1.18}$$

which can be proved by mathematical induction. For example, in the induction step,

$$G_{(k+1)/n} = \max\left\{\left(1 + \frac{\rho}{n}\right)^{k+1} \max_{j=0,\cdots,k}\left\{\left(1 + \frac{\rho}{n}\right)^{-j} F_{j/n}\right\}, F_{(k+1)/n}\right\}$$

$$= \left(1 + \frac{\rho}{n}\right)^{k+1} \max\left\{\max_{j=0,\cdots,k}\left\{\left(1 + \frac{\rho}{n}\right)^{-j} F_{j/n}\right\}, \left(1 + \frac{\rho}{n}\right)^{-(k+1)} F_{(k+1)/n}\right\},$$

which agrees with (1.18) with k replaced with $k + 1$.

There are also other combinations in the market. For example, a common practice is to offer the greater of a step-up option and a roll-up option:

$$G_{k/n} = \max\left\{G_0\left(1 + \frac{\rho}{n}\right)^k, \max_{j=0,1,\cdots,k}\{F_{j/n}\}\right\}.$$

While discrete time models are easy to explain, their continuous time counterparts are often more elegant in representations and more mathematically tractable in advanced modeling. If we divide each time unit into n subintervals and let n go to infinity in all models above, then we can obtain their continuous time analogues. Many of these representations use the elementary identity in (1.2).

- Roll-up option:
$$G_t = \lim_{n\to\infty} G_{\lceil nt\rceil/n} = G_0 e^{\rho t},$$

where $\lceil x\rceil$ is the integer ceiling of x.

- Lifetime high step-up option:

$$G_t = \sup_{0 \le s \le t} \{F_s\}, \qquad (1.19)$$

where the supremum is defined in Appendix C.2.

- Combination of roll-up and step-up #1:

$$G_t = e^{\rho t} \sup_{0 \le s \le t} \{e^{-\rho s} F_s\}.$$

- Combination of roll-up and step-up #2:

$$G_t = \max \left\{ G_0 e^{\rho t}, \sup_{0 \le s \le t} \{F_s\} \right\}.$$

The continuous-time analogue of annual high step-up option requires the concept of positive variation, which is to be introduced in Section 2.4. The continuous-time analogue of (1.16) is given by

$$\frac{dG_t}{G_t} = \frac{d\langle F \rangle_t^+}{F_t},$$

where $\langle F \rangle_t^+$ is the positive variation process of the underlying model for F.

1.2.3 Guaranteed minimum maturity benefit

The guaranteed minimum maturity benefit (GMMB) guarantees the policyholder a minimum monetary amount G at the maturity T. As the insurer is only possibly liable for the amount by which the guarantee exceeds the policyholder's account balance at maturity, the present value of the gross liability to the insurer is

$$e^{-rT}(G - F_T)_+ I(T_x > T), \qquad (1.20)$$

where $(x)_+ = \max\{x, 0\}$. Consider the *individual net liability* of the guaranteed benefits from the insurer's perspective, which is the gross liability of guaranteed benefits less the fee incomes. The present value of the GMMB net liability is given by

$$L_e^{(n)}(T_x) := e^{-rT}(G - F_T)_+ I(T_x > T) - M_{T \wedge T_x},$$

where $x \wedge y = \min\{x, y\}$ and the margin offset is given by (5.55).

We shrink the valuation period to zero by taking n to ∞, thereby reaching the limiting continuous-time model. Recall that

$$\lim_{n \to \infty} \left(1 - \frac{m}{n} \right)^n = e^{-m}, \qquad (1.21)$$

where m in this case should be interpreted as the continuously compounded annual rate of total charges. As a result, for each sample path, the continuous-time analogue of (1.13) is given by

$$F_t = \lim_{n \to \infty} F_{\frac{[nt]}{n}} = \frac{F_0}{S_0} \lim_{n \to \infty} S_{\frac{[nt]}{n}} \left[\left(1 - \frac{m}{n}\right)^n \right]^{\frac{[nt]}{n}} = F_0 \frac{S_t}{S_0} e^{-mt}. \quad (1.22)$$

Using the definition of Riemann integral, we observe that the limit of the margin offset is given by

$$M_t = \lim_{n \to \infty} M_{\frac{[nt]}{n}} = \lim_{n \to \infty} \sum_{j=1}^{[nt]} \frac{1}{n} e^{-r(j-1)/n} m_e F_{(j-1)/n} = \int_0^t e^{-rs} m_e F_s \, ds$$

where m_e is interpreted as the continuously compounded annual rate of rider charge allocated to the GMMB rider.

The limit of L leads to a continuous time model. In the case of the GMMB,

$$L_e^{(\infty)}(T_x) = e^{-rT}(G - F_T)_+ I(T_x > T) - \int_0^{T \wedge T_x} e^{-rs} m_e F_s \, ds. \quad (1.23)$$

The net liabilities L should be negative with a sufficiently high probability, as the products are designed to be profitable. However, in adverse scenarios, the net liabilities can become positive.

1.2.4   Guaranteed minimum accumulation benefit

It is increasingly common that GMMB riders are designed to be automatically renewed at the end of their fixed terms. Such a rider is often referred to as the guarantee minimum accumulation benefit (GMAB).

Consider a two-period GMAB for an example. Suppose that the original GMMB matures at the end of T_1 periods, when the policyholder is guaranteed to receive a minimum of a pre-determined guarantee amount, say G_0. In other words, the investment account is worth $\max(G_0, F_{T_1})$, at which the new guarantee is reset. Let T_2 be the maturity of the renewed contract. There are two cases to be considered, as shown in Figures 1.2 and 1.3.

1. The equity performs so poorly in the first period that the policyholder's account investment F_{T_1} drops below G_0 at the renewal date. Then the insurer is responsible for injecting the additional cash $(G_0 - F_{T_1})$ into the policyholder's account and the new guaranteed level G_1 remains the same as G_0.

2. The equity performs so well in the first period that F_{T_1} exceeds G_0. Then there is no payment from the insurer. However, the guaranteed level for the second period is reset to F_{T_1}.

In other words, the policyholder should never lose what has been accumulated from the previous period

$$G_{T_1} = \max(G_0, F_{T_1}),$$

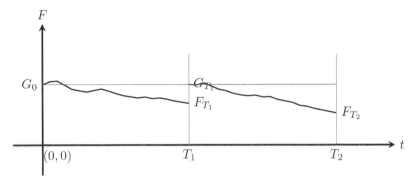

FIGURE 1.2: GMAB gross liability - Case 1

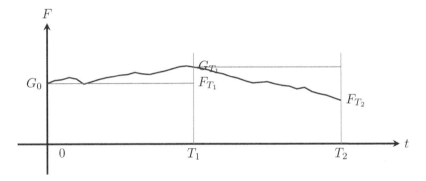

FIGURE 1.3: GMAB gross liability - Case 2

for which the account value fluctuates in sync with equity index,

$$F_{T_1} = F_0 \frac{S_{T_1}}{S_0} e^{-mT_1}.$$

In both of the above-described cases, the policyholder is guaranteed to receive at least the new guaranteed amount at the maturity T_2, i.e.

$$G_{T_2} = \max(G_{T_1}, F_{T_2}),$$

where F_{T_2} is the accumulation of the guaranteed amount from the first period

$$F_{T_2} = G_{T_1} \frac{S_{T_2}}{S_{T_1}} e^{-m(T_2-T_1)}.$$

Note, however, that in practice there is a different version of the rider, also commonly referred to as a GMAB, in which the guarantee base is reset every few years (see Section 1.2.2 for reset options) but the account value is never adjusted.

$$G_{T_2} = \max(G_{T_1}, F_{T_2}),$$

where F_{T_1} is the accumulation of account value from the the first period,

$$F_{T_2} = F_{T_1} \frac{S_{T_2}}{S_{T_1}} e^{-m(T_2-T_1)}.$$

Careful readers would notice that this version of the GMAB can be viewed as an ordinary GMMB with a step-up option on the guarantee base.

1.2.5 Guaranteed minimum death benefit

The GMDB guarantees the policyholder a minimum monetary amount G upon death payable at the end of the $1/n$-th period following his/her death. In other words, the insurer is responsible the difference between the guaranteed amount G and the actual account value at the time of payment, should the former exceed the latter. Figure 1.4 shows a particular scenario of account value falling below a guaranteed level at the time of death T_x, which represents a liability for the insurer.

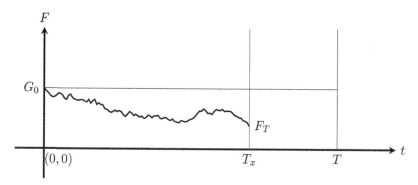

FIGURE 1.4: GMDB gross liability

We denote by K_x the future lifetime of the policyholder rounded to the lower $1/n$-th of a year

$$K_x^{(n)} = \frac{1}{n} \lfloor nT_x \rfloor.$$

It is fairly common that the guarantee amount accumulates interest at a fixed rate $\rho > 0$, which is known as a roll-up option. The present value of the gross liability to the insurer is

$$e^{-r(K_x^{(n)}+1/n)} \left(G \left(1 + \frac{\rho}{n} \right)^{nK_x^{(n)}} - F_{K_x^{(n)}+1/n} \right)_+ I(K_x^{(n)} < T).$$

The present value of the GMDB net liability is given by

$$L_d^{(n)}(T_x) := e^{-r(K_x^{(n)}+1/n)} \left(G \left(1 + \frac{\rho}{n}\right)^{nK_x^{(n)}} - F_{K_x^{(n)}+1/n} \right)_+ I(K_x^{(n)} < T)$$

$$- \sum_{j=1}^{n(T \wedge K_x^{(n)})} e^{-r(j-1)/n} \left(\frac{m_d}{n}\right) F_{(j-1)/n},$$

where m_d is the rate of fees per period allocated to fund the GMDB rider. Bear in mind that the rider fees are not charged separately, but rather as part of the M&E fees, i.e. $m > m_d$. Similarly, it is easy to use limiting arguments to show that in case of the GMDB,

$$L_d^{(\infty)}(T_x) = e^{-rT_x}(Ge^{\rho T_x} - F_{T_x})_+ I(T_x \leq T) - \int_0^{T \wedge T_x} e^{-rs} m_d F_s \, ds. \quad (1.24)$$

Compare (1.7) and (1.24) for their similarities. The GMDB rider is in essence an equity-linked extension of a term life insurance.

1.2.6 Guaranteed minimum withdrawal benefit

The GMWB guarantees the policyholder the return of initial premium, typically through systematic withdrawals, regardless of the performance of the underlying equity funds. The policyholder is allowed to withdraw up to a maximal percentage of the initial premium per year out of the sub-account without penalty. The withdrawals are guaranteed to last until the initial premium is fully refunded, at which point any remaining balance of the investment account would be returned to the policyholder. Figure 1.5 shows a scenario where the guarantee amount, represented by the stair-step graph on the top, decreases each year with systematic withdrawals. Even though the account value, represented by the stair-step graph on the bottom, is depleted early, systematic withdrawals continue until the premium is full returned.

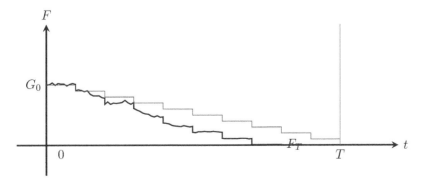

FIGURE 1.5: GMWB gross liability

Example 1.11. A contract starts with an initial premium of $100 and the policyholder elects to withdraw the maximum amount 7% of the initial premium without penalty each year. Suppose that, due to the poor performance of the funds in which the policyholder invests, the account value is depleted at the end of five years. By this time, the policyholder would have only withdrawn $7 × 5 = $35 in total. There is no more fund in the policyholder's account to pay for the requisite $7 per year. Then the GMWB kicks in to sustain the annual withdrawal $7 until the entire initial premium is returned, which means it pays until the maturity at the end of $100/$7 = 14.28 years. In contrast, if the underlying equity index/fund performs well and the account values remain positive throughout the entire 14.28 years, then all withdrawals literally are taken out of the policyholder's own account and the insurer is relieved of its obligation. The policyholder is also entitled to the remaining balance at the end of 14.28 years.

In practice, most policyholders choose to withdraw the maximum amount without penalty, denoted by w, which is typically a fixed percentage of the initial premium. Then it takes $T = F_0/w$ periods before the initial premium is fully refunded, at which point the GMWB rider expires. We denote this fixed amount per time unit by w, the total fees per time unit by m. The margin offset per time unit used to fund the GMWB rider is denoted by m_w.

To build up a model for the GMWB rider, we consider the incremental change of the policyholder's investment account over each period,

$$F_{(k+1)/n} - F_{k/n} = \frac{S_{(k+1)/n} - S_{k/n}}{S_{k/n}} F_{k/n} - \frac{m}{n} F_{k/n} - \frac{w}{n}, \qquad (1.25)$$

which consists of the financial return from the equity-linking mechanism less the management fee and the withdrawal for that period. Note that this recursive relation does not seem to have a simple explicit solution. To be more precise, however, one needs to make sure that the account does not go below zero and hence

$$F_{(k+1)/n} = \max\left\{\frac{S_{(k+1)/n}}{S_{k/n}} F_{k/n} - \frac{m}{n} F_{k/n} - \frac{w}{n}, 0\right\}. \qquad (1.26)$$

Let us first consider the GMWB liability from a policyholder's point of view. The systematic withdrawals in the initial periods are typically taken directly out of the policyholder's account. When the equity performs badly, there is a chance that the account is depleted prior to time T. In that case, the insurer would have to continue to fund the systematic withdrawals out of its own general account. Therefore, the insurer's liability starts at the first time when the policyholder's sub-account is exhausted, called *ruin time*, i.e.

$$\tau := \min\left\{\frac{k}{n} > 0 : F_{k/n} = 0\right\}.$$

Note that the ruin time is a random variable and can be greater than T. For simplicity, we consider the case where the policyholder starts to withdraw immediately after the purchase of the contract. There would possibly be two sources of income for the policyholder. (1) The collection of all guaranteed withdrawals until the initial premium is returned. The present value of all withdrawals is given by

$$\sum_{k=1}^{\lceil nT \rceil} e^{-rk/n} \frac{w}{n}.$$

(2) The balance of the policyholder's investment account, if there is any remaining at the maturity T. This can be easily represented by $e^{-rT}F_T$. Therefore, the total sum of financial returns from the investment in the variable annuity contract can be written as

$$\sum_{k=1}^{\lceil nT \rceil} e^{-rk/n} \frac{w}{n} + e^{-rT}F_T I(F_T > 0). \tag{1.27}$$

From an insurer's point of view, the cash flows would look somewhat different. First of all, one has to keep in mind that the policyholder withdraws from his/her own account as long as it remains sufficient, and that the insurer only picks up the bill after the account plunges to zero prior to T. On one hand, the total present value of the insurer's liabilities (guaranteed withdrawals) would be the sum of present values of all withdrawals after ruin time and before the maturity T,

$$\sum_{k=n\tau}^{(n\tau-1)\vee\lceil nT \rceil} e^{-rk/n} \frac{w}{n},$$

with the convention that $\sum_{k=m}^{m-1} = 0$ for any integer m. On the other hand, the insurer collects M&E fees from the start of the contract until the policyholder's account is exhausted and hence the present value of its income stream is given by

$$\sum_{k=1}^{(n\tau-1)\wedge\lceil nT \rceil} e^{-r(k-1)/n} F_{(k-1)/n} \frac{mw}{n}.$$

Piecing together both sides of the benefit outgo and the fee income, we obtain the individual net liability of a GMWB rider

$$L_w^{(n)} := \sum_{k=n\tau}^{(n\tau-1)\vee\lceil nT \rceil} e^{-rk/n} \frac{w}{n} - \sum_{k=1}^{(n\tau-1)\wedge\lceil nT \rceil} e^{-r(k-1)/n} F_{(k-1)/n} \frac{mw}{n}. \tag{1.28}$$

The continuous-time model is obtained by shrinking the valuation period to zero in the discrete time model. The continuous-time analogue of the recursive relation (1.25) is provided by a differential equation

$$dF_t = \frac{F_t}{S_t} dS_t - mF_t \, dt - w \, dt, \tag{1.29}$$

for some suitable interpretation of "differentials" to be discussed in Section 2.12.2. The restriction (1.26) implies in the continuous-time model that the process F is absorbed at zero once it reaches zero.

From a policyholder's point of view, we obtain the total worth of investment with the variable annuity contract with the GMWB rider in continuous-time by taking the limit of (1.27) as $n \to \infty$,

$$\int_0^T e^{-rt} w \, dt + e^{-rT} F_T I(F_T > 0).$$

Similarly, the continuous-time individual net liability of a GMWB rider from an insurer's point of view is given by the limit of (1.28) as $n \to \infty$,

$$L_w^{(\infty)} := \int_\tau^{\tau \vee T} e^{-rt} w \, dt - \int_0^{\tau \wedge T} e^{-rt} m_w F_t \, dt,$$

where the ruin time is defined by

$$\tau := \inf\{t > 0 : F_t \le 0\}.$$

1.2.7   Guaranteed lifetime withdrawal benefit

The guaranteed lifetime withdrawal benefit (GLWB) can be viewed as an extension of the GMWB. Instead of allowing a policyholder to withdraw a certain amount until the initial premium is refunded, the GLWB guarantees systematic withdrawals for the policyholder's whole life.

Example 1.12. Let us consider a numerical example on the dynamics of cash flows with a GLWB rider in Table 1.1. The first two columns represent a particular sequence (also known as a sample path in Section 2.4) of yearly yield rates of some equity fund over the 20 year period. Suppose that an initial purchase payment of $\$10,000$ is made with a variable annuity contract, which is linked to the equity fund, and the guarantee base is set equal to the initial purchase payment. Assume that the policyholder elects a systemic withdrawal scheme to withdraw 5% of the guarantee base every year. At the end of each policy year, a rate of investment return is reported on the underlying equity fund and also applied to the policyholder's account value from the previous year. For example, the equity index increases by 5% in the first year and so does the account value. Then 5% of the guarantee base from the previous year, $5\% \times \$10,000 = \$500$, is withdrawn from the account and passed on to the policyholder for consumption. The same mechanism applies each year for the remaining lifetime of the policyholder. Note that the policyholder's account receives a boost of financial return in the second year resulting in an account value after withdrawal, $\$10,500$, which is higher than the benefit base from the previous year, $\$10,000$. Then the "step-up" option kicks in and the benefit base is automatically reset to the account value. In other words, the step-up option allows the policyholder to lock in the maximum account value to date as the basis of withdrawals. Note that

Policy year	Investment return	AV before withdrawal	Annual withdrawal	AV after withdrawal	Benefit base
0	-	-	-	10000.00	10000.00
1	5%	10500.00	500.00	10000.00	10000.00
2	10%	11000.00	500.00	10500.00	10500.00
3	5%	11025.00	525.00	10500.00	10500.00
4	10%	11550.00	525.00	11025.00	11025.00
5	-20%	8820.00	551.25	8268.75	11025.00
6	-10%	7441.88	551.25	6890.63	11025.00
7	-10%	6201.56	551.25	5650.31	11025.00
8	5%	5932.83	551.25	5381.58	11025.00
9	10%	5919.74	551.25	5368.49	11025.00
10	20%	6442.18	551.25	5890.93	11025.00
11	-5%	5596.39	551.25	5045.14	11025.00
12	-15%	4288.37	551.25	3737.12	11025.00
13	-10%	3363.40	551.25	2812.15	11025.00
14	10%	3093.37	551.25	2542.12	11025.00
15	-15%	2160.80	551.25	1609.55	11025.00
16	5%	1690.03	551.25	1138.78	11025.00
17	-10%	1024.90	551.25	473.65	11025.00
18	-5%	449.97	551.25	0.00	11025.00
19	-	0.00	551.25	0.00	11025.00
20	-	0.00	551.25	0.00	11025.00

TABLE 1.1: GLWB with a step-up option

when the policyholder dies, the remaining balance of his/her account would be paid to a designated beneficiary. For example, if the person dies at the end of 6th year, then the beneficiary is entitled to $6890.63. If the person dies at the end of 20th year, then there is no remaining balance to be paid. However, the death benefit is usually considered as the GMDB rider, not a part of the GLWB rider.

Under the GLWB, the amount of systematic withdrawals per period is typically determined by a pre-specified percentage of a guarantee base. We shall denote the value of the guarantee base at any point of time t by G_t. It is typical that the starting value of the guarantee base matches with the initial premium $G_0 = F_0$ and the evolution of the guarantee base over time $\{G_t, t \geq 0\}$ is determined by various options of policyholders' choosing. See Section 1.2.2 for details. Keep in mind, however, that the guarantee base is a nominal account which only serves as a base for determining withdrawal amounts. The actual withdrawals, which are typically a fixed percentage, denoted by h, of the then-current guarantee base, are taken out of the policyholder's own investment account (not the guarantee base!). Recall that there are two common types of fees that appear in various versions of the product, namely, account-value based fees and guarantee based fees.

With an analogy to the GMWB model in (1.25), we observe that the incremental change per period for the GLWB model is given by

$$F_{(k+1)/n} - F_{k/n} = \frac{S_{(k+1)/n} - S_{k/n}}{S_{k/n}} F_{k/n} - \frac{m_w + h}{n} G_{k/n} - \frac{m}{n} F_{k/n}. \quad (1.30)$$

Again we need a similar operation as in (1.26) to ensure that the process modeling the policyholder's account value does not go below zero. The guarantee base grows in accordance with the step-up option described in (1.15).

The payoffs from the GLWB are similar to those from a GMWB except that systematic withdrawals are guaranteed to last until the policyholder's death. The present value of all withdrawals would be given by

$$\sum_{k=0}^{\lfloor nT_x \rfloor} e^{-r(k+1)/n} \frac{hG_{k/n}}{n}.$$

In addition, a beneficiary is entitled to the balance of the policyholder's investment account upon his/her death due to the GMDB rider. The present value of the account value payable upon death is given by $e^{-rT_x} F_{T_x}$. The combined value of the GLWB and the policyholder's investment is given by

$$\sum_{k=0}^{\lfloor nT_x \rfloor} e^{-r(k+1)/n} \frac{hG_{k/n}}{n} + e^{-rT_x} F_{T_x}.$$

From the insurer's perspective, the GLWB rider incurs cost when the policyholder continues to withdraw after the account is depleted. Hence, the present value of GMWB gross liability is given by

$$\sum_{k=n\tau}^{(n\tau-1)\vee\lfloor nT_x \rfloor} e^{-r(k+1)/n} \frac{h}{n} G_{k/n}.$$

In the discrete time case, there is the possibility that the last withdrawal payment before the account is depleted comes partly from the the policyholder's account and partly from the insurer's general account. We shall ignore the small payment from the insurer for simplicity. Similar to any other benefit, the GMWB is funded by the collection of rider charges, which can be account-value based or guarantee based. The present value of total rider charges is given by

$$\sum_{k=0}^{(n\tau-1)\wedge\lfloor nT_x \rfloor} e^{-rk/n} G_{k/n} \frac{m_w}{n}.$$

The insurer's net liability (present values of outgoes less present values of incomes) for the GLWB rider is given by

$$L_{lw}^{(n)} := \sum_{k=n\tau}^{(n\tau-1)\vee\lfloor nT_x\rfloor} e^{-r(k+1)/n} G_{k/n} \frac{h}{n} - \sum_{k=0}^{(n\tau-1)\wedge\lfloor nT_x\rfloor} e^{-rk/n} G_{k/n} \frac{m_w}{n}.$$

When the valuation period $1/n$ shrinks to zero, we can consider the continuous-time version of the GMWB model. For example, the analogue of the recursive relation (1.30) is driven by

$$dF_t = \frac{F_t}{S_t} dS_t - (m_w + h)G_t \, dt - mF_t \, dt,$$

with the precise interpretation of "differentials" to be introduced in Section 2.12.2. Similarly, the insurer's net liability for the GLWB rider in the continuous time model is given by

$$L_{lw}^{(\infty)} := \int_{\tau}^{\tau\vee T_x} e^{-rt} G_t h \, dt - \int_0^{\tau\wedge T_x} e^{-rt} G_t m_w \, dt.$$

1.2.8 Mechanics of immediate variable annuity

The funding mechanism of immediate variable annuities is very similar to that of deferred variable annuities. For example, they can be either tax-qualified or non-tax-qualified. Insurers transfer to third-party vendors policyholders' investments, which appear as separate accounts on insurers' balance sheets. The main difference is that the accumulation phase of deferred variable annuity precedes the income phase but the two phases coincide for immediate variable annuity. We illustrate the payout mechanics with an example on how a policyholder's annuity incomes are calculated.

Let us digress to the issue of a fixed annuity as opposed to a variable annuity for the moment. Suppose that a policyholder intends to purchase from an insurer an annuity that pays 1 dollar at the beginning of each year for 3 years and that the current yield rate on the insurer's portfolio of fixed-income securities is 5% effective per annum. Then the present value of such a fixed annuity is given by

$$\ddot{a}_{\overline{3}|} = 1 + \frac{1}{1+5\%} + \frac{1}{(1+5\%)^2} = 2.85941.$$

In other words, if the policyholder pays $2,859.41$ for an initial premium, the insurer can invest the premium with fixed-income securities and accumulate enough to pay for $1,000$ at the beginning of each year for 3 years. We shall call the yield rate the *assumed interest rate* (AIR) to be denoted by i.

Immediate variable annuity benefits are often quoted by the initial payout rate per $1,000$ of purchase payment (premium). For example, consider a 3-year immediate variable annuity and the initial payout rate with the AIR of 5% is $1,000/2.85941 = 349.72$ per thousand of purchase payment. Only the initial payout rate is known

with certainty. Consider the case where the policyholder makes an initial purchase
payment of $\$2,859.41$. Then the initial payout is given by

$$P_0 = 2.85941 \times 349.72 = 1,000.$$

Subsequent payout rates fluctuate with the performance of the equity fund in which
the remaining purchase payment is invested. Similar to deferred annuities, immediate
annuity benefits are measured in terms of the number of *annuity units* and *annuity
unit value*. Let us denote the annuity unit value (AUV) at time k by V_k for $k = 0, 1, 2$.
The initial annuity unit value is often set arbitrarily, say $V_0 = 10$. Then the number of
annuity units is determined by $P_0/V_0 = 1,000/10 = 100$. In each of the subsequent
years $k = 1, 2, 3$, the AUV is calculated by the formula

$$V_k = V_{k-1} \times \frac{I_k}{1+i}, \tag{1.31}$$

where I_k represents the net investment factor (NIF) for the k-th year and is often
determined by

$$I_k = \frac{(a) + (b) - (c)}{(a)}$$

and

(a) the policyholder's asset value at the end of the $k - 1$-th period,

(b) investment income and capital gains credited during the k-th period,

(c) capital losses and deduction of daily charges during the k-th period.

Suppose that the NIFs for the first two years are given by $I_1 = 1.1$ and $I_2 = 0.9$
respectively. Then we can determine the AUV in the second year according to (1.31)

$$V_1 = V_0 \times \frac{1.1}{1.05} = 10.47619.$$

Assume that there are no additional deposits into the sub-account or withdrawals
from the sub-account. Then the number of annuity units remains the same throughout
the two years. The second variable payment is given by

$$P_1 = V_1 \times 100 = 1,047.62.$$

Similarly, the third payment is determined as follows.

$$V_2 = V_1 \times \frac{0.9}{1.05} = 8.97959,$$
$$P_2 = V_2 \times 100 = 897.96.$$

Observe that the annuity payments are reflective of changes in equity values.
More is paid when the sub-account performs wells. A natural question to ask is

whether the policyholder bears all the risk with the sub-account investment. To answer this question, let us take a look at the evolution of sub-account values. Initially the policyholder's purchase payment is known to be

$$F_0 = 2,859.41.$$

After the first annuity payment to the policyholder, the remaining in the sub-account grows by the NIF over the first period.

$$F_1 = (F_0 - P_0) \times I_1 = (2,859.41 - 1,000) \times 1.1 = 2,045.35.$$

The same process holds for the second period.

$$F_2 = (F_1 - P_1) \times I_2 = (2,045.35 - 1047.62) \times 0.9 = 897.96.$$

Note that the insurer takes no responsibility for any benefit payment throughout the term, as the balance of the sub-account is the exact amount to make the last annuity payment to the policyholder. In other words, the balance of the sub-account at the end of the term of the variable annuity is $F_3 = 0$. This is not a coincidence, as we shall demonstrate through a more general mathematical formulation.

1.2.9 Modeling of immediate variable annuity

Let us formulate the example in the previous section in more general terms. Assume that a policyholder buys an immediate variable annuity with annual benefit payments for N years with an AIR denoted by i per year. Note that the first payment upon the purchase of the annuity is always determined with certainty by the initial payout rate per $\$1,000$ of purchase payment, F_0,

$$P_0 = \frac{F_0}{1,000} \times \frac{1,000}{\ddot{a}_{\overline{N}|}} = \frac{F_0}{\ddot{a}_{\overline{N}|}}, \tag{1.32}$$

where $\ddot{a}_{\overline{N}|}$ is the present value of a fixed annuity with the same payment frequency as the variable annuity

$$\ddot{a}_{\overline{N}|} = 1 + (1+i)^{-1} + \cdots + (1+i)^{-(N-1)}.$$

Recall that all variable annuity payments are determined by the number of annuity units, $\# = P_0/V_0$, and varying annuity unit values, i.e. for $k = 0, 1, \cdots, N$,

$$P_k = \# \times V_k.$$

Since AUVs are determined by the recursive formula (1.31), we note that

$$P_k = \frac{P_0}{V_0} \frac{V_0 \prod_{i=1}^{k} I_k}{(1+i)^k} = \frac{P_0 \prod_{i=1}^{k} I_k}{(1+i)^k},$$

which justifies the fact that the initial AUV does not matter and is often chosen arbitrarily. Roughly speaking, the NIFs can be represented by

$$I_k = \frac{(a) + (b) - (c)}{(a)} = \frac{S_{k-1} + (S_k - S_{k-1})}{S_{k-1}}(1 - m),$$

where item (a) is represented by equity value S_{k-1}, (b) is represented by total capital gains on equities $S_k - S_{k-1}$ and (c) is represented by total amount of asset-based-charges, mS_k. It follows immediately that

$$P_k = P_0 \frac{S_k}{S_0} \left(\frac{1-m}{1+i} \right)^k.$$

The balance of policyholder's subaccount is also determined recursively by

$$F_k = I_k(F_{k-1} - P_{k-1}) = \frac{S_k}{S_{k-1}}(1-m)(F_{k-1} - P_{k-1}). \tag{1.33}$$

Note that (1.33) is in fact the immediate variable annuity analogue of the equity-linking mechanism (1.22) for deferred variable annuity. We shall show by mathematical induction that for $k = 0, 1, \cdots, N$

$$F_k = \frac{S_k}{S_0}(1-m)^k (F_0 - P_0 \ddot{a}_{\overline{k}|}). \tag{1.34}$$

It is obvious that (1.33) agrees with (1.34) for $k = 1$. Suppose that (1.34) holds for $k - 1$. Then it follows that

$$
\begin{aligned}
F_k &= \frac{S_k}{S_{k-1}}(1-m) \left(\frac{S_{k-1}}{S_0}(1-m)^{k-1}(F_0 - P_0 \ddot{a}_{\overline{k-1}|}) - P_{k-1} \right) \\
&= \frac{S_k}{S_0}(1-m)^k \left(F_0 - P_0 \ddot{a}_{\overline{k-1}|} \right) - P_0 \frac{S_k}{S_0} \frac{(1-m)^k}{(1+i)^{k-1}} \\
&= \frac{S_k}{S_0}(1-m)^k \left(F_0 - P_0 \ddot{a}_{\overline{k-1}|} - P_0 \frac{1}{(1+i)^{k-1}} \right),
\end{aligned}
$$

which agrees with (1.34) since $\ddot{a}_{\overline{k}|} = \ddot{a}_{\overline{k-1}|} + 1/(1+i)^{k-1}$. This proves the earlier claim that there is always exactly enough fund to pay for the variable annuity payments regardless of equity performance, i.e. owing to (1.32),

$$F_N = \frac{S_N}{S_0}(1-m)^N (F_0 - P_0 \ddot{a}_{\overline{N}|}) = 0.$$

Therefore, an insurer merely acts as a steward of policyholder's own investment option in this case and the policyholder takes all the investment risk.

While the previous example assumed annual benefit payments and considered no mortality, the same process holds for life-contingent annuities with other frequencies. However, in general, the investment risk cannot be entirely passed on to policyholders. For example, in the case of a whole-life immediate variable annuity with annual payments, we would expect the initial payout to be determined by the analogue of (1.32)

$$P_0 = \frac{F_0}{\ddot{a}_x},$$

where $\ddot{a}_x$ is the present value of a whole-life fixed annuity

$$\ddot{a}_x = \sum_{k=0}^{\infty}(1+i)^{-k}\,{}_kp_x.$$

Following the same calculation, we can show that a living policyholder's subaccount after k periods would have the balance of

$$F_k = \frac{S_k}{S_0}(1-m)^k(F_0 - P_0\ddot{a}_{\overline{k}|}).$$

If a policyholder dies early in the sense that $\ddot{a}_{\overline{K_x}|} \leq \ddot{a}_x$, then the insurer makes a profit of

$$F_{K_x} = \frac{S_{K_x}}{S_0}(1-m)^{K_x}F_0\left(1 - \frac{\ddot{a}_{\overline{K_x}|}}{\ddot{a}_x}\right).$$

If a policyholder survives so long that $\ddot{a}_{\overline{K_x}|} > \ddot{a}_x$, then the insurer is liable for the benefit payments

$$\sum_{k=1}^{K_x} P_k I(\ddot{a}_{\overline{k}|} > \ddot{a}_x) = P_0\sum_{k=1}^{K_x}\frac{S_k}{S_0}\left(\frac{1-m}{1+i}\right)^k I(\ddot{a}_{\overline{k}|} > \ddot{a}_x).$$

In other words, like a traditional life annuity, the profits made from those annuitants who die early can be used to cover losses from benefit payments to annuitants who live long. However, in contrast with traditional life annuity, even if actual mortality experience matches up exactly with the mortality assumption made by the insurer when determining the fixed life annuity $\ddot{a}_x$, the mechanics of immediate life-contingent variable annuity does not guarantee the insurer to break even or make a net profit due to the interaction of mortality risk and investment risk.

1.2.10   Single premium vs. flexible premium annuities

As the name suggests, a single-premium annuity is funded by a single purchase payment. The payment may be invested for a long period of time, known as an accumulation phase, typical in single-premium deferred annuity, or used immediately for income benefits, as in single-premium immediate annuity. In contrast, a flexible premium annuity is designed to be funded by multiple purchase payments prior to the payout of benefits. They are always deferred annuities which allow the accumulation of sufficient base to suppose withdrawals or other income benefits.

The modeling of guaranteed benefit for flexible premium annuity is similar to that for single premium annuity. An insurer has to keep track of deposits, their investment returns and accrual of guaranteed benefits. For example, it is very typical to sign up for an automatic deposit plan where a certain amount of contribution is made regularly to a variable annuity account. Let c be the annualized rate of additional purchase payments (contributions). In a discrete-time model, the incremental change of the policyholder's investment account over each period is given by

$$F_{(k+1)/n} - F_{k/n} = \frac{S_{(k+1)/n} - S_{k/n}}{S_{k/n}}F_{k/n} - \frac{m}{n}F_{k/n} + \frac{c}{n}.$$

Note that the computation of quantities pertaining to the evolution of such an account is not much different from that of (1.25), as deposits may be viewed as negative withdrawals. Similarly, if the contract comes with a roll-up option, then the guarantee base grows in the following way

$$G_{k/n} = G_{k/n}\left(1 + \frac{\rho}{n}\right) + \frac{c}{n}.$$

In the corresponding continuous-time model, the instantaneous change of the policy-holder's account is determined by

$$\mathrm{d}F_t = \frac{F_t}{S_t}\,\mathrm{d}S_t - mF_t\,\mathrm{d}t + c\,\mathrm{d}t, \tag{1.35}$$

and that of the guarantee base with a roll-up option is given by

$$\mathrm{d}G_t = \rho G_t\,\mathrm{d}t + c\,\mathrm{d}t.$$

Due to the similarity between regular contributions and systematic withdrawals, we only consider single-premium deferred annuities with withdrawals and corresponding results can be easily found for flexible-premium annuities.

1.3 Equity-indexed annuities

Equity-indexed annuities, also known as fixed indexed annuities, provide policyholders with financial returns on their investments linked to some equity indices with minimum guaranteed rates. The idea is to allow policyholders to earn more than traditional fixed annuities, such as deferred life annuity in Example 1.8, when the market performs well while not losing their investment balance when the market performs poorly. While this sounds similar to variable annuities, equity-indexed annuities function in many ways differently from variable annuities. Here we outline a few differences between the two product lines.

- (Cash flows) There is no separate account for equity-indexed annuities. All premiums are deposited into the insurer's general account and benefit payments are paid out of general account, in manners similar to traditional life insurance. Equity risk lies largely with the insurer. Policyholders' investments under variable annuities are deposited in separate accounts. The insurer merely acts as the steward of policyholders' assets and takes no equity risk unless guaranteed benefits are involved.

- (Risk and reward) Equity-indexed annuities only offer a certain percentage of participation in financial returns from equity indices while policyholders can choose their own investment and fully benefit from equity returns. The upside returns for equity-indexed annuities are often capped at certain rates whereas there is no limit on the upside for variable annuities.

- (Fees) Equity indexed annuities do not charge fees. The cost is typically controlled through setting participation rate, return cap and guaranteed floor. The insurer is expected to earn more on its assets backing up the equity-indexed returns to policyholders. Like mutual funds, fees are charged by insurers to manage variable annuities and to provide minimum guaranteed benefits.

- (Regulation) In the US, equity-indexed annuities are sold as fixed annuities which are not registered with the Securities and Exchange Commission (SEC) whereas variable annuities are considered securities and regulated by the SEC.

Actual product designs of equity-indexed annuities vary from contract to contract. Similar to variable annuity products, equity indexed annuities may be offered with a single premium or flexible premiums. We shall only consider the single premium annuity for simplicity. Here we provide a summary of a few common index crediting options.

1.3.1 Point-to-point option

Given a single premium P, the product often offers a guaranteed minimum annual continuously compounding interest rate g on the premium up to maturity T. For example, the guarantee base accumulates at maturity T to

$$G_T := Pe^{gT}.$$

Point-to-point index crediting option is a method of crediting interest on the policyholder's premium based on percentage changes of a linked equity index. The contract typically specifies a participation rate $\alpha \in (0, 1)$, which determines the proportion of financial returns on equity index to be received by the policyholder. From a policyholder's point of view, the benefit from the equity-indexed annuity is given by

$$\max \left(P \left(1 + \alpha \frac{S_T - S_0}{S_0} \right), G_T \right). \tag{1.36}$$

In the literature, there is also another popular version of the PTP design given by

$$\max \left(P \left(\frac{S_T}{S_0} \right)^\alpha, G_T \right). \tag{1.37}$$

The difference between (1.36) and (1.37) is similar to that of simple interest and compound interest in a fractional year, i.e. the accumulation of investment according to $1 + rt$ versus $(1 + r)^t$ for annual interest rate r and a fraction of a year $t \in (0, 1)$. Using the binomial theorem, we can show that $(1 + x)^\alpha = 1 + \alpha x + o(x)$ as $x \to 0$. Then the two PTP designs are very close in value when the percentage change in equity index value is very small.

1.3.2 Cliquet option

Another popular index crediting option for equity-indexed annuities is the so-called the *cliquet*, which is ratchet in French. The interest credited to policyholders is determined by the greater of return rate on the equity index and a guaranteed minimum rate. It allows policyholders to lock in interest credits from previous periods while keeping the potential of upside returns.

Suppose that an equity-indexed annuity with an annual cliquet design allows a participation rate $\alpha \in (0,1)$ and the guaranteed minimum rate $g \in (0,1)$. The value of the policy at maturity T is given by

$$P \prod_{k=1}^{T} \max\left(1 + \alpha \frac{S_k - S_{k-1}}{S_{k-1}}, e^g\right). \tag{1.38}$$

In some design, the contract caps the annual rate at a maximum rate c where $g < c < 1$. The value of such a policy at maturity T is given by

$$P \prod_{k=1}^{T} \max\left(\min\left(1 + \alpha \frac{S_k - S_{k-1}}{S_{k-1}}, e^c\right), e^g\right). \tag{1.39}$$

With analogy to (1.37), the values of annual cliquet designs (1.38) and (1.39) can also be determined by

$$P \prod_{k=1}^{T} \max\left(\left(\frac{S_k}{S_{k-1}}\right)^{\alpha}, e^g\right). \tag{1.40}$$

$$P \prod_{k=1}^{T} \max\left(\min\left(\left(\frac{S_k}{S_{k-1}}\right)^{\alpha}, e^c\right), e^g\right). \tag{1.41}$$

1.3.3 High-water mark option

Perhaps the most generous index crediting option to policyholders is the high-water mark method, for which interest credited is based on percentage change of the highest of index values on policy anniversaries from the original index value. Again assume that the product design offers some guarantee minimum maturity value G_T. The value of such a policy at maturity T is given by

$$\max\left(P\left(1 + \alpha\left(\frac{\max\{S_k : k = 1, \cdots, T\}}{S_0} - 1\right)\right), G_T\right).$$

With analogy to (1.37), the value of another version of high-water mark design is given by

$$\max\left(P\left(\frac{\max\{S_k : k = 1, \cdots, T\}}{S_0}\right)^{\alpha}, G_T\right). \tag{1.42}$$

As it shall be clear later, such an option is most easily valued in a continuous-time model where the analogue of (1.42) is given by

$$\max\left(P\left(\frac{\sup_{0\leq t\leq T}\{S_t\}}{S_0}\right)^{\alpha}, G_T\right). \tag{1.43}$$

1.4 Fundamental principles of equity-linked insurance

As alluded to earlier, the most fundamental principles for traditional insurance pricing and management are laws of large numbers, which dictate that the uncertainty in insurance liabilities can be reduced or eliminated by diversification among a large pool of policies. However, with the market innovation of equity-linked insurance, the basic assumptions of laws of large numbers, such as independence and identical distribution of policies, are under challenge.

Consider the insurance liability from the GMMB rider for example. Suppose that an insurer can sell the GMMB rider to n policyholders of the same age. Note that each policyholder may contribute different amount of initial premium due to varying needs for financial planning. We denote the initial premium from the i-th policyholder by $F_0^{(i)}$. It is reasonable to assume that policyholders make independent decisions on how much to invest and hence $\{F_0^{(1)}, \cdots, F_n^{(i)}\}$ are independent of each other. The minimum guarantee is typically proportional to initial premium. Here we set the guarantee to be $\gamma > 1$ times the initial premium, i.e. $G^{(i)} = \gamma F_0^{(i)}$. For $i = 1, 2, \cdots, n$,

$$X_i = e^{-rT}(G^{(i)} - F_T^{(i)})_+ I(T_x^{(i)} > T) = e^{-rT} F_0^{(i)}\left(\gamma - \frac{S_T}{S_0}e^{-mT}\right)_+ I(T_x^{(i)} > T).$$

A quick examination of the structure quickly reveals that the law of large numbers in (1.3) does not apply to the average liability even if the sample size n increases to infinity,

$$\frac{1}{n}\sum_{i=1}^{n} X_i \nrightarrow \mathbb{E}[X_i].$$

There are a number of ways in which equity-linked insurance models violate the assumptions of Theorem 1.1. First of all, it is immediately clear that random variables $\{X_1, \cdots, X_n\}$ are not mutually independent. As all contracts are linked to the same equity index or fund $\{S_t, t \geq 0\}$, all contracts require payments from the insurer when the equity index or fund underperforms over the term of the rider. Second, the mean of insurance liabilities $\mathbb{E}(X_1), \cdots, \mathbb{E}(X_n)$ may not necessarily be the same. A wealthy policyholder is more likely to make a larger purchase payment than an average policyholder. Due to varying contract sizes, we cannot expect the insurance claims from all contracts to have the same mean.

In other words, no matter how many contracts are included in the insurance pool, one can not completely eliminate the uncertainty with the financial risk arising from the equity-linking mechanism. Nonetheless, the insurer can expect to observe that there are roughly the percentage $_Tp_x$ of policyholders who survive to maturity. The insurer would have to pay the GMMB benefits to all survivors if $S_T/S_0e^{-mT} < \gamma$, or none of them otherwise. In contrast with the diversifiable mortality risk, we say the financial risk is *nondiversifiable* or *systematic*, as the insurer cannot eliminate uncertainty of claims through taking on more policies.

However, we could expect an extension of the law of large numbers. If all initial premiums are i.i.d. with the same mean $\overline{F}_0$ and the future lifetimes of all policyholders are mutually independent, then under some mild integrability condition we have

$$\frac{1}{n}\sum_{i=1}^{n}X_i \longrightarrow \overline{X} := e^{-rT}\overline{F}_0\left(\gamma - \frac{S_T}{S_0}e^{-mT}\right)_+ {}_Tp_x.$$

Observe that the limiting random variable contains no uncertainty with regard to mortality risk. Its randomness is driven by the performance of the underlying equity index only. We shall examine in greater details such laws of large numbers for the pricing and risk management of equity-linked insurance in Section 5.4.3.

1.5   Bibliographic notes

The first section in this chapter collects essential elements of material typically taught in courses for two related actuarial subjects, *the theory of interest* and *life contingent actuarial mathematics*. A classic treatise on the theory of interest is Kellison [70]. Pricing and reserving of traditional life insurance and annuities are covered in great details in well-known texts including Bowers et al. [11], Dickson, Hardy and Waters [33], etc.

The emergence of the topic on stochastic modeling of equity-linked insurance in the actuarial literature dates back to early years of market development with pioneering works including Brennan and Schwartz [15], Boyle and Schwartz [13], etc. A well-known text that popularized the subject is Hardy [61]. A comprehensive coverage of stochastic modeling techniques can be found in an encyclopedia-like publication by the International Actuarial Association [66] as well as a white paper by the Geneva Association [60]. An informative rich book on variable annuities for researchers and practitioners is Dellinger [24], which covers a wide range of practical issues. Readers can find more variety of product features for equity-indexed annuities in Tiong [99], Lin and Tan [75], Boyle and Tian [12], Gerber, Shiu and Yang [55], etc.

Most equity-linked insurance products are linked to certain equity indices or equity funds managed by third-party vendors. To protect their own proprietary trading strategies, third party vendors do not typically disclose the composition of indices or their investment portfolios to the insurer who underwrites the equity-linked insurance products. Since an insurer bears certain equity risk with the various types of investment guarantees, it is critical that the insurer develops investment portfolios to track the underlying equity index/fund. Tools developed to map between an underlying index/fund and insurer's investment portfolio are referred to *fund mapping* in the insurance industry. Note that most of models in this book are based on a single equity index/fund. Since this book is intended to serve as an introduction to the theoretical underpinning of equity-linked insurance, we choose not to dive into multi-dimensional stochastic models. Interested readers are referred to Fredricks, Ingalls and McAlister [50] for an introduction to fund mapping techniques.

1.6 Exercises

1. The portfolio percentile premium principle in (1.12) is based on the approximation of aggregate net liability by a normal distribution. In many cases, however, we can obtain exact distribution of L and subsequently compute the portfolio percentile premium from (1.10) without using the normal approximation. Suppose an insurer sells identical policies to $n = 100$ policyholders. Compute the premium with which the probability of the portfolio making a profit is $p = 90\%$, under the assumptions that all insurance claims $\{X_1, \cdots, X_n\}$ follow

   (a) Gamma distribution with the probability density function

   $$f(x) = \frac{(x/\theta)^\kappa e^{-x/\theta}}{x\Gamma(\kappa)}, \qquad x > 0,$$

   where $\kappa = 1$ and $\theta = 2$.

   (b) Compare the result from part (a) with that from the normal approximation.

   (c) Poisson distribution with the probability mass function

   $$p_k = \frac{e^{-\lambda}\lambda^k}{k!}, \qquad k = 0, 1, \cdots,$$

   where $\lambda = 1$.

   (d) Compare the result from part (c) with that from the normal approximation.

2. Google search "variable annuity prospectus" and look up the prospectus of an actual variable annuity product offered in the market. Identify the following items and create a fact sheet about the product.

   •Investment options;

   •Fee and charges;

   •Death benefit;

•Withdrawal options;

•Additional features and benefits.

Explain whether any of the guaranteed minimum benefits discussed in
Chapter 1 is present with the product under consideration. If so, create
a numerical example to show how each guaranteed minimum benefit or
their combination works.

2

Elementary Stochastic Calculus

In the first course of probability, we learned that a random variable is a variable that takes on a set of possible different values by chance. While this intuitive definition is sufficient for simple computations with stand-alone random variables, the analysis of stochastic processes, which are collections of random variables, requires a different way of thinking, which is to treat random variables as functions. Then we could use calculus of functions to compute interesting random variables arising from applications of stochastic processes.

2.1 Probability space

We use some elementary notations from set theory throughout this section. Readers who are not familiar with set theory are referred to Appendix C for a brief introduction.

Let us investigate the construction of a random variable. We often use random variables to model outcomes of phenomena in the physical world. Consider the set of all possible outcomes of the phenomenon under consideration, denoted by Ω. The set is often referred to as a *full set* or a *sample set*. If we model the outcome of a coin toss, then the sample set of outcomes can be written as $\Omega = \{H, T\}$ where H stands for the outcome that the coin lands on a head and T stands for the outcome that it lands on a tail. If we model the health status of an individual in an epidemic, then we can divide the whole population into three compartments $\Omega = \{$healthy, infected, deceased$\}$. We often use ω as a generic variable for an outcome.

Definition 2.1 (Information Set). Consider a collection of subsets of Ω, denoted by $\mathcal{F}$, that satisfies the following properties.

1. The empty set $\varnothing \in \mathcal{F}$;
2. (closed under complement) If $A \in \mathcal{F}$, then $A^c := \Omega \backslash A \in \mathcal{F}$;
3. (closed under union) If $A_1, A_2, \cdots \in \mathcal{F}$, then

$$\bigcup_{k=1}^{\infty} A_k \in \mathcal{F}.$$

The sets belonging to $\mathcal{F}$ are called *events* and $\mathcal{F}$ is called an *information set*[*].

Remark 2.2. If $A_1, A_2, \cdots \in \mathcal{F}$ then $A_1^c, A_2^c, \cdots \in \mathcal{F}$ by Property 2. Observe that according to Property 3,

$$\bigcap_{k=1}^{\infty} A_k = \left(\bigcup_{k=1}^{\infty} A_k^c \right)^c \in \mathcal{F}.$$

Hence we can replace Property 3 by the following alternative.

4. (closed under intersection) if $A_1, A_2, \cdots \in \mathcal{F}$, then

$$\bigcap_{k=1}^{\infty} A_k \in \mathcal{F}.$$

Example 2.3 (Borel sets). Here we illustrate the most commonly used information set in probability theory. Consider the collection of all closed intervals on the real line, i.e. $\mathbf{C} := \{[a, b] : a, b \in \mathbb{R}\}$. This set alone would not satisfy the requirements of Definition 2.1. For example, since $A := [0, 1]$ is in $\mathbf{C}$, one would expect A^c to be included as well according to Property 2. However, $A^c = (-\infty, 0) \cup (1, \infty)$ is clearly not a closed interval, which means that A^c is not in $\mathbf{C}$. Therefore, we need to put in additional sets such as A^c to fulfill the requirements of an information set. The minimum collection of all closed sets and additional sets necessary to meet all requirements is said to be the information set generated by $\mathbf{C}$. Due to its importance in applications, we give it a special name called Borel σ-algebra, denoted by $\mathbb{B}$. Such an information set is incredibly rich to include almost all sets one might encounter in applications, such as $(a, \infty), (-\infty, b), (a, b), [a, b), (a, b]$, etc. For instance, by Property 3,

$$(a, b) = \bigcup_{n=1}^{\infty} \left[a + \frac{1}{n}, b - \frac{1}{n} \right] \in \mathbb{B}.$$

All elements in $\mathbb{B}$ are called Borel sets. Sometimes, we consider the Borel σ-algebra generated by the collection of closed intervals between 0 and 1, or written as, $\{[a, b] : a, b \in [0, 1]\}$ and denote the information set by $\mathbb{B}_{[0,1]}$.   □

Example 2.4. Let us consider the simplest possible information set generated by outcomes of a coin toss. Since there are only two elements in the full set $\Omega = \{H, T\}$, the collection of sets that satisfy all requirements in Definition 2.1 is given by

$$\mathcal{F}_1 = \{\varnothing, \{H\}, \{T\}, \{H, T\}\}.$$

---

[*]In most mathematical books, this collection of sets is also called a σ-algebra. Since we do not actually make use of its algebraic structure, we use the term *information set* throughout the book for its convenient interpretation.

For instance, we first include all elements of Ω, i.e. $\{H\}, \{T\}$, in the collection $\mathcal{F}_1$. By definition the empty set $\varnothing$ must also be included. If we set $A_1 = \{H\}, A_2 = \{T\}, A_3 = A_4 = \cdots = \varnothing$, then the union $\bigcup_{k=1}^{\infty} A_k = \Omega = \{H, T\}$, which should also be included. With the four elements in $\mathcal{F}_1$, all requirements in Definition 2.1 are met. That completes the construction of the information set generated by outcomes of a coin toss. $\qquad\square$

Readers who are new to set theory should be reminded that the information set is a collection of sets. For example, while the set $\{H\}$ is an element of $\mathcal{F}_1$, $\{H\}$ is not considered a subset of $\mathcal{F}_1$, as any subset of $\mathcal{F}_1$ has to be a set of sets as well. We can say $\{\{H\}\} \subset \mathcal{F}_1$, where $\{\{H\}\}$ is the set of a single element $\{H\}$.

Example 2.5. Now let us move on to the information set generated by a sequence of coin tosses. Let Ω_n denote the set of all possible outcomes in the first n coin tosses. For example, $\Omega_2 = \{HH, HT, TH, TT\}$, and $\Omega_3 = \{HHH, HHT, HTH, HTT, THH, THT, TTH, TTT\}$. The construction of information sets based on these set of finite elements is similar to that in Example 2.4 and left as an exercise. We can write down the information set generated by the two first coin tosses, denoted by $\mathcal{F}_2$,

$$\mathcal{F}_2 = \Big\{\varnothing, \{HH, HT\}, \{TH, TT\}, \{HH, TH\}, \{HT, TT\}, \{HH\}, \{HT\}, \{TH\},$$
$$\{TT\}, \{HH\}^c, \{HT\}^c, \{TH\}^c, \{TT\}^c, \{HT, TH\}, \{HH, TT\}, \Omega_2\Big\}.$$

Suppose we have a magic machine that tosses out one coin at a time and never ends. Let Ω_∞ denote the set of all possible sequences of outcomes generated by this machine. Mathematically, we can write

$$\Omega_\infty = \{\omega_1\omega_2\omega_3\cdots : \omega_n = H \text{ or } T, n \in \mathbb{Z}\},$$

where ω_n represents the outcome of the n-th coin toss. In this case, there are infinitely many sets in the information set. For example, let A_k^H and A_k^T be the sets of sequences for which the k-th toss results in a head and a tail respectively, i.e.

$$A_k^H = \{\omega_1\omega_2\cdots\omega_{k-1}H\omega_{k+1}\cdots : \omega_n = H \text{ or } T, n \in \mathbb{Z}, n \neq k\};$$
$$A_k^T = \{\omega_1\omega_2\cdots\omega_{k-1}T\omega_{k+1}\cdots : \omega_n = H \text{ or } T, n \in \mathbb{Z}, n \neq k\}.$$

It is clear that they are complements of each other. If we include one, the other is also included in the information set. Observe that we can use these sets to represent information sets generated by any finite coin tosses. For example,

$$\mathcal{F}_1 = \{\varnothing, A_1^H, A_1^T, \Omega_\infty\}.$$

Observe that all possible outcomes of the first two coin tosses can be represented as intersections of these sets. For example, if the first coin lands on a head and the second on a tail, there are infinitely many sequences which would begin with these two outcomes and which can all be described by the set $A_1^H \cap A_2^T$, which we shall write as A^{HT} for short. If we include $A_1^H, A_1^T, A_2^H, A_2^T$, then all possible outcomes of two tosses, $A^{HH}, A^{HT}, A^{TH}, A^{TT}$, should also be included according to Property 4. According to Property 2 and 3, their complements and unions are also included. Therefore, we determine the information set by the first two coins,

$$\mathcal{F}_2 = \qquad \Big\{ \varnothing, A_1^H, A_1^T, A_2^H, A_2^T, A^{HH}, A^{HT}, A^{TH}, A^{TT},$$

$$(A^{HH})^c, (A^{HT})^c, (A^{TH})^c, (A^{TT})^c, A^{HT} \cup A^{TH}, A^{HH} \cup A^{TT}, \Omega_\infty \Big\}.$$

By continuing this process, we can determine information set $\mathcal{F}_n$ generated by any finite many coin tosses Ω_n. If we collect all elements in $\mathcal{F}_n$ for any $n \in \mathbb{N}$ and include all necessary elements to meet the requirements in Definition 2.1, we obtain a new information set, denoted by $\mathcal{F}$. Note that all events in $\mathcal{F}$ are subsets of outcomes of infinitely many coin tosses in Ω_∞. $\square$

Definition 2.6 (Filtration). An increasing sequence of information sets, i.e. $\{\mathcal{F}_1, \mathcal{F}_2, \cdots\}$, in which $\mathcal{F}_n \subset \mathcal{F}_m$ for any $1 \leq n \leq m$, is called a filtration.

In financial and insurance applications, a filtration often represents the evolution of information over time. Observe that the above-mentioned sequence of information sets generated by finitely many coin tosses is an example of a filtration. As we observe more coin tosses, we learn more and more about the evolution of history with regard to this coin.

Now that events and information sets are defined, we introduce a device to measure the chance of their occurrences.

Definition 2.7 (Probability measure). A probability measure is a set function $\mathbb{P} : \mathcal{F} \mapsto [0, 1]$ that satisfies

    1. $\mathbb{P}(\Omega) = 1$;

    2. For mutually disjoint events $A_1, A_2, \cdots \in \mathcal{F}$,

$$\mathbb{P}\left(\bigcup_{k=1}^{\infty} A_k \right) = \sum_{k=1}^{\infty} \mathbb{P}(A_k). \qquad (2.1)$$

The symbol $\mapsto$ means "maps to". The function $\mathbb{P}$ maps elements in $\mathcal{F}$, which are sets, to points in the interval $[0, 1]$. Note the probability measure $\mathbb{P}$ is by definition associated with a sample set Ω and an information set $\mathcal{F}$. Note that by

Property 1 the total probability mass of 1 is assigned to the sample set Ω. Since Ω contains all possible outcomes, we can distribute different probability mass to each element. In Example 2.8, we shall further elaborate on the distribution of probability masses. The collection of sets $\mathcal{F}$ specifies for what events the probability measure can actually measure. We call the triplet $(\Omega, \mathcal{F}, \mathbb{P})$ a probability space.

If the sample set Ω consists of only finitely many elements, then the information set $\mathcal{F}$ generated by these elements also has finitely many events. One of such examples is provided in Example 2.4. The probability measure can be easily defined by specifying the probability mass assigned to $\{\omega\}$ for each element ω in Ω. Then the probability of any other event in $\mathcal{F}$ can be determined by (2.1), as we shall see in the next example.

Example 2.8. Consider the simplest possible information set $\mathcal{F}_1$ generated by a single toss of a coin in Example 2.4. We want to define a probability measure on the set of all possible outcomes $\Omega_1 = \{H, T\}$ to reflect our understanding of the randomness associated with the coin. Say the probability of landing on a head is p and that of landing a tail is $q = 1 - p$. Then we can complete the construction of the probability space $(\Omega_1, \mathcal{F}_1, \mathbb{P})$ by setting *

$$\mathbb{P}(\varnothing) = 0, \mathbb{P}(H) = p, \mathbb{P}(T) = q, \mathbb{P}(\Omega_1) = 1. \qquad (2.2)$$

Keep in mind that the probability measure $\mathbb{P}$ specified by (2.2) is only well-defined on the information set containing as much information as $\mathcal{F}_1$. Note that $\mathcal{F}_1$ is a subset of $\mathcal{F}_2$, which is generated by the outcomes of two coin tosses in Example 2.4. That means the information in $\mathcal{F}_2$ is richer than that in $\mathcal{F}_1$. However, the probability measure $\mathbb{P}$ is not fine enough to measure sets of events such as A^{TH} unless we extend its definition to the larger information set $\mathcal{F}_2$ as shown in Example 2.5. □

Definition 2.9 (Independence). On a probability space $(\Omega, \mathcal{F}, \mathbb{P})$, two information sets $\mathcal{G}$ and $\mathcal{H}$, which are subsets of $\mathcal{F}$, are said to be independent if

$$\mathbb{P}(A \cap B) = \mathbb{P}(A)\mathbb{P}(B), \qquad \text{for all } A \in \mathcal{G}, B \in \mathcal{H}.$$

Consider a sequence of information sets $\mathcal{G}_1, \mathcal{G}_2, \cdots, \mathcal{G}_n$, which are all subsets of $\mathcal{F}$. They are said to be independent if for all $A_1 \in \mathcal{G}_1, A_2 \in \mathcal{G}_2, \cdots, A_n \in \mathcal{G}_n$

$$\mathbb{P}(A_1 \cap A_2 \cap \cdots \cap A_n) = \mathbb{P}(A_1)\mathbb{P}(A_2) \cdots \mathbb{P}(A_n).$$

---

*Technically we should write the probability as a function of a set such as $\mathbb{P}(\{H\}) = p$ and $\mathbb{P}(\{T\}) = q$. But we often omit the brackets for brevity.

Example 2.10. Let us define the probability space $(\Omega_2, \mathcal{F}_2, \mathbb{P})$ by setting

$$\mathbb{P}(\varnothing) = 0, \mathbb{P}(HH) = p^2, \mathbb{P}(HT) = pq, \mathbb{P}(TH) = pq, \mathbb{P}(TT) = q^2. \qquad (2.3)$$

Note that the information set $\mathcal{G}_2$ generated by the second coin toss is given by

$$\mathcal{G}_2 = \{\varnothing, \{HH, TH\}, \{HT, TT\}, \Omega_2\}.$$

Clearly both $\mathcal{F}_1$ and $\mathcal{G}_2$ are subsets of $\mathcal{F}_2$. Observe that the two information subsets are independent, i.e. the two coin tosses are independent, as we check through the definition. For example, let $A = \{HH, HT\} \in \mathcal{F}_1$ and $B = \{HT, TT\} \in \mathcal{G}_2$. It is clear that $A \cap B = \{HT\}$ and by definition of probability measure

$$
\begin{aligned}
\mathbb{P}(A) &= \mathbb{P}(HH) + \mathbb{P}(HT) = p^2 + pq = p, \\
\mathbb{P}(B) &= \mathbb{P}(HT) + \mathbb{P}(TT) = pq + q^2 = q.
\end{aligned}
$$

Observe that

$$\mathbb{P}(A \cap B) = \mathbb{P}(HT) = pq = \mathbb{P}(A)\mathbb{P}(B),$$

which meets the definition of the independence. Similarly, one can verify that $\mathbb{P}(A \cap B) = \mathbb{P}(A)\mathbb{P}(B)$ for all $A \in \mathcal{F}_1$ and $B \in \mathcal{G}_2$. $\qquad \square$

We have so far only seen examples of probability measure defined on a probability space where the sample set Ω only has finitely many outcomes. Complication arises when Ω has infinitely many outcomes. Unlike the case of Ω with finitely many outcomes, it is no longer sufficient to only define a probability measure by specifying probability mass to any set of the form $\{\omega\}$ in the case of Ω with infinitely many outcomes. For example, if a set A in $\mathcal{F}$ is uncountable, then it cannot be written as $A = \bigcup_{k=1}^{\infty}\{\omega_k\}$. Therefore, one cannot determine $\mathbb{P}(A)$, even if $\mathbb{P}(\{\omega\})$ is known for any $\omega \in \Omega$. Instead, we need to **define the probability measure on a collection of sets which can be used to generate the entire information set**, as shown in Examples 2.11 and 2.15.

Example 2.11. Consider the sample set of all outcomes of infinitely many coin tosses Ω_∞ in Example 2.5. Recall that $\mathcal{F}$ is generated by all sets in the information sets from finitely many coin tosses, $\mathcal{F}_1, \mathcal{F}_2, \cdots$. Therefore, we first define the probability measure $\mathbb{P}$ on sets in $\mathcal{F}_n$ for $n = 1, 2, \cdots$. The procedure is similar to that of finite coin tosses space in Examples 2.8 and 2.10. For sets in $\mathcal{F}_1$, we define

$$\mathbb{P}(\varnothing) = 0, \mathbb{P}(A^H) = p, \mathbb{P}(A^T) = q, \mathbb{P}(\Omega_\infty) = 1.$$

For sets in $\mathcal{F}_2$, we define

$$\mathbb{P}(A^{HH}) = p^2, \mathbb{P}(A^{HT}) = pq, \mathbb{P}(A^{TH}) = pq, \mathbb{P}(A^{TT}) = q^2.$$

Following the notation introduced in Example 2.5, we write $A^{\omega_1\omega_2\cdots\omega_n}$ as the set of coin toss sequences that begin $\omega_1\omega_2\cdots\omega_n$. Then for sets in $\mathcal{F}_n$, we always define

$$\mathbb{P}(A^{\omega_1\omega_2\cdots\omega_n}) = p^h q^{n-h}, \tag{2.4}$$

where h is the number of heads in $\omega_1\omega_2\cdots\omega_n$. For instance, consider any set in $\mathcal{F}_5$, say $A^{HटHTT}$, we would define $\mathbb{P}(HTHTT) = p^2 q^3$ according to (2.4).

Note that if we only observe the outcome of a single coin toss, say the k-th toss, then the information set generated by this particular phenomenon can be written as

$$\mathcal{G}_k = \{\varnothing, \Omega, A_k^H, A_k^T\}.$$

It is easy to show (Exercise 2.1.2) by the definition of probability measure that

$$\mathbb{P}(\varnothing) = 0, \mathbb{P}(A_k^H) = p, \mathbb{P}(A_k^T) = q, \mathbb{P}(\Omega) = 1. \tag{2.5}$$

Then one can show that $\mathcal{G}_k$ is independent of $\mathcal{G}_m$ if $k \neq m$. For example, for $A_2^H \in \mathcal{G}_2$ and $A_3^T \in \mathcal{G}_3$, observe that

$$\mathbb{P}(A_2^H \cap A_3^T) = \mathbb{P}(HHT) + \mathbb{P}(THT) = p^2 q + pq^2 = pq = \mathbb{P}(A_2^H)\mathbb{P}(A_3^T).$$

Hence, the coin tosses are independent of each other on the probability space $(\Omega, \mathcal{F}, \mathbb{P})$ with $\mathbb{P}$ defined in (2.4). $\qquad\square$

2.2 Random variable

As alluded to earlier, a random variable X is viewed as a real-valued function that maps every point ω in a sample set Ω to a point on the real line $\mathbb{R}$. We often use the symbol $X : \Omega \mapsto \mathbb{R}$ to indicate such a function. The sample set is often equipped with a probability space $(\Omega, \mathcal{F}, \mathbb{P})$.

Figure 2.1 provides a visualization of a random variable as a mapping from an abstract sample set Ω to the real line $\mathbb{R}$. For example, the point ω_1 is mapped to a number x_1 whereas points ω_2 and ω_3 are mapped to the same number x_2. We are often concerned with what subset in the abstract sample set is mapped to an interval on the real line. For example, all points in the square S are mapped to numbers in the first interval B. In mathematical terms, $B := \{x : x = X(\omega), \omega \in S\}$ is called the *image* of S whereas $S := \{\omega \in \Omega : X(\omega) \in B\}$ is considered the *pre-image* of B. If we know how the probability is assigned to S, then X transfers the same probability mass to B. Since we are interested in the probability distribution of outcomes of X, it is critical that the pre-image of intervals of the form B is measurable, i.e. the pre-images must be in $\mathcal{F}$.

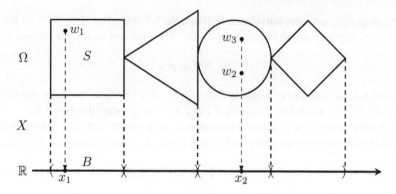

FIGURE 2.1: Random variable: a mapping from an abstract space to real line

---

Definition 2.12 (Random variable). Let $(\Omega, \mathcal{F}, \mathbb{P})$ be a probability space. The function $X : \Omega \mapsto \mathbb{R}$ is said to be a random variable if for every Borel set $B \in \mathbb{B}$,

$$\{X \in B\} := \{\omega \in \Omega : X(\omega) \in B\} \in \mathcal{F}.$$

Throughout the book, the symbol ":=" means "is defined by".

Since $\mathbb{B}$ is generated by sets of the form (a, b) and everything else arises from combinations of unions and complements, it suffices for us to verify the membership of $\{X \in (a, b)\}$ and everything else in $\mathcal{F}$ also follows from unions and complements.

Example 2.13. Consider $\Omega = [0, 1]$ and $\mathcal{F} = \mathbb{B}_{[0,1]}$. Define a function X such that

$$X(\omega) = 1 - \omega.$$

Let $B = (a, b) \subset [0, 1]$. It follows that $\{X \in B\} = \{\omega \in \Omega | X(\omega) \in (a, b)\} = (1 - b, 1 - a) \in \mathbb{B}_{[0,1]}$. Therefore, X is indeed a random variable.   □

Definition 2.14 (Distribution function). The distribution function F of a random variable X is defined by

$$F(x) := \mathbb{P}(X \leq x) = \mathbb{P}\left(\{\omega : X(\omega) \in (-\infty, x]\}\right), \qquad \text{for any } x \in \mathbb{R}.$$

If F is differentiable, i.e. the random variable X is continuous, then we often call its derivative $f(x) = F'(x)$ a probability density function.

Note that $(-\infty, x]$ is a Borel set, as defined in Example 2.3. By Definition 2.12, its pre-image $A := \{\omega : X(\omega) \leq x\} \in \mathcal{F}$ and thereby $\mathbb{P}(A)$ is well-defined. Therefore, knowing the definition of the probability measure $\mathbb{P}$, we should be able to infer the value of $\mathbb{P}(X \leq x)$.

The key point in the definition of a random variable as a real-valued function is that all the probabilities with regard to the "randomness" of X is really defined by a priori assignments of probability mass to subsets on Ω. In other words, the function X merely translates the assignment of probability on an abstract sample space to one on a real line.

Here we present two constructions of uniform random variable on different sample spaces. In other words, two mappings are constructed in such a way that probability distributions on distinct sample spaces are mapped to the same probability distribution on a real line.

Example 2.15 (Uniform random variable # 1). Consider the probability space in Example 2.13 with the probability measure defined by $\bar{\mathbb{P}}[a, b] = b - a$, where the probability given to an interval is the length of the interval. Then it is clear that, for any $x \in [0, 1]$, the distribution function of X is given by

$$
\begin{aligned}
F(x) &= \bar{\mathbb{P}}(\{\omega \in [0,1] : 1 - \omega \leq x\}) = \bar{\mathbb{P}}(\{\omega \in [0,1] | \omega \geq 1 - x\}) \\
&= \bar{\mathbb{P}}(\{\omega : \omega \in [1-x, 1]\}) = \bar{\mathbb{P}}([1-x, 1]) = x.
\end{aligned}
$$

Therefore, we know from elementary probability that X must be a uniform random variable on $[0, 1]$. $\qquad\square$

Example 2.16 (Uniform random variable # 2). We can also define a uniform random variable on the infinite coin toss space $(\Omega_\infty, \mathcal{F}, \mathbb{P})$. Define a sequence of random variables $\{Y_1, Y_2, \cdots\}$ for which

$$
Y_n(\omega) := \begin{cases} 1, & \text{if } \omega_n = H; \\ 0, & \text{if } \omega_n = T. \end{cases} \tag{2.6}
$$

Furthermore, we define a random variable

$$
X := \sum_{n=1}^{\infty} \frac{Y_n}{2^n}.
$$

Since the probability measure defined in Example 2.11 is constructed in such a way that coin tosses are mutually independent, we obtain that $\mathbb{P}(A_k^H) = \mathbb{P}(A_k^T) = 1/2$. In the following we show that X is also a uniform random variable. Suppose $x \in [0, 1]$. Then it can always be written in binary number $x = \sum_{n=1}^{\infty} y_n/2^n = 0.y_1 y_2 \cdots$ where $y_n = 0$ or 1. For example, 0.75 can be written as $1/2 + 1/4$ or 0.11 in binary system. Say, we want to sort three decimal numbers, $0.413, 0.276, 0.472$, from the smallest to the largest. We first consider the order of their first digits, identifying the smallest number 0.276. If two numbers have the same first digit, then we order them according to the second digit, leading to $0.276 < 0.413 < 0.472$. We apply the same idea to compare binary numbers by comparing one digit at a time. Hence,

$$
\begin{aligned}
F(x) &= \mathbb{P}(X \leq x) = \mathbb{P}\left(\sum_{n=1}^{\infty} \frac{Y_n}{2^n} \leq \sum_{n=1}^{\infty} \frac{y_n}{2^n}\right) \\
&= \mathbb{P}(\{Y_1 < y_1\}) + \mathbb{P}(\{Y_1 = y_1\} \cap \{Y_2 < y_2\}) + \cdots \\
&= \frac{y_1}{2} + \frac{y_2}{2^2} + \cdots = \sum_{n=1}^{\infty} \frac{y_n}{2^n} = x.
\end{aligned}
$$

Thus X defined in such a way is also a uniform random variable on $[0, 1]$. □

Readers may find it surprising that a uniform random variable is not uniquely defined, as we are often taught in elementary probability courses that any random variable is fully characterized by a single distribution function. This is not contradictory, because even though the two random variables are defined on different abstract spaces, $([0, 1], \mathbb{B}_{[0,1]}, \bar{\mathbb{P}})$ in Example 2.15 and $(\Omega_\infty, \mathcal{F}, \mathbb{P})$ in Example 2.16, they are both mapped via X to the same probability space $(\mathbb{R}, \mathbb{B}, \mathbb{M}_X)$ where $\mathbb{M}_X$ is a probability measure to be introduced. For computational purposes, we almost always only use the probability measure $\mathbb{M}_X$ and its distribution function F on the real line, which have a unique correspondence with the random variable.

Definition 2.17 (Induced measure). A probability measure $\mathbb{M}_X$ is induced by a random variable X, if for any given $B \in \mathbb{B}$,

$$
\mathbb{M}_X(B) := \mathbb{P}(\{\omega : X(\omega) \in B\}).
$$

Example 2.18. (1) The probability measure $\mathbb{P}$ defined on $\Omega = [0, 1]$ in Example 2.16 is in fact the measure induced by the random variable X defined on the infinite coin toss space Ω_∞ in Example 2.16.

(2) Consider the random variable Y_n defined on the infinite coin toss space Ω_∞. It is clear that the probability measure induced by Y_n only assigns a probability mass of p to 1 and a probability mass of q to 0, i.e. for any $B \in \mathbb{B}$,

$$
\mathbb{M}_{Y_n}(B) = pI(\{1\} \in B) + qI(\{0\} \in B),
$$

where the indicator function $I(A) = 1$ if A is true and $I(A) = 0$ if A is false. In general, for any discrete random variable X taking values $\{x_1, x_2, \cdots\}$, the induced measure can be written as

$$
\mathbb{M}_X(B) = \sum_{i=1}^{\infty} p_i I(\{x_i\} \in B), \qquad p_i = \mathbb{P}(X = x_i).
$$

In other words, the induced measure only assigns positive probability masses to discrete points.

Sometimes we wish to be more specific on the information set $\mathcal{F}$ with which the random variable is defined.

Definition 2.19 (Information from random variables). The information set generated by a random variable X is the collection of all sets of the form $\{\omega : X(\omega) \in B\}$ where $B \in \mathbb{B}$. We often denote such an information set by $\sigma(X)$. If there is a sequence of random variables $X_1, X_2, \cdots, X_n$, then the information set generated by the sequence is the smallest information set containing all sets of the form $\{\omega : X_k(\omega) \in B\}$ for $k = 1, 2, \cdots, n$. We denote such an information set by $\sigma(X_1, X_2, \cdots, X_n)$.

Example 2.20. Let Y_k be a random variable indicating the number of heads in the k-th coin toss, which is formulated in (2.6). It is clear that the information set generated by Y_k is given by $\sigma(Y_k) = \mathcal{G}_k$, which is defined in Example 2.11. Note that the information set generated by $\{Y_k : k = 1, 2, \cdots, n\}$ is equivalent to the information set generated by all first n coin tosses. Thus it is intuitive to understand that

$$\sigma(Y_1, Y_2, \cdots, Y_n) = \mathcal{F}_n.$$

However, one should note that $\mathcal{F}_n$ is a bigger collection than the simple collection of all elements in $\mathcal{G}_k$ where $k = 1, 2, \cdots, n$, i.e.

$$\bigcup_{k=1}^{n} \mathcal{G}_k \subset \mathcal{F}_n.$$

For example, the event $\{HHT\} = A_1^H \cap A_2^H \cap A_3^T$ is not a member of $\cup_{k=1}^{3} \mathcal{G}_k$.

2.3 Expectation

In an elementary probability course, we often define the expectation of a discrete random variable by

$$\mathbb{E}[X] = \sum x_k \mathbb{P}(X = x_k), \tag{2.7}$$

where the sum is taken over all possible values of X. The expectation of a continuous random variable is defined as

$$\mathbb{E}[X] = \int_{\mathbb{R}} x f(x)\,\mathrm{d}x. \tag{2.8}$$

While both continue to hold in more advanced setting here, we want to unify the two seemingly different formulas, which hinges on an abstract concept of Lebesgue integral.

Let us first review the concept of Riemann integral from ordinary calculus. Consider a positive continuous function defined on an interval $[a, b]$. We typically visualize the integral

$$I = \int_a^b f(x)\,\mathrm{d}x$$

as the area underneath the graph of the function f and above the interval $[a, b]$. To quantify the concept, we determine the integral by the following procedure.

1. Partition $[a, b]$ into subintervals $[x_0, x_1], [x_1, x_2], \cdots, [x_{n-1}, x_n]$ where the partition points $\Pi = \{x_0 = a, x_1, \cdots, x_n = b\}$ are ordered from the smallest to the largest. From this, we denote the length of the longest subinterval by $\| \Pi \| = \max(x_k - x_{k-1})$.

2. Approximate the area underneath the graph of f over every subinterval $[x_{k-1}, x_k]$ by the area of a rectangle of height $f(x_{k-1})$ based on each subinterval. Therefore, the integral I is approximated by

$$\mathrm{RS}_\Pi(f) = \sum_{k=1}^{n} f(x_{k-1})(x_k - x_{k-1}).$$

3. We can achieve better and better approximations by cutting $[a, b]$ into more subintervals of smaller lengths. Passing to the limit as the maximum length goes to zero, we obtain the Riemann integral

$$I = \lim_{\|\Pi\| \to 0} \mathrm{RS}_\Pi(f).$$

Before introducing the notion of Lebesgue integral, we need a standardized measurement of "length", known as Lebesgue measure, which is a special case of σ-finite measure.

Definition 2.21 (Partition). A *partition* of a set Ω is a collection of mutually disjoint nonempty subsets of Ω whose union is the full set Ω.

Definition 2.22 (σ-finite measure). Let $\mathcal{F}$ be an information set generated by sets in Ω. A set function $\mathbb{M} : \mathcal{F} \mapsto [-\infty, \infty]$ is called *countably additive* if for mutually disjoint events $A_1, A_2, \cdots \in \mathcal{F}$,

$$\mathbb{M}\left(\bigcup_{k=1}^{\infty} A_k\right) = \sum_{k=1}^{\infty} \mathbb{M}(A_k).$$

A countably additive non-negative set function $\mathbb{M} : \mathcal{F} \mapsto [0, \infty]$ is called a *measure*. In addition, *σ-finite measure* is a measure for which there exists a partition $\{A_1, A_2, \cdots\} \subset \mathcal{F}$ such that $\mathbb{M}(A_k) < \infty$ for all $k = 1, 2, \cdots$. The triplet $(\Omega, \mathcal{F}, \mathbb{M})$ is considered a *measure space*.

Example 2.23 (σ-finite measure). (1) By definition, a probability measure is countably additive. Since $\mathbb{P}(\Omega) = 1 < \infty$, it must be true that $\mathbb{P}(A_k) < \infty$ for A_k in any partition of Ω. Therefore, any probability measure $\mathbb{P}$ is a special case of σ-finite measure.

(2) Lebesgue measure, denoted by $\mathbb{L}$, measures length of sets on the real line $\mathbb{R}$. For example, given an interval $I = [a, b]$, $\mathbb{L}(I) = b - a$. Note that Lebesgue measure is clearly countably additive, as the length of the union of non-overlapping intervals is clearly the sum of lengths of all intervals. There also exists a partition for which all subsets have finite measures. For example, set $A_k = [k - 1, k) \cup [-k, -k + 1)$ for $k = 1, 2, \cdots$. Observe that $\bigcup_{k=1}^{\infty} A_k = \mathbb{R}$ and $\mathbb{L}(A_k) = [k - (k - 1)] + [(-k + 1) - (-k)] = 2 < \infty$ for all $k = 1, 2, \cdots$.

(3) We also commonly use a counting measure in daily life, which assigns 1 to each object. For example, if there are three quarters, two dimes, one nickel and one penny on the table, then the counting measure gives 3 to the set of quarters, 2 to the set of dimes, 1 to each of the set of nickels and the set of pennies. It is trivial that such a counting measure is also a σ-finite measure.

Whenever a Riemann integral exists, the corresponding Lebesgue integral has the exactly same value. In contrast with Riemann integral, we can determine Lebesgue integral by the following procedure.

1. Find the maximum M and minimum m of the function f over $[a, b]$. Partition $[m, M]$ into subintervals $[y_0, y_1], [y_1, y_2], \cdots, [y_{n-1}, y_n]$ where the partition points $\Pi = \{y_0 = m, y_1, \cdots, y_n = M\}$ are ordered from the smallest to the largest. We denote the length of the longest subinterval by $\| \Pi \| = \max(y_k - y_{k-1})$.

2. For each subinterval $[y_{k-1}, y_k]$, find the set $B_k = \{x \in \mathbb{R} | y_{k-1} \leq f(x) < y_k\}$, which is a union of many intervals on x-axis. Determine the Lebesgue measure of the set B_k, denoted by $\mathbb{L}(B_k)$, which is the total

length of all corresponding intervals on the x-axis. Then the integral I is approximated by

$$\text{LS}_\Pi(f) = \sum_{k=1}^{n} y_k \mathbb{L}(B_k).$$

3. We can achieve better approximations by cutting $[m, M]$ into more subintervals of smaller lengths. Passing to the limit as the maximum length goes to zero, we obtain the Lebesgue integral if

$$I = \lim_{\|\Pi\| \to 0} \text{LS}_\Pi(f).$$

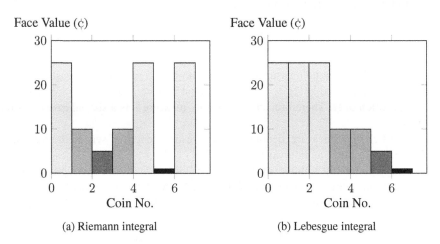

(a) Riemann integral   (b) Lebesgue integral

FIGURE 2.2: Coin counting using Riemann integral and Lebesgue integral

Example 2.24. The distinction between Riemann integral and Lebesgue integral can be easily explained by two methods of counting. Suppose your mother gives you a handful of coins to count for their total value. One way to do this is to line them up on a table and count from the left to right. As shown in Figure 2.2a, each bar represents the value of a coin. The total sum would be

$$25¢ + 10¢ + 5¢ + 10¢ + 25¢ + 1¢ + 25¢ = 101¢.$$

Alternatively, one could put all coins of the same kind in a pile, count all coins within each pile and add values of all piles. To demonstrate separating coins into four piles, we move all bars with the same height in Figure 2.2a together and rearrange them from the largest to the smallest in Figure 2.2b. The total sum can again be calculated by

$$25¢ \times 3 + 10¢ \times 2 + 5¢ \times 1 + 1¢ \times 1 = 101¢.$$

The first approach is in essence the way of Riemann integral whereas the second approach is in spirit the way of Lebesgue integral.

Note that Riemman integral is defined on a real line where partition points can be ordered from smallest to largest on a given interval. The notion of Riemann integral is difficult to use when it comes to defining an integral of a function defined on an abstract sample set Ω, which may not possess a particular order. Instead, we extend the notion of the Lebesgue integral to define the integral of any measurable function f, denoted by $\int_\Omega f(\omega) \, d\mathbb{M}(\omega)$, where the range of f $\mathbb{R}$ rather than its domain in the abstract space Ω is partitioned.

> **Definition 2.25.** Consider a measure space $(\Omega, \mathcal{F}, \mathbb{M})$. A function $f : \Omega \mapsto \mathbb{R}$ is called $(\mathcal{F}\text{-})measurable$ if $\{\omega : f(\omega) \in B\} \in \mathcal{F}$ for any Borel set B.

Observe that this definition of measurable function is no different from Definition 2.12, except that X is associated with a probability space whereas f is defined with a more general measure space.

We now generalize the three-step procedure of constructing a Lebesgue integral in the earlier discussion.

1. (Simple function) Suppose that $f(\omega)$ is a simple function, i.e. $f(\omega) = \sum_{i=1}^n a_i I_{A_i}(\omega)$ where $\{a_1, a_2, \cdots, a_n\}$ are distinct real numbers and $\{A_1, \cdots, A_n\}$ is a partition of Ω. Then

$$\int_\Omega f(\omega) \, d\mathbb{M}(\omega) = \sum_{i=1}^n a_i \mathbb{M}(A_i). \tag{2.9}$$

2. (Positive function) If $f(\omega) \geq 0$, then it can be approximated by simple functions. Then

$$\int_\Omega f(\omega) \, d\mathbb{M}(\omega) = \sup \left\{ \int_\Omega g(\omega) \, d\mathbb{M}(\omega) : \begin{array}{l} g \text{ is simple} \\ 0 \leq g(\omega) \leq f(\omega) \text{ for all } \omega \end{array} \right\},$$

where sup means supremum, the smallest real number greater than or equal to all elements in the set (See Appendix C.2).

3. (General) Any function can be broken down as the sum of two positive functions $f_+(\omega) = \max\{f(\omega), 0\}$ and $f_-(\omega) = -\min\{f(\omega), 0\}$. Then

$$\int_\Omega f(\omega) \, d\mathbb{M}(\omega) = \int_\Omega f_+(\omega) \, d\mathbb{M}(\omega) - \int_\Omega f_-(\omega) \, d\mathbb{M}(\omega),$$

provided that both integrals on the right exist.

In the case of Lebesgue measure $\mathbb{L}$ defined on $\mathbb{R}$, we often do not distinguish the symbol of Lebesgue integral (LHS) and that of Riemman integral (RHS)

$$\int_\mathbb{R} f(\omega) \, d\mathbb{L}(\omega) = \int_\mathbb{R} f(\omega) \, d\omega,$$

due to the fact that Lebesgue integral agrees with Riemann integral whenever the latter exists. Since any probability measure $\mathbb{P}$ is a special case of a σ-finite measure, we can use the three-step procedure above to define an expectation

$$\mathbb{E}[X] := \int_\Omega X(\omega)\, d\mathbb{P}(\omega). \tag{2.10}$$

If the integral in (2.10) exists, we say that the random variable X is integrable.

2.3.1   Discrete random variable

As we shall see in the next two subsections, both familiar formulas (2.7) and (2.8) are indeed examples of the general definition of expectation in (2.10).

Example 2.26. When computing an expectation, it is often more convenient to treat it as an integral with respect to the induced measure on the real line, rather than an integral with respect to the original probability measure on an abstract space. One can apply the three-step procedure to show that

$$\mathbb{E}[X] = \int_\Omega X(\omega)\, d\mathbb{P}(\omega) = \int_\mathbb{R} x\, d\mathbb{M}_X(x).$$

For example, consider a piecewise defined function $X(\omega) = \sum x_i I_{A_i}(\omega)$ where $\{A_1, A_2, \cdots\}$ is a partition of the sample space Ω. For convenience, we often write $I_{A_i}(\omega)$ for the indicator function $I(\omega \in A_i)$. Then

$$\begin{aligned}
\int_\Omega X(\omega)\, d\mathbb{P}(\omega) &= \sum x_i \mathbb{P}(A_i) = \sum x_i \mathbb{P}(\{\omega : X(\omega) = x_i\}) \\
&= \sum x_i \mathbb{M}_X(\{x_i\}) = \int_\mathbb{R} x\, d\mathbb{M}_X(x),
\end{aligned}$$

where the proof of last equality is left as Exercise 2.3.1.

Example 2.27 (Discrete random variable). Since a discrete random variable X takes only countably many values, it can always be written as

$$X(\omega) = \sum_{i=1}^\infty x_i I_{A_i}(\omega), \text{ for some } A_i, \bigcup_{i=1}^\infty A_i = \Omega,$$

which can be approximated by a sequence of simple functions. Passing to the limit on both sides[*] of (2.9), we obtain the familiar formula for the expectation of a discrete random variable

$$\mathbb{E}[X] = \sum_{i=1}^\infty x_i \mathbb{P}(A_i) = \sum_{i=1}^\infty x_i \mathbb{P}(X = x_i),$$

where the event $X = x_i$ is interpreted as the set $\{\omega : X(\omega) = x_i\} = A_i$.

---

[*]The existence of the limit is a result of Monotone Convergence Theorem.

2.3.2 Continuous random variable

Definition 2.28. We say $\mathbb{M}_1$ is absolutely continuous with respect to $\mathbb{M}_2$ if $\mathbb{M}_1(A) = 0$ for all $A \in \mathcal{F}$ such that $\mathbb{M}_2(A) = 0$.

Example 2.29 (Beta random variable). Let $\Omega = [0, 1]$ and define the probability measure

$$\tilde{\mathbb{P}}([a, b]) = \frac{b^{n+1} - a^{n+1}}{n} = \frac{(b-a)(b^n + b^{n-1}a + \cdots + ba^{n-1} + a^n)}{n}.$$

Consider the probability measure $\mathbb{P}$ defined by $\mathbb{P}([a, b]) = b - a$. It can be shown that $\tilde{\mathbb{P}}(A) = 0$ whenever $\mathbb{P}(A) = 0$. Therefore, by Definition 2.28, $\tilde{\mathbb{P}}$ is absolutely continuous with respect to $\mathbb{P}$.

We state without a proof a well-known result that connects the two measures, which is the last piece to connect the general formula (2.10) and its special case for a continuous random variable.

Theorem 2.30 (Radon-Nikodym). *Let $\mathbb{M}_1$ and $\mathbb{M}_2$ be two σ-finite measures such that $\mathbb{M}_1$ is absolutely continuous with respect to $\mathbb{M}_2$. Then there exists a function $f : \Omega \mapsto [0, \infty]$ such that*

$$\mathbb{M}_1(A) = \int_A f(\omega) \, d\mathbb{M}_2(\omega), \text{ for all } A \in \mathcal{F}.$$

The function f is known as the Radon-Nikodym derivative and often denoted by $d\mathbb{M}_1 / d\mathbb{M}_2$.

Example 2.31 (Beta random variable). Recall Example 2.29 in which $\Omega = [0, 1]$, $\mathbb{P}$ is the Lebesgue measure and $\tilde{\mathbb{P}}$ is absolutely continuous with respect to $\mathbb{P}$. Observe that

$$\tilde{\mathbb{P}}([a, b]) = \int_a^b \omega^n \, d\omega = \int_a^b \omega^n \, d\mathbb{P}(\omega),$$

where the last equality follows from the fact that $\mathbb{P}$ is a Lebesgue measure on $[0, 1]$. Therefore, $f(\omega) = \omega^n$ is the Radon-Nikodym derivative.

Example 2.32 (Continuous random variable). The probability measure induced by a continuous random variable $\mathbb{M}_X$ is always absolutely continuous with respect to the

Lebesgue measure $\mathbb{L}$. According to the Radon-Nikodym theorem, there must exists a function f such that

$$\mathbb{M}_X(A) = \int_A f(\omega)\,\mathrm{d}\mathbb{L}(\omega) = \int_A f(x)\,\mathrm{d}x.$$

Therefore,

$$\mathbb{E}[X] = \int_\Omega X(\omega)\,\mathrm{d}\mathbb{P}(\omega) = \int_\mathbb{R} x\,\mathrm{d}\mathbb{M}_X(x) = \int_\mathbb{R} xf(x)\,\mathrm{d}x,$$

which produces the familiar formula for the expectation of a continuous random variable. In particular, the Radon-Nikodym derivative f is also known as the probability density function.

Now we conclude the section by pointing out that the Lebesgue integral definition of expectation enables us to unify both formulas (2.7) and (2.8).

2.4   Stochastic process and sample path

Definition 2.33 (Stochastic process). Suppose that I is a set on $[0, \infty)$. A stochastic process is a collection of random variables $\{X_t : t \in I\}$, all of which are defined on a probability space $(\Omega, \mathcal{F}, \mathbb{P})$.

Stochastic processes are often used to model the evolution of a physical or economic phenomenon over time. In Definition 2.33, the index t admits the convenient interpretation as time and X_t is viewed as an observation of the process at time t. If I is a discrete set, then the process is called a *discrete-time process*. If I is an interval being either open, closed or half-closed, and either finite or infinite in length, the process is referred as a *continuous-time process*. A visual illustration of a discrete-time process is to be shown in Figure 2.3 of Example 2.35 whereas a continuous-time process will be pictured in Figure 2.9 in Section 2.9.

Example 2.34 (Markov chain). In many applications, the phenomenon to be modeled is characterized by a sequence of categorical variables. For example, the health status of an insured may include "healthy", "sick", "recovered", or even "deceased", which are called *states*. We can number them by $1, 2, 3, 4$. As time elapses, her health status moves through these states randomly from year to year, which forms a stochastic process.

In general, we consider a sequence of these categorical variables, denoted by

$\{X_1, X_2, \cdots\}$, taking values from a finite set E. We assume that whenever the process at time k, X_k, is in state $i \in E$ there is a fixed probability, $p_{ij} \in [0, 1]$, that the process at the next period, X_{k+1}, is in state j, i.e.

$$\mathbb{P}(X_{k+1} = j | X_k = i, X_{k-1} = i_{k-1}, X_{k-2} = i_{k-2}, \cdots, X_0 = i_0) = p_{ij},$$

for all states $i, j, i_{k-1}, i_{k-2}, \cdots, i_0 \in E$ and $k \geq 0$. In other words, given the history of the process up to the present, the conditional distribution of future state X_{k+1} only depends on the present state X_k, not on its past states $\{X_{k-1}, \cdots, X_0\}$. Such a stochastic process is known as a *Markov chain*. In the earlier case of the health status of an insured, $E = \{1, 2, 3, 4\}$ and the Markov chain is determined by defining the 16 probability masses $\{p_{11}, p_{12}, \cdots, p_{43}, p_{44}\}$.

Here we consider a special case of Markov chain, known as a random walk, which is of particular interest in this chapter, as it can be used to construct a continuous-time process in Section 2.7.

Example 2.35. (Random walk) To construct a random walk, we repeatedly toss a fair coin independently of its past. In other words, we consider the probability space $(\Omega_\infty, \mathcal{F}, \mathbb{P})$ defined in Examples 2.5 and 2.11. A random walk describes the position of an object after a succession of random steps. In each step, the object either moves up by one unit or down by one unit. To define the random walk on the infinite coin tosses space, the direction of movement is governed by the binary outcomes of coin tosses. Define a sequence of new random variables as follows. For $k = 1, 2, \cdots$, let X_k represent a change of position at time k,

$$X_k = \begin{cases} 1, & \text{if } \omega_k = H, \\ -1, & \text{if } \omega_k = T. \end{cases} \tag{2.11}$$

Suppose the random walk starts off at 0. Let M_n represent the position of the object at time n, which is the sum of position changes since time 0,

$$M_k = \sum_{j=1}^{k} X_j, \qquad k = 1, 2, \ldots \tag{2.12}$$

Let $M_0 = 0$. Then the collection of random variables $\{M_k, k = 0, 1, 2, \ldots\}$ is called a *random walk*. If $\mathbb{P}(H) = \mathbb{P}(T) = 1/2$, then the random walk is considered symmetric. If we capture the outcomes of a particular sequence of coin tosses, say $\omega = HTHHT \ldots$, we can determine the trajectory of the random walk $\{M_0 = 0, M_1 = 1, M_2 = 0, M_3 = 1, M_4 = 2, M_5 = 1, \ldots\}$.

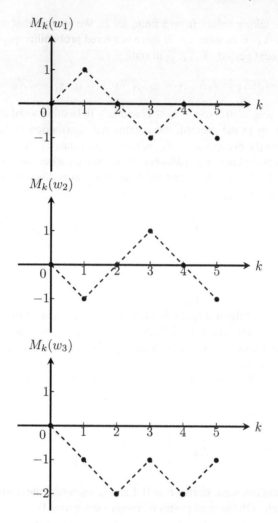

FIGURE 2.3: Sample paths of random walk

When we visualize the notion of a stochastic process, the best we can do is to picture a limited number of possible trajectories, which are often called *sample paths*.
For example, Figure 2.3 shows the first five steps for three different sample paths
of a symmetric random walk, which correspond to three sequences of coin tosses,
namely, $\omega_1 = HTTHT, \omega_2 = THHTT, \omega_3 = TTHTH$. To describe the randomness of the process, we have to specify the probability with which each path may
occur. If we can only observe the symmetric random walk up to five steps, then there
are only $2^5 = 32$ distinguishable paths, each of which has the equal probability $1/32$
of occurrence. Not only is this a valid approach for visualization, it is also a useful
way of characterizing a stochastic process. Again, using the example of a random
walk, instead of defining the process as the partial sum of the sequence of indepen-

dent variables in (2.12), we can also view the process $\{M_k, k = 0, 1, 2, \cdots, 5\}$ as a mapping from the sample space Ω to a set of sequences of numbers (or equivalently a set of "discrete functions")

$$M.(\omega) = \begin{cases} 0,1,0,1,2,1 & \omega = HTTHT, \\ 0,-1,0,1,0,-1 & \omega = THHTT, \\ 0,-1,-2,-1,-2,-1 & \omega = TTHTH, \\ \vdots & \vdots \end{cases}$$

Instead of defining all random variables $X_1, \cdots, X_5$, we could simply describe the "randomness" of the stochastic process $\{M_k, k = 0, 1, 2, \cdots, 5\}$ by assigning the probability mass to the sample space Ω_5 or equivalently assigning the probability mass to a set of sequences of numbers ("discrete functions").

In general, a stochastic process can be viewed as a mapping from a sample space $(\Omega, \mathcal{F}, \mathbb{P})$ to a space of functions (sample paths). We often speak of the "variation" of a process, which refers to the behavioral properties of the sample paths. Hence, here we introduce different notations of variations for functions.

Total variation

In simple words, the total variation of a function over an interval is the sum of the absolute values of all vertical changes of its graph. For example, consider the function shown in Figure 2.4(a). We wish to compute the total amount of up and down oscillation undergone by this function between 0 and T, with the down moves adding to the up moves. Denote the total variation by $\langle f \rangle_T$. For the function f in Figure 2.4(a), the total variation is given by

$$\langle f \rangle_T = |f(t_1) - f(t_0)| + |f(t_2) - f(t_1)| + |f(t_3) - f(t_2)|. \tag{2.13}$$

In other words, we first look at a fixed partition by points $\{t_0, t_1, t_2, t_3\}$ and add the absolute values of changes of the function over all subintervals. In general, a fixed partition is not sufficient to capture all variations. For example, compare functions f_1 and f_2 in Figures 2.4(a) and 2.4(b). Since the graph of f_2 tends to shift more than that of f_1, then f_2 has more variations than f_1. However, if we were to use the formula in (2.13) with a fixed partition, the two functions would have the same measurement of total variation, which is incorrect. Therefore, the definition of the total variation cannot be based on a fixed partition but rather a dynamic process of searching for partitions that capture all ups and downs.

Definition 2.36. Consider a *partition* of $[0, T]$, denoted by Π, which is a collection of intervals,

$$\Pi := \{[t_0, t_1), [t_1, t_2), \cdots, [t_{n-1}, t_n]\}, \tag{2.14}$$

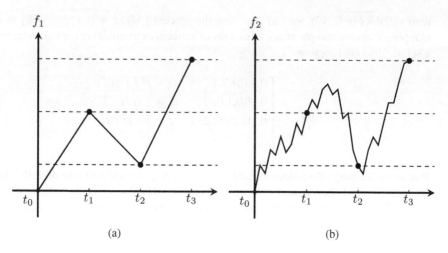

FIGURE 2.4: Motivation of total variation

where end points are given by a set of (not necessarily equally spaced) points

$$0 = t_0 < t_1 < \ldots < t_n = T.$$

The maximum step size of the partition is denoted $\|\Pi\| = \max_{j=0,\ldots,n-1}(t_{j+1} - t_j)$. The total variation of the function f from 0 to T is defined by

$$\langle f \rangle_T = \lim_{\|\Pi\| \to 0} \sum_{j=0}^{n-1} |f(t_{j+1}) - f(t_j)|. \tag{2.15}$$

The positive variation of the function from 0 to T is defined by

$$\langle f \rangle_T^+ = \lim_{\|\Pi\| \to 0} \sum_{j=0}^{n-1} (f(t_{j+1}) - f(t_j))_+. \tag{2.16}$$

While (2.15) is a precise definition, it is inconvenient to compute with a limit. In some cases, the total variation can be calculated using a simple formula. If the function f has a continuous derivative everywhere, then we know from the Mean Value Theorem of Calculus that

$$f(t_{j+1}) - f(t_j) = f'(t_j^*)(t_{j+1} - t_j),$$

for some point $t_j^* \in [t_j, t_{j+1}]$. Therefore, it follows immediately that

$$\langle f \rangle_T = \lim_{\|\Pi\| \to 0} \sum_{j=0}^{n-1} |f'(t_j^*)|(t_{j+1} - t_j) = \int_0^T |f'(t)|\, \mathrm{d}t. \tag{2.17}$$

Similarly, one can determine its positive variation by

$$\langle f \rangle_T = \lim_{\|\Pi\| \to 0} \sum_{j=0}^{n-1} f'(t_j^*))_+(t_{j+1} - t_j) = \int_0^T (f'(t))_+ \, dt.$$

These formulas can be extended to a function with continuous derivatives everywhere on an interval except for finite many points. Then variations of the function on the interval is the sum of variations of the function on all subintervals separated by the points. See the following example.

Example 2.37. Compute the total variation of the triangle function $f(t) = 1 - |t - 1|$ for $0 \leq t \leq 2$. It is easy to observe from its picture that the total amount of up and down movements between 0 and 2 must be 2. We can also verify this using (2.17). Observe that $f'(t) = 1$ for $0 \leq t \leq 1$ and $f'(t) = -1$ for $1 \leq t \leq 2$. Hence

$$\langle f \rangle_2 = \int_0^1 |f'(t)| \, dt + \int_1^2 |f'(t)| \, dt = \int_0^1 1 \, dt + \int_1^2 1 \, dt = 2.$$

Similarly, one can show that $\langle f \rangle_2^+ = 1$. In general, for any $T \in [0, 2]$,

$$\langle f \rangle_T = \int_0^{\min\{1,T\}} |f'(t)| \, dt + \int_{\min\{1,T\}}^T |f'(t)| \, dt = \int_0^T 1 \, dt = T,$$

and similarly $\langle f \rangle_T^+ = \min\{T, 1\}$.

Although most functions we learned in ordinary calculus have finite first-order variations, i.e. $\langle f \rangle_T < \infty$ for any $T \in \mathbb{R}$, there are also many functions that do not fit into this category. Here is an example of a function which wobbles too much near zero.

Example 2.38. Consider $f : [0, 1] \to \mathbb{R}$ such that $f(0) = 0$ and

$$f\left(\frac{1}{n}\right) = \frac{(-1)^n}{n}, \qquad n = 1, 2, \cdots.$$

Between any two points $1/n$ and $1/(n-1)$, the function interpolates linearly. As shown in Figure 2.5, $f(1) = -1$, $f(1/2) = 1/2$, $f(1/3) = -1/3$, $\cdots$ and the graph of $f(x)$ for non-integer x is defined by a straight line connecting its values at neighboring integer points. Show that $\langle f \rangle_1 = \infty$.
Solution: Observe that

$$[0, 1] = \bigcup_{n=1}^{\infty} \left[\frac{1}{n+1}, \frac{1}{n}\right],$$

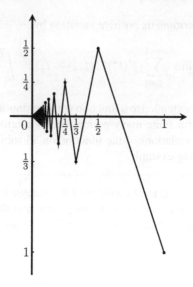

FIGURE 2.5: Plot of a function with infinite total variation

and f has continuous derivatives everywhere on each interval $(1/(n+1), 1/n)$. Hence, it follows immediately from the definition that

$$\langle f \rangle_1 = \lim_{n \to \infty} \sum_{i=1}^{n} \int_{\frac{1}{i+1}}^{\frac{1}{i}} |f'(x)| \, dx$$

Note that $|f'(x)| = \frac{(1/i) + 1/(i+1)}{(1/i) - 1/(i+1)}$. Thus,

$$\langle f \rangle_1 = \lim_{n \to \infty} \sum_{i=1}^{n} \left(\frac{1}{i} + \frac{1}{i+1} \right) = 2 \lim_{n \to \infty} \sum_{i=1}^{n} \frac{1}{i} - 1.$$

Since the harmonic series is divergent, we obtain that $\langle f \rangle_1 = \infty$.

Quadratic variation

As a measurement of "variations", the total variation is not informative when it comes to functions of erratic behavior such as the one in Example 2.38. If we think of time as the independent variable, then these functions generally fluctuate "too fast" to have a finite total variation. Keep in mind that the limit in (2.17) is in essence an infinite sum of infinitely small amounts of changes. If the sum of absolute values explodes, one may hope for a more meaningful measurement by squaring the changes. Indeed this is the notion of quadratic variation.

Definition 2.39 (Quadratic variation). Let $f(t)$ be a function defined for $0 \leq t \leq T$. The *quadratic variation* of f up to time T is

$$[f, f]_T = \lim_{\|\Pi\| \to 0} \sum_{j=0}^{n-1} [f(t_{j+1}) - f(t_j)]^2, \tag{2.18}$$

where the partition Π is defined in (2.14).

Example 2.40. If a function f has a continuous derivative everywhere on $[0, T]$, then $[f, f]_T = 0$.

Proof. Since f is continuously differentiable, the Mean Value Theorem tells us that

$$\sum_{j=0}^{n-1} [f(t_{j+1}) - f(t_j)]^2 = \sum_{j=0}^{n-1} |f'(t_j^*)|^2 (t_{j+1} - t_j)^2 \leq \|\Pi\| \cdot \sum_{j=0}^{n-1} |f'(t_j^*)|^2 (t_{j+1} - t_j),$$

and thus

$$[f, f]_T \leq \lim_{\|\Pi\| \to 0} \left[\|\Pi\| \cdot \sum_{j=0}^{n-1} |f'(t_j^*)|^2 (t_{j+1} - t_j) \right]$$

$$= \lim_{\|\Pi\| \to 0} \|\Pi\| \cdot \lim_{\|\Pi\| \to 0} \sum_{j=0}^{n-1} |f'(t_j^*)|^2 (t_{j+1} - t_j)$$

$$= \lim_{\|\Pi\| \to 0} \|\Pi\| \cdot \int_0^T |f'(t)|^2 dt = 0.$$

In the last step, note that $f'(t)$ is continuous and hence $\int_0^T |f'(t)|^2 dt$ is finite. $\square$

An extension of the concept of quadratic variation is the cross-variation.

Definition 2.41 (Cross variation). Let $f(t)$ and $g(t)$ be two functions defined for $0 \leq t \leq T$. The *cross variation* of f and g up to time T is

$$[f, g]_T = \lim_{\|\Pi\| \to 0} \sum_{j=0}^{n-1} [f(t_{j+1}) - f(t_j)][g(t_{j+1}) - g(t_j)], \tag{2.19}$$

where the partition Π is defined in (2.14).

If f is continuously differentiable and g is continuous for $0 \le t \le T$, then $[f, g]_T = 0$. The proof is left to Exercise 2.4.3.

2.5 Conditional expectation

Conditional expectation is an important concept that arises in financial and insurance applications, although not often explicitly stated. Here is an example how conditional expectation is used in pricing an insurance policy.

Suppose there are 200 men and 100 women among an insurer's policyholders. It is known that 70 of the men are smokers and 50 of the women are smokers. If a policyholder is chosen at random, note that the probability that the person is a smoker is in fact a random variable. This probability is known as a *conditional probability*. To be precise, we are considering a probability model defined on a sample space $\Omega = \{\male\approx, \male\oslash, \female\approx, \female\oslash\}$ where $\male$, $\female$ represent male and female, $\approx$, $\oslash$ represent smoker and nonsmoker. Since we have exact data on each combination of gender and smoking habit, the full information set would be[*]

$$
\mathcal{F} = \Big\{\varnothing, \Omega, \male\approx, \male\oslash, \female\approx, \female\oslash, \male, \female, \oslash, \approx,
$$
$$
\male\approx \cup \female\oslash, \male\oslash \cup \female\approx, \male\approx^c, \male\oslash^c, \female\approx^c, \female\oslash^c\Big\}
$$

The probability $\mathbb{P}$ is defined naturally by their proportions. However, if a policyholder is chosen at random, the insurer could easily identify the person's gender but would not know without any investigation whether he/she is a smoker. Hence the information set prior to investigation is given by

$$
\mathcal{G} = \{\varnothing, \Omega, \male, \female\}.
$$

What is the likelihood that a policyholder is a smoker? If the person is female, then the chance is $50/100 = 0.5$. If the person is male, then the chance is $70/200 = 0.35$. However, if we only have the information that the person is a policyholder, then this question is best answered by the probability of being a smoker given the information set $\mathcal{G}$,

$$
\mathbb{P}(\approx|\mathcal{G})(\omega) = (0.35)I_{\male}(\omega) + (0.50)I_{\female}(\omega), \qquad \text{for } \omega \in \Omega.
$$

In order to provide a health insurance coverage, the insurer estimates that the cost of the coverage is given in Table 2.1.

Let's introduce the cost of insurance as a random variable to be defined on $(\Omega, \mathcal{G}, \mathbb{P})$. Then it follows immediately that

$$
X(\omega) = 100I_{\male\approx}(\omega) + 80I_{\male\oslash}(\omega) + 90I_{\female\approx}(\omega) + 60I_{\female\oslash}(\omega).
$$

---

[*]For brevity, we use symbols of elements to denote sets with a slight abuse of notation. For example, $\male\oslash$ in $\mathcal{F}$ refers to the set $\{\male\oslash\}$ and $\male$ in $\mathcal{F}$ represents the set $\{\male\oslash, \male\approx\}$.

	Female	Male
Smoker	90	100
Nonsmoker	60	80

TABLE 2.1: Cost of coverage per person

Suppose the insurer is allowed to charge differential premiums on males and females given the information set $\mathcal{G}$. How should the insurer determine its premium, denoted by $P(\omega)$, based on the equivalence principle?

Let p_1, p_2 be differential premiums for males and for females respectively.

$$P(\omega) \;=\; p_1 I_{\sigma}(\omega) + p_2 I_{\varphi}(\omega)$$

It would only make sense to charge the average cost given that the person is a male.

$$
\begin{aligned}
p_1 &\;=\; \mathbb{E}\left[X|\sigma\right] = \frac{\mathbb{E}\left[X\mathbb{I}_{\sigma}\right]}{\mathbb{P}(\sigma)} = X(\sigma\approx)\frac{\mathbb{P}(\sigma\approx)}{\mathbb{P}(\sigma)} + X(\sigma\oslash)\frac{\mathbb{P}(\sigma\approx)}{\mathbb{P}(\sigma)} \\
&\;=\; 100 \times 0.35 + 80 \times 0.65 = 87.
\end{aligned}
$$

Similarly, we can show that $p_2 = \mathbb{E}\left[X|\varphi\right] = 75$. Putting both pieces together, we obtain the insurance premium

$$P(\omega) = 87 I_{\sigma}(\omega) + 75 I_{\varphi}(\omega).$$

In practice, we would always present insurance premiums in the form of a table. Nonetheless, the insurance premium P of such a form is in fact known mathematically as the conditional expectation of insurance cost given the information set, often denoted by $\mathbb{E}[X|\mathcal{G}]$. As this example illustrates, conditional expectation can be viewed as a coarse estimate of a random variable given limited information. A visualization of random variable and its conditional expectation is shown in Figure 2.6. Here we present a general definition of conditional expectation. The verification of P being a conditional expectation will be left as Exercise 2.5.2.

Definition 2.42 (Conditional expectation). Let X be a random variable defined on $(\Omega, \mathcal{F}, \mathbb{P})$ and $\mathcal{G}$ be a subset of $\mathcal{F}$. The *conditional expectation* of X given $\mathcal{G}$ is a random variable P that satisfies the following properties:

1. The random variable P is $\mathcal{G}$-measurable.

2. $\int_A P(\omega)\, d\mathbb{P}(\omega) = \int_A X(\omega)\, d\mathbb{P}(\omega)$ for all $A \in \mathcal{F}$.

To emphasize its dependency on $\mathcal{G}$, we often write P as $\mathbb{E}[X|\mathcal{G}]$. For any $A \in \mathcal{F}$, the *conditional probability* given $\mathcal{G}$ denoted by $\mathbb{P}(A|\mathcal{G})$ is a special case of $\mathbb{E}[X|\mathcal{G}]$ where $X = I_A$.

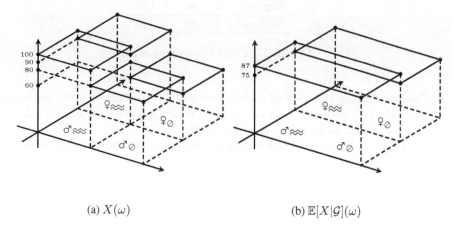

(a) $X(\omega)$ (b) $\mathbb{E}[X|\mathcal{G}](\omega)$

FIGURE 2.6: Visualization of random variable and its conditional expectation

As the second property in the definition involves expectations, it is implicitly assumed that both X and P are integrable random variables. Therefore, we implicitly assume throughout the lecture note that a random variable is integrable whenever we speak of its conditional expectation. The first property guarantees that the random variable P is well-defined on the probability space $(\Omega, \mathcal{G}, \mathbb{P})$, according to remarks immediately following Definition 2.14. The fact that P is based on the information set $\mathcal{G}$, which is a subset of the information set $\mathcal{F}$ on which X is based, implies that the loss of information makes P a coarse estimate of X. The second property ensures that P has the same average as X on each event in the information set $\mathcal{G}$.

Example 2.43 (Conditional expectation given an information set with finite events). Suppose that there is a partition of the sample space for which all sets have positive probabilities, i.e.

$$\Omega = \bigcup_{k=1}^{n} B_k, \qquad \mathbb{P}(B_k) > 0, \text{ for } k = 1, 2, \cdots, n.$$

Let $\mathcal{G}$ be the information set generated by these sets. Then the conditional expectation of X given $\mathcal{G}$ has an explicit representation

$$\mathbb{E}[X|\mathcal{G}](\omega) = \sum_{k=1}^{n} b_k I_{B_k}(\omega), \qquad b_k = \mathbb{E}[X|B_k].$$

Proof. Let us verify the two properties of the conditional expectation. (1) It is clear by definition that $\{\omega : Y(\omega) \leq a\}$ is the union of some B_i's for which $b_i \leq a$. Then $\{\omega : Y(\omega) \leq a\} \in \mathcal{G}$. (2) For any set $C \in \mathcal{G}$, we want to show that

$$\mathbb{E}[PI_C] = \mathbb{E}[XI_C],$$

where $P = \mathbb{E}[X|\mathcal{G}]$. If $C = B_i$ for some i, then

$$\mathbb{E}[PI_C] = \int_{B_i} \sum_{k=1}^{n} b_k I_{B_k} \, d\mathbb{P} = \frac{\mathbb{E}[XI_{B_i}]}{\mathbb{P}(B_i)} \mathbb{P}(B_i) = \mathbb{E}[XI_C].$$

Since $\mathcal{G}$ is a finite space, then any arbitrary C can be represented as $B_{k_1} \cup B_{k_2} \cup \cdots \cup B_{k_j}$ for some $j \leq n$. Summing over the k_j's gives the same identity. □

A very important application of conditional expectation will be shown in Section 4.2 of Chapter 4.

In general, we do not always have the luxury of writing a conditional expectation in explicit form as in Example 2.43. Nonetheless, the two fundamental properties of conditional expectation lead to a number of additional useful properties.

Example 2.44. [Properties of conditional expectation] Let $(\Omega, \mathcal{F}, \mathbb{P})$ be a probability space and $\mathcal{G}$ be a smaller information set than $\mathcal{F}$.

    1. (Linearity) If X and Y are both defined on the probability space and a, b are constants, then

$$\mathbb{E}[aX + bY|\mathcal{G}] = a\mathbb{E}[X|\mathcal{G}] + b\mathbb{E}[Y|\mathcal{G}].$$

    2. (Pulling out known factor) If X is $\mathcal{G}$-measurable, then

$$\mathbb{E}[XY|\mathcal{G}] = X\mathbb{E}[Y|\mathcal{G}].$$

    3. (Tower property) If $\mathcal{H}$ is a smaller information set than $\mathcal{G}$, then

$$\mathbb{E}[\mathbb{E}[X|\mathcal{G}]|\mathcal{H}] = \mathbb{E}[X|\mathcal{H}].$$

    4. (Ordinary expectation by independence) If X is independent of $\mathcal{G}$, then
$$\mathbb{E}[X|\mathcal{G}] = \mathbb{E}[X].$$

    5. (Jensen's inequality) Let ϕ be a convex function. For any random variable X and information set $\mathcal{G}$,

$$\phi(\mathbb{E}[X|\mathcal{G}]) \leq \mathbb{E}[\phi(X)|\mathcal{G}]. \tag{2.20}$$

Proof. Here we take Property 2 as an example. Properties 1, 3, 4 can be proved in a similar manner.

Since both X and $\mathbb{E}[Y|\mathcal{G}]$ are $\mathcal{G}$-measurable, the product must also be $\mathcal{G}$-measurable. Suppose $X(\omega) = I_B(\omega)$ for any $B \in \mathcal{G}$. Then for any $A \in \mathcal{G}$ we must have

$$\int_A \mathbb{E}[XY|\mathcal{G}](\omega)\,d\mathbb{P}(\omega) = \int_A X(\omega)Y(\omega)\,d\mathbb{P}(\omega)$$

$$= \int_{A \cap B} Y(\omega)\,d\mathbb{P}(\omega)$$

$$= \int_{A \cap B} \mathbb{E}[Y|\mathcal{G}](\omega)\,d\mathbb{P}(\omega)$$

$$= \int_A X(\omega)\mathbb{E}[Y|\mathcal{G}](\omega)\,d\mathbb{P}(\omega),$$

which shows the second fundamental property of conditional expectation. Although only the case of $X = I_B$ is proven here, we can use the standard three-step procedure in Section 2.3 to show the identity for all measurable function X.

The proof of Property 5 is based on the property of convex function stated in Theorem C.4. Consider any linear function $l(x) = a + bx$ lying below ϕ. It is clear from the linearity of conditional expectation that

$$\mathbb{E}[\phi(X)|\mathcal{G}] \geq \mathbb{E}[l(X)|\mathcal{G}] = l(\mathbb{E}[X|\mathcal{G}]).$$

Since the inequality holds for every linear function lying below ϕ, then we can take the supremum of all such functions. Then

$$\mathbb{E}[\phi(X)|\mathcal{G}] \geq \sup\{l(\mathbb{E}[X|\mathcal{G}]) : l(y) = a + by, l(y) \leq \phi(y) \text{ for all } y \in \mathbb{R}\}$$
$$= \phi(\mathbb{E}[X|\mathcal{G}]),$$

which yields the Jensen's inequality. $\square$

Theorem 2.45. *Let $(\Omega, \mathcal{F}, \mathbb{P})$ be a probability space and $\mathcal{G}$ be a smaller information set than $\mathcal{F}$. Suppose that X is adapted to $\mathcal{G}$ and Y is independent of $\mathcal{G}$. Let $f : \mathbb{R} \times \mathbb{R} \mapsto \mathbb{R}$ be a measurable function. Then*

$$\mathbb{E}[f(X,Y)|\mathcal{G}] = h(X) \tag{2.21}$$

where h is a measurable function and $h(x) = \mathbb{E}[f(x,Y)]$.

The proof is left as Exercise 2.5.3.

Remark 2.46. When the information set is generated by a random variable, say $\mathcal{G} = \sigma(X)$, we often write $\mathbb{E}[\cdot|\sigma(X)]$ as $\mathbb{E}[\cdot|X]$ for short. Another way to write such a conditional expectation is $\mathbb{E}[\cdot|X] = h(X)$ where

$$h(x) = \mathbb{E}[\cdot|X = x].$$

When the information set $\mathcal{G} = \sigma(X)$ in Theorem 2.45, the identity (2.21) reduces the familiar formula from the first course of probability $\mathbb{E}[f(X,Y)|X] = h(X)$ where

$$h(x) = \mathbb{E}[f(x,Y)|X = x] = \mathbb{E}[f(x,Y)].$$

Example 2.47. Consider the probability space in Example 2.10. Let X be the number of heads in the first coin toss and Y be the number of heads in the second coin toss. We are interested in an estimate of the number of heads in the first two coin tosses based on the information up to the first coin toss, i.e. $\mathbb{E}[f(X, Y)|\mathcal{F}_1]$ where $f(a, b) = a + b$. If we only know the information from the first coin, then there are only two possible outcomes. If it lands on a head, the probability of having another head from the second coin and thereby having two heads in total is p and the probability of having another tail from the second toss and thereby having only one head in total is q. In this case, the average number of heads is $2p + q$. If it lands on a tail, the probability of having a head from the second coin and thereby having only one head in total is p and the probability of no head at all is q. In this case, the average number of heads is p. Therefore, according to the result from Example 2.43, we obtain

$$
\begin{aligned}
\mathbb{E}[X + Y|\mathcal{F}_1](\omega) &= (2p + q)I_{\{H\}}(\omega) + pI_{\{T\}}(\omega) \\
&= (1 + p)I_{\{H\}}(\omega) + pI_{\{T\}}(\omega) \quad\quad (2.22) \\
&= I_{\{H\}}(\omega) + p. \quad\quad (2.23)
\end{aligned}
$$

Since Y is clearly independent of $\mathcal{F}_1$, we can apply (2.21) instead to produce the expression

$$
\mathbb{E}[X + Y|\mathcal{F}_1](\omega) = h(X(\omega)), \quad\quad (2.24)
$$

where for any arbitrary $x \in \mathbb{R}$

$$
h(x) = \mathbb{E}[x + Y] = (x + 1)p + (x + 0)q = x(p + q) + p = x + p.
$$

Recall that X is the number of heads in the first coin toss and hence can be written as

$$
X(\omega) = 1 \cdot I_{\{H\}}(\omega) + 0 \cdot I_{\{T\}}(\omega) = I_{\{H\}}(\omega).
$$

Substituting this expression for X in (2.24) yields (2.23).

2.6 Martingale vs. Markov processes

There are two categories of stochastic processes that are of crucial importance to stochastic analysis. The first category is known as martingale, which originally refers to a class of popular betting strategies from France in the 18th century. Its mathematical definition was later introduced in the probability literature as follows.

Definition 2.48 (Martingale). Let $(\Omega, \mathcal{F}, \mathbb{P})$ be a probability space with a filtration $\{\mathcal{F}_t, 0 \leq t \leq T\}$ on which an adapted process $\{M_t, 0 \leq t \leq T\}$ is defined for a fixed $T > 0$. The process is said to be a martingale if

$$\mathbb{E}[M_t | \mathcal{F}_s] = M_s \text{ for all } 0 \leq s \leq t \leq T.$$

Example 2.49. (1) Consider a fair game in which the chances of winning and losing equal amounts are the same, i.e. if we denote X_k the outcome of k-th trial at the game, then it is known that $\mathbb{E}[X_k] = 0$. Suppose that the initial wealth of a gambler is 0 and he is allowed to borrow as much as possible at no extra cost to play. Then his total wealth after k trials is determined by

$$M_k = \sum_{n=1}^{k} X_n.$$

Denote the information set generated by the first k trials by $\mathcal{F}_k = \sigma(X_1, X_2, \cdots, X_k)$. Then it is clear that his wealth process $\{M_1, M_2, \cdots, M_T\}$ is a discrete time martingale for T trials. For $k = 1, 2, \cdots, T$,

$$
\begin{aligned}
\mathbb{E}[M_{k+1} | \mathcal{F}_k] &= \mathbb{E}\left[\sum_{n=1}^{k} X_n + X_{k+1} \,\middle|\, \mathcal{F}_k \right] \\
&= \sum_{n=1}^{k} X_n + \mathbb{E}[X_{k+1} | \mathcal{F}_k] \\
&= \sum_{n=1}^{k} X_n + \mathbb{E}[X_{k+1}] = M_k.
\end{aligned}
$$

The second equality follows from pulling out known factor, while the conditional expectation becomes an ordinary expectation in the third equality as X_{k+1} is independent of $\mathcal{F}_k$.

(2) Consider another betting strategy called "double or nothing". The gambler starts with an initial wealth of 1 dollar and she always bets all of her wealth on the head of a fair coin. If the coin lands on a head, she doubles her wealth. Otherwise, she goes broke. This process is defined on the infinite coin toss probability space $(\Omega_\infty, \mathcal{F}, \mathbb{P})$ which is defined in Example 2.11. Since the game is based on a fair coin, we let $p = q = 1/2$. Define a sequence of random variables by setting

$$
X_n = \begin{cases} 2, & \omega_n = H \\ 0, & \omega_n = T. \end{cases}
$$

Then it is clear that her wealth process $\{M_1, M_2, \cdots, M_T\}$ defined by

$$M_k = \prod_{n=1}^{k} X_n,$$

is a martingale, since

$$
\begin{aligned}
\mathbb{E}[M_{k+1}|\mathcal{F}_k] &= \mathbb{E}\left[M_k X_{k+1}| \mathcal{F}_k\right] \\
&= M_k \mathbb{E}\left[X_{k+1}| \mathcal{F}_k\right] \\
&= M_k \mathbb{E}[X_{k+1}] = M_k.
\end{aligned}
$$

The derivation is again based on applying the same set of properties of conditional expectation as in the previous example.

Another very important class of stochastic processes for applications is known as *Markov process*.

Definition 2.50 (Markov process). Let $(\Omega, \mathcal{F}, \mathbb{P})$ be a probability space with a filtration $\{\mathcal{F}_t, 0 \leq t \leq T\}$. A real-valued stochastic process $\{X_t, 0 \leq t \leq T\}$ adapted to the filtration is said to possess the Markov property, if for each $B \in \mathbb{B}$ and each $0 \leq s < t \leq T$ such that

$$\mathbb{P}(X_t \in B|\mathcal{F}_s) = \mathbb{P}(X_t \in B|X_s).$$

Or equivalently, for any measurable function f, there exists another measurable function g such that
$$\mathbb{E}[f(X_t)|\mathcal{F}_s] = g(X_s).$$

Another way to interpret the Markov property is that

$$\mathbb{E}[f(X_t)|\mathcal{F}_s] = \mathbb{E}[f(X_t)|X_s] = g(X_s)$$

where $g(x) = \mathbb{E}[f(X_t)|X_s = x]$. Note that the information set $\mathcal{F}_s$ is richer than the information set $\sigma(X_s)$, as the former includes all information regarding the behavior of the process between 0 and s, which is not in the latter. The Markov property can be interpreted as a statement that its stochastic behavior in the future only depends on its current value, not on its past. Markov process is an extension of the notion of Markov chain in Example 2.34.

Example 2.51. The two examples above are in fact both Markov processes, as the gamblers' future wealth only depends on their current wealth. Take the "double or nothing" strategy for example. For any integers $0 \leq s < t \leq T$, it is clear that

$M_t = M_s Y$ where $Y = \prod_{i=s+1}^{t} X_i$ which is independent of M_s. Using (2.21), we find that

$$\mathbb{E}[f(M_t)|\mathcal{F}_s] = \mathbb{E}[f(M_sY)|\mathcal{F}_s] = g(M_s),$$

where

$$g(x) = \mathbb{E}[f(xY)] = f(2^{t-s}x)2^{s-t} + f(0)(1 - 2^{s-t}).$$

2.7 Scaled random walks

To better understand its stochastic nature, we shall consider Brownian motion as a limit of scaled random walks, which is much easier to analyze and explain.

Recall the construction of a random walk in Example 2.35 defined on the infinite coin toss space $(\Omega_\infty, \mathcal{F}, \mathbb{P})$. The random walk is the sum of position changes to a moving object over consecutive periods.

$$M_k = \sum_{j=1}^{k} X_j, \qquad k = 1, 2, \cdots$$

where in each period the object moves up or down by one step in accordance with the outcome of an independent coin toss,

$$X_j(\omega) = \begin{cases} 1, & \text{if } \omega = H, \\ -1, & \text{if } \omega = T. \end{cases}$$

If the coin is fair, i.e. $p = q = 1/2$, then the random walk is considered to be symmetric. It is easy to show that any symmetric random walk is both a martingale and a Markov process (Exercise 2.7.1).

There are two properties of symmetric random walk that are important to our discussion.

1. **Independent increments**

   An increment of the random walk refers to the change in its position over a certain time period. Choose nonnegative integers $0 < k_0 < k_1 < \ldots < k_m$. These increments of the random walk over all non-overlapping time periods

   $$(M_{k_1} - M_{k_0}), (M_{k_2} - M_{k_1}), \ldots, (M_{k_m} - M_{k_{m-1}})$$

   are mutually independent.

This is because increments over non-overlapping time intervals depend on different coin tosses, i.e.

$$M_{k_{i+1}} - M_{k_i} = \sum_{j=k_i+1}^{k_{i+1}} X_j. \tag{2.25}$$

For example, $M_3 - M_1 = X_2 + X_3$ and $M_4 - M_3 = X_4$. By construction, the random variables X_i's are mutually independent and hence $M_3 - M_1$ is independent of $M_4 - M_3$. Note, however, when the time periods overlap, the independence does not hold. For example, $M_3 - M_1 = X_2 + X_3$ would not be independent of $M_4 - M_2 = X_3 + X_4$.

2. **Stationary increments**

Choose any two nonnegative integers $0 < s < t$, the increment $M_t - M_s$ has the same distribution as M_{t-s}.

Observe that $M_t - M_s$ is a sum of $t - s$ independent and identically distributed random variables, as is $M_{t-s} = M_{t-s} - M_0$. Therefore, they must have exactly the same distribution.

To approximate a Brownian motion, we speed up time and scale down the step size of a symmetric random walk. More precisely, we fix a positive integer n and define the *scaled symmetric random walk*

$$W_t^{(n)} = \frac{1}{\sqrt{n}} M_{nt}, \tag{2.26}$$

provided nt is itself an integer. If nt is not an integer, we define $W_t^{(n)}$ by linear interpolation between its values at the nearest points s and u to the left and right of t for which ns and nu are integers. As we shall see next, $\{W_t^{(n)} : t \geq 0\}$ becomes a continuous-time process known as a Brownian motion as $n \to \infty$.

Similar to the random walk, the scaled random walk has independent and stationary increments. If $0 < t_0 < t_1 < \ldots < t_m$ are such that each nt_j is an integer, then

$$(W_{t_1}^{(n)} - W_{t_0}^{(n)}), W_{t_2}^{(n)} - W_{t_1}^{(n)}), \ldots, (W_{t_m}^{(n)} - W_{t_{m-1}}^{(n)})$$

are independent. Furthermore, for any j, the increment $W_{t_j}^{(n)} - W_{t_{j-1}}^{(n)}$ would have the same distribution as $W_{t_j - t_{j-1}}^{(n)}$. We leave the proofs to Exercise 2.7.1.

Figure 2.7 shows sample paths of several scaled random walks all determined by the same event in the sample space. In other words, we have fixed a sequence of coin tosses $\omega = \omega_1 \omega_2 \ldots$ and drawn corresponding sample paths of resulting processes according to (2.26) for $n = 1, 5, 20, 100$. As n increases, one would observe more rapid up and down moves over time.

To understand the limiting behavior of the scaled random walk as n goes to infinity, we investigate the randomness of the process evaluated at a fixed time t. Keep in mind that different sequences of coin tosses would lead to various paths of the resulting random walk, reaching different values at time t. Consider all possible values of

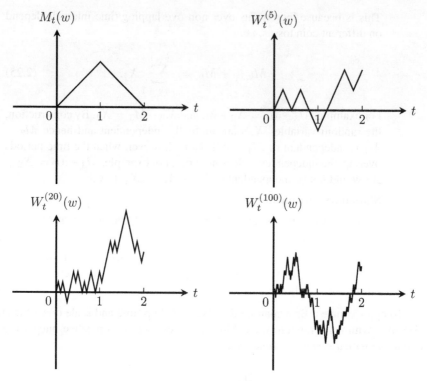

FIGURE 2.7: Sample paths of scaled symmetric random walks

$W_t^{(n)} = \frac{1}{\sqrt{n}} M_{nt}$ at some fixed t such that nt is an integer. Since every up move can be cancelled by another down move, we can find all possible values of the unscaled random walk M_{nt} by listing

$$(+1)h + (-1)(nt - h) = 2h - nt, \qquad h = 0, 1, \cdots, nt$$

where h is the number of heads in nt coin tosses. Therefore, we can determine the probability mass function of a scaled random walk at a fixed time t

$$\mathbb{P}\left(W_t^{(n)} = \frac{1}{\sqrt{n}}(2h - nt)\right) = \mathbb{P}(M_{nt} = 2h - nt) = \binom{nt}{h}\left(\frac{1}{2}\right)^{nt}.$$

For example, set $n = 100$ and $t = 0.1$. The random variable M_{10} is determined by ten coin tosses and can take values of $-10, -8, -6, \cdots, 6, 8, 10$, corresponding to a total of $h = 0, 1, 2, \cdots, 8, 9, 10$ heads. Therefore, the scaled random walk can only take values of $-1, -0.8, -0.6, \cdots, 0.6, 0.8, 1$. Let us consider the probability of $W_{0.1}^{(100)}$ taking the value 0,

$$\mathbb{P}\left(W_{0.1}^{(100)} = 0\right) = \binom{10}{5}\left(\frac{1}{2}\right)^{10} \approx 0.24609375.$$

Let us compare the probability mass function of $W_t^{(n)}$ with the probability density of a normal random variable with mean 0 and variance t. Figure 2.8 shows the histogram of $W_{0.1}^{(n)}$ with various choices of n. The dotted line in each plot in Figure 2.8 represents the density function of a standard normal random variable. To make a fair comparison with the normal density, we shall scale the histogram so that the area of each bar is equal to the probability mass assigned to the value covered in its base. As each bar has a width of 0.2, the height of the bar is $0.24609/0.2 = 1.230468750$. The corresponding value on the normal density is

$$f(0) = \frac{1}{\sqrt{0.2\pi}} \approx 1.128379167.$$

As the pattern shows in Figure 2.8, the histogram looks more like the density of a normal density as n gets bigger.

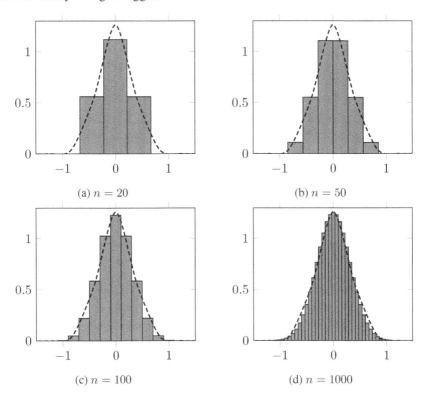

(a) $n = 20$

(b) $n = 50$

(c) $n = 100$

(d) $n = 1000$

FIGURE 2.8: Histograms of sample from scaled random walk

This phenonmenon can be easily justified by the fact that the scaled random walk, in essence, acts as a normalized sample average of changes in every step, i.e.

$$W_t^{(n)} = \frac{1}{\sqrt{n}} \sum_{j=1}^{nt} X_j = \sqrt{t} \frac{\overline{X}_{nt} - \mathbb{E}[\overline{X}_{nt}]}{\sqrt{\mathbb{V}(\overline{X}_{nt})}}, \qquad \overline{X}_k = \sum_{j=1}^{k} X_j.$$

Central Limit Theorem (Theorem 1.9) tells us that the normalized sample average converges to a standard normal random variable. Therefore, $W_t^{(n)}$ behaves roughly like a normal random variable with mean 0 and variance t.

2.8 Brownian motion

As shown in the previous section, Brownian motion can be obtained as the limit of the scaled random walks $W_t^{(n)}$ of (2.26) as $n \to \infty$. In fact, Brownian motion inherits many properties from random walks, which lead to the following definition.

Definition 2.52. A real-valued stochastic process $W = \{W_t : t \geq 0\}$ is said to be a *Brownian motion* if the following conditions hold:

1. $\mathbb{P}(W_0 = 0) = 1$;

2. The paths of W are continuous with probability 1;

3. For any $0 \leq s \leq t$, $W_t - W_s$ is equal in distribution to W_{t-s};

4. For any $0 \leq s \leq t$, $W_t - W_s$ is independent of $\{W_u : u \leq s\}$;

5. For any $t > 0$, W_t is normally distributed with mean 0 and variance t.

While the Brownian motion is the limit of the scaled random walks, there are several key differences between the two processes. The sample path of a random walk is the succession of a series of up and down movements and hence has a finite total variation up to any finite time. In contrast, the sample path of a Brownian motion cannot have finite variation no matter how small is the time horizon (Exercise 2.8.3). In view of (2.12) and (2.26), we know that the random walk at a fixed time $W_t^{(n)}$ is a sum of independent Bernoulli random variables, which has a binomial distribution. However, the Brownian motion at any fixed time W_t is normally distributed.

When necessary, we often identify the information set generated by a Brownian motion up to time t, $\mathcal{F}_t := \sigma\{W_s : 0 \leq s \leq t\}$. The sequence of information set generated by the Brownian motion over time is called the natural filtration of the Brownian motion, $\{\mathcal{F}_t : t \geq 0\}$.

The definition of Brownian motion leads to several important properties that are used frequently for applications.

Example 2.53 (Martingale property). The Brownian motion $W = \{W_t : 0 \leq t \leq T\}$ is a martingale. To show the martingale property, observe that for $0 \leq s \leq t \leq T$ we have

$$\begin{aligned}
\mathbb{E}[W_t|\mathcal{F}_s] &= \mathbb{E}[W_t - W_s + W_s|\mathcal{F}_s] = \mathbb{E}[W_t - W_s|\mathcal{F}_s] + W_s \\
&= \mathbb{E}[W_t - W_s] + W_s = W_s.
\end{aligned}$$

Example 2.54 (Markov property). For any measurable function f, we can apply Theorem 2.45 to show that

$$\mathbb{E}[f(W_t)|\mathcal{F}_s] = \mathbb{E}[f(W_t - W_s + W_s)|\mathcal{F}_s] = g(W_s),$$

where

$$g(x) = \mathbb{E}[f(W_t - W_s + x)] = \int_{-\infty}^{\infty} f(x+y)\frac{1}{\sqrt{2\pi}}e^{-y^2/2}\,\mathrm{d}y.$$

Therefore, W is indeed a Markov process.

Example 2.55. Let W be a standard Brownian motion. Observe the Brownian motion at three time points $0 < s < u < t$. Find:

1. The distribution of $W_t - W_s$.
2. The distribution of $W_t + W_s$.
3. $\mathbb{C}(W_s, W_t)$.
4. The conditional distribution of W_t given that $W_s = x$.
5. The conditional distribution of W_s given that $W_t = y$.
6. The conditional distribution of W_u given that $W_s = x, W_t = y$.

Solutions: 1. By definition, the increment of the Brownian motion over time period $[s, t]$ has mean zero and variance $t - s$.
2. Observe that $W_t + W_s = 2W_s + (W_t - W_s)$, which is the sum of two independent normal random variables and which is again normal with mean $\mathbb{E}[W_t + W_s] = 2\mathbb{E}[W_s] + \mathbb{E}[W_t - W_s] = 0$ and variance

$$\mathbb{V}[2W_s + (W_t - W_s)] = 4\mathbb{V}[W_s] + \mathbb{V}[W_t - W_s] = 4s + (t - s) = t + 3s.$$

3. By definition,

$$\mathrm{Cov}[W_s, W_t] = \mathbb{E}[W_s W_t] = \mathbb{E}[W_s(W_t - W_s + W_s)] = \mathbb{E}[W_s(W_t - W_s)] + \mathbb{E}[W_s^2] = s,$$

where we used the independence of W_s and $W_t - W_s$ in the last equality.
5. Observe that (W_s, W_t) is a bivariate normal random vector with mean zero and covariance matrix

$$\begin{bmatrix} s & s \\ s & t \end{bmatrix}$$

Then we can apply the conditional normal result from Exercise 2.8.2 to obtain

$$\mathbb{E}[W_s|W_t = y] = 0 + \frac{s}{t}(y - 0) = \frac{s}{t}y$$

and variance

$$\mathbb{V}[W_s|W_t = y] = s - \frac{s}{t}s = \frac{s(t - s)}{t}.$$

6. Note that (W_u, W_s, W_t) has mean zero and covariance matrix

$$\begin{bmatrix} u & s & u \\ s & s & s \\ u & s & t \end{bmatrix}$$

It follows from Exercise 2.8.2 that the conditional distribution is normal with mean

$$\mathbb{E}[W_u|W_s = x, W_t = y] = \begin{bmatrix} s & u \end{bmatrix} \begin{bmatrix} s & s \\ s & t \end{bmatrix}^{-1} \begin{bmatrix} x \\ y \end{bmatrix} = \frac{(t - u)x + (u - s)y}{t - s}$$

and variance

$$\mathbb{V}[W_u|W_s = x, W_t = y] = u - \begin{bmatrix} s & u \end{bmatrix} \begin{bmatrix} s & s \\ s & t \end{bmatrix}^{-1} \begin{bmatrix} u \\ s \end{bmatrix} = \frac{(u - s)(t - u)}{t - s}.$$

Throughout the next few sections, we consider increments of Brownian motion over the time periods

$$[t_0, t_1), [t_1, t_2), \cdots, [t_{n-1}, t_n],$$

where $t_0 = 0 < t_1 < t_2 < \cdots < t_n = T < \infty$. For brevity, we denote

$$\Delta W_j := W_{t_j} - W_{t_{j-1}}, \Delta t_j = t_j - t_{j-1}, \text{ for } j = 1, \cdots, n. \quad (2.27)$$

When applying the definition of quadratic variation in (2.19) to a Brownian motion, a cautious reader may notice that the sum of squares is a rather complex random variable by itself. For example, if the partition of $[0, t)$ is equidistant, i.e. $\Delta t_j = T/n$ for all $j = 1, \cdots, n$, then

$$\frac{1}{\Delta t} \sum_{j=1}^{n} (\Delta W_j)^2 \sim \chi_n^2,$$

meaning that the sum of squares has a Chi-squared distribution with n degrees of freedom. Applying the Law of Large Numbers (Theorem 1.1), we observe that

$$\frac{1}{n} \sum_{j=1}^{n} \frac{(\Delta W_j)^2}{\Delta t} \to 1, \qquad n \to \infty,$$

since $\mathbb{E}[(\Delta W_j)^2] = \Delta t$ and all increments are mutually independent. Recall that $\Delta t = T/n$ and therefore we can expect that

$$\sum_{j=1}^{n} (\Delta W_j)^2 \to T, \qquad \text{as } \|\Pi\| \to 0.$$

As we speak of the convergence of random variables, we need to measure the size of "distance" between two random variables. A commonly used measure is known as the L^2 norm, which is defined for any random variable X on $(\Omega, \mathcal{F}, \mathbb{P})$

$$\|X\| := \left[\mathbb{E}(X^2)\right]^{1/2}.$$

Then we say a sequence of random variables $\{X_1, X_2, \cdots\}$ converges to X in the L^2 norm if the distance between X_n and X shinks to zero as n goes to infinity, i.e.

$$\|X_n - X\| \longrightarrow 0, \qquad \text{as } n \to \infty.$$

Theorem 2.56. *The quadratic variation of a standard Brownian motion is given by*

$$[W, W]_T = T \qquad \text{for all } T \geq 0 \text{ almost surely.}$$

Proof. To prove that $[W, W]_T = T$, we need to show that as $\|\Pi\| \to 0$,

$$\left\| \sum_{j=1}^{n} \Delta W_j^2 - T \right\| \longrightarrow 0.$$

Note that

$$\mathbb{E}\left[\left(\sum_{j=1}^{n} (\Delta W_j)^2 - \sum_{j=1}^{n} \Delta t_j \right)^2 \right] = \mathbb{E}\left[\sum_{j=1}^{n} \left((\Delta W_j)^2 - \Delta t_j \right)^2 \right],$$

which follows from the fact that all cross terms have mean zero, i.e.

$$\mathbb{E}[((\Delta W_j)^2 - \Delta t_j)((\Delta W_k)^2 - \Delta t_k)] = \mathbb{E}[(\Delta W_j)^2 - \Delta t_j]\mathbb{E}[(\Delta W_k)^2 - \Delta t_k] = 0.$$

Observe that

$$\begin{aligned} \mathbb{E}[(\Delta W_j^2 - \Delta t_j)^2] &= \mathbb{E}[(\Delta W_j)^4 - 2(\Delta W_j)^2 \Delta t_j + (\Delta t_j)^2] \\ &= 3(\Delta t_j)^2 - 2(\Delta t_j)^2 + (\Delta t_j)^2 = 2(\Delta t_j)^2. \quad (2.28) \end{aligned}$$

In the second equality, the first term comes from the fact that the fourth moment of a normal random variable with zero mean is three times its variance squared (see Exercise 2.8.2). Therefore, as $\|\Pi\| \to 0$,

$$\left\| \sum_{j=1}^{n} \Delta W_j^2 - T \right\|^2 = 2 \sum_{j=1}^{n} (\Delta t_j)^2 \leq 2(\max \Delta t_j) \sum_{j=1}^{n} \Delta t_j = 2\|\Pi\|T \to 0.$$

$\square$

Remark 2.57. Note that the quadratic variation $[W, W]_T = T$ for all $T \geq 0$ can be expressed in the differential form $d[W, W]_t = dt$. Many books use mnemonics such as

$$dW_t \, dW_t = dt. \tag{2.29}$$

to help readers remember the "differentiation rules" of the quadratic variation. Similarly, since W_t is continuous in t and the linear function $l(t) = t$ has continuous derivatives everywhere, it follows from Exercise 2.4.3 that $[W, l]_t = 0$ and $[l, l]_t = 0$. The mnemonics can be conveniently expressed in differential forms according to the following multiplication table.

	dW_t	dt
dW_t	dt	0
dt	0	0

One should note that Theorem 2.56 implies that W_t is not continuously differentiable with respect to any t. This is because its quadratic variation would be zero otherwise as shown in Example 2.40.

2.9   Stochastic integral

The stochastic integral to be introduced in this section is a natural concept that arises in financial modeling. Suppose that the profits and losses from holding a unit of a certain financial instrument are modeled by a Brownian motion $\{W_t, t \geq 0\}$. An investor invests in such an instrument with a trading strategy up to a finite time represented by $\{\Gamma_t, 0 \leq t \leq T\}$, which means that the investor holds Γ_t units of the instrument at time t. Since the investor can only buy or sell every so often, we assume that trading occurs at the following discrete time points

$$0 = t_0 < t_1 < \cdots < t_k \to T < \infty.$$

Then the investor would be interested in the evolution of her accumulated wealth over time, to be denoted by $\{I_t, 0 \leq t \leq T\}$ with I_t representing her wealth at time t. It is easy to see that the investor's gain or loss over each period $[t_j, t_{j+1}]$ is determined by the number of units held multiplied by the gain/loss per unit, i.e. $\Gamma_{t_j}[W_{t_{j+1}} - W_{t_j}]$. Therefore, the accumulated wealth at present is in fact a sum of gains and losses from all periods in the past. That means, for $t_k \leq t < t_{k+1}$ with $k = 0, 1, \cdots$, her wealth is given by

$$I_t = \sum_{j=1}^{k} \Gamma_{t_{j-1}}[W_{t_j} - W_{t_{j-1}}] + \Pi_{t_k}[W_t - W_{t_k}]. \tag{2.30}$$

This is in fact the idea of a stochastic integral which we shall denote by

$$I_t = \int_0^t \Gamma_s \, dW_s.$$

Definition 2.58 (Adaptedness and square integrability). Let $\{\mathcal{F}_t, t \geq 0\}$ be a given filtration. A stochastic process $\{\Gamma_t, t \geq 0\}$ is adapted if for each $t \geq 0$ the random variable Γ_t is $\mathcal{F}_t$-measurable, i.e. for every Borel set $B \in \mathbb{B}$,

$$\{\Gamma_t \in B\} \in \mathcal{F}_t. \tag{2.31}$$

A stochastic process $\{\Gamma_t, t \geq 0\}$ is square integrable if for each $t \geq 0$,

$$\mathbb{E}\left[\int_0^t \Gamma_s^2 \, ds\right] < \infty.$$

Throughout this section, we work with the filtration $\{\mathcal{F}_t : t \geq 0\}$ where $\mathcal{F}_t = \sigma(W_s : 0 \leq s \leq t)$, which is often called the *natural filtration* generated by the Brownian motion.

In this book, we only consider stochastic integrals of adapted square integrable processes. However, the concept can be extended for a larger class of processes, which goes beyond the scope of this book. The interested reader may consult Harrison [62] and McKean [76] for the construction of stochastic integrals in generality.

Intuitively speaking, the condition (2.31) means that we know how to assign probabilities to events of Γ_t (of the form $\{\Gamma_t \leq a\}$ for all $a \in \mathbb{R}$) necessary to determine its distribution using the information up to time t. In the context of trading, a strategy of holding one unit only when the current price is within a range $[a, b]$, i.e. $\Gamma_t = I_{[a,b]}(W_t)$, is clearly adapted, but a trading strategy based on a future price, say $\Gamma_t = I_{[a,b]}(W_{t+1})$, is not.

Definition 2.59 (Simple process). A square-integrable and adapted stochastic process $\{\Gamma_t, 0 \leq t \leq T\}$ is called simple if there exists a partition of $[0, T]$ as defined in (2.14) such that $\Gamma_t(\omega) = \Gamma_{t_j}(\omega)$ for all $t \in [t_j, t_{j+1}), j = 0, 1, \cdots, n-1$ and all $\omega \in \Omega$.

Figure 2.9 shows several sample paths of a simple process. For any given sample path ω, $\Gamma_t(\omega)$ is a constant for $t \in [t_j, t_{j+1})$. However, keep in mind that Γ_t is a random variable by itself.

An example of a simple process is already given by an investor's trading strategy at the beginning of this section. Since the investor's trading decisions can only be made based on historical returns on the instrument (nobody has a crystal ball to predict future with certainty!), then it is reasonable to assume that $\{\Gamma_t, t \geq 0\}$ is adapted to the natural filtration of the Brownian motion. Square integrability is a technical condition that is met in most applications. For instance, Γ_t's often have second moments for all $t \geq 0$. For such a simple process, it is easy to define a stochastic integral.

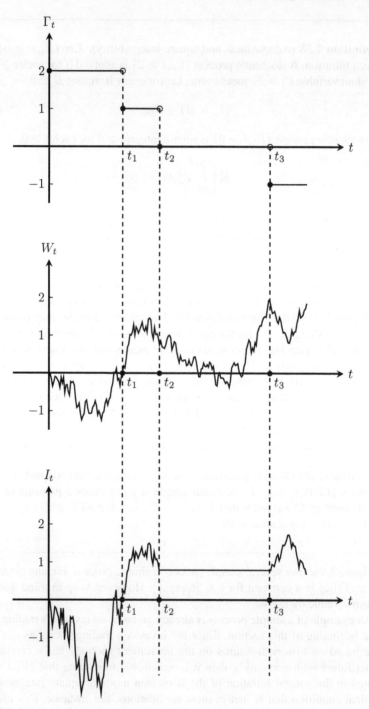

FIGURE 2.9: Sample paths of stochastic integral and corresponding simple process and Brownian motion

---

Definition 2.60 (Stochastic integral for simple process). For any simple process $\{\Gamma_t, 0 \le t \le T\}$, its stochastic integral is defined pathwise by (2.30) for all $t \in [t_j, t_{j+1})$ and $j = 0, 1, \cdots, n-1$.

As we shall see in the proof of following properties of stochastic integral, it is essential that the increments of Brownian motion in (2.30) are forward differences in relation to the time point of the integrand.

Theorem 2.61 (Itô isometry). *If $\{\Gamma_t, 0 \le t \le T\}$ is a simple process, then the stochastic integral $I_t = \int_0^t \Gamma_s \, dW_s$ defined by (2.30) has the following properties:*

1. $\{I_t, 0 \le t \le T\}$ *is a mean zero martingale.*

2. *Itô's isometry:*

$$\mathbb{E}\left[\left(\int_0^t \Gamma_s \, dW_s\right)^2\right] = \mathbb{E}\left[\int_0^t \Gamma_s^2 \, ds\right].$$

3. *The quadratic variation of the stochastic integral*

$$[I, I](t) = \int_0^t \Gamma_s^2 \, ds.$$

Proof. (1) Consider $0 \le t_j \le s < t_{j+1} \le t_k \le t < t_{k+1} \le T$ for some integers j and k. Then

$$
\begin{aligned}
\mathbb{E}[I_t | \mathcal{F}_s] &= \mathbb{E}\left[\sum_{i=1}^k \Gamma_{t_i} \Delta W_i + \Gamma_{t_k} \Delta W_{k+1} \middle| \mathcal{F}_s\right] \\
&= \sum_{i=1}^j \Gamma_{t_i} \Delta W_i + \Gamma_{t_j}(W_s - W_{t_j}) \\
&\quad + \mathbb{E}\left[\Gamma_{t_j}(W_{t_{j+1}} - W_s) + \sum_{i=j+2}^k \Gamma_{t_i} \Delta W_i + \Gamma_{t_k} \Delta W_k \middle| \mathcal{F}_s\right] \\
&= \sum_{i=1}^j \Gamma_{t_i} \Delta W_i + \Gamma_{t_j}(W_s - W_{t_j}) = I_s,
\end{aligned}
$$

where ΔW_i is defined in (2.27) for $i = 1, 2, \cdots, k$ and $\Delta W_{k+1} = W_t - W_{t_k}$. It is easy to show that the conditional expectation in the second equality is zero. For example,

$$\mathbb{E}\left[\Gamma_{t_j}(W_{t_{j+1}} - W_s) \middle| \mathcal{F}_s\right] = \mathbb{E}\left[\Gamma_{t_j} \mathbb{E}[(W_{t_{j+1}} - W_s)] \middle| \mathcal{F}_s\right] = 0.$$

(2) Without loss of generality, we assume that $t = t_{k+1}$ for some integer k. Otherwise, one can carry out similar arguments as in (1). Observe that

$$\mathbb{E}\left[\left(\int_0^t \Gamma_s \, dW_s\right)^2\right] = \mathbb{E}\left[\left(\sum_{i=1}^{k+1} \Gamma_{t_i} \Delta W_i\right)^2\right] = \sum_{i=1}^{k+1} \mathbb{E}\left[\Gamma_{t_i}^2 (\Delta W_i)^2\right].$$

Note that Γ_{t_i} is $\mathcal{F}_{t_i}$-measurable and ΔW_i is independent of $\mathcal{F}_{t_i}$. Thus,

$$\begin{aligned}
\mathbb{E}\left[\Gamma_{t_i}^2 (\Delta W_i)^2\right] &= \mathbb{E}\left[\mathbb{E}\left[\Gamma_{t_i}^2 (\Delta W_i)^2 \big| \mathcal{F}_{t_i}\right]\right] \\
&= \mathbb{E}\left[\Gamma_{t_i}^2 \mathbb{E}\left[(\Delta W_i)^2\right]\right] = \mathbb{E}\left[\Gamma_{t_i}^2\right] \mathbb{E}\left[(\Delta W_i)^2\right].
\end{aligned}$$

Therefore,

$$\mathbb{E}\left[\left(\int_0^t \Gamma_s \, dW_s\right)^2\right] = \sum_{i=1}^{k+1} \mathbb{E}\left[\Gamma_{t_i}^2\right](t_{i+1} - t_i) = \int_0^t \mathbb{E}[\Gamma_s^2] \, ds = \mathbb{E}\left[\int_0^t \Gamma_s^2 \, ds\right].$$

(3) By definition, we know that the quadratic variation of the stochastic integral (2.30) over the interval $[0, t]$ is the sum of its quadratic integral over all subintervals $[t_j, t_{j+1})$ for $j = 0, \cdots, k - 1$ and $[t_k, t)$. Over the interval $[t_j, t_{j+1})$, the quadratic variation is given by $\Gamma_{t_j}^2 (t_{j+1} - t_j)$. $\qquad\qquad\square$

However, in applications we often have to deal with processes beyond simple processes. For example, the trading strategy $\Gamma_t = I_{[a,b]}(W_t)$ is not simple. **How does one define a stochastic integral of a general process?** Recall from Section 2.3 that we always define integrals of simple functions and then extend the definition of general functions by taking limit of approximations. For example, in the case of Riemann integral, the standard procedure is first to find a sequence of approximating step functions $\{f_n, n = 1, 2, \cdots\}$ that can get arbitrarily close to the general function f and then to the integral of the general function $\int f(x) \, dx$ is taken as the limit of those of the approximating functions $\{\int f_n(x) \, dx : n = 1, 2, \cdots\}$. We can measure the "closeness" of an approximating function to the true function by the maximum distance between their graphs, i.e. $\sup_x |f(x) - f_n(x)|$. Similarly, we want to approximate the integral of a general stochastic process by a sequence of integrals of approximating simple process that can be arbitrarily close to the general process. To this end, we have to define what we mean by "closeness" of two stochastic processes. Here we use a "length" measure

$$\|\Gamma\| := \mathbb{E}\left[\int_0^T \Gamma_t^2 \, dt\right]^{1/2}.$$

We say the sequence of processes $\{\Gamma^{(n)}, n = 1, 2, \cdots\}$ with $\Gamma^{(n)} = \{\Gamma_t^{(n)}, 0 \le t \le T\}$ converges to a process $\Gamma = \{\Gamma_t, 0 \le t \le T\}$, if the "length" of the difference between $\Gamma^{(n)}$ and Γ decreases with n, i.e.

$$\|\Gamma^{(n)} - \Gamma\| \to 0, \qquad \text{as } n \to \infty.$$

Example 2.62 (Approximation of Brownian motion). We choose a large n to create an equidistant partition of $[0, T]$ and approximate the Brownian motion $\{W_t, 0 \le t \le T\}$ by a sequence of simple processes $\{W^{(n)}, n = 1, 2, \cdots\}$ where

$$W_t^{(n)} := \begin{cases} W_0, & 0 \le t < \frac{T}{n}; \\ W_{T/n}, & \frac{T}{n} \le t < \frac{2T}{n}; \\ \vdots & \vdots \\ W_{(n-1)T/n}, & \frac{(n-1)T}{n} \le t < T. \end{cases}$$

Consider the "distance" ("length" of the difference) of $W^{(n)}$ from W

$$\begin{aligned} \|W^{(n)} - W\|^2 &= \mathbb{E}\left[\int_0^T (W_t - W_t^{(n)})^2 \, dt\right] \\ &= \int_0^T \mathbb{E}\left[(W_t - W_t^{(n)})^2\right] \, dt \\ &= \sum_{j=0}^{n-1} \int_0^{T/n} \mathbb{E}\left[(W_{jT/n+t} - W_{jT/n})^2\right] \, dt \\ &= \sum_{j=0}^{n-1} \int_0^{T/n} t \, dt = \sum_{j=0}^{n-1} \frac{T^2}{2n^2} = \frac{T^2}{2n}. \end{aligned}$$

Thus $\|W^{(n)} - W\| \to 0$ as $n \to \infty$, which implies that the sequence of simple process $\{W^{(n)}, n = 1, 2, \cdots\}$ does converge to the Brownian motion.

Theorem 2.63. *For any square-integrable adapted process* $\Gamma := \{\Gamma_t, 0 \le t \le T\}$, *there always exists a sequence of simple processes* $\{\Gamma^{(n)}, n = 1, 2, \cdots\}$ *for which*

$$\|\Gamma^{(n)} - \Gamma\| \to 0, \qquad \text{as } n \to \infty.$$

Keep in mind that the stochastic integral of a simple process for each fixed t as shown in (2.30) is a random variable.

Theorem 2.64. *For each square-integrable adapted process* $\{\Gamma_t, 0 \le t \le T\}$, *there always exists a random variable* I_t *for each fixed* t *such that* $I_t^{(n)} := \int_0^t \Gamma_s^{(n)} \, ds$ *converges to* I_t, *i.e.*

$$\|I_t^{(n)} - I_t\| \to 0, \qquad \text{as } n \to \infty, \tag{2.32}$$

where $\{\Gamma^{(n)}, n = 1, \cdots\}$ *is a sequence of simple processes that converges to* Π.

Definition 2.65 (Stochastic integral for general process). For any square-integrable adapted process $\{\Gamma_t, 0 \le t \le T\}$, its stochastic integral is defined by the limit process $\{I_t, 0 \le t \le T\}$ in (2.32) and often denoted by $I_t = \int_0^t \Gamma_s \, dW_s$.

For brevity, we sometimes write the convergence in (2.32) in the following way

$$\int_0^t \Gamma_s^{(n)} \, dW_s \xrightarrow{L^2} \int_0^t \Pi_s \, dW_s.$$

Example 2.66. Show that

$$\int_0^t W_s \, dW_s = \frac{1}{2} W_t^2 - \frac{t}{2}.$$

As shown in Example 2.62, the sequence of simple processes $\{W^{(n)}, n = 1, 2, \cdots\}$ converges to a Brownian motion W. Then it follows immediately from Theorem 2.64 that

$$\int_0^t W_s^{(n)} \, dW_s \xrightarrow{L^2} \int_0^t W_s \, dW_s.$$

Suppose that $t_k \le t < t_{k+1}$ and denote $\Delta W_{k+1} = W_t - W_{t_k}$. Following the notation in (2.27), we obtain on the left side

$$\int_0^t W_s^{(n)} \, dW_s = \sum_{j=1}^{k+1} W_{t_{j-1}} \Delta W_j.$$

Observe that

$$\begin{aligned}
\Delta W_j^2 &= W_{t_j}^2 - W_{t_{j-1}}^2 = (\Delta W_j)^2 + 2W_{t_{j-1}}(W_{t_j} - W_{t_{j-1}}) \\
&= (\Delta W_j)^2 + 2W_{t_{j-1}} \Delta W_j.
\end{aligned}$$

Therefore,

$$W_t^2 = \sum_{j=1}^{k+1} \Delta W_j^2 = \sum_{j=1}^{k+1} (\Delta W_j)^2 + 2 \sum_{j=1}^{k+1} W_{t_{j-1}} \Delta W_j,$$

or equivalently,

$$\sum_{j=1}^{k+1} W_{t_{j-1}} \Delta W_j = \frac{1}{2} W_t^2 - \frac{1}{2} \sum_{j=1}^{k+1} (\Delta W_j)^2. \tag{2.33}$$

Since the left side of (2.33) converges to $\int_0^t W_s \, dW_s$ in L^2-norm and the right side converges to $(1/2)W_t^2 - t/2$ by Theorem 2.56, we obtain the desired identity.

The following properties of stochastic integrals are of crucial importance to our applications.

1. I_t is continuous in t.
2. If $I_t = \int_0^t \Gamma_u \, dW_u$ and $J_t = \int_0^t \Delta_u \, dW_u$, then

$$I_t + J_t = \int_0^t \Gamma_u + \Delta_u \, dW_u.$$

3. I_t is a mean-zero martingale.
4. (Itô isometry) $\mathbb{E}[I_t^2] = \mathbb{E}\left[\int_0^t \Gamma_u^2 \, du\right]$.
5. $[I, I]_t = \int_0^t \Gamma_u^2 \, du$.

Example 2.67. For each fixed t, we can compare two random variables

$$I_t := \int_0^t \sqrt{u} \, dW_u, \qquad J_t := \int_0^t W_u \, dW_u.$$

Note that both are mean-zero martingales. It follows from Itô isometry that

$$\mathbb{E}[I_t^2] = \int_0^t u \, du = \frac{u^2}{2};$$

$$\mathbb{E}[J_t^2] = \int_0^t \mathbb{E}[W_u^2] \, du = \int_0^t u \, du = \frac{u^2}{2}.$$

Hence both random variables have the same mean and variance. However, they have different distributions. It is clear from Example 2.66 that $J_t = W_t^2/2 - t/2$ and hence it follows a scaled and shifted chi-squared distribution with one degree of freedom. In contrast, we can show that I_t follows a normal distribution. Following the result in Exercise , we know that

$$\mathbb{E}\left[\exp\left\{sI_t - \frac{1}{2}s^2 \int_0^t \Gamma_u^2 \, du\right\}\right] = 1.$$

Therefore, the moment generating function of I_t is given by

$$\mathbb{E}[e^{sI_t}] = \exp\left\{\frac{s^2}{2} \int_0^t \Gamma_u^2 \, du\right\},$$

which implies that I_t is a normal random variable.

In most applications, we often work with a class of stochastic processes known as Itô's process, which is defined by

$$X_t = X_0 + \int_0^t \Theta_u \, du + \int_0^t \Gamma_u \, dW_u, \tag{2.34}$$

where X_0 is a constant and $\{\Theta_t, t \geq 0\}$ is an adapted process. We often write the dynamics of the process X in the differential form

$$dX_t = \Theta_t \, dt + \Gamma_t \, dW_t. \tag{2.35}$$

Note, however, (2.35) is purely symbolic. Recall from calculus that if a function f is differentiable then we can define the total differential

$$df(x, y) = f_x(x, y) \, dx + f_y(x, y) \, dy.$$

It is not possible to define the differential "dX_t" in the sense of ordinary calculus since its sample paths, in general, are not differentiable. One should always keep in mind that (2.35) is a shortcut of the integral form, in which all integrals are well-defined.

Suppose that $\{\Delta_t, 0 \leq t \leq T\}$ is an adapted process. Its stochastic integral with respect to X_t is defined as follows

$$\int_0^t \Delta_u \, dX_u = \int_0^t \Delta_u \Theta_u \, du + \int_0^t \Delta_u \Gamma_u \, dW_u, \tag{2.36}$$

provided that both integrals on the right hand side are well-defined.

Example 2.68. The quadratic variation of the Itô process (2.36) is

$$[X, X]_t = \int_0^t \Gamma_u^2 \, du.$$

Again this result can be "proved by symbols" in terms of the mnemonics described in Remark 2.57. Note that

$$dX_t = \Gamma_t \, dW_t + \Theta_t \, dt.$$

Then it follows from the differential multiplication table that

$$dX_t \, dX_t = \Gamma_t^2 \, dW_t \, dW_t + 2\Gamma_t \Theta_t \, dW_t \, dt + \Theta_t^2 \, dt \, dt = \Gamma_t^2 \, dt.$$

2.10 Itô formula

Theorem 2.69. *Let $X = \{X_t, 0 \leq t \leq T\}$ be an Itô process and $f(t, x)$ be continuously differentiable with respect to t and twice continuously differentiable with respect to x. Then $\{f(t, X_t), 0 \leq t \leq T\}$ is also an Itô process and*

$$f(T, X_T) = f(0, X_0) + \int_0^T f_t(t, X_t) \, dt + \int_0^T f_x(t, X_t) \, dX_t$$

$$+ \frac{1}{2} \int_0^T f_{xx}(t, X_t) \, d[X, X]_t.$$

Proof. Consider the change of $f(t, X_t)$ over the time interval $[0, T]$ as the sum of incremental changes over subintervals in the partition (2.14). For brevity, we shall write

$$\Delta t_j = t_j - t_{j-1}, \Delta X_j = X_{t_j} - X_{t_{j-1}}, \Delta f_j = f(t_j, X_{t_j}) - f(t_{j-1}, X_{t_{j-1}}),$$

Using Taylor's expansion, we see that

$$
\begin{aligned}
\Delta f_j &= f_t(t_j, X_{t_j}) \Delta t_j + f_x(t_j, X_{t_j}) \Delta X_j + \frac{1}{2} f_{tt}(t_j, X_{t_j})(\Delta t_j)^2 \\
&\quad + f_{tx}(t_j, X_{t_j}) \Delta t_j \Delta X_j + \frac{1}{2} f_{xx}(t_j, X_{t_j})(\Delta X_j)^2 + \text{HOT},
\end{aligned}
$$

where "HOT" stands for higher order terms of $\Delta t, \Delta X_j$ and their products. We first consider the case where Θ_t and Γ_t are simple functions with the same partition (2.14). Then it is clear that

$$\Delta X_j = \Theta_{t_j} \Delta t_j + \Pi_{t_j} \Delta W_j.$$

Making the substitution for each Δf_j and looking at the sum gives

$$
\begin{aligned}
f(T, X_T) - f(0, X_0) &= \sum_{j=1}^{n} \Delta f_j = \sum_{j=1}^{n} [f_t(t_j, X_{t_j}) + f_x(t_j, X_{t_j}) \Theta_{t_j}] \Delta t_j \\
&\quad + \sum_{j=1}^{n} f_x(t_j, X_{t_j}) \Pi_{t_j} \Delta W_j + \sum_{j=1}^{n} f_{xx}(t_j, X_{t_j}) \Pi_{t_j}^2 (\Delta W_j)^2 + \text{HOT}.
\end{aligned}
$$

All terms involving HOT converge to zero. Based on the definition of Riemann-integral, we see that as $\| \Pi \| \to 0$,

$$\sum_{j=1}^{n} f_t(t_j, X_{t_j}) \Delta t_j \to \int_0^T f_t(t, x) \, dt.$$

Similarly, it follows from (2.36) that as $\| \Pi \| \to 0$,

$$\sum_{j=1}^{n} f_x(t_j, X_{t_j}) [\Theta_{t_j} \Delta t_j + \Gamma_{t_j} \Delta W_j] \xrightarrow{L^2} \int_0^T f_x(t, X_t) \, dX_t.$$

Lastly, we can show that

$$\sum_{j=1}^{n} f_{xx}(t_j, X_{t_j}) \Gamma_{t_j}^2 (\Delta W_j)^2 \xrightarrow{L^2} \int_0^T f_{xx}(t, X_t) \Gamma_t^2 \, dt = \int_0^T f_{xx}(t, X_t) \, d[X, X]_t.$$

For brevity, we shall write $a_j = f_{xx}(t_j, X_{t_j}) \Gamma_{t_j}^2$. In order to prove the above convergence, we show that

$$\mathbb{E}\left[\left(\sum_{j=1}^{n} a_j (\Delta W_j)^2 - \sum_{j=1}^{n} a_j \Delta t_j \right)^2 \right] = \sum_{i,j=1}^{n} \mathbb{E}\left[a_i a_j \left((\Delta W_i)^2 - \Delta t_i \right) \left((\Delta W_j)^2 - \Delta t_j \right) \right]$$

Note that if $i < j$ then

$$
\begin{aligned}
&\mathbb{E}\left[a_i a_j \left((\Delta W_i)^2 - \Delta t_i\right)\left((\Delta W_j)^2 - \Delta t_j\right)\right] \\
={} &\mathbb{E}[\mathbb{E}\left[a_i a_j \left((\Delta W_i)^2 - \Delta t_i\right)\left((\Delta W_j)^2 - \Delta t_j\right)|\mathcal{F}_{t_j}\right] \\
={} &\mathbb{E}\left[a_i a_j \left((\Delta W_i)^2 - \Delta t_i\right)\mathbb{E}\left[\left((\Delta W_j)^2 - \Delta t_j\right)|\mathcal{F}_{t_j}\right]\right] \\
={} &\mathbb{E}\left[a_i a_j \left((\Delta W_i)^2 - \Delta t_i\right)\right]\mathbb{E}\left[(\Delta W_j)^2 - \Delta t_j\right] = 0.
\end{aligned}
$$

Similarly, one can show that $\mathbb{E}\left[a_i a_j \left((\Delta W_i)^2 - \Delta t_i\right)\left((\Delta W_j)^2 - \Delta t_j\right)\right] = 0$ for $i > j$. Thus,

$$
\begin{aligned}
\mathbb{E}\left[\left(\sum_{j=1}^{n} a_j (\Delta W_j)^2 - \sum_{j=1}^{n} a_j \Delta t_j\right)^2\right] &= \sum_{j=1}^{n}\mathbb{E}\left[a_j^2\left((\Delta W_j)^2 - \Delta t_j\right)^2\right] \\
= \sum_{j=1}^{n}\mathbb{E}\left[a_j^2\mathbb{E}\left[\left((\Delta W_j)^2 - \Delta t_j\right)^2\Big|\mathcal{F}_{t_j}\right]\right] &= 2\sum_{j=1}^{n}\mathbb{E}[a_j^2](\Delta t_j)^2 \to 0,
\end{aligned}
$$

where the last equality is derived in the same manner as in (2.28).   □

Remark 2.70. The Itô formula is often written for convenience in the differential form

$$
\mathrm{d}f(t, X_t) = f_t(t, X_t)\,\mathrm{d}t + f_x(t, X_t)\,\mathrm{d}X_t + \frac{1}{2}f_{xx}(t, X_t)\,\mathrm{d}[X, X]_t.
$$

Note that

$$
\mathrm{d}[X, X]_t = \Gamma_t^2\,\mathrm{d}t, \qquad \mathrm{d}X_t = \Theta_t\,\mathrm{d}t + \Gamma_t\,\mathrm{d}W_t.
$$

It follows immediately that

$$
\mathrm{d}f(t, X_t) = \left[f_t(t, X_t) + f_x(t, X_t)\Theta_t + \frac{1}{2}f_{xx}(t, X_t)\Gamma_t^2\right]\mathrm{d}t + f_x(t, X_t)\Gamma_t\,\mathrm{d}W_t,
$$

which clearly shows that $f(t, X_t)$ is also an Itô process.

   We consider a special case of the Itô formula which is used in many applications in this book.

Theorem 2.71. *Let* $W = \{W_t, 0 \le t \le T\}$ *be a standard Brownian motion and* $f(t, x)$ *be continuously differentiable with respect to* t *and twice continuously differentiable with respect to* x. *Then* $\{f(t, W_t), 0 \le t \le T\}$ *is also an Itô process and*

$$
f(T, W_T) = f(0, 0) + \int_0^T \left[f_t(t, W_t) + \frac{1}{2}f_{xx}(t, W_t)\right]\mathrm{d}t + \int_0^T f_x(t, W_t)\,\mathrm{d}W_t.
$$

Example 2.72. (Geometric Brownian motion) For reasons to be seen, a stochastic process known as the geometric Brownian motion is widely used in the financial and insurance industries for modeling equity returns. For each fixed $t \geq 0$, the process $\{S_t : t \geq 0\}$ is defined by

$$S_t = S_0 \exp \left\{ (\mu - \frac{\sigma^2}{2})t + \sigma W_t \right\}. \tag{2.37}$$

We can use the Itô formula to analyze the dynamics of the geometric Brownian motion. Think of

$$S_t = f(t, W_t), \qquad \text{where } f(t, x) = S_t \exp \left\{ \sigma x + (\mu - \frac{\sigma^2}{2})t \right\}.$$

Then we have

$$f_t(t, x) = (\mu - \frac{\sigma^2}{2})f(t, x);$$
$$f_x(t, x) = \sigma f(t, x);$$
$$f_{xx}(t, x) = \sigma^2 f(t, x).$$

Applying the Itô formula,

$$\begin{aligned} f(T, W_T) =& f(0, W_0) + \int_0^T (\mu - \frac{\sigma^2}{2})f(t, W_t)\, dt \\ &+ \int_0^T \sigma f(t, W_t)\, dW_t + \int_0^T \frac{\sigma^2}{2} f(t, W_t)\, dt \\ =& f(0, W_0) + \int_0^T \mu f(t, W_t)\, dt + \int_0^T \sigma f(t, W_t)\, dW_t. \end{aligned}$$

In other words,

$$S_T = S_0 + \int_0^T \mu S_t\, dt + \int_0^T \sigma S_t\, dW_t. \tag{2.38}$$

This is known as the stochastic differential equation for the geometric Brownian motion $\{S_t, 0 \leq t \leq T\}$. It is sometimes written symbolically in a differential form

$$dS_t = \mu S_t\, dt + \sigma S_t\, dW_t.$$

Observe that μ measures the intensity with which the equity process increases with respect to time. If $\mu > 0 (< 0)$, the process tends to drift upwards (downwards). Hence μ is often called a drift parameter. The other parameter σ measures the intensity with which the process changes with respect to changes in the underlying Brownian motion. A high (low) value σ often leads to more volatile (stable) behavior of the process. Therefore, σ is called a volatility parameter.

Multivariate Itô formula can also be obtained using similar arguments as in the proof of univariate Itô formula.

Theorem 2.73. *Let $X = \{X_t : 0 \le t \le T\}$ and $Y = \{Y_t : 0 \le t \le T\}$ both be Itô processes and $f(t, x, y)$ be continuously differentiable with respect to t and twice continuously differentiable with respect to x and y. Then $\{f(t, X_t, Y_t) : 0 \le t \le T\}$ is also an Itô process and*

$$
\begin{aligned}
f(T, X_T, Y_T) \quad = \quad & f(0, X_0, Y_0) + \int_0^T f_t(t, X_t, Y_t) \, \mathrm{d}t + \int_0^T f_x(t, X_t, Y_t) \, \mathrm{d}X_t \\
& + \int_0^T f_y(t, X_t, Y_t) \, \mathrm{d}Y_t + \frac{1}{2} \int_0^T f_{xx}(t, X_t) \, \mathrm{d}[X, X]_t \\
& + \frac{1}{2} \int_0^T f_{yy}(t, X_t) \, \mathrm{d}[Y, Y]_t + \int_0^T f_{xy}(t, X_t) \, \mathrm{d}[X, Y]_t.
\end{aligned}
$$

A special case of the multivariate Itô formula, known as *product rule*, is obtained by setting $f(t, x, y) = xy$ in Theorem 2.73.

Theorem 2.74 (Product rule). *Let $X = \{X_t : 0 \le t \le T\}$ and $Y = \{Y_t : 0 \le t \le T\}$ be two Itô processes. Then $Z = \{Z_t = X_t Y_t : 0 \le t \le T\}$ is also an Itô process and given by*

$$
Z_T = Z_0 + \int_0^T X_t \, \mathrm{d}Y_t + \int_0^T Y_t \, \mathrm{d}X_t + [X, Y]_T. \tag{2.39}
$$

2.11   Stochastic differential equation

When applying Itô's formula, we often encounter equations in the differential form

$$
\mathrm{d}X_t = a(t, X_t) \, \mathrm{d}t + b(t, X_t) \, \mathrm{d}W_t,
$$

under some functions $a(t, x)$ and $b(t, x)$. When X_t appears on both sides, this is known as a stochastic differential equation, often abbreviated by SDE. If there is a stochastic process $\{X_t : 0 \le t \le T\}$ where X_t has an explicit representation in terms of t and the Brownian motion $\{W_t : 0 \le t \le T\}$ and which satisfies the SDE, such as the case of geometric Brownian motion in Example 2.72, we call it a solution to the SDE. More often than not, SDEs do not have explicitly known solutions. Therefore, it is important to keep in mind that some necessary technical conditions for $a(t, x)$ and $b(t, x)$ are known in order to guarantee the existence of such a solution. All SDEs that we shall encounter in the lecture notes satisfy these conditions, which are hence omitted for brevity.

An important property of any stochastic process driven by an SDE is that it always has the Markov property. While it is fairly technical to prove this property, which goes beyond the scope of this text and hence is omitted, we can explain the intuition behind the property. Observe that for $u \ge t$,

$$
X_u = X_t + \int_t^u a(s, X_s) \, \mathrm{d}s + \int_t^u b(s, X_s) \, \mathrm{d}W_s.
$$

Suppose that a and b are step functions defined on a partition with points $t_0 = t < t_1 < t_2 < \cdots < t_n = u$. Then

$$X_{t_1} = X_t + a(t, X_t)(t_1 - t) + b(t, X_t)(W_{t_1} - W_t).$$

Similarly, one can show that for $j = 1, 2, \cdots, n$

$$X_{t_j} = X_t + \sum_{i=1}^{j} \left[a(t_{i-1}, X_{t_{i-1}})(t_i - t_{i-1}) + b(t_{i-1}, X_{t_{i-1}})(W_{t_i} - W_{t_{i-1}}) \right].$$

Hence one can tell that X_u for $u > t$ depends only on X_t through $X_t, a(t, X_t), b(t, X_t)$ and that X_u does not depend on the state of the process prior to t. In fact, if we fix $X_t = x$, then it is clear that X_u is independent of the information set $\mathcal{F}_t$ which is generated by $\{W_s : 0 \leq s \leq t\}$. Therefore, for any measurable function h, we expect there to be a measurable function g such that

$$\mathbb{E}[X_u | \mathcal{F}_t] = g(t, X_t),$$

which implies the Markov property.

2.12 Applications to equity-linked insurance

2.12.1 Stochastic equity returns

Let us briefly recall the concept of time value of money in Section 1.1.1. The mechanism of compound interest is based on the assumption that the term of investment has no bearing on the underlying interest rate, i.e. an investment of five years bears the same interest rate per time per dollar as an investment of one year. This is sometimes referred as the flat yield curve. Under this assumption, the time value of money, represented by the accumulated function $a(t)$, is argued to satisfy the equation

$$a(t + s) = a(t)a(s), \qquad t, s \geq 0.$$

It follows from the solution that

$$\mathrm{d}a(t) = ra(t)\,\mathrm{d}t, \qquad t \geq 0, \tag{2.40}$$

where r is the force of interest.

Now, we intend to generalize this model to include random investment return. In reality, the assumption of flat yield curve makes the model inadequate to capture the true dynamics in a bond market. In contrast, the time commitment of investment has very little impact on the stock market. In an efficient stock market, the prices are determined by the balance of supply and demand regardless of any investor's decision as to how long one holds the stock. For this precise reason, in keeping with the essence of the previous model, we are interested in a suitable generalization to model random investment returns in the stock market. We now think of $\{a_t, t \geq 0\}$ as a stochastic process since a_t, at any time t, is a random variable reflecting the uncertainty with the proceeds from an investment of one dollar in the stock market for t periods.

Assume that all investors are rational and the market is perfectly efficient in that every investor is fully aware of the riskiness of their investment measured by distribution functions. Following the same logic as in the discussion of (1.1), we consider constraints on reasonable model setup:

1. For any $s, t \geq 0$, it should never occur that $a_{t+s} \succ a_t a_s$;

2. For any $s, t \geq 0$, it should never occur that $a_t a_s \succ a_{t+s}$,

where for two nonnegative random variables $a_1 \succ a_2$ means a_1 is greater than a_2 in stochastic order, i.e. $\mathbb{P}(a_1 > x) > \mathbb{P}(a_2 > x)$ for all $x \in [0, \infty)$. Note that when offered choices at any time, rational investors will always choose accumulations that have higher chances of positive investment returns. As discussed before, when the first assumption is violated, one could argue that no investor will enter the stock market. If the second assumption is violated, there will be an infinite number of transactions which eventually crushes the market.

Therefore, we postulate two criteria on what may be perceived as a good model of the investment of one unit with random returns.

1. In order to avoid any of these above-mentioned erratic behaviors in the stock market, it is reasonable to assume that for any $t, s \geq 0$,

$$a_{t+s} \sim a_t a_s \qquad (2.41)$$

   where $\sim$ means equality in distribution.

2. If two periods have no overlap, the growth of unit investment over one period should have no bearing on that of another period. In other words, a_t should be independent of a_{t+s}/a_s for any $t, s \geq 0$.

If we introduce a new stochastic process, $\{X_t, t \geq 0\}$, defined by $X_t = \ln a(t)$, then it follows immediately from the two criteria that for any $t > 0$, we must have

$$
\begin{aligned}
X_t &= \ln a_t = \ln\left(\frac{a_{t/n}}{a_0}\right) + \ln\left(\frac{a_{2t/n}}{a_{t/n}}\right) + \cdots + \ln\left(\frac{a_t}{a_{(n-1)t/n}}\right) \\
&= (X_{t/n} - 0) + (X_{2t/n} - X_{t/n}) + \cdots + (X_t - X_{(n-1)t/n}), \quad (2.42)
\end{aligned}
$$

where all random variables in brackets on the right-hand side are independent and identically distributed. This clearly shows that for any $t > 0$ X_t has an infinitely divisible distribution.

Definition 2.75 (Infinitely divisible distribution). A real-valued random variable Θ is said to have an infinitely divisible distribution if for each $n = 1, 2, \cdots$ there exist a sequence of i.i.d. random variables $\Theta_{1,n}, \Theta_{2,n}, \cdots, \Theta_{n,n}$ such that $\Theta \sim \Theta_{1,n} + \Theta_{2,n} + \cdots + \Theta_{n,n}$.

Examples of infinitely divisible distributions include Poisson, negative binomial, gamma, normal, etc. It is well-known in probability theory that there is a one-to-one correspondence between infinitely divisible distributions and Lévy processes.

Definition 2.76 (Lévy process). A stochastic process $X = \{X_t : t \geq 0\}$ is said to be a Lévy process if the following hold:

    1. $\mathbb{P}(X_0 = 0) = 1$;

    2. The paths of X are right-continuous with left limits with probability 1;

    3. For any $0 \leq s \leq t$, $X_t - X_s$ is equal in distribution to X_{t-s};

    4. For any $0 \leq s \leq t$, $X_t - X_s$ is independent of $\{X_u : u \leq s\}$.

Therefore, a good candidate model for the log-return process is Lévy process. Let us consider the logarithm of the moment generating function of the Lévy process at any time $t > 0$

$$\Psi_t(u) = \ln \mathbb{E}[e^{uX_t}].$$

Then using (2.42) twice we obtain for any positive integers m, n such that

$$m\Psi_1(u) = \Psi_m(u) = n\Psi_{m/n}(u),$$

and hence for any rational number $t > 0$,

$$\Psi_t(u) = t\Psi_1(u). \tag{2.43}$$

Using some continuity arguments, one can show that (2.43) holds true for all real number $t > 0$. In conclusion, any Lévy process has the property that

$$\mathbb{E}[e^{uX_t}] = e^{t\Psi_1(u)},$$

for some function Ψ_1, often known as the *Laplace exponent*.

Comparing Definitions 2.76 and 2.52, one can tell that Brownian motion is a special case of Lévy process. In particular, since the Brownian motion at a fixed time B_t is normally distributed, it follows that the Laplace exponent is given by

$$\psi_1(u) = \ln \mathbb{E}[e^{uB_1}] = \frac{u^2}{2}.$$

There are also many other interesting examples of Lévy processes such as Poisson process, compound Poisson, stable processes, etc. However, we refrain from discussing other Lévy processes beyond Brownian motion in this introductory book. Nonetheless, nearly all topics in the book can be further extended to more general models involving Lévy processes.

From now on, we consider a well-studied model for equity returns, known as the geometric Brownian motion or independent log-normal model in the insurance industry. Denote the evolution of values of the underlying equity fund or index by $\{S_t : t \geq 0\}$,

$$S_t = S_0 a_t = S_0 e^{X_t}, \qquad X_t = \left(\mu - \frac{\sigma^2}{2}\right)t + \sigma W_t, \qquad t \geq 0.$$

It follows immediately from Example 2.72 that $\{S_t : t \geq 0\}$ satisfies the stochastic differential equation

$$dS_t = \mu S_t \, dt + \sigma S_t \, dW_t. \tag{2.44}$$

There is also another reason why the geometric Brownian motion or geometric Lévy processes are popular in practice. Recall the Taylor expansion that

$$\ln(1 + x) = x + o(x).$$

Therefore, for very small $\Delta t > 0$, the logarithm of the growth of a unit investment over the period $[t, t + \Delta t]$ is roughly the percentage change in values of each unit investment over that period, i.e.

$$\ln\left(\frac{S_{t+\Delta t}}{S_t}\right) = \ln\left(1 + \frac{S_{t+\Delta t} - S_t}{S_t}\right) \approx \frac{S_{t+\Delta t} - S_t}{S_t}.$$

In other words, the geometric Brownian motion model adopts a convenient assumption that percentage changes of unit investment are normally distributed.

2.12.2   Guaranteed withdrawal benefits

If the equity value process is driven by the geometric Brownian motion determined by (2.44), then a policyholder's sub-account also follows a geometric Brownian motion. Observe that $F_t = f(t, S_t)$ where $f(t, x) = (F_0/S_0)x e^{-mt}$. Then applying Itô formula to (1.22) shows

$$
\begin{aligned}
dF_t &= f_t(t, S_t) \, dt + f_x(t, S_t) \, dS_t + \frac{1}{2} f_{xx}(t, S_t) \, d[S, S]_t \\
&= -mF_t \, dt + \frac{F_t}{S_t} \, dS_t \\
&= (\mu - m)F_t \, dt + \sigma F_t \, dW_t. \tag{2.45}
\end{aligned}
$$

In the theory of interest, annuity-certain is a type of financial arrangement in which payments of fixed amount are made periodically. Suppose that an investor invests x dollars with a savings account earning r dollars per time unit. Every dollar invested at time 0 would have grown to e^{rt} at the end of t periods. Assume that every dollar works like every other dollar, i.e. the investment is proportional to its principal. Had there not been any additional deposits or withdrawals, her investment would have accumulated to $e^{rt}x$. Now assume that she makes continuous withdrawals for consumption at the rate of one dollar per time unit from the savings account. Then she would have lost the accumulation of ds dollars every instant s up to time t, which is equal to $e^{r(t-s)} ds$. The total amount of lost accumulated values would be $\int_0^t e^{r(t-s)} ds$. Therefore, the outstanding balance at time t of the account is

$$\bar{s}_t := e^{rt}x - \int_0^t e^{r(t-s)} ds, \qquad (2.46)$$

or equivalently by the ODE

$$d\bar{s}_t = (r\bar{s}_t - 1) dt, \qquad \bar{s}_0 = x.$$

If the accumulation of investor's payments is unit-linked to an equity index driven by a Brownian motion, then the accumulated value at time t of one dollar deposited or withdrawn at u should be proportional to the financial return of holding one share of the equity index over the period $[u, t]$, i.e. S_t/S_u, for any time $0 \le u \le t$. Deducted by continuous fee payments, every dollar at time u is worth $e^{-m(t-u)}S_t/S_u$ at the end of t periods. With analogy to (2.46), if the account begins with an endowment of F_0 dollars and the investor withdraws w per time unit continuously for consumption, then the outstanding balance in the equity-linked account at t should be

$$F_t = \frac{S_t}{S_0}e^{-mt}F_0 - w\int_0^t \frac{S_t}{S_u}e^{-m(t-u)} du. \qquad (2.47)$$

The first term in (2.47) represents the potential balance had the investor not withdrawn at all, while the second term represents the loss of revenue due to the continuous withdrawals. We can rewrite F_t as $X_t Y_t$ where

$$X_t := S_t e^{-mt},$$
$$Y_t := \frac{F_0}{S_0} - w\int_0^t \frac{e^{mu}}{S_u} du.$$

It follows immediately from Theorem 2.74 that the dynamics of the subaccount follows the SDE

$$dF_t = X_t dY_t + Y_t dX_t$$
$$= S_t e^{-mt}\left(-w\frac{e^{mt}}{S_t}\right) dt + Y_t[-mX_t dt + X_t(\mu dt + \sigma dW_t)].$$

Rearranging terms yields the SDE with $F_0 > 0$ and $\mu^* = \mu - m$,

$$dF_t = (\mu^* F_t - w) dt + \sigma F_t dW_t, \qquad (2.48)$$

which was also obtained in (1.29) as an interpretation of the limit of the discrete-time recursive relation (1.25). This stochastic process is sometimes referred as the geometric Brownian motion with affine drift.

2.12.2.1 Laplace transform of ruin time

As alluded to in Section 1.2.6, we are interested in the ruin time of a policyholder's investment account in the analysis of an insurer's GMWB liability. Ideally we would like to know its probability distribution. However, it is much easier to determine the Laplace transform of the ruin time, which has a one-to-one correspondence with its distribution function,

$$L(x; s) := \mathbb{E}[e^{-s\tau}] = \int_0^\infty e^{-st}\mathbb{P}(\tau \in dt), \qquad s > 0, \qquad (2.49)$$

where the expectation implicitly depends on the initial value of the process F, i.e. $\mathbb{E}[\cdot] = \mathbb{E}[\cdot|F_0 = x]$. It is intuitive that the bigger the initial account value x the longer it takes for the account value to reach zero. Therefore, $L(x; s)$ must be a decreasing function of x.

Suppose that there exists a decreasing solution, $L(x)$, to an ordinary differential equation (ODE)

$$\frac{\sigma^2 x^2}{2}L''(x) + (\mu^* x - w)L'(x) - sL(x) = 0, \qquad x > 0, \qquad (2.50)$$

subject to the condition that

$$L(0) = 1. \qquad (2.51)$$

We can show that $L(x)$ must have the stochastic representation (2.49). Applying Itô's formula and product rule to $f(t, F_t) = e^{-st}L(F_t)$ gives

$$e^{-sT}L(F_T) = L(x) + \sigma \int_0^T e^{-st}L'(F_t)F_t \, dW_t$$

$$+ \int_0^T e^{-st}\left\{\frac{\sigma^2}{2}F_t^2 L''(F_t) + (\mu^* F_t - w)L'(F_t) - sL(F_t)\right\} dt. \quad (2.52)$$

Observe that

$$\mathbb{E}\left[\int_0^{T\wedge\tau} e^{-st}L'(F_t)F_t \, dW_t\right] = \mathbb{E}\left[\int_0^T e^{-st}L'(F_t)F_t I(F_t > 0) \, dW_t\right] = 0.$$

Replacing T with $T \wedge \tau$ in (2.52) and taking expectations on both sides yields

$$\mathbb{E}[e^{-s(T\wedge\tau)}L(F_{T\wedge\tau})] = L(x)$$

$$+ \mathbb{E}\left[\int_0^{T\wedge\tau} e^{-st}\left\{\frac{\sigma^2}{2}F_t^2 L''(F_t) + (\mu^* F_t - w)L'(F_t) - sL(F_t)\right\} dt\right].$$

Recall that L satisfies the ODE 2.50 and $F_\tau = 0$. Then it follows that

$$
\begin{aligned}
L(x) &= \mathbb{E}[e^{-s(T \wedge \tau)} L(F_{T \wedge \tau})] \\
&= \mathbb{E}[e^{-sT} L(F_T) I(T < \tau)] + \mathbb{E}[e^{-s\tau} L(F_\tau) I(\tau < T)] \\
&= \mathbb{E}[e^{-sT} L(F_T) I(T < \tau)] + \mathbb{E}[e^{-s\tau} I(\tau < T)]. \quad (2.53)
\end{aligned}
$$

Since $L(F_T) \le L(0) = 1$, the first term must be bounded by e^{-sT}. As we take $T \to \infty$ on both sides of (2.53), it is clear that the first term on the right-hand side vanishes and

$$
L(x) = \mathbb{E}[e^{-s\tau}].
$$

It is known that the ODE (2.50) has two real-valued fundamental solutions

$$
\begin{aligned}
L_1(x) &= x^{-k} \exp\left\{-\frac{2w}{\sigma^2 x}\right\} M\left(b - k, b, \frac{2w}{\sigma^2 x}\right) = x^{-k} M\left(k, b, -\frac{2w}{\sigma^2 x}\right), \\
L_2(x) &= x^{-k} \exp\left\{-\frac{2w}{\sigma^2 x}\right\} U\left(b - k, b, \frac{2w}{\sigma^2 x}\right),
\end{aligned}
$$

where M and U are known as Kummer's functions whose definitions can be found in Appendix D and

$$
k := \frac{2\mu^* - \sigma^2 + \sqrt{(2\mu^* - \sigma^2)^2 + 8\sigma^2 s}}{2\sigma^2}, \qquad b := 2k + 2 - \frac{2\mu^*}{\sigma^2}.
$$

It is known that L_1 is a decreasing function whereas L_2 is an increasing function. Therefore, the desired solution for L must be a multiple of L_1. It follows from D.1 that as $x \to 0+$,

$$
x^{-k} M\left(b - k, b, \frac{2w}{\sigma^2 x}\right) \exp\left(-\frac{2w}{\sigma^2 x}\right) \to \frac{\Gamma(b)}{\Gamma(b - k)} \left(\frac{2w}{\sigma^2}\right)^{-k}.
$$

In view of the boundary condition (2.51), we obtain the solution

$$
L(x; s) = \mathbb{E}[e^{-s\tau}] = \frac{\Gamma(b - k)}{\Gamma(b)} \left(\frac{2w}{\sigma^2 x}\right)^k M\left(k, b, -\frac{2w}{\sigma^2 x}\right). \quad (2.54)
$$

2.12.2.2 Present value of fee incomes up to ruin

Since asset-value-based fees are often taken as a fixed percentage of policyholders' account values, we often encounter quantities pertaining to the present value of fee incomes up to ruin of the following form

$$
D(x; s) := \mathbb{E}\left[\int_0^\tau e^{-st} F_t \, dt\right], \quad (2.55)
$$

where s is interpreted as the continuously compounding interest rate for discounting. Again the expectation depends on the initial account value $F_0 = x$ and can be interpreted as $\mathbb{E}[\cdot] = \mathbb{E}[\cdot | F_0 = x]$. Note that for $s > \mu - m$,

$$
D(x) \le \mathbb{E}\left[F_0 \int_0^\infty e^{-st} \frac{S_t}{S_0} e^{-mt} \, dt \,\middle|\, F_0 = x\right] = \frac{x}{s - \mu^*}.
$$

Suppose that there exists a solution $D(x)$ to the inhomogeneous ODE

$$\frac{\sigma^2 x^2}{2} D''(x) + (\mu^* x - w)D'(x) - sD(x) + x = 0, \qquad x > 0, \qquad (2.56)$$

subject to the boundary condition

$$D(0) = 0. \qquad (2.57)$$

We can also show that $D(x)$ must have the stochastic representation (2.55). By similar arguments to those used in the previous subsection, we can obtain

$$\mathbb{E}[e^{-s(T \wedge \tau)} D(F_{T \wedge \tau})] = D(x)$$

$$+ \mathbb{E}\left[\int_0^{T \wedge \tau} e^{-st}\left\{\frac{\sigma^2}{2} F_t^2 D''(F_t) + (\mu^* F_t - w)D'(F_t) - sD(F_t)\right\} dt\right].$$

In view of (2.56), we must have

$$\mathbb{E}[e^{-s(T \wedge \tau)} D(F_{T \wedge \tau})] = D(x) - \mathbb{E}\left[\int_0^{T \wedge \tau} e^{-st} F_t \, dt\right]. \qquad (2.58)$$

Note that for some constant $C > 0$

$$\mathbb{E}[e^{-sT} D(F_T)I(\tau > T)] \leq C\mathbb{E}[e^{-sT} F_T I(\tau > T)]$$

$$\leq C\mathbb{E}\left[e^{-sT}\frac{S_T}{S_0} e^{-mT}\right] = Ce^{-(s-\mu^*)T}.$$

Therefore, for $s > \mu - m$, as $T \to \infty$,

$$\mathbb{E}[e^{-s(T \wedge \tau)} D(F_{T \wedge \tau})] = \mathbb{E}[e^{-sT} D(F_T)I(\tau > T)] + \mathbb{E}[e^{-s\tau} D(F_\tau)I(\tau \leq T)] \to 0.$$

Taking $T \to \infty$ on both sides of (2.58) gives the representation (2.55).

Note that the ODE (2.56) has a particular solution

$$\frac{x}{s - \mu^*} + \frac{w}{s(\mu^* - s)}.$$

Given that D is finite near zero, D must be given by

$$D(x) = \frac{x}{s - \mu^*} + \frac{w}{s(\mu^* - s)} + Cx^{-k} M\left(k, b, -\frac{2w}{\sigma^2 x}\right),$$

for some constant C. Using the boundary condition (2.57), we obtain

$$\mathbb{E}\left[\int_0^\tau e^{-st} F_t \, dt\right] = \frac{x}{s - \mu^*} + \frac{w}{s(\mu^* - s)}$$

$$+ \frac{w}{s(s - \mu^*)} \frac{\Gamma(b - k)}{\Gamma(b)}\left(\frac{2w}{\sigma^2 x}\right)^k M\left(k, b, -\frac{2w}{\sigma^2 x}\right). \qquad (2.59)$$

2.12.3 Stochastic interest rates

While no mathematical model would be able to fully describe all market phenomena, a useful model should be able to capture important features. When developing mathematical models, people often seek models addressing stylized facts, which generally refer to qualitative empirical findings that are regarded as facts. For example, it is generally accepted that interest rates should fluctuate around its average over long term, which is known as *mean reversion*. In this introductory note, we consider two commonly used mean-reverting interest rate models.

2.12.3.1 Vasicek model

The model specifies that the instantaneous interest rate follows the SDE

$$\mathrm{d}r_t = \alpha(\gamma - r_t)\,\mathrm{d}t + \eta\,\mathrm{d}W_t, \tag{2.60}$$

where $\gamma > 0$ is called the long term mean, $\alpha > 0$ is called the speed of reversion and η is the instantaneous volatility. Note that when r_t is below (above) γ the process has a tendency to move upwards (downwards), as the non-stochastic term is positive (negative). Either way the process is driven towards the long-term mean γ, which is why the process is mean-reverting. The parameter α controls the intensity at which the process moves towards γ. Next, we can show by Itô's formula that the SDE admits the following explicit solution

$$r_t = r_0 e^{-\alpha t} + \gamma(1 - e^{-\alpha t}) + \eta e^{-\alpha t}\int_0^t e^{\alpha s}\,\mathrm{d}W_s. \tag{2.61}$$

Rewrite r_t as $X_t + Z_t U_t$ where

$$X_t := r_0 e^{-\alpha t} + \gamma(1 - e^{-\alpha t}),\, U_t := \int_0^t e^{\alpha s}\,\mathrm{d}W_s,\, Z_t := \eta e^{-\alpha t}.$$

Applying the one-dimensional Itô's formula shows that

$$\mathrm{d}X_t = [-\alpha r_0 e^{-\alpha t} - (-\alpha)\gamma e^{-\alpha t}]\,\mathrm{d} = -\alpha(X_t - \gamma)\,\mathrm{d}t.$$

Using the product rule, we obtain

$$\mathrm{d}Z_t U_t = Z_t\,\mathrm{d}U_t + U_t\,\mathrm{d}Z_t = \eta\,\mathrm{d}W_t - \alpha Z_t U_t\,\mathrm{d}t.$$

Putting the two pieces together, we manage to show that r_t defined in (2.61) indeed satisfies the SDE (2.60), since

$$
\begin{aligned}
\mathrm{d}r_t &= \mathrm{d}X_t + \mathrm{d}Z_t U_t \\
&= -\alpha(X_t + Z_t U_t)\,\mathrm{d} + \alpha\gamma\,\mathrm{d}t + \eta\,\mathrm{d}W_t \\
&= \alpha(\gamma - r_t)\,\mathrm{d}t + \eta\,\mathrm{d}W_t.
\end{aligned}
$$

Thus it is obvious that

$$\mathbb{E}[r_t] = \mu(r_0, t) := r_0 e^{-\alpha t} + \gamma(1 - e^{-\alpha t}), \tag{2.62}$$

$$\mathbb{V}[r_t] = \sigma^2(t) := \frac{\eta^2}{2\alpha}(1 - e^{-2\alpha t}). \tag{2.63}$$

Therefore, it is easy to see that γ is the long term mean and $\eta^2/(2\alpha)$ is the long term variance.

2.12.3.2 Cox-Ingersoll-Ross model

A "disadvantage" of the Vasicek model is that its interest rates can become negative, which is an undesirable feature of model. However, keep in mind that in recent years there are many developed countries with stagnant economies where negative interest rates have been observed. The perceived drawback may actually be a realistic feature. Nonetheless, if negative interest rates are to be avoided, a well-known model to address this issue is the Cox-Ingersoll-Ross (CIR) model, which stipulates that instantaneous interest rates follow the SDE

$$\mathrm{d}r_t = \alpha(\gamma - r_t)\,\mathrm{d}t + \eta\sqrt{r_t}\,\mathrm{d}W_t. \tag{2.64}$$

Note that the CIR model is also mean-reverting as it shares the same non-stochastic term with the Vasicek model. However, unlike Vasicek model, the SDE in the CIR model does not have an explicit solution. Nonetheless, the distribution of the CIR process determined by the SDE can still be calculated.

Here we illustrate how to calculate the mean of the CIR process in explicit form. To do this, we use the function $f(t, x) = e^{\alpha t}x$. It follows immediately from Itô formula that

$$\begin{aligned} \mathrm{d}e^{\alpha t}r_t &= \alpha e^{\alpha t}r_t\,\mathrm{d}t + e^{\alpha t}\,\mathrm{d}r_t \\ &= \alpha\gamma e^{\alpha t}\,\mathrm{d}t + \eta e^{\alpha t}r_t\,\mathrm{d}W_t. \end{aligned}$$

In other words,

$$r_t = e^{-\alpha t}\left(r_0 + \gamma(1 - e^{\alpha t}) + \eta\int_0^t e^{\alpha s}r_s\,\mathrm{d}W_s\right).$$

Note, however, that this is not a solution to the SDE, as the right-hand side involves the unknown r_t. Nonetheless, the unknown term is a stochastic process, which is known to have mean zero. Therefore,

$$\mathbb{E}[r_t] = e^{-\alpha t}\left(r_0 + \gamma(1 - e^{\alpha t})\right).$$

2.13   Bibliographic notes

The writing of this chapter is largely inspired by well-crafted texts and class notes for readers with diverse backgrounds including Shreve [97], Björk [10], Harrison [62] and Bass [6]. It is intended to offer a brief introduction to a rather advanced subject matter without diving into too heavy technical details. Readers williing to learn the material with more mathematical rigor are referred to the classic text of Karatzas and Shreve [69]. While this book only briefly touches on Lévy processes, most of the analysis can be extended to more general classes of Lévy processes. Well-known texts on Lévy process and other Markov processes are Kyprianou [72] and Rolski et al. [90].

Much of the material on applications to equity-linked insurance are drawn from Feng and Volkmer[48, 49]. Many results for applications to variable annuity guaranteed benefits have been extended to Lévy models in Feng, Kuznetsov and Yang [44].

2.14 Exercises

Section 2.1

1. Explain how many sets are there in the information set generated by the outcomes of three coin tosses, Ω_3.

2. Prove (2.5) in Example 2.11.

Section 2.2

1. There are six possible outcomes of rolling a die, $\{1, 2, 3, 4, 5, 6\}$. Suppose that we can roll a die infinitely many times and consider the sample space

   $\Omega_\infty = $ the set of infinite sequence of integers between 1 and 6.

   We assume that the probability of landing on each of the six numbers on a roll is $1/6$ and that the different rolls are independent. Then we can define a probability measure $\mathbb{P}$ on every set that can be described in terms of finitely many rolls. (The same procedure as the coin-toss space is defined in Example 2.11.) Describe how you can construct a uniformly distributed random variable taking values in $[0, 1]$ and defined on the infinite die-rolling space Ω_∞. Justify why it is uniformly distributed on $[0, 1]$.

2. Construct an exponential random variable on the probability space defined in Example 2.13.

3. A random variable maps all points inside and on a unit circle (a circle with radius 1) to numbers on the interval $[0, 1]$, as illustrated in Figure 2.10. For any point $(x, y) \in \{(x, y) : x^2 + y^2 = r^2\}$ with any $r \in [0, 1]$, $X(x, y) = r$. Suppose a probability measure $\mathbb{P}$ is defined on the unit circle by $\mathbb{P}(A) = $ area of A. Find the distribution function of the random variable X.

4. Independence of random variables can be affected by changes of measure. To illustrate this point, consider the space of two coin tosses $\Omega_2 = \{HH, HT, TH, TT\}$, and let stock prices be given by

$$S_0 = 4, S_1(H) = 8, S_1(T) = 2, S_2(HH) = 16,$$
$$S_2(HT) = S_2(TH) = 4, S_2(TT) = 1.$$

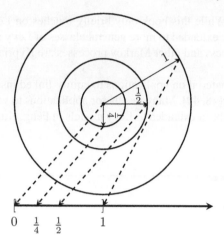

FIGURE 2.10: A mapping from unit circle to unit interval

Consider two probability measures given by

$$\tilde{\mathbb{P}}(HH) = 1/4, \tilde{\mathbb{P}}(HT) = 1/4, \tilde{\mathbb{P}}(TH) = 1/4, \tilde{\mathbb{P}}(TT) = 1/4.$$
$$\mathbb{P}(HH) = 4/9, \mathbb{P}(HT) = 2/9, \mathbb{P}(TH) = 2/9, \mathbb{P}(TT) = 1/9.$$

Define the random variable

$$X = \begin{cases} 1, & \text{if } S_2 = 4, \\ 0, & \text{if } S_2 \neq 4. \end{cases}$$

(a) List all the sets in $\sigma(X)$.

(b) List all the sets in $\sigma(S_1)$.

(c) Show that $\sigma(X)$ and $\sigma(S_1)$ are independent under the probability measure $\tilde{\mathbb{P}}$.

(d) Show that $\sigma(X)$ and $\sigma(S_1)$ are not independent under the probability measure $\mathbb{P}$.

Section 2.3

1. Use the definition of Lebesgue integral to show that for any discrete random variable X and its induced probability measure $\mathbb{M}_X$,

$$\int_{\mathbb{R}} x \, d\mathbb{M}_X(x) = \sum_{i=1}^{\infty} x_i \mathbb{M}_X(\{x_i\}).$$

Section 2.4

1. Compute the total variation between 0 and 2π of the function $f(t) = \sin(t)$ (i) using the intuitive formula (2.13) and (ii) using the alternative definition (2.17).

2. Consider the function

$$f(t) = \begin{cases} 0, & t = 0; \\ t^a \sin\left(\frac{1}{t}\right), & 0 < t \le 1. \end{cases}$$

Show that

(a) The function has finite total variation if $a > 1$;

(b) The function has finite quadratic variation if $a > 1/2$.

3. Show that if f has continuous derivative and g is continuous on $[0, T]$, then $[f, g]_T = 0$.

Section 2.5

1. An automobile insurance company classifies each of its policyholders as being of one of two types. It supposes that the number of accidents that a policyholder has in successive years are independent binomial random variables. The number of accidents for a low risk policyholder has mean 1 and variance 0.9 and that for a high risk policyholder has mean 4 and variance 2.4. The probability that a newly insured policyholder is the low risk type is 80% and the probability that she is the high risk type is 20%. Given the information an insurer obtains from a newly insured policyholder's first year accident report, what is the expected number of accidents in her second year?

2. Verify that the insurance premium P defined in Section 2.5 satisfies the following two properties:

(a) The premium P is $\mathcal{G}$-measurable.

(b) In all cases, the expectation of the premium P is equal to the expectation of the cost of coverage X, i.e.

$$\int_A P(\omega)\, d\mathbb{P}(\omega) = \int_A X(\omega)\, d\mathbb{P}(\omega) \qquad \text{for all } A \in \mathcal{G}.$$

3. Prove equation (2.21) in Theorem 2.45.

4. If X is a random variable and a predictor Z is another random variable measurable to a σ-algebra $\mathcal{G}$ (i.e. we know the distribution of Z given the information set $\mathcal{G}$), then the goodness of the prediction will be measured by $\mathbb{E}[(X - Z)^2]$, known as *the mean squared error*. This exercise is to demonstrate that the conditional expectation $Y = \mathbb{E}[X|\mathcal{G}]$ is the best predictor among the collection of all $\mathcal{G}$ measurable random variables.

(a) Suppose Z is any $\mathcal{G}$ measurable random variable. Show that

$$\mathbb{E}[(X - Z)^2|\mathcal{G}] = \mathbb{E}[(X - Y)^2|\mathcal{G}] + (Y - Z)^2.$$

(b) Use the above equation to show that $\mathbb{E}[(X - Z)^2]$ is minimized if and only if $Z = Y$.

(c) We can always write

$$X = Y + (X - Y).$$

Show that Y and $X - Y$ are uncorrelated. (i.e. $\mathbb{E}[Y(X - Y)] = 0$.)
*(Comments) We can think of the collection of all random variables as
a linear space and the collection of all $\mathcal{G}$-measurable random variables as a subspace. Given X, the conditional expectation $\mathbb{E}[X|\mathcal{G}]$ is
a projection of X onto the subspace of $\mathcal{G}$-measurable random variables. If we define the inner product of X_1 and X_2 to be $\mathbb{E}[X_1 X_2]$,
then the above result tells us that Y and $X - Y$ are orthogonal to
each other.*

Section 2.6

1. Let $\{X_1, X_2, \cdots, X_N\}$ be a sequence of independent random variables
    with mean 0 and variance 1. Let $S_k = \sum_{n=1}^{k} X_n$ and $M_k = S_k^2 - k$ for
    any $k = 1, 2, \cdots, N$. Show that $\{S_k, k = 1, 2, \cdots, N\}$ is a martingale.

2. Let $\{\mathcal{F}_t, t \geq 0\}$ be a given filtration and X be a given random variable
    with $\mathbb{E}|X| < \infty$. Let $M_t = \mathbb{E}[X|\mathcal{F}_t]$. Prove that $\{M_t, t \geq 0\}$ is martingale.

3. This exercise is intended to show that Markov processes and martingales
    are not subsets of each other.

    (a) Let X_0 be a given random variable and $\{\epsilon_n, n = 1, 2, \cdots\}$ be a sequence of i.i.d. mean 0 random variables and is independent of X_0.
         Define $X_{n+1} = X_n + \epsilon_{n+1} X_0$ for $n = 1, 2, \cdots, N$. Show that
         $\{X_n, n = 1, 2, \cdots\}$ is a martingale but not a Markov process.

    (b) Consider the "double or nothing" strategy. You start with one dollar
         and bet on the outcomes of independent coin tosses. If the coin turns
         up heads you double your wealth. Otherwise, you go broke. If the
         coin has a $1/3$ chance of turning up heads, then you can show that
         your wealth is not a martingale. Nonetheless, your wealth process is
         a Markov process.

Section 2.7

1. Show that the scaled random walk is

    (a) a process with independent and stationary increments;
    (b) a martingale;
    (c) a Markov process.

2. As the name suggests, a moment generating function $\psi(u) := \mathbb{E}(e^X)$
    yields all finite moments, provided that they exist, in the following way.

$$\left.\frac{d^k \psi(u)}{du^k}\right|_{u=0} = \mathbb{E}(X^k e^{uX})|_{u=0} = \mathbb{E}(X^k).$$

The *kurtosis* of a random variable is defined to be the ratio of its fourth central moment to the square of its variance. Let X be a normal random variable with mean μ and variance σ^2. Use the moment generating function of $X - \mu$ to show that $\mathbb{E}[(X - \mu)^4] = 3\sigma^4$. Therefore, the kurtosis of a normal random variable is 3.

Section 2.8

1. Consider the Brownian motion with drift for $t \geq 0$,

$$B_t = \mu t + \sigma W_t. \tag{2.65}$$

Show that for all $t \geq 0$, the quadratic variation of B up to time t is

$$[B, B]_t = \sigma^2 t.$$

2. A random vector $\mathbf{X}$ is said to have an n-dimensional multivariate normal distribution with mean $\boldsymbol{\mu}$ and covariance matrix $\boldsymbol{\Sigma}$ if its probability density function is of the form

$$f_{\mathbf{X}}(\mathbf{x}) = \frac{1}{\sqrt{(2\pi)^n |\boldsymbol{\Sigma}|}} \exp \left\{ -\frac{1}{2} (\mathbf{x} - \boldsymbol{\mu})^\top \boldsymbol{\Sigma}^{-1} (\mathbf{x} - \boldsymbol{\mu}) \right\}.$$

Suppose that two random vectors $\mathbf{X}_1, \mathbf{X}_2$ both have multivariate normal distributions with mean $\boldsymbol{\mu}_1$ and $\boldsymbol{\mu}_2$ and covariance matrix

$$\begin{bmatrix} \boldsymbol{\Sigma}_{11} & \boldsymbol{\Sigma}_{12} \\ \boldsymbol{\Sigma}_{21} & \boldsymbol{\Sigma}_{22} \end{bmatrix}$$

with a full rank matrix $\boldsymbol{\Sigma}_{22}$. Then the conditional distribution of $\mathbf{X}_1$ given that $\mathbf{X}_2 = \mathbf{x}$ is also normal with mean $\boldsymbol{\mu}_1 + \boldsymbol{\Sigma}_{12}\boldsymbol{\Sigma}_{22}^{-1}(\mathbf{x} - \boldsymbol{\mu}_2)$ and covariance matrix $\boldsymbol{\Sigma}_{11} - \boldsymbol{\Sigma}_{12}\boldsymbol{\Sigma}_{22}^{-1}\boldsymbol{\Sigma}_{21}$. Prove this result when both X_1 and X_2 are one-dimensional normal random variables.

3. Show that

   (a) for any stochastic process with continuous sample paths, if it has finite (total) variation, then its quadratic variation is constantly zero.

   (b) Brownian motion cannot have finite variation, i.e. $\langle W \rangle_t = \infty$ for any $0 < t < \infty$.

4. (a) Show that any stochastic process with continuous and monotonic sample paths must have finite (total) variation.

   (b) Consider the running supremum process of Brownian motion, $\{\overline{W}_t, 0 \leq t \leq T\}$, where

$$\overline{W}_t = \sup_{0 \leq s \leq t} \{W_s\}.$$

   Determine the total variation of the supremum up to time T.

Section 2.9

1. Consider the stochastic integral $J_t = \int_0^t \Delta_s \, dX_s$ defined in (2.36). Determine its quadratic variation $[J, J]_t$.

2. Let $\{W_t : 0 \le t \le T\}$ be a Brownian motion with an associated filtration $\{\mathcal{F}_t : 0 \le t \le T\}$ and $\{\Gamma_t : 0 \le t \le T\}$ be another adapted and square integrable process. Define a new stochastic process $\{S_t : 0 \le t \le T\}$ by

$$S_t := S_0 \exp\left\{\int_0^t \Gamma_s \, dW_s - \frac{1}{2} \int_0^t \Gamma_s^2 \, ds\right\},$$

    where S_0 is a fixed positive number. Show that the process $\{S_t : 0 \le t \le T\}$ is a martingale.

3. Suppose that $\{S_t : 0 \le t \le T\}$ is a geometric Brownian motion defined by (2.37). Determine its quadratic variation $[S, S]_t$ for each $t \in [0, T]$.

Section 2.10

1. Use Itô's formula to prove that

$$\int_t^{t+h} [W_s - W_t] \, dW_s = \frac{1}{2} (W_{t+h} - W_t)^2 - \frac{1}{2} h.$$

    Observe this approach also verifies the result in Example 2.66, which was obtained by definition.

2. Use the one-dimensional Itô formula to show that the process $\{X(t), t \ge 0\}$,

$$X(t) = e^{at} X(0) + \sigma \int_0^t e^{a(t-s)} \, dW(s), \qquad t > 0,$$

    where $X(0)$ is a constant, is a solution to the stochastic differential equation

$$dX(t) = aX(t) \, dt + \sigma \, dW(t).$$

3. Consider the geometric Brownian motion $\{S_t : 0 \le t \le T\}$ defined in Example 2.72. Show that the new process defined by $\{S_t^\alpha : 0 \le t \le T\}$ satisfies the stochastic differential equation for $0 < t < T$

$$dS_t^\alpha = \left(\alpha\mu + \frac{1}{2}\alpha(\alpha - 1)\sigma^2\right) S_t^\alpha \, dt + \alpha\sigma S_t^\alpha \, dW_t.$$

Section 2.12

1. Suppose that a policyholder makes deposits into her sub-account continuously at the rate of d per time unit and that the account value is linked to an equity index whose dynamics is driven by the geometric Brownian motion defined by (2.37). Show that the dynamics of the sub-account is driven by

$$dF_t = (\mu^* F_t + d) \, dt + \sigma F_t \, dW_t.$$

2. Consider the dynamics of a policyholder's sub-account given by the geometric Brownian motion in (2.45). We are often interested in a stochastic process pertaining to the present value of fee incomes, denoted by $\{A_t : t \geq 0\}$ where for all $t \geq 0$

$$A_t := \int_0^t e^{-st} F_s \, \mathrm{d}s.$$

(a) Find the total variation of the process up to time T, i.e. $\langle A \rangle_T$.

(b) Find the quadratic variation of the process up to time T, i.e. $[A, A]_T$.

(c) Show that the bivariate process $\{(F_t, A_t) : t \geq 0\}$ has the Markov property.

3

Monte Carlo Simulations of Investment Guarantees

Monte Carlo methods are computational algorithms that estimate deterministic quantities by repeated sampling of random events. These deterministic quantities often admit representations in terms of random variables. For example, when an actuary intends to compute the expected value, $\mathbb{E}[L]$, of an insurance liability, L, it is typically very difficult, if not impossible, to determine the exact distribution of L as it often arises from a complex asset and liability structure. The principle of a Monte Carlo approach is to draw samples from independent experiments of L (e.g. by setting different economic scenarios), denoted by $L^{(1)}, L^{(2)}, \cdots, L^{(n)}$, and to rely on the strong law of large numbers which implies that as $n \to \infty$,

$$\frac{1}{n} \left(L^{(1)} + L^{(2)} + \cdots + L^{(n)} \right) \longrightarrow \mathbb{E}[L].$$

While the convergence is guaranteed in theory, there are at least two issues arising from its implementation in practice. (1) It is impossible to run infinite experiments in reality, therefore, one has to settle with a sufficiently large sample of finite size n. (2) We can only obtain observed values, sometimes referred as realizations, of random variables. To distinguish the two concepts, we follow the convention of upper letters for random variables and lower letters for their realizations. A random sample means a collection of observed values from independent copies of the same random variable. For example, a random sample of the insurance liability is denoted by $\{l_1, l_2, \cdots, l_n\}$ where l_k is a realization of the k-th experiment $L^{(k)}$. Therefore, a Monte Carlo algorithm effectively computes an estimate based on realizations from a finite sample. For instance, we can use $(l_1 + l_2 + \cdots + l_n)/n$ to estimate $\mathbb{E}[L]$.

3.1 Simulating continuous random variables

Most statistical software packages provide built-in algorithms to generate common discrete and continuous random variables such as uniform, normal and exponential random variables. However, for life insurance applications, we often want to simulate policyholders' remaining lifetimes, which are modeled by distributions that are usually not pre-programmed. Therefore, we provide a brief summary of several well-known methods for generating more "sophisticated" random variables from common random variables.

3.1.1   Inverse transformation method

Suppose that the desired random variable T has a known distribution function F with an explicit inverse function F^{-1}. Then, we can generate random samples $\{t_1, t_2, \cdots, t_n\}$ as follows. Throughout this chapter, we shall refer to a uniform random variable on the interval $[0,1]$ simply as a uniform random variable, denoted by U.

Algorithm of inverse transformation method: For $j = 1, 2, \cdots, n$,

Step 1: Generate a realization u_j of a uniform random variable.
Step 2: Set $t_j = F^{-1}(u_j)$.

This algorithm is based on the well-known result that $F^{-1}(U)$ has the same distribution as T.

$$\mathbb{P}(F^{-1}(U) \le t) = \mathbb{P}(F(F^{-1}(U)) \le F(t)) = \mathbb{P}(U \le F(t)) = F(t).$$

Equivalently, one can replace the inverse function F^{-1} in Step 2 by the inverse function of its survival function $S(t) = 1 - F(t)$. This is because

$$\mathbb{P}(S^{-1}(U) \le t) = \mathbb{P}(U \ge S(t)) = \mathbb{P}(1 - U \ge S(t)) = \mathbb{P}(U \le F(t)) = F(t),$$

where the first equality is due to S being non-increasing and the second equality comes from the fact that $1 - U$ is identically distributed as U.

Example 3.1 (Gompertz's law of mortality).   Let T_x be the random variable for future lifetime of a policyholder at age x. The Gompertz's law of mortality is characterized by the hazard rate function

$$\mu(t) := \frac{f(t)}{S(t)} = Bc^t, \qquad t \ge 0,$$

where $0 < B < 1, c > 1$, $S(t) = \mathbb{P}(T_0 > t)$ is the survival function of a newborn T_0 and $f(t) = -S'(t)$ is the corresponding density function. It is easy to show that the probability that a policyholder at age x will survive t years:

$$S_x(t) := \mathbb{P}(T_x > t) = \mathbb{P}(T_0 > x + t | T_0 > x) = \exp\left\{ -\frac{B}{\ln c} c^x (c^t - 1) \right\}.$$

Therefore, if we generate a random sample $\{u_1, u_2, \cdots, u_n\}$ of the $[0,1]$-uniform random variable, then a random sample from the Gompertz's law of mortality is obtained by $g(u_1), g(u_2), \cdots, g(u_n)$ where g is the inverse function of the survival function $S_x(t)$ and given by

$$g(u) = \frac{\ln\left(1 - \frac{\ln u \ln c}{Bc^x}\right)}{\ln c}.$$

Example 3.2 (Rayleigh distribution). Given that a standard Brownian motion $\{W_t : 0 \leq t \leq 1\}$ hits the level b at time 1, its maximum over the period $[0, 1]$

$$M_1 := \sup_{t \in [0,1]} \{W_t\}$$

has the following distribution function

$$F(x) = 1 - e^{2x(x-b)}, \qquad x \geq b.$$

If we can generate a random sample $\{u_1, u_2, \cdots, u_n\}$ of the uniform random variable, then a random sample $\{m_1, m_2, \cdots, m_n\}$ of the maximum can be determined by

$$m_j = \frac{b}{2} + \frac{\sqrt{b^2 - 2\ln(u_j)}}{2}.$$

3.1.2 Rejection method

When an explicit form of F^{-1} is not available, it is not easy to apply the inverse transform method. Therefore, we often consider an alternative approach known as the rejection method. Suppose that the desired random variable T has a known density function f and we know how to generate a random sample of an auxiliary random variable Y with a known positive density function g. It is also known that the ratio f/g is bounded, i.e. there exists a constant $C \neq 0$ such that

$$\frac{f(t)}{g(t)} \leq C \qquad \text{for all } t.$$

Algorithm of rejection method: For $j = 1, 2, \cdots, n$

Step 1: Generate a realization, y, of the auxiliary random variable Y and a realization, u, of an independent uniform random variable.
Step 2: Set $t_j = y$ if $u \leq f(y)/Cg(y)$. Return to Step 1 otherwise.

We can show that the algorithm does produce the desired random variable. Observe that

$$\mathbb{P}\left(Y \leq t \,\Big|\, U \leq \frac{f(Y)}{Cg(Y)}\right) = \frac{1}{K}\mathbb{P}\left(Y \leq t, U \leq \frac{f(Y)}{Cg(Y)}\right) \tag{3.1}$$

$$= \frac{1}{K}\int_{-\infty}^{t} \mathbb{P}\left(U \leq \frac{f(Y)}{Cg(Y)}\,\Big|\, Y = y\right) g(y)\,dy$$

$$= \int_{-\infty}^{t} \frac{f(y)}{KCg(y)}g(y)\,dy$$

$$= \frac{1}{KC}\int_{-\infty}^{t} f(y)\,dy, \tag{3.2}$$

where $K = \mathbb{P}(U \le f(Y)/Cg(Y))$. Furthermore, letting $t \to \infty$ on the right hand side of (3.1) shows that

$$\lim_{t\to\infty} \frac{1}{K}\mathbb{P}\left(Y \le t, U \le \frac{f(Y)}{Cg(Y)}\right) = \frac{1}{K}\mathbb{P}\left(U \le \frac{f(Y)}{Cg(Y)}\right) = 1.$$

Letting $t \to \infty$ in (3.2) leads to

$$\lim_{t\to\infty} \frac{1}{KC}\int_{-\infty}^{t} f(y)\,\mathrm{d}y = \frac{1}{KC}.$$

Since both (3.1) and (3.2) are equivalent, it follows that $K = 1/C$. In conclusion,

$$\mathbb{P}\left(Y \le t \,\middle|\, U \le \frac{f(Y)}{Cg(Y)}\right) = \int_{-\infty}^{t} f(y)\,\mathrm{d}y = \mathbb{P}(T \le t).$$

Keep in mind that the number of random numbers sampled from T and U in order to generate one random number for Y is uncertain due to the selection criterion. In fact, since we know that the chance of acceptance is $1/C$, i.e. $\mathbb{P}(U \le f(Y)/cg(Y)) = K = 1/C$, then the number of random numbers from Y until the first y is accepted is a geometric random variable with the probability of success being $1/C$. This implies that the number of trials until the first success, the sample size of Y to produce one realization of X, is given by C. Hence, in order to develop an efficient simulation algorithm, we want the constant C to be as small as possible.

Example 3.3 (Makeham's law of mortality). Makeham's law of mortality is an extension of Gompertz's law with the hazard rate function

$$\mu(t) = A + Bc^t, \qquad t \ge 0,$$

where the constant term $A > 0$ is added to account for the rate of deaths due to accidents and the exponential term is interpreted as the rate of deaths due to aging. It can be shown that under Makeham's law

$$S_x(t) = \exp\left\{-At - \frac{B}{\ln c}c^x(c^t - 1)\right\}.$$

Note that in this case it is impossible to obtain an explicit expression for S^{-1}. Hence, we sort to the rejection method to generate a random sample from Makeham's law given that a random sample from Gompertz's law. Let

$$f(t) = (A + Bc^t)\exp\left\{-At - \frac{B}{\ln c}c^x(c^t - 1)\right\}, \tag{3.3}$$

and

$$g(t) = Bc^t \exp\left\{-\frac{B}{\ln c}c^x(c^t - 1)\right\}.$$

Recall that $c > 1$ and $A > 0$. Then it is clear that

$$\frac{f(t)}{g(t)} = \left(\frac{A}{B} e^{-(\ln c)t} + 1\right) e^{-At} \leq C := \frac{A}{B} + 1.$$

Now that f, g and C are all identified, we can proceed as described in the algorithm to carry out the simulation based on the rejection method.

Example 3.4 (Mixture of exponentials). It is sometimes convenient to approximate mortality density by a mixture of exponentials. We shall provide an application in the pricing of GLWB in Section 4.7.5. Here we demonstrate how to simulate a probability density given by a mixture of exponentials using the rejection method. Suppose that we are interested in generating a random sample from the following *hyperexponential* density function

$$f(t) = \frac{4}{3} e^{-2t} + \frac{4}{3} e^{-4t}, \qquad t \geq 0.$$

It is common to use an exponential auxiliary random variable with parameter $\lambda > 0$ and density function

$$g(t) = \lambda e^{-\lambda t}, \qquad t \geq 0.$$

It is clear that if $\lambda > 2$ then the ratio $f(t)/g(t) \to \infty$ as $t \to \infty$. In order to find a constant C such that $f(t)/g(t) \leq C$ for all $t \geq 0$, we have to use $\lambda \leq 2$, in which case the derivative of $f(t)/g(t)$ is negative and hence $f(t)/g(t)$ must be a decreasing function of t. Therefore,

$$\frac{f(t)}{g(t)} \leq \frac{f(0)}{g(0)} = \frac{8}{3\lambda}.$$

We can achieve the smallest possible C by setting $\lambda = 2$.

In general, if we want to draw a random sample of a hyperexponential distribution with density

$$f(t) = \sum_{i=1}^{N} p_i \lambda_i e^{-\lambda_i t}, \qquad t \geq 0,$$

where $0 < p_i < 1$ and λ_i for all i's and $\sum_{i=1}^{N} p_i = 1$, then the best choice of auxiliary exponential distribution for the rejection method is always given by the one with parameter $\lambda = \min_{1 \leq i \leq N}\{\lambda_i\}$.

3.2 Simulating discrete random variables

In practice, we often rely on non-parametric distributions for building survival models, as they naturally arise from industry mortality data or company experience. For example, Appendix A.3 provides a life table required by the NAIC for statutory reserving of the GMDB. Since survival probabilities $_kp_0$'s are only available for integer ages $k \in \mathbb{N}$, each life table corresponds to a discrete random variable, known as the curtate future lifetime of a newborn, K_0, for which $\mathbb{P}(K_0 > k) = {}_kp_0$. We could determine the cumulative distribution function of K_0 by tabulating the pairs $(k, {}_kq_0)$ where $_kq_0 = 1 - {}_kp_0$ for $k = 1, 2, \cdots, 115$. Similarly, we can extract information from the life table to determine the cumulative distribution function of K_x for $x = 0, 1, 2, \cdots, 114$. While the methods for simulating discrete random variables in this section apply to general discrete random variables, we shall focus on random variables with finite support only on nonnegative integers, due to insurance applications of future lifetime random variable K_x.

3.2.1   Bisection method

The most natural approach to generate a discrete random variable is the analogue of the inverse transformation method in Section 3.1.1. In principle, one could draw a realization u of a uniform random variable U and locate its position on the table relative to death probabilities, i.e. find row k for which

$$_kq_x < u \le {}_{k+1}q_x. \tag{3.4}$$

Then the desired realization of the curtate future lifetime K_0 is given by k. It is easy to see that such an intuitive method indeed produces the correct random variable, as

$$\mathbb{P}(K_0 = k) = \mathbb{P}\left({}_kq_x < U \le {}_{k+1}q_x\right) = {}_{k+1}q_x - {}_kq_x.$$

Similarly, one can produce a realization of the end of the year of death, $k + 1$, or a realization of the time of death based on the uniform distribution of death (UDD) assumption

$$\frac{\left({}_{k+1}q_x - u\right)k + (u - {}_kq_x)(k + 1)}{{}_{k+1}q_x - {}_kq_x}.$$

While the idea is quite straightforward, the search of k in (3.4) is easier said than done. The brute force approach is the sequential linear search, in which the algorithm starts at $k = 1$ (or $k = w$ where w is the maximum value) on a table of distribution function such as Table 3.1 and move downward (upward) one row at a time on the table until $u > {}_kq_x$ ($u \le {}_kq_x$). However, the linear search can be quite time consuming, as it moves through all adjacent entries on the table. Here we intend to introduce a few more efficient approaches to produce a random sample $\{k_1, k_2, \cdots, k_n\}$ of the curtate future lifetime K_x.

Bisection search algorithm: For $j = 1, 2, \cdots, n$

Step 1: Generate a realization, u_j, from a uniform random variable. Set the left pointer $l = 0$ and the right pointer $r = w$.
Step 2: While $l < r - 1$, do the following.

1. Set $m = \lfloor (l + r)/2 \rfloor$;

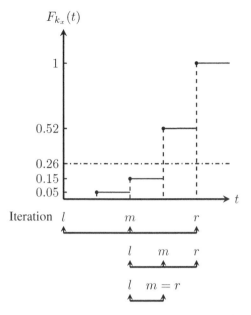

FIGURE 3.1: An illustration of bisection search algorithm

2. If $u_j > {}_mq_x$, set $l = m$. Otherwise, set $r = m$.

Step 3: Set $k_j = l$.

The algorithm is best explained with a simple example.

Example 3.5. Suppose that we can extract the following information from a life table to develop a survival model for an individual at an advanced age and that the maximum number of years of survival is $w = 4$.

k	${}_kq_x$
1	0.05
2	0.15
3	0.52
4	1.00

TABLE 3.1: Distribution function of a future lifetime random variable

Suppose a realization $u = 0.26$ is drawn from a uniform random variable in Step 1. As illustrated by Figure 3.1, we can determine the sample k in three iterations in Step 2. In the first iteration, the pointers $l = 0, m = 2$ and $r = 4$. Since $0.26 > {}_mq_x = 0.15$, the first half interval $[0, 2]$ is eliminated. The left pointer is moved to

$l = 2$. In the second iteration, the middle pointer is reset to $m = 3$. Since $_m q_x = 0.52 > 0.26$, the second half interval $[3, 4]$ is ruled out. The right pointer is shifted to $r = 3$. The while loop terminates at the third iteration as $l = r - 1 = 2$. Therefore, the corresponding realization of a curtate future lifetime is $k = 2$.

3.2.2   Narrow bucket method

While a bisection search does cut down the number of steps in a linear search, it cannot compete with human intuition. For example, any layman could quickly locate the position of 0.26 between 0.15 and 0.52 in one step. A careful thinking would reveal that the first step in our thought process is to compare the first decimal place of all numbers in the table and that of 0.26, which one can immediately identify as a number between 0.2 and 0.3. Therefore, anyone would quickly point out that the number should be placed between 0.15 and 0.52. To make this strategy operational for a computer, we can utilize the idea of curtate lifetime. For example, divide the interval $[0, 1]$ into 10 subintervals of equal length, $[0, 0.1], [0.1, 0.2], \cdots, [0.9, 1.0]$, indexed by $1, 2, \cdots, 10$. Then we can quickly identify that it belongs to the third interval $[0.2, 0.3]$ by calculating the index $\lceil 0.26 \times 10 \rceil = 3$. This is the set-up of the so-called "narrow bucket" method.

Before starting the search process, we divide $[0, 1]$ into m buckets indexed by $1, 2, \cdots, m$, each of width $1/m$. Although m is an arbitrary parameter, it is usually sufficient when m is chosen between w and $3w$. For each bucket $i = 1, 2 \cdots, m$, set l_i to be the maximum value at which the cumulative distribution function is less than the lower boundary of the i-th bucket and r_i to be the maximum value at which the cumulative distribution function is less than the upper boundary of the i-th bucket, i.e.

$$l_i = \max \left\{ j : {}_j q_x \le \frac{i-1}{m} \right\}, \qquad r_i = \max \left\{ j : {}_j q_x < \frac{i}{m} \right\}.$$

One has to look at an illustration such as Example 3.6 to better understand the purpose of setting up the pointers. Roughly speaking, if a random number between 0 and 1 falls in the i-th bucket, then the left pointer l_i and the right pointer r_i indicate the range of possible integers for a realization of the random variable. We can then proceed in two cases.

1. $l_i = r_i$

   The entire bucket is contained within the range of cumulative probabilities for two integer ages. If a number u drawn from a uniform random variable falls in the i-th bucket, then there is no doubt that the realization of the curtate lifetime is l_i.

2. $l_i < r_i$

   If u lies in the i-th bucket, there is ambiguity as to which of $l_i, l_i +$

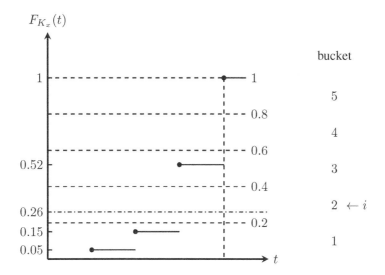

FIGURE 3.2: An illustration of narrow bucket algorithm

$1, \cdots, r_i$ is the realization of the desired random variable. Then we perform a linear search to find the k such that $l_i \leq k \leq r_i$ and $_kq_x \leq u <\; _{k+1}q_x$. To prepare for the search algorithm, we first develop a table $\{b_1, b_2, \cdots, b_m\}$ to record the integer from which to begin the search in each bucket. If $l_i = r_i$, then set $b_i = l_i$. Otherwise, set $b_i = -l_i$, where the negative value is to be used to invoke a linear search within the bucket.

Narrow bucket algorithm: For $j = 1, 2, \cdots, n$

Step 1: Generate a realization, u_j, from a uniform random variable. Set $i = \lceil mu_j \rceil$.

Step 2: If $b_i > 0$, then set $k_j = b_i$. Otherwise, set $k_j = -b_i$ and do the following: While $_{k_j+1}q_x < u_j$, set $k_j = k_j + 1$.

Let us continue with the previous example to illustrate the narrow bucket algorithm.

Example 3.6. Consider generate a realization of the random variable defined by the distribution function in Table 3.1. We summarize all values of l_i, r_i, b_i in Table 3.2.

Once the table is set up, we begin the algorithm by drawing a realization from a uniform random variable, say $u = 0.26$. The search process is illustrated in Figure 3.2. Note that the index of the narrow bucket containing u is given by $i = \lceil 5 \times 0.26 \rceil = 2$. Searching through Table 3.2, we observe that $b_2 = 2 > 0$. Then there is only one possibility that the realization k of the desired random variable must be 2.

---

i	1	2	3	4	5
l_i	0	2	2	3	4
r_i	2	2	3	3	4
b_i	0	2	-2	3	4

TABLE 3.2: Bucket table

3.3 Simulating continuous-time stochastic processes

3.3.1 Exact joint distribution

Both Brownian motions and geometric Brownian motions are relatively easy to simulate, as their finite time distributions are well known.

3.3.1.1 Brownian motion

Suppose we want to generate a sample path of Brownian motion with drift $\{B_0, B_{t_1}, \cdots, B_{t_n}\}$ defined in (2.65) at time points where $t_0 = 0 < t_1 < t_2 < \cdots < t_n$. For brevity, we shall denote the sample path by $\{b_0, b_1, \cdots, b_n\}$ where b_j is a realization of B_{t_j}. Given that $B_{t_{j-1}} = b_{j-1}$, it follows from definition that B_{t_j} is normally distributed with mean $b_{j-1} + \mu(t_j - t_{j-1})$ and variance $\sigma^2(t_j - t_{j-1})$. Therefore, a common approach is first to generate random increments and then to determine resulting positions in a chronological order.

Algorithm for generating a sample path of Brownian motion:

Step 0: Set $t = 0, j = 0$ and $w_j = 0$.
Step 1: Generate a realization, z_j, of a standard normal random variable.
Step 2: Set $t = t_j$ and $w_j = w_{j-1} + b(t_j - t_{j-1}) + \sigma\sqrt{t_j - t_{j-1}}z_j$. Unless $j = n$, return to Step 1 .

3.3.1.2 Geometric Brownian motion

Similarly, we can also generate a sample path of geometric Brownian motion by its representation in terms of a Brownian motion. Recall that for any fixed $t \geq 0$ and $S_0 > 0$,

$$S_t = S_0 \exp\left\{(\mu - \frac{\sigma^2}{2})t + \sigma W_t\right\}.$$

Here we shall denote the sample path by $\{s_0, s_1, \cdots, s_n\}$ where s_j is a realization of S_{t_j}. Suppose that the geometric Brownian motion starts off at $S_0 > 0$.

Algorithm for generating a sample path of geometric Brownian motion:

Step 0: Set $t = 0, j = 0$ and $s_j = S_0$.

Step 1: Randomly generate a number, z_j, from a standard normal random variable.

Step 2: Set $t = t_j$ and $s_j = s_{j-1} \exp\{(\mu - \sigma^2/2)(t_j - t_{j-1}) + \sigma\sqrt{t_j - t_{j-1}} z_j\}$. Unless $j = n$, return to Step 1 .

3.3.1.3 Vasicek process

Consider generating a random sample of instantaneous interest rates from the Vasicek model at time points $t_0 = 0 < t_1 < t_2 < \cdots < t_n$. It follows immediately from (2.61) that for $j = 1, 2, \cdots, n$

$$r_{t_j} = e^{-\alpha(t_j - t_{j-1})} r_{t_{j-1}} + \gamma \left[1 - e^{-\alpha(t_j - t_{j-1})}\right] + \eta \int_{t_{j-1}}^{t_j} e^{-\alpha(t_j - s)} \, dW_s.$$

Observe that given a known value of $r_{t_{j-1}}$, the random variable r_{t_j} is normally distributed with mean $\mu(r_{t_{j-1}}, t_j - t_{j-1})$ and variance $\sigma^2(t_j - t_{j-1})$ where functions μ and σ^2 are given by (2.62) and (2.63) respectively.

Algorithm for generating a sample path of instantaneous interest rates from the Vasicek model:

Step 0: Set $t = 0, j = 0$ and $r_j = r_0$.

Step 1: Generate a realization, z_j, of a standard normal random variable.

Step 2: Set $t = t_j$ and $r_j = e^{-\alpha(t_j - t_{j-1})} r_{j-1} + \gamma \left[1 - e^{-\alpha(t_j - t_{j-1})}\right] + \eta\sqrt{\frac{1}{2\alpha}\left(1 - e^{-2\alpha(t_{j+1} - t_j)}\right)} z_j$. Unless $j = n$, return to Step 1.

3.3.2 Euler discretization

Since we know that the geometric Brownian motion is a solution to the SDE

$$dS_t = \mu S_t \, dt + \sigma S_t \, dW_t,$$

one would attempt to simulate a sample path by the approximate recursive relation

$$s_j = s_{j-1} + \mu s_{j-1}(t_j - t_{j-1}) + \sigma s_{j-1}(w_j - w_{j-1}). \tag{3.5}$$

This method is known as the Euler discretization, which is very useful for simulating stochastic processes determined by stochastic differential equations with no explicit solution. However, one should keep in mind that the method based on exact joint distribution in Section 3.3.1 is superior in terms of accuracy. Observe that $(s_0, s_1, \cdots, s_n)$ is a sample generated from the exact distributions of the random variables $(S_0, S_1, \cdots, S_n)$, whereas the Euler discretization produces an approximation that contains discretization errors. A cautious reader would notice that (3.5) can in fact produce negative values for s_j's, as $w_j - w_{j-1}$ is generated from a normal random variable and can be a negative number with large absolute value. This clearly contradicts the fact that S_j's are strictly positive random variables.

3.3.2.1 Euler method

Let us consider the Euler discretization and its refinement for Itô's process determined by

$$dX_t = a(X_t)\, dt + b(X_t)\, dW_t.$$

The idea of the Euler discretization is to approximate increments of the process

$$X_{t+\Delta t} - X_t = \int_t^{t+\Delta t} a(X_s)\, ds + \int_t^{t+\Delta t} b(X_s)\, dW_s$$

using the notion of integrals with simple processes

$$\int_t^{t+\Delta t} a(X_s)\, ds \;\approx\; \int_t^{t+\Delta t} a(X_t)\, ds = a(X_t)\Delta t. \tag{3.6}$$

$$\int_t^{t+\Delta t} b(X_s)\, dW_s \;\approx\; \int_t^{t+\Delta t} b(X_t)\, dW_s = b(X_t)[W_{t+\Delta t} - W_t]. \tag{3.7}$$

Algorithm for Euler method:

Step 0: Set $t = 0, j = 0$ and $x_j = x_0$.

Step 1: Randomly generate a number, z_j, from a standard normal random variable.

Step 2: Set $t = t_j$ and $x_j = x_{j-1} + a(x_{j-1})(t_j - t_{j-1}) + b(x_{j-1})\sqrt{t_j - t_{j-1}}\, z_j$. Unless $j = n$, return to Step 1.

A disadvantage of the Euler discretization is that (3.6) is considered $O(\Delta t)$ whereas (3.7) behaves like $O(\sqrt{\Delta t})$ as $W_{t+\Delta t} - W_t \sim \sqrt{\Delta t}\, Z$ where Z is a standard normal random variable. The mismatch in the rate of convergence seems to suggest that the approximation of (3.7) can be improved with the consideration of $O(t)$ terms.

3.3.2.2 Milstein method

To find a better approximation of (3.7), we expand $b(X_s)$ using Itô's formula

$$
\begin{aligned}
db(X_s) &= b'(X_s)\, dX_s + \frac{1}{2} b''(X_s)\, d[X, X]_s \\
&= \left[b'(X_s)a(X_s) + \frac{1}{2} b''(X_s) b^2(X_s) \right] ds \\
&\quad + b'(X_s)b(X_s)\, dW_s,
\end{aligned}
$$

which suggests the approximation for $t < s < t + \Delta t$

$$
\begin{aligned}
b(X_s) &\approx b(X_t) + \left[b'(X_t)a(X_t) + \frac{1}{2}b''(X_t)b^2(X_t) \right] (s - t) \\
&\quad + b'(X_t)b(X_t)(W_s - W_t) \\
&\approx b(X_t) + b'(X_t)b(X_t)[W_s - W_t],
\end{aligned}
$$

where in the second step of approximation $O(s - t)$ term is omitted. Therefore,

$$
\begin{aligned}
\int_t^{t+\Delta t} b(X_s)\,dW_s &\approx \int_t^{t+\Delta t} \left[b(X_t) + b'(X_t)b(X_t)(W_s - W_t) \right] dW_s \\
&= b(X_t)[W_{t+\Delta t} - W_t] \\
&\quad + \frac{1}{2}b'(X_t)b(X_t)\left[(W_{t+\Delta t} - W_t)^2 - \Delta t \right], \quad (3.8)
\end{aligned}
$$

where in the second step we use the result from Exercise 2.10.1.

Combining (3.6) and (3.8), we obtain the Milstein method

$$
\begin{aligned}
X_{t+\Delta t} &\approx X_t + a(X_t)\Delta t + b(X_t)[W_{t+\Delta t} - W_t] \\
&\quad + \frac{1}{2}b'(X_t)b(X_t)\left[(W_{t+\Delta t} - W_t)^2 - \Delta t \right].
\end{aligned}
$$

Algorithm for Milstein method:

Step 0: Set $t = 0, j = 0$ and $x_j = x_0$.

Step 1: Randomly generate a number, z_j, from a standard normal random variable.

Step 2: Set $t = t_j$ and $x_j = x_{j-1} + a(x_{j-1})(t_j - t_{j-1}) + b(x_{j-1})\sqrt{t_j - t_{j-1}}z_j + (1/2)b'(x_{j-1})b(x_{j-1})(t_j - t_{j-1})(z_j^2 - 1)$. Unless $j = n$, return to Step 1 .

Example 3.7. (1) Geometric Brownian motion. A simple application of the Milstein method with $a(x) = \mu x$ and $b(x) = \sigma x$ shows that a more accurate discretization of the geometric Brownian motion should be based on the following recursive relation, which is an improvement of (3.5).

$$
s_j = s_{j-1} + \mu s_{j-1}(t_j - t_{j-1}) + \sigma s_{j-1}(w_j - w_{j-1}) + \frac{\sigma^2}{2}s_{j-1}[(w_j - w_{j-1})^2 - (t_j - t_{j-1})].
$$

(2) Cox-Ingersoll-Ross model. Although it is impossible to solve the SDE (2.64), the conditional distribution of r_t given r_0 is in fact implicitly known and hence the simulation method described in the previous section still applies. Nonetheless, let

us develop a simple but useful approximation algorithm based on Milstein method where $a(x) = \alpha(\gamma - x)$ and $b(x) = \eta\sqrt{x}$. Thus, the recursive relation is given by

$$
\begin{aligned}
r_j &= r_{j-1} + \alpha(\gamma - r_{j-1})(t_j - t_{j-1}) + \eta\sqrt{(r_{j-1})_+(t_j - t_{j-1})}z_j \\
&\quad -(\eta^2/2)(t_j - t_{j-1})(z_j^2 - 1),
\end{aligned}
$$

where z_j is a number generated from a standard normal random variable.

3.4   Economic scenario generator

An economic scenario generator is a collection of interactive computer algorithms that project scenarios of joint movements of economic variables and risk factors. The scenarios generated are usually fed into valuation frameworks for various applications such as pricing of interest-sensitive insurance products, market-consistent valuation of insurance contracts with embedded options, setting regulatory capital requirements, etc.

Most economic scenario generators would include modeling economic variables such as government bond yield rates, corporate bond yield rates, equity returns, inflation rates, foreign exchange rates, etc. While many models used in the industry for interest rates and equity rates can be more sophisticated than those introduced in this book, readers can already develop a simple economic scenario generator based on simulation methods developed in this chapter.

While there is no consensus in the insurance industry on what constitutes a good economic scenario generator, there are common desirable features developed in the industrial best practices.

1. A comprehensive economic scenario generator should be able to capture stylized facts on market data, such as equities tend to exhibit higher expected returns and higher volatility than fixed-income instruments, etc.

2. A comprehensive economic scenario generator should be able to accommodate a wide range of applications involving with market-consistent risk neutral scenarios and real-world scenarios and to produce simulation results consistent with historical market dynamics.

3. A comprehensive economic scenario generator should be computational efficient and numerically stable.

We shall see that a comprehensive economic scenario generator is a critical component of stochastic modeling and analysis with Monte Carlo methods. Several applications shall be observed in this book, including actuarial pricing in Section 4.8, risk aggregation in Section 5.3, nested stochastic modeling for various purposes in Section 7.3.

3.5 Bibliographic notes

Detailed accounts of simulation methods for discrete and continuous random variables can be found in Ross [91, Chapter 11], Bratley, Fox and Schrage [14]. An authoritative text on the simulation of stochastic processes and their financial applications is Glasserman [56].

An in-depth primer on economic scenario generator is the research study published by the Society of Actuaries [82]. The American Academy of Actuaries and the Society of Actuaries (SOA) provide sample economic scenario generators used in regulatory reserve and capital calculations. Interested readers can find an economic scenario generator at the following web link.

https://www.soa.org/tables-calcs-tools/research-scenario/.

An extensive overview of the modeling of a wide range of variable annuity minimum guarantees using Monte Carlo simulation methods can be seen in Bauer, Kling and Russ [7], Bacinello et al. [4].

3.6 Exercises

Section 3.1

1. It is well-known in the analysis literature that any continuous distribution can be approximated arbitrarily closely by a combination of exponential distributions. For example, it is often convenient in many applications to approximate the future lifetime random variable by a combination of exponential random variables, known as hyperexponential random variable. Consider the problem of generating a random sample from the following hyperexponential exponential random variable with the probability density function

$$f(t) = \sum_{i=1}^{N} a_i \lambda_i e^{-\lambda_i t}, \qquad t \geq 0,$$

where $\lambda_i > 0, a_i > 0$ for $i = 1, 2, \cdots, N$ and $\sum_{i=1}^{N} a_i = 1$.

(a) Describe your algorithm.

(b) Implement the algorithm to generate a random sample with size $N = 1000$ of a hyperexponential distribution where $a_1 = 0.3, a_2 = 0.7, \lambda_1 = 5, \lambda_2 = 3$.

(c) Test the accuracy of a sample mean based on your algorithm against the theoretical mean $\sum_{i=1}^{N} a_i / \lambda_i$.

2. Consider the Pareto random variable with the density function

$$f(t) = \frac{\alpha \theta^\alpha}{(x + \theta)^{\alpha+1}}, \qquad \alpha, \theta, x > 0.$$

   (a) Develop a method to generate a random sample of the Pareto random variable using the inverse transformation method;

   (b) Develop a method to generate a random sample of the Pareto random variable using the rejection method.

Section 3.2

1. Develop a method for simulating a binomial random variable with parameters $n = 5$ and $p = 0.3$.

2. Consider an individual model in which we need to simulate the future lifetime of a life age 85. The distribution of future time should be based on the GMDB life table in Appendix A.3.

   (a) Generate a random sample of size 100 using a computer algorithm based on the narrow bucket method with 50 buckets. Report on the number of search steps for each sample point.

   (b) Propose an improvement on the algorithm to speed up the simulation.

Section 3.3

1. Since the distribution of W_t is known for each fixed time t, it may be tempting to simulate a sample path of the Brownian motion in the following way. Let $\{z_1, z_2, \cdots, z_n\}$ be a random sample drawn from a standard normal random variable. Set $w_{t_j} = \sqrt{t_j} z_j$ for all $j = 1, 2, \cdots, n$. Explain why $\{w_{t_j}, j = 1, 2, \cdots, n\}$ is not a sample path of the Brownian motion.

2. Develop two computer algorithms to generate sample paths of a geometric Brownian motion $\{S_t, 0 \le t \le 1\}$ with the drift parameter $\mu = 0.3$ and the volatility parameter $\sigma = 0.5$. The first algorithm should be based on the exact joint distribution, while the second algorithm should be based on the Milstein method. The time step is chosen to be $\Delta t = 0.01$.

   (a) Compute the theoretical value $\mathbb{E}[S_1]$.

   (b) Utilize random samples of S_1 with size 1000 generated by the two algorithms to estimate $\mathbb{E}[S_1]$, denoted by $\widehat{\mathbb{E}[S_1]}$ and $\widetilde{\mathbb{E}[S_1]}$ respectively.

   (c) Generate 100 estimates for each of $\widehat{\mathbb{E}[S_1]}$ and $\widetilde{\mathbb{E}[S_1]}$ and compare their sample variances.

4

Pricing and Valuation

No-arbitrage pricing was first discovered in 1970s in the Nobel-Prize winning work of American economists Fischer Black and Myron Scholes, which laid out a mathematical model for pricing financial derivatives. Over the past few decades, the theory has evolved and has been widely used in the financial industry for pricing and risk managing financial products. Their ground breaking work led to the rapid development of quantitative modeling for innovative products in the financial industry and, some would argue, created the profession of quantitative analysts around the world.

Although the Black-Scholes framework of pricing was not directly used in the insurance industry for various reasons to be discussed in Section 4.8, hedging techniques, which are inseparable from the no-arbitrage pricing theory, nonetheless proved to be critical tools of mitigating and managing market risks embedded in equity-linked investment guarantees.

4.1 No-arbitrage pricing

We begin with a review of basic financial derivatives - forwards, futures and options. Then we introduce the fundamental principle of modern financial theory - the no-arbitrage arguments, also known as the "law of one price".

> **Definition 4.1.** A *derivative* is a financial instrument (an agreement between two parties) that has a value determined by the price of something else (typically commodities and stocks).

The price of a bushel of corn is not a derivative but a bet on its price is. The value of your auto insurance depends on the price of your car and hence is also a derivative.

Example 4.2. (Forwards and Futures)

A *forward* contract is an agreement to buy or sell an asset at a certain future time for a certain price. It is often a private contract customized to address the trade between two parties (a buyer and a seller). A *futures* contract is similar to a forward contract but it is standardized and traded in exchanges. We do not distinguish them for the purpose of this introductory book.

There is no cost to enter into a forward. The price at which two parties agree to buy or sell an asset is called *forward price*. In contrast, the market price for immediate delivery of the asset is called *spot price*. The party who agrees to buy the underlying asset is said to assume a *long position* and the other party who agrees to sell is said to assume a *short position*. The date on which the delivery of the asset occurs is known as the *maturity*. The *payoff* of a contract is the value of its position at maturity.

We shall denote the maturity by $T > 0$, the spot price of one unit of an underlying asset by S_t for any time $0 \leq t \leq T$, and the forward price by F. In general, the payoff from a long position in a forward contract on one unit of an asset is

$$S_T - F. \tag{4.1}$$

This is because the holder of the contract is obligated to buy an asset worth S_T for F. Similarly, the payoff from a short position in a forward contract on one unit of an asset is

$$F - S_T.$$

The payoffs can be either positive or negative. We typically consider a positive payoff as a *gain* and a negative payoff as a *loss*.   □

Example 4.3. (Options) A *call option* gives the holder *the right but not obligation* to buy the underlying asset (commodities or stocks) by a certain date for a certain price. A *put option* gives the holder *the right but not obligation* to sell the underlying asset by a certain date for a certain price. The price in the contract is known as the *exercise price* or *strike price*. We often say that the buyer of the option takes a *long position* and the seller takes a *short position*. Selling an option is also known as *writing the option*.

An option that can only be exercised at maturity is often referred to as a *European option* . There are other types of options with more flexible exercise dates. Most of the options traded in exchanges are in fact *American options*, which can be exercised at any time up to maturity.

We denote the strike price of an option on one unit of an asset by K. In general, the payoff from a long position in a European call option contract on one unit of an asset is

$$(S_T - K)_+, \tag{4.2}$$

where $(x)_+ = \max\{x, 0\}$. This is because a rational holder of the option would only choose to exercise when the payoff is positive.

Similarly, the payoff from a long position of a put option contract on one unit of an asset is

$$(K - S_T)_+. \tag{4.3}$$

This is because a rational holder of the put option would only choose to exercise when the payoff is positive.

Observe that the payoffs from both the long call and the long put are always nonnegative, meaning the option holders are guaranteed to make gains at maturity. Therefore, one must have to pay a certain price to enter into such a contract. The price of a call option is often called a *call premium* and that of a put option is called a *put premium*. □

Example 4.4. If the payoff from a financial derivative depends only on the value of the underlying asset at maturity, not on its sample path prior to maturity, it is called a *path-dependent derivative*. Otherwise, it is called a *path-dependent derivative*. Clearly European call and put options with payoffs in (4.2) and 4.3 respectively are both path-independent. As the point-to-point index crediting option for equity-indexed annuity (1.37) closely resembles that of a European call option, it is also considered a path-independent derivative. In contrast, the payoffs from cliquet index crediting options (1.38) and (1.39) are determined by the highest equity return up to maturity and hence cliquet options are path-dependent. Similarly, since the payoff from the high-water mark option (1.43) relies on the highest value of equity index up to maturity, the option is also considered path-dependent. We shall address pricing methods of both path-independent and path-dependent derivatives in Section 4.5. □

Definition 4.5. An *arbitrage* is a trading strategy that

  1. begins with no money,

  2. has zero probability of losing money,

  3. has a positive probability of making money.

An essential feature of an efficient market is that if a trading strategy can turn nothing into a profit, then it must also run the risk of losses. Otherwise, there would be an arbitrage. It is believed that in an efficient market any arbitrage can be detected immediately and such trading strategies should be in such a high demand that their costs are pushed up immediately to the level at which the arbitrages are no longer possible. Therefore, in an efficient market, there should be no place for an arbitrage.

The fundamental principle of derivatives pricing in an efficient market is that pricing should be done in such a way that no arbitrage can exist. In this section, we use a forward contract as a model example to demonstrate the use of no-arbitrage arguments.

Example 4.6. Consider two ways of purchasing a unit of an asset, namely, an outright purchase and a forward contract. In an outright purchase at present, say time t, a unit of the asset is transferred from the seller to the buyer upon the payment of the spot price S_t. In contrast, a forward price F is set at the time of inception t and the buyer pays F at the maturity of the forward T and receives one unit of the asset from the seller. Note that both transactions give the investor the ownership of one unit of the asset after T periods and the only difference is the timing of the payment. Therefore, they are considered different but equivalent transactions. To make the two transactions comparable, we assume that the cost of an outright purchase is entirely financed by borrowing. Suppose that the continuously compounding interest rate is r per time unit, which means each dollar at time t accumulates to $e^{r(T-t)}$ at time T.

Portfolio Cash Flow Statement

	time t	time T
Portfolio #1: Outright Purchase		
Buy and hold asset	$-S_t$	0
Borrow to fund purchase	$+S_t$	$-S_t e^{r(T-t)}$
Net Cash Flow	0	$-S_t e^{r(T-t)}$
Portfolio #2: Forward Contract		
Enter into a forward contract	0	$-F$
Net Cash Flow	0	$-F$

TABLE 4.1: No-arbitrage argument to determine forward price

Comparing cash flows for an outright purchase and a prepaid forward in Table 4.1, we note that the two transactions both start at time t with zero cost. Therefore, they should produce exactly the same outcome at time T, i.e. $S_0 = Fe^{-rT}$. If that is not the case, then there would be an arbitrage in the market. For example, if $S_t > Fe^{-r(T-t)}$, an investor can shortsell[*] one unit of the underlying asset, invest the proceeds of S_t in the money market account and also enter into a forward contract. Note that this trading strategy matches the defining properties of an arbitrage. (1) The net cost of such a transaction is 0 at time t. (2) When the contract matures, the investor takes the principal and interest from the money market account, which would have accumulated to $S_t e^{r(T-t)}$, pays the forward price F. The newly acquired asset is then returned to the lender. Since the proceeds from the money market account exceed the forward price, there is no chance for the investor to lose money. (3) In fact, the investor makes a profit of $S_t e^{r(T-t)} - F$ with certainty. Similarly, one can always create an arbitrage if $S_t < Fe^{-r(T-t)}$. (Exercise 4.1.1.) Therefore, in the absence of arbitrage, the forward price must be set at the level

$$F = S_t e^{r(T-t)}. \tag{4.4}$$

---

[*]Short-sell refers to the sale of stocks borrowed by the investor. Such a transaction is often motivated by the speculation that the current market price is higher than the price at which the stock is bought back and returned to the lender, enabling the investor to make a profit from the price difference.

Readers should not confuse the forward price with the initial cost of the forward contract, which is zero. □

The argument above is an application of the no-arbitrage principle, also known as the law of one price, means that two transactions with equivalent cash flows should have the same price. If two equivalent transactions do not have the same price, one can always create an arbitrage by a "buy low and sell high" strategy, meaning that an investor can take a long position in the cheaper transaction and a short position in the more expensive transaction.

4.2 Discrete time pricing: binomial tree

4.2.1 Pricing by replicating portfolio

Let us first consider a simple one-period model for option pricing under which the underlying asset is a stock. Suppose the initial stock price is S_0 and the stock price only experiences a binary movement. To introduce random variables to model stock prices, we consider the probability space $(\Omega_1, \mathcal{F}_1, \mathbb{P})$ defined in Example 2.8. Suppose that there is a magic coin that determines the outcome of the stock price's binary movement. If the coin lands on a head (with the probability p), the stock price goes up by a factor of u. If the coin lands on a tail (with the probability q), the stock price goes down by a factor of d. In other words,

$$\frac{S_1(H)}{S_0} = u, \qquad \frac{S_1(T)}{S_0} = d.$$

There is also a money market account in which cash deposits earn interests at the force of interest r per period. Any investor is allowed to borrow from or lend to a money market account with unlimited amounts. Similarly, the investor can buy or short-sell unlimited shares of the underlying stock without occurring any transaction costs. In the absence of arbitrage, it must be true that

$$u > e^r > d. \tag{4.5}$$

We shall leave as Exercise 4.2.1 the existence of an arbitrage when the condition (4.5) is violated.

We intend to price a financial derivative at the beginning of the period which pays off V_1 at the end of the period. For example, if the financial derivative is a European call option, then $V_1 = (S_1 - K)_+$. Note that this expression in fact includes two cases:

$$\begin{aligned} V_1(H) &= (S_1(H) - K)_+ = (uS_0 - K)_+ \\ V_1(T) &= (S_1(T) - K)_+ = (dS_0 - K)_+. \end{aligned}$$

In order to utilize the no-arbitrage principle, we want to construct a portfolio consisting of only stocks and money market account which can replicate the outcomes of the financial derivative to be priced. Such a portfolio is often known as a *replicating* portfolio. The no-arbitrage principle tells that two equivalent transactions with the same outcomes should cost exactly the same. Since the price of stock and the cost of setting up money market account are known at the beginning, we can infer the price of the option from the cost of the replicating portfolio.

To this end, we introduce variables to be determined for the replicating portfolio. Suppose that the initial cost of the replicating portfolio is X_0, which is to be determined. To construct the portfolio, we assume that the investor

- holds Δ_0 shares of the underlying stock;

- invests $B_0 = X_0 - \Delta_0 S_0$ in the money market account.

The quantity Δ_0 to be determined may be positive or negative. A positive Δ_0 implies buying shares from the stock market whereas a negative Δ_0 means shortselling shares to the market. Similarly, a positive B_0 indicates lending to the money market and a negative B_0 leads to borrowing from the market.

Consider all possible outcomes of the replicating portfolio at the end of the period, to be denoted by X_1. Since there is no certainty with the money market account, it accumulates to $B_1 = B_0 e^r$ at the end the period. If the stock price goes up, then the portfolio is worth

$$X_1(H) = \Delta_0 S_1(H) + e^r B_0.$$

If the stock price goes down, then it is worth

$$X_1(T) = \Delta_0 S_1(T) + e^r B_0.$$

Matching the outcomes of the replicating portfolio with those of the option produces the system of equations

$$X_1(H) = \Delta_0 S_1(H) + e^r(X_0 - \Delta_0 S_0) = V_1(H). \tag{4.6}$$
$$X_1(T) = \Delta_0 S_1(T) + e^r(X_0 - \Delta_0 S_0) = V_1(T). \tag{4.7}$$

Subtracting (4.7) from (4.6) gives that

$$\Delta_0 = \frac{V_1(H) - V_1(T)}{S_1(H) - S_1(T)}.$$

For the ease of presentation, we introduce some constants

$$\tilde{p} = \frac{e^r - d}{u - d}, \qquad \tilde{q} = \frac{u - e^r}{u - d}. \tag{4.8}$$

Note that

$$e^{-r}\left[\tilde{p}S_1(H) + \tilde{q}S_1(T)\right] = e^{-r}\left[\frac{e^r - d}{u - d}uS_0 + \frac{u - e^r}{u - d}dS_0\right] = S_0. \tag{4.9}$$

Multiplying (4.6) by $e^{-r}\tilde{p}$ and (4.7) by $e^{-r}\tilde{q}$ yields

$$X_0 = e^{-r}\left[\tilde{p}V_1(H) + \tilde{q}V_1(T)\right].$$

Recall the no-arbitrage principle that two transactions with the same outcomes should cost the same to begin with. Therefore, the no-arbitrage price of the financial derivative should also be given by

$$V_0 = e^{-r}\left[\tilde{p}V_1(H) + \tilde{q}V_1(T)\right]. \tag{4.10}$$

Note that $0 < \tilde{p}, \tilde{q} < 1$ due to (4.5) and $\tilde{p} + \tilde{q} = 1$. Therefore, one can think of a probability measure $\tilde{\mathbb{P}}$ under which S_1 takes the value $S_1(H)$ (V_1 takes the value $V_1(H)$) with the probability $\tilde{p}$ and S_1 take the value $S_1(H)$ (V_1 takes the value $V_1(T)$) with the probability $\tilde{q}$. Hence the no-arbitrage price of a financial derivative can be written as the expected present value of payoffs at maturity under the probability measure $\tilde{\mathbb{P}}$,

$$V_0 = e^{-r}\tilde{\mathbb{E}}[V_1],$$

where the expectation $\tilde{\mathbb{E}}$ is taken with respect to the probability measure $\tilde{\mathbb{P}}$. Observe that (4.9) also implies

$$S_0 = e^{-r}\tilde{\mathbb{E}}[S_1].$$

A quick comparison of all three instruments shows that

$$B_1 = B_0 e^r, \qquad \tilde{\mathbb{E}}[S_1] = S_0 e^r, \qquad \tilde{\mathbb{E}}[V_1] = V_0 e^r,$$

which implies that under the probability measure $\tilde{\mathbb{P}}$, on average, the continuously compound yield rates on all financial instruments are the same. In other words, an investor would be indifferent about investing as they all return the same on average. This is why the measure $\tilde{\mathbb{P}}$ is often referred to as the risk neutral measure.

Example 4.7. Consider a particular one-period European put option written on a stock. Suppose that the spot price $S_0 = 100$, the up factor $u = 1.5$, the down factor $d = 0.5$, one-period discount factor $e^{-r} = 0.8$ and the strike price is $K = 110$. When the stock price goes up, the payoff from the put option is given by

$$V_1(H) = (K - uS_0)_+ = (110 - 150)_+ = 0.$$

When the stock price goes down, the payoff from the put option is given by

$$V_1(T) = (K - dS_0)_+ = (110 - 50)_+ = 60.$$

Risk-neutral probabilities $\tilde{p}, \tilde{q}$ can be determined by

$$\tilde{p} = \frac{e^r - d}{u - d} = \frac{3}{4}, \qquad \tilde{q} = 1 - \tilde{p} = \frac{1}{4}.$$

Therefore, we can determine the no-arbitrage price of the put option by (4.10),

$$V_0 = e^{-r}[\tilde{p}V_1(H) + \tilde{q}V_1(T)] = 0.8(0.75 \times 0 + 0.25 \times 60) = 12.$$

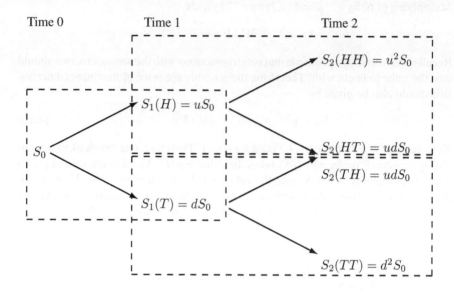

FIGURE 4.1: Two-period binomial tree model

The notion of binomial tree pricing can be easily extended to multi-period models. For example, consider a two-period model defined on the two coin tosses probability space $(\Omega_2, \mathcal{F}_2, \mathbb{P})$ and stock price random variables S_1 and S_2 are defined in Figure 4.1. Note that stock price either goes up by a factor of u or down by a factor of d at any point of time, i.e. for $k = 0, 1$,

$$\frac{S_{k+1}}{S_k} = \begin{cases} u, & \text{with probability } p \\ d, & \text{with probability } q. \end{cases}$$

Suppose that a financial derivative which pays off V_2 at the end of two periods is sold for V_0 at time 0, where V_0 is to be determined. We can keep the European call option in mind as an example where $V_2 = (S_2 - K)_+$ and K is the strike price at maturity. Note that there are two branches of the tree at time 1 in Figure 4.1, each of which resembles the structure of a one-period model with two nodes. For each of the two branches, since we know the payoffs from the option at time 2, the no-arbitrage price at time 1 of the two-period option can be determined in the same way as that at time 0 of the one-period option with everything else being equal. Therefore, using exactly the same arguments as done earlier, we can construct a replicating portfolio for the model in the upper branch that

- buys $\Delta_1(H) = [V_2(HH) - V_2(HT)]/[S_2(HH) - S_2(HT)]$ shares of the underlying stock;

- invests $X_1(H) - \Delta_1(H)S_1(H)$ in the money market account.

In doing so, we can determine the no-arbitrage price of the financial derivative by matching the outcomes of the replicating portfolio with those of the financial derivative

$$
\begin{aligned}
X_2(HH) &= \Delta_1(H)S_2(HH) + e^r(X_1(H) - \Delta_1(H)S_1(H)) = V_2(HH), \\
X_2(HT) &= \Delta_1(H)S_2(HT) + e^r(X_1(H) - \Delta_1(H)S_1(H)) = V_2(HT).
\end{aligned}
$$

Solving the system for the two unknowns $\Delta_1(H)$ and $X_1(H)$, we obtain the no-arbitrage price of the financial derivative when the stock price is at $S_1(H)$,

$$
V_1(H) = e^{-r}[\tilde{p}V_2(HH) + \tilde{q}V_2(HT)]. \tag{4.11}
$$

Similarly, we can also determine the no-arbitrage price of the financial derivative of the one-period model in the lower branch. We can construct a similar replicating portfolio for the model in the lower branch that

- buys $\Delta_1(T) = [V_2(TH) - V_2(TT)]/[S_2(TH) - S_2(TT)]$ shares of the underlying stock;

- invests $X_1(T) - \Delta_1(T)S_1(T)$ in the money market account.

When the stock price is at $S_1(T)$, we can show that the no-arbitrage price is given by

$$
V_1(T) = X_1(T) = e^{-r}[\tilde{p}V_2(TH) + \tilde{q}V_2(TT)]. \tag{4.12}
$$

Going backward in time, we can also treat $V_1(H)$ and $V_1(T)$ as the outcomes of the financial derivative at the end of the first period. A similar replicating portfolio is constructed for the first period, which

- holds $\Delta_0 = [V_1(H) - V_1(T)]/[S_1(H) - S_1(T)]$ shares of the underlying stock;

- invests $B_0 = X_0 - \Delta_0 S_0$ in the money market account.

Then applying the one-period pricing arguments gives the no-arbitrage price at the beginning of the first period

$$
V_0 = X_0 = e^{-r}[\tilde{p}V_1(H) + \tilde{q}V_1(T)]. \tag{4.13}
$$

Example 4.8. Consider a two-period European put option written on a stock. Suppose that the spot price $S_0 = 100$, the up factor $u = 1.5$, the down factor $d = 0.5$, one-period discount factor $e^{-r} = 0.8$ and the strike price is $K = 110$. As in Example 4.7, risk-neutral probabilities are known to be $\tilde{p} = 0.75, \tilde{q} = 0.25$. The three possible payoffs from the put option at the end of two periods are as follows.

$$
\begin{aligned}
V_2(HH) &= (K - u^2 S_0)_+ = (110 - 225)_+ = 0, \\
V_2(HT) &= V_2(TH) = (K - ud S_0)_+ = (110 - 75)_+ = 35, \\
V_2(TT) &= (K - d^2 S_0)_+ = (110 - 25)_+ = 85.
\end{aligned}
$$

We now work backward in time to figure out the no-arbitrage price of the option at each time point. If we treat stock movement from time 1 to time 2 as a one period model, there are two cases to consider. When the stock price at time 1 is $S_1(H)$ (top right corner in Figure 4.1), the corresponding price of the put option is given by (4.11), i.e.

$$V_1(H) = e^{-r}[\tilde{p}V_2(HH) + \tilde{q}V_2(HT)] = 7.$$

When the stock price at time 1 is $S_1(T)$ (bottom right corner in Figure 4.1), the corresponding price of the put option is given by (4.12), i.e.

$$V_1(T) = e^{-r}[\tilde{p}V_2(TH) + \tilde{q}V_2(TT)] = 38.$$

Considering the period from time 0 to time 1, we can determine the no-arbitrage price of the put option by (4.13),

$$V_0 = e^{-r}[\tilde{p}V_1(H) + \tilde{q}V_1(T)] = 0.8(0.75 \times 7 + 0.25 \times 38) = 11.8.$$

Comparing formulas (4.11), (4.12) and (4.13), we can quickly identify a pattern that governs pricing formulas under binomial tree models for n periods. Consider the probability space $(\Omega_\infty, \mathcal{F}, \mathbb{P})$ defined in 2.5. Let $\omega_1\omega_2\cdots\omega_n$ represent outcomes of the first n coin tosses corresponding to stock movements in an N-period binomial tree model $(0 \leq n \leq N)$. In other words, stock prices for each period either go up by a factor of u or down by a factor of d from the previous period, i.e. for $n = 1, 2, \cdots, N$,

$$\frac{S_n}{S_{n-1}} = \begin{cases} u, & \text{with probability } p \\ d, & \text{with probability } q. \end{cases}$$

In a manner similar to that in the two-period model, we can derive risk-neutral probabilities by (4.8). Then no-arbitrage prices can be determined backwards in time by the recursive formula

$$V_{n-1}(\omega_1\omega_2\cdots\omega_{n-1}) = e^{-r}[\tilde{p}V_n(\omega_1\omega_2\cdots\omega_{n-1}H) + \tilde{q}V_n(\omega_1\omega_2\cdots\omega_{n-1}T)],$$

$$(4.14)$$

for all $n = 1, 2, \cdots, N$ and the terminal value of the financial derivative is typically known from its payoff at maturity. For example, the terminal value of an N-period European call option would be given by

$$V_N(\omega_1\omega_2\cdots\omega_N) = (S_N(\omega_1\omega_2\cdots\omega_N) - K)_+,$$

and that of an N-period European put option would be given by

$$V_N(\omega_1\omega_2\cdots\omega_N) = (K - S_N(\omega_1\omega_2\cdots\omega_N))_+.$$

4.2.2   Representation by conditional expectation

In each of the three one-period models under the two-period binomial tree, there is a common risk neutral measure $\tilde{\mathbb{E}}$ under which for $n = 0, 1$

$$\frac{S_{n+1}}{S_n} = \begin{cases} u, & \text{with probability } \tilde{p} \\ d, & \text{with probability } \tilde{q}. \end{cases}$$

Therefore, we can view no-arbitrage prices at the end of the first period as

$$V_1(H) = e^{-r}\tilde{\mathbb{E}}[V_2|H] = e^{-r}\frac{\tilde{\mathbb{E}}[V_2 \mathbf{1}_H]}{\tilde{\mathbb{P}}(H)} = e^{-r}\frac{\tilde{p}^2 V_2(HH) + \tilde{p}\tilde{q}V_2(HT)}{\tilde{p}},$$

where H here stands for the set $\{HH, HT\}$, and

$$V_1(T) = e^{-r}\tilde{\mathbb{E}}[V_2|T] = e^{-r}\frac{\tilde{\mathbb{E}}[V_2 \mathbf{1}_T]}{\tilde{\mathbb{P}}(T)} = e^{-r}\frac{\tilde{p}\tilde{q}V_2(TH) + \tilde{q}^2 V_2(TT)}{\tilde{q}}.$$

In view of the result in Example 2.43, the no-arbitrage price at time 1 of the financial derivative can be rewritten as

$$V_1 = e^{-r}\tilde{\mathbb{E}}[V_2|\mathcal{F}_1]. \tag{4.15}$$

We can also rewrite the no-arbitrage price at time 0 of the financial derivative in (4.13) as

$$V_0 = e^{-r}\tilde{\mathbb{E}}[V_1|\mathcal{F}_0] = e^{-r}\tilde{\mathbb{E}}[e^{-r}\tilde{\mathbb{E}}[V_2|\mathcal{F}_1]|\mathcal{F}_0] = e^{-2r}\tilde{\mathbb{E}}[V_2|\mathcal{F}_0], \tag{4.16}$$

where $\mathcal{F}_0$ is the trivial information set at time 0, i.e. $\mathcal{F}_0 = \{\varnothing, \Omega_2\}$.

The similarity between (4.15) and (4.16) is no coincidence. In general, for an N-period binomial tree model, the no-arbitrage price at time n of the financial derivative given by the recursive formula (4.14) can be rewritten as

$$V_{n-1}(\omega_1\omega_2\cdots\omega_{n-1}) = e^{-r}\tilde{\mathbb{E}}[V_n|\omega_1\omega_2\cdots\omega_{n-1}],$$

for every possible event $\omega_1\omega_2\cdots\omega_{n-1} \in \Omega_n$. Again, using the result in Example 2.43, we can conclude that the no-arbitrage price at time n can be rewritten as a conditional expectation

$$V_{n-1} = e^{-r}\tilde{\mathbb{E}}[V_n|\mathcal{F}_{n-1}],$$

for $n = 1, 2, \cdots, N$. Applying the tower property in Example 2.44, we can always write the no-arbitrage price at time n concisely as the conditional expectation of its terminal value with respect to the information up to time n, i.e.

$$V_n = e^{-r(N-n)}\tilde{\mathbb{E}}[V_N|\mathcal{F}_n]. \tag{4.17}$$

Using arguments in Example 2.51, one can show that the binomial tree model is a Markov process. Then we can also write (4.17) as

$$V_n(\omega_1\omega_2\cdots\omega_n) = e^{-r(N-n)}\tilde{\mathbb{E}}[V_N|S_n(\omega_1\omega_2\cdots\omega_n)], \tag{4.18}$$

for every possible event $\omega_1\omega_2\cdots\omega_n \in \Omega_n$.

4.3   Dynamics of self-financing portfolio

In the binomial tree model, we have already used the notion of self-financing portfolio in discrete time,

$$X_{n+1} = \Delta_n S_{n+1} + (1+r)(X_n - \Delta_n S_n), \qquad (4.19)$$

which means that this period's portfolio value is equal to the proceeds from selling last period's portfolio, including both equities and money market account, at today's prices. A self-financing portfolio requires no additional cash injection from an investor. As we shall see later, many embedded options in equity-linked insurance can be hedged with self-financing portfolios with net cash flows (fee incomes less benefit outgoes). While binomial tree models can be used for hedging equity-linked insurance, one often gains additional insights looking at continuous-time models. Now we want to find out the analogue of the "self-financing" portfolio in (4.19) in continuous time with net outgoing cash flows.

Consider a portfolio with multiple assets using the following notation.

- X_t – the wealth at the start of period t.

- N – the number of different types of assets.

- $h_t^{(i)}$ – the number of shares of type i held at time t for $i = 1, \cdots, N$.

- $S_t^{(i)}$ – the price of one share of type i held at time t for $i = 1, \cdots, N$.

- c_t – net outgoing cash flow per time unit at time t from the portfolio.

Throughout the section, we use $\mathbf{x} \cdot \mathbf{y}$ where $\mathbf{x}$ and $\mathbf{y}$ are both vectors of dimension N to indicate their dot product, i.e. $\mathbf{x} \cdot \mathbf{y} = \sum_{i=1}^{N} x_i y_i$.

Theorem 4.9. *Let* $\{X_t = \mathbf{h}_t \cdot \mathbf{S}_t : t \geq 0\}$ *be the wealth process of a self-financing portfolio consisting of N assets where* $\mathbf{h}_t = (h_t^{(1)}, h_t^{(2)}, \ldots, h_t^{(N)})$ *and* $\mathbf{S}_t = (S_t^{(1)}, S_t^{(2)}, \ldots, S_t^{(N)})$ *with all components being Ito processes. If the portfolio is self-financing, then it must satisfy the SDE*

$$d X_t = \mathbf{h}_t \cdot d\mathbf{S}_t - c_t \, dt, \qquad t \geq 0 \qquad (4.20)$$

which means for any $T \geq 0$,

$$X_T - X_0 = \int_0^T \mathbf{h}_t \cdot d\mathbf{S}_t - \int_0^T c_t \, dt. \qquad (4.21)$$

Proof. Consider a partition of interval $[0, T]$ such as (2.14) where the portfolio rebalanced at points $t_0, t_1, \cdots, t_n$. This idea of this proof is to utilize the notion of self-financing in the discrete time model and then to obtain the corresponding result in continuous time by letting $\|\Pi\| \to 0$. Note that the total wealth of the portfolio at time t_j prior to rebalancing is given by $X_{t_j} = \mathbf{h}_{t_{j-1}} \cdot \mathbf{S}_{t_j}$ and the outgoing cash flow is set at $c_{t_{j-1}}$ per time unit over the period $[t_{j-1}, t_j)$. Suppose that we now decide to rebalance the portfolio at time t_j resulting in a new mix of assets represented by h_{t_j}. The cost of the new portfolio, which has to be evaluated at then-current prices at time t_j, is given by $\mathbf{h}_{t_j} \cdot \mathbf{S}_{t_j}$. Since the new portfolio and net outgoing cash flow have to be financed solely by selling assets already in the portfolio, we must require that for all $j = 1, 2, \cdots, n$

$$\mathbf{h}_{t_{j-1}} \cdot \mathbf{S}_{t_j} = \mathbf{h}_{t_j} \cdot \mathbf{S}_{t_j} + c_{t_{j-1}}(t_j - t_{j-1}) \tag{4.22}$$

For notational brevity, we write $\Delta X_{t_j} = X_{t_j} - X_{t_{j-1}}$ for X being either $\mathbf{h}$ or $\mathbf{S}$ and $\Delta t_j = t_j - t_{j-1}$. Then (4.22) can be rewritten as

$$\mathbf{S}_{t_j} \cdot \Delta \mathbf{h}_{t_j} + c_{t_j} \Delta t_j = 0. \tag{4.23}$$

For reasons to be seen soon, we compare $\mathbf{S}_{t_j} \cdot \Delta \mathbf{h}_{t_j}$ with the definition of stochastic integral in (2.30). Recall that the increments of Brownian motion in (2.30) are forward differences. Note, however, that (4.23) only contains backward differences. Then we add and subtract $\mathbf{S}_{t_{j-1}} \cdot \Delta \mathbf{h}_{t_j}$ and get

$$\mathbf{S}_{t_j} \cdot \Delta \mathbf{h}_{t_j} - \mathbf{S}_{t_{j-1}} \cdot \Delta \mathbf{h}_{t_j} + \mathbf{S}_{t_{j-1}} \cdot \Delta \mathbf{h}_{t_j} + c_{t_j} \Delta t_j = 0$$

which can be rewritten as

$$\Delta \mathbf{S}_{t_j} \cdot \Delta \mathbf{h}_{t_j} + \mathbf{S}_{t_{j-1}} \cdot \Delta \mathbf{h}_{t_j} + c_{t_j} \Delta t_j = 0.$$

Therefore,

$$\sum_{i=1}^{n} \Delta \mathbf{S}_{t_i} \cdot \Delta \mathbf{h}_{t_i} + \sum_{i=1}^{n} \mathbf{S}_{t_i} \cdot \Delta \mathbf{h}_{t_i} + \sum_{i=1}^{n} c_{t_j} \Delta t_j = 0. \tag{4.24}$$

Letting $\|\Pi\| \to 0$, the limit of the first term in (4.24) is exactly the cross-variation of $\mathbf{S}$ and $\mathbf{h}$ and the limit of the second term is a stochastic integral. Hence, we obtain

$$\int_0^T S(t) \cdot \mathrm{d}\mathbf{h}_t + [\mathbf{S}, \mathbf{h}]_t + \int_0^T c_t \, \mathrm{d}t = 0. \tag{4.25}$$

Since $X_t = \mathbf{h}_t \cdot \mathbf{S}_t$, applying product rule (Theorem 2.74) yields that

$$X_T - X_0 = \int_0^T \mathbf{h}_t \cdot \mathrm{d}\mathbf{S}_t + \int_0^T \mathbf{S}_t \cdot \mathrm{d}\mathbf{h}_t + [\mathbf{S}, \mathbf{h}]_t,$$

which leads to (4.21) after using the identity in (4.25).

$\square$

Remark 4.10. The equation (4.19) can be treated as the discrete time analogue of (4.20) with no net cash flow ($c_t = 0$ for $t \geq 0$). Think of $\mathbf{S}_t = (S_t, B_t)$

where S_t represents equity value and B_t represents bond value at time t and $h_t = \left(\Delta_t, (X_t - \Delta_t S_t)/B_t \right)$. Recall that $dB_t = rB_t\, dt$ (because $B_t = B_0 e^{rt}$). Therefore, $dX_t = \mathbf{h} \cdot d\mathbf{S}_t$ implies that

$$
\begin{aligned}
dX_t &= \Delta_t\, dS_t + \frac{X_t - \Delta_t S_t}{B_t}\, dB_t \\
     &= \Delta_t dS_t + r(X_t - \Delta_t S_t)\, dt.
\end{aligned}
$$

This is the continuous-time analogue of incremental change of the portfolio over integer periods

$$
X_{n+1} - X_n = \Delta_n (S_{n+1} - S_n) + r(X_n - \Delta_n S_n),
$$

which implies that

$$
X_{n+1} = \Delta_n S_{n+1} + (1 + r)(X_n - \Delta_n S_n).
$$

Example 4.11. Suppose that a policyholder invests the amount of F_0 in a balanced portfolio consisting of both non-dividend paying stock and bonds. The portfolio is constantly rebalanced to maintain its fixed asset mix. In other words, there is a fixed real number φ, such that, at every point of time, $100\varphi\%$ of the fund's assets are invested in a stock and $100(1 - \varphi)\%$ in a bond earning a continuously compounded rate of return r per time unit. The price of the stock, $S(t)$, follows a geometric Brownian motion described in (2.44). What is the policyholder's account value F_t at time t where $t \geq 0$?

Solution: We first break down the portfolio into the stock portion and bond portion.

$$
F_t = \varphi F_t + (1 - \varphi)F_t = \frac{\varphi F_t}{S_t} S_t + \frac{(1-\varphi)F_t}{B_t} B_t
$$

where $dS_t = \mu S_t\, dt + \sigma S_t\, dW_t$ and $dB_t = rB_t\, dt$. Using (4.20), we see that

$$
\begin{aligned}
dF_t &= \frac{\varphi F_t}{S_t}\, dS_t + \frac{(1 - \varphi)F_t}{B_t}\, dB_t \\
     &= \frac{\varphi F_t}{S_t}(\mu S_t\, dt + \sigma S_t\, dW_t) + \frac{(1 - \varphi)F_t}{B_t}(rB_t\, dt) \\
     &= [\mu\varphi + r(1 - \varphi)]F_t\, dt + \sigma\varphi F_t\, dW_t,
\end{aligned}
$$

which implies that F_t is still driven by a geometric Brownian motion.

4.4   Continuous time pricing: Black-Scholes model

Let us consider the value of a European call option in the continuous time model, which was originally developed in the work of Black and Scholes. The model makes a number of simplifying assumptions. For simplicity, we consider here a financial market with only two types of assets:

- A non-dividend paying stock whose price dynamics is driven by a geometric Brownian motion as defined in (2.44);

- A money market account that pays interest continuously at the so-called "risk-free" rate r per time unit.

Similar to the binomial tree model, we also assume that investors can borrow from money market account or short-sell stocks with no limitation. While the assumptions are not realistic, the model provides mathematical convenience that permits explicit solutions to option prices. Unfortunately, any departure from the model assumptions often makes the model difficult to analyze. This is often the compromise we make between model complexity and its usefulness in practice.

4.4.1 Pricing by replicating portfolio

We shall denote the time-t no-arbitrage price of the European call option by $\{f(t, S_t) : 0 \leq t \leq T\}$ where T is the maturity of the option and the option price is assumed to depend only on time t and the current stock price S_t. Furthermore, we assume the function $f(t, s)$ is continuously differentiable with respect to t and twice so with respect to s. Then it follows immediately from the Itô's formula that

$$
\begin{aligned}
\mathrm{d}f(t, S_t) &= \frac{\partial f}{\partial t}(t, S_t)\,\mathrm{d}t + \frac{\partial f}{\partial s}(t, S_t)\,\mathrm{d}S_t + \frac{1}{2}\frac{\partial^2 f}{\partial s^2}(t, S_t)\,\mathrm{d}[S, S]_t \\
&= \left[\frac{\partial f}{\partial t}(t, S_t) + \mu S_t \frac{\partial f}{\partial s}(t, S_t) + \frac{1}{2}\sigma^2 S_t^2 \frac{\partial^2 f}{\partial s^2}(t, S_t)\right]\,\mathrm{d}t \quad (4.26) \\
&\quad + \sigma S_t \frac{\partial f}{\partial s}(t, S_t)\,\mathrm{d}W_t.
\end{aligned}
$$

$$(4.27)$$

We want to construct a self-financing replicating portfolio that exactly matches the value of the call option. The replicating portfolio is assumed to consist of Δ_t shares of the underlying stock and an amount of B_t invested in a money market account. With a slight abuse of notation, we shall use $f(t, S_t)$ as the value of the replicating portfolio as well.

$$f(t, S_t) = \Delta_t S_t + B_t,$$

where the dynamics of stock prices and money market account are given by

$$
\begin{aligned}
\mathrm{d}S_t &= \mu S_t\,\mathrm{d}t + \sigma S_t\,\mathrm{d}W_t, \quad (4.28) \\
\mathrm{d}B_t &= r B_t\,\mathrm{d}t.
\end{aligned}
$$

In view of the self-financing property (4.20), the dynamics of the replicating portfolio is hence given by

$$
\begin{aligned}
\mathrm{d}f(t, S_t) &= \Delta_t \, \mathrm{d}S_t + \mathrm{d}B_t = [\mu \Delta_t S_t + r B_t] \, \mathrm{d}t + \sigma S_t \Delta_t \, \mathrm{d}W_t \\
&= [\mu \Delta_t S_t + r(f(t, S_t) - \Delta_t S_t)] \, \mathrm{d}t + \sigma S_t \Delta_t \, \mathrm{d}W_t. \quad (4.29)
\end{aligned}
$$

Comparing the two SDEs (4.27) and (4.29), we see that the dynamics of the replicating portfolio would exactly match that of the option value if the number of shares is constantly adjusted according to

$$
\Delta_t = \frac{\partial f}{\partial s}(t, S_t) \quad (4.30)
$$

and the function f also satisfies

$$
\frac{\partial f}{\partial t}(t, S_t) + \frac{1}{2} \sigma^2 S_t^2 \frac{\partial^2 f}{\partial s^2}(t, S_t) = r \left[f(t, S_t) - S_t \frac{\partial f}{\partial s}(t, S_t) \right].
$$

Since the SDE above holds true for all $t \in (0, T)$ and values of S_t, it also implies that the function f has to satisfy the partial differential equation (PDE)

$$
\frac{\partial f}{\partial t}(t, s) + rs \frac{\partial f}{\partial s}(t, s) + \frac{1}{2} \sigma^2 s^2 \frac{\partial^2 f}{\partial s^2}(t, s) - r f(t, s) = 0. \quad (4.31)
$$

Recall that the value of the call option at maturity T is given by the amount by which the stock price at maturity exceeds the strike, as shown in (4.2). Hence the terminal value of the function f is known explicitly as

$$
f(T, s) = (s - K)_+, \qquad \text{for all } s \in \mathbb{R}. \quad (4.32)
$$

The PDE together with the terminal condition (4.32) is known as the Black-Scholes-Merton pricing equation.

Note that the derivation of the Black-Scholes-Merton PDE is in fact independent of the payoffs of the financial derivative under consideration, except for the terminal condition. In general, the same arguments carry through for any *path-independent* financial derivative, i.e. the type of derivatives whose payoffs depend only on the terminal stock price, not on its paths prior to maturity. Therefore, the no-arbitrage price of any path-independent derivative is also determined by (4.31) with the terminal condition

$$
f(T, s) = h(s), \qquad \text{for all } s \in \mathbb{R},
$$

where the function h is the payoff from the derivative at maturity.

Example 4.12. Consider the forward contract in Example 4.2 whose price depends on a particular stock. If the spot price at time t is given by S_t and the forward price to be paid at the maturity T is F. Determine the price of the forward at time t.

It is clear that the forward is a path-independent derivative and hence its price has to be a solution to the Black-Scholes-Merton pricing equation (4.31) subject to the terminal condition

$$
f(T, s) = s - F.
$$

Consider the function

$$f(t, s) = s - Fe^{-r(T-t)}, \qquad 0 \leq t \leq T. \tag{4.33}$$

Observe that

$$\frac{\partial f}{\partial t} = -rFe^{-r(T-t)}, \qquad \frac{\partial f}{\partial s} = 1, \qquad \frac{\partial^2 f}{\partial s^2} = 0. \tag{4.34}$$

It is easy to check that f indeed satisfies (4.31) as well as (4.33) and hence provides the no-arbitrage price of a forward contract. Note that the forward price is in fact determined by the spot price in (4.4). Therefore, the no-arbitrage price of the forward at the inception (time t) can be written as

$$f(t, S_t) = S_t - Fe^{-r(T-t)} = 0,$$

which is consistent with the market practice that there is no cost to enter into a forward. However, at any other point prior to maturity $u \in (t, T)$, the no-arbitrage price is given by

$$f(u, S_u) = S_u - Fe^{-r(T-u)}.$$

4.4.2 Representation by conditional expectation

Theorem 4.13 (Feymann-Kac Formula). *Consider the stochastic differential equation*

$$dX_t = a(t, X_t)\, dt + b(t, X_t)\, dW_t.$$

The function f defined by

$$f(t, x) = \mathbb{E}[e^{-r(T-t)} h(X_T)|X_t = x] \tag{4.35}$$

satisfies the partial differential equation (PDE)

$$f_t(t, x) + a(t, x)f_x(t, x) + \frac{1}{2}b(t, x)^2 f_{xx}(t, x) = rf(t, x) \tag{4.36}$$

with the terminal condition

$$f(T, x) = h(x) \qquad \text{for all } x. \tag{4.37}$$

Conversely, if a function f solves the PDE (4.36) with the terminal condition (4.37), then it has the stochastic representation (4.35).

While the rigorous proof of this theorem is fairly technical, we can briefly demonstrate the main idea of the proof of the forward statement. Since it is known from Section 2.11 that the process X has the Markov property, there must be a function g such that

$$g(t, X_t) := \mathbb{E}[e^{-rT} h(X_T)|\mathcal{F}_t] = e^{-rt} f(t, X_t).$$

It follows from Exercise 2.6.2 that $\{g(t, X_t) : 0 \leq t \leq T\}$ is a martingale. It follows immediately from Itô formula that

$$g(t, X_t) = g(0, X_0) + \int_0^t e^{-rs}\left[-rf(s, X_s) + f_t(s, X_s) + a(s, X_s)f_x(s, X_s) \right.$$
$$\left. +\frac{1}{2}b(s, X_s)^2 f_{xx}(s, X_s) \right] ds + \int_0^t e^{-rs}b(s, X_s)f_x(s, X_s)\, dW_s.$$

Since $\{g(t, X_t) : 0 \leq t \leq T\}$ is a martingale, the first integral must be constantly zero, which implies the integrand is zero for all paths of $x = \{X_s : 0 \leq s \leq t\}$. Therefore, f must satisfy (4.36) for every pair of (t, x) attainable by (t, X_t). It is trivial that $f(T, x) = \mathbb{E}[e^{-r(T-T)}h(X_T)|X_T = x] = h(x)$.

Similarly, we can sketch the idea behind the proof of the backward statement. Since f satisfies the PDE (4.36), we have by Itô's formula that

$$e^{-rT}f(T, X_T) = e^{-rt}f(t, X_t) + \int_t^T e^{-rs}b(s, X_s)f_x(s, X_s)\, dW_s.$$

Conditioning on $\{X_t = x\}$ and taking the expectation on both sides yields

$$f(t, x) = \mathbb{E}[e^{-r(T-t)}f(T, X_T)|X_t = x] = \mathbb{E}[e^{-r(T-t)}h(X_T)|X_t = x],$$

where the last equality results from (4.37).

4.5 Risk-neutral pricing

4.5.1 Path-independent derivatives

One of the most important findings of modern financial theory is the application of the Feymann-Kac formula for option pricing. Observe that the Black-Scholes-Merton PDE (4.31) is a special case of (4.36) with $a(t, x) = rx$ and $b(t, x) = \sigma x$ and the terminal condition (4.32) also conforms to (4.37) with $h(x) = (x - K)_+$. Therefore, Feymann-Kac formula tells us that the no-arbitrage price at time t of any path-independent financial derivative with maturity at time T is given by $f(t, S_t)$ where

$$f(t, s) = \tilde{\mathbb{E}}\left[e^{-r(T-t)}h(S_T)\Big| S_t = s \right], \tag{4.38}$$

where the price process is determined under some probability measure $\tilde{\mathbb{P}}$ by

$$dS_t = rS_t\, dt + \sigma S_t\, d\tilde{W}_t, \tag{4.39}$$

where $\{\tilde{W}_t : 0 \leq t \leq T\}$ is a Brownian motion under the probability measure $\tilde{P}$.

Note that the dynamics of the stock price process in (4.28) has a different drift coefficient than that of the stock price process in (4.39). This shows that the no-arbitrage price is only represented as an expected present value of the payoff function under an artificial probability measure $\tilde{\mathbb{P}}$ under which the price process is given by (4.39). It shows that the average instantaneous rate of return on stock prices is the same as the risk-free rate of return r on the money market account, i.e.

$$d\tilde{\mathbb{E}}[S_t] = r\tilde{\mathbb{E}}[S_t]\,dt, \qquad dB_t = rB_t\,dt.$$

A peculiar phenomenon is that under the probability measure $\tilde{\mathbb{P}}$ not only does the stock price process have the risk-free average rate of return, any financial derivative would have the same average rate of return. For example, consider any financial derivative with a replicating portfolio

$$H_t = \Delta_t S_t + B_t.$$

It follows immediately that under the probability measure $\tilde{\mathbb{P}}$

$$dH_t = \Delta_t\,dS_t + dB_t = r(\Delta_t + B_t)\,dt + \sigma\Delta_t S_t\,d\tilde{W}_t = rH_t\,dt + \sigma\Delta_t S_t\,d\tilde{W}_t,$$

which again implies that

$$d\tilde{\mathbb{E}}[H_t] = r\tilde{\mathbb{E}}[H_t]\,dt.$$

Under this artificial probability measure, all financial instruments would have the same risk-free average rate of return and hence the investor would be indifferent about which instrument to invest with, which is consistent with the notation of the absence of arbitrage. Therefore, the probability measure $\tilde{\mathbb{P}}$ is often called *risk-neutral* probability measure and the option pricing formula (4.38) the *risk-neutral pricing formula*. In contrast, the probability measure under which stock prices and money market account are observable and their dynamics are modeled by (4.28) is often referred to as *real-world or physical* probability measure.

It should be pointed out that the risk neutral pricing formula (4.38) is the continuous-time analogue of the pricing formula (4.18) in the binomial tree model.

Example 4.14 (Black-Scholes formula). Consider the European call option with the payoff function

$$h(t, s) = (s - K)_+.$$

The no-arbitrage price of the option is therefore given by $c(t, S_t)$ where

$$c(t, s) = \tilde{\mathbb{E}}\left[e^{-r(T-t)}(S_T - K)_+ \Big| S_t = s\right]. \tag{4.40}$$

Since the stock price process is a geometric Brownian motion, we know that S_T is lognormally distributed with location parameter $(r - \sigma^2/2)(T - t)$ and scale parameter $\sigma\sqrt{T - t}$. It is easy to show that

$$c(t, s) = s\Phi\big(d_1(T - t, s/K)\big) - Ke^{-r(T-t)}\Phi\big(d_2(T - t, s/K)\big), \tag{4.41}$$

where Φ is the cumulative distribution function of a standard normal random variable and

$$d_1(t, u) = \frac{\ln u + (r + \sigma^2/2)t}{\sigma\sqrt{t}} \tag{4.42}$$

$$d_2(t, u) = d_1(t, u) - \sigma\sqrt{t}. \tag{4.43}$$

The proof is left as Exercise 4.5.2. We can also determine the no-arbitrage price of the European put option with the payoff function

$$p(t, s) = \tilde{\mathbb{E}}\left[e^{-r(T-t)}(K - S_T)_+ | S_t = s\right]. \tag{4.44}$$

Recall that

$$(x)_+ - (x)_- = x.$$

Therefore,

$$c(t, s) - p(t, s) = \tilde{\mathbb{E}}\left[e^{-r(T-t)}(S_T - K) | S_t = s\right] = s - e^{-r(T-t)}K.$$

This identity is known as the *put-call parity*. Therefore, we obtain

$$p(t, s) = Ke^{-r(T-t)}\Phi\big(-d_2(T - t, s/K)\big) - s\Phi\big(-d_1(T - t, s/K)\big). \tag{4.45}$$

4.5.2   Path-dependent derivatives

We further extend the notion of risk-neutral pricing to path-dependent financial derivative. Keep in mind that the no-arbitrage value of a path-dependent derivative typically depends on more than just the current asset value. Take the high-water mark option for equity-indexed annuity as an example. When attempting to find the time-t value of such an option with t being an integer, we known the information set up to time t and recognize the known and unknown components of its payoff

$$\max\left(PS_0^{-\alpha} \max\left\{ \underbrace{\max\{S_1, S_2, \cdots, S_t\}}_{\text{known by time } t}, \underbrace{S_{t+1}, \cdots, S_T}_{\text{unknown but depend on } S_t} \right\}^\alpha, G_T \right).$$

Even if the underlying process $\{S_t : t = 1, 2, \cdots, T\}$ is Markov, the option value at time t clearly depends on not only the current index value S_t but also the maximum of annual index values $\max\{S_1, S_2, \cdots, S_t\}$.

Hence, it is no longer appropriate to start with the assumption of time-t derivative price in the form of $f(t, S_t)$. Nonetheless, we assume that there exists a risk neutral probability measure $\tilde{\mathbb{P}}$ under which the stock price has the same average rate of return as the risk-free money market account. Here we consider a more general case of stochastic interest rates driven by the process $\{r_t : 0 \leq t \leq T\}$. Therefore, the dynamics of the stock price and the money market account are given by

$$
\begin{aligned}
dS_t &= r_t S_t \, dt + \sigma S_t \, d\tilde{W}_t, \\
dB_t &= r_t B_t \, dt,
\end{aligned}
$$

where $\{\tilde{W}_t : 0 \leq t \leq T\}$ is a Brownian motion under the probability measure $\tilde{\mathbb{P}}$. Suppose that we can construct a self-financing replicating portfolio that consists of Δ_t shares of the underlying stock and an investment of B_t in the money market account. Denote the time-t value of the replicating portfolio by X_t. Then

$$
X_t = \Delta_t S_t + B_t, \qquad 0 \leq t \leq T.
$$

In view of the self-financing property (4.20), it follows immediately that

$$
\begin{aligned}
dX_t &= \Delta_t \, dS_t + dB_t = \Delta_t (r_t S_t \, dt + \sigma S_t \, d\tilde{W}_t) + r_t B_t \, dt \\
&= r_t \Delta_t S_t \, dt + \sigma \Delta_t S_t \, d\tilde{W}_t + r_t (X_t - \Delta_t S_t) \, dt \\
&= r_t X_t \, dt + \sigma \Delta_t S_t \, d\tilde{W}_t.
\end{aligned}
$$

Applying Itô's formula to the present value of X_t, $Y_t := e^{-\int_0^t r_s \, ds} X_t$, yields

$$
dY_t = e^{-\int_0^t r_s \, ds} \, dX_t - r_t e^{-\int_0^t r_s \, ds} X_t \, dt = \sigma e^{-\int_0^t r_s \, ds} \Delta_t S_t \, d\tilde{W}_t,
$$

which implies that the present value process $\{Y_t : 0 \leq t \leq T\}$ is a martingale.

Since the economic outcome of the replicating portfolio should match that of the financial derivative, then it must be true that

$$
X_T = H_T.
$$

Since $\{Y_t : 0 \leq t \leq T\}$ is a martingale, it follows by martingale property that

$$
e^{-\int_0^t r_s \, ds} X_t = \tilde{\mathbb{E}} \left[e^{-\int_0^T r_s \, ds} X_T \,\middle|\, \mathcal{F}_t \right] = \tilde{\mathbb{E}} \left[e^{-\int_0^T r_s \, ds} H_T \,\middle|\, \mathcal{F}_t \right].
$$

By the principle of no-arbitrage, two portfolios that end with the same outcome should cost the same at any time. Therefore,

$$
H_t = X_t = \tilde{\mathbb{E}} \left[e^{-\int_t^T r_s \, ds} H_T \,\middle|\, \mathcal{F}_t \right]. \tag{4.46}
$$

It is worthwhile pointing out that (4.46) is in fact the continuous-time analogue of the risk-neutral pricing formula (4.17) in the binomial tree model. Furthermore, if the underlying process $\{S_t : 0 \leq t \leq T\}$ is Markov, then

$$
H_t = X_t = \tilde{\mathbb{E}} \left[e^{-\int_t^T r_s \, ds} H_T \,\middle|\, S_t \right].
$$

4.6   No-arbitrage costs of equity-indexed annuities

We are ready to develop solutions to the no-arbitrage costs of embedded options in equity-indexed annuities. Like Black-Scholes formula for European call/put options, these formulas are derived under the geometric Brownian motion model. Most solutions discussed in this book can be further extended to other equity return models.

4.6.1   Point-to-point index crediting option

Suppose that the equity index underlying the annuity product is driven by a geometric Brownian motion defined by (2.44). Recall from Section 1.3.1 that the benefit from the equity-indexed annuity with point-to-point design (1.37) resembles the payoff from a European put option and hence is a path-independent derivative. It follows immediately from the principle of risk-neutral pricing in Section 4.5.1 that its time-t no-arbitrage value is given by $f(t, S_t)$ where

$$f(t, s) := \tilde{\mathbb{E}}\left[e^{-r(T-t)} \max\left(P\left(\frac{S_T}{S_0}\right)^\alpha, P e^{gT} \right) \middle| S_t = s \right],$$

where the expectation $\tilde{\mathbb{E}}$ is taken under the risk-neutral probability measure $\tilde{\mathbb{P}}$. Note that the dynamics of the geometric Brownian motion is given by (4.39) under the measure $\tilde{\mathbb{P}}$. Multiplying the result in Exercise 4.5.1 by $PS_0^{-\alpha}$ and setting $K = e^{gT} S_0^\alpha$ yields

$$\begin{aligned}
f(t, s) =& P\left(\frac{s}{S_0}\right)^\alpha \exp\left\{ \left[(\alpha - 1)r + \alpha(\alpha - 1)\frac{\sigma^2}{2} \right](T - t) \right\} \\
& \times \Phi\left(\frac{\ln(s/S_0) + (r - \sigma^2/2 + \alpha\sigma^2)(T - t) - gT/\alpha}{\sigma\sqrt{T - t}} \right) \\
& + P e^{gT - r(T-t)} \Phi\left(\frac{gT/\alpha - \ln(s/S_0) - (r - \sigma^2/2)(T - t)}{\sigma\sqrt{T - t}} \right).
\end{aligned}$$

Recall that equity indexed annuities do not charge fees. As the insurer is expected to retain financial returns beyond credited interest to the policyholder's assets, the cost is managed by setting participation rate, return cap and guarantee floor at appropriate levels. For example, given fixed return cap and floor, one can determine the "fair" participation rate α by setting

$$f(0, S_0) = P,$$

or equivalently, solving the following equation for α,

$$\begin{aligned}
& e^{[(\alpha-1)r+\alpha(\alpha-1)\frac{\sigma^2}{2}]T} \Phi\left(\frac{(r - \frac{\sigma^2}{2} + \alpha\sigma^2)T - \frac{gT}{\alpha}}{\sigma\sqrt{T}} \right) \\
& + e^{(g-r)T} \Phi\left(\frac{\frac{gT}{\alpha} - (r - \frac{\sigma^2}{2})T}{\sigma\sqrt{T}} \right) = 1.
\end{aligned}$$

4.6.2 Cliquet index crediting option

Recall from Section 1.3.2 that the equity indexed annuity with a cliquet index crediting option has a payoff function given by (1.40), which resembles a sequence of options written on each dollar of investment with a staggered start. One can also show by the principle of risk-neutral pricing in Section 4.5.2 that its time-t no-arbitrage value is given by

$$V_t := \tilde{\mathbb{E}} \left[P \prod_{k=1}^{T} \max \left(\left(\frac{S_k}{S_{k-1}} \right)^{\alpha}, e^g \right) \middle| \mathcal{F}_t \right].$$

Suppose that t is an integer. It follows from Exercise 4.5.1 that

$$V_t = P \prod_{k=1}^{t} \max \left\{ \left(\frac{S_k}{S_{k-1}} \right)^{\alpha}, e^g \right\}$$

$$\times \left[e^{(\alpha-1)r + \frac{1}{2}\alpha(\alpha-1)\sigma^2} \Phi \left(\frac{r - \frac{1}{2}\sigma^2 + \alpha\sigma^2 - \frac{g}{\alpha}}{\sigma} \right) + e^{-(r-g)} \Phi \left(\frac{\frac{g}{\alpha} - r + \frac{1}{2}\sigma^2}{\sigma} \right) \right]^{T-t}.$$

Similarly, we can also determine the time-t no-arbitrage value of the equity-indexed annuity with a cliquet index crediting option (1.41) by

$$V_t := \tilde{\mathbb{E}} \left[P \prod_{k=1}^{T} \max \left(\min \left(\left(\frac{S_k}{S_{k-1}} \right)^{\alpha}, e^c \right), e^g \right) \middle| \mathcal{F}_t \right].$$

Using similar arguments, we can show that

$$V_t = P \prod_{k=1}^{t} \max \left\{ \min \left\{ \left(\frac{S_k}{S_{k-1}} \right)^{\alpha}, e^c \right\}, e^g \right\}$$

$$\times \left\{ e^{-(r-g)} \Phi \left(\frac{\frac{g}{\alpha} - r + \frac{1}{2}\sigma^2}{\sigma} \right) + e^{c-r} \Phi \left(\frac{r - \frac{1}{2}\sigma^2 - \frac{c}{\alpha}}{\sigma} \right) \right.$$

$$\left. + e^{(\alpha-1)r + \frac{1}{2}\alpha(\alpha-1)\sigma^2} \left[\Phi \left(\frac{\frac{c}{\alpha} - r + \frac{1}{2}\sigma^2 - \alpha\sigma^2}{\sigma} \right) - \Phi \left(\frac{\frac{g}{\alpha} - r + \frac{1}{2}\sigma^2 - \alpha\sigma^2}{\sigma} \right) \right] \right\}^{T-t}.$$

4.6.3 High-water mark index crediting option

The equity indexed annuity with high-water mark index crediting option is introduced in Section 1.3.3. Consider the simple case with the payoff given by (1.43), which is clearly a path-dependent financial derivative. The time-t no-arbitrage value of such an annuity product is given by

$$V_t := \tilde{\mathbb{E}} \left[\max \left(P \left(\frac{\overline{S}_T}{S_0} \right)^{\alpha}, G_T \right) \middle| \mathcal{F}_t \right], \qquad (4.47)$$

where

$$\overline{S}_T := \sup_{0 \le t \le T} \{S_t\}.$$

It is also shown in Exercise 4.6.2 that the time-t no-arbitrage value can be determined in two cases. On one hand, when $\overline{S}_t \ge S_0(1+r)^T$, the time-$t$ no-arbitrage value of the equity indexed annuity is given by

$$
V_t = P\left(\frac{\overline{S}_t}{S_0}\right)^\alpha e^{-r(T-t)}\left\{ e^{h(\alpha)}\Phi\big(d_1(\alpha) + \alpha\sigma\sqrt{T-t}\big)\right.
$$

$$
- \frac{2r-\sigma^2}{g(\alpha)\sigma^2}\left[-e^{g(\alpha)\frac{\ln(\overline{S}_t/S_t)}{\alpha}}\Phi(d_2(\alpha)) + e^{m(\alpha)}\Phi(d_2(\alpha) + g(\alpha)\sigma\sqrt{T-t})\right]
$$

$$
\left. + e^{m(\alpha)}\Phi\big(d_2(\alpha) + g(\alpha)\sigma\sqrt{T-t}\big) + \Phi(-d_1(\alpha)) - e^{\frac{(2r-\sigma^2)\ln(\overline{S}_t/S_t)}{\sigma^2\alpha}}\Phi(d_2(\alpha))\right\}
$$

$$(4.48)$$

where

$$
\begin{aligned}
d_1(\alpha) &= \frac{(r-\sigma^2/2)(T-t) - \ln(\overline{S}_t/S_t)/\alpha}{\sigma\sqrt{T-t}}, \\[2mm]
d_2(\alpha) &= \frac{-(r-\sigma^2/2)(T-t) - \ln(\overline{S}_t/S_t)/\alpha}{\sigma\sqrt{T-t}}, \\[2mm]
g(\alpha) &= \alpha - 1 + \frac{2r}{\sigma^2}, \\[2mm]
h(\alpha) &= \alpha r(T-t) + \frac{\sigma^2}{2}\alpha(\alpha-1)(T-t), \\[2mm]
m(\alpha) &= -g(\alpha)r(T-t) + \frac{\sigma^2}{2}g(\alpha)(g(\alpha)-1)(T-t).
\end{aligned}
$$

On the other hand, when $\overline{S}_t < S_0(1+r)^T$, the time-$t$ no-arbitrage value of the equity indexed annuity is given by

$$
V_t = Pe^{-r(T-t)}\left\{ e^{h(\alpha)}\left(\frac{S_t}{S_0}\right)^\alpha \Phi(d_1(\alpha) + \alpha\sigma\sqrt{(T-t)})\right.
$$

$$
+ e^{m(\alpha)}\left(\frac{S_t}{S_0}\right)^\alpha \Phi(d_2(\alpha) + g(\alpha)\sigma\sqrt{(T-t)})
$$

$$
- \left(\frac{S_t}{S_0}\right)^\alpha \frac{2r-\sigma^2}{g(\alpha)\sigma^2}\left[-e^{g(\alpha)(\frac{T\ln(1+r)}{\alpha} - \ln(\frac{S_t}{S_0}))}\Phi(d_2(\alpha))\right.
$$

$$
\left. + e^{m(\alpha)}\Phi(d_2(\alpha) + g(\alpha)\sigma\sqrt{(T-t)})\right]
$$

$$
\left. + (1+r)^T\left[\Phi(-d_1(\alpha)) - e^{\frac{2r-\sigma^2}{\sigma^2}(\frac{T\ln(1+r)}{\alpha} - \ln(\frac{S_t}{S_0}))}\Phi(d_2(\alpha))\right]\right\}, \quad (4.49)
$$

where

$$d_1(\alpha) = \frac{(r - \frac{1}{2}\sigma^2)(T - t) - (\frac{T\ln(1+r)}{\alpha} - \ln(\frac{S_L}{S_0}))}{\sigma\sqrt{T-t}},$$

$$d_2(\alpha) = \frac{-(r - \frac{1}{2}\sigma^2)(T - t) - (\frac{T\ln(1+r)}{\alpha} - \ln(\frac{S_L}{S_0}))}{\sigma\sqrt{T-t}}.$$

4.7 No-arbitrage costs of variable annuity guaranteed benefits

We can also derive the no-arbitrage value of investment guarantees from variable annuities in a similar fashion. While guaranteed benefits are viewed as financial options in this section, one should keep in mind a few unique features that set the investment guarantees apart from exchange-traded financial instruments.

1. While most exchange-traded options are short-lived with typical terms ranging from a few months to a year, variable annuities last for many many years as an investment vehicle for retirement planning. The long-term nature of the products require projections of cash flows that can be affected by many economic factors.

2. Unlike most financial instruments that require an up-front fee, the costs of variable annuity guaranteed benefits are compensated by collections of asset-based fees from policyholder's investment accounts. Therefore, the financial risks embedded in the insurer's liability side are also present on the income side. In adverse economic scenarios, high liabilities may be accompanied by low incomes, which exacerbate the severity of potential losses to the insurers.

3. Financial options are typically traded by institutional investors. Guaranteed minimum benefits, however, are sold to individual investors and therefore often involves the interaction of both financial risks and mortality risk, a unique feature to equity-linked insurance products.

4.7.1 Guaranteed minimum maturity benefit

Recall from Section 1.2.3 that the cost of GMMB from an insurer's perspective is given by

$$(G - F_T)_+ I(T_x > T),$$

where G is the minimum guarantee at maturity and the policyholder's nominal account is driven by the geometric Brownian motion in (2.45). Following Feymann-Kac formula, we can quickly recognize that its no-arbitrage cost can be determined by $B_e(t, F_T)$ where

$$B_e(t, F) := \tilde{\mathbb{E}}[e^{-r(T-t)}(G - F_T)_+ I(T_x > T)|F_t = F], \qquad 0 \le t \le T, F > 0.$$

Under the assumption that mortality is independent of equity returns, we know from Theorem 2.45 that

$$B_e(t, F) = {}_{T}p_x\tilde{\mathbb{E}}[e^{-r(T-t)}(G - F_T)_+ | F_t = F].$$ (4.50)

Recall from (1.22) that the policyholder's subaccount is linked to the equity index in the following way

$$F_t = F_0 \frac{S_t}{S_0} e^{-mt}, \qquad 0 \le t \le T.$$ (4.51)

Since the Feymann-Kac formula shows that the no-arbitrage value should be determined with the dynamics of stock price process given by (4.39) under the risk-neutral measure $\tilde{\mathbb{P}}$. Therefore, applying Itô formula to (4.51), we obtain the dynamics of the policyholder's subaccount under the measure $\tilde{\mathbb{P}}$

$$dF_t = (r - m)F_t \, dt + \sigma F_t \, dW_t, \qquad 0 < t < T.$$ (4.52)

Comparing (4.39) and (4.52), we observe that the cost of GMMB in (4.50) resembles the price of a European put option in (4.44). Replacing r with $r - m$ and K with G in (4.44), we obtain immediately from the Black-Scholes formula (4.45) that

$$B_e(t, F) = {}_{T}p_x\left[Ge^{-r(T-t)}\Phi\left(-d_2\left(T - t, \frac{F}{G}\right)\right)\right.$$

$$\left. - Fe^{-m(T-t)}\Phi\left(-d_1\left(T - t, \frac{F}{G}\right)\right)\right],$$ (4.53)

where

$$d_1(t, u) = \frac{\ln u + (r - m + \sigma^2/2)t}{\sigma\sqrt{t}}$$ (4.54)

$$d_2(t, u) = d_1(t, u) - \sigma\sqrt{t}.$$ (4.55)

Recall from Section 1.2.3 that the insurer is always compensated by rider charges. While the quantities were expressed in Section 1.2.3 at policy issue, we can similarly derive the time-t value of all rider charges up to the earlier of maturity or the policyholder's death, i.e.

$$\int_t^T e^{-r(s-t)} m_e F_s I(s < T_x) \, ds.$$

Note that the insurer's fee incomes can be viewed as a series of financial derivatives on the policyholder's subaccount, which pay off the amount $m_e F_s I(s < T_x)$ per time unit at any time $s \in (t, T)$. Therefore, we can naturally extend the no-arbitrage price of a single financial derivative in (4.38) to that of a series of derivatives, which we denote by $P_e(t, F_t)$ where

$$
\begin{aligned}
P_e(t, F) &= \tilde{\mathbb{E}}\left[\int_t^T e^{-r(s-t)} m_e F_s I(s < T_x)\,\mathrm{d}s \,\Big|\, F_t = F\right] \\
&= \int_t^T e^{-r(s-t)} m_e \tilde{\mathbb{E}}[F_s I(s < T_x)\,|\, F_t = F]\,\mathrm{d}s \\
&= \int_t^T e^{-r(s-t)} m_e\, {}_sp_x F e^{(r-m)(s-t)}\,\mathrm{d}s \\
&= m_e\, {}_tp_x F \int_0^{T-t} e^{-ms}\, {}_sp_{x+t}\,\mathrm{d}s = m_e\, {}_tp_x F \bar{a}_{x+t:\overline{T-t}|m},
\end{aligned}
$$

where $\bar{a}_{x:\bar{t}|m}$ is the actuarial symbol for the present value of an annuity continuously payable at the rate of 1 per period lasting for t periods computed with the force of interest m per period.

Based on the no-arbitrage principle, the risk-neutral value of insurer's benefit payments should be equal to that of insurer's fee incomes at time of issue in the absence of arbitrage. We consider any pair of total fee rate and rider charge rate (m, m_e) that matches the risk-neutral values of the insurer's incomes and outgoes as *fair rates*. Therefore, the fair rates (m, m_e) should be determined by the identity

$$
B_e(0, F_0) = P_e(0, F_0). \tag{4.56}
$$

Since the guarantee level is often proportional to the initial purchase payment, i.e. $G = F_0 e^{\rho T}$ with a roll-up option, then the identity is in fact independent of the initial purchase payment, i.e.

$$
{}_Tp_x\left[e^{(\rho-r)T}\Phi\left(\frac{\rho - (r - m - \sigma^2/2)}{\sigma}\sqrt{T}\right) \right. \\
\left. -e^{-mT}\Phi\left(\frac{\rho - (r - m + \sigma^2/2)}{\sigma}\sqrt{T}\right)\right] = m_e \bar{a}_{x:\bar{T}|m}
$$

4.7.2 Guaranteed minimum accumulation benefit

Since the benefit payment of the GMAB at the end of the first period is same as that of the GMMB, the no-arbitrage cost from the the first period is also given by (4.53) except that T is replaced by T_1. Hence we shall only discuss the no-arbitrage cost of the benefit from the second period. Note that the policyholder's account may receive a cash injection due to the maturity benefit at time T_1 and hence should be represented by G_{T_1} immediately after T_1. Therefore, the benefit payment from the second period is given by

$$
(G_{T_1} - F_{T_2})_+ = G_{T_1}\left(1 - \frac{F_{T_2}}{G_{T_1}}\right)_+ = \max\{G_0, F_{T_1}\}\left(1 - \frac{F_{T_2}}{G_{T_1}}\right)_+. \tag{4.57}
$$

Since the payoff from the GMAB in (4.57) is clearly path-dependent, it follows from (4.46) that the no-arbitrage cost of the second period benefit payment for $0 \leq t \leq T_1$

is given by

$$\tilde{\mathbb{E}}\left[e^{-r(T_2-t)}\max(G_0, F_{T_1})\left(1-\frac{F_{T_2}}{G_{T_1}}\right)_+ I(T_x > T_2)\middle| \mathcal{F}_t\right].$$

Due to the Markov property of $\{F_t : 0 < t < T_1\}$ and $\{F_t/G_{T_1} : T_1 < t < T_2\}$, the above quantity can be written as $B_a^{(2)}(t, F_t)$ where

$$
\begin{aligned}
B_a^{(2)}(t, F) &= \tilde{\mathbb{E}}\left[e^{-r(T_2-t)}\max(G_0, F_{T_1})\left(1-\frac{F_{T_2}}{G_{T_1}}\right)_+ I(T_x > T_2)\middle| F_t = F\right] \\
&= {}_{T_2}p_x\, e^{-r(T_2-t)}\tilde{\mathbb{E}}\left[\max(G_0, F_{T_1})\middle| F_t = F\right]\tilde{\mathbb{E}}\left[\left(1-\frac{F_{T_2}}{G_{T_1}}\right)_+\right],
\end{aligned}
$$

where in the last step we use the fact that F_{T_1} is independent of F_{T_2}/G_{T_1}. The two factors can both be calculated using no-arbitrage price of European options. Since $\max(a, b) = a + (b - a)_+$, we have

$$
\begin{aligned}
&\tilde{\mathbb{E}}\left[\max(G_0, F_{T_1})\middle| F_t = F\right] = G_0 + \tilde{\mathbb{E}}\left[(F_{T_1} - G_0)_+\middle| F_t = F\right] \\
&= G_0 + Fe^{(r-m)(T_1-t)}\Phi(d_1(T_1 - t, F/G_0)) - G_0\Phi(d_2(T_1 - t, F/G_0)) \\
&= G_0\Phi(-d_2(T_1 - t, F/G_0)) + Fe^{(r-m)(T_1-t)}\Phi(d_1(T_1 - t, F/G_0)),
\end{aligned}
$$

where d_1 and d_2 are given by (4.54) and (4.55) respectively. Similarly,

$$
\begin{aligned}
\tilde{\mathbb{E}}\left[\left(1-\frac{F_{T_2}}{G_{T_1}}\right)_+\right] &= \Phi\left(\frac{m + \sigma^2/2 - r}{\sigma}\sqrt{T_2 - T_1}\right) \\
&- e^{(r-m)(T_2-T_1)}\Phi\left(\frac{m - r - \sigma^2/2}{\sigma}\sqrt{T_2 - T_1}\right).
\end{aligned}
$$

The no-arbitrage cost of the second period benefit for $T_1 < t < T_2$ can be computed in a similar manner to that of the GMMB.

$$
\begin{aligned}
&\tilde{\mathbb{E}}\left[e^{-r(T_2-t)}(G_{T_1} - F_{T_2})_+ I(T_x > T_2)\middle| \mathcal{F}_t\right] \\
&= {}_{T_2}p_x e^{-r(T_2-t)}\Big[G_{T_1}\Phi\big(-d_2(T_2 - t, F_t/G_{T_1}) \\
&\quad - F_t e^{(r-m)(T_2-t)}\Phi\big(-d_1(T_2 - t, F_t/G_{T_1})\big)\Big].
\end{aligned}
$$

4.7.3 Guaranteed minimum death benefit

The GMDB rider offers the greater of the guarantee base G_{T_x} and the balance of the policyholder's account value F_{T_x} at the time of the policyholder's death. The guarantee base may accrue interest under a roll-up option, i.e. $G_t = G_0 e^{\rho t}$ where ρ is the annualized roll-up rate. As shown in Section 1.2.5, the continuous-time version of the gross liability is given by

$$e^{-rT_x}(G_{T_x} - F_{T_x})_+ I(T_x < T).$$

Then the no-arbitrage cost of the gross liability can be determined by $B_d(t, F_t)$ where

$$B_d(t, F) := \tilde{\mathbb{E}}[e^{-r(T_x - t)}(G_{T_x} - F_{T_x})_+ I(T_x < T)|F_t = F], \qquad 0 \leq t \leq T, F > 0.$$

It is known from Section 2.11 that the stochastic process $\{F_t : t \geq 0\}$ defined by (4.52) has the Markov property. Hence, the new process $\{\tilde{F}_s := F_{t+s} : s > 0, F_t = F\}$ is equivalent to the process $\{F_s : s > 0, F_0 = F\}$. In view of this fact and the independence of mortality and equity returns, we observe that

$$B_d(t, F) = \tilde{\mathbb{E}}[e^{-rT_{x+t}}(G_{t+T_{x+t}} - F_{T_{x+t}})_+ I(T_x < T)|F_0 = F]. \qquad (4.58)$$

Suppose that the future lifetime is modeled by a continuous random variable with the survival function $_t p_x = \mathbb{P}(T_x > t)$ and force of mortality

$$\mu_{x+t} = -\frac{\mathrm{d}\,_t p_x/\,\mathrm{d}t}{_t p_x}. \qquad (4.59)$$

Then

$$\begin{aligned}
B_d(t, F) &= \tilde{\mathbb{E}}\left[\int_0^{T-t} e^{-rs}(G_{t+s} - F_s)_+ \,_{t+s}p_x \mu_{x+t+s}\,\mathrm{d}s \,\middle|\, F_0 = F\right] \\
&= \int_0^{T-t} \tilde{\mathbb{E}}\left[e^{-rs}(G_{t+s} - F_s)_+ \,\middle|\, F_0 = F\right] {}_{t+s}p_x \mu_{x+t+s}\,\mathrm{d}s
\end{aligned}$$

where the conditional expectation is obtained earlier in (4.50),

$$\begin{aligned}
&\tilde{\mathbb{E}}\left[e^{-rs}(G_{t+s} - F_s)_+ \,\middle|\, F_0 = F\right] \\
&= G_{t+s}e^{-rs}\Phi(-d_2(s, F/G_{t+s})) - Fe^{-ms}\Phi(-d_1(s, F/G_{t+s})).
\end{aligned}$$

Similarly, the present value of GMDB rider charges is given by

$$\int_t^{T \wedge T_x} e^{-r(s-t)}m_d F_s \,\mathrm{d}s.$$

Its no-arbitrage value can be written as

$$\begin{aligned}
P_d(t, F) &:= \tilde{\mathbb{E}}\left[\int_t^{T \wedge (T_x \vee t)} e^{-r(s-t)}m_d F_s \,\mathrm{d}s \,\middle|\, F_t = F\right] \\
&= \tilde{\mathbb{E}}\left[I(T_x > t)\int_0^{(T-t) \wedge T_{x+t}} e^{-rs}m_d F_s \,\mathrm{d}s \,\middle|\, F_0 = F\right] \\
&= \tilde{\mathbb{E}}\left[\int_0^{T-t} e^{-rs}m_d \,_{t+s}p_x F_s \,\mathrm{d}s \,\middle|\, F_0 = F\right] \\
&= m_d F \int_0^{T-t} e^{-ms} \,_{t+s}p_x \,\mathrm{d}s = m_d F \,_t p_x \bar{a}_{x+t:\overline{T-t}|m}.
\end{aligned}$$

In general, the no-arbitrage cost of the GMDB net liability at time 0 is given by

$$N_d(0, F_0) := B_d(0, F_0) - P_d(0, F_0)$$

$$= \tilde{\mathbb{E}}\left[\int_0^T e^{-rt} {}_tp_x\mu_{x+t}(G_t - F_t)_+ \, dt - \int_0^T e^{-rt}m_d \, {}_tp_x F_t \, dt\right]$$

(4.60)

4.7.4 Guaranteed minimum withdrawal benefit

Recall from Section 1.2.6 that the formulation of the GMWB from a policyholder's perspective is different than that from an insurer's perspective. Let us formulate and compare no-arbitrage costs of the GMWB from both perspectives.

4.7.4.1 Policyholder's perspective

A policyholder who elects the GMWB rider is entitled to (1) a guaranteed stream of incomes that provide a full refund of initial purchase payment and (2) outstanding balance in the sub-account at expiry. Here we consider the case where the policyholder chooses a systematic withdrawal plan where the maximal amount without any penalty w is withdrawn continuously. Formulated mathematically, the no-arbitrage time-t value of the policyholder's investment with the GMWB rider is given by $B_w(t, F_t)$ where

$$
\begin{aligned}
B_w(t, F) &= \tilde{\mathbb{E}}\left[e^{-r(T-t)}F_T I(F_T > 0)] + w\int_t^T e^{-r(s-t)} \, ds \,\Big|\, F_t = F\right] \\
&= \tilde{\mathbb{E}}[e^{-r(T-t)}F_T I(F_T > 0)|F_t = F] + \frac{w}{r}(1 - e^{-r(T-t)}),
\end{aligned}
$$

where the dynamics of the sub-account is given by (2.48). Recall that the new process $\{\tilde{F}_s := F_{t+s} : s > 0, F_t = F\}$ is equivalent to the process $\{F_s : s > 0, F_0 = F\}$. Therefore,

$$B_w(t, F) = \tilde{\mathbb{E}}[e^{-r(T-t)}F_{T-t} I(F_{T-t} > 0)|F_0 = F] + \frac{w}{r}(1 - e^{-r(T-t)}) \quad (4.61)$$

In the absence of any arbitrage, an investor should be indifferent at the inception about whether to hold the initial purchase payment F_0 (in cash or other assets) or to invest in a variable annuity contract with the GMWB rider, which has the time-0 value $B_w(0, F_0)$. Note that the annualized fee rate m is hidden in $B_w(0, F_0)$ through the stochastic differential equation (4.52). In other words, by no-arbitrage principle, the fair fee rate m is set such that

$$F_0 = B_w(0, F_0). \quad (4.62)$$

4.7.4.2 Insurer's perspective

For the purpose of pricing, an insurer would be concerned with the balance of incomes and outgoes. On one hand, the time-t value of out-of-pocket costs for the insurer over the period $[t, T]$ is that of guaranteed payments after the sub-account is depleted prior to maturity T,

$$w \int_{\tau \vee t}^{\tau \vee T} e^{-r(s-t)} \, \mathrm{d}s = \frac{w}{r} \left(e^{-r(\tau \vee t - t)} - e^{-r(\tau \vee T - t)} \right).$$

One the other hand, the time-t value of total fee incomes for the insurer is determined by GMWB rider charges

$$m_w \int_{\tau \wedge t}^{\tau \wedge T} e^{-r(s-t)} F_s \, \mathrm{d}s,$$

where m_w is the rate per time unit of fees allocated to fund the GMWB. Note that in general $m > m_w$ as part of fees and charges are used to cover overheads and other expenses.

Assuming all cash flows can be securitized as tradable assets. We can obtain the risk-neutral value of the insurer's net liability by $N_w(t, F_t)$ where

$$N_w(t, F) := \tilde{\mathbb{E}} \left[w \int_{\tau \vee t}^{\tau \vee T} e^{-r(s-t)} \, \mathrm{d}s - m_w \int_{\tau \wedge t}^{\tau \wedge T} e^{-r(s-t)} F_s \, \mathrm{d}s \, \middle| \, F_t = F \right].$$

When $F_t > 0$, it is clear that $\tau \vee t = \tau$. Using the same arguments as earlier, we observe that

$$
\begin{aligned}
N_w(t, F) &= \tilde{\mathbb{E}} \left[w \int_{\tau - t}^{(\tau \vee T) - t} e^{-rs} \, \mathrm{d}s - m_w \int_{(\tau \wedge t) - t}^{(\tau \wedge T) - t} e^{-rs} \tilde{F}_s \, \mathrm{d}s \, \middle| \, \tilde{F}_0 = F \right] \\
&= \tilde{\mathbb{E}} \left[w \int_{\tau}^{\tau \vee (T-t)} e^{-rs} \, \mathrm{d}s - m_w \int_{0}^{\tau \wedge (T-t)} e^{-rs} F_s \, \mathrm{d}s \, \middle| \, F_0 = F \right],
\end{aligned}
$$

(4.63)

where τ refers to the time of ruin for its respective stochastic process.

In the absence of any arbitrage, the insurer's cash inflows and cash outflows should be considered equivalent transactions. Therefore, by no-arbitrage principle, the fair fee rates (m, m_w) should be set such that the risk-neutral value of the GWMB net liability is zero,

$$N_w(0, F_0) = 0. \tag{4.64}$$

Readers may notice from 4.61 and (4.63) that $B_w(t, F)$ and $N_w(t, F)$ both have t-dependence only through the time to maturity $T - t$. Therefore, if one can compute $B_w(0, F_0)$ and $N_w(0, F_0)$, then the results for $B_w(t, F_t)$ and $N_w(t, F_t)$ follow immediately by replacing T with $T - t$ and F_0 with F_t.

4.7.4.3 Equivalence of pricing

For financial derivatives with up front costs such as exotic options, there is no difference between the pricing from a buyer's perspective and that from a seller's perspective. However, that is not the case with a variable annuity product where fees are

collected throughout the lifecycle of the product. We shall demonstrate that only under the assumption of no friction cost (i.e. $m = m_w$) the two pricing approaches are
equivalent, i.e. the fair fee rate m from the buyer's perspective is exactly the same as
that from the seller's perspective, provided that there are no other expenses allowed
in the model beyond the actual cost of the GMWB.

To see their differences, we can summarize the cash flows for the buyer (policyholder) and the seller (insurer) of the GMWB. From a buyer's standpoint, the present
value of net financial return (the payoff less the premium) is given by

$$e^{-rT} F_T I(\tau > T) + \frac{w}{r}(1 - e^{-rT}) - F_0.$$

From an insurer's standpoint, the present value of loss (benefit outgoes less fee incomes) is given by

$$w \int_{\tau \wedge T}^{T} e^{-rs}\, ds - m_w \int_0^{\tau \wedge T} e^{-rs} F_s\, ds.$$

Note that on the insurer's income side, there is an extra parameter m_w which does
not appear in the policyholder's cash flows. To make the two viewpoints comparable,
we assume $m = m_w$, which implies all charges are only used to fund the guarantee.
Observe that, unlike ordinary financial derivative, the buyer's financial return from
the variable annuity contract does not exactly offset the seller's profit, which appears
to be an asymmetric structure.

In the case where $m = m_w$, we can reveal the equivalence of the two pricing
equations (4.62) and (4.64) despite the asymmetric structure of payoffs. Note that
(4.62) can be rewritten as

$$\mathbb{E}[e^{-rT} F_T I(\tau > T)] + w \int_0^T e^{-rs}\, ds = F_0, \qquad (4.65)$$

and (4.64) can be rewritten as

$$\mathbb{E}\left[m \int_0^{\tau \wedge T} e^{-rs} F_s\, ds \right] = \mathbb{E}\left[w \int_{\tau \wedge T}^{T} e^{-rs}\, ds \right]. \qquad (4.66)$$

We subtract (4.66) from (4.65) to obtain

$$\mathbb{E}\left[e^{-rT} F_T I(\tau > T) + \int_0^{\tau \wedge T} e^{-rs}(mF_s + w)\, ds \right] = F_0. \qquad (4.67)$$

It is easy to see that (4.62) and (4.64) are equivalent if and only if (4.67) holds true
for all $m \in \mathbb{R}, T \in \mathbb{R}^+$. Applying Itô's formula to $f(t, F_t)$ where $f(t, x) = e^{-rt}x$,
we obtain that for any $t \geq 0$,

$$e^{-rt} F_t = F_0 - \int_0^t e^{-rs}(mF_s + w)\, ds + \sigma \int_0^t e^{-rs} F_s\, dW_s.$$

Letting $t = \tau \wedge T$ and taking expectation on both sides gives

$$
\mathbb{E}\left[e^{-r(\tau \wedge T)} F_{\tau \wedge T}\right] = F_0 - \mathbb{E}\left[\int_0^{\tau \wedge T} e^{-rs}(mF_s + w)\,\mathrm{d}s\right]
$$
$$
+ \sigma \mathbb{E}\left[\int_0^{\tau \wedge T} e^{-rs} F_s\,\mathrm{d}W_s\right]. \tag{4.68}
$$

Recall that a stochastic integral is a mean-zero martingale. Observe that

$$
\mathbb{E}\left[\int_0^{\tau \wedge T} e^{-rs} F_s\,\mathrm{d}W_s\right] = \mathbb{E}\left[\int_0^{T} e^{-rs} F_s I(F_s > 0)\,\mathrm{d}W_s\right] = 0.
$$

Therefore, the last term in (4.68) vanishes. Rearranging the remaining terms in (4.68) and using the fact that $F_\tau = 0$ gives

$$
F_0 - \mathbb{E}\left[\int_0^{\tau \wedge T} e^{-rs}(mF_s + w)\,\mathrm{d}s\right] = \mathbb{E}[e^{-r(\tau \wedge T)} F_{\tau \wedge T}] = \mathbb{E}\left[e^{-rT} F_T I(\tau > T)\right],
$$

which yields (4.67) after rearrangement. Therefore, (4.62) and (4.64) are equivalent and the implied fair charges must be the same.

Readers should bear in mind that total fees typically allow insurers to be compensated for overheads, commissions and other policy-related expenses. In practice, we expect the total fee rate to be higher than the rider charge, i.e. $m > m_w$. While the two pricing methods are shown to be equivalent in the case where $m = m_w$, they do not in general yield the same set of fair fee rates (m, m_w).

4.7.5 Guaranteed lifetime withdrawal benefit

While explicit solutions for (4.61) and (4.63) are known in the literature, they are not so easy to present in this introductory book. Instead, we shall present solutions to explicit solutions to their counterparts for the pricing of the GLWB rider.

As discussed in Section 1.2.7, the GLWB rider is a natural extension of the GMWB rider where the policyholder is entitled to withdrawals up to a maximal amount per year for lifetime. To better compare with the GMWB rider in Section 4.7.4, we consider a "plain vanilla" GLWB rider with the following product specification:

• The guarantee base is set equal to the initial purchase payment, i.e. $G_t = F_0$ for all $t \geq 0$;

• The rider charge rate m_w is contained in the total fee rate m, rather than a separate fee rate.

In this case, the dynamics of the sub-account $\{F_t : t \geq 0\}$ is given by (2.48) as in the previous section. One can obtain similar results when modeling separately guarantee-based rider charges and asset-value-based management fees (Exercise 4.7.1).

Let us consider for simplicity the case of constant force of mortality for all ages, i.e. $\mu_x = \delta$ for all $x \geq 0$. In other words, the future lifetime random variable follows an exponential distribution

$$\mathbb{P}(T_x \in \mathrm{d}t) = \delta e^{-\delta t}\, \mathrm{d}t, \qquad t \geq 0.$$

It is unrealistic to assume the future lifetime to have "memoryless" property, i.e., a 18-year-old would have the same likelihood to die as a 81-year-old. Nevertheless, it allows us to obtain explicit solutions which can be easily implemented with any computational software platform. We shall demonstrate later that any real life mortality model can be well approximated by a mixture of exponential distributions. Due to "memoryless" property of exponential lifetime, the no-arbitrage cost of the GLWB would be independent of the time of evaluation. Therefore, we shall simply consider the no-arbitrage cost at time 0 in this section.

4.7.5.1 Policyholder's perspective

The policyholder of a GLWB rider and his/her beneficiaries are entitled to two types of payments throughout the term of the variable annuity contract. (1) Living benefits of guaranteed withdrawals. A policyholder under a systematic withdrawal plan would take withdrawals up to the time of death, regardless of whether his/her investment account is depleted. The withdrawal rate w is typically a fixed percentage γ of the guarantee base. Therefore, the present value of all withdrawals up to the policyholder's death is given by

$$\int_0^{T_x} we^{-rs}\, \mathrm{d}s, \tag{4.69}$$

(2) Return to beneficiaries of remaining positive account value upon the policyholder's death. Its present value is given by

$$e^{-rT_x} F_{T_x} I(F_{T_x} > 0). \tag{4.70}$$

Therefore, the no-arbitrage cost of the GLWB rider is determined under the risk-neutral measure by

$$B_{lw}(F_0) := \tilde{\mathbb{E}}\left[\int_0^{T_x} we^{-rs}\, \mathrm{d}s + e^{-rT_x} F_{T_x} I(F_{T_x} > 0)\right]$$

$$= \frac{w}{r} - \frac{\delta w}{r(\delta + r)} + \delta\tilde{\mathbb{E}}\left[\int_0^\tau e^{-(\delta+r)t} F_t\, \mathrm{d}T\right].$$

Note that the third term is already obtained in (2.59). Hence, the no-arbitrage cost of the GLWB rider admits the explicit solution

$$B_{lw}(F_0) = \frac{w}{r} - \frac{\delta w}{r(\delta + r)} + \frac{\delta F_0}{\delta + r - \mu^*} - \frac{\delta w}{(\delta + r)(\mu^* - \delta - r)}$$

$$+ \frac{\delta w}{(\delta + r)(\delta + r - \mu^*)} \frac{\Gamma(b-k)}{\Gamma(b)} \left(\frac{2w}{\sigma^2 F_0}\right)^k M\left(k, b, -\frac{2w}{\sigma^2 F_0}\right),$$

where

$$k := \frac{2\mu^* - \sigma^2 + \sqrt{(2\mu^* - \sigma^2)^2 + 8\sigma^2(\delta + r)}}{2\sigma^2}, \qquad b := 2k + 2 - \frac{2\mu^*}{\sigma^2}. \qquad (4.71)$$

Following the no-arbitrage principle, the fair rate m should be set in such a way that a policyholder would be indifferent about whether to invest the initial purchase payment F_0 in any other financial instruments or in a variable annuity with a GLWB rider, i.e.

$$F_0 = B_l(F_0). \qquad (4.72)$$

Note that (4.72) is in essence the same as (4.62) where the fixed time of maturity $T = F_0/w$ for the GMWB is replaced with the random time of maturity for the GLWB, which is the time of policyholder's death T_x.

4.7.5.2 Insurer's perspective

While the policyholder receives a guaranteed stream of withdrawals throughout his/her lifetime, not all withdrawals are necessarily the liabilities of the insurer. Keep in mind that withdrawals are taken from the policyholder's investment account when the balance is positive. The true GLWB benefit only kicks in when the investment account is exhausted prior to the policyholder's death. Thus the present value of the insurer's liability is represented by

$$\int_{\tau \wedge T_x}^{T_x} w e^{-ru} \, du. \qquad (4.73)$$

The GLWB rider is compensated by the collection of rider charges m_w per annum per dollar of account value from the policy issue to the earlier of the time of ruin and the policyholder's time of death. Therefore, the present value of the insurer's fee income is represented by

$$\int_0^{\tau \wedge T_x} e^{-ru} m_w F_u \, du. \qquad (4.74)$$

Therefore, the no-arbitrage value of the GLWB net liability is given by

$$N_{lw}(F_0) := \tilde{\mathbb{E}} \left[\int_{\tau \wedge T_x}^{T_x} w e^{-ru} \, du - \int_0^{\tau \wedge T_x} e^{-ru} m_w F_u \, du \right].$$

We shall leave it as Exercise 4.7.3 to show that

$$N_{lw}(F_0) = \frac{w}{r + \delta} \tilde{\mathbb{E}}[e^{-(\delta + r)\tau}] + m_w \tilde{\mathbb{E}} \left[\int_0^\tau e^{-(\delta + r)u} F_u \, du \right]. \qquad (4.75)$$

Since both terms are already known in (2.54) and (2.59), the solution to the no-arbitrage value of the GLWB net liability is given by

$$
\begin{aligned}
N_{lw}(F_0) &= \frac{m_w F_0}{\delta + r - \mu^*} - \frac{m_w w}{(\delta + r)(\mu^* - \delta - r)} \\
&\quad + \frac{w(\delta + r - \mu^* + m_w)}{\delta + r - \mu^*} \frac{\Gamma(b - k)}{\Gamma(b)} \left(\frac{2w}{\sigma^2 F_0} \right)^k M\left(k, b, -\frac{2w}{\sigma^2 F_0} \right),
\end{aligned}
$$

where k and b are given in (4.71).

From the insurer's perspective, the absence of an arbitrage implies to the equivalence of the risk-neutral values of the insurer's benefit outgoes and its fee incomes, i.e. m and m_w should be set so that

$$N_{lw}(F_0; \delta) = 0. \tag{4.76}$$

Again (4.76) is the analogue of (4.64) where the fixed time T is replaced with the random time T_x.

In general cases of survival model, we can still utilize the analytical results for the exponential mortality. Suppose that the density function of T_x for a general survival model can be approximated by an exponential sum, i.e. $\mathbb{P}(T_x \, dt) = q_x(t) \, dt$ where

$$q_x(t) \approx \sum_{k=1}^{n} \lambda_k e^{-s_k t},$$

where $\operatorname{Re} s_k > 0$ for all $k = 1, \cdots, n$. Note that all parameters λ_k's and s_k's depend implicitly on the policyholder's age x. We recommend a numerical technique for the approximation of mortality density by an exponential sum in Appendix E.

Using the Markov property, we can show that the no-arbitrage cost of the GLWB rider at time t is given by $B_{lw}(t, F_t)$ where

$$
\begin{aligned}
B_{lw}(t, F) &= \tilde{\mathbb{E}} \left[\int_t^{T_x} w e^{-r(s-t)} \, ds + e^{-r(T_x - t)} F_{T_x} I(F_{T_x} > 0) \,\middle|\, F_t = F, T_x > t \right] \\
&= \tilde{\mathbb{E}} \left[\int_0^{T_{x+t}} w e^{-rs} \, ds + e^{-rT_{x+t}} F_{T_{x+t}} I(F_{T_{x+t}} > 0) \,\middle|\, F_0 = F \right].
\end{aligned}
$$

Note the dependency of B_{lw} on t is only through the model for the current future life time T_{x+t}. It is easy to show that

$$B_{lw}(t, F) = \frac{w}{r} (1 - \tilde{q}_{x+t}(r)) + \tilde{\mathbb{E}} \left[\int_0^{\tau} e^{-rs} F_s q_{x+t}(s) \, ds \right],$$

where $\tilde{q}_{x+t}$ is the Laplace transform of the mortality density either known explicitly or approximated by

$$\tilde{q}_{x+t}(r) = \int_0^{\infty} e^{-rs} q_{x+t}(s) \, ds \approx \sum_{k=1}^{n} \frac{\lambda_k}{r + s_k}.$$

Then we can approximate B_{lw} by

$$
\begin{aligned}
B_{lw}(t, F) &\approx \frac{w}{r} (1 - \tilde{q}_{x+t}(r)) + \sum_{k=1}^{n} \tilde{\mathbb{E}} \left[\int_0^{\tau} e^{-(r+s_k)u} F_u \, du \right] \\
&= \frac{w}{r} (1 - \tilde{q}_{x+t}(r)) + \sum_{k=1}^{n} D(F; r + s_k),
\end{aligned}
$$

where the explicit solution to D is known in (2.59).

Similarly, we can compute the no-arbitrage value at time t of the GLWB net liability from the insurer's perspective given by $N_{lw}(t, F_t)$ where

$$N_{lw}(t, F) := \tilde{\mathbb{E}} \left[\int_{\tau \wedge T_x}^{T_x} we^{-r(u-t)}\, \mathrm{d}u - \int_t^{\tau \wedge T_x} e^{-r(u-t)} m_w F_u\, \mathrm{d}u \,\middle|\, F_t = F, T_x > t \right]$$

$$= \tilde{\mathbb{E}} \left[\int_{\tau \wedge T_{x+t}}^{T_{x+t}} we^{-ru}\, \mathrm{d}u - \int_0^{\tau \wedge T_{x+t}} e^{-ru} m_w F_u\, \mathrm{d}u \,\middle|\, F_0 = F \right].$$

Due to the independence of mortality and equity returns, we can show that

$$N_{lw}(t, F) = \frac{w}{r} \tilde{\mathbb{E}} \left[e^{-r\tau} \overline{Q}_{x+t}(\tau) \right] - \frac{w}{r} \tilde{\mathbb{E}} \left[\int_\tau^\infty e^{-ru} q_{x+t}(u)\, \mathrm{d}u \right]$$
$$+ m_w \tilde{\mathbb{E}} \left[\int_0^\tau e^{-ru} \overline{Q}_{x+t}(u) F_u\, \mathrm{d}u \right]$$

where $\overline{Q}$ is the survival function of the future lifetime T_{x+t}. Therefore, we find the approximation of N_{lw} by

$$N_{lw}(t, F) \approx \sum_{k=1}^n \frac{w\lambda_k}{(r + s_k)s_k} L(F; r + s_k) + \sum_{k=1}^n m_w \lambda_k D(F; r + s_k),$$

where the explicit solution to L is known in (2.54).

4.8 Actuarial pricing

As alluded to earlier, no-arbitrage pricing is not directly used in the insurance industry for at least two reasons.

- The principle of no-arbitrage pricing does not explicitly allow for expenses and profits. Although one may forcefully add in these components under the risk-neutral valuation, it is fundamentally inconsistent with the theoretical framework;

- No-arbitrage pricing is based on the assumption that the underlying assets and financial derivatives are freely tradable and short-selling is allowed for any amount. An insurer typically transfers policyholders' purchase payments to competing third-party fund managers, who do not disclose proprietary information regarding the exact mix of their assets. Therefore, the opaqueness of underlying assets does not allow an investor to develop a replicating portfolio. In addition, an investor can buy investment guarantees from an insurer but cannot sell them to the insurer. Therefore, short-selling of investment guarantees are not possible either.

Nonetheless, the insurance industry has seen applications of the corresponding hedging theory, which provides a means of financial risk management of embedded options, as we shall demonstrate in Chapter 6.

In practice, an actual pricing model for equity linked insurance is usually based on the projection of cash flows emerging from individual contracts from period to period under a range of economic scenarios (under a physical measure). A critical measure of the healthy operation of a business is *profit*, which the amount of revenue gained from its business activities less the expenses, costs and taxes needed to sustain the activities. The end goal of each cash flow projection is to identify the profit (or loss) an insurer can expect from the contract over the projection period. This actuarial practice is commonly referred to as *profit testing*. The procedure allows an insurer to quantify its loss or gain under each set of assumptions including fees and charges. By testing various assumptions, an insurer can identify the "sweet spot" of fees and charges which meets specified profit measures with a certain level of confidence.

4.8.1   Mechanics of profit testing

We shall demonstrate the practice of profit testing with an example of single premium variable annuity (SPVA) with the GMDB, from which a policyholder's beneficiary is guaranteed to receive the greater of the sub-account value at death or the guarantee base with a combination of ratchet option and 5% annual roll-up option.

Since fees are charged on a daily basis, one may desire to project cash flows involving fee incomes at monthly intervals. However, an insurer may have hundreds and thousands of contracts and it is too costly and time consuming to run such projections for all contracts. As a compromise in practice, it is very common to project cash flows at monthly or quarterly intervals. In order for us to illustrate the mechanism of profit testing more clearly with limited space, we only project the cash flows at yearly intervals for the first seven years.

Readers should keep in mind that cash flow projections are often carried out at the level of a line of business. Even with the simple example of the SPVA, we assume that there are thousands of policyholders in the insurance pool for the contract with the same product specification. One may consider the following calculations as profit testing for the average of a large pool of contracts. We shall discuss the distinction between an individual model and an aggregate model in more detail in Section 5.4.

Actuarial assumptions

In order to carry out projections, the profit testing requires a set of assumptions on the following items driving cash flows, many of which are illustrated in Table 4.2 and Table 4.3.

- **Equity returns**: As all policyholders are offered a set of investment funds to choose from, the growth of their purchase payments are determined by financial returns of these investment funds. Hence, stochastic models are necessary to project the evolution of equity returns, interest rates, etc. This is typically done with a economic scenario generator developed internally by the insurer or externally by a third software vendor. Some regulators also provide pre-packaged scenarios for insurers to use for statutory pricing and reserving. In this example, we list percentage returns of the investment funds in Item A.

- **Fees and charges**: As discussed in Section 1.2, there are many types of fees and charges deducted from subaccounts for various purposes. For simplicity, we consider in this example an asset-value-based risk charges and fixed policy fees.

  - Risk charges: 1.5% of sub-account value per year. (Item B)
  - Policy fees: 30 per policy per year.

- **Surrenders**: Policyholders may voluntarily give up their policies prior to maturity. Lapse rates, given in Item D, provide estimates of likelihood that a policyholder surrenders year by year. In this example, all lapse rates are considered deterministic. It is also common in practice to introduce dynamic lapse rates, which fluctuate with equity values. Readers are referred to Section 7.3.4 for an example of dynamic lapse rates. As it takes time to recover initial expenses, an insurer typically tries to discourage early surrenders by levying high surrender charges in early years. As a result, surrender charges, as shown in Item G, form a declining schedule.

- **Annuitization**: Policyholders may voluntarily convert their investments to an annuity prior to maturity. Such a process is irreversible. The annuitization rates, which are estimates of likelihood that a policyholder exits the contract by annuitization, are given in Item E.

- **Survival model**: In the case that a policyholder dies prior to maturity, a death benefit is provided to beneficiaries. Therefore, estimations of death benefit also require mortality rates, which are typically taken from an industrial life table. To make conservative assumptions, an insurer may incorporate a safety margin by multiplying standard mortality rates by some factor great than one. Item F shows an example of mortality rates by year.

- **Fund values**: As the insurer sets up a large fund from all policyholders' purchase payments, the aggregate nature ensures predicability of mortality and expenses, as demonstrated by the law of large numbers. As the cash flow projection is based on the average of similar contracts, we use the term fund value as opposed to account value often used for an individual contract.

- **Expenses**: There are several types of expenses associated with insurance policies – administrative expenses, commissions and claim expenses. Administrative expenses are occurred by an insurer throughout the term of the policy to cover overheads, staff salaries, etc. The initial administrative expense is typically higher than administrative expenses in subsequent years, as the former include underwriting expenses. In this example, we assume

  - Initial administrative expenses: 100 per policy and 1% of sub-account value;
  - Renewal administrative expenses: 30 per policy per year;
  - Commission: 6.5% of first year's purchase payment;

– Claim expenses (GMDB cost): 0.40% of sub-account value.

Note, however, the renewal administrative expenses are estimated by the insurer's current conditions. We consider 2% inflation every year afterward on renewal expenses.

- **Interest on surplus**: From an insurer's point of view, the policyholder's purchase payment, fee incomes, and surrender charges are considered incoming cash flows, while expenses and death benefits are considered outgoing cash flows. As the opposing cash flows often do not offset each other, we expect surplus (profit) emerging at the end of each year, which are invested in liquid assets. Here, we assume that surplus accrues interest at the annual rate of 5.00% for all years.

- **Statutory reserve**: In this example we consider cash flows from both an insurer's general account and separate account. An insurer is expected to transfer to beneficiaries the balance of subaccounts (shown as separate account on the insurer's balance sheet) at the end of the year of the policyholder's death. As we shall discuss in more details in Section 5.1, an insurer typically sets aside assets, known as reserves, to cover expected future payments. Since the insurer is expected to transfer sub-account balance for policies still inforce, we set the reserve to be the same as sub-account value after decrements by lapses and annuitization.

- **Tax on surplus**: All profits are subject to federal income tax, which is assumed to be 37.00%.

- **Target surplus**: After profits are realized, an insurer may set aside additional assets from the profits to ensure long-term capital adequacy. Note that target surplus is the amount of capital held beyond statutory reserve. In this example, we assume target surplus to be 0.85% of statutory reserve for each year.

Profit testing

To illustrate the mechanism of profit testing more clearly, we separate the procedure into several components. While all calculations are illustrated here in the format of an Excel spreadsheet, such exercise can be done in any other computational platform.

Section 1 - projected account values

Due to the equity-linking mechanism, most cash flows are dependent on projected account values and guarantee bases, which are themselves determined by projected economic scenarios of equity return rates and interest rates, etc. The calculations of account values are summarized in Table 4.2. Throughout the section, the abbreviation BOY stands for the beginning of year while EOY stands for the end of year. Items A–C and D–H are all specified in actuarial assumptions mentioned above, whereas Items I–V are determined by the following recursive relations. For the ease of presentation, we use the notation $X[t]$ to denote the t-th year for Item X for $t = 1, 2, 3, 4, 5$.

- Investment Income

$$I[t] = A[t] \times \left(H[t] + U[t] - \frac{1}{2}L[t] \right)$$

	Proj. Year	1	2	3	4	5	6	7
A	Earned Rate	6.25%	6.25%	6.25%	6.25%	6.25%	6.25%	6.25%
B	Risk Charges	1.50%	1.50%	1.50%	1.50%	1.50%	1.50%	1.50%
C	Credited Rate	4.75%	4.75%	4.75%	4.75%	4.75%	4.75%	4.75%
	Decrements							
D	Lapses by Year	3.00%	3.00%	3.00%	4.00%	4.00%	5.00%	6.00%
E	Annuitizations by Year	1.00%	1.00%	1.00%	1.00%	1.00%	1.00%	1.00%
F	Mortality	0.41%	0.44%	0.48%	0.52%	0.56%	0.60%	0.64%
G	Surrender Charge	8.00%	7.00%	6.00%	5.00%	4.00%	3.00%	2.00%
H	Premium Collected	25,000	0	0	0	0	0	0
	Incomes							
I	Investment Income	1,559	1,562	1,564	1,566	1,551	1,535	1,503
J	Credited to Policyholder Account	1,185	1,187	1,189	1,190	1,178	1,167	1,142
K	Risk Charges	374	375	375	376	373	368	361
	Decrements							
L	Mortality	101	111	121	131	139	148	155
M	Lapses	775	776	777	1,037	1,026	1,270	1,492
N	Surrender Charge	62	54	47	52	41	38	30
O	Annuitizations	261	261	262	262	259	257	251
P	Current Inforce	95.59%	91.35%	87.25%	82.44%	77.85%	72.72%	67.16%
Q	Policyholder Fund Value (BOY)	25,000	25,048	25,087	25,116	24,876	24,630	24,122
R	– before Lapses & Anntzns (EOY)	26,084	26,124	26,155	26,175	25,915	25,649	25,109
S	– before Lapses after Anntzns (EOY)	25,823	25,863	25,893	25,913	25,656	25,392	24,858
T	– after Lapses & Anntzns (EOY)	25,048	25,087	25,116	24,876	24,630	24,122	23,366
U	Statutory Reserve (BOY)	0	25,048	25,087	25,116	24,876	24,630	24,122
V	Statutory Reserve (EOY)	25,048	25,087	25,116	24,876	24,630	24,122	23,366
W	GMDB Benefit Base	25,000	25,094	25,178	25,252	25,051	24,841	24,362
X	GMDB Benefit	101	0	0	1	1	1	2

TABLE 4.2: Profit testing - section 1 - projected account values

- Credited to Policyholder Account

$$J[t] = C[t] \times \left(Q[t] - \frac{1}{2} \times L[t] \right)$$

- Risk Charges

$$K[t] = B[t] \times \left(Q[t] - \frac{1}{2} \times L[t] \right)$$

- Mortality

$$L[t] = Q[t] \times F[t]$$

- Lapses

$$M[t] = S[t] \times D[t]$$

- Surrender Charge

$$N[t] = M[t] \times G[t]$$

- Annuitization

$$O[t] = R[t] \times E[t]$$

- Current Inforce (as % of initial)

$$P[t] = P[t-1] \times (1 - D[t] - E[t] - F[t])$$

- Policyholder Fund Value (BOY)

$$Q[t] = T[t-1] + H[t]$$

- Policyholder Fund Value before Lapses & Annuitizations (EOY)

$$R[t] = Q[t] + J[t] - L[t]$$

- Policyholder Fund Value before Lapses & after Annuitizations(EOY)

$$S[t] = R[t] - O[t]$$

- Policyholder Fund Value after Lapses & Annuitizations (EOY)

$$T[t] = S[t] - M[t]$$

- Statutory Reserve (BOY)

$$U[t] = V[t-1]$$

- Statutory Reserve (EOY)

$$V[t] = T[t]$$

- GMDB Benefit Base (5% – roll-up rate)

$$W[t] = P[t-1] \times \max\left(Q[t], H[1] \times (1+5\%)^t\right)$$

- GMDB Benefits

$$X[t] = (W[t] - U[t])_+ \times F[t]$$

Section 2 - projected cash flows

The calculations of cash flows emerging from the contract at the end of each year are set out in Table 4.3, which can be viewed as an income statement with three main components – (1) Revenues: the amount an insurer receives as gross income; (2) Expenses: the business costs an insurer incurs excluding the costs of insurance liabilities; (3) Benefits: the amount an insurer pays or prepares to set aside as the costs of insurance liabilities.

The key elements of cash flow projection are determined by recursive relations as follows. Numbers in brackets in Table 4.3 are considered negative.

- Policy Fee Income (30 – annual policy fee)

$$AG[t] = 30 \times AD[t-1]$$

- Total Revenues

$$AH[t] = AE[t] + AF[t] + AG[t]$$

- Premium-Based Administrative Expenses

$$AO[t] = AE[t] \times AJ[t]$$

- Per Policy Administrative Expenses (2% – inflation rate)

$$AP[t] = AK[t] \times AM[t] \times (1+2\%)^{t-1}$$

	Proj. Year	1	2	3	4	5	6	7
	Revenues							
AA	Earned Rate	6.25%	6.25%	6.25%	6.25%	6.25%	6.25%	6.25%
AB	Risk Charges	1.50%	1.50%	1.50%	1.50%	1.50%	1.50%	1.50%
AC	Credited Rate	4.75%	4.75%	4.75%	4.75%	4.75%	4.75%	4.75%
AD	Current Inforce	95.59%	91.35%	87.25%	82.44%	77.85%	72.72%	67.16%
AE	Premium	25,000	0	0	0	0	0	0
AF	Investment Inc.	1,559	1,562	1,564	1,566	1,551	1,535	1,503
AG	Pol Fee Inc.	29	27	26	25	23	22	20
AH	**Total Revenues**	26,588	1,589	1,590	1,591	1,574	1,557	1,523
	Expenses							
AI	Admin rate							
AJ	% of Premium	1.00%	0.00%	0.00%	0.00%	0.00%	0.00%	0.00%
AK	Per Policy	100	30	30	30	30	30	30
AL	Commission	4.50%	0.00%	0.00%	0.00%	0.00%	0.00%	0.00%
AN	Admin expenses							
AO	Prem-based	250	0	0	0	0	0	0
AP	Per Policy	96	28	27	26	25	24	23
AQ	Commissions	1,000	0	0	0	0	0	0
AR	GMDB Cost	100	100	100	100	100	99	96
AS	**Total Expenses**	1,446	128	127	126	125	123	119
	Benefits							
AT	Death Claims	101	111	121	131	139	148	155
AU	Annuitizations	261	261	262	262	259	257	251
AV	Surrender Benefit	713	722	730	985	985	1,232	1,462
AW	Increase in Resv	25,048	39	30	(239)	(246)	(507)	(755)
AX	GMDB Benefit	101	0	0	0	1	1	2
AY	**Total Benefits**	26,224	1,133	1,143	1,140	1,138	1,131	1,115
AZ	**Profits (pre-tax)**	(1,082)	328	320	325	311	303	289

TABLE 4.3: Profit testing - section 2 - projected cash flows from general and separate accounts

- Commissions
$$AQ[t] = AE[t] \times AL[t]$$

- GMDB Cost (0.4% of account value – GMDB cost)
$$AR[t] = T[t] \times 0.4\%$$

- Total Expenses
$$AS[t] = AO[t] + AP[t] + AQ[t] + AR[t]$$

- Death Claims
$$AT[t] = L[t]$$

- Annuitization
$$AU[t] = O[t]$$

- Surrender Benefit
$$AV[t] = M[t] - N[t]$$

- Increase in Reserve
$$AW[t] = V[t] - V[t-1]$$

- GMDB Benefit

$$AX[t] = (W[t] - U[t])_+ \times F[t]$$

- Total Benefits

$$AY[t] = AT[t] + AU[t] + AV[t] + AW[t] + AX[t]$$

- Book Profit Before Tax

$$AZ[t] = AH[t] - AS[t] - AY[t]$$

Table 4.3 shows a common practice of cash flow projections involving both the insurer's general account and separate account. For example, on the revenues side, policyholders have ownerships of Items AE and AF, which should be accounted for in a separate account, whereas, on the benefits side, Items AU, AV, AW correspond to payments from the separate account to policyholders or their beneficiaries or assets withheld for future payments. From an insurer's point of view, these are not real incomes and outgoes in the same way as claims and expenses, but rather accounting transfers. The insurer does not take ownership of policyholders' funds, nor does it take any responsibility for their losses. One should note confuse this with investment guarantees due to various guaranteed benefits, which are considered add-ons to a base contract and are genuine costs to the insurer and paid out of the general account.

If we only consider an insurer's general account, then the cash flows in and out of the separate account can be cancelled. Observe that, on the revenues side,

> Premium Collected + Investment Income
>
> = Risk Charges and Surrender Charges (allocated to general account)
>
> +Premium and Credited Interest (allocated to separate account),

on the benefits side,

> Death Claim + Annuitization + Surrender Benefit + Increase in Reserve
>
> = Assets in separate account
>
> GMDB Benefit = Assets in general account.

Note that the death claim refers to the return of policyholders' fund values to beneficiaries, whereas the GMDB benefit records the actual cost for the insurer to match policyholders' total incomes to guaranteed minimums.

If the accounting transfers are removed from consideration, then we can obtain an alternative version of the income statement in Table 4.4. Observe that the book profits before tax in Table 4.4 still match those in Table 4.3, due to the cancellation of payments in and out of the separate account. Although it is less common to use the income statement in Table 4.4 in practice, its simplified calculations reveal the mathematical structure of profit testing, which shall be compared with no-arbitrage pricing in the next section.

Section 3: projected distributable earnings

Projection Year	1	2	3	4	5	6	7
Revenues							
Surrender Charge	62	54	47	52	41	38	30
Policy Fee Income	29	27	26	25	23	22	20
Risk Charges	374	375	375	376	373	368	361
Total Revenues	26,588	1,589	1,590	1,591	1,574	1,557	1,523
Expenses							
Administrative rate							
% of Premium	1.00%	0.00%	0.00%	0.00%	0.00%	0.00%	0.00%
Per Policy	100	30	30	30	30	30	30
Commission	4.50%	0.00%	0.00%	0.00%	0.00%	0.00%	0.00%
Administrative expenses							
Premium-based	250	0	0	0	0	0	0
Per Policy	96	28	27	26	25	24	23
Commissions	1,000	0	0	0	0	0	0
GMDB Cost	100	100	100	100	100	99	96
Total Expenses	1,446	128	127	126	125	123	119
Benefits							
GMDB Benefit	101	0	0	0	1	1	2
Total Benefits	101	0	0	0	1	1	2
Book Profits Before Tax	(1,082)	328	320	325	311	303	289

TABLE 4.4: Profit testing - section 2 - projected cash flows with general account

Both book profit and distributable earning are both measures of the profitability of insurance business. As shown earlier, book profit is determined by total revenues less total expenses and total benefits. The distributable earning is the amount that an insurance business can distribute while retaining the level of capital required to support its ongoing operations. The difference between book profit and the distributable earning is due to taxation and withholding of additional capital required to support ongoing operations, which is beyond statutory reserves.

The calculations of book profit, target surplus and distributable earnings are set out in Table 4.5 and recursive relations among various entries are described in more detail below.

- Taxes on Book Profit (37% – federal income tax rate)

$$BF[t] = BE[t] \times 37\%$$

- Book Profits after Tax

$$BD[t] = BE[t] - BF[t]$$

- Target Surplus (BOY)

$$BI[t] = BJ[t-1]$$

- Target Surplus (EOY) (0.85% – target surplus rate)

$$BI[t] = V[t] \times 0.85\%$$

- Increase in Target Surplus

$$BG[t] = BI[t] - BH[t]$$

	Proj. Year	1	2	3	4	5	6	7
BA	Total Revenues	26,588	1,589	1,590	1,591	1,574	1,557	1,523
BB	Total Expenses	1,446	128	127	126	125	123	119
BC	Total Benefit	26,224	1,133	1,143	1,140	1,138	1,131	1,115
BD	Book Profits after Tax	(682)	207	201	205	196	191	182
BE	Profit Before Tax	(1,082)	328	320	325	311	303	289
BF	Taxes on Profit	(400)	121	118	120	115	112	107
	Target Surplus							
BG	Incr. in Target Sur.	213	0	0	(2)	(2)	(4)	(6)
BH	Target Sur. (BOY)	0	213	213	213	211	209	205
BI	Target Sur. (EOY)	213	213	213	211	209	205	199
BJ	Int. on Sur. (post-tax)	0	7	7	7	7	7	6
BK	Int. on Target Sur.	0	11	11	11	11	10	10
BL	Taxes on Interest	0	4	4	4	4	4	4
BM	Distributable Earnings	(895)	213	208	214	205	202	195

TABLE 4.5: Profit testing - section 3 - projected distributable earnings

- Interest on Target Surplus (5% – interest rate on surplus)

$$BK[t] = BH[t] \times 5\%$$

- Taxes on Interest on Target Surplus

$$BL[t] = BK[t] \times 37\%$$

- After Tax Interest on Target Surplus

$$BJ[t] = BK[t] - BL[t]$$

- Distributable Earnings

$$BM[t] = BD[t] + BJ[t] - BG[t]$$

The bottom line of 4.5 shows the distributable earnings emerging at the end of each year under the current actuarial assumptions. Table 4.5 reveals a common feature of cash flow projections where a large deficit emerges in the first year. This is commonly referred to as *new business strain*. A careful examination of Table 4.4 shows that expenses start off high in the first year and taper off in subsequent years whereas the insurer's genuine incomes tend to be flat over time. It takes a few years before the initial expenses are paid off gradually by the small but steady stream of incomes. This is why insurers often impose high surrender charges in the first few policy years to discourage early lapsation.

As income statements present the pattern of profits emerging from year to year, it is up to investors to interpret by various profit measures the financial condition of the companies which report the income statements. These profit measures allow investors to compare across companies and lines of business. Likewise, to determine whether or not a product line generates sufficient profits, an insurer often resorts to simple metrics for measuring its profitability. There are a number of profit measures commonly used in insurance practice.

1. Net present value (NPV) – The difference between the present value of all distributable earnings/deficits. Since distributable earnings are considered incomes for shareholders, the interest rate for discounting surplus should be the yield rate required by shareholders on its capital to support the product line, which is commonly referred as the *hurdle rate*. Here we assume the hurdle rate to be $j = 8\%$ effective per year. Then the NPV is given by

$$\text{NPV} = \sum_{t=1}^{7} \frac{BM[t]}{(1+j)^t} = 56.29.$$

A positive number indicates a net profit for the insurer, whereas a negative number suggests a net loss.

2. Internal rate of return (IRR) – The IRR is the discounting interest rate that makes the NPV of all distributable earnings zero. It reflects the average annual yield rate realized for the investor. For example, we can determined the IRR denoted by i by solving the equation for i

$$\sum_{t=1}^{7} \frac{BM[t]}{(1+i)^t} = 0,$$

which implies $i = 10.24\%$. Since the IRR is higher than the hurdle rate, the product line is considered profitable.

3. Profit margin (PM) – Net present value of distributable earnings as a percentage of premiums. In the case of the SPVA example, there is only a single purchase payment and hence

$$\text{PM} = \frac{\text{NPV}}{H[1]} = 0.23\%.$$

One should keep in mind that the purchase payment is transferred to an insurer's separate account and should not be considered as the insurer's revenue. Therefore, an alternative definition of the profit margin can be the NPV of distributable earnings as a percentage of the present value of the insurer's total revenues (in Table 4.4).

The profit testing was originally developed for traditional life insurance products which are mostly subject to mortality risk that can be diversified through a large pool of policyholders according to the law of large numbers. Therefore, the standard practice for pricing traditional products is to use "best estimates" for various actuarial assumptions including expenses, mortality rates, interest rates, etc. The profit testing allows an insurer to obtain ballpark estimates of its profits over long term. Actuarial assumptions used to project cash flows can be adjusted to test the impact of adverse experience to the profitability. As alluded to in Section 1.4, investment risk associated with equity-linked insurance products is not diversifiable. Hence it is impossible to use a single scenario to capture the uncertainty with equity returns. For instance, we assume the constant annualized equity return rate of 6.25% for all seven years

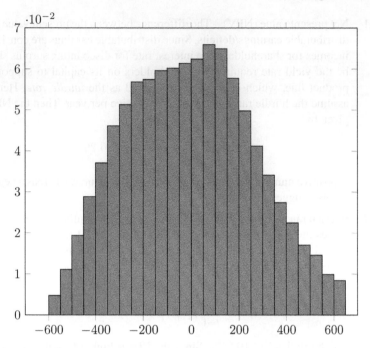

FIGURE 4.2: Histogram of NPV profit

in the example studied earlier. It begs the question of whether the profit still holds if the equity returns turn out differently over time. Hence, the profit testing technique is extended in the actuarial practice to allow for stochastic scenarios. As discussed in Section 3.4, a common approach to do this is to replace deterministic scenario in actuarial assumptions by stochastic scenarios using Monte Carlo simulations. For example, simulated equity returns from a geometric Brownian motion model calibrated to market data can be used in place of the constant equity return assumption. The profit testing proceeds exactly as described above and a different value of the profit measure is determined for each economic scenario. Then the collection of all profit measures from all scenarios forms an empirical distribution of the insurer's profit measure. For example, Figure 4.2 shows the histogram (empirical density function) of the NPV of distributable earnings with annual equity returns generated from a geometric Brownian motion model with parameters $\mu = 0.060625$ and $\sigma = 0.10$.

Having developed a mechanism for identifying the distribution of profits, we can combine the stochastic profit testing with various premium principles. A common approach is to utilize the portfolio percentile premium principle introduced in Chapter 1. For example, we might be willing to write the contract if the NPV of distributable earnings turns out positive for 70% of scenarios. One cannot expect to solve for the exact fee rate explicitly. However, we can gradually adjust the fee rate as well as other actuarial assumptions until we reach the target NPV level with a specified probability.

4.8.2 Actuarial pricing vs. no-arbitrage pricing

In Table 4.4, we have shown how revenues are generated, expenses and benefits are taken out, the remaining are transformed into profits from year to year. It is in the calculation of profit measure that the overall profitability is assessed over the entire projection horizon. Therefore, it makes sense to investigate the attribution of profit measure to various components over time.

To get the big picture of profit testing and make a comparison with no-arbitrage pricing, let us bring out essential elements of the insurer's cash flows and formulate the mechanism in a mathematical model. While we present all recursive relations at yearly intervals in previous sections, these ideas can be extended to projections with shorter time intervals. Consider the cash flow projection over integer T years at discrete intervals of length $\Delta t = 1/n$. Later on we intend to find its continuous-time analogue by shrinking Δt to zero. Denote policyholder fund values by $\{A_t : t = 0, \Delta t, \cdots\}$.

- Decrements: Let $_{\Delta t}q^d_{x+t}$, $_{\Delta t}q^l_{x+t}$, $_{\Delta t}q^a_{x+t}$ be the mortality rate, lapse rate and annuitization rate respectively over the period $[t, t+\Delta t]$. The policyholder fund value before decrements (EOY) is given by $A_t S_{t+\Delta t}/S_t(1 - m\Delta t)$ [*]. Roughly speaking, the decrements to policyholder fund due to mortality, lapses and annuitization (Items L, M, O) are determined by the fund value before decrements multiplied by $_{\Delta t}q^d_{x+t}$, $_{\Delta t}q^l_{x+t}$, $_{\Delta t}q^a_{x+t}$ respectively. We ignore the nuance of the order of decrements, as they make no difference in continuous-time.

- Surrender charge (Item N): Let k_t be the annualized rate of surrender charge at time t as a percentage of account value (Item G). Then the total surrender charge over the period $[t, t + \Delta t]$ is given by $k_t \,_{\Delta t}q^l_{x+t}A_t$.

- Expenses: All expenses are either premium-based, per policy or account-value-based. Therefore, expenses can be formulated either as a deterministic function of time or a time-varying percentage of policyholder fund value, both of which are commonly seen in other items. To provide concise formulation, we avoid identifying separate expenses but instead use E_t to denote the annualized rate of expenses at time t.

- Risk charge (Item K): Let m be the annualized rate of fee as a percentage of account value. Then the total amount of risk charge over the period $[t, t + \Delta t]$ is $m\Delta t A_t$.

- GMDB benefit (Item AX): The GMDB benefit base (Item U) after decrements at time t, denoted by B_t, is given by

$$B_t = \max\left(A_t, B_{t-\Delta t}\left(1 + \frac{\rho}{n}\right)\,_{\Delta t}p_{t-\Delta t}\right),$$

where the annualized roll-up rate is denoted by ρ. Hence the total GMDB benefit over the period $[t, t + \Delta t]$ is given by $_{\Delta t}q^d_{x+t}(B_t - A_t)_+$.

---

[*]In Table 4.2, rider charge is shown as a portion of the investment return. Therefore, the more precise formulation of fund value should be $A_t(S_{t+\Delta t}/S_t - m\Delta t)$. However, the two expressions are equivalent with slightly different interpretation of the fee rate m.

Policyholder fund values in Table 4.2 are determined recursively by investment returns, deductions due to benefit claims, expenses, charges, i.e.

$$A_{t+\Delta t} = A_t \frac{S_{t+\Delta t}}{S_t} (1 - m\Delta t)(1 - \Delta t q_{x+t}^l - \Delta t q_{x+t}^a - \Delta t q_{x+t}^d)$$

$$= A_t \frac{S_{t+\Delta t}}{S_t} (1 - m\Delta t) \, \Delta t p_{x+t}. \tag{4.77}$$

A quick comparison of (1.22) and (4.77) shows that policyholder fund value in an aggregate model is in fact an individual account value multiplied by survival probability, i.e.

$$A_t = {}_t p_x F_t.$$

Similarly, one can show that the GMDB base in an aggregate model is also given by that in an individual model multiplied by survival probability, i.e.

$$B_t = {}_t p_x G_t, \qquad G_t = F_0 \left(1 + \frac{\rho}{n}\right)^{t/\Delta t}.$$

The profit emerging at the end of each period in Table 4.4 is determined by the following relationship

$$\text{Profit} \quad = \quad \text{Surrender Charge} + \text{Policy Fee Income} + \text{Risk Charges}$$
$$-\text{Expenses} - \text{GMDB benefit},$$

which translates to

$$P_{t+\Delta t} \quad = \quad k_t \,_{\Delta t} q_t^l A_t + m\Delta t A_t - E_t \Delta t - \,_{\Delta t} q_{x+t}^d (B_t - A_t)_+$$

or equivalently,

$$P_{t+\Delta t} = k_t \,_t p_x \,_{\Delta t} q_t^l F_t + m \,_t p_x F_t \Delta t - E_t \Delta t - \,_t p_x \,_{\Delta t} q_{x+t}^d (G_t - F_t)_+.$$

Summing over all periods, we can determine the net present value of profits by

$$\mathfrak{P} = \sum_{k=1}^{nT} \left(1 + \frac{r}{n}\right)^k P_{k/n}, \tag{4.78}$$

where r is the annualized discounting rate/hurdle rate required by shareholders for their capital investments. Here we do not distinguish between book profit and distributable earning as their differences due to interests and taxes do not make significant difference in terms of mathematical modeling.

Let us now consider the continuous-time version of profit testing. Observe that as $\Delta t \to 0$,

$$\frac{\Delta t q_{x+t-\Delta t}^d}{\Delta t} = \frac{\mathbb{P}(t - \Delta t < T_x < t)}{\Delta t} = \frac{\mathbb{P}(T_{x+t-\Delta t} < \Delta t)}{\Delta t \mathbb{P}(T_x > t - \Delta t)} \to {}_t p_x \mu_{x+t}^d,$$

where μ_t^d is the force of mortality at the instant t. Similarly, one can show that

$_{\Delta t}q^l_{x+t-\Delta}/\Delta t \rightarrow {}_tp_x\mu^l_{x+t}$ where μ^l_t is the force of lapsation at the instant t. Lapse rates may not be age-dependent, in which case one could model μ^l as a function of current time t alone. Therefore, letting $n \rightarrow \infty$ (i.e. $\Delta t \rightarrow 0$) in (4.78) gives the continuous-time stochastic representation

$$
\begin{aligned}
\mathfrak{P} &= \int_0^T e^{-rt}P_t\,\mathrm{d}t \\
&= \int_0^T e^{-rt}k_t\mu^l_{x+t}\,{}_tp_xF_t\,\mathrm{d}t + m\int_0^T e^{-rt}\,{}_tp_xF_t\,\mathrm{d}t \\
&\quad - \int_0^T e^{-rt}E_t\,\mathrm{d}t - \int_0^T e^{-rt}\mu^d_{x+t}\,{}_tp_x(G_t - F_t)_+\,\mathrm{d}t.
\end{aligned}
\tag{4.79}
$$

The percentile premium principle based on profit testing is to look for the fair fee rate m such that

$$\mathbb{P}(\mathfrak{P} > 0) > \alpha,$$

for some confident level $0 < \alpha < 1$. In other words, an insurer may want to make sure that with the probability of at least α the product is guaranteed to generate a profit of at least $V \geq 0$,

$$\mathbb{P}(\mathfrak{P} > V) > \alpha.$$

In the framework of no-arbitrage pricing, we ignore expenses, surrender charges and taxes. In the absence of these cash flows, we can easily recognize by comparing (4.60) and (4.79) that the net present value of profits is in fact the opposite of the net liability, i.e. $\mathfrak{P} = -L$. Although derived from entirely different theoretical basis, no-arbitrage pricing is very similar to equivalence premium principle, which is to find the fair fee rate m such that

$$\tilde{\mathbb{E}}[L] = 0.$$

In essence, the actuarial pricing practice is based on the quantile of L under the real-world measure, whereas the no-arbitrage pricing is based on the expectation of L under the risk-neutral measure.

4.9 Bibliographic notes

There are many well-known texts on the pricing and hedging of financial derivatives. Readers are referred to Shreve [96] for detailed account of binomial tree model, Shreve [97] and Björk [10] for continuous-time models. Vecer [104] addresses the subject using a rather intuitive numeraire approach. Jeanblanc, Yor and Chesney [67] offers an overview of stochastic processes and fundamental properties for applications to option pricing and hedging.

Milevsky and Posner [79], Gerber and Shiu [54] are among the first to lay the groundwork of no-arbitrage pricing for guaranteed minimum benefits. A number of subsequent papers have extended that framework by either enriching the underlying price process and/or including additional state and control variables, including Ulm [101, 102], Gerber, Shiu and Yang [55], etc. The connection between guaranteed minimum maturity benefit and exotic (Asian) put options is first recognized and modeled formally in Milevsky and Salisbury [80], which is further explored in more general models such as Peng, Leung and Kwok [83], Feng and Volkmer [49], etc. The discussion of no-arbitrage pricing for equity indexed annuities is largely based on the work of Tiong [99].

Actuarial pricing of investment guarantees in equity-linked insurance is largely based on stochastic extension of pricing models for traditional life insurance. Readers are referred to Sun [98] for detailed account of market practice on pricing and risk management of variable annuities. More discussions on actuarial pricing methods for universal life insurance and equity-linked insurance can be found in Dickson, Hardy and Waters [33].

4.10   Exercises

Section 4.1

1. Use a money market account earning the continuously compounding interest rate of r per year and a T-period forward contract to create an arbitrage opportunity in the case where $S_0 < Fe^{-rT}$.

Section 4.2

1. Construct an arbitrage opportunity in the binomial tree model where

   (a) $u > d > e^r$;
   (b) $e^r > u > d$.

2. Consider a two-period European call option written on a stock. Under a binomial tree model, the spot price $S_0 = 100$, the strike price $K = 110$, the up factor $u = 1.5$, the down factor $d = 0.5$ and the discount factor for each period is $e^{-r} = 0.8$. Determine the no-arbitrage price of this call option.

Section 4.5

1. Show that the discounted stock price process $\{e^{-rt}S_t : 0 \le t \le T\}$, which satisfies the stochastic differential equation (4.39), is a martingale under the risk-neutral measure, i.e. for all $0 \le t \le T$,

$$\tilde{\mathbb{E}}\left[e^{-rT}S_T \mid \mathcal{F}_t\right] = e^{-rt}S_t.$$

2. We can prove the Black-Scholes formula for the European call option in Example 4.14 in two different ways.

    (a) Use the stochastic representation in (4.40) to prove (4.41).

    (b) Verify that the Black-Scholes formula (4.41) satisfies the Black-Scholes-Merton PDE (4.31).

    (c) Show that $c(t, s)$ also satisfies the terminal condition by taking the limit of (4.41) as $t \to T$.

3. In this exercise, we consider the Black-Scholes formula for a European call option written on a dividend-paying stock. Consider an investment portfolio that consists of simply one share of a dividend-paying stock at time 0. Denote the evolution of the portfolio values by $\{M_t : 0 \le t \le T\}$. Suppose that dividends are paid continuously at the rate of q per time unit per dollar worth of stock, i.e. during the instantaneous moment dt the amount of dividend $qM_t \, dt$ is received. To make the portfolio self-financing, the investor does not inject cash into or take any withdrawal from the portfolio. Any dividend payments will be reinvested in the purchase of additional shares of the stock. Under the real-world measure, it is easy to see that the instantaneous change in portfolio value is due to the sum of instantaneous change of stock prices and dividend payments,

$$dM_t = \frac{M_t}{S_t} \, dS_t + qM_t \, dt.$$

    (a) Regardless of the underlying model for the stock price, show that

$$M_t = e^{qt} S_t, \qquad 0 \le t \le T.$$

    (b) Suppose that the stock prices follow a geometric Brownian motion given in (4.28). Recall that all self-financing portfolio have the same expected rate of return under the risk-neutral probability measure $\tilde{\mathbb{P}}$. Thus,

$$dM_t = rM_t \, dt + \sigma M_t \, dW_t.$$

    Show that under $\tilde{\mathbb{P}}$

$$dS_t = (r - q)S_t \, dt + \sigma S_t \, dW_t.$$

    (c) Use the no-arbitrage pricing formula (4.40) to show that the Black-Scholes formula for a European call on a dividend-paying stock is given by $c(t, S_t)$ where

$$
\begin{aligned}
c(t, s) \;=\; & se^{-q(T-t)}\Phi\Big(d_1\big(T - t, se^{-q(T-t)}\big)\Big) \\
& - Ke^{-r(T-t)}\Phi\Big(d_2(T - t, se^{-q(T-t)})\Big),
\end{aligned}
$$

    where d_1 and d_2 are given by (4.42) and (4.43) respectively.

Section 4.6

1. Consider a stock whose price dynamics is given by (4.39) under the risk-neutral measure $\tilde{\mathbb{P}}$. Suppose that there is a financial derivative whose pay-off at maturity T is

$$\max\{S_T^\alpha, K\},$$

where the strike price K is pre-determined. Using the result in Exercise 2.10.3 to show that the time-t no-arbitrage price of the derivative is given by

$$\exp\left\{\left[(\alpha-1)r + \frac{1}{2}\alpha(\alpha-1)\sigma^2\right](T-t)\right\}S_t^\alpha$$

$$\times \Phi\left(\frac{\ln S_t + (r - \frac{1}{2}\sigma^2 + \alpha\sigma^2)(T-t) - \ln K/\alpha}{\sigma\sqrt{T-t}}\right)$$

$$+ \exp\left\{-r(T-t)\right\}K\Phi\left(\frac{\ln K/\alpha - \ln S_t - (r - \frac{1}{2}\sigma^2)(T-t)}{\sigma\sqrt{T-t}}\right).$$

2. This exercise is intended to derive the no-arbitrage value of the equity indexed annuity with the high-water mark index crediting option given in (4.47).

   (a) Show that if X is normally distributed with mean μ and variance σ^2. Then for any real numbers a and z,

   $$\mathbb{E}[e^{zX}I(X > a)] = e^{\mu z + \sigma^2 z^2/2}\Phi\left(\frac{\mu + \sigma^2 z - a}{\sigma}\right).$$

   (b) Define the running supremum of a Brownian motion

   $$\overline{B}_t := \sup_{0 \le s \le t}\{B_s\}, \qquad B_t := \mu_* t + \sigma W_t,$$

   where μ_*, σ are the drift parameter and the volatility parameter of the Brownian motion. Its cumulative distribution function is given in (7.24). Show that its density function is given by

   $$f_{\overline{B}_t}(y) = \frac{1}{\sigma\sqrt{t}}\phi\left(\frac{y - \mu_* t}{\sigma\sqrt{t}}\right) + e^{\frac{2\mu_* y}{\sigma^2}}\frac{1}{\sigma\sqrt{t}}\phi\left(\frac{-y - \mu_* t}{\sigma\sqrt{t}}\right)$$
   $$- \frac{2\mu_*}{\sigma^2}e^{\frac{2\mu_* y}{\sigma^2}}\Phi\left(\frac{-y - \mu_* t}{\sigma\sqrt{t}}\right),$$

   where $\mu^* = r - \sigma^2/2$ under the risk-neutral measure $\tilde{\mathbb{P}}$.

   (c) Show that $\{(S_t, \overline{S}_t) : 0 \le t \le T\}$ is a Markov process. Hence,

   $$V_t := \tilde{\mathbb{E}}\left[\max\left(P\left(\frac{\overline{S}_t}{S_0}\frac{\overline{S}_T}{\overline{S}_t}\right)^\alpha, G_T\right)\bigg|(S_t, \overline{S}_t)\right],$$

   $$= \tilde{\mathbb{E}}\left[\max\left(P\left(\frac{\max\{\overline{S}_t, \sup_{t \le u \le T}\{S_u\}\}}{S_0}\right)^\alpha, G_T\right)\bigg|(S_t, \overline{S}_t)\right].$$

(d) Use the results above to prove the no-arbitrage values (4.48) and (4.49).

Section 4.7

1. Consider the no-arbitrage value of the GLWB rider in the continuous-time model described in Section 1.2.7. Suppose that the dynamics of the underlying equity index is driven by the geometric Brownian motion defined in (2.44) and the guarantee base is set to the initial purchase payment.

    (a) Show that the dynamics of the policyholder's sub-account is given by

    $$dF_t = [\mu^* F_t - w - (m_w + h)F_0] \, dt + \sigma F_t \, dW_t.$$

    (b) Determine the no-arbitrage value of the variable annuity contract with the GLWB rider from the policyholder's viewpoint.

    (c) Determine the no-arbitrage value of the GLWB net liability from the insurer's view point.

2. Suppose that a policyholder signs up with an automatic deposit plan where contributions are made continuously into the investment account at the rate of c per year. In other words, the evolution of the policyholder's account is driven by the SDE (1.35). In the absence of any withdrawal, explain why the policyholder's account always stays positive. Calculate the average amount of fee incomes for an insurer up to the end of accumulation phase T, i.e. $\mathbb{E}\left[\int_0^T e^{-rt} F_t \, dt\right]$.

3. Suppose that a policyholder's future lifetime is independent of the performance of equity fund, i.e. T_x is independent of the information set $\{\mathcal{F}_t : t \geq 0\}$. Use Theorem 2.45 to prove (4.75).

4. There are sometimes alternative ways to compute the no-arbitrage cost of the GMDB rider (4.58). Assume that there is no roll-up option and T_x follows an exponential distribution with mean $1/\delta$. Show that

$$\mathbb{E}[e^{-rT_x} u(W_{T_x}) I(T_x < T)] = \int_{-\infty}^{\infty} u(w) f(w) \, dw,$$

where

$$
f(w) = \frac{\delta}{2\sqrt{2(r+\delta)}} \left[e^{-\sqrt{2(r+\delta)}|w|} \operatorname{erfc}\left(\frac{\sqrt{|w|}}{\sqrt{2T}} - \sqrt{(r+\delta)T}\right) \right.
$$
$$
\left. - e^{\sqrt{2(r+\delta)}|w|} \operatorname{erfc}\left(\sqrt{(r+\delta)T} + \frac{|w|}{\sqrt{2T}}\right) \right].
$$

Use this result to compute (4.58).

5

Risk Management - Reserving and Capital Requirement

Insurance is a business of dealing with risks. The art of the business is to split the risks involved between the insurer and the insured so that the financial impacts of losses are acceptable to both parties. As shown in Chapter 1, insurance companies offer a dazzling variety of product designs to policyholders. Without any investment guarantee, an insurer merely acts as a steward of its policyholders' investment funds and hence equity risk lies entirely with policyholders. When certain investment guarantee is offered, a portion of equity risk is transferred from policyholders to the insurer. Therefore, how to manage risk is a critical component of an insurance business.

In general, all techniques of risk management in the financial industry fall into one or more of the four categories:

1. **Risk avoidance**: This includes not engaging in any activity that carries risk. Issuing a variable annuity contract with no investment guarantee is an example of an insurer's avoidance of equity risk. While this approach avoids any chance of loss, it also gives up the potential of making a profit.

2. **Risk reduction**: This may include a variety of approaches to reduce risk, such as providing policyholders with coverage or incentives for preventive healthcare in expectation of lowering the likelihood of health problems for policyholders and expensive bills for the insurer. However, in this book, we do not consider any external factor that may influence the probability distribution of risks involved. Instead we are interested in the reduction of uncertainty due to the aggregation of contracts. As shown in Example 1.2, the diversification of mortality risk among a large pool of contracts makes the average loss much more predictable and manageable.

3. **Risk sharing**: This includes any design of insurance or financial product where certain risk is packaged and transferred from one party to another. An example would be the GMDB rider, where the down side of equity risk on a policyholder's assets is transferred from the policyholder to the insurer, while the policyholder retains the up side of the equity risk, leading to high financial returns.

4. **Risk retention**: This means to accept a risk and absorb any loss from the risk with one's own resources. In the insurance industry, a common approach of risk retention is to set aside some resources, known as reserve or capital, to cover potential losses in the future.

In Chapters 5 and 6, we shall see how various types of risk management techniques are applied to equity-linked insurance. To be specific, we shall discuss the assessment and quantification of risk retention through reserves and capitals in Chapter 5. We also consider a common method of risk reduction by diversification in Section 5.4. In contrast, dynamic hedging in Chapter 6 is considered as a method of risk sharing. Readers should be reminded that a minimalist approach is taken throughout the book to focus on core elements in order to bring out the essence of computational models.

5.1 Reserve and capital

Like any business, an insurance company has a financial structure. A standardized tool to understand a company's financial structure is a balance sheet which summarizes its assets, liabilities and net worth. A simplified example of a balance sheet is shown in Table 5.1. Income statement discussed in Section 4.8 is another tool to understand a company's financial conditions.

Balance Sheet (in thousands)

Assets		Liabilities	
General Account Assets	607,258	General Account Reserve	519,107
Separate Account Assets	1,376,968	Separate Account Liabilities	1,376,968
		Net Worth	
		Capital	15,492
		Surplus	72,660
Total Assets	1,984,226	Total Liabilities & Net Worth	1,984,226

TABLE 5.1: Illustrative balance sheet

Assets include all things the insurer owns. Although not fully shown in Table 5.1, assets are typically listed in categories, such as cash, bonds, stocks, mortgage loans, premiums, real estate, etc. In the case of variable annuities, assets can be broken into general account and separate accounts.

Liabilities reflect all the money the insurer owes to others. This includes amounts owed to policyholders (reserves and separate accounts) and those to debtholders, etc.

Reserves are what an insurer sets aside to provide for future claims. The purpose is to ensure that together with future incomes there is sufficient fund to cover expected claims and benefits to be paid in the future. Since reserve is often matched with certain classes of assets backing up the liabilities, there is often a misconception that a reserve is a part of asset. One should keep in mind that reserves are liabilities rather than assets. By definition, a reserve is equal to the expected present value of all future incomes less the expected present value of all future benefit payments. Here we provide a few simple examples of determining reserves for traditional life insurance products.

Example 5.1. Consider the reserve at time $t \in (0, T)$ of the pure endowment introduced in Example 1.2. Since it is a single premium policy, there is no more future payment, the reserve, denoted by V_t, should be set to the expected present value of the survival payment. Take the i-th contract as an example.

$$V_t := \mathbb{E}[BI(T_x^{(i)} \geq T)|T_x^{(i)} > t] = \mathbb{E}[BI(T_{x+t}^{(i)} \geq T - t)] = B\,_{T-t}p_{x+t}.$$

It is clear in this case that the reserve starts with $B\,_T p_x$ and eventually increases to B at the maturity of the contract T, which is exactly enough to pay benefit to the survivor.

Example 5.2. Consider the whole life insurance in Example 1.7 where a lump sum B is payable immediately upon the policyholder's death and level premiums are collected continuously at the rate of P per year. The reserve at time $t \in (0, T)$ should be the expected present value of death benefit less the expected present value of all future premiums.

$$
\begin{aligned}
V_t \quad &:= \quad \mathbb{E}\left[Be^{-r(T_x^{(i)} - t)} - P \int_t^{T_x^{(i)}} e^{-r(s-t)}\,\mathrm{d}s \,\middle|\, T_x^{(i)} > t \right] \\
&= \quad B \int_0^\infty e^{-rs}\,{}_s p_{x+t} \mu_{x+t+s}\,\mathrm{d}s - P \int_0^\infty e^{-rs}\,{}_s p_{x+t}\,\mathrm{d}s,
\end{aligned}
$$

where the force of mortality μ_{x+t} is defined in (4.59).

The two examples above are sometimes referred to as net premium reserves, as they are determined on the basis of providing sufficient funding for future benefit payments. While net premium reserves provide a clear view of basic principle, the determination of reserves can be far more complicated in practice as expenses, taxes, lapses, and other factors in actuarial assumptions are considered. In fact, different reserves are determined by financial reporting actuaries for various purposes and different audiences. Their differences arise from different accounting conventions.

1. Generally accepted accounting principles (GAAP) reserves: GAAP are a common set of standardized accounting principles, standards and procedures that all companies follow when compiling financial statements. As the audience are investors, the primary objective is to provide an accurate reporting of the value of the business on a going-concern basis. Thus, "best estimates" of risk factors are used in actuarial assumptions.

2. Statutory accounting practices (SAP) reserves: An insurer must hold minimum reserves in accordance with statutory provisions of insurance laws.

As the primary objective is to safeguard the insurer's solvency, SAP reserves are typically determined with conservatism on actuarial assumptions and accounting procedures.

3. Tax reserves: These liabilities are estimated for the purpose of determining income taxes.

Net worth represents the excess of the value of an insurer's assets over the value of its liabilities. In addition to reserve, insurers typically also earmark part of the net worth, often called *capital* to provide additional resources to cover losses. The allocated fund becomes unavailable for other corporate purposes. One key difference between reserve and capital is that the former is intended to cover "expected" liabilities that arise under moderately adverse conditions whereas the latter is established to provide a cushion to absorb "unexpected" severe losses that arise under extremely adverse conditions.

Like reserves, different definitions of capital arise from different accounting conventions (e.g. GAAP, statutory, fair value, economic, etc.), which prescribe different assumptions and methodologies of valuations applied to assets and liabilities. Accounting standards and procedures also vary greatly in different jurisdictions and are constantly evolving. There are many solvency/risk capital frameworks such as the U.S.'s NAIC Risk-Based Capital (RBC), Europe's Solvency II and Basel II, UK's Individual Capital Assessment (ICA), Canada's OSFI Minimum Continuing Capital and Surplus Requirements (MCCSR), etc. Since the main purpose of this book is to convey common principles, we shall refrain from getting into details of specific accounting convention. Nonetheless, we shall summarize at a high level the general procedure of RBC requirement as an example of how capital requirement is determined in practice.

Example 5.3. Risk-based capital (RBC) was established by the National Association of Insurance Commissioners (NAIC) in 1993 as an early warning system for US insurance regulation and has been updated on an annual basis. The RBC requirement specifies the minimum amount of capital an insurer is required to hold in order to support its overall business operation in consideration of its size and risk profile. If an insurer does not meet the RBC requirement, then regulators have the legal authority to take preventive and corrective measures in order to protect policyholders and the stability of the insurance market.

Here we only consider the life RBC formulas. For the most part of the current RBC model, the amount of capital required to be held for each item from the insurer's balance sheet, e.g. various asset, premium, claim expense and reserve items, etc., is calculated by applying various factors. In principle, the factor is higher for those items with greater underlying risk and lower for those with less risk. Table 5.2 gives an example of a worksheet for calculating RBC requirements for various bonds.

After the RBC requirements for all items are determined, they are grouped in the following five main categories of risks.

Bonds (C-1o)			
Rating Category	Book/Adjusted Carrying Value	**Factor**	RBC Requirement
Long Term Bonds			
Exempt Obligations		× 0.000 =	
Asset Class 1		× 0.004 =	
⋮			
Total Long-Term Bonds			
Short Term Bonds			
Exempt Obligations		× 0.000 =	
Asset Class 1		× 0.004 =	
⋮			
Total Short-Term Bonds			
Credit for Hedging			
⋮			
Total Bonds			

TABLE 5.2: RBC formula worksheet

C-0 **Asset Risk – Affiliates:** The risk of assets' default for certain affiliated investments.

C-1 **Asset Risk – Other:** The risk of assets' default of principle and interest or fluctuation in fair value. This includes two subcategories: Asset Risk – Unaffiliated Common Stock and Affiliated Non-Insurance Stock (C-1cs) and Asset Risk – All Other (C-1o).

C-2 **Insurance Risk:** The risk of underestimating liabilities from business already written or inadequately pricing business to be written in the coming year.

C-3 **Interest Rate Risk, Health Credit Risk and Market Risk:** The risk of losses due to changes in interest rate levels and the risk that health benefits prepaid to providers become the obligation of the health insurer once again, and risk of losses due to changes in market levels associated with variable products with guarantees. The three types of risks are assessed in subcategories C-3a, C-3b, C-3c respectively.

C-4 **Business Risk:** The risk of general business including mismanagement, lawsuits, fraud, regulatory changes, etc. It is assessed based on premium incomes, annuity considerations and separate account liabilities.

This category is further broken down into Premium and Liability (C-4a) and Health Administrative Expense (C-4b).

While RBC requirements for most risk categories are calculated by a factor-based approach, a notable exception is the C-3 risk, for which the NAIC implemented the RBC requirements in two phases. Implemented in 2001, Phase I addressed asset/liability mismatch risk for single premium life insurance and annuities including deferred and immediate annuities, guaranteed investment certificates, etc. Since 2003, NAIC has adopted several revisions for Phase II capital standards for variable annuities and other products with equity-related risks. Due to the complexity of these approaches, we shall defer the discussion to Section 5.2.7.

All RBC requirement data are then aggregated on a worksheet to determine the authorized control level RBC. It is assumed that each risk category is either completely independent of other risk categories, or completely correlated with other risk categories. Using a statistical adjustment, known as "covariance adjustment", the authorized control level RBC is determined by

$$50\% \times \Big[\text{C-0} + \text{C-4a} + $$

$$\sqrt{(\text{C-1o} + \text{C-3a})^2 + (\text{C-1cs} + \text{C-3c})^2 + (\text{C-2})^2 + (\text{C-3b})^2 + (\text{C-4b})^2}\Big]. \quad (5.1)$$

We shall offer some technical explanation of the formula in Section 5.3. The authorized control level of RBC is then compared with the Total Adjusted Capital, which is given by

$$\text{TAC} = \text{unassigned surplus} + \text{asset valuation reserve} + 50\% \times \text{dividend liability}.$$

Again all these items for the TAC calculation are determined by formulas prescribed by the NAIC. For more details, readers are encouraged to read an annual statement of a life insurance company based in the US, which is typically available in a public domain. Then the level of regulatory attention depends on the RBC ratio which is given by

$$\text{RBC ratio} = \frac{\text{Total adjusted capital}}{\text{Authorized control level of RBC}}.$$

Five levels of regulatory action may be triggered depending on the RBC ratio:

• None (RBC ratio > 200%) requires no action.

• Company action level (150% ≤ RBC ratio < 200%) requires the company to prepare and submit an RBC Plan to the commissioner of the state of domicile. After review, the commissioner will notify the company if the plan is satisfactory.

• Regulatory action level (100% ≤ RBC ratio < 150%) requires the insurer to submit an RBC Plan. After examination or analysis, the commissioner will issue an order specifying corrective actions to be taken.

• Authorized control level (70% ≤ RBC ratio < 100%) authorizes the commissioner to take regulatory actions considered necessary to protect the best interests of the policyholders and creditors of the insurer.

- Mandatory control level (RBC ratio $\leq 70\%$) authorizes the commissioner to take actions necessary to place the company under regulatory control (i.e. rehabilitation or liquidation).

5.2 Risk measures

Since risks are often quantified by random variables, it is important to develop metrics to assess the impact of taking on risks for a business. The idea of using a metric to summarize information of uncertainty level is very prevalent in everyday life. For example, the highest and lowest temperature in daily weather forecast are metrics of temperature random variables; a university ranking offers a metric to measure the quality of university education in comparison of its peer institutes. These simple metrics allow an average person to prepare for the weather without understanding complicated atmospheric chemistry and physics, and give a prospective student a sense of the relative competitiveness of a university saving them from time consuming research on their own. In the same spirit, a risk measure is intended to offer a summary on the nature of a risk random variable in order for a decision maker to take an action with regard to the risk.

We interpret risk as the uncertainty of losses. Hence we use the terms risk and loss interchangeably. For brevity, we also call a random variable representing a risk or loss as a risk for short.

Definition 5.4. A risk measure is a mapping from a random variable X to a risk $\rho(X)$.

Different university rankings may give different ranks to a university. Meteorologists from various TV stations can have different forecasts for the same area. Likewise, different risk measures reflect different aspects of a risk. For example, the mean measures the central tendency of randomness whereas the variance measures how far the outcomes of a risk are spread out from their average value.

Here we introduce a few risk measures that are used for the purpose of capital requirement.

5.2.1 Value-at-risk

In many areas of risk management practice and regulation, the concept of *Value-at-Risk* (VaR) is introduced to measure the likelihood of severe losses to a business. It is also referred as a *quantile function* or *inverse distribution function*.

Definition 5.5. Consider a loss random variable X whose distribution function is denoted by F. Given a probability level $p \in (0, 1)$, the corresponding VaR is defined as

$$\text{VaR}_p[X] = \inf\{x : F(x) \geq p\} = \sup\{x : F(x) < p\},$$

where inf A is the infimum of a set A and sup A is the supremum of the set. To emphasize its functional relationship with p, we sometimes write $\text{VaR}_p[X] = F^{-1}(p)$.

In simple words, $\text{VaR}_p[X]$ is the smallest threshold exceeded by X with the probability of at most p. There are essentially three different cases that one needs to consider when computing the VaR, as shown in Figure 5.1. When the value p corresponds to a flat piece on the graph of the cumulative distribution function, $\text{VaR}_p[X]$ is always defined to be the left endpoint of the interval on which the flat piece appears. It is also clear from Figure 5.1 that $\text{VaR}_p[X]$ as a function of p is left-continuous.

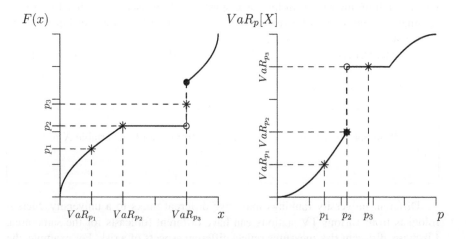

FIGURE 5.1: Value-at-risk and cumulative distribution function

Example 5.6. Consider the value-at-risk of a normal random variable X with mean μ and variance σ^2. Denote a standard normal random variable (with mean 0 and variance 1) by N. It is easy to see that

$$F(x) = \mathbb{P}(X \leq x) = \mathbb{P}(\mu + \sigma N \leq x) = \mathbb{P}\left(N \leq \frac{x - \mu}{\sigma}\right) = \Phi\left(\frac{x - \mu}{\sigma}\right),$$

where Φ is the standard normal distribution function given by

$$\Phi(x) = \int_{-\infty}^{x} \frac{1}{\sqrt{2\pi}} e^{-t^2/2} \, dt.$$

Since F in this case is a continuous and strictly increasing function, then the value-at-risk is the ordinary inverse function, which can be written as

$$\text{VaR}_p[X] = \mu + \sigma \Phi^{-1}(p), \tag{5.2}$$

where Φ^{-1} is the inverse function of Φ.

Example 5.7. Consider two loss random variables L_1 and L_2 from an insurer's point of view. The random variable L_1 is exponentially distributed with the cumulative distribution function given by

$$F(x) = 1 - e^{-\lambda x}, \qquad x \geq 0.$$

It is clear that the value-at-risk of L_1 is given by

$$\text{VaR}_p[L_1] = -\frac{1}{\lambda} \ln(1 - p), \qquad p \in (0, 1).$$

The random variable $L_2 := \max\{L_1, u\}$, which represents the loss L_1 subject to a policy limit of $u = \text{VaR}_{0.9}(L_1) = \ln 10/\lambda$. As indicated in Figure 5.2, it follows

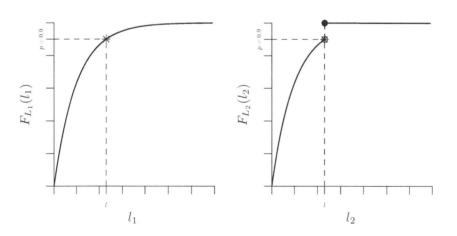

FIGURE 5.2: VaR does not capture information in the tail

by definition that $\text{VaR}_p[L_1] = \text{VaR}_p[L_2]$ for all $p \leq 0.9$ and $\text{VaR}_p[L_1] > \text{VaR}_p[L_2]$ for all $p > 0.9$. Even though the unbounded loss L_1 can be more dangerous than the capped loss L_2, the insurer would receive the same amount of capital if $VaR_{0.9}$ is the chosen risk measure as the basis of capital requirement. The shortcoming of VaR as a risk measure gives arguments from an alternative risk measure to be introduced in the next section.

It is well-known that $VaR_{1-\epsilon}[X]$ is a solution to the following minimization problem.

$$\min_{c \in \mathbb{R}} \left\{ \mathbb{E}[(X - c)_+] + c\epsilon \right\}, \qquad 0 < \epsilon < 1. \tag{5.3}$$

Here we provide an economic interpretation of the quantity in curly brackets. Note that if c is interpreted as an insurer's total capital, then the first term is the expected value of shortfall in capital after taking on the loss X. Of course, if the sole purpose is to minimize the expected shortfall, then the capital c should be set as high as possible. Note, however, holding capital incurs a cost to an insurer, as the allocated fund is unavailable for any other corporate purposes. The second term is to penalize the use of capital by imposing the cost of capital at the rate of ϵ per unit, say the borrowing interest rate of 5% per unit. The greater amount of capital, the higher the cost. The goal of the minimization problem (5.3) is to strike a balance between minimal capital shortfall and minimal cost of capital. Observe that

$$
\begin{aligned}
g(c) \quad &:= \quad \mathbb{E}[(X - c)_+] + c\epsilon = \mathbb{E}\left[\int_c^\infty I(X > x)\, dx \right] + c\epsilon \\
&= \quad \int_c^\infty \mathbb{P}(X > x)\, dx + c\epsilon = \int_c^\infty \overline{F}(x)\, dx + c\epsilon,
\end{aligned}
\tag{5.4}
$$

where $\overline{F}$ is the survival function of X. Setting the derivative of g with respect to c to zero yields

$$g'(c) = \epsilon - \overline{F}(c) = 0.$$

Since $g'(c)$ is an increasing function of c, it is clear that $c^* = VaR_{1-\epsilon}[X]$ is the global minimum of the function $g(c)$. In other words, $VaR_{1-\epsilon}$ is the minimizer of the optimal capital requirement problem (5.3). Note that, if we let $p = 1 - \epsilon$, then the minimal value in (5.3) is given by

$$\mathbb{E}[(X - VaR_p[X])_+] + VaR_p[X](1 - p). \tag{5.5}$$

5.2.2   Conditional tail expectation

As demonstrated in Example 5.6, a shortcoming of VaR as a risk measure is that it does not say much about the severity of losses beyond the threshold. In many jurisdictions, capital requirements are based on another risk measure called the conditional tail expectation (CTE).

Definition 5.8. Given a probability level $p \in (0, 1)$, the corresponding CTE is defined as

$$\text{CTE}_p[X] = \mathbb{E}[X|X > \text{VaR}_p[X]].$$

In simple words, the $\text{CTE}_p[X]$ is the average of losses exceeding the threshold $\text{VaR}_p[X]$, which is considered an improvement over VaR, as it contains information on both likelihood and severity of losses beyond the threshold $\text{VaR}_p[X]$.

Example 5.9. Let X be a Bernoulli random variable with the probability of success being p. In other words,

$$X = \begin{cases} 0, & \text{with probability } 1 - p; \\ 1, & \text{with probability } p. \end{cases}$$

Then it is clear that $\text{VaR}_q[X] = I(q > 1 - p)$ for $q \in (0, 1)$. Therefore, if $q \leq 1 - p$, $\text{CTE}_q[X] = \mathbb{E}[X|X > 0] = 1$; if $q > 1 - p$, $\text{CTE}_q[X] = \mathbb{E}[X|X > 1] = 0$. Therefore, $\text{CTE}_q[X] = I(q \leq 1 - p)$.

Example 5.10. Consider the random variable X being uniformly distributed on the interval (α, β). It is easy to show that

$$\text{VaR}_p[X] = (1 - p)\alpha + p\beta.$$

Then by definition

$$
\begin{aligned}
\text{CTE}_p[X] &= \frac{1}{\overline{F}(\text{VaR}_p[X])} \mathbb{E}[XI(X > \text{VaR}_p[X])] \\
&= \frac{1}{1 - p} \int_{(1-p)\alpha + p\beta}^{\beta} \frac{x}{\beta - \alpha} \, \mathrm{d}x \\
&= \frac{1}{2}[(1 - p)\alpha + (1 + p)\beta].
\end{aligned}
$$

5.2.3 Coherent risk measure

While Definition 5.4 offers little restriction on what constitutes a risk measure, there are certain common properties of risk measures that guide a decision maker's search for a desirable risk measure. An concept well-accepted in the financial literature is the *coherent risk measure*.

Definition 5.11. A risk measure ρ is said to be coherent if it satisfies the following properties for all random variables X, Y

- (Translativity) $\rho[X + c] = \rho[X] + c$ for any constant c;

- (Positive homogeneity) $\rho[cX] = c\rho[X]$ for any constant $c > 0$;

- (Subadditivity) $\rho[X + Y] \le \rho[X] + \rho[Y]$;

- (Monotonicity) If $\mathbb{P}(X \le Y) = 1$, then $\rho[X] \le \rho[Y]$.

It is helpful to keep in mind that risk measures are often used for regulatory purposes. The primary objective of a regulator is to ensure market stability by requiring financial institutions in its jurisdiction to hold sufficient funds, e.g. reserve and capital, to cover its liability even under adverse economic conditions. The quantification and assessment of risk through risk measure serves as the basis of setting up capital requirement. Here we explain why these properties are reasonable requirements in the context of capital requirement.

- (Translativity) This property means that if the loss of the business increases (decreases) by a fixed amount then the business should raise (lower) its capital by the same amount to account for the increased (decreased) risk. Since there is no added uncertainty, the amount of increase (decrease) in capital should exactly match the amount of increase (decrease) in loss.

- (Positive homogeneity) This property means that if the loss is inflated by a factor c then the capital should increase by the same factor.

- (Subadditivity) This property can be roughly translated as "diversification reduces risk". The capital required for the sum of two risks should be less than the sum of stand-alone capital requirements for the two risks. The amount of reduction in capital by combining two risks is viewed as the benefit of "diversification".

- (Monotonicity) This property means that capital requirement should be commensurate with the size of the underlying risk. Larger risk requires higher capital.

If a decision maker is willing to accept coherence as a guiding principle of risk management, then there are a number of well-known coherent risk measures available for applications. Before showing examples of coherent risk measure, let us first consider the earlier mentioned risk measures.

Example 5.12. In general, the Value-at-Risk is not coherent. To see this, we look at various properties of a coherent risk measure.

(a) *VaR is translative, positive homogeneous and monotonic.* Let $\rho[X] =$

$\mathrm{VaR}_p[X]$. Observe that for any real number c,

$$
\begin{aligned}
\rho[X+c] &= \inf\{x : \mathbb{P}(X+c \le x) \ge p\} = \inf\{x : \mathbb{P}(X \le x-c) \ge p\} \\
&= \inf\{y+c : \mathbb{P}(X \le y) \ge p\} = \inf\{y : \mathbb{P}(X \le y) \ge p\} + c \\
&= \rho[X] + c.
\end{aligned}
$$

Similarly, one can show its homogeneity. For any constant $c > 0$,

$$
\begin{aligned}
\rho[cX] &= \inf\{x : \mathbb{P}(cX \le x) \ge p\} = \inf\{x : \mathbb{P}(X \le x/c) \ge p\} \\
&= \inf\{cy : \mathbb{P}(X \le y) \ge p\} = c\inf\{y : \mathbb{P}(X \le y) \ge p\} = c\rho[X].
\end{aligned}
$$

Suppose that $\mathbb{P}(X \le Y) = 1$. If $Y \le y$ for any fixed y, then it is obvious that $X \le y$. Therefore, the set $\{Y \le y\} \subseteq \{X \le y\}$, implying that $\mathbb{P}(Y \le y) \le \mathbb{P}(X \le y)$. Consequently, $\mathbb{P}(Y \le y) \ge p$ implies $\mathbb{P}(X \le y) \ge p$, which means that $\{y : \mathbb{P}(Y \le y) \ge p\} \subseteq \inf\{y : \mathbb{P}(X \le y) \ge p\}$. Since the infimum of a smaller set is no smaller than that of a larger set, then

$$
\rho[Y] = \inf\{y : \mathbb{P}(Y \le y) \ge p\} \ge \inf\{y : \mathbb{P}(X \le y) \ge p\} = \rho[X],
$$

which proves its monotonicity.

(b) However, *VaR is not subadditive.* To provide an example where VaR is not subadditive, let us revisit the pure endowment insurance in Example 1.6. Recall that the net liability from a single contract is given for any arbitrary policyholder i by

$$
L_i = \begin{cases} 81, & \text{with probability } 0.1; \\ -9, & \text{with probability } 0.9. \end{cases}
$$

If VaR is subadditive, then by induction we would expect that for any $p \in (0,1)$,

$$
\mathrm{VaR}_p[\overline{L}] = \frac{1}{1000}\mathrm{VaR}_p\left[\sum_{i=1}^{1000} L_i\right] \le \frac{1}{1000}\sum_{i=1}^{1000}\mathrm{VaR}_p[L_i] = \mathrm{VaR}_p[L_1]. \qquad (5.6)
$$

On one hand, it is easy to see that $\mathrm{VaR}_{0.9}[L_1] = -9$. On the other hand, we note that $L_i = 90B_i - 9$ where B_i is a Bernoulli random variable with the rate of success 0.1 and hence $\overline{L} = 0.09B - 9$ where B is a binomial random variable with parameters $(1000, 0.1)$. One can use a computer algorithm to determine that $\mathrm{VaR}_{0.9}[B] = 112$. This implies that $\mathrm{VaR}_{0.9}[\overline{L}] = 1.08 > \mathrm{VaR}_{0.9}[L_1]$, which contradicts the subadditivity in (5.6). Therefore, VaR cannot be subadditive.

Example 5.13. The conditional tail expectation is not coherent either. It is easy to show that CTE is also translative, positive homogeneous and monotonic, which is left as Exercise 5.2.1. However, CTE is not subadditive in general. The following is an example to show its lack of subadditivity.

Consider a pair of risks (X, Y) where X is uniformly distributed on (α, β) and

$$
Y = \alpha + \theta - X + (\beta - \alpha)I(X > \theta)
$$

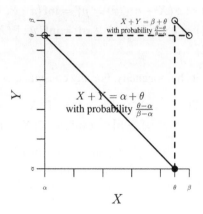

FIGURE 5.3: The support of a bivariate risk

with $\alpha < \theta < \beta$. We shall prove that for $0 < q < (\theta - \alpha)/(\beta - \alpha)$,

$$\mathrm{CTE}_q[X + Y] > \mathrm{CTE}_q[X] + \mathrm{CTE}_q[Y].$$

First, observe that

$$X + Y = \begin{cases} \alpha + \theta, & \text{if } X \leq \theta \quad \left(\text{with probability } \dfrac{\theta - \alpha}{\beta - \alpha}\right) \\[2ex] \beta + \theta, & \text{if } X > \theta \quad \left(\text{with probability } \dfrac{\beta - \theta}{\beta - \alpha}\right). \end{cases}$$

The support of (X, Y) is shown in Figure 5.3. It is immediately clear that $X+Y$ takes either the value $\alpha+\theta$ or the value $\beta+\theta$. In other words, $X+Y = (\alpha+\theta)+(\beta-\alpha)B$ where B follows a Bernoulli distribution with parameter $p := (\beta-\theta)/(\beta-\alpha)$. Using the result in Example 5.9, positive homogeneity and translational invariance, we can conclude that

$$\mathrm{CTE}_q[X + Y] = (\alpha + \theta) + (\beta - \alpha)I(q \leq 1 - p).$$

Note that we can determine the cumulative distribution function of Y by

$$F_Y(y) = \mathbb{P}(\alpha + \theta - X \leq y, X \leq \theta) + \mathbb{P}(\beta + \theta - X \leq y, X > \theta) = \frac{y - \alpha}{\beta - \alpha},$$

where the last equality can be shown for both cases of $y \leq \theta$ and $y > \theta$. This result implies that Y is uniformly distributed on (α, β). It follows immediately from Example 5.10 that

$$\mathrm{CTE}_p[X] = \mathrm{CTE}_p[Y] = \frac{1}{2}(1 - p)\alpha + \frac{1}{2}(1 + p)\beta.$$

Therefore, we can conclude that for $0 < q < (\theta - \alpha)(\beta - \alpha)$,

$$
\begin{aligned}
\text{CTE}_q[X] + \text{CTE}_q[Y] &= \alpha + \beta + (\beta - \alpha)q \\
&< \alpha + \beta + (\beta - \alpha)\frac{\theta - \alpha}{\beta - \alpha} = \beta + \theta = \text{CTE}_q[X + Y].
\end{aligned}
$$

In the next two sections, we offer a few examples of commonly used risk measures that are indeed coherent.

5.2.4 Tail value-at-risk

Recall that a single VaR does not offer any information on the tail of the underlying risk. While the CTE remedies this shortcoming, it lacks the subadditivity. When used as a basis of capital requirement, CTE does not reward risk diversification. A similar quantity, known as the tail-value-at-risk, addresses both shortcomings of the VaR and the CTE.

Definition 5.14. The Tail-Value-at-Risk (TVaR) of a loss random variable X at a probability level $p \in (0, 1)$ is defined by

$$
\text{TVaR}_p[X] = \frac{1}{1-p} \int_p^1 \text{VaR}_q[X] \, dq.
$$

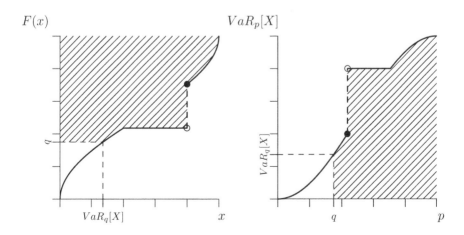

FIGURE 5.4: Visualization of an integral of value-at-risk

Recall that the graph of the inverse function $\text{VaR}_p[X]$ is a reflection of the distribution function $F_X(x)$ across the line $y = x$. As shown in Figure 5.4, the shaded areas in the two graphs are the same, which implies that

$$
\begin{aligned}
\int_p^1 \text{VaR}_q[X]\,dq &= \text{VaR}_p[X](1-p) + \int_{\text{VaR}_p[X]}^\infty \overline{F}_X[q]\,dq \\
&= \text{VaR}_p[X](1-p) + \mathbb{E}[(X - \text{VaR}_p[X])_+].
\end{aligned}
$$

where the last equality is obtained using an argument similar to that for (5.4). Then it is clear that

$$
\text{TVaR}_p[X] = \text{VaR}_p[X] + \frac{1}{1-p}\mathbb{E}[(X - \text{VaR}_p[X])_+]. \tag{5.7}
$$

Since TVaR_p is by definition the "arithmetic" average of VaR_q's at all levels between p and 1, TVaR inherits many properties of VaR. We leave it as Exercise 5.2.3 to show that TVaR is translative, positively homogeneous and monotonic. However, in contrast with VaR, TVaR is subadditive and hence a coherent risk measure. To prove the subadditivity, first recall the minimization problem (5.3) and its minimum value (5.5), which implies that

$$
\text{TVaR}_p[X] = \min_{c\in\mathbb{R}}\left\{\frac{1}{1-p}\mathbb{E}[(X-c)_+] + c\right\}. \tag{5.8}
$$

Therefore, choosing a constant $c = \text{VaR}_p[X] + \text{VaR}_p[Y]$, we must have

$$
\begin{aligned}
\text{TVaR}_p[X + Y] &\le \frac{1}{1-p}\mathbb{E}[(X + Y - c)_+] + c \\
&\le \frac{1}{1-p}\mathbb{E}[(X - \text{VaR}_p[X])_+ + (Y - \text{VaR}_p[Y])_+] + c \\
&= \text{TVaR}_p[X] + \text{TVaR}_p[Y],
\end{aligned}
$$

where the second inequality comes from the elementary inequality $(a+b)_+ \le (a)_+ + (b)_+$ for any $a, b \in \mathbb{R}$.

Remark 5.15. The TVaR can be viewed as an "improved" version of the CTE in some sense. Because of the identity

$$
\mathbb{E}[X I(X > d)] = \mathbb{E}[(X - d)_+] + d\overline{F}(d),
$$

it follows by definition that

$$
\begin{aligned}
\text{CTE}_p[X] &= \frac{\mathbb{E}[X I(X > \text{VaR}_p[X]]}{\overline{F}(\text{VaR}_p[X])} \\
&= \text{VaR}_p[X] + \frac{1}{\overline{F}(\text{VaR}_p[X])}\mathbb{E}[(X - \text{VaR}_p[X])_+]. \tag{5.9}
\end{aligned}
$$

Note that in general $F(\text{VaR}_p[X]) \geq p$ (inequality appears in the case of p_3 in Figure 5.1). Due to (5.8), we observe that

$$\text{CTE}_p[X] \geq \text{VaR}_p[X] + \frac{1}{1-p}\mathbb{E}[(X - \text{VaR}_p[X])_+] = \text{TVaR}_p[X].$$

If the underlying risk X is a continuous random variable, then $F(\text{VaR}_p[X]) = p$ and hence $\text{CTE}_p[X] = \text{TVaR}_p[X]$ for all $p \in (0,1)$.

Example 5.16. Consider the bivariate risk (X, Y) in Example 5.13 where X and Y are both uniformly distributed on (α, β) and

$$X + Y = \begin{cases} \alpha + \theta, & \text{with probability } (\theta - \alpha)/(\beta - \alpha); \\ \beta + \theta, & \text{with probability } (\beta - \theta)/(\beta - \alpha), \end{cases}$$

for a fixed $\theta \in (\alpha, \beta)$. It follows from Example 5.10 and Remark 5.15 that

$$\text{TVaR}_q[X] = \text{CTE}_q[X] = \frac{1}{2}[(1 - q)\alpha + (1 + q)\beta].$$

It is easy to show that

$$\text{VaR}_q[X + Y] = \begin{cases} \alpha + \theta, & 0 < q < \frac{\theta - \alpha}{\beta - \alpha}; \\ \beta + \theta, & \frac{\theta - \alpha}{\beta - \alpha} \leq q < 1. \end{cases}$$

Hence it follows from the definition that

$$\text{TVaR}_q[X + Y] = \begin{cases} \frac{1}{q}[\alpha + \beta - q(\alpha + \theta)], & 0 < q < \frac{\theta - \alpha}{\beta - \alpha}; \\ \beta + \theta, & \frac{\theta - \alpha}{\beta - \alpha} \leq q < 1. \end{cases}$$

We leave it as Exercise 5.2.5 to show that $\text{TVaR}_q[X + Y] \leq \text{TVaR}_q[X] + \text{TVaR}_q[Y]$.

5.2.5 Distortion risk measure

Definition 5.17. A function g defined on $[0, 1]$ is called a *distortion function* if it is non-decreasing, $g(0) = 0$ and $g(1) = 1$. Given any random variable X, the *distortion risk measure* of X associated with a distortion function g is defined by

$$\rho_g[X] = \int_0^\infty g(\overline{F}_X(x))\,dx - \int_{-\infty}^0 \left(1 - g(\overline{F}_X(x))\right)\,dx. \tag{5.10}$$

There is an equivalent expression that is also useful for the analysis of its properties.

$$\rho_g[X] = \int_0^1 \text{VaR}_{1-p}[X] \, dg(p). \tag{5.11}$$

This identity (5.11) is most easily seen for positive random variables. Observe that for a positive random variable X

$$\rho_g[X] = \int_0^\infty g(\overline{F}_X(x)) \, dx = \int_0^1 \overline{F}_X^{-1}(p) \, dg(p), \tag{5.12}$$

where the inverse function of $\overline{F}$ is defined by $\overline{F}_X^{-1}(p) = \sup\{x : \overline{F}_X(x) > p\}$. Here we provide a visual interpretation of the identity (5.12) in Figure 5.5. The top panel of two graphs shows the effect of a distortion function $g(p) = 1 - \sqrt{1-p}$ applied to a survival function. In particular, the dark shaded regions in both graphs correspond to $p \in (0.45, 0.55)$. In other words, the top right graph is obtained from the top left graph by changing the scale of the vertical axis. The bottom left graph is the reflection of the top left graph about the line "$y = x$", as they are inverse functions of each other. Similarly, the bottom right graph is also the reflection of the top right graph about the line "$y = x$". The shaded regions in the left panel of graphs are exactly the same, whereas the shaded regions in right panel of graphs match each other. Note that the scale of the horizontal axis is also changed by the distortion function g in the bottom right graph. Therefore, the area of the shaded region in the bottom right graph should be represented by the Lebesgue integral $\int_0^1 \overline{F}_X^{-1}(p) \, dg(p)$. Since it is the same as the area of the shaded region in the top right graph, which is given by the integral $\int_0^\infty g(\overline{F}_X(x)) \, dx$, we must have the identity (5.12).

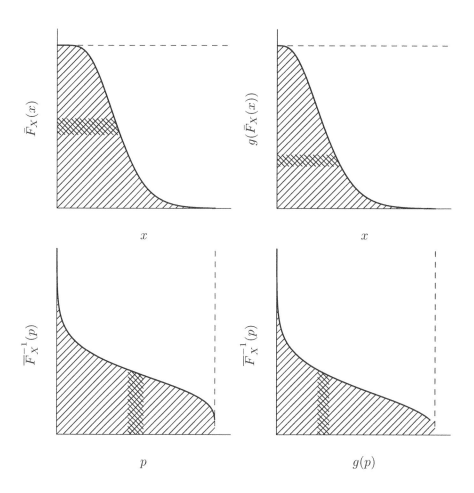

FIGURE 5.5: Visual illustration of the identity (5.12)

Furthermore, observe that

$$\overline{F}_X^{-1}(p) = \sup\{x : F_X(x) < 1 - p\} = \text{VaR}_{1-p}[X],$$

which shows the equivalence of (5.11) and (5.12).

Example 5.18. There are many well-known examples of distortion risk measures.

    1. (Expectation) If we let $g(x) = x$ in (5.10), it is easy to see that the distortion risk measure of X becomes its expectation by the formula

$$\rho_g[X] = \int_0^\infty \overline{F}_X(x)\, \mathrm{d}x - \int_{-\infty}^0 \left(1 - \overline{F}_X(x)\right)\, \mathrm{d}x = \mathbb{E}[X].$$

2. (Value-at-Risk) In the case that the distortion function is given by

$$g(x) = I(x > 1 - p),$$

for any fixed $p \in (0,1)$, then it follows from (5.12) that $\rho_g[X] = \text{VaR}_p[X]$.

3. (Tail-Value-at-Risk) In the case that the distortion function is given by

$$g(x) = \min\left\{\frac{x}{1-p}, 1\right\},$$

then it follows from (5.12) that

$$\rho_g[X] = \frac{1}{1-p}\int_0^{1-p} \text{VaR}_{1-q}[X]\,dq = \text{TVaR}_p[X].$$

It is clear from Example 5.18 that not all distortion risk measures are convex risk measures. Since (5.11) shows that the distortion risk measure is in essence a weighted average of VaRs, then, like TVaR, it also inherits properties such as positive homogeneity, translativity and monotonicity. Here is a sufficient and necessary condition for which a distortion risk measure is coherent. For brevity, we only sketch the proof of the sufficiency.

Theorem 5.19. *Distortion risk measure ρ_g is subadditive if g is concave.*

Proof. Assume that the distortion function g has a continuous second derivative, i.e. $g''(x) \leq 0$ for all $x \in (0,1)$. Using integration by parts, we obtain that

$$\int_0^1 \text{VaR}_{1-p}[X]\,dg(p) = g'(1)\mathbb{E}[X] - \int_0^1\left(\int_0^p \text{VaR}_{1-q}[X]\,dq\right)g''(p)\,dp.$$

Then it follows that

$$\rho_g[X] = g'(1)\mathbb{E}[X] - \int_0^1 \text{TVaR}_{1-p}[X](1-p)g''(p)\,dp. \tag{5.13}$$

Since both TVaR and expectation are subadditive, it follows immediately from (5.13) that ρ_g must also be subadditive. If g is concave but not necessarily twice continuously differentiable, then we can always approximate g by linear combinations of concave piecewise linear functions. It is known from Example 5.18 that a linear distortion function corresponds to a TVaR. Hence ρ_g can also be approximated by linear combinations of TVaRs. Thus the subadditivity can be shown by limiting arguments. □

5.2.6 Comonotonicity

Although not required for a coherent risk measure, there are other desirable properties of risk measure that are also useful in practice.

> **Definition 5.20.** A random vector $(X_1, X_2, \cdots, X_n)$ is said to be comonotonic if there exists a random variable Z and non-decreasing functions $t_1, t_2, \cdots, t_n$ such that $(t_1(Z), t_2(Z), \cdots, t_n(Z))$ has the same joint distribution as $(X_1, X_2, \cdots, X_n)$.

The intuition behind the comonotonicity is that these random variables tend to be small or large all together and there is a single "force" that drives the values of all random variables.

Example 5.21. Stop-loss insurance is a policy that limits claim coverage to a specified maximum amount. It is a form of insurance to protect the insurer from unlimited liability, commonly seen in health insurance, property and casualty insurance, reinsurance, etc. Here we use as an example excess-of-loss reinsurance, where a primary insurer transfers a portion of its insured risk to a reinsurer. For instance, if the policy limit of a stop-loss insurance is u and the total amount of insurance claims to the primary insurer is represented by X, then the reinsurer reimburses the primary insurer the amount by which the aggregate claim exceeds the policy limit, i.e.

$$X_1 = (X - u)_+,$$

and hence the primary insurer only suffers the total loss of

$$X_2 = X - X_1 = \max\{X, u\}.$$

Note that in this case the pair of losses for primary insurer and reinsurer, (X_1, X_2), is clearly comonotonic.

Example 5.22. Another common form is proportional insurance, or sometimes referred to as co-insurance or pro-rata insurance, where the policyholder and the insurer share the loss under coverage proportionally. In the context of healthcare insurance, for example, co-insurance is developed as a mechanism to discourage "moral hazard", which occurs when policyholders opt for unnecessarily expensive treatments or medicine in expectation of insurance full coverage. If the policyholder is subject to cost sharing, it is expected that caution would be taken resulting in more necessary and cost efficient treatment options. Suppose that the total loss from the policyholder is represented by X and the coinsurance rate is $\alpha \in (0, 1)$, then the policyholder pays a portion of the loss, i.e.

$$X_1 = \alpha X,$$

and the insurer pays the rest of the loss, i.e.

$$X_2 = X - X_1 = (1 - \alpha)X.$$

Hence, in this case, the total losses for the policyholder and the insurer (X_1, X_2) is also comonotonic.

Readers should be reminded that the two examples above are clear examples of risk sharing as an important tool of risk management. We will see in Section 5.5 an example of variable annuity guarantee benefit where risk sharing is mixed with risk reduction.

Definition 5.23. A risk measure ρ is said to be comonotonic additive if, for any comonotonic vector (X_1, X_2),

$$\rho(X_1 + X_2) = \rho(X_1) + \rho(X_2).$$

Example 5.24. VaR is comonotonic additive, i.e. for $0 < p < 1$ and any comonotonic random vector (X_1, X_2),

$$\text{VaR}_p(X_1 + X_2) = \text{VaR}_p(X_1) + \text{VaR}_p(X_2).$$

Here we prove the identity when (X_1, X_2) have continuous and strictly increasing marginal distributions F_1 and F_2. In this case, the inverse functions of F_1 and F_2, denoted by F_1^{-1} and F_2^{-1}, are also continuous and strictly increasing in p. Let t be any continuous and strictly increasing function. Then

$$
\begin{aligned}
F_{t(X)}^{-1}(p) &= \inf\{x \in \mathbb{R} : \mathbb{P}(t(X) \le x) > p\} \\
&= \inf\{x \in \mathbb{R} : \mathbb{P}(X \le t^{-1}(x)) > p\} \\
&= \inf\{t(y) \in \mathbb{R} : \mathbb{P}(X \le y) > p\} \\
&= t(F_X^{-1}(p)). \tag{5.14}
\end{aligned}
$$

Since the vector (X_1, X_2) is comonotonic, we must have

$$
\begin{aligned}
\mathbb{P}(X_1 \le x_1, X_2 \le x_2) &= \mathbb{P}(t_1(Z) \le x_1, t_2(Z) \le x_2) \\
&= \min\{\mathbb{P}(t_1(Z) \le x_1), \mathbb{P}(t_2(Z) \le x_2)\} \\
&= \min\{\mathbb{P}(X_1 \le x_1), \mathbb{P}(X_2 \le x_2)\} \\
&= \min\{\mathbb{P}(F_1^{-1}(U) \le x_1), \mathbb{P}(F_2^{-1}(U) \le x_2)\} \\
&= \mathbb{P}(F_1^{-1}(U) \le x_1, F_2^{-1}(U) \le x_2),
\end{aligned}
$$

where U is a uniform random variable on $(0, 1)$. The above identity shows that (X_1, X_2) has the same distribution as $(F_1^{-1}(U), F_2^{-1}(U))$. Let $t(u) = F_1^{-1}(u) + F_2^{-1}(u)$. Using (5.14), we obtain

$$
\begin{aligned}
\text{VaR}_p(X_1 + X_2) &= \text{VaR}_p(t(U)) = F_{t(U)}^{-1}(p) \\
&= t(F_U^{-1}(p)) = t(p) = \text{VaR}_p(X_1) + \text{VaR}_p(X_2).
\end{aligned}
$$

Example 5.25. TVaR is also comonotonic additive. To see this, we let (X_1, X_2) be a comonotonic random vector and hence

$$
\begin{aligned}
\text{TVaR}_p(X_1 + X_2) &= \frac{1}{1-p} \int_p^1 \text{VaR}_q(X_1 + X_2) \, dq \\
&= \frac{1}{1-p} \int_p^1 \text{VaR}_q(X_1) + \text{VaR}_q(X_2) \, dq \\
&= \text{TVaR}_p(X_1) + \text{TVaR}_p(X_2).
\end{aligned}
$$

We shall illustrate applications of comonotonicity in the context of equity-linked insurance in Section 7.2.

5.2.7 Statistical inference of risk measures

In practice it is often the case that the exact distribution of a risk is not known and a sample of observations can be collected. Therefore, we cannot apply definitions of risk measures directly due to the lack of information on the underlying distribution. Instead, we often consider the estimation of risk measures.

Suppose that a sample of independent observations $(x_1, x_2, \cdots, x_n)$ is drawn from a random variable X with the distribution function F. The empirical distribution function is given by

$$
\hat{F}(x) = \frac{1}{n} \sum_{i=1}^n 1(x_i \leq x).
$$

Then the *empirical quantile function* is given by

$$
\widehat{\text{VaR}}_p = \inf\{x : \hat{F}(x) \geq p\}.
$$

As the symbol suggests, $\widehat{\text{VaR}}$ is a nonparametric estimator of the value-at-risk. If we order the sample from the smallest to the largest and denoted the k-th largest observation by $x_{(k)}$, then it is clear that

$$
\widehat{\text{VaR}}_p = x_{(\lceil np \rceil)}.
$$

It is known in the literature that empirical distribution function and empirical quantile function converge asymptotically to the distribution function and the quantile function (VaR).

The shortcoming of the above-mentioned approach is that the empirical quantile function is a step function. There are other nonparametric or parametric methods to smooth the empirical quantile function.

Example 5.26. (Nonparametric method) As p is often known in advance, we can always choose a large enough n such that np becomes an integer. When it is not possible to collect a sample of large enough size, we can use a linear interpolation between two order statistics, i.e. for any $p \in (0, 1)$,

$$\widehat{\text{VaR}}_p = (\lceil np \rceil - np)x_{(\lfloor np \rfloor)} + (np - \lfloor np \rfloor)x_{(\lceil np \rceil)}. \quad (5.15)$$

As shown in Figure 5.6, such an estimator is piecewise-linear as a function of p.

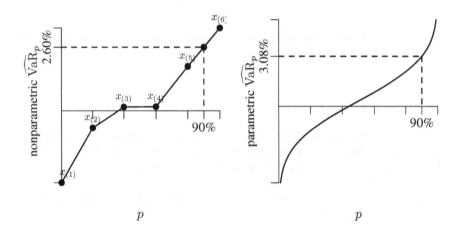

FIGURE 5.6: Two methods of estimating VaR

(Parametric method) If the sample of observation is used to fit a parametric probability distribution model, then quantile risk measure can be determined by the fitted distribution. For example, if the random sample is assumed to follow a normal distribution with unknown parameters μ and σ^2. Then one can first estimate the parameters using unbiased estimators:

$$\hat{\mu} = \frac{1}{n} \sum_{i=1}^{n} l_i \text{ and } \widehat{\sigma^2} = \frac{1}{n-1} \sum_{i=1}^{n} (l_i - \hat{\mu})^2.$$

Recall that the VaR of a normal random variable is given by (5.2). Then the VaR can be estimated by

$$\widehat{\text{VaR}}_p = \hat{\mu} + \Phi^{-1}(p)\hat{\sigma}$$
$$= \frac{\sum_{i=1}^{n} x_i}{n} + \Phi^{-1}(p) \cdot \sqrt{\frac{\sum_{i=1}^{n} x_i^2}{n-1} - \frac{(\sum_{i=1}^{n} x_i)^2}{n(n-1)}}. \quad (5.16)$$

Consider a random sample from a normal random variable with mean 0.01 and standard deviation 0.03.

$$x_1 = 15.478\%, x_2 = -2.938\%, x_3 = 3.386\%,$$
$$x_4 = 1.810\%, x_5 = 0.168\%, x_6 = -0.698\%$$

The nonparametric estimate of VaR in (5.15) is given by $\widehat{\text{VaR}}_{0.9} = 2.60\%$ whereas the parametric estimator based on normal model assumption in (5.16) is given by $\widehat{\text{VaR}}_{0.9} = 3.08\%$. The graphs of the two estimators as functions of p are given in Figure 5.6.

The analogue of nonparametric estimator (5.15) for TVaR is given by

$$\widehat{\text{TVaR}}_p = \frac{1}{n - \lceil np \rceil + 1} \sum_{i=\lceil np \rceil}^{n} x_{(i)}, \tag{5.17}$$

which is in essence an arithmetic average of empirical estimators of VaR at various levels.

Similarly, the analogue of nonparametric estimator (5.15) for distortion risk measure is given by

$$\hat{\rho}_g = \sum_{i=1}^{n} x_{(n-i+1)} \left[g\left(\frac{i}{n}\right) - g\left(\frac{i-1}{n}\right) \right], \tag{5.18}$$

where g is the underlying distortion function. As the TVaR is a special case of distortion risk measure, the nonparametric estimator of TVaR (5.17) can also be obtained from that of distortion risk measure (5.18) by setting

$$g(x) = \min\left\{ \frac{nx}{n - \lceil np \rceil + 1}, 1 \right\}.$$

Recall that CTE risk measure can be written as

$$\text{CTE}_p[X] = \frac{\mathbb{E}[XI(X > \text{VaR}_p[X])]}{\mathbb{E}[I(X > \text{VaR}_p[X])]}.$$

With similar interpretation, a nonparametric estimator for CTE is given by

$$\widehat{\text{CTE}}_p = \frac{\sum_{i=1}^{n} x_i I(x_i \geq \widehat{\text{VaR}}_p)}{\sum_{i=1}^{n} I(x_i \geq \widehat{\text{VaR}}_p)}.$$

Example 5.27. (Cash flow testing for C-3 RBC) The nature of equity-linked insurance and annuities makes these business lines sensitive to market and interest rate risks. A factor-based approach, such as described in Example 5.3, is deemed inadequate to quantify and assess market and interest rate risks. Cash flow testing requires the valuation of an entire portfolio of business, including assets and liabilities, under various economic scenarios. It is an approach to analyze the impact of interest rate and equity market sensitivity of asset and liability cash flows.

Here we provide a description of the cash flow testing for C-3 RBC methodology. It requires a valuation actuary to run 12 or 50 scenarios produced from the interest-rate scenario generator provided by the American Academy of Actuaries. For each business line, the accumulated surplus/deficiency U_t should be evaluated for every scenario for each year over the projection horizon $t = 1, \cdots, T$. A more detailed example of the accumulated surplus/deficiency can be found in Section 5.7. Let us denote the scenarios by $\{\omega_1, \cdots, \omega_{50}\}$. Under the i-th scenario, the C-3 measure, denoted by x_i, is determined by the most negative of present values of accumulated surplus/deficiency at all times,

$$x_i = - \min_{t=1,\cdots,T} \{p_t(\omega_i)U_t(\omega_i)\},$$

where p_t is the accumulated discount factor for t years using 105% of the after-tax one-year treasury rates $\{i_k, i = 1, 2, \cdots, T\}$ for that scenario, i.e.

$$p_t(\omega_i) = \prod_{k=1}^{t} \frac{1}{1 + i_k(\omega_i)}.$$

Scenario specific C-3 measures are ranked in descending order with scenario #1 being the positive capital necessary to cover the worst possible present value of deficiency.

Scenario Rank (i)	17	16	15	14	13	12	
Weight c_i	0.02	0.04	0.06	0.08	0.10	0.12	
Scenario Rank (i)	11	10	9	8	7	6	5
Weight c_i	0.16	0.12	0.10	0.08	0.06	0.04	0.02

TABLE 5.3: Weighting table for 50 scenario set

Then the C-3 after-tax factor is determined by the weighted average of a subset of the scenario specific C-3 measures. The weights for C-3 measures for the 50 scenario set are given by Table 5.3. In other words,

$$\text{C-3 factor} = \sum_{i=5}^{17} c_i x_{(i)}. \tag{5.19}$$

Comparing (5.18) and (5.19), we note that the C-3 after-tax factor is in fact based on the nonparametric estimator of a distortion risk measure.

For the 12 scenario set, the C-3 after-tax factor is determined by the maximum of the average of C-3 measures under scenarios #2 and #3 and the C-3 measure under scenario #1. In other words,

$$\text{C-3 factor} = \max \left\{ \frac{1}{2}(x_{(2)} + x_{(3)}), \frac{1}{2}x_{(1)} \right\}.$$

The C-3 factor is then entered into the RBC worksheet for interest rate risk and market risk with some technical adjustment. Details can be found in the NAIC's annual publication of *Risk-Based Capital Forecasting and Instructions.*

5.3 Risk aggregation

The basic principle of risk retention is that one sets aside enough assets now to absorb potential losses in the future resulting from retaining the underlying risk. The challenge is often to decide how much to set aside. As alluded to earlier in the optimization problem (5.3), the decision maker has to balance costs and benefits of setting aside capitals. In order to quantify and assess costs and benefits, one has to acquire a thorough understanding of the risk profile of the business under scrutiny.

Risk aggregation refers to the process of consolidating risk exposures from the bottom level (e.g. individual risks, contracts or business lines) of a business hierarchy to a risk profile at the top level (e.g. corporate total). Such an exercise can provide the quantitative basis for setting reserves and capitals for internal risk management and regulatory purposes.

In a static setting, risk aggregation boils down to a question of quantifying the financial impact of the aggregate loss. For example, if random variables $X_1, X_2, \cdots, X_n$ represent potential losses resulted from n individual risks, then the aggregate loss is given by $S = X_1 + X_2 + \cdots + X_n$. Keep in mind that the purpose of setting capital is to ensure sufficient funds for the business to survive economic adversity. A common approach to determine capital is to estimate a certain risk measure of the aggregate loss S. For example, one might evaluate how much capital is needed to cover the maximum amount of loss under "doomsday" scenarios, say, the worst possible in 100 years.

5.3.1 Variance-covariance approach

This approach is commonly used in banking and insurance industries. It is developed under the following assumptions.

1. All risks $\{X_1, X_2, \cdots, X_n\}$ are normally distributed with mean 0;

2. Minimal capital is determined by a risk measure of the aggregate risk which is proportional to its standard deviation.

For example, VaR can be used to determine minimal capital under this approach. Because of (5.2), we know that

$$\mathrm{VaR}_p(S) = \sigma(S)\Phi^{-1}(p), \qquad p \in (0,1), \tag{5.20}$$

where σ is the standard deviation. Since the sum of normal random variables is also normal, we must have

$$\sigma(S) = \sqrt{\sum_{i=1}^{n}\sum_{j=1}^{n} r_{ij}\sigma(X_i)\sigma(X_j)}, \tag{5.21}$$

where r_{ij} is the correlation coefficient of X_i and X_j. Similarly, TVaR can also be used under the variance-covariance approach, due to the fact (Exercise 5.2.4) that

$$\text{TVaR}_p(S) = \sigma(S)\frac{\phi(\Phi^{-1}(p))}{1-p}, \qquad p \in (0,1).$$

Let ρ be any risk measure which is proportional to the standard deviation of the underlying normal random variable. Then we can rewrite (5.21) in terms of the risk measure

$$\rho(S) = \sqrt{\sum_{i=1}^{n}\sum_{j=1}^{n} r_{ij}\rho(X_i)\rho(X_j)}. \tag{5.22}$$

If all random variables $X_1, X_2, \cdots, X_n$ are mutually independent, then $r_{ij} = 0$ for $i \neq j$ in (5.22) and hence the formula simplifies to

$$\rho(S) = \sqrt{\rho(X_1)^2 + \cdots + \rho(X_n)^2}. \tag{5.23}$$

If $X_1, X_2, \cdots, X_n$ are perfectly correlated with each other, i.e. $r_{ij} = 1$ for all i, j, then

$$\rho(S) = \rho(X_1) + \cdots + \rho(X_n). \tag{5.24}$$

As in this case the random variables are comonotonic (Exercise 5.3.4), the above result for VaR and TVaR can also be obtained from their comonotonic additivity.

Example 5.28. Many capital regulatory frameworks, such as the NAIC risk-based capital in Example 5.3, use an extended version of the variance-covariance approach to determine the total capital required for undertaking on a variety of risks. Standalone capital is calculated for individual risk factors (e.g. C-0, C-1o, C-1cs, C-2, C-3a, C-3b, C-3c, C-4a, C-4b, etc). Then certain risk categories are grouped first and aggregated at the group level by applying the "variance adjustment" formula in (5.22). The purpose of such adjustment is to take into account the potential diversification across different risks. For example, the risks C-1o, C-1cs, C-2, C-3a, C-3b, C-3c, C-4a are considered in a group and it is assumed that the perfectly correlated pairs (C-1o, C-3a) and (C-1cs, C-3c) are independent of other mutually independent risks. The capital for aggregate risk in this group is given by the formula 5.23,

$$\sqrt{(\text{C-1o} + \text{C-3a})^2 + (\text{C-1cs} + \text{C-3c})^2 + (\text{C-2})^2 + (\text{C-3b})^2 + (\text{C-4b})^2}.$$

The risks C-0 and C-4b are considered mutually independent in another group and aggregated at the group level by the formula (5.24),

$$C\text{-}0 + C\text{-}4b.$$

Last, the two groups are considered independent of each other and aggregated at the corporate level according to the formula for the authorized control level RBC (5.1). However, a word of caution is needed here. The variance-covariance approach is based on the assumptions that all capitals are measured by VaR and all risks are assumed to be normally distributed. In contrast, Section 5.7 will show an application of scenario aggregation application in practice for stochastic reserving and the procedures for determining C-3a and C-3c risks can be carried out in a similar manner. As shown in Example 5.27, cash flow testing for RBC requirements are also determined by other risk measures. Therefore, as complex as the regulatory framework, there is some incoherence in the treatment of different risks and modeling assumptions.

5.3.2 Model uncertainty approach

If individual risks are mutually independent, then the VaR of aggregate risk may be calculated by the formula (5.23), or by convolution, as seen in Exercise 1.1. However, independence is actually rare in practice. While it is easy to build models for standalone risks, it is often difficult to model their dependence, especially when the number of risks is large. Suppose that the marginal distributions of risks $X_1, \cdots, X_n$ are known (or can be estimated) and the capital requirement is also based on the VaR of the aggregate risk. A well-studied theoretical approach is to assume model uncertainty regarding the dependence and estimate the distribution of the aggregate risk $F(s) := \mathbb{P}(S \leq s)$ where $S = X_1 + X_2 + \cdots + X_n$ merely using information of marginal distributions.

Theorem 5.29. *Let* $(X_1, X_2, \cdots, X_n)$ *be a random vector with known marginal distributions* $F_i(x) = \mathbb{P}(X_i \leq x)$ *with left limit* $F_i^-(x) = \mathbb{P}(X_i < x)$ *for* $i = 1, 2, \cdots, n$. *Then, for any* $s \in \mathbb{R}$,

$$F_*^-(s) \leq F(s) \leq F^*(s), \tag{5.25}$$

where F_*^- *and* F^* *are lower and upper bounds of* F *defined respectively by*

$$F_*^-(s) = \sup\left\{ \max\left(\sum_{i=1}^n F_i^-(x_i) - (n-1), 0 \right) \middle| x_1 + \cdots + x_n = s \right\},$$

$$F^*(s) = \inf\left\{ \min\left(\sum_{i=1}^n F_i(x_i), 1 \right) \middle| x_1 + \cdots + x_n = s \right\}.$$

Proof. (Upper bound) For any events $A_1, A_2, \cdots, A_n, B$, if $\cap_{i=1}^n A_i \subseteq B$, then

$B^c \subseteq \cup_{i=1}^n A_i^c$ and due to the subadditivity of probability measure

$$\mathbb{P}(B^c) \leq \mathbb{P}\left(\bigcup_{i=1}^n A_i^c\right) \leq \sum_{i=1}^n \mathbb{P}(A_i^c). \tag{5.26}$$

Let $B = \{S > s\}$ and $A_i = \{X_i > x_i\}$ for $i = 1, \cdots, n$, where $x_1, x_2, \cdots, x_n$ are arbitrary numbers for which $x_1 + x_2 + \cdots + x_n = s$. Then it follows from (5.26) that

$$F(s) = \mathbb{P}(S \leq s) \leq \sum_{i=1}^n \mathbb{P}(X_i \leq x_i) = \sum_{i=1}^n F_i(x_i).$$

Since $x_1, \cdots, x_n$ are arbitrary subject to the constraint on their sum, we can take the supremum on both sides the inequality. Together with the fact that $F(s) \leq 1$, we obtain the upper bound in (5.25).

(Lower bound) Using the countable additivity (2.1) of any probability measure, we observe that, for any event $A_1, A_2, \cdots, A_n$,

$$\mathbb{P}\left(\bigcup_{i=1}^n A_i^c\right) \leq \sum_{i=1}^n \mathbb{P}(A_i^c),$$

where the superscript c indicates the compliment of the underlying set. Since $\mathbb{P}(A^c) = 1 - \mathbb{P}(A)$, it follows that

$$\mathbb{P}\left(\bigcap_{i=1}^n A_i\right) \geq \sum_{i=1}^n \mathbb{P}(A_i) - n + 1.$$

Setting $A_i = \{X_i < x_i\}$ for $i = 1, 2, \cdots, n$ and for which $x_1 + \cdots + x_n = s$, we obtain

$$F(s) \geq \sum_{i=1}^n F_i^-(x_i) - (n - 1).$$

Since $x_1, \cdots, x_n$ are arbitrary as long as they sum up to s, then we can take the infimum on both sides of the inequality. Together with the fact that $F(s) \geq 0$, we also obtain the lower bound in (5.25). $\qquad\qquad\square$

A careful reader may notice the choices of symbols F_*^- and F^*. They are in fact used to indicate that there exist two random variables S_* and S^* for which $F_*^-(s) = \mathbb{P}(S_* < s)$ and $F^*(s) = \mathbb{P}(S^* \leq s)$. It is not difficult to verify that F_*^- and F^* are left-continuous and right-continuous versions of some distribution functions, which guarantees the existence of S_* and S^*.

Example 5.30. Suppose that two insurance claims X_1, X_2 from a particular insurance policy both follow shifted exponential distributions. In other words, the distribution function of the i-th claim where $i = 1, 2$ is given by

$$F_i(x) = 1 - \exp\left\{-\frac{x - \theta_i}{\alpha_i}\right\}, \qquad \alpha_i > 0, x \geq \theta_i.$$

For notational brevity, we can write $X_i \sim \mathrm{SE}(\alpha_i, \theta_i)$. Without any information on their dependence, we can at least provide bounds on the distribution of the aggregate claim $S = X_1 + X_2$. According to Theorem 5.29, the lower bound of F is given by

$$
\begin{aligned}
F_*(s) &= \sup_{x \in \mathbb{R}} \left(1 - \exp\left\{ -\frac{x - \theta_1}{\alpha_1} \right\} - \exp\left\{ -\frac{s - x - \theta_2}{\alpha_2} \right\} \right)_+ \\
&= \left(\sup_{x \in \mathbb{R}} \left[1 - \exp\left\{ -\frac{x - \theta_1}{\alpha_1} \right\} - \exp\left\{ -\frac{s - x - \theta_2}{\alpha_2} \right\} \right] \right)_+ \quad (5.27)
\end{aligned}
$$

where we exchange the order of supremum and maximum. In order to simplify the expression for the supremum, we set the derivative of the quantity inside square brackets in (5.27) to zero and find the critical point of x,

$$
x^* = \frac{\alpha_1 \alpha_2}{\alpha_1 + \alpha_2} \left[\ln \frac{\alpha_2}{\alpha_1} + \frac{\theta_1}{\alpha_1} + \frac{s - \theta_2}{\alpha_2} \right].
$$

It is easy to see that the second derivative of the quantity inside square brackets in (5.27) is negative. Therefore, x^* must also be the global maximum. After some simple algebra, we can show that

$$
e^{-(x^* - \theta_1)/\alpha_1} = C_1 e^{-s/(\alpha_1 + \alpha_2)}, \quad C_1 = \exp\left[-\frac{\alpha_2}{\alpha_1 + \alpha_2} \ln \frac{\alpha_2}{\alpha_1} + \frac{\theta_1 + \theta_2}{\alpha_1 + \alpha_2} \right];
$$

$$
e^{-(s - x^* - \theta_2)/\alpha_2} = C_2 e^{-s/(\alpha_1 + \alpha_2)}, \quad C_2 = \exp\left[\frac{\alpha_1}{\alpha_1 + \alpha_2} \ln \frac{\alpha_2}{\alpha_1} + \frac{\theta_1 + \theta_2}{\alpha_1 + \alpha_2} \right].
$$

It follows immediately that the expression inside square brackets in (5.27) is also in the family of shifted exponential distribution. After some arrangement, we can show that

$$
F_*(s) = 1 - \exp\left\{ 1 - \frac{s - \theta_*}{\alpha_*} \right\}, \quad s \geq \theta_*,
$$

where $\alpha_* = \alpha_1 + \alpha_2$ and

$$
\theta_* = \theta_1 + \theta_2 + (\alpha_1 + \alpha_2) \ln(\alpha_1 + \alpha_2) - \alpha_1 \ln \alpha_1 - \alpha_2 \ln \alpha_2.
$$

In other words, there exists such as a pair (X_1^*, X_2^*) such that $X_i^* \sim \mathrm{SE}(\alpha_i, \theta_i)$ for $i = 1, 2$ and $S^* = X_1^* + X_2^* \sim \mathrm{SE}(\alpha_*, \theta_*)$.

Similarly, one can show that the upper bound is also given by a shifted exponential distribution

$$
F^*(s) = 1 - \exp\left\{ 1 - \frac{s - \theta^*}{\alpha^*} \right\}, \quad s \geq \theta^*,
$$

where $\theta^* = \theta_1 + \theta_2, \alpha^* = \max\{\alpha_1, \alpha_2\}$. In other words, there exists such as a pair (X_{*1}, X_{*2}) such that $X_{*i} \sim \mathrm{SE}(\alpha_i, \theta_i)$ for $i = 1, 2$ and $S_* = X_{*1} + X_{*2} \sim \mathrm{SE}(\alpha_*, \theta_*)$.

Note that in this example, both S^* and S_* can be identified as shifted exponential random variables and we can identify explicitly the bounds for the value-at-risk as well, i.e.

$$\underline{\text{VaR}}_p(S) \leq \text{VaR}_p(S) \leq \overline{\text{VaR}}_p(S)$$

where

$$\underline{\text{VaR}}_p(S) = \text{VaR}_p(S^*) = \theta^* - \alpha^* \ln(1 - p);$$
$$\overline{\text{VaR}}_p(S) = \text{VaR}_p(S_*) = \theta_* - \alpha_* \ln(1 - p).$$

If the capital requirement is based on some subadditive and comonotonic additive risk measure, say, TVaR or concave distortion risk measure, then it is relatively easy to find upper bounds of these risk measures. For example, recall that TVaR is subadditive, i.e.

$$\text{TVaR}_p \left(\sum_{i=1}^n X_i \right) \leq \sum_{i=1}^n \text{TVaR}_p(X_i), \tag{5.28}$$

and that if $X_1, \cdots, X_n$ are comonotonic then by comonotonic additivity

$$\text{TVaR}_p \left(\sum_{i=1}^n X_i \right) = \sum_{i=1}^n \text{TVaR}_p(X_i).$$

Hence it is clear that the risk capital by TVaR is maximal when the underlying risks are comonotonic. If no information about the dependence is known, then (5.28) provides a tight upper bound of the capital requirement, which can be attained in the case of comonotonicity. Some more results on lower bounds of risk measures of aggregate risk can be found in Exercises 5.3.1.

However, it is also worth pointing out that, while comonotonic dependence between X_1 and X_2 leads to upper bounds of comonotonic additive and subadditive risk measures, it is not the extremal case for VaR due to its lack of subadditivity. Let us revisit Example 5.30 and consider the VaR of the comonotonic sum $S^c := X_1^c + X_2^c$ where (X_1^c, X_2^c) has the same marginal distributions as (X_1, X_2) but (X_1^c, X_2^c) is comonotonic. We can set $X_1^c = F_1^{-1}(U)$ and $X_2^c = F_2^{-1}(U)$ where U is a uniform random variable (see proof in Example 5.24). Then the VaR of the comonotonic sum $S = F_1^{-1}(U) + F_2^{-1}(U)$ is also known explicitly,

$$\text{VaR}_p(S^c) = F_1^{-1}(p) + F_2^{-1}(p) = \theta_1 + \theta_2 - (\alpha_1 + \alpha_2) \ln(1 - p),$$

and it can be shown that

$$\underline{\text{VaR}}_p(S) \leq \text{VaR}_p(S^c) \leq \overline{\text{VaR}}_p(S).$$

The reason that comonotonicity does not correspond to the extremal case of $\mathbb{P}(X_1 + X_2 > s)$ is that, while it increases the probability that $X_1 + X_2$ exceeds some high thresholds (as both can be very big), the comonotonicity decreases the exceedance probabilities of low thresholds (both can be very small).

Example 5.31. Consider an extension of Example 5.30 where there are n insurance policies with potential losses $\{X_1, \cdots, X_n\}$. Suppose that each loss X_i follows a shifted exponential distribution with parameters (θ_i, α_i) for $i = 1, \cdots, n$. In order to assess the likelihood of severe losses, we are interested in the distribution of the aggregate loss from all n policies, i.e.

$$F(s) = \mathbb{P}\left(\sum_{i=1}^{n} X_i \leq s\right).$$

If we do not have any information regarding the dependence among these loss random variables, the model uncertainty approach enables us to identify the best possible and worst possible cases. It is easy to show by induction that both the upper bound F^* and the lower bound F_* are given by shifted exponential distributions with parameters

$$\alpha_* = \sum_{i=1}^{n} \alpha_i, \quad \theta_* = \sum_{i=1}^{n} \theta_i + \left(\sum_{i=1}^{n} \alpha_i\right) \ln\left(\sum_{i=1}^{n} \alpha_i\right) - \sum_{i=1}^{n} \alpha_i \ln \alpha_i;$$

$$\alpha^* = \max_i \alpha_i, \quad \theta^* = \sum_{i=1}^{n} \theta_i.$$

However, an issue with this approach is that the difference between upper and lower bounds often increases drastically with the number of variables. Consider the difference between the upper and lower bounds of value-at-risk

$$\overline{\mathrm{VaR}}_p[S] - \underline{\mathrm{VaR}}_p[S] = (\theta_* - \theta^*) - (\alpha_* - \alpha^*)\ln(1-p)$$

$$= \left(\sum_{i=1}^{n} \alpha_i\right) \ln\left(\sum_{i=1}^{n} \alpha_i\right) - \sum_{i=1}^{n} \alpha_i \ln \alpha_i - \left(\sum_{i=1}^{n} \alpha_i - \max_i \alpha_i\right) \ln(1-p)$$

For example, if $\alpha_i = \alpha$ for all $i = 1, 2, \cdots, n$, then

$$\overline{\mathrm{VaR}}_p[S] - \underline{\mathrm{VaR}}_p[S] = n\ln(n\alpha) - (n-1)\alpha\ln(1-p).$$

which shows that the difference grows roughly at the rate of $n \ln n$.

The top left graph in Figure 5.7 shows upper and lower bounds of the distribution function of $S = X_1 + X_2$ where both X_1 and X_2 follow the same shifted exponential distribution with $\theta = 1$ and $\alpha = 3$. The top right graph shows the upper and lower bounds of their VaRs. Similarly, the bottom panel shows those of $S = X_1 + X_2 + X_3$ where all X_i for $i = 1, 2, 3$ follow the same shifted exponential distribution. It is not surprising that the difference between upper and lower bounds widens for both distribution function and value-at-risk as the number of risks increases, as more uncertainty is included in the aggregate risk. However, Figure 5.7 also reveals a shortcoming of the model uncertainty approach, which is that the bounds may be too wide to provide useful estimates for risk measures of the aggregate risk. Note that, even for the sample size of 3, the bounds of the probability distribution function are already as wide as $(0, 1)$ in some region.

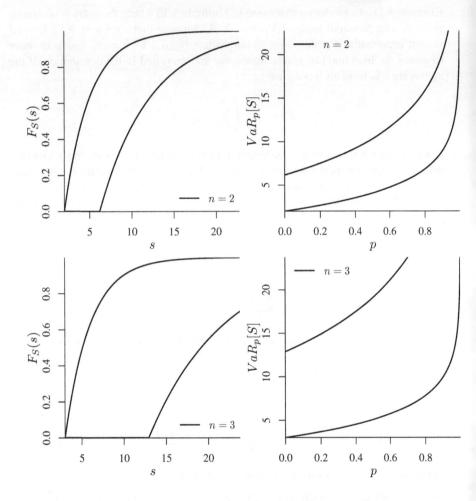

FIGURE 5.7: Upper and lower bounds of distribution function and value-at-risk of the sum of n shifted exponentials.

5.3.3 Scenario aggregation approach

While the variance-covariance approach makes simplistic assumptions and the model uncertainty approach utilizes little information on the dependence of risks, the scenario aggregation approach attempts to capture often complex dependence among risk factors through the simulation of the value creation process of the underlying business.

Take the equity-linked insurance as an example. While all contracts depend on common risk factors, such as interest rate risk, equity risk, etc., the extent to which these product lines are affected may vary greatly. The purpose of scenario aggregation approach is to quantify and assess the losses/profits by projection of cash flows over a time horizon under various scenarios of the underlying risk factors. The capital requirement calculated from the loss distribution at the corporate level is implicitly determined by the dependence structure among various quantities, such as fees, benefits, expenses, investment incomes, etc., which are all affected by risk factors. Figure 5.8 illustrates the idea of dependence in the situation of a typical equity-linked insurance product.

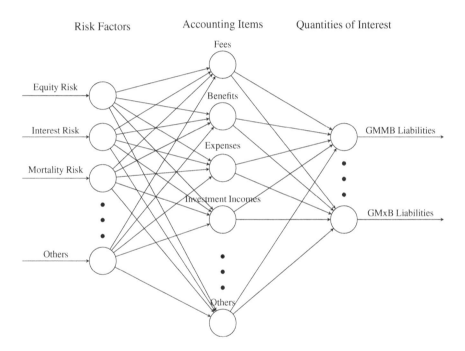

FIGURE 5.8: Network representation of dependence

Here we discuss two common approaches of capital modeling in practice.

5.3.3.1 Liability run-off approach

Under this approach, the capital requirement is typically determined by certain risk measure of projections of required assets to pay all future liabilities (benefits, expenses, taxes, etc.) less the current value of liabilities on a best estimate basis. While details may vary in practice, the liability run-off approach can be summarized in three steps. The logic flow of the liability run-off approach is shown in Figure 5.9.

1. Use either pre-packaged scenarios or internally built stochastic models, a.k.a. **economic scenario generators**, for all risk factors driving the insurer's asset and liability portfolio under the real-world measure. These stochastic models often need to be calibrated to meet regulatory standards. Generate a variety of sample paths of risk factors for the runoff of the business.

2. Project asset and liability cash flows from all product lines according to certain accounting practice under each scenario and determine the accumulated profit/deficiency for the entire projection length.

3. Amounts of required assets (or accumulated surplus/deficiency) are ranked to form an empirical distribution. Use order statistics to estimate certain risk metrics, such as value-at-risk, conditional tail expectation etc., which form the basis of determining reserve or capital.

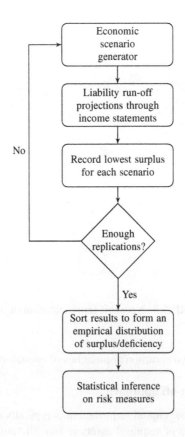

FIGURE 5.9: Logic flow of the liability run-off approach

5.3.3.2 Finite horizon mark-to-market approach

Under this approach, the capital requirement is determined by certain risk measure of projections of required assets to cover liabilities marked to market value at a finite time point in the future (typically one year) less the current value of liabilities. The approach is typically performed as follows. Its logic flow is shown in Figure 5.10.

1. Generate a number of scenarios of risk factors under the real world measure up to a finite horizon (typically one year).

2. Under each of the real-world scenarios, assets of all kinds and liabilities of all product lines are projected and a balance sheet is developed at the end of the finite horizon. As many product lines involve investment guarantees and options, the market-consistent valuation of liabilities often require the use of risk neutral valuations. The asset required to to ensure solvency is determined by the net liability for that scenario discounted to the valuation date using project investment returns over the finite horizon.

3. The level of required assets are then ranked to form an empirical distribution. A certain risk measure is applied to determine the capital requirement.

The key difference between liability run-off approach and finite horizon mark-to-market approach lies in the valuation of liability. The former investigates the runoff of the business over a long period (typically 30-50 years), whereas the latter is more concerned with short-term sustainability. Keep in mind that embedded options in insurance products are often long-term and there are no matching hedging instruments available to determine their market values. Therefore, even under the finite horizon approach, a run-off of liability is necessary under the risk-neutral measure to determine its market-consistent value.

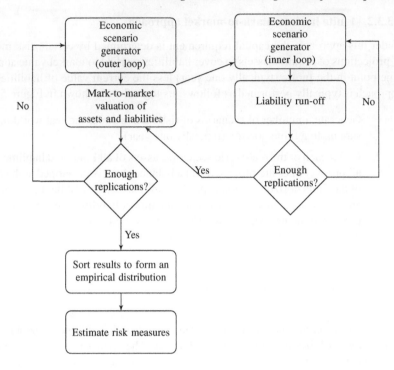

FIGURE 5.10: Logic flow of the finite horizon mark-to-market approach

---

Example 5.32. We shall elaborate on the application of scenario aggregation approach for the guaranteed minimum death benefit in Section 5.7. Nonetheless, we provide here a simplified model for quantitative-minded readers to compare the difference in the target quantities of the two approaches. Consider the individual net liability of the GMMB rider in a continuous-time model introduced in Section 1.2.3. If treated on a stand-alone basis, the risk measure of the GMMB rider under the liability run-off approach can be formulated mathematically as

$$\rho(L_{[0,T]}),$$

where the net liability is denoted with a slight change in the subscript to emphasize its time horizon

$$L_{[0,T]} := e^{-rT}(G - F_T)_+ I(T_x > T) - \int_0^{T \wedge T_x} e^{-rs} m_e F_s \, ds.$$

Note that all projections are typically performed and risk measures are calculated under real world/physical measure, under which model parameters are estimated from observable market data on equity returns, yield rates, etc. In contrast, the finite-horizon mark-to-market approach is to project the values of assets and liabilities at a future time point, say time t, and assess the risk involved with that time point. The risk measure of the individual net liability of the GMMB rider at time t can be written as

$$\rho\left(\tilde{\mathbb{E}}[L_{[t,T]}|\mathcal{F}_t]\right),$$

where $\tilde{\mathbb{E}}$ indicates the expectation taken under the risk-neutral measure, $\mathcal{F}_t$ represents the information set up to time t, the time t value of the net liability is given by

$$L_{[t,T]} := e^{-r(T-t)}(G - F_T)_+ I(T_{x+t} > T - t) - \int_t^{T \wedge T_{x+t}} e^{-r(s-t)} m_e F_s \, ds.$$

In this formulation, the risk measure is assessed under the real world/physical measure whereas the projected net liability at a future time is estimated under the risk-neutral measure. Keep in mind that in practice an insurer's overal liability can be much more complex and contain several product lines with hundreds of thousands of policies. It is also worthwhile to point out that, compared with the liablility run-off approach, the mark-to-market approach can be much more sophisticated and time consuming as it requires nested simulation, which shall be discussed in Section 7.3.

5.4 Risk diversification

5.4.1 Convex ordering

In many financial and insurance applications, ordering of random variables plays a critical role in understanding the differences between comparable risks. We shall use the concept of convex ordering to demonstrate the effect of diversification later in this section.

Definition 5.33. Given two random variables X and Y, X is said to be less than or equal to Y in convex order, denoted by $X \leq_{cx} Y$ if

$$\mathbb{E}[v(X)] \leq \mathbb{E}[v(Y)], \tag{5.29}$$

for any convex function v such that the expectations exist.

Convex ordering is used to compare random variables with identical means. Note that $x \mapsto x$ and $x \mapsto -x$ are both convex functions. It follows from the definition that if $X \leq_{cx} Y$ then $\mathbb{E}[X] \leq \mathbb{E}[Y]$ and $\mathbb{E}[X] \geq \mathbb{E}[Y]$, which implies $\mathbb{E}[X] = \mathbb{E}[Y]$. Convex order also implies the comparison of dispersion between two random variables. If $X \leq_{cx} Y$ then $\mathbb{V}[X] \leq \mathbb{V}[Y]$. It follows from the definition by letting

$v(x) = x^2$ and using the fact that $\mathbb{E}[X] = \mathbb{E}[Y]$. However, the convex order is much stronger than the order of variances, because the inequality (5.29) has to hold for more than just linear and quadratic functions.

It is in general difficult to check the convex order by attempting to verify (5.29) for all convex functions. Therefore, we often resort to a number of other equivalent or sufficient conditions for convex order.

Theorem 5.34. *Given two random variables X and Y, $X \leq_{cx} Y$ if and only if, for all $d \in R$,*

$$\mathbb{E}[(X - d)_+] \leq \mathbb{E}[(Y - d)_+], \qquad \mathbb{E}[(d - X)_+] \leq \mathbb{E}[(d - Y)_+]. \qquad (5.30)$$

It is easy to see that (5.30) is a necessary condition for convex order, because $x \mapsto (x - d)_+$ and $x \mapsto (d - x)_+$ are both convex functions. One can also prove that (5.30) is sufficient because any convex function can be approximated as closely as desired by a linear combination of functions of the form $(x - d)_+$ and $(d - x)_+$.

5.4.1.1 Thickness of tail

The following theorem gives a sufficient condition for a convex order, which is that distribution functions of X and Y cross each other exactly once.

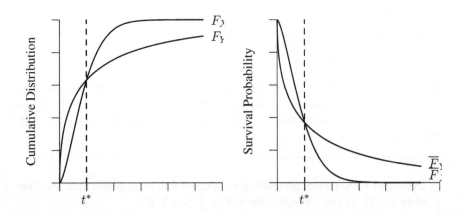

FIGURE 5.11: Comparison on thickness of tail

Theorem 5.35. *If there exists $t^* \in R$ for which*

$$\begin{cases} \mathbb{P}(X \leq t) \leq \mathbb{P}(Y \leq t), & t < t^*; \\ \mathbb{P}(X \leq t) \geq \mathbb{P}(Y \leq t), & t > t^*. \end{cases}$$

and $\mathbb{E}[X] = \mathbb{E}[Y]$, then $X \leq_{cx} Y$.

Proof. Denote distribution functions of X and Y by F_X and F_Y respectively. By assumption, $F_X(t) \leq F_Y(t)$ for $t \leq t^*$ and $F_X(t) \geq F_Y(t)$ for $t > t^*$. Consider the difference

$$\Delta(d) := \mathbb{E}[(Y - d)_+] - \mathbb{E}[(X - d)_+]. \tag{5.31}$$

Using the identity (5.4), we obtain that

$$\Delta(d) = \int_d^\infty (F_X(t) - F_Y(t)) \, dt.$$

When $d < 0$, we can rewrite

$$
\begin{aligned}
\Delta(d) &= \left(d + \int_d^\infty \overline{F}_Y(t) \, dt \right) - \left(d + \int_d^\infty \overline{F}_X(t) \, dt \right) \\
&= \left(\int_0^\infty \overline{F}_Y(t) \, dt - \int_d^0 F_Y(t) \, dt \right) - \left(\int_0^\infty \overline{F}_X(t) \, dt - \int_d^0 F_X(t) \, dt \right).
\end{aligned}
\tag{5.32}
$$

Recall that using integration by parts one can write that

$$\mathbb{E}[X] = \int_0^\infty \overline{F}_X(t) \, dt - \int_{-\infty}^0 F_X(t) \, dt.$$

Therefore, as we let $d \to -\infty$ in (5.32), it must be true that

$$\Delta(d) \to \mathbb{E}[Y] - \mathbb{E}[X] = 0.$$

It is also obvious from (5.31) that $\Delta(d) \to 0$ as $d \to \infty$. By assumption, we know that $\Delta'(d) = F_X(d) - F_Y(d) \geq 0$ for $d \leq t^*$ and $\Delta'(d) \leq 0$ for $d > t^*$. Therefore, the function Δ is non-decreasing over $(-\infty, t^*]$ and non-increasing over (t^*, ∞), which implies that $\Delta(d) \geq 0$ for all $d \in \mathbb{R}$. Using similar arguments, one can also show that for all $d \in \mathbb{R}$,

$$\nabla(d) := \mathbb{E}[(d - Y)_+] - \mathbb{E}[(d - X)_+] \geq 0.$$

Applying Theorem 5.34, we obtain $X \leq_{cx} Y$. □

As shown in Figure 5.11, the graph of the survival function of Y lies above that of X to the right of t^*. In simple words, it is more likely to observe large values of Y than it is large values of X. Sometimes, this relationship is referred to in the literature as Y being *thicker-tailed* than X. From an insurer's point of view, a thicker-tailed risk is more costly than otherwise. For example, the cost of a stop-loss insurance for a reinsurer in Example 5.21 is typically estimated by $\mathbb{E}[(X - u)_+]$ where u is the policy limit of the primary insurance company. If Y has a thicker tail than X, then Theorem 5.35 implies that $\mathbb{E}[(X - u)_+] \leq \mathbb{E}[(Y - u)_+]$ for any $u \in \mathbb{R}$, which implies that a stop-loss insurance policy costs less on average to cover the risk X than it is to cover Y.

Example 5.36. Let $\mathcal{X}$ be a collection of random variables with the same support $[0, b]$ where $0 < a < b < \infty$ and the same mean μ. Consider the distribution function of any arbitrary random variable in $\mathcal{X}$, whose graph is represented in solid line in Figure 5.12. Since $\int_0^b \overline{F}(x)\, dx = \mathbb{E}[X]$, the area of the shaded region should be equal to μ. To determine their convex order, we can use the concept of thicker-tailedness in Theorem 5.35.

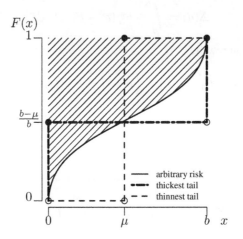

FIGURE 5.12: Random variables with the same finite support and mean

(Random variable with thinnest tail) As we look for such a random variable X_* that

$$X_* \leq_{cx} X, \qquad \text{for all } X \in \mathcal{X},$$

its distribution function must lie above all other distribution functions starting from the smallest possible point t^*. It is obvious that the largest possible value for a distribution function is 1. Keep in mind that the area above its distribution function and the horizontal line $F(x) = 1$ must be equal to μ. To make t^* as small as possible, the distribution of X_* must jump from 0 to 1 at t^*. Note that the total area between such a distribution function and the top horizontal line must be t^*. Hence, it must be the case that $t^* = \mu$. In other words, the random variable is in fact a constant,

$$X_* = \mu \qquad \text{with probability 1.}$$

The graph of the distribution function of X_* is shown in Figure 5.12.

(Random variable with thickest tail) We turn to the other extreme case where

$$X \leq_{cx} X^*, \qquad \text{for all } X \in \mathcal{X},$$

its distribution function must lie below all other distribution functions starting from the smallest possible point t^{**}. For t^{**} to be as small as possible, the distribution function of X^* should have a jump from 0 to some constant c at 0. The total area between such a distribution function and the top horizontal line must be $b(1 - c)$. Since all random variables have the same mean, we must have $c = (b - \mu)/b$. In other words, the random variable X^* can be represented by

$$X^* = \begin{cases} a, & \text{with probability } \frac{b-\mu}{b}; \\ b, & \text{with probability } \frac{\mu}{b}. \end{cases}$$

The graph of the distribution function X^* is also shown in Figure 5.12. According to Theorem 5.35, for any arbitrary random variable $X \in \mathcal{X}$,

$$X_* \leq_{cx} X \leq_{cx} X^*.$$

5.4.1.2 Conditional expectation

Another important sufficient condition for a convex order is that a random variable is always no less than its conditional expectation in convex order.

Theorem 5.37. *If* $X = \mathbb{E}[Y|\mathcal{F}]$ *for some information set* $\mathcal{F}$, *then*

$$X \leq_{cx} Y.$$

Proof. This is a straightforward application of Jensen's inequality (2.20). For any arbitrary convex function u,

$$\mathbb{E}[u(X)] = \mathbb{E}\left[u\big(\mathbb{E}[Y|\mathcal{F}]\big)\right] \leq \mathbb{E}\left[\mathbb{E}[u(Y)|\mathcal{F}]\right] = \mathbb{E}[u(Y)],$$

provided that the integrals exist. By definition, $X \leq_{cx} Y$. □

Example 5.38. Let X and Y be two independent random variables with $\mathbb{E}[X] < \infty$ and $\mathbb{E}[Y] = 0$. Show that

$$X \leq_{cx} X + Y.$$

Proof. Observe that $X = \mathbb{E}[X + Y|X] = X + \mathbb{E}[Y]$. It follows immediately from Theorem 5.37 that $X \leq_{cx} X + Y$. □

5.4.2 Diversification and convex order

The importance of convex order in the understanding of diversification lies in the fact that tail risk can be measured by risk measures such as TVaR and that convex order and its relationship with TVaR can be used to quantify the effect of diversification.

Theorem 5.39. *Given two random variables* X *and* Y, *if* $X \leq_{cx} Y$ *then for all* $p \in (0, 1)$

$$\mathrm{TVaR}_p[X] \leq \mathrm{TVaR}_p(Y).$$

Proof. Recall the representation of TVaR in (5.8). Then

$$\mathrm{TVaR}_p[X] \leq \mathrm{VaR}_p(Y) + \frac{1}{1-p}\mathbb{E}[(X - \mathrm{VaR}_p[Y])_+]$$

$$\leq \mathrm{VaR}_p(Y) + \frac{1}{1-p}\mathbb{E}[(Y - \mathrm{VaR}_p[Y])_+] = \mathrm{TVaR}_p[Y],$$

where the second inequality is due to the fact that $x \mapsto (x - \mathrm{VaR}_p[X])_+$ is a convex function. □

Definition 5.40. The random vector $(X_1, X_2, \cdots, X_n)$ is *exchangeable* if it has the same joint distribution as $(X_{j_1}, X_{j_2}, \cdots, X_{j_n})$ for all permutations $(j_1, j_2, \cdots, j_n)$ of $\{1, 2, \cdots, n\}$.

Theorem 5.41. *Let $(X_1, X_2, \cdots, X_{n+1})$ be an exchangeable random vector for any positive integer n. Then*

$$\frac{1}{n+1}\sum_{i=1}^{n+1} X_i \leq_{cx} \frac{1}{n}\sum_{i=1}^{n} X_i, \tag{5.33}$$

Proof. For notational brevity, we write $\overline{X}^{(n)} := (1/n)\sum_{i=1}^{n} X_i$ for any positive integer n. Observe that, due to the exchangeability, for any arbitrary $i, j = 1, 2, \cdots, n$,

$$\mathbb{E}\left[X_i|\overline{X}^{(n)}\right] = \mathbb{E}\left[X_j|\overline{X}^{(n)}\right].$$

Therefore,

$$\mathbb{E}\left[X_i|\overline{X}^{(n)}\right] = \frac{1}{n}\sum_{j=1}^{n}\mathbb{E}\left[X_j|\overline{X}^{(n)}\right] = \overline{X}^{(n)}.$$

This also implies that

$$\mathbb{E}\left[\overline{X}^{(n-1)}\Big|\overline{X}^{(n)}\right] = \frac{1}{n-1}\sum_{i=1}^{n-1}\mathbb{E}\left[X_i|\overline{X}^{(n)}\right] = \overline{X}^{(n)}.$$

The convex order (5.33) follows immediately from Theorem 5.37. □

The TVaR of the sample mean of exchangeable random vectors decreases with the sample size, which can be translated as "diversification reduces risk".

Corollary 5.42. *Let $(X_1, X_2, \cdots, X_{n+1})$ be an exchangeable random vector for any positive integer n. Then, for any $p \in (0, 1)$,*

$$\mathrm{TVaR}_p\left[\frac{1}{n+1}\sum_{i=1}^{n+1} X_i\right] \leq \mathrm{TVaR}_p\left[\frac{1}{n}\sum_{i=1}^{n} X_i\right]. \tag{5.34}$$

5.4.3 Law of large numbers for equity-linked insurance

5.4.3.1 Individual model vs. aggregate model

In this section, we take the guaranteed minimum maturity benefit (GMMB) as a model example to show the diversification of mortality risk. However, as shown in Feng and Shimizu [45], similar results can also be obtained for all other types of equity-linked insurance introduced in Chapter 1.

Recall from Section 1.2.3 that the individual net liability of the GMMB is defined to be the present value of future outgo less the present value of future income on a stand-alone contract basis. Unlike standardized exchange-traded financial derivatives with unit contract sizes, variable annuities are sold to individual investors as a retirement planning vehicle. Individuals may choose to purchase annuities with different payments. To introduce an aggregate model, let us re-formulate the individual net liability so as to distinguish different policies in a large pool.

We can write the individual net liability of the GMMB rider for the i-th policyholder where $i = 1, 2, \cdots, n$ as

$$L(T_x^{(i)}) := e^{-rT}(G^{(i)} - F_T^{(i)})_+ I(T_x^{(i)} > T) - \int_0^{T \wedge T_x^{(i)}} e^{-rs} m_e F_s^{(i)} \, \mathrm{d}s, \quad (5.35)$$

where

- $T_x^{(i)}$ – the future lifetime of the i-th policyholder of age x at issue;

- $F_0^{(i)}$ – the initial purchase payment of the i-th policyholder;

- $F_t^{(i)} := e^{-mt} F_0^{(i)} S_t / S_0$ – the evolution of the i-th policyholder's investment account;

- $G^{(i)} := \gamma F_0^{(i)}$ – the guaranteed minimum amount at maturity for the i-th policyholder, where γ determines the guaranteed amount $G^{(i)}$ as a percentage of the i-th policyholder's initial purchase payment.

Then the *aggregate net liability* of the GMMB rider for all n policies is determined by

$$\sum_{i=1}^n L(T_x^{(i)}) = \sum_{i=1}^n e^{-rT}(G^{(i)} - F_T^{(i)})_+ I(T_x^{(i)} > T) - \sum_{i=1}^n \int_0^T e^{-rt} m_e F_t^{(i)} I(T_x^{(i)} > t) \, \mathrm{d}t.$$

While we are interested in the tail risk of the aggregate net liability, it is clear that the total liability scales up with the size of the policy pool. To consider the diversification effect, we need to "normalize" the total liability by introducing the *average net liability*

$$\overline{L}^{(n)} := \frac{1}{n} \sum_{i=1}^n L(T_x^{(i)}).$$

If the individual net liabilities $(L(T_x^{(1)}), L(T_x^{(2)}), \cdots, L(T_x^{(n)}))$ are exchangeable, then it follows from Corollary 5.42 that

$$\text{TVaR}_p \left(\overline{L}^{(n+1)} \right) \leq \text{TVaR}_p \left(\overline{L}^{(n)} \right).$$

The TVaR of the average net liability is a decreasing function of the sample size n. In other words, the tail risk of average net liability can always be reduced by diversification through a large pool of policies. Furthermore, if $(L(T_x^{(1)}), L(T_x^{(2)}), \cdots, L(T_x^{(n)}))$ are independent, then the strong law of large numbers implies that as $n \to \infty$

$$\text{TVaR}_p \left[\overline{L}^{(n)} \right] \to \mathbb{E} \left[L(T_x^{(i)}) \right].$$

However, as alluded to in Section 1.4, individual net liabilities $\left(L(T_x^{(1)}), L(T_x^{(2)}), \cdots, L(T_x^{(n)}) \right)$ are not mutually independent. Nonetheless, we shall show in Theorem 5.46 that there is a limit, denoted by $\overline{L}^{(\infty)}$, such that as $n \to \infty$

$$\overline{L}^{(n)} \longrightarrow \overline{L}^{(\infty)}. \tag{5.36}$$

In Corollary 5.47, we shall prove that tail risks of averages decrease with the sample size and eventually converge to that of an average model, i.e. as $n \to \infty$,

$$\text{TVaR}_p \left(\overline{L}^{(n)} \right) \downarrow \text{TVaR}_p \left(\overline{L}^{(\infty)} \right).$$

In other words, the uncertainty of L^* is entirely attributable to financial risk whereas the mortality risk is fully diversified.

If we know how to approximately compute the TVaR of the average net liability, then it is trivial to provide an estimate for the TVaR of the aggregate net liability for any $p \in (0, 1)$

$$\text{TVaR}_p \left[\sum_{i=1}^{n} L(T_x^{(i)}) \right] = n\text{TVaR}_p \left[\overline{L}^{(n)} \right] \approx n\text{TVaR}_p \left[\overline{L}^{(\infty)} \right].$$

In Section 5.7, an example will be provided to show how risk measures of the average net liability of the GMDB are roughly determined in practice.

5.4.3.2 Identical and fixed initial payments

Let us first consider the simple case where all initial purchase payments are fixed and exactly the same

$$F_0^{(1)} = F_0^{(2)} = \cdots = F_0^{(n)} = \cdots,$$

and hence the minimum guarantee at maturity is the same for all policies. We shall drop the subscript for $F_t^{(i)}$ and $G^{(i)}$ as they are the same for all policyholders. In other words,

$$L(T_x^{(i)}) = e^{-rT}(G - F_T^{(i)})_+ I(T_x^{(i)} > T) - \int_0^{T \wedge T_x^{(i)}} e^{-rs} m_e F_s \, ds, \tag{5.37}$$

Before we show a law of large numbers for equity-linked insurance, we digress to show an important result that is needed to derive the limit of sample means for the net liabilities.

Theorem 5.43. *(Glivenko-Cantelli Theorem) Assume that $X_1, X_2, \cdots$ are independent and identically distributed random variables with common distribution function F. Define the empirical distribution function*

$$F_n(x) = \frac{1}{n} \sum_{i=1}^{n} I(X_i \leq x).$$

Then F_n converges uniformly to F, i.e.

$$\sup_{x \in \mathbb{R}} |F_n(x) - F(x)| \longrightarrow 0 \qquad almost\ surely.$$

Note that $\{F_1(x), F_2(x), \cdots\}$ is a sequence of binomial random variables for each fixed $x \in \mathbb{R}$. We know from the law of large numbers (Theorem 1.1) that, as $n \to \infty$, for all $x \in \mathbb{R}$,

$$F_n(x) \longrightarrow \mathbb{E}[F_n(x)] = F(x).$$

Glivenko-Cantelli theorem extends this result further and shows convergence in a stronger sense.

Theorem 5.44. *Assume that (i) all initial purchase payments are of equal size and their growths are driven by the same fund $\{F_t : t \geq 0\}$; (ii) the future lifetimes of policyholders are independent and identically distributed; (iii) $\int_0^T |e^{-rs} F_s|\, ds < \infty$ almost surely. Then the convergence in (5.36) is true almost surely where*

$$
\begin{aligned}
\overline{L}^{(\infty)} &:= \mathbb{E}\left[L(T_x^{(i)}) \middle| \mathcal{F}_T \right] \\
&= {}_T p_x e^{-rT} (G - F_T)_+ - \int_0^T {}_s p_x e^{-rs} m_e F_s\, ds. \quad (5.38)
\end{aligned}
$$

Proof. Recall that

$$\frac{1}{n} \sum_{i=1}^{n} L(T_x^{(i)}) := e^{-rT}(G - F_T)_+ \bar{I}_n^x(T) - \int_0^T e^{-rs} m_e F_s \bar{I}_n^x(s)\, ds,$$

where $\bar{I}_n^x$ is the empirical survival function given by

$$\bar{I}_n^x(t) := \frac{1}{n} \sum_{i=1}^{n} I(T_x^{(i)} > t).$$

Since $T_x^{(i)}$ $(i = 1, \ldots, n)$ are i.i.d., it follows from the *Glivenko-Cantelli theorem* that, for almost every $\omega \in \Omega$,

$$\left| \int_0^T e^{-rs} m_e F_s \bar{I}_n^x(s) \, ds - \int_0^T e^{-rs} m_e F_s \, {}_s p_x \, ds \right|$$

$$\leq \sup_{s \in [0,T]} |\bar{I}_n^x(s) - {}_s p_x| m_e \int_0^T |e^{-rs} F_s| \, ds \to 0,$$

almost surely, if $\int_0^T |e^{-rs} F_s| \, ds < \infty$ almost surely.   □

Remark 5.45. Observe that there are two sources of randomness, namely $T_x^{(i)}$ and $\{F_t : t \geq 0\}$ in the formulation of net liability in (5.37), whereas only financial risk is present in the formulation of net liability in (5.38). The disappearance of $T_x^{(i)}$ is owing to the full diversification of mortality risk. In other words, there is no uncertainty with respect to the timing of payments due to policyholder's survivorship in (5.38), but rather the average contract size shrinks in a deterministic fashion according to the survival function of mortality.

5.4.3.3   Identically distributed initial payments

As pointed out earlier, part (i) of Proposition 5.44 does not hold true in practice. A more realistic assumption on policies with different contract sizes is to randomize the initial payments. That is to say, without any a priori knowledge of particular policyholders, we assume that their contributions all come from a general distribution of a "random generator" determined by social economic development of the general population. Even though policyholders come in with different initial payments, their payment sizes are drawn from the same "random generator".

Theorem 5.46. *Suppose that (i) $F_0^{(i)}$, $(i = 1, \ldots, n)$ are i.i.d., independent of $T_x^{(i)}$; (ii) the future lifetimes of policyholders are independent and identically distributed; (iii) $\int_0^T |e^{-rs} F_s| \, ds < \infty$ almost surely; (iv) $\bar{F}_0 := \mathbb{E}[F_0^{(i)}] < \infty$. Then the average of liabilities converges almost surely:*

$$\lim_{n \to \infty} \frac{1}{n} \sum_{i=1}^n L(T_x^{(i)}) = \bar{L}^{(\infty)},$$

where

$$\bar{L}^{(\infty)} := e^{-rT}(\gamma \bar{F}_0 - \bar{F}_T)_+ \, {}_T p_x - \int_0^T e^{-rt} \, {}_t p_x m_e \bar{F}_t \, dt \tag{5.39}$$

with

$$\bar{F}_t := e^{-mt} \bar{F}_0 S_t / S_0.$$

Corollary 5.47. *Under the assumptions of Proposition 5.46, for all $p \in (0,1)$,*

$$\lim_{n \to \infty} \text{TVaR}_p\left[\bar{L}^{(n)}\right] = \text{TVaR}_p\left[\bar{L}^{(\infty)}\right]. \tag{5.40}$$

5.4.3.4 Other equity-linked insurance products

The general results of equity-linked insurance are more complex to state in a rigorous manner. Nonetheless, we can illustrate the general principle of such laws of large numbers.

Suppose that $L(T_x^{(i)})$ represents the individual net liability over the time horizon $[t, T]$ of any equity-linked insurance on a contract with the i-th policyholder and that the vector $(L(T_x^{(1)}), L(T_x^{(2)}), \cdots, L(T_x^{(n)}))$ are exchangeable. The evolution of equity index and other investment returns are all driven by stochastic processes defined on a general probability space $(\Omega, \mathbb{P}, \{\mathcal{F}_t\})$. If the future lifetimes of all policyholders and purchase payments are all i.i.d., then we can expect that, as the sample size $n \to \infty$, the average net liability converges almost surely

$$\overline{L}^{(n)} = \frac{1}{n} \sum_{i=1}^{n} L(T_x^{(i)}) \longrightarrow \overline{L}^{(\infty)} := \mathbb{E}\left[L(T_x^{(i)}) \middle| \mathcal{F}_T \right].$$

While this principle is not explicitly stated, it is used widely in the insurance literature and industrial practice. For example, in the framework of Gaillardetz and Lakhmiri [52], equity-indexed annuities under consideration can provide both death and survival benefits, for which the present value of payoffs can be written as

$$L^{(i)} := e^{-r(T_x^{(i)} \wedge T)} D(T_x^{(i)} \wedge T),$$

with $D(t)$ representing product features which may vary from company to company. The point-to-point index crediting option with capped and floored interests can be written as

$$D(t) = \max\left\{ \min\left[1 + \alpha\left(\frac{S_t}{S_0} - 1 \right), (1 + \eta)^t \right], \beta(1 + g)^t \right\},$$

where α is known as the participation rate and determines the percentage of profit sharing with policyholders, β represents the percentage of the initial premium that is guaranteed to receive the minimum return of g per dollar, η provides a upper bound on credited interests. sWe can expect from the law of large numbers for equity-linked insurance that as $n \to \infty$,

$$\bar{L}^n \longrightarrow \int_0^T e^{-rt} D(t) \, {}_t p_x \, \mathrm{d}t + e^{-rT} \, {}_T p_x D(T), \qquad \text{almost surely.}$$

5.5 Risk engineering of variable annuity guaranteed benefits

The risk management of equity-linked insurance is as much an art as a science. It can be a fairly complex system with financial arrangements between multiple parties in the insurance market or more broadly the financial industry. As described in the

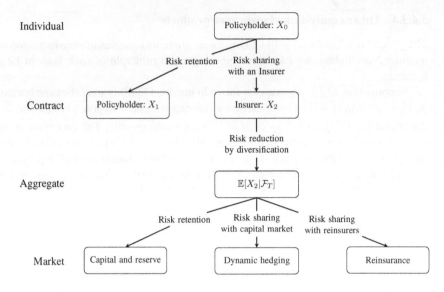

FIGURE 5.13: Risk management techniques embedded in equity-linked insurance

beginning of this chapter, three most important tools of risk management, namely, risk reduction, risk sharing, risk retention, are present for different participants at various levels of product design and development.

Take the guaranteed minimum maturity benefit as an example. There are two parties involved at the individual contract level – a policyholder and an insurer underwriting the variable annuity contract. There are two types of risks associated with the contract – equity risk and mortality risk. Consider a policyholder's investment in two cases.

- Without investment guarantee

  Had a policyholder not purchased variable annuity, he or she would use the initial purchase payment F_0 to buy equity directly and hence be completely exposed to the equity risk with the uncertainty of financial returns. For easy comparison, we shall use the same notation as in earlier chapters with variable annuity modeling. With an analogy to (1.22), an investment without any guarantee will end up at time T with

  $$F_0 \frac{S_T}{S_0} = F_T e^{mT},$$

  or written in terms of time-0 value as the risk $X_0 := F_T e^{-(r-m)T}$. Here we assume that the original investment of F_0 in equity can continue with a heir of the policyholder until time T.

- With investment guarantee

  In contrast, the equity risk is shared between the policyholder and the insurer once a contract with the GMMB rider is in force. The policyholder or beneficiary (heir) is now entitled to the balance in the sub-account and additional guarantee benefit in time-0 value

  $$X_1 := e^{-rT} \max\{F_T, G\} I(T_x \geq T) + e^{-rT_x} F_{T_x} I(T_x < T),$$

  whereas the insurer collects equity-linked fees and covers the downside of equity risk

  $$X_2 := \int_0^{T \wedge T_x} e^{-rs} m_e F_s \, ds - e^{-rT}(G - F_T)_+ I(T_x > T).$$

  Note that with the variable annuity contract the split of risk is complicated by the additional uncertainty with the policyholder's mortality risk.

- Equivalence

  We shall demonstrate below that the split of risks is justifiable in the sense that the combination of the risk retained by the policyholder and the risk ceded to the insurer is equivalent to the original equity risk. In other words, under a risk-neutral measure $\tilde{\mathbb{P}}$

  $$\tilde{\mathbb{E}}[X_0] = \tilde{\mathbb{E}}[X_1] + \tilde{\mathbb{E}}[X_2]. \tag{5.41}$$

  Although this result holds true in more general model setting, we shall only provide the proof for the Black-Scholes model where the dynamics of the policyholder's sub-account is driven by (2.45). On the left hand side of (5.41), it follows from Exercise 4.5.1 that

  $$\tilde{\mathbb{E}}[X_0] = F_0.$$

  In view of the fact that $\max\{F_T, G\} - (G - F_T)_+ = F_T$, we must have that

  $$X_1 + X_2 = e^{-r(T \wedge T_x)} F_{T \wedge T_x} + \int_0^{T \wedge T_x} e^{-rs} m_e F_s \, ds.$$

  Using arguments similar to those in Section 4.7.4.3, we can show that

  $$\tilde{\mathbb{E}}\left[e^{-r(T \wedge T_x)}\right] = F_0 - \tilde{\mathbb{E}}\left[\int_0^{T \wedge T} e^{-rs} m F_s \, ds\right].$$

  Therefore, on the right hand side of (5.41), we also have

  $$\tilde{\mathbb{E}}[X_1 + X_2] = F_0,$$

  which proves the identity (5.41) for the decomposition of risks on an individual contract.

  As the insurance product is designed to transfer certain amount of equity and mortality risks from individual policyholders to the insurer, the risks from individual contracts are pooled together in the insurer's "melting pot", otherwise known as a line of business. As explained in Section 5.4.3, the insurer's average liability at the corporate level is in essence a conditional expectation of its individual liability at the contract level. It is also know that the tail risk of the average liability is reduced compared with that of the individual liability due to the diversification of mortality risk, i.e., for any $p \in (0, 1)$,

$$\text{TVaR}_p \left[\tilde{\mathbb{E}}[-X_2 | \mathcal{F}_T] \right] \leq \text{TVaR}_p \left[-X_2 \right].$$

The remaining undiversifiable aggregate risk is then processed in three ways. As described in Section 5.1, the insurer may choose to retain the aggregate risk by the traditional approach of setting up reserves and capitals. Under adverse circumstances, the insurer can use reserves and capitals to absorb losses from underwriting the risks. Another common approach, which we shall discuss in more details in Section 6.2, is to set up a hedging program to offset losses. Under this approach, the aggregate risk is effectively transferred to the capital market. The third approach is for the insurer to enter into a reinsurance contract, which effectively further splits the aggregate risk between the insurer and its reinsurer.

5.6   Capital allocation

Overall capital is often determined at the corporate level by the process of risk aggregation, as described in Section 5.2. Capital allocation refers to the process of dividing overall capital to more granular levels of the business. For example, to provide incentives for areas of potential growth, management may develop a mechanism to allocate large capital to units with high risk and small capital to units with little uncertainty. For insurance companies, allocation may also be needed for reserves and other resources. As shown as an example in Section 5.7, it is a statutory requirement to allocate reserves to policies for tax purposes. The decision-making process behind allocation can be quite complex in practice, taking into account risk management policies, regulatory requirements, internal performance measures, etc. In this section, we provide an introduction to a few common approaches based on simple quantitative methods.

Definition 5.48. An *allocation principle* is a mapping from a random vector $(X_1, X_2, \cdots, X_n)$ to a real-valued vector $(K_1, K_2, \cdots, K_n)$ such that the sum $K_1 + K_2 + \cdots + K_n = K$ for a given total amount K.

Sometimes the total amount of allocation is determined by a risk measure of the aggregate risk, i.e. $K = \rho(S)$ where $S = X_1 + \cdots + X_n$. A naive choice of allocation may be based on the risk measure of individual risk,

$$K_i = \rho(X_i).$$

However, such an allocation lacks the additivity. For example, if ρ is a coherent risk measure, then

$$K \leq K_1 + K_2 + \cdots + K_n.$$

To provide a remedy for additivity, we consider two sets of principles known in practice and in the literature.

5.6.1 Pro-rata principle

It is a common practice to measure stand-alone risks by risk measures such as VaR and TVaR. In line with such a practice, a simple allocation method is to split the overall capital among individual risks in proportion to their stand-alone risk measures.

(**Allocation by proportion**) Given any risk measure ρ and the total amount K, the allocation to the i-th risk is given by

$$K_i = \frac{\rho(X_i)}{\sum_{i=1}^{n} \rho(X_i)} K. \tag{5.42}$$

Haircut allocation principle: A common choice of risk measure in (5.42) for capital requirement is

$$\rho(X_i) = \mathrm{VaR}_p(X_i).$$

While this principle is straightforward and easy to implement, a disadvantage is that it does not depend on the dependence among risks and hence ignores any diversification effect.

Quantile allocation principle: If the overall capital is set at $K = \mathrm{VaR}_p(S)$, then the capital offers a level of security that it is sufficient to absorb losses with the probability p. However, with the haircut allocation principle, it is unclear at what level of security the allocated capital K_i offers to cover the i-th risk. The quantile allocation principle is based on the idea of dividing capital to offer equal level of security for all risks. Here we describe the quantile allocation principle with the assumption that all risks are represented by continuous random variables, although it can be extended for all random variables with some technical nuances. The objective is to set the allocated amount for each risk by the same risk measure at the same probability level, i.e.

$$K_i = \mathrm{VaR}_{\beta p}(X_i),$$

where β is to be determined so that $\sum_{i=1}^{n} K_i = K = \mathrm{VaR}_p(S)$.

(**Allocation by marginal contribution**) Given any risk measure ρ and the total amount K, the allocation to the i-th risk is given by

$$K_i = \frac{\rho_i^m}{\sum_{i=1}^n \rho_i^m} K, \qquad (5.43)$$

where

$$\rho_i^m = \rho(S) - \rho(S - X_i).$$

We shall illustrate calculations under the various capital allocation principles introduced earlier with a concrete example.

Example 5.49. Suppose that an insurer possesses a portfolio of n risks with which the potential losses follow a multi-dimensional normal distribution, i.e.

$$\mathbf{X} = (X_1, X_2, \cdots, X_N)^\top \sim N(\mu, \Sigma),$$

where we denote $\mu_i = \mathbb{E}[X_i]$, $\sigma_i{}^2 = \mathbb{V}[X_i]$, and r_{ij} is the correlation coefficient of X_i and X_j, $\mu = (\mu_1, \mu_2, \cdots, \mu_N)^\top$ and $\Sigma = (r_{ij}\sigma_i\sigma_j)_{i,j}$.

In the case of multivariate normal risks, we can compute the distribution of aggregate risk $S = \sum_{i=1}^n X_i = \mathbf{1}^\top \mathbf{X}$, where $\mathbf{1}$ is a column vector of ones with size n. We know from elementary probability class that any linear combination of normal random variables still follows normal distribution. Hence, it suffices to compute $\mathbb{E}[S]$ and $\mathbb{V}[S]$ to determine its distribution. Therefore, S is a normal random variable with

$$\mu_S := \mathbb{E}[S] = \mathbb{E}[\mathbf{1}^\top \mathbf{X}] = \mathbf{1}^\top \mathbb{E}[\mathbf{X}] = \mathbf{1}^\top \mu = \sum_{i=1}^n \mu_i$$

$$\sigma_S^2 := \mathbb{V}[S] = \mathbb{V}[\mathbf{1}^\top \mathbf{X}] = \mathbf{1}^\top \mathbb{V}[\mathbf{X}]\mathbf{1} = \mathbf{1}^\top \Sigma \mathbf{1} = \sum_{i=1}^n \sum_{j=1}^n r_{ij}\sigma_i\sigma_j.$$

Now consider the situation where the insurer is required to set aside a total capital based on VaR risk measure of its aggregate risk, i.e.

$$K = \mathrm{VaR}_p[S] = \mu_S + \sigma_S \Phi^{-1}(p).$$

The question is how to distribute the total capital to individual risks in an objective way. We can work out the allocations based on various principles.

Allocation by Proportion - Haircut Allocation Principle

In view of (5.2) and (5.42),

$$\begin{aligned}
K_i :&= \frac{\rho(X_i)}{\sum_{i=1}^n \rho(X_i)} K = \frac{\mathrm{VaR}_p[X_i]}{\sum_{i=1}^n \mathrm{VaR}_p[X_i]} K \\
&= \frac{\sigma_i \Phi^{-1}(p) + \mu_i}{(\sum_{j=1}^n \sigma_j)\Phi^{-1}(p) + (\sum_{j=1}^n \mu_j)} K.
\end{aligned}$$

As we pointed out earlier, this allocation principle does not depend on the dependence among risks and hence ignores any diversification effect.

Allocation by Proportion - Quantile Allocation Principle

By definition, to guarantee the equal level of safety for all risks, there must exist a percentage β such that

$$K_i = VaR_{\beta p}[X_i] = \mu_i + \sigma_i \Phi^{-1}(\beta p) \text{ and } \sum_{i=1}^{n} K_i = K = \mu_S + \sigma_S \Phi^{-1}(p).$$

To solve for β, we note that

$$\Phi^{-1}(\beta p) = \frac{\sigma_S}{\sum_{i=1}^{n} \sigma_i} \Phi^{-1}(p),$$

which implies that

$$\beta = \frac{1}{p} \Phi \left(\frac{\sigma_S}{\sum_{i=1}^{n} \sigma_i} \Phi^{-1}(p) \right).$$

In general, as long as $p \geq 1/2$, since

$$\sigma_S^2 = \sum_{i=1}^{n} \sum_{j=1}^{n} r_{ij} \sigma_i \sigma_j \leq \left(\sum_{i=1}^{n} \sigma_i \right)^2 = \sum_{i=1}^{n} \sum_{j=1}^{n} \sigma_i \sigma_j,$$

we must have

$$\beta \leq \frac{1}{p} \Phi(\Phi^{-1}(p)) = 1,$$

which means that the level of security with the aggregate risk is always no less than that with individual risks. In other words, such an allocation principle takes into account diversification effect among individual normal risks when $p \geq 1/2$. This is not surprising due to the fact that VaR is indeed subadditive for normal risks when $p \geq 1/2$. (Exercise 5.6.3) However, when $p < 1/2$, it is easy to see that

$$\beta > \frac{1}{p} \Phi(\Phi^{-1}(p)) = 1,$$

which means that the level of security with the aggregate risk is less than that with individual risks. In other words, under such an allocation principal, the capital requirement for the aggregate risk is higher than the sum of those for individual risks treated separately.

Allocation by Marginal Contribution

First, note that $S - X_i = \sum_{j \neq i} X_j$. Therefore, $S - X_i$ follows a normal distribution with mean $\mu_{S-X_i} = \sum_{j \neq i} \mu_j$ and variance $\sigma_{S-X_i}^2 = \sum_{k \neq i, l \neq i} r_{kl} \sigma_k \sigma_l$. Hence, $\rho(S - X_i) = VaR_p[S - X_i] = \mu_{S-X_i} + \sigma_{S-X_i} \Phi^{-1}(p)$ and

$$\rho^m(X_i) = \rho(S) - \rho(S - X_i) = \mu_i + \left(\sqrt{\sum_{k,l} r_{kl} \sigma_k \sigma_l} - \sqrt{\sum_{k \neq i, l \neq i} r_{kl} \sigma_k \sigma_l} \right) \Phi^{-1}(p).$$

It follows from (5.43) that

$$K_i := \frac{\rho^m(X_i)}{\sum_{i=1}^{n} \rho^m(X_i)} K$$

$$= \frac{\mu_i + \left(\sqrt{\sum_{k,l} r_{kl}\sigma_k\sigma_l} - \sqrt{\sum_{k\neq i, l\neq i} r_{kl}\sigma_k\sigma_l}\right)\Phi^{-1}(p)}{\sum_{i=1}^{n} \mu_i + \left(n\sqrt{\sum_{k,l} r_{kl}\sigma_k\sigma_l} - \sum_{i=1}^{n}\sqrt{\sum_{k\neq i, l\neq i} r_{kl}\sigma_k\sigma_l}\right)\Phi^{-1}(p)} K$$

5.6.2 Euler principle

The Euler's principle follows the same line of logic as the allocation by marginal contribution. The key difference is that the former measures the marginal contribution by the rate of change with the exposure to a particular risk whereas the latter measures the marginal contribution by incremental change with the addition of a full unit of risk.

> **(Euler allocation)** Given any positive homogeneous risk measure ρ for which $\rho[S + hX_i]$ is differentiable with respect to h for all $i = 1, \cdots, n$ and the total amount $K = \rho[S]$, the allocation to the i-th risk is given by
>
> $$K_i = \left. \frac{\partial\rho[S + hX_i]}{\partial h} \right|_{h=0}. \tag{5.44}$$

The Euler principle is based on the Euler's theorem for homogeneous functions, which we shall illustrate here. Suppose that ρ is positively homogeneous and $\rho(\lambda)$ is differentiable with respect to $\lambda \in \mathbb{R}$. Define a multivariate function

$$f(\mathbf{c}) = \rho(c_1 X_1 + c_2 X_2 + \cdots + c_n X_n),$$

where the vector $\mathbf{c} = (c_1, \cdots, c_n)$ represents numbers of units invested in all n risks. It is clear that $f(\mathbf{1}) = S$ for the vector of 1's of dimension n. Since ρ is positively homogeneous, then for any $\lambda > 0$,

$$f(\lambda\mathbf{c}) = \lambda f(\mathbf{c}).$$

Euler's theorem for homogeneous function implies that

$$f(\mathbf{c}) = \sum_{i=1}^{n} c_i \frac{\partial f(\mathbf{c})}{\partial c_i}. \tag{5.45}$$

Here we provide a simple proof of (5.45). On one hand, we apply positive homogeneity to show that

$$\frac{\mathrm{d}}{\mathrm{d}\lambda} f(\lambda\mathbf{c}) = \frac{\mathrm{d}}{\mathrm{d}\lambda} \lambda f(\mathbf{c}) = \rho[c_1 X_1 + c_2 X_2 + \cdots + c_n X_n]. \tag{5.46}$$

On the other hand, we use the differentiability of f and obtain

$$\frac{d}{d\lambda}f(\lambda\mathbf{c}) = \sum_{i=1}^{n} c_i \frac{\partial}{\partial(\lambda c_i)} f(\lambda\mathbf{c}) = \sum_{i=1}^{n} c_i \frac{\partial}{\partial c_i} f(\mathbf{c}). \tag{5.47}$$

Equating both (5.46) and (5.47) gives the identity (5.45). Setting $\mathbf{c} = \mathbf{1}$ gives the Euler's allocation principle

$$\rho[S] = \sum_{i=1}^{n} \left. \frac{\partial\rho[X_1 + \cdots + c_i X_i + \cdots + X_n]}{\partial c_i} \right|_{c_i=1} = \sum_{i=1}^{n} \left. \frac{\partial\rho[S + hX_i]}{\partial h} \right|_{h=0}.$$

It may be difficult sometimes to determine an explicit expression for K_i in (5.44), in which case the finite difference approximation may be used.

$$\left. \frac{\partial\rho[S + hX_i]}{\partial h} \right|_{h=0} \approx \frac{\rho[S + hX_i] - \rho[S]}{h},$$

where h is a suitable choice of small number. Keep in mind that risk measures are often estimated from Monte Carlo simulations. If h is too small, then the ratio may not be accurate due to sampling errors of estimators. If h is too large, then the finite difference may not be a good approximation of the derivative.

Example 5.50. (Value-at-Risk) It can be shown (Exercise 5.6.1) that for any continuous random variables X and S,

$$\frac{\partial}{\partial h}\mathrm{VaR}_p[S + hX] = \mathbb{E}[X|S + hX = \mathrm{VaR}_p[S + hX]]. \tag{5.48}$$

Suppose that the total amount of capital requirement is determined by

$$K = \mathrm{VaR}_p[S],$$

for some $p \in (0, 1)$, and that all risks and the aggregate risk are continuous random variables. Now we can use Euler's principle to allocate the total capital among all individual risks. Since VaR is positively homogeneous, then we can use (5.48) to determine the Euler allocation for the i-th risk

$$K_i = \mathbb{E}[X_i|S = \mathrm{VaR}_p[S]].$$

It is easy to see that

$$\sum_{i=1}^{n} K_i = \sum_{i=1}^{n} \mathbb{E}[X_i|S = \mathrm{VaR}_p[S]] = \mathrm{VaR}_p[S] = K.$$

Example 5.51. (Tail Value-at-Risk) It can be shown (Exercise 5.6.1) that for any continuous random variables X and S,

$$\frac{\partial}{\partial h}\mathrm{TVaR}_p[S + hX] = \mathbb{E}[X|S + hX \geq \mathrm{VaR}_p[S + hX]]. \tag{5.49}$$

Suppose that the total amount of capital requirement is determined by

$$K = \text{TVaR}_p[S],$$

for some $p \in (0,1)$, and that all risks and the aggregate risk are continuous random variables. In view of (5.49), we can determine the allocation for the i-th risk is given by

$$K_i = \mathbb{E}[X_i | S \geq \text{VaR}_p[S]].$$

It is easy to see that

$$\sum_{i=1}^n K_i = \sum_{i=1}^n \mathbb{E}[X_i | S \geq \text{VaR}_p[S]] = \mathbb{E}[S | S \geq \text{VaR}_p[S]] = K.$$

Example 5.52. We can now apply Euler allocation principles to the problem of multivariate normal risks in Example 5.49.

Euler Allocation Principle with VaR

Under Euler allocation principle with Value-at-Risk as the underlying risk measure, we know that $K_i = \mathbb{E}[X_i | S = \text{VaR}_p[S]]$. Recall from (2.8.2) that for any two normal random variables X_1, X_2 with mean μ_1, μ_2, variance σ_1^2, σ_2^2 and correlation coefficient r, the distribution of X_1 conditioning on $X_2 = x_2$ is also normal with

$$X_1 | X_2 = x_2 \sim N\left(\mu_1 + r\frac{\sigma_1}{\sigma_2}(x_2 - \mu_2), \sigma_1^2(1 - r^2)\right).$$

Observe that $\mathbb{C}[X_i, S] = \mathbb{C}[X_i, \sum_j X_j] = \sum_j \mathbb{C}[X_i, X_j] = \sum_j r_{ij}\sigma_i\sigma_j$. It follows that

$$K_i = \mathbb{E}[X_i | S = \text{VaR}_p[S]] = \mathbb{E}[X_i] + \frac{\mathbb{C}[X_i, S]}{\mathbb{V}[S]}(\text{VaR}_p[S] - \mathbb{E}[S])$$

$$= \mu_i + \frac{\sum_j r_{ij}\sigma_i\sigma_j}{\sqrt{\sum_{i,j} r_{ij}\sigma_i\sigma_j}}\Phi^{-1}(p).$$

Also note that the total capital is indeed the sum of allocations to individual risks,

$$K = \sum_{i=1}^n K_i = \text{VaR}_p[S] = \mu_s + \sigma_S \Phi^{-1}(p).$$

Euler Allocation Principle with TVaR

It follows from Exercises 5.6.4 and 5.2.4 that

$$
\begin{aligned}
K_i &= \mathbb{E}[X_i|S \geq \mathrm{VaR}_p[S]] = \frac{1}{1-p} \int_{\mathrm{VaR}_p[S]}^{+\infty} \mathbb{E}[X_i|S=s] f_S(s) \, \mathrm{d}s \\
&= \frac{1}{\mathbb{P}(S \geq \mathrm{VaR}_p[S])} \int_{VaR_p[S]}^{+\infty} \left(\mu_i + \frac{\mathbb{C}[X_i, S]}{\sigma_S^2}(s - \mu_S) \right) f_S(s) ds \\
&= \mu_i + \frac{Cov[X_i, S]}{\sigma_S^2}(\mathrm{TVaR}_p[S] - \mu_S) = \mu_i + \frac{\mathbb{C}[X_i, S]}{(1-p)\sigma_S}\phi(\Phi^{-1}(p)) \\
&= \mu_i + \frac{\sum_j r_{i.j}\sigma_i\sigma_j}{(1-p)\sqrt{\sum_{i,j} r_{i,j}\sigma_i\sigma_j}}\phi(\Phi^{-1}(p)).
\end{aligned}
$$

Note that in this case the total capital is also the sum of allocations,

$$
K = \sum_{i=1}^{n} K_i = \mu_S + \frac{\sigma_S}{1-p}\phi(\Phi^{-1}(p)) = \mathrm{TVaR}_p[S] = K.
$$

5.7 Case study: stochastic reserving

In this section, we shall illustrate the implementation of risk aggregation and allocation methods with a practical example. While we present it as a procedure of stochastic reserving, RBC requirements of C-3a and C-3c risks are determined in a very similar way in practice.

For many years, regulators and the insurance industry in the U.S. have struggled with the issue of applying a uniform reserve standard for variable annuity products, which involve significantly higher market risks than traditional life insurance products due to the complex guaranteed benefit riders. After years of deliberation, the American Academy of Actuaries (AAA) proposed in 2008 Actuarial Guideline XLIII (AG-43), which essentially established a new industrial standard of reserving based on stochastic modeling and simulations, replacing older guidelines based on deterministic and formula-based calculations.

Under AG-43, the AAA provides a set of pre-packaged economic scenarios for equity returns, yield rates on government and cooperate bonds, etc. Insurance companies are permitted to run their own internal stochastic models to simulate fund performances as long as the models meet the calibration criteria set by the AAA. Examples of such pre-packaged economic scenarios as well as detailed accounts of calibration criteria can be found in [59].

While the industrial practice on reserve calculation varies greatly by product lines, and even AG-43 itself has been revised from year to year, we shall again take the minimalistic approach and only investigate the basic principles and embedded quantitative relations of essential components in the AG-43 regulation using illustrative spreadsheet calculations. For the ease of presentation, we deliberately exclude expenses, taxes, reinsurance from consideration, which are arguably critical components from a practitioner's point of view. Nevertheless, expenses are often modeled by deterministic projections and taxes often act as scaling factors, which do not significantly alter the stochastic nature of the model. Hence, we shall focus on the simplified model, although more realistic features can also be incorporated.

5.7.1   Recursive calculation of surplus/deficiency

Let us first consider the so-called **Stochastic Scenario Method** described by AG-43. We shall run cash flow analysis through a particular scenario of the underlying fund's performance on a representative single contract (also called model cell in practice). The calculations can be summarized in three sections.

Section 1: Projected values before decrements

In this example, we consider the AG-43 reserve valuation one year after the policy is issued. To shorten the presentation, we only present the first two quarters of projection in Tables 5.4 through 5.6 to illustrate the recursive relation in a typical spreadsheet calculation.

	A	B	C	D	E	F	G	H
	Proj. Year	Quarterly Contract Duration	Projected Attained Age	Annualized Gross Returns	Asset Based Charges	Quarterly Net Returns	Projected Account Values	Projected GMDB Benefit Base
1	0	4.00	71	-	-	-	2,350,000	1,850,000
2	1	4.25	71	-7.77%	2.20%	-2.54%	2,290,323	1,850,000
3	1	4.50	71	43.40%	2.20%	8.83%	2,492,556	1,850,000

TABLE 5.4: Reserve valuation method - projected values before decrements

As shown in Table 5.4, the starting account value is $2,350,000$ (cell G1) and benefit base is $1,850,000$ (cell H1). Annualized equity returns (Column D) are extracted from a simulated scenario for the whole projection period of 10 years. We only show the first two quarters as an example. For each projection period, the percentage of net returns (Column F) is calculated by the percentage of equity return less the percentage of fees and charges (Column E). Then the net returns are added to the projected account value from the previous period to produce the projected account value for the current period. For instance, the Excel function would be used to define Columns F and G: $F2 = ((1+D2) \wedge (1/360) - E2/360) \wedge (360/4) - 1, G2 =$ IF(C1 $>=$ maturity, $0, G1 * (1 + F1)$). In this case, the GMDB benefit base is assumed to remain constant. In terms of the notation introduced in the previous section, the calculations (from Columns D to G) can be characterized by the equity-linking mechanism in (1.13) and projected account values are thus described by F_t on time points $t = 4.00, 4.25, 4.50, \cdots$ and the GMDB benefit base is denoted by G.

Section 2: Projected values after decrements

Decrements due to deaths, lapses and annuitization are introduced in this part of the projection. Here, we do not consider dynamic lapses due to policyholder behavior (such as low lapse during periods of high growth and high lapse during periods of low growth), although the model can be extended to incorporate this feature. In Table 5.5, the calculations in Columns F through H can be described as follows.

Projected account value inforce = Survivorship × Projected account value = $_tp_xF_t$,

Projected benefit base inforce = Survivorship × Projected benefit base = $_tp_xG$,

Projected net amount at risk = max{0, Projected benefit base inforce

$-$Projected account value inforce} = $_tp_x(G - F_t)_+$.

A	B	C	D	E	F	G	H
Proj. Year	Quarterly Contract Duration	Quarterly Death Rate	Quarterly Lapse Annuitzn	Projected Survivor- ship	Projected Account Inforce	Projected Benefit Inforce	Projected Net Amt at Risk
0	4.00	-	-	100%	2,350,000	1,850,000	0
1	4.25	0.527%	1.535%	97.946%	2,243,285	1,850,000	0
1	4.50	0.527%	1.535%	95.935%	2,391,223	1,812,005	0

TABLE 5.5: Reserve valuation method - projected values after decrements

Section 3: Projected income statement and accumulated surplus

All incoming and outgoing cash flows are considered in the last section in order to generate the income statement based on this particular scenario. As shown in Table 5.6, the M&E charges income (Column C) is given by a quarter of the annual M&E rate ($m_d = 1.435\%$) times the mid-quarter fund value (the average of fund values from previous quarter and current quarter). The GMDB benefit (Column D) is calculated by the death rate times mid-quarter GMDB net amount at risk (the average of net amounts at risk from previous quarter and current quarter). The pre-tax income (Column F) is determined by the fee income (Column C) less the GMDB benefit (Column D) plus the investment income (Column E). In other words, if we denote the accumulated surplus by U_t, then the incremental change in the accumulated surplus is determined quarter-to-quarter by the following recursive relation:

$$\Delta U_t = U_{t+\Delta t} - U_t = m_d \Delta t \,_{t+\Delta t}p_x \frac{F_{t+\Delta t} + F_t}{2}$$
$$- \,_{\Delta t}q_{x+t}\,_tp_x \frac{(G - F_{t+\Delta t})_+ + (G - F_t)_+}{2} + r\Delta t U_t. \qquad (5.50)$$

In this example, the quarterly interest rate on surplus is $r = 1.412\%$. The investment income on surplus is typically generated from post-tax surplus. However, for simplicity, we do not distinguish the pre-tax and post-tax basis here. For the same reason, the maintenance and overhead expenses, and the surrender charges are all omitted.

	A	B	C	D	E	F	G	H
	Proj. Year	Quarterly Contract Duration	M&E Charges Income	GMDB Benefits	Investment Income on Surplus	Adjust Pre-tax Income	Pre-tax Accumulated Surplus	Present Value Surplus
1	0	4.00	-	-	-	-	-	-
2	1	4.25	8,325	0	-	8,325	8,325	8,209
3	1	4.50	8,400	0	118	8,518	16,961	15,645

TABLE 5.6: Reserve valuation method - projected income statement

In most cases, as indicated in this example, the accumulated surplus stays positive as the product is designed to be profitable. However, due to the random nature of investment return, there are extreme cases in which the accumulated surplus becomes negative and the insurer may not have sufficient funds to cover its liabilities. The measurement on the likelihood and severity of such as extreme events is in fact what the model is designed to capture for the purpose of risk management. After the income statement is generated for each scenario, the worst case present value of surplus (the smallest, sometimes negative, entry in Column H), also known as the greatest present value of accumulated deficiency (GPVAD) in AG-43, is determined and recorded. In other words, the GPVAD for each scenario is defined by

$$\mathcal{L} := - \min_{k=0,1,\cdots,n} e^{-rt_k} U_{t_k}, \tag{5.51}$$

where $\{t_0 = 0, t_1, \cdots, t_n = T\}$ are the time points of projection, which is on a quarterly basis in the spreadsheet example. Then the so-called Scenario Greatest Present Value (SGPV) is the sum of the GPVAD and the starting asset amount[*], F_0. This concludes the procedure of a single scenario calculation.

Conditional tail expectation (CTE) amount:

The single scenario procedure is repeated for 1,000-2,000 randomly generated scenarios for equity returns either from an insurance company's own internal model or the AAA pre-packaged cases. The SGPV for all scenarios are gathered and ranked to form an empirical distribution of the insurer's net liability (surplus/deficiency). In order to identify the worst $100p\%$ scenarios, practitioners first estimate the quantile risk measure, also known as value at risk in finance literature, defined for any loss random variable X as

$$\text{VaR}_p[X] := \inf\{V : \mathbb{P}(X \leq V) > p\}.$$

Observe that

$$\text{VaR}_p[\text{SGPV}] = \text{VaR}_p[\mathcal{L} + F_0] = \text{VaR}_p[\mathcal{L}] + F_0.$$

As the starting asset is a fixed amount at the valuation date, we shall only consider the

---

[*]Here we consider the policyholder invests all purchase payments in separate accounts.

GPVAD $\mathcal{L}$ without loss of generality. After obtaining the quantile risk measure, one can further determine the mean of $100(1 - p)\%$ worst scenarios by the conditional tail expectation risk measure

$$\text{CTE}_p[\mathcal{L}] := \mathbb{E}[\mathcal{L}|\mathcal{L} > \text{VaR}_p(\mathcal{L})].$$

These risk measures are usually estimated by $100(1 - p)\%$ largest order statistics and their averages in practice. Under AG-43, the **CTE amount** is determined by 70%-CTE of the SGPV.

In principle, the reserve calculation should be done on a contract-by-contract basis. However, given the large volume of contracts in their portfolios, it is considered impractical for insurance companies to carry out the procedure for all individual contracts. Therefore, AG-43 stipulated that in the calculation of CTE amount, contracts can be sub-grouped "into representative cells of model plans using all characteristics and criteria having a material impact on the size of the reserve". The practice of sub-grouping contracts with similar characteristics is effectively a reflection of risk reduction by diversification as illustrated in Figure 5.13. We shall illustrate next that the recursive calculation of surplus/deficiency can be translated to the formulation of average net liability discussed in Section 5.4.3.

5.7.2   Average net liability

Although one may not realize this, the above-mentioned spreadsheet calculation is in fact based on a difference equation from a mathematical point of view, which is concisely expressed in the recursive relation (5.50). We shall investigate the continuous-time analogue of (5.50), which defines a differential equation, for several reasons. First, bear in mind that practicing actuaries often make a compromise to use a modestly small valuation period such as a quarter in order to simplify the calculations, even though fee incomes are collected on a daily basis. Therefore, it actually makes the calculation more accurate to investigate smaller valuation periods. Second, we can use the differential equation to identify a stochastic representation of the net liability, enabling us to determine its risk measures by the connection between stochastic differential equations and partial differential equations (PDE). Third, we can make a clear comparison of the spreadsheet calculations and the individual model presented in the previous section, which sheds light on their different treatment of mortality risks.

Dividing both sides of (5.50) by Δt gives

$$\frac{U_{t+\Delta t} - U_t}{\Delta t} = m_d \; {}_{t+\Delta t}p_x \frac{F_{t+\Delta t} + F_t}{2}$$

$$- \frac{\Delta t q_{x+t}}{\Delta t} \; {}_t p_x \frac{(G - F_{t+\Delta t})_+ + (G - F_t)_+}{2} + rU_t.$$

Letting the time difference Δt (a quarter in previous example) shrink to zero yields the differential equation

$$U'_t = m_d \; {}_t p_x F_t - \mu_{x+t} \; {}_t p_x (G - F_t)_+ + rU_t. \tag{5.52}$$

Using the method of integrating factors, we obtain the following representation of the present value of the accumulated surplus for $t \in [0, T]$

$$e^{-rt}U_t = \int_0^t e^{-rs}m_d \, {}_sp_x F_s \, ds - \int_0^t e^{-rs}\mu_{x+s} \, {}_sp_x(G - F_s)_+ \, ds.$$

In other words, the present value of the accumulated deficiency up to maturity T, which we denote by $\overline{L}_T^{(\infty)}$, can be written as

$$\overline{L}_T^{(\infty)} := \int_0^T e^{-rs}\mu_{x+s} \, {}_sp_x(G - F_s)_+ \, ds - \int_0^T e^{-rs}m_d \, {}_sp_x F_s \, ds. \qquad (5.53)$$

Note that in this model the only source of randomness arises from financial returns.

Let us revisit the modeling of the GMDB rider on a contract basis in Section 1.2.5. The individual net liability of the GMDB rider for the i-th policyholder is given by

$$L(T_x^{(i)}) = e^{-rT_x^{(i)}}(G - F_{T_x^{(i)}})_+ I(T_x^{(i)} \leq T) - \int_0^{T \wedge T_x^{(i)}} e^{-rs}m_d F_s \, ds.$$

One should note that the present value of accumulated surplus up to maturity $\overline{L}^{(\infty)}$ is in fact the conditional expectation of the individual net liability $L(T_x^{(i)})$ with respect to the natural filtration of asset price process (the market information up to time T).

$$\mathbb{E}[L(T_x^{(i)})|\mathcal{F}_T]$$

$$= \int_0^T e^{-rs}(G - F_s)_+ \, d\mathbb{P}(T_x^{(i)} \in s) - \int_0^T \int_0^s e^{-ru}m_d F_u \, du \, d\mathbb{P}(T_x^{(i)} \in s)$$

$$\quad - \mathbb{P}(T_x^{(i)} > T) \int_0^T e^{-rs}m_d F_s \, ds$$

$$= \int_0^T e^{-rs} \, {}_sp_x\mu_{x+s}(G - F_s)_+ \, ds - \int_0^T ({}_up_x - {}_Tp_x) e^{-ru}m_d F_u \, du$$

$$\quad - {}_Tp_x \int_0^T e^{-rs}m_d F_s \, ds$$

$$= \int_0^T e^{-rs} \, {}_sp_x\mu_{x+s}(G - F_s)_+ \, ds - \int_0^T {}_sp_x e^{-rs}m_d F_s \, ds = \overline{L}_T^{(\infty)},$$

where we exchange the order of integration in the last equality. This result is consistent with that of the law of large numbers in Section 5.4.3.

Let us recall the distinction and connection between an individual model and an aggregate model. Suppose there are a total of n policyholders of the same age to which the same death benefit has been issued. Suppose that

1. the future lifetimes of all policyholders are mutually independent and identically distributed;

2. all contracts are of equal size*, i.e. $F_0^{(i)} = F_0^{(j)}$ for all $i, j = 1, \cdots, n$.

Then a true aggregate model for the whole block of the GMDB business is given by

$$\overline{L}_T^{(n)} := \sum_{i=1}^{n} L(T_x^{(i)}).$$

It is shown in Feng and Shimizu [46] that as $n \to \infty$,

$$\overline{L}^{(n)} \longrightarrow \overline{L}_T^{(\infty)} = \mathbb{E}[L(T_x^{(i)})|\mathcal{F}_T], \qquad \text{almost surely.} \qquad (5.54)$$

This means that when the number of i.i.d. policies is large enough, the average of the insurer's net liability for each contract is roughly the average net liability in an aggregate model.

In this continuous-time model, the greatest present value of accumulated deficiencies (GPVAD) with analogy to (5.51) is given by the running supremum of net liabilities,

$$M_T := - \inf_{0 \le t \le T} \left\{ e^{-rt} U_t \right\} = \sup_{0 \le t \le T} \left\{ \overline{L}_t^{(\infty)} \right\}. \qquad (5.55)$$

Thus, in the continuous-time model, the quantile risk measure is determined by

$$\text{VaR}_p(M_T) := \inf\{V : \mathbb{P}(M_T \le V) = p\}.$$

After obtaining the quantile risk measure, we can determine the conditional tail expectation by

$$\text{CTE}_p(M_T) := \mathbb{E}[M_T | M_T > \text{VaR}_p(M_T)].$$

5.7.3 Aggregate reserve

Aggregate reserve is in principle the total amount of reserves to be held by an insurer for its overall product portfolio in accordance with statutory standards. The **aggregate reserve** for all contracts falling within the scope of AG-43 is equal to the greater of (1) the **standard scenario amount** and (2) the **CTE amount**. The standard scenario amount is the sum of reserves determined by applying a **Standard Scenario Method** to each individual contract. The Standard Scenario Method is in essence similar to the **Stochastic Scenario Method** described above, except for some technical treatments of surrender charge amortization and that the calculations in the above-mentioned three sections are done only under a single scenario (typically sharp losses in financial return in early years and modest returns in later years), which is prescribed by the AG-43 regulation. As it does not involve any stochastic

---

*One can replace the assumption of fixed identical amount by a more relaxed assumption that (**A2'**) $F_0^{(i)}$ are i.i.d. In this case, the process $\{F_t, t \ge 0\}$ in the formulation (5.53) should be interpreted as account values of an average account and F_0 should be equal to $\mathbb{E}(F_0^{(i)})$. Then the law of large numbers (5.54) still holds in this case.

component, we do not discuss the Standard Scenario Method here in details. One should keep in mind that the main purpose of the standard scenario amount is for the regulator to put a floor on calculated reserves to prevent potential abuse of actuarial assumptions and methodology to reduce the CTE amount under stochastic projections.

For VA contracts with GMDB only, which is generally perceived as a relatively low-risk rider, a company can choose to use the **Alternative Methodology** described in AG-43 in place of the stochastic reserving approach. Since the Alternative Methodology is a factor-based formula approach, which does not involve stochastic components, we will not discuss it in this paper.

Example 5.53. Here we formulate the aggregate reserve using the example of the GMDB rider. The aggregate reserve for all VA contracts with the GMDB rider can be determined by

$$\max\{\text{SS}, \text{CTE}\},$$

where SS is the standard scenario amount at the aggregate level and CTE is the conditional tail expectation amount.

- Standard scenario amount (SS):

  Consider the model of equity index $\{S_t, t \geq 0\}$ to be defined a probability space $(\Omega, \mathbb{P}, \{\mathcal{F}_t, t \geq 0\})$. A standard scenario $\omega \in \Omega$ is specified by the regulator. For each contract, the evolution of the equity index $\{S_t(\omega) : 0 \leq t \leq T\}$ becomes a deterministic function of time t (say, 30% loss in the first three years and 5% steady returns in the next twenty-seven years). Then the standard scenario reserve (SSR) for i-th contract is determined by

  $$\text{SSR}_i := \overline{L}_T^{(\infty)}(\omega), \tag{5.56}$$

  where $\overline{L}_T^{(\infty)}$ is a random variable defined in (5.53) and $\overline{L}_T^{(\infty)}(\omega)$ is a number determined by evaluating the integrals in (5.53) with F_t replaced with deterministic function $F_t(\omega) = F_0 S_t(\omega)/S_0$ for any time $t \in [0, T]$.

- Conditional tail expectation amount (CTE):

  In consideration of a wide range of economics scenarios in addition to the standard scenario ω, insurers are required to calculate the CTE amount. To reduce computational burden, most companies sub-group contracts with similar characteristics (e.g. age of policyholder, contract size) and make stochastic projections to determine the CTE for each group. For example, we divide n contracts into m subgroups with k-th group having n_k contracts of similar characteristics. Then the CTE for the k-th group would be

  $$\text{CTE}_k := \text{TVaR}_p\left(\sum_{i=1}^{n_k} \mathbb{E}[L(T_x^{(i)})|\mathcal{F}_T]\right),$$

  where p is set at 70% by the AG-43. Since the net liabilities are typically modeled by continuous random variables, we do not distinguish CTE and TVaR for the purpose of this discussion (see Remark 5.15). If all policyholders are of similar ages and all contracts are of similar sizes and have similar features in this group, then one can expect that

$$\text{TVaR}_p \left(\sum_{i=1}^{n_k} \mathbb{E}[L^{(i)}|\mathcal{F}_T] \right) \approx \sum_{i=1}^{n_k} \text{TVaR}_p \left(\mathbb{E}[L^{(i)}|\mathcal{F}_T] \right).$$

The approximation becomes an exact identity due to the positive homogeneity of TVaR, if the policyholders are of the same age and all contracts are identical.

• Aggregation

The next step is to add up standard scenario amounts from all contracts and CTE amounts from all groups, i.e.

$$\text{SS} = \sum_{i=1}^{n} \text{SSR}_i, \qquad \text{CTE} = \sum_{k=1}^{m} \text{CTE}_k.$$

The greater of the two should be the total reserve to be held by the insurer as the statutory reserve at the aggregate level.

5.7.4 Reserve allocation

AG-43 states that the aggregate reserve shall be allocated to the contracts falling within the scope of the guideline. The allocation is done in two steps. Each step is illustrated with a numerical example from a policy practice note by the AAA [58].

The first step is to allocate the aggregate excess to the sub-grouping level. The excess of the aggregate CTE amount over the standard scenario amount is allocated, in proportion to the difference between CTE amount and standard scenario amount, only to the sub-groupings whose CTE amount is greater than standard scenario amount.

Example 5.54. for a company with three sub-groupings with the following results:

Sub-grouping i	1	2	3	Total
CTE_i	84	120	156	360
SS_i	60	135	90	285
Aggregate reserve				360
$\text{CTE}_i - \text{SS}_i$	24	-15	66	75
Allocation of excess	20	0	55	75
Aggregate	80	135	145	360

The excess of the CTE amount over the standard scenario amount is allocated in such a way that the sub-group 1 receives $75 \times 24/(24+66) = 20$ and the sub-group 2 receives $75 \times 66/(24+66) = 55$.

Formulated mathematically, the allocation to sub-groupings can be written as

$$\text{Sub-group reserve} = \text{SS}_i + \frac{\text{CTE}_i - \text{SS}_i}{\sum_{k=1}^{m} (\text{CTE}_k - \text{SS}_k)_+} (\text{CTE} - \text{SS}).$$

The second step is to allocate the allocated amount of each sub-grouping to the contract level. The excess of aggregate reserve over standard scenario amount is allocated to each contract on the basis of the difference between the standard scenario reserve and the cash surrender value on the valuation date for the contract[*]. If CSV is not defined or not available, the standard scenario reserve will be the basis of allocation.

Example 5.55. Consider a sub-group of two contracts A and B with the following data:

- The standard scenario reserve for each contract is 100 and the standard scenario amount is 200 for the sub-group.

- The CTE amount for the sub-group is 240, which is determined by stochastic projection.

- The cash surrender value for the contract A is 40, but that for the contract B is not defined/available.

The allocation basis for contract A is $60 - 40 = 20$ and for B is the same as the standard scenario reserve 100. Therefore, the excess of $240-200 = 40$ is allocated $40 \times 60/(60+100) = 15$ to A and $40 \times 100/(60+100) = 25$ to B. The reserves for A and B are $100 + 15 = 115$ and $100 + 25 = 125$, respectively.

Since it is theoretically possible to have no contracts with an excess of standard scenario reserve over cash surrender value, some actuaries deal with that situation by allocating the excess of the aggregate reserve over standard scenario amount using the standard scenario reserve as a basis.

Formulated mathematically, the allocation of reserve for the k-th sub-group to contracts can be written as

$$\text{Contract reserve} = \text{SS}_i + \frac{(\text{CSV}_i - \text{SS}_i)_+}{\sum_{i=1}^{n_k} (\text{CSV}_i - \text{SS}_i)_+} (\text{CTE}_i - \text{SS}_i)_+,$$

or if none of the contracts has an excess of standard scenario reserve over cash surrender value, then

$$\text{Contract reserve} = \text{SS}_i + \frac{\text{SS}_i}{\sum_{i=1}^{n_k} \text{SS}_i} (\text{CTE}_i - \text{SS}_i)_+.$$

---

[*]Cash surrender value is determined by the current account value less surrender charges on the valuation date.

While the purpose of this case study is to showcase risk aggregation and reserve allocation in practice, it is worthwhile to point out some potential shortcomings of the methodology. Note that the aggregate reserve is the sum of the CTE amount $(\text{CTE}_{70\%}(M_T))$ and aggregate starting asset amounts for all groups in the whole block of business, unless the standard scenario amount is greater. The allocation of aggregate reserves to individual contracts in proportion to their standard scenario amounts appears to be based on expert opinions, rather than probabilistic reasoning. Because the CTE does not have additive property, this approach of aggregating reserves from all sub-groups and then allocating to individual contracts no longer guarantees that the contract reserves are sufficient to cover the contract liabilities with the confidence level of 70%. If the purpose of reserving is to ensure the confidence level of 70% at the sub-grouping level, then the allocation of reserves to individual contracts may be unnecessarily complicated.

5.8 Bibliographic notes

Risk measure is a topic of active research in the financial literature. Many seminal works on the subject matter include coherent risk measures introduced by Artzner et al. [3], Acerbi and Tasche [1], Rockafellar and Uryasev [88], etc., distortion risk measures by Wang [105], etc. Comonotonicity is well-studied in the actuarial literature in a series of papers including Dhaene et al. [30, 29], Deelstra et al. [23], Dhaene et al. [32], Wang and Dhaene [106], etc. Classic texts on risk measures, dependence modeling and more general quantitative risk management techniques are McNeil, Frey and Embrechts [77], Denuit et al. [27], Rüschendorf [92].

This chapter touches on three main approaches of risk aggregation. The variance-covariance approach and the scenario aggregation approach are largely developed and popularized in the banking and insurance industries, whereas the model uncertainty approach is created in the academia with its limitation pointed out earlier. Readers can find out more details about variance-covariance approach in Resti and Sironi [86] and scenario aggregation approach in Farr et al. [38], Farr, Koursaris and Mennemeyer [37]. An overiew of the model uncertainty approach can be found in Embrechts, Puccetti and Rüschendorf [36].

An extensive survey and comparison of capital allocation methods can be seen in Bauer and Zanjani [8]. Many more advanced capital allocation methods can be found in Kalkbrener [68], Tsanakas and Barnett [100], Dhaene, Tsanakas, Valdez and Vanduffel [31], Bargés, Cossette and Marceau [5], Denault [26], etc.

Resources on accounting procedures and practices for equity-linked insurance include Gorski and Brown [58, 59], American Academy of Actuaries [74], National Associate of Insurance Commissioners' annual publications [81], etc. A review of actuarial guidelines and reserve valuation methods can be found in Sharp [95, 94] and a detailed mathematical formulation of quantitative principles behind the actuarial guidelines is given in Feng [39]. The distinction of individual versus aggregate models of variable annuity guaranteed benefits has been exploited in Feng and Huang [41]. A new methodology of contract sub-grouping using functional data analysis can be found in Gan and Lin [53].

Laws of large numbers have long been viewed as the fundamental theoretical underpinning of insurance business. While they have been discussed in virtually all texts of traditional insurance, few books address the issue of laws of large numbers for equity-linked insurance. A discussion of systematic versus diversifiable risks can be found in Busse, Dacorogna and Kratz [17] with detailed numerical examples. Hardy [61] was among the first to touch on the subject. The theoretical development of laws of large numbers for equity-linked insurance is introduced in Feng and Shimizu [46].

5.9 Exercises

Section 5.2

1. Show that CTE is translative, positively homogeneous and monotonic.

2. Although CTE is not subadditive in general, it is for the class of continuous random variables.

   (a) Consider a loss random variable X and any x for which $\mathbb{P}(X > x) > 0$. For any event A such that $\mathbb{P}(A) = \mathbb{P}(X > x)$. Prove that

   $$\mathbb{E}[X|A] \leq \mathbb{E}[X|X > x].$$

   (b) Note that when X is continuous we must have $\mathbb{P}(X > \text{VaR}_p[X]) = p$. Use this fact and part (a) to prove that

   $$\text{CTE}_p[X + Y] \leq \text{CTE}_p[X] + \text{CTE}_p[Y],$$

   when X, Y and $X + Y$ are all continuous random variables.

3. Show that TVaR is translative, positively homogeneous and monotonic.

4. Consider a normal random variable X with mean μ and variance σ^2. Show that

   $$\text{TVaR}_p[X] = \mu + \sigma \frac{\phi(\Phi^{-1}(p))}{1 - p}, \qquad p \in (0, 1).$$

5. Prove $\text{TVaR}_p[X + Y] \leq \text{TVaR}_p[X] + \text{TVaR}_p[Y]$ for the special case of bivariate risk (X, Y) in Example 5.13.

6. A nonnegative risk X can be decomposed to different layers. Consider a partition of $[0, \infty)$ given by $[x_0, x_1), [x_1, x_2), \ldots$, where $x_0 = 0 < x_1 < x_2 < \cdots$. Define for $i = 1, 2, \cdots$

$$X_i = \begin{cases} 0, & 0 \leq X < x_{i-1}; \\ X - x_{i-1}, & x_{i-1} \leq X < x_i; \\ x_i - x_{i-1}, & X \geq x_i. \end{cases}$$

Therefore, $X = \sum_{i=1}^{\infty} X_i$. Show that, for any distortion risk measure ρ_g, we must have

$$\rho_g[X] = \sum_{i=1}^{\infty} \rho_g[X_i].$$

7. Consider a risk measure, known as the exponential premium principle, defined by

$$\Pi_a[X] = \frac{1}{a} \log \mathbb{E}[e^{aX}]$$

for a risk X with $\mathbb{E}[e^{a_0 X}] < \infty$ for some $a_0 > 0$.

(a) Show that the premium principle $\Pi_a[X]$ is a strictly increasing function of $a \in (0, a_0]$ provided that F_X is not concentrated on a single point.

(b) $\lim_{a \to 0+} (1/a) \log \mathbb{E}[e^{aX}] = \mathbb{E}[X]$.

(c) If $\mathbb{E}[e^{aX}] < \infty$ for all $a > 0$,

$$\lim_{a \to \infty} \Pi_a[X] = F_X^{-1}(1).$$

8. Consider a risk measure, known as the absolute deviation principle, defined by

$$\Pi[X] = \mathbb{E}[X] + a\kappa_X, \qquad \kappa_X = \mathbb{E}|X - F_X^{-1}(1/2)|.$$

Show that

(a) the risk measure is positively homogenous;

(b) the risk measure is subadditive.

9. Consider a risk measure, known as the absolute deviation principle, which is defined by

$$\Pi[X] = \mathbb{E}[X] + a\kappa_X, \qquad \kappa_X = \mathbb{E}|X - F_X^{-1}(1/2)|, \qquad 0 \leq a \leq 1.$$

Show that

(a) the absolute deviation principle is a special case of the distortion risk measure ρ_g where

$$g(x) = \begin{cases} (1+a)x, & 0 \leq x < 1/2 \\ a + (1-a)x, & 1/2 \leq x \leq 1. \end{cases}$$

(b) if a non-negative risk has less than $1/2$ chance of being positive, i.e. $S_X(0) < 1/2$, then the absolute deviation principle applied to this risk reduces to the usual expected value principle

$$\Pi[X] = (1+a)\mathbb{E}[X].$$

Section 5.3

1. (consider the lower bound of TVaR of the sum of rvs.

2. Although CTE is not a coherent risk measure in general, it is subadditive for continuous random variables.

   (a) Consider a loss random variable X and any x for which $\mathbb{P}(X > x) > 0$. For any event A such that $\mathbb{P}(A) = \mathbb{P}(X > x)$. Prove that

   $$\mathbb{E}[X|A] \leq \mathbb{E}[X|X > x].$$

   (b) Note that when X is continuous we must have $\mathbb{P}(X > \mathrm{VaR}_p[X]) = p$. Use this fact and part (a) to prove that

   $$\mathrm{CTE}_p[X + Y] \leq \mathrm{CTE}_p[X] + \mathrm{CTE}_p[Y].$$

3. Show that TVaR is translative, positively homogeneous and monotonic.

4. Let X, Y be any two real-valued random variables. Denote the covariance of X and Y by $\mathbb{C}(X, Y)$ and the variance of Y by $\mathbb{V}(Y)$.

   (a) Show that the regression coefficients a_R and b_R that minimize the squared distance

   $$\mathbb{E}[(Y - (aX + b))^2]$$

   are given by

   $$a^* = \frac{\mathbb{C}[X, Y]}{\sigma^2(X)}$$
   $$b^* = \mathbb{E}[Y] - a^*\mathbb{E}[X].$$

   (b) Show that

   $$\rho(X, Y)^2 = \frac{\sigma^2(Y) - \min_{a,b} \mathbb{E}[(Y - (aX + b))^2]}{\sigma^2(Y)}.$$

   (c) Show that if X and Y are perfectly correlated, then (X, Y) must be comonotonic.

   (d) Given an example to show that the converse of part (c) is false.

5. Show that

   $$\mathrm{CTE}_p[X] = \mathrm{VaR}_p[X] + \frac{1}{\overline{F}(\mathrm{VaR}_p[X])}\mathbb{E}[(X - \mathrm{VaR}_p[X])_+].$$

   Compare this expression with (5.8) and explain why CTE agrees with TVaR for all continuous random variables.

Section 5.4

1. We can provide an alternative proof to Theorem 5.41 in the following steps.

   (a) Show that for any convex function g and $x_1, x_2, \cdots, x_{n+1} \in \mathbb{R}$,

   $$\frac{1}{n+1}\sum_{i=1}^{n+1} x_i = \frac{1}{n+1}\sum_{i=1}^{n+1}\frac{1}{n}\sum_{j=1, j\neq i}^{n+1} x_j.$$

   (b) Show that for any convex function g and $x_1, x_2, \cdots, x_n \in \mathbb{R}$,

   $$\frac{1}{n}\sum_{i=1}^{n} g(x_i) \geq g\left(\frac{1}{n}\sum_{i=1}^{n} x_i\right).$$

   (c) Show that for any exchangeable random vector $(X_1, X_2, \cdots, X_{n+1})$

   $$\mathbb{E}\left[g\left(\frac{1}{n+1}\sum_{i=1}^{n+1} X_i\right)\right] \leq \mathbb{E}\left[g\left(\frac{1}{n}\sum_{j=1}^{n} X_j\right)\right],$$

   which establishes the convex order in (5.33).

2. Let X and Y be independent random variables. Show that

   $$X\mathbb{E}[Y] \leq_{cx} XY.$$

Section 5.6

1. Show that for any continuous random variables S and X

   $$\frac{\partial}{\partial h}\mathrm{VaR}_p[S + hX] = \mathbb{E}[X|S + hX = \mathrm{VaR}_p[S + hX]].$$

2. Show that for any continuous random variables S and X

   $$\frac{\partial}{\partial h}\mathrm{TVaR}_p[S + hX] = \mathbb{E}[X|S + hX \geq \mathrm{VaR}_p[S + hX]].$$

3. Suppose that X and Y are both normally distributed. Show that for any $p \in [1/2, 1]$,

   $$\mathrm{VaR}_p[X + Y] \leq \mathrm{VaR}_p[X] + \mathrm{VaR}_p[Y].$$

4. Consider two random variables X and Y with the density function of Y denoted by f. Show that for any $t \in (-\infty, \infty)$

   $$\mathbb{E}[X|Y \geq t] = \frac{1}{\mathbb{P}(Y \geq t)}\int_t^\infty \mathbb{E}[X|Y = y]f(y)\,\mathrm{d}y.$$

6

Risk Management - Dynamic Hedging

Hedging is a trading strategy that aims to offset potential losses of a particular financial position. For example, if a financial institution sells a call option, it may hedge the position by buying a synthetic call that has almost the same cash flows. When the call option is exercised, the loss from the short position in the option can be recovered from the long position in the synthetic call. The composition of such a synthetic option is exactly the topic to be investigated in this chapter.

In general, while it can be used for speculative purposes, hedging is also considered a type of risk management, particularly in the category of risk sharing, where the underwritten risk is partially or fully transferred from a business to another party in the capital market. It is increasingly common that insurance companies develop hedging strategies to protect themselves from exposures to market and interest rate risks when underwriting equity-indexed insurance.

6.1 Discrete time hedging: binomial tree

A *replicating portfolio* for a given financial instrument is a collection of assets structured to produce the same cash flows as the financial instrument. The purpose of constructing a replicating portfolio is to determine the unknown price of the financial instrument. Since the underlying assets of a replicating portfolio are typically tradable and their prices are observable in the market, it is often argued in the no-arbitrage theory that the price of the replicated financial instrument should be the same as the value of a replicating portfolio.

In contrast, a *hedging portfolio* is constructed to reduce risk exposure of a business from a product or a portfolio. If a business underwrites a financial instrument, then it can buy other instruments with opposite cash flows to minimize the uncertainty or negative impact of losses from the underwritten contract.

While many texts do not treat these two types of portfolios separately, their technical nuances may cause confusion for beginners. Hence we take a moment to distinguish them for better clarity.

6.1.1   Replicating portfolio

The by-product of no-arbitrage pricing under the binomial tree model is the construction of replicating portfolio. Let us recapitulate how to create such a portfolio under the N-period binomial tree model in Section 4.2. Recall that the value of a replicating portfolio at the end of time n is denoted by X_n and that of the financial derivative is denoted by V_n. The portfolio starts with the initial value of the financial derivative to be replicated, $X_0 = V_0$. At the beginning of each period, time $n = 0, 1, \cdots, N - 1$, the portfolio is always rebalanced and invested in two types of assets including

- Δ_n shares of the underlying stock

- $B_n = X_n - \Delta_{n-1} S_{n-1}$ in the money market account

where Δ_n is determined for $n = 1, 2, \cdots, N - 1$ by

$$\Delta_n(\omega_1 \cdots \omega_n) = \frac{V_{n+1}(\omega_1 \cdots \omega_n H) - V_{n+1}(\omega_1 \cdots \omega_n T)}{S_{n+1}(\omega_1 \cdots \omega_n H) - S_{n+1}(\omega_1 \cdots \omega_n T)}.$$

The portfolio value at the end of each period is determined recursively for $n = 1, 2, \cdots, N$ by

$$X_n = \Delta_{n-1} S_n + e^r B_{n-1}.$$

We have demonstrated through calculations in Section 4.2 that the value of such a portfolio at any time point exactly matches that of the financial derivative under consideration, i.e., for all $n = 1, \cdots, N$,

$$X_n = V_n.$$

Example 6.1. Recall the replicating portfolio developed in Example 4.8 under a binomial tree model. To begin with, the replicating portfolio is set up with an initial value of $X_0 = V_0 = 11.8$. As an example, we consider the scenario where the stock price goes up in the first year and goes down in the second year, i.e. $\omega_1 = H, \omega_2 = T$. We can follow the algorithm outlined above to determine

$$\begin{aligned} \Delta_0 &= \frac{V_1(H) - V_1(T)}{S_1(H) - S_1(T)} = \frac{7 - 38}{150 - 50} = -0.31, \\ B_0 &= X_0 - \Delta_0 S_0 = 11.8 + 0.31 \times 100 = 42.8. \end{aligned}$$

The replicating portfolio at the beginning of the first year is created by shortselling 0.31 shares of the underlying stock and investing the proceeds of shortsale as well as initial value, 42.8, all in a money market account. When the stock price goes up at the end of the first year, the portfolio value is given by

$$X_1(H) = \Delta_0 S_1(H) + e^r B_0 = -0.31 \times 150 + 1.25 \times 42.8 = 7,$$

which agrees with the no-arbitrage price of the put option $V_1(H) = 7$. The replicating portfolio is rebalanced at the beginning of the second year. As determined by the formula

$$\Delta_1(H) = \frac{V_2(HH) - V_2(HT)}{S_2(HH) - S_2(HT)} = \frac{0 - 35}{225 - 75} = -\frac{7}{30},$$

we buy back $\Delta_1(H) - \Delta_0 = -7/30 - (-0.31) = 23/300$ shares of the underlying stock at the cost of

$$(\Delta_1(H) - \Delta_0)S_1(H) = 23/300 \times 150 = 11.5.$$

The cost of buying stocks is withdrawn from the money market account, which has a balance after the balancing of

$$B_1(H) = e^r B_0 - (\Delta_1(H) - \Delta_0)S_1(H) = 1.25 \times 42.8 - 11.5 = 42,$$

which agrees with the formula

$$B_1(H) = X_1(H) - \Delta_1(H)S_1(H) = 7 + \frac{7}{30} \times 150 = 42.$$

When the stock price goes down at the end of the second year, the replicating portfolio is now worth

$$X_2(HT) = \Delta_1(H)S_2(HT) + e^r B_1(H) = -\frac{7}{30} \times 75 + 1.25 \times 42 = 35,$$

which is again in agreement with the no-arbitrage price of the put option $V_2(HT) = 35$. We can summarize the evolution of the replicating portfolio under this particular scenario in Table 6.1.

TABLE 6.1: Simulation of replicating portfolio

t (time)	S_t (stock price)	$\Delta_t S_t$ (stock)	B_t (cash)	X_t (portfolio)	V_t (option)
0	100	-31	42.8	11.8	11.8
1	150	-35	42	7	7
2	75	-17.5	52.5	35	35

Similarly, one can also work out the evolution of the replicating portfolio under other scenarios. It comes at no surprise that the portfolio values always match those of the European put option under consideration.

6.1.2   Hedging portfolio

As the replicating portfolio exactly reproduces cash flows of a financial derivative or a portfolio to be replicated, it can also be used to offset cash flows from a short position of the financial instrument in question. Hence, in principle, a replicating portfolio can also be viewed as a hedging portfolio. However, in practice, since hedging is not necessarily used to completely offset cash flows, but rather to reduce uncertainty of fluctuations with market conditions, the hedging portfolio is often described in a slightly different manner than the replicating portfolio.

Consider the same N-period binomial tree model as in Section 6.1.1. An investor is assumed to **take a short position** in the financial derivative and intends to hedge the position. A hedging portfolio is assembled by holding Δ_n shares of the underlying stock at any point of time and financing the trading via the money market account. Here we denote the balance of the money market account by B_n^* and the value of the hedging portfolio by X_n^*, for $n = 0, 1, \cdots, N$. Formulated formally, the portfolio starts with Δ_0 shares of the underlying stock and holding $B_0^* = -\Delta_0 S_0$ in the money market account. Then the money market account evolves according to the recursive relation

$$B_{n+1}^* = e^r B_n^* - (\Delta_{n+1} - \Delta_n)S_{n+1},$$

for $n = 0, 1, 2, \cdots, N - 1$. Let us show the hedging strategy with an example.

Example 6.2.   Consider the same model and stock movement scenario as in Example 6.1. The insurer sells one unit of the two period European put option. In other words, the insurer holds a short position in the put option. A hedging portfolio is set up to protect the insurer from the uncertainty of payoff at maturity. Assume that the hedging portfolio is separated from the put option to be hedged. The portfolio begins with an initial cost of zero. Since $\Delta_0 = -0.31$, the portfolio is created by shortselling 0.31 shares of the underlying stock and investing the proceeds $B_0^* = -\Delta_0 S_0 = 0.31 \times 100 = 31$ in the money market account. When the stock goes up at the end of the first year, the delta rises from $\Delta_0 = -0.31$ to $\Delta_1(H) = -7/30$ and hence the portfolio is rebalanced with additional $\Delta_1(H) - \Delta_0 = 23/300$ shares of the underlying stock, which costs 11.5 and is paid from the money market account. Hence the balance of the money market account after the rebalancing is

$$B_1^* = e^r B_0^* - (\Delta_1(H) - \Delta_0)S_1(H) = 27.25.$$

When the stock goes down in the second year, the hedging portfolio is worth

$$X_2^* = e^r B_1^* + \Delta_1(H)S_2(HT) = 1.25 \times 27.25 - \frac{7}{30} \times 75 = 16.5625.$$

How does this portfolio reduce the risk with the put option? Look at the insurer's liability of the put option and its proceeds from selling the option. Since the option sells for 11.8 at time 0, the proceeds are worth $e^{2r}V_0 = 1.25^2 \times 11.8 = 18.4375$ at the end of two years. Under the assumed scenario, the stock price ends up lower than the strike price. It is clear that the optionholder/buyer would choose to exercise the option and the insurer would incur a loss of $(K - S_2(HT))_+ = 35$. Therefore, the net liability of the put option is worth

$$e^{2r}V_0 - (K - S_2(HT))_+ = -16.5625.$$

This shows that the profit from the hedging portfolio is exactly enough to offset the loss from selling the put option. Here we can also summarize the evolution of the hedging portfolio in Table 6.2.

TABLE 6.2: Simulation of hedging portfolio

t (time)	S_t (stock price)	$\Delta_t S_t$ (stock)	B_t^* (cash)	X_t^* (portfolio)	$e^{rt}V_0 - V_t$ (net loss/profit)
0	100	-31	31	0	0
1	150	-35	27.25	-7.75	-7.75
2	75	-17.5	34.0625	16.5625	16.5625

It is in fact possible to show analytically that the difference between a replicating portfolio and a hedging portfolio under the binomial tree model is the accumulated value of the no-arbitrage price of the financial derivative at time 0.

Theorem 6.3. *In the N-period binomial tree model, it is true for $n = 0, 1, 2, \cdots, N$ that*

$$X_n - X_n^* = e^{rn}V_0.$$

Proof. A replicating portfolio is always made up of two components at time n immediately following the rebalancing

$$X_n = \Delta_n S_n + B_n. \tag{6.1}$$

The value of the portfolio at time $n - 1$ prior to rebalancing is given by

$$X_{n+1} = \Delta_n S_{n+1} + e^r B_n. \tag{6.2}$$

Similar expressions are true for the hedging portfolio.

$$X_n^* = \Delta_n S_n + B_n^*. \tag{6.3}$$
$$X_{n+1}^* = \Delta_n S_{n+1} + e^r B_n^*. \tag{6.4}$$

It is clear by comparing (6.2) and (6.4) that

$$X_{n+1} - X_{n+1}^* = e^r(B_n - B_n^*). \tag{6.5}$$

It follows from the comparison of (6.1) and (6.3) that

$$B_n - B_n^* = X_n - X_n^*. \tag{6.6}$$

Inserting (6.6) into (6.5) and applying the resulting recursive formula repeatedly gives

$$X_n - X_n^* = e^{nr}(B_0 - B_0^*) = e^{nr}V_0.$$

$\square$

6.2 Continuous time hedging: Black-Scholes model

6.2.1 Replicating portfolio

Although not stated explicitly, the replication of a financial derivative in the Black-Scholes model is known as a result of the derivation for the Black-Scholes-Merton pricing equation (4.31) in Section 4.5.

Denote the value at time t of a replicating portfolio by X_t. The portfolio is constructed with the initial value of the financial derivative $X_0 = f(0, S_0)$ where f is known to be a solution to the PDE (4.31) subject to a terminal condition. In this continuous-time model, the replicating portfolio is constantly rebalanced to include

- Δ_t shares of the underlying stock;

- $B_t = X_t - \Delta_t S_t$ invested in the money market account,

where at any time $t \in [0, T]$,

$$\Delta_t = \frac{\partial}{\partial s} f(t, S_t).$$

It is known in Section 4.5 that the value of such a portfolio would exactly match that of the financial derivative at all time $t \in [0, T]$, i.e.

$$X_t = f(t, S_t).$$

Example 6.4. Let us revisit the risk-neutral pricing of the European call option in Example 4.14. It can be shown (Exercise 6.2.1) that

$$\frac{\partial}{\partial s} c(t, s) = \Phi\left(d_1(T - t, s/K)\right).$$

According to (4.30), the number of shares in the hedging portfolio should be set to $\Delta_t = \Phi\left(d_1(T - t, S_t/K)\right)$. Observe that the option value at time t is given by

$$c(t, S_t) = \underbrace{\Phi\left(d_1(T - t, S_t/K)\right)}_{\Delta_t} S_t \underbrace{-Ke^{-r(T-t)}\Phi\left(d_2(T - t, S_t/K)\right)}_{B_t}.$$

Hence it is clear that the Black-Scholes formula not only presents the no-arbitrage price of the European call option, but also provides explicit breakdown of components for a replicating portfolio. In theory, if the replicating portfolio is constantly rebalanced with Δ_t shares of the underlying stock and the portfolio is kept self-financing, then there would always be exactly the amount B_t invested in the money market account.

6.2.2 Gross liability hedging portfolio

In the literature on the dynamic hedging of equity-linked insurance, it is often the case that only the gross liability is hedged against while equity-linked income is left out of consideration. For example, the GMMB rider is often viewed as a life-contingent put option and hence treated as such in the construction of hedging portfolio. As alluded to at the beginning of Section 4.7, unlike an exchange-traded put option, the GMMB rider is compensated not by an up-front fee but rather a stream of equity-linked fees. The problem with hedging only the gross liability is that the equity risk lingers on the income side. When equity returns are low, even if one creates a synthetic hedge against the GMMB gross liability, the fee incomes may not be sufficient to cover the hedging cost of the gross liability. Hence, we shall begin the discussion with the more classic approach of gross liability hedging, followed by the approach of net liability hedging in the next section.

6.2.2.1 Continuous hedging in theory

We start with the assumption that an insurer underwrites an embedded option with its insurance product. The purpose of the hedge is to remove the uncertainty with the insurer's gross liability. As in the discrete-time model, a hedging portfolio in a continuous time model, whose value at time t is denoted by X_t^*, is also constructed to contain Δ_t shares of the underlying stock where

$$\Delta_t = \frac{\partial}{\partial s} f(t, S_t).$$

The hedging portfolio is self-financing by definition. If the calculation of Δ_t indicates that the number of shares needs to be reduced, then the proceeds from selling stock is invested in the money market account. If the number of shares is to be increased, then the cost of additional shares of the stock is borrowed from the money market account. The portfolio begins with no value, i.e. just enough is borrowed from the money market to finance the stock portion of the portfolio,

$$B_0^* = -\Delta_0 S_0.$$

Afterward, the money market account accumulates interest at the risk-free rate, i.e.

$$dB_t^* = r B_t^* \, dt.$$

Keep in mind that the hedging portfolio consists of two parts at all time, i.e. $X_t^* = \Delta_t S_t + B_t^*$, and that it is self-financing. Therefore, the dynamics of the portfolio values is given by

$$dX_t^* = \Delta_t \, dS_t + dB_t^* = \Delta_t \, dS_t + r(X_t^* - \Delta_t S_t) \, dt. \tag{6.7}$$

Remark 6.5. As in the discrete-time model, the difference between a replicating portfolio and a hedging portfolio is also given by the accumulated value of the no-arbitrage price of the financial derivative in the continuous-time model. To show this, we observe that the dynamics of the replicating portfolio is given by

$$dX_t = \Delta_t \, dS_t + dB_t = \Delta_t \, dS_t + r(X_t - \Delta_t S_t) \, dt. \tag{6.8}$$

Subtracting (6.8) from (6.7) yields that

$$d(X_t - X_t^*) = r(X_t - X_t^*) \, dt.$$

The solution to this differential equation is given by

$$X_t - X_t^* = e^{rt}(X_0 - X_0^*) = e^{rt}V_0, \qquad 0 \le t \le T, \tag{6.9}$$

which is consistent with similar result in Theorem 6.3 for the discrete-time model.

6.2.2.2 Discrete hedging in practice

While the dynamics of the hedging portfolio is known in theory by (6.7), it is impractical to constantly rebalance the portfolio at all times. Even if it is possible to enforce a nearly continuous trading strategy, it would be too costly to be useful due to the accumulation of transaction cost associated with each trade. Therefore, a hedging program is typically implemented in a way similar to that in a discrete time model, which can be summarized as follows.

- Begin with zero value. Estimate Δ_0 and hold Δ_0 shares of the underlying stock. (If Δ_0 is positive, purchase stock shares with enough borrowing from the money market account. Otherwise, short-sell stock shares and deposit proceeds in the money market account.)

- Update Δ_t periodically and adjust your stock holdings accordingly. Increase stock shares by borrowing from the money market account, or decrease stock shares with proceeds sent to the money market account.

We shall illustrate the procedure with an example of hedging the GMMB rider for a variable annuity contract.

Example 6.6. Consider a variable annuity contract with the GMMB rider described in Section 4.7.1. According to (4.53), the no-arbitrage cost of the GMMB rider at any time $t \in [0, T]$ is given by

$$B_e(t, F_t) = {}_T p_x$$
$$\times \left[Ge^{-r(T-t)} \Phi\left(-d_2\left(T - t, \frac{F_t}{G}\right) \right) - F_t e^{-m(T-t)} \Phi\left(-d_1\left(T - t, \frac{F_t}{G}\right) \right) \right],$$

where d_1, d_2 are defined in (4.54) and (4.55) respectively. One can create a hedging portfolio by investing in the underlying stock or index futures and risk-free assets such as bonds.

The following numerical example is based on model assumptions and parameters of the GMMB rider listed in Appendix A.1. We establish a hedging portfolio $\tilde{X}_t$ according to the discrete hedging algorithm described above. It is not hard to show that the Δ_t^* for this hedging portfolio is given by

$$\Delta_t^* = -{}_T p_x \frac{F_t}{S_t} e^{-m(T-t)} \Phi\left(-d_1(T-t, \frac{F_t}{G})\right).$$

We shall illustrate the effectiveness of the above-described hedging program under a particular scenario of equity returns, which is shown in Figure 6.1.

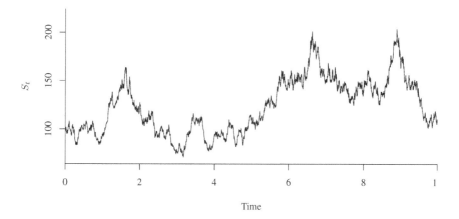

FIGURE 6.1: Sample path of equity index value

We can now inspect the result of the hedging strategy in Figure 6.2. The grey line represents the evolution of the hedging portfolio $\{\tilde{X}_t^* : 0 \leq t \leq T\}$ while the black line shows the path of $\{\tilde{V}_t := B_e(t, F_t) - e^{rt} B_e(0, F_0) : 0 \leq t \leq T\}$. Note that this quantity is chosen as a benchmark for the value of the gross liability hedging portfolio due to (6.9). If the GMMB were to be compensated by a single up-front fee $B_e(0, F_0)$, then the value V_t would represent the net profit or loss of the GMMB rider at time t. One can hardly distinguish one line from the other in Figure 6.2, which implies that the daily rebalanced hedging strategy closely offsets the GMMB gross liability. However, one should be reminded that the GMMB rider is funded by a stream of equity-based fees. As we shall discuss later, such a hedging portfolio cannot eliminate the uncertainty with equity risk remaining on the income side.

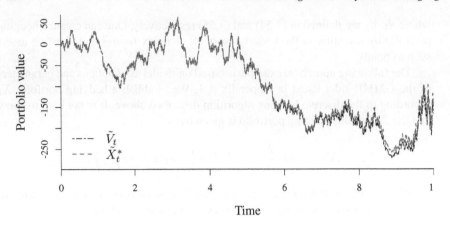

FIGURE 6.2: A sample path of gross liability hedging portfolio

6.2.3   Net liability hedging portfolio

Gross liabilities and fee incomes of variable annuity guaranteed benefits are viewed separately as path-independent or path-dependent financial derivatives and priced accordingly using theory of no-arbitrage in Chapter 4. While the approach suffices to determine no-arbitrage costs of these investment guarantees, we have not addressed the issue of hedging with fee incomes. It should be pointed out that in Section 4.5 the replicating portfolios are all assumed to be self-financing with no withdrawal or deposit. However, equity-linked annuity products are often structured with intermediate cash flows over their policy terms. For example, all embedded options with variable annuities are compensated by equity-based fees charged on a regular basis. Certain benefits, such as the GMWB, the GLWB and the immediate variable annuity, etc, pay living benefits to policyholders periodically for consumption. In this section, we extend the idea of self-financing portfolio in Section 4.5 to develop a hedging program with exogenous cash flows.

6.2.3.1   Pricing and hedging of derivatives with exogenous cash flows

Consider an insurer's hedging portfolio that consists of two components at all times, namely, the underlying stock*, and investment in a money market account. For any time t between 0 and the maturity T, we use the following notation:

- X_t^* – the value of the hedging portfolio;

---

*If the underlying asset is an equity index, then the hedging portfolio could be constructed with index futures. If the underlying asset is a portfolio with undisclosed asset mix, an insurer may use fund mapping to develop a similar portfolio and the analysis in this section can be extended to hedging with the fund mapping portfolio.

- B_t^* – the value of the money market account;

- h_t – the number of shares invested in the underlying stock;

- C_t – the annualized rate of net cash flow (incomes less outgoes).

In the following, we shall extend similar arguments as in Section 4.3 to determine the dynamics of a self-financing portfolio with the presence of exogenous cash flows. It is clear that at any time $t \in [0, T]$ the value of the hedging portfolio should be given by

$$X_t^* = h_t S_t + B_t^*.$$

Suppose that the portfolio is rebalanced periodically at time intervals of length Δt. For notational brevity, we denote the marginal increments by $\Delta X_t = X_{t+\Delta t} - X_t$ for $X = h, B$. Since the portfolio is self-financing with the exogenous net cash flow, we expect that

$$\underbrace{\Delta_{t-\Delta t} S_t + e^{r\Delta t} B_{t-\Delta t}}_{\text{portfolio value of last period}} + \underbrace{C_{t-\Delta t}\Delta t}_{\text{net cash flow}} = \underbrace{\Delta_t S_t + B_t^*}_{\text{portfolio value of current period}},$$

which implies that

$$\Delta h_t S_t + \Delta B_t^* - (e^{r\Delta t} - 1)B_{t-\Delta t} - C_{t-\Delta t}\Delta t = 0. \tag{6.10}$$

To avoid backward difference, we add and subtract $\Delta_t S_{t-\Delta t}$ in (6.10) and obtain

$$\Delta h_t \Delta S_t + S_{t-\Delta}\Delta h_t + \Delta B_t^* - (e^{r\Delta t} - 1)B_t^* - C_{t-\Delta t}\Delta t. = 0$$

Dividing both sides by Δt and letting Δt go to zero, we obtain the continuous-time version of the self-financing condition

$$\mathrm{d}h_t\,\mathrm{d}S_t + S_t\,\mathrm{d}h_t + \mathrm{d}B_t^* = rB_t^*\,\mathrm{d}t + C_t\,\mathrm{d}t = 0.$$

It follows immediately that

$$\begin{aligned} \mathrm{d}X_t^* &= \mathrm{d}(h_t S_t + B_t^*) = h_t\,\mathrm{d}S_t + S_t\,\mathrm{d}h_t + \mathrm{d}S_t\,\mathrm{d}h_t + \mathrm{d}B_t^* \\ &= h_t\,\mathrm{d}S_t + rB_t^*\,\mathrm{d}t + C_t\,\mathrm{d}t = h_t\,\mathrm{d}S_t + r(X_t^* - h_t S_t)\,\mathrm{d}t + C_t\,\mathrm{d}t. \end{aligned} \tag{6.11}$$

Under the Black-Scholes model, we know that

$$\mathrm{d}X_t^* = \mu h_t S_t\,\mathrm{d}t + \sigma h_t S_t\,\mathrm{d}W_t + rX_t^*\,\mathrm{d}t - rh_t S_t\,\mathrm{d}t + C_t\,\mathrm{d}t$$

Suppose that the value of the embedded option to be hedged can be determined by $f(t, S_t)$ for some function f to be determined. Recall from (4.27) that

$$\mathrm{d}f(t, S_t) = \left[\frac{\partial f}{\partial t}(t, S_t) + \mu S_t \frac{\partial f}{\partial s}(t, S_t) + \frac{1}{2}\sigma^2 S_t^2 \frac{\partial^2 f}{\partial s^2}(t, S_t)\right]\mathrm{d}t + \sigma S_t \frac{\partial f}{\partial s}(t, S_t)\,\mathrm{d}W_t.$$

If we can match the dynamics of the embedded option value $f(t, S_t)$ and that of the hedging portfolio X_t^*, i.e. $f(t, S_t) = X_t^*$ for all $0 < t < T$, then it is clear that

$$h_t = \frac{\partial f}{\partial s}(t, S_t),$$

and

$$\frac{\partial f}{\partial t}(t, S_t) + \frac{1}{2}\sigma^2 S_t^2 \frac{\partial^2 f}{\partial s^2}(t, S_t) = rf(t, S_t) - rS_t \frac{\partial f}{\partial s}(t, S_t) + C_t.$$

Let us further assume that the rate of net cash flow can be represented by $c(t, S_t)$ for some function c. The analysis indicates that the hedging portfolio should keep $\partial f(t, S_t)/\partial s$ shares of the underlying stock at all times and the no-arbitrage cost of the embedded option can be determined by the partial differential equation

$$\frac{\partial f}{\partial t}(t, s) + \frac{1}{2}\sigma^2 x^2 \frac{\partial^2 f}{\partial s^2}(t, s) = rf(t, s) - rs\frac{\partial f}{\partial s}(t, s) + c(t, s). \tag{6.12}$$

Equity-linked insurance does not typically require an up-front fee. Therefore, the initial condition of (6.12) is given by

$$f(0, S_0) = 0. \tag{6.13}$$

Example 6.7. Recall from Section 4.7.1 that the no-arbitrage value of the GMMB net liability from an insurer's perspective is given by

$$f(t, S_t) := B_e(t, F(t, S_t)) - P_e(t, F(t, S_t)), \tag{6.14}$$

where B_e denotes the no-arbitrage value of the GMMB gross liability,

$$B_e(t, F) = {}_Tp_x\left[Ge^{-r(T-t)}\Phi\left(-d_2\left(T-t, \frac{F}{G}\right)\right) - Fe^{-m(T-t)}\Phi\left(-d_1\left(T-t, \frac{F}{G}\right)\right)\right]$$

and P_e denotes the no-arbitrage value of the insurer's fee incomes,

$$P_e(t, F) = mF \int_t^T e^{-m(s-t)} {}_sp_x \, ds. \tag{6.15}$$

Since the net liability is valued under the assumption on the absence of arbitrage, we set $m_e = m$ in (6.19) to avoid any friction cost in the model. (See similar arguments in Section 4.7.4.3.) While policyholders' accounts are not tradable, the underlying assets or equity index futures are. Therefore, we view these no-arbitrage values as functions of equity value through the dependence of policyholders' sub-accounts on equity, i.e. $F_t = F(t, S_t)$ where

$$F(t, s) = \frac{F_0}{S_0} se^{-mt}.$$

Since the function f must satisfy the PDE (6.12), we can show (Exercise 6.2.2) that the function $c(t, s)$ is given by

$$c(t, s) = -\left(\frac{\partial}{\partial t} + rs\frac{\partial}{\partial s} + \frac{1}{2}\sigma^2 s^2 \frac{\partial^2}{\partial s^2} - r\right) f(t, s) = m_t p_x F(t, s), \quad (6.16)$$

which implies that the net cash flow at any time $t \in (0, T)$ required to support the self-financing portfolio should be

$$c(t, S_t) = m_t p_x F_t.$$

Observe that the required cash flow is exactly the rate of GMMB fees charged in proportion to the survivorship of policyholders. □

6.2.3.2 Discrete hedging in practice

While continuous hedging works in theory, we can only implement the strategy on a discrete basis. We can summarize the procedure for hedging with exogenous cash flows as follows.

- Begin with zero value. Estimate Δ_0 and hold Δ_0 shares of the underlying stock. Deposit net cash flow C_0 in the money market account (If Δ_0 is positive, purchase stock shares with the initial net cash flow and necessary borrowing from the money market account. Otherwise, short-sell stock shares and deposit proceeds in the money market account.)

- Collect and deposit net cash flows C_t in the money market account. Update Δ_t periodically and adjust your stock holdings accordingly. Increase stock shares by borrowing from the money market account, or decrease stock shares with proceeds sent to the money market account.

Example 6.8. Let us consider the hedging of the GMMB net liability as opposed to that of the GMMB gross liability in Example 6.6. In theory, one can set up a self-financing portfolio with the GMMB fee incomes to completely hedge the GMMB net liability. Recall from Example 6.7 that the hedge is rebalanced at every instant with the dynamics

$$dX_t^* = \Delta_t \, dS_t + r(X_t^* - \Delta_t S_t) \, dt + m_t p_x F_t \, dt$$

where Δ_t denotes the number of shares of the underlying asset,

$$\begin{aligned}
\Delta_t &= \frac{\partial}{\partial s} f(t, S_t) \\
&= -\frac{F_t}{S_t}\left[{}_T p_x e^{-m(T-t)} \Phi\left(-d_1\left(T - t, \frac{F_t}{G}\right)\right) + m \int_t^T e^{-m(s-t)} {}_s p_x ds\right].
\end{aligned}$$

In practice, since continuous hedging is not feasible, a discrete-time approximation is required. Suppose that the GMMB rider matures in T years with T being an
integer and that the hedging portfolio can rebalanced periodically with time intervals
of length $\Delta t = T/N$. For brevity, we write $X_n = X^*_{t_n}$ for $X = H^*, B^*, S, F, \Delta$ at
discrete time points

$$\{t_0 = 0, t_1 = \Delta t, t_2 = 2\Delta t \cdots, t_N = T\}.$$

The portfolio is set to maintain Δ_n shares of the underlying asset at the end of each
period. The cost of change in stock shares should always be financed by fee incomes
and the money market account. Hence, the balance of the money account is changed
according to

$$B^*_{n+1} \quad = \quad e^{r\Delta t} B^*_n - (\Delta_{n+1} - \Delta_n) S_{n+1} + m\,_{t_n} p_x F_n.$$

Let us demonstrate the effectiveness of the hedging portfolio with numerics. Consider a GMMB contract with the product specification listed in Appendix A.1. The
survivorship is based on the Illustrative Life Table in Appendix A.3. Survival probabilities for fractional ages are estimated using the uniform distribution of deaths
assumption, i.e. $_s q_x = s\,_1 q_x$ for any integer x and $0 \le s \le 1$. To avoid any friction
cost, we set $m_e = m$ in the model. The fee rate m is determined by the equivalence
principle (4.56) under the risk-neutral measure. In other words, the no-arbitrage value
of the insurer's gross liability would exactly match that of the insurer's fee incomes.

All illustrations will be based on the sample path of the equity index/fund $\{S_t :
0 \le t \le T\}$ in Figure 6.1. Following this particular scenario, we develop three
hedging portfolios based on the above-described method which are rebalanced on
yearly, monthly and daily bases respectively, i.e. $\Delta t = 1, 1/12, 1/252$. Pathwise
comparison of portfolio values and GMMB net liability values at all time points for
all three hedging portfolios can be seen in Figure 6.3. In each graph, the dashed line
shows the fluctuation of hedging portfolio whereas the dash-dotted line represents the
fluctuation of GMMB net liability. Portfolio values of a least active hedging program,
which is rebalanced on an annual basis and depicted in the bottom graph, generally
follow the pattern of fluctuation with net liability values. The path of the hedging
portfolio and that of the net liability are almost indistinguishable for the most active
hedging portfolio, which is rebalanced on a daily basis and depicted in the top graph.
It is not surprising that hedging errors reduce with the frequency of rebalancing.
However, a word of caution should be made. There is a trade-off between hedging
error and transaction cost of running a hedging program. A prudent insurer strives to
strike a balance and develop an affordable and effective hedging strategy.

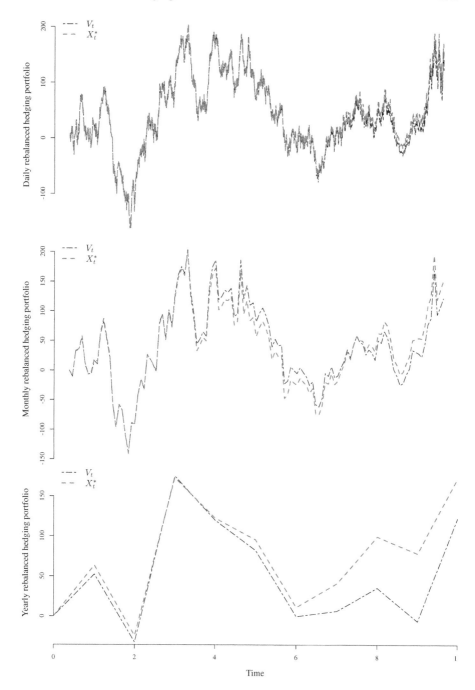

FIGURE 6.3: Effectiveness of hedging portfolios with various rebalancing frequencies

We can further compare the net liability hedging strategy with the gross liability hedging strategy developed in Example 6.6. In the top graph of Figure 6.4, the dark line represents the evolution of the GMMB net liability whereas the light grey line illustrates the evolution of gross liability hedging portfolio. This graph should be compared with the top graph in Figure 6.3. The bottom graph of Figure 6.4 shows hedging errors from the two portfolios. The maximum absolute hedging error of the net liability hedging portfolio X_t^* is around \$17 while that for the gross liability hedging portfolio $\tilde{X}_t^*$ is clearly greater than \$100. It is not surprising that the gross liability hedging portfolio does not perform as well as the net liability hedging portfolio to hedge against the net liability. The reason is that the equity risk lingers with fee incomes and is not accounted for in the gross liability hedging portfolio.

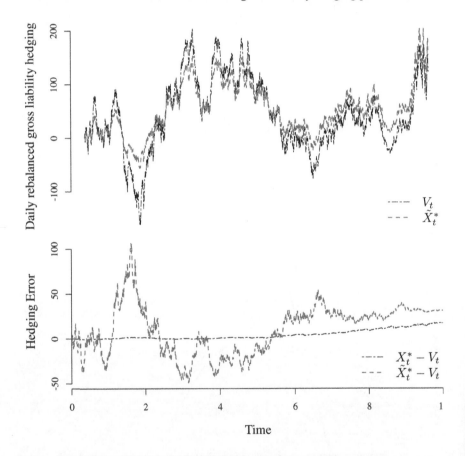

FIGURE 6.4: Comparison of gross and net liability hedging strategies

Example 6.8 shows that fee incomes, if not hedged properly, can cause large fluctuation with an insurer's cash flows. Although gross liability hedging is most common in practice, the best practice for managing investment guarantees is to conduct the net liability hedging portfolio.

6.3 Greek letters hedging

In theory, if one is able to continuously rebalance a hedging portfolio and to maintain the exact value of delta according to the algorithm described in the previous section, any equity risk can be completely hedged against in the Black-Scholes framework. However, continuous hedging is not possible in reality. It in fact may not necessarily be a good idea to hedge as frequently as possible due to transaction costs with hedging instruments. Facing the reality of imperfect and infrequent hedging, practitioners extended the notion of delta-hedging to a more general framework of hedging, which we shall discuss in this section.

Recall Taylor's theorem from multivariate calculus. If a function f is differentiable at (x, y, z), then

$$f(x + \Delta x, y + \Delta y, z + \Delta z) - f(x, y, z)$$
$$= \frac{\partial}{\partial x} f(x, y, z) \Delta x + \frac{\partial}{\partial y} f(x, y, z) \Delta y + \frac{\partial}{\partial z} f(x, y, z) \Delta z + \epsilon_1 \Delta x + \epsilon_2 \Delta y + \epsilon_3 \Delta z,$$

where $\epsilon_1, \epsilon_2, \epsilon_3 \to 0$ as $(\Delta x, \Delta y, \Delta z) \to (0, 0, 0)$. In other words, when changes in the arguments $\Delta x, \Delta y, \Delta z$ are very small, we have a good approximation

$$f(x + \Delta x, y + \Delta y, z + \Delta z) - f(x, y, z) \approx \frac{\partial}{\partial x} f(x, y, z) \Delta x + \frac{\partial}{\partial y} f(x, y, z) \Delta y$$
$$+ \frac{\partial}{\partial z} f(x, y, z) \Delta z. \tag{6.17}$$

Traders view the value of a hedging portfolio as the output of a trading strategy with many uncertain inputs, such as the stock prices, the time to maturity, volatility, etc. Hence, the total change to the portfolio value can be approximated by the sum of changes caused by each input which can be explained by (6.17). Put in another way, if the partial derivatives with respect to each input can be set near zero, then the output of the portfolio is less sensitive to changes due to small variation in the inputs. This is why traders often look at other sensitivity measures beyond deltas, known as the *greek letters*, which are partial derivatives of the portfolio value with respect to various parameters.

For simplicity, we consider the Greek letters of any path-independent financial derivative. It is known from Section 4.5.1 that the no-arbitrage value of such an instrument can be written as $f(t, s)$ given that the underlying asset value is s at time t. Although not identified explicitly, the function f also depends on other model parameters such as volatility coefficient σ, etc.

Delta

The *delta* (Δ) of a portfolio is the rate of change of the value of the portfolio with respect to the change in underlying asset price with all else remaining the same. In other words, given that the underlying asset value is s at time t, the delta is defined as

$$\Delta_t := \frac{\partial}{\partial s} f(t, s).$$

Gamma

The *gamma* (Γ) of a portfolio on an underlying asset is the rate of change of the portfolio's delta with respect to the price of the underlying asset. It is the second partial derivative of the portfolio with respect to asset price. Translated mathematically, given that the underlying asset value is s at time t, the gamma is defined as

$$\Gamma_t := \frac{\partial^2}{\partial s^2} f(t, s).$$

Theta

The *theta* (Θ) of a portfolio of options is the rate of change of the value of the portfolio with respect to the passage of time with all else remaining the same. Theta is sometimes referred to as the *time decay* of the portfolio. Given that the underlying asset value is s at time t, , the theta is defined as

$$\Theta_t := \frac{\partial}{\partial t} f(t, s).$$

Vega

In the Black-Scholes model, it is assumed that the volatility of the asset underlying a derivative is constant. However, in practice, the *implied volatility* is often estimated by setting a Black-Scholes formula to the observable market price of an option and solving the equation for the volatility coefficient σ. As mentioned before, the geometric Brownian motion is a convenient tool for modeling asset prices. Since actual prices may not always follow a geometric Brownian motion, it is not surprising that the implied volatility obtained by inverting the Black-Scholes formula is not always constant. Nevertheless, for simplicity, rather than abandoning the Black-Scholes model completely, practitioners treat it as if the model is correct but with random volatility. Hence, the sensitivity measure of portfolio value with respect to the volatility is needed. While there is some logical flaw in such an application, it has been widely acceptable in practice. The *vega* of a portfolio of derivatives, $\mathcal{V}$, is the rate of change of the value of the portfolio with respect to the volatility of the underlying asset. In other words, given that the underlying asset value is s at time t,

$$\mathcal{V}_t := \frac{\partial}{\partial \sigma} f(t, s).$$

Example 6.9 (Greeks of the GMMB net liability). Recall from Section 4.7.1 that the no-arbitrage value of the GMMB net liability from an insurer's perspective is given by

$$f(t, S_t) := B_e(t, F(t, S_t)) - P_e(t, F(t, S_t)), \tag{6.18}$$

where B_e denotes the no-arbitrage value of the GMMB gross liability,

$$B_e(t, F) = {}_Tp_x\left[Ge^{-r(T-t)}\Phi\left(-d_2\left(T-t, \frac{F}{G}\right)\right) - Fe^{-m(T-t)}\Phi\left(-d_1\left(T-t, \frac{F}{G}\right)\right)\right]$$

and P_e denotes the no-arbitrage value of the insurer's fee incomes,

$$P_e(t, F) = mF\int_t^T e^{-m(s-t)}{}_sp_x\,ds, \tag{6.19}$$

and the dependence of policyholders' sub-accounts on equity, i.e. $F_t = F(t, S_t)$, is given by

$$F(t, s) = \frac{F_0}{S_0}se^{-mt}.$$

Since the gross liability of the GMMB rider resembles a put option, we can use the results from Exercise 6.3.1 and 6.3.2 to find the Greeks of the GMMB net liability. Given that the time t value of the underlying equity index is s and that of the policyholder's subaccount is F, its Greeks are given by

$$\Delta_t = -{}_Tp_x\frac{F}{s}e^{-m(T-t)}\Phi\left(-d_1\left(T-t, \frac{F}{G}\right)\right) - \frac{P_e}{s};$$

$$\Gamma_t = {}_Tp_x\frac{F}{s^2}e^{-m(T-t)}\frac{\phi\left(d_1\left(T-t, \frac{F}{G}\right)\right)}{\sigma\sqrt{T-t}};$$

$$\Theta_t = {}_Tp_x\left[rGe^{-r(T-t)}\Phi\left(-d_2\left(T-t, \frac{F}{G}\right)\right) - mFe^{-m(T-t)}\Phi\left(-d_1\left(T-t, \frac{F}{G}\right)\right)\right.$$

$$\left. - e^{-m(T-t)}\frac{\sigma F\phi\left(d_1\left(T-t, \frac{F_t}{G}\right)\right)}{2\sqrt{T-t}}\right] + m\,{}_tp_xF;$$

$$\mathcal{V}_t = {}_Tp_xFe^{-m(T-t)}\phi\left(d_1\left(T-t, \frac{F}{G}\right)\right)\sqrt{T-t}.$$

With a given portfolio with known Greeks, the hedging strategy is developed by adding additional financial derivatives with opposite Greeks. Suppose that the current time is t and current value of the underlying asset is s. Denote the value of the current portfolio by $f(t, s)$ and those of other hedging instruments by $f^1(t, s), f^2(t, s), \cdots$. Their deltas and the number of shares invested for the hedging purpose are denoted by $\Delta_t^1, \Delta_t^2, \cdots$ and $h_t^1, h_t^2, \cdots$, respectively.

We say a hedging portfolio is delta neutral if its delta is zero. In other words, we can add to the hedging portfolio h_1 shares of the first hedging instrument so that

$$\frac{\partial}{\partial s}\left\{f(t,s) + h_t^1 f^1(t,s)\right\} = 0.$$

In other words, the portfolio is delta neutral if

$$h_t^1 = -\frac{\Delta_t}{\Delta_t^1}.$$

Similarly, if we want to make the portfolio delta and gamma neutral, then we set

$$\frac{\partial^2}{\partial s^2}\left\{f(t,s) + h_t^1 f^1(t,s) + h_t^2 f^2(t,s)\right\} = 0,$$

which implies that

$$h_t^2 = -\frac{\Gamma_t + h_t^1 \Gamma_t^1}{\Gamma_t^2}.$$

The same approach extends further to other Greeks. Suppose there are n different Greeks to be made neutral in the hedging portfolio. A total of n different hedging instruments are needed to construct the Greeks-neutral portfolio. Since differentiation is a linear operation, we can always determine the make-up of the hedging portfolio by solving a system of linear equations, i.e.

$$\begin{cases} h_t^1 \Delta_t^1 + h_t^2 \Delta_t^2 + \cdots + h_t^n \Delta_t^n = 0; \\ h_t^1 \Gamma_t^1 + h_t^2 \Gamma_t^2 + \cdots + h_t^n \Gamma_t^n = 0; \\ \cdots \\ h_t^1 \mathcal{V}_t^1 + h_t^2 \mathcal{V}_t^2 + \cdots + h_t^n \mathcal{V}_t^n = 0. \end{cases}$$

Example 6.10. Imagine that you are at a trading desk for a risk management team and that you are asked to trade options so that the position of a newly issued GMMB rider will be delta-gamma-vega neutral. Consider the GMMB rider with product features outlined in Appendix A.1. As the Greeks are known in Example 6.9, we obtain that $\Delta_0 = 4.06048$, $\Gamma_0 = -0.02239$ and $\mathcal{V}_0 = -671.82079$ at the issuance of contract.

Suppose that the underlying equity fund is invested entirely on the Apple stock. You may look up the information on option greeks through certain financial data system. Here we retrieved data from NASDAQ website [*]. The dates below are maturity dates of the corresponding options. The data was downloaded after trading hours on March 6, 2018 and the closing stock price was roughly $178 per share.

Greeks for Apple Inc. (AAPL)														
Calls	Delta	Gamma	Rho	Theta	Vega	IV	Root	Strike	Puts	Delta	Gamma	Rho	Theta	Vega	IV
Mar 09 2018	0.65431	0.04862	0.00694	-0.74956	0.05330	0.21044	AAPL	172.50	Mar 09 2018	-0.19666	0.08369	-0.00206	-0.22411	0.03450	0.24974

[*] Apple Inc. Option Greeks, https://www.nasdaq.com/symbol/aapl/option-chain/greeks

We summarizes the information in the following table.

Security	Delta	Gamma	Vega
Current portfolio - short GMMB	4.06048	-0.02239	-671.82079
Underlying asset - Apple stock	1.00000	0.00000	0.00000
Option 1 - call	0.65431	0.04862	0.05330
Option 2 - put	-0.19666	0.08369	0.03450

To make the portfolio gamma and vega neutral, we use both option 1 and option 2. Let w_1, w_2, and w_3 be the quantities of the Apple stock, option 1, and option 2 to be added to the portfolio. We can set the delta, gamma and vega of the overall hedging portfolio to zero and solve for the three unknowns (w_1, w_2, w_3).

Delta Neutral: $\quad 4.06048 + 1 \cdot w_1 \quad +0.65431 \cdot w_2 - 0.19666 \cdot w_3 \quad = 0$

Gamma Neutral: $\quad -0.02239 + 0 \cdot w_1 \quad +0.04862 \cdot w_2 + 0.08369 \cdot w_3 \quad = 0$

Vega Neutral: $\quad -671.82079 + 0 \cdot w_1 \quad +0.05330 \cdot w_2 + 0.03450 \cdot w_3 \quad = 0$

The solution to this system of linear equations is

$$w_1 = -15,529.34$$
$$w_2 = 20,200.54$$
$$w_3 = -11,735.31$$

Hence, the trader needs to shortsell 15,529 shares of Apple stock (underlying asset), buy 20,201 contracts of call options (option 1), and shortsell 11,735 contracts of put options (option 2) to achieve an approximately *delta-gamma-vega neutral* portfolio.

$\square$

6.4 Bibliographic notes

The material on pricing and hedging in the binomial tree model is largely based on the excellent reference by Shreve [96]. The purpose of the discussion in the binomial tree model is for readers to get a good grasp of the distinction between a replicating portfolio and a hedging portfolio before we show a similar result in the continuous-time Black-Scholes model. Most texts on the subject matter do not distinguish the two portfolios as their difference is in essence a risk-free asset. However, it is often a source of confusion for beginners from the author's own experience with students. Therefore, we can spell out as much detail as possible for their commonality and differences.

Detailed account of market practice and risk management of financial derivatives can be found in Hull [65]. The discussion of continuous-time hedging in this book is tailored to the features of equity-linked insurance products. While most work in the current literature focus largely on gross liability hedging, this chapter explores in great details the net liability hedging adapted to the unique equity-linking funding mechanism. Readers are also referred to Delong [25], Fung, Ignatieva and Sherris [51], for pricing and hedging of variable annuities in more general stochastic models.

This book focuses on the so-called complete hedging methods, which in theory can completely eliminate any equity risk with embedded options in insurance products. These methods are well accepted in the financial industry and adopted for hedging equity-linked insurance. However, readers should be reminded that this are many other hedging methods beyond the scope of this introductory book. A new text on partial hedging methods is Melnikov and Nosrati [78].

6.5 Exercises

Section 6.2

1. Consider no-arbitrage price formulas for European call and put options in Example 4.14. Show that

   (a) $\frac{\partial}{\partial s} c(t, s) = \Phi\left(d_1(T - t, s/K)\right);$

   (b) $\frac{\partial}{\partial s} p(t, s) = -\Phi\left(-d_1(T - t, s/K)\right).$

2. According to the analysis in Section 6.2.3, the no-arbitrage value of the GMMB net liability is given by (6.18) where f must satisfies the PDE (6.12). Verify that both (6.13) and (6.16) hold when the fee rate m is determined by equivalence principle in (4.56).

Section 6.3

1. This exercise is intended to show the computation of Greeks for an European put option defined in Example 4.14. Denote by $p(t, s)$ the no-arbitrage price at time t of the European put option with the strike price K, the maturity T given that the time t price of the underlying asset is s. Show that

   (a) its gamma is given by

$$
\frac{\partial^2}{\partial s^2} p(t, s) = e^{-m(T-t)} \frac{\phi\left(d_1(T - t, s/K)\right)}{s\sigma\sqrt{T - t}}
$$
$$
= K e^{-r(T-t)} \frac{\phi\left(d_2(T - t, s/K)\right)}{s^2\sigma\sqrt{T - t}};
$$

(b) its vega is given by

$$
\begin{aligned}
\frac{\partial}{\partial \sigma} p(t, s) &= F e^{-m(T-t)} \phi\big(d_1(T-t, s/K)\big)\sqrt{T-t} \\
&= K e^{-r(T-t)} \phi\big(d_2(T-t, s/K)\big)\sqrt{T-t};
\end{aligned}
$$

(c) its theta is given by

$$
\begin{aligned}
\frac{\partial}{\partial t} p(t, s) &= r K e^{-r(T-t)} \Phi\big(-d_2(T-t, s/K)\big) \\
&\quad -m s e^{-m(T-t)} \Phi\big(-d_1(T-t, s/K)\big) \\
&\quad -e^{-m(T-t)} \frac{\sigma s \phi\big(d_1(T-t, s/K)\big)}{2\sqrt{T-t}}.
\end{aligned}
$$

2. Consider the stream of fee incomes from the GMMB rider as a financial derivative of its own. It is shown that the no-arbitrage value of fee incomes is given by $P_e(t, F)$ in (6.19). Show that

(a) its first derivative with respect to F is given by

$$
\frac{\partial}{\partial F} P_e(t, F) = \frac{P_e(t, F)}{F};
$$

(b) its second derivative with respect to F is given by

$$
\frac{\partial^2}{\partial F^2} P_e(t, F) = 0;
$$

(c) its derivative with respect to t is given by

$$
\frac{\partial}{\partial t} P_e(t, F) = -mF \, {}_t p_x.
$$

Calculate the Greeks of fee incomes using the results shown above.

3. Greeks are related to each other in the Black-Scholes model. Suppose that the time t no-arbitrage value of the GMMB net liability is V_t, the time t value of the equity index is S_t and the time t account value is F_t. Then the Greeks must satisfy the following equation for any time t:

$$
\Theta_t + r S_t \Delta_t + \frac{1}{2}\sigma^2 S_t^2 \Gamma_t - r V_t + m \, {}_t p_x F_t = 0.
$$

7

Advanced Computational Methods

While many earlier chapters provide an overview of product management for equity-linked insurance with plain-vanilla product designs, we investigate in this chapter more complex features that warrant more advanced computational techniques.

In this chapter, we shall take a problem-solving approach. Each computational technique is introduced and illustrated with a model problem to solve. While model problems may seem relatively simple compared with full scale risk management problems in the industry, they contain essential elements with applicability for applications in more general setting.

7.1   Differential equation methods

As shown in Section 4.5, differential equation methods are fundamental to the derivation of risk-neutral price in the no-arbitrage framework. We shall demonstrate in this section the same techniques can also be extended for more general risk management problems involving evaluation of risk measures. Readers are encouraged to compare the techniques to be introduced here with those in Section 4.5 and find their commonalities.

Suppose that the risk management problem is defined on a probability space $(\Omega, \mathbb{P}, \{\mathcal{F}_t : 0 \leq t \leq T\})$ where $\{\mathcal{F}_t : 0 \leq t \leq T\}$ represents the filtration with which a stochastic process $\{X_t : 0 \leq t \leq T\}$ is defined. The process may be multivariate and should possess the Markov property. We can summarize a common problem-solving process as follows.

1. Represent the quantity of interest as a special case of a conditional expectation of the form $Y_t := \mathbb{E}[\cdot | \mathcal{F}_t]$;

2. Use Markov property of the underlying process to write the conditional expectation Y_t as a function of time and the underlying process, i.e. $Y_t = f(t, X_t)$ for some function f to be determined, and apply Itô formula to identify the stochastic differential equation satisfied by the process $\{Y_t : 0 \leq t \leq T\}$.

3. Use martingale property of the process $\{Y_t : 0 \leq t \leq T\}$ (Exercise 2.6.2) to identify the partial differential equation and associated boundary conditions satisfied by f.

4. The rest of the calculation boils down to the problem of solving the resulting differential equation for f. Once $f(t, x)$ is determined analytically or numerically for all (t, x), the quantity of interest is also obtained as a special case of $f(t, X_t)$.

We begin this section with an example where various computational tools can be used to tackle the same problem.

(**Background of a model problem**) Consider the running supremum of a Brownian motion

$$\overline{B}_t := \sup_{0 \le s \le t} \{B_s\}, \qquad B_t := \mu_* t + \sigma W_t,$$

where μ_*, σ are the drift parameter and the volatility parameter of the Brownian motion. As shown in Section 1.2.2, the running supremum plays a critical role in the modeling of step-up option in various guaranteed benefits. For example, the payoff from the guaranteed minimum maturity benefit with a lifetime high step-up option, which is an extension of (1.20) in conjunction with (1.19), is given by

$$e^{-rT}(G_T - F_T)_+ I(T_x > T) = e^{-rT} \left(\sup_{0 \le t \le T} \{F_t\} - F_T \right)_+ I(T_x > T).$$

Observe that

$$\sup_{0 \le t \le T} \{F_t\} = \frac{F_0}{S_0} e^{-mt} \sup_{0 \le t \le T} \{S_t\} = \frac{F_0}{S_0} e^{\overline{B}_t},$$

where $\mu_* = \mu - m$. For the rest of this section, the value of μ^* is irrelative and can be treated as an arbitrary parameter.

With this application in mind, we shall illustrate differential equation methods in this section by investigating the distribution of the running supremum,

$$\mathbb{P}(\overline{B}_t \le m).$$

We shall leave it as Exercise 7.1.1 to derive the joint distribution of $(\overline{B}_t, B_t)$.

Consider the conditional expectation

$$\mathbb{E}[I(\overline{B}_T \le m)|\mathcal{F}_t]$$

where $\{\mathcal{F}_t : 0 \le t \le T\}$ is the natural filtration of the Brownian motion. Due to the Markov property of the bivariate process $\{(B_t, \overline{B}_t) : 0 \le t \ge T\}$, we know that there exists a function $f(t, x, y)$ such that

$$\mathbb{E}[I(\overline{B}_T \le m)|\mathcal{F}_t] = f(t, B_t, \overline{B}_t), \qquad 0 \le t \le T. \tag{7.1}$$

It is clear from its definition that $\mathbb{P}(\overline{B}_T \le m) = f(0, 0, 0)$. In other words, if we can find such a function f, then $\mathbb{P}(\overline{B}_T \le m)$ can be obtained by evaluating f at the origin.

Here is a formal derivation of the PDE satisfied by the function f. Applying Itô's formula, we have

$$df(t, B_t, \overline{B}_t) = \frac{\partial}{\partial t} f(t, B_t, \overline{B}_t)\, dt + \frac{\partial}{\partial x} f(t, B_t, \overline{B}_t)\, dB_t + \frac{\partial}{\partial y} f(t, B_t, \overline{B}_t)\, d\overline{B}_t$$

$$+ \frac{\sigma^2}{2} \frac{\partial^2}{\partial x^2} f(t, B_t, \overline{B}_t)\, d[W, W]_t.$$

The cross variation term vanishes because the running supremum is a process of finite variation (Exercise 2.8.4). Hence,

$$df(t, B_t, \overline{B}_t) = \left[\frac{\partial}{\partial t} f(t, B_t, \overline{B}_t) + \mu_* \frac{\partial}{\partial x} f(t, B_t, \overline{B}_t) + \frac{1}{2} \frac{\partial^2}{\partial x^2} f(t, B_t, \overline{B}_t) \right] dt$$

$$+ \sigma \frac{\partial}{\partial x} f(t, B_t, \overline{B}_t)\, dW_t + \frac{\partial}{\partial y} f(t, B_t, \overline{B}_t)\, d\overline{B}_t.$$

Or written in an integral form,

$$f(t, B_t, \overline{B}_t) - f(0, 0, 0)$$

$$= \int_0^t \left[\frac{\partial}{\partial s} f(s, W_s, \overline{B}_s) + \mu_* \frac{\partial}{\partial x} f(s, W_s, \overline{B}_s) + \frac{\sigma^2}{2} \frac{\partial^2}{\partial x^2} f(s, W_s, \overline{B}_s) \right] ds$$

$$+ \int_0^t \mu_* \frac{\partial}{\partial x} f(s, W_s, \overline{B}_s)\, dW_s + \int_0^t \frac{\partial}{\partial y} f(s, W_s, \overline{B}_s)\, d\overline{B}_s. \tag{7.2}$$

Since $f(t, B_t, \overline{B}_t)$ is a martingale by its definition in (7.1), the expectation of both sides of (7.2) must be zero for all $0 \le t \le T$. Hence it must be true that

$$\frac{\partial}{\partial t} f(t, x, y) + \mu_* \frac{\partial}{\partial x} f(t, x, y) + \frac{\sigma^2}{2} \frac{\partial^2}{\partial x^2} f(t, x, y) = 0, \qquad t \ge 0, y \ge x. \tag{7.3}$$

Similarly, it must be true that for all $0 \le t \le T$

$$\int_0^t \frac{\partial}{\partial y} f(s, B_s, \overline{B}_s)\, d\overline{B}_s = 0.$$

Note that the integrator $\{\overline{B}_t, 0 \le t \le T\}$ only increases when the Brownian motion is at its maximum, i.e. $\overline{B}_t = B_t$. Therefore, it implies

$$\left. \frac{\partial}{\partial y} f(t, x, y) \right|_{x=y} = 0. \qquad \textbf{(\emph{y}-boundary cond'n 1)} \tag{7.4}$$

The rest of boundary conditions can be determined from the probabilistic interpretation of the conditional expectation in (7.1). Keep in mind that the function f can be written as

$$f(t, x, y) = \mathbb{E}[I(\overline{B}_T \le m) | B_t = x, \overline{B}_t = y], \qquad 0 \le t \le T. \tag{7.5}$$

If $\overline{B}_t = y > m$, then $\overline{B}_T > m$ and hence

$$\lim_{y \downarrow m} f(t, x, y) = 0, \qquad x \leq m, 0 \leq t \leq T. \qquad \text{(y-boundary cond'n 2)} \qquad (7.6)$$

Similarly, if $B_t = x$ approaches $-\infty$, it is unlikely that the Brownian motion will reach a new maximum within a finite amount of time and hence the running supremum $\overline{B}_T$ will stay at y.

$$\lim_{x \to -\infty} f(t, x, y) = 1, \qquad y < m, 0 \leq t \leq T. \qquad \text{(x-boundary cond'n 1)} \quad (7.7)$$

If B_t approaches m from the above, then the running supremum stays above m and hence

$$\lim_{x \downarrow m} f(t, x, y) = 0, \qquad m \leq y, 0 \leq t \leq T. \qquad \text{(x-boundary cond'n 2)} \quad (7.8)$$

Finally, when t is set to the terminal time T, we must have

$$f(T, B_T, \overline{B}_T) = \mathbb{E}[I(\overline{B}_T \leq m)|\mathcal{F}_T] = I(\overline{B}_T \leq m),$$

which implies that

$$\lim_{t \uparrow T} f(t, x, y) = I(y \leq m), \qquad x < y. \qquad \text{(terminal cond'n)} \qquad (7.9)$$

Now we have shown that f satisfies the PDE (7.3) subject to terminal and boundary conditions (7.4), (7.6), (7.7), (7.8) and (7.9).

7.1.1 Reduction of dimension

In many financial applications, one may reduce the dimension of the PDE under consideration. An apparent advantage of working with the PDE (7.3) is that its solution has a known probabilistic representation (7.5). Note that

$$\overline{B}_T = \max\left\{\overline{B}_t, \sup_{t \leq s \leq T} B_s\right\}.$$

Hence,

$$
\begin{aligned}
f(t, x, y) &= \mathbb{E}\left[I\left(\overline{B}_t + \left(\sup_{t \leq s \leq T} B_s - \overline{B}_t\right)_+ \leq m\right)\middle| B_t = x, \overline{B}_t = y\right] \\
&= \mathbb{E}\left[I\left(y + \left(\sup_{t \leq s \leq T} B_s - y\right)_+ \leq m\right)\middle| B_t = x\right],
\end{aligned}
$$

where $(x)_+ = \max\{x, 0\}$. Since the increments of Brownian motion are independent and stationary, we see that

$$
\begin{aligned}
f(t, x, y) &= \mathbb{E}\left[I\left((\overline{B}_{T-t} + x - y)_+ \leq m - y\right)|B_0 = 0\right] \\
&= I(y \leq m)\mathbb{P}(\overline{B}_{T-t} \leq m - x),
\end{aligned}
$$

where in the last equality we use the fact that $I((x)_+ \leq y) = I(x \leq y)I(y > 0)$.

Observe that the dependency of f on y is only through the indicator. In other words, for some unknown function h,

$$f(t, x, y) = I(y \leq m)h(T - t, m - x). \tag{7.10}$$

With this composition of f, boundary conditions (7.4) and (7.6) are trivially satisfied.

We are now ready to convert terminal and boundary conditions of f to those of h. Let $s = T - t$ and $z = m - x$. Then it is clear that (7.3) becomes

$$\frac{\partial}{\partial s}h(s, z) + \mu_* \frac{\partial}{\partial z}h(s, z) = \frac{\sigma^2}{2} \frac{\partial^2}{\partial z^2}h(s, z), \qquad 0 < s < T. \tag{7.11}$$

The terminal condition (7.9) is now turned into an initial condition

$$h(0, z) = 1, \qquad z > 0. \qquad \textbf{(initial cond'n)} \tag{7.12}$$

The boundary conditions (7.7) and (7.8) correspond to

$$\lim_{z \to \infty} h(s, z) = 1, \qquad 0 \leq s \leq T. \qquad \textbf{(\textit{z}-boundary cond'n 1)} \tag{7.13}$$

$$\lim_{z \to 0} h(s, z) = 0, \qquad 0 \leq s \leq T. \qquad \textbf{(\textit{z}-boundary cond'n 2)} \tag{7.14}$$

In the next two sections, we present an analytical method and a numerical method to solve the PDE (7.11). Analytical approaches often have limited applicability due to their reliance on particular structure of the PDE whereas numerical methods tend to be suitable for more complex and realistic models.

7.1.2 Laplace transform method

7.1.2.1 General methodology

> **Definition 7.1.** The *Laplace transform* of a function $f(s)$ defined for all $s \geq 0$ is given by
>
> $$\mathcal{L}\{f\}(r) = \int_0^\infty e^{-rs} f(s) \, ds, \qquad r \geq 0,$$
>
> provided that the integral exists.

The popularity of the Laplace transform method for solving differential equations is due to its differentiation property, which is derived from integration by parts,

$$\mathcal{L}\{f\}(r) = \frac{e^{-rs} f(s)}{-r} \bigg|_0^\infty - \int_0^\infty \frac{e^{-rs} f'(s)}{-s} \, ds = \frac{f(0)}{r} + \frac{1}{r}\mathcal{L}\{f'\}(r).$$

Applying this result repeatedly one can obtain the general result for any positive integer n

$$\mathcal{L}\{f^{(n)}\}(r) = r^n \mathcal{L}\{f\}(r) - r^{n-1} f(0) - \cdots - f^{(n-1)}(0),$$

where $f^{(n)}$ is the nth derivative of f. Therefore, the Laplace transform can turn a differential equation of f with respect to s into an algebraic equation of $\mathcal{L}\{f\}$ with respect to r. It is often easier to work with an algebraic equation than a differential equation.

7.1.2.2 Application

The partial differential equation (7.11) provides a perfect example of the Laplace transform method. Consider the Laplace transform of h with respect to s, which we denote by

$$\tilde{h}(r, z) := \mathcal{L}\{h\}(r) = \int_0^{+\infty} e^{-rs} h(s, z)\, ds, \qquad r > 0.$$

For notational brevity, we sometimes suppress the parameter r when viewing h as a function of z, i.e. $\tilde{h}(z) = \tilde{h}(r, z)$.

Taking Laplace transform on both sides of (7.11) and using the initial condition (7.12) leads to

$$\frac{\sigma^2}{2}\tilde{h}''(z) - \mu_*\tilde{h}'(z) - r\tilde{h}(z) = -1, \qquad z > 0. \tag{7.15}$$

Note that (7.15) is no longer a partial differential equation, because it is now an algebraic equation with respect to r. The boundary conditions (7.13) and (7.14) now become

$$\lim_{z \to \infty} \tilde{h}(z) = \frac{1}{r},$$

$$\lim_{z \to 0} \tilde{h}(z) = 0.$$

The fundamental solutions to (7.15) are given by

$$\tilde{h}_1(z) = e^{\rho_1 z}; \tag{7.16}$$

$$\tilde{h}_2(z) = e^{\rho_2 z}, \tag{7.17}$$

where ρ_1, ρ_2 are solutions to

$$\frac{\sigma^2}{2}\rho^2 - \mu_*\rho - r = 0.$$

In other words,

$$\rho_1 = \frac{\mu_* + \sqrt{\mu_*^2 + 2r\sigma^2}}{\sigma^2}, \qquad \rho_2 = \frac{\mu_* - \sqrt{\mu_*^2 + 2r\sigma^2}}{\sigma^2}.$$

Since $r, \sigma > 0$, it is clear that $\rho_1 > 0$ and $\rho_2 < 0$. Note that $\tilde{h}(z) = 1/r$ is a particular solution to (7.15). Therefore, its general solution must be given by

$$\tilde{h}(z) = \frac{1}{r} + c_1 e^{\rho_1 z} + c_2 e^{\rho_2 z} \qquad z > 0, \tag{7.18}$$

with coefficients c_1 and c_2 to be determined. In view of boundary conditions (7.16) and (7.17), we obtain

$$c_1 = 0, \qquad c_2 = -\frac{1}{r}.$$

Inserting the values for c_1 and c_2 in (7.18), we have

$$\tilde{h}(z) = \frac{1}{r} - \frac{1}{r} \exp\left\{ \frac{\mu_* - \sqrt{\mu_*^2 + 2r\sigma^2}}{\sigma^2} z \right\}, \qquad z > 0. \tag{7.19}$$

The rest of the calculation is to invert the Laplace transform in (7.19) with respect to r and to obtain an explicit expression of h, which is provided in Theorem 7.2.

Theorem 7.2. *The solution to the PDE* (7.11) *with initial and boundary conditions* (7.13), (7.14) *and* (7.12) *is given by*

$$h(s, z) = \Phi\left(\frac{z - \mu_* s}{\sigma\sqrt{s}} \right) - e^{2\mu_* z/\sigma^2} \Phi\left(\frac{-z - \mu_* s}{\sigma\sqrt{s}} \right),$$

where Φ is the standard normal distribution function.

Proof. It suffices to show that

$$\int_0^{+\infty} e^{-rs} \left[\Phi\left(\frac{-z + \mu_* s}{\sigma\sqrt{s}} \right) + e^{2\mu_* z/\sigma^2} \Phi\left(\frac{-z - \mu_* s}{\sigma\sqrt{s}} \right) \right] ds$$

$$= \frac{1}{r} \exp\left\{ (\mu_* - \sqrt{\mu_*^2 + 2r\sigma^2}) \frac{z}{\sigma^2} \right\}.$$

Applying integrations by parts gives

$$\int_0^{+\infty} e^{-rs} \Phi\left(\frac{-z + \mu_* s}{\sigma\sqrt{s}} \right) ds = \frac{1}{r\sqrt{2\pi}} \int_0^{+\infty} e^{-rs} e^{-\frac{(z - \mu_* s)^2}{2s\sigma^2}} \frac{\mu_*\sqrt{s} + \frac{z}{\sqrt{s}}}{2s\sigma} ds$$

$$\int_0^{+\infty} e^{-rs} e^{2\mu_* z} \Phi\left(\frac{-z - \mu_* s}{\sigma\sqrt{s}} \right) ds = \frac{1}{r\sqrt{2\pi}} \int_0^{+\infty} e^{-rs} e^{-\frac{(z - \mu_* s)^2}{2s\sigma^2}} \frac{-\mu_*\sqrt{s} + \frac{z}{\sqrt{s}}}{2s\sigma} ds.$$

Thus it remains to show that

$$\int_0^{+\infty} e^{-rs} e^{-\frac{(z - \mu_* s)^2}{2s\sigma^2}} \frac{z}{\sigma s^{\frac{3}{2}}} ds = \sqrt{2\pi} e^{(\mu_* - \sqrt{\mu_*^2 + 2r\sigma^2})z/\sigma^2}. \tag{7.20}$$

By letting $1/(\sigma\sqrt{s}) = t$, we can rewrite the left-hand side of (7.20) as

$$2z e^{\mu_* z/\sigma^2} I(a, b), \tag{7.21}$$

where $a = z/\sqrt{2}, b = \sqrt{r + \mu_*^2/(2\sigma^2)}/\sigma$ and

$$I(a, b) = \int_0^{+\infty} e^{-a^2 t^2 - \frac{b^2}{t^2}} dt. \tag{7.22}$$

Making a change of variables $y = b/(at)$ gives

$$I(a, b) = \frac{b}{a} \int_0^{+\infty} \frac{1}{y^2} e^{-a^2 y^2 - \frac{b^2}{y^2}} \, dy \qquad (7.23)$$

Adding (7.22) and (7.23) and dividing by 2 yields the identity

$$I(a, b) = \frac{1}{2a} \int_0^{+\infty} (a + \frac{b}{t^2}) e^{-a^2 t^2 - \frac{b^2}{t^2}} \, dt.$$

Making another change of variable $t = ax - b/x$ leads to

$$I(a, b) = \frac{\sqrt{\pi}}{2a} e^{-2ab} \int_{-\infty}^{+\infty} \frac{1}{\sqrt{\pi}} e^{-t^2} \, dt = \frac{\sqrt{\pi}}{2a} e^{-2ab}.$$

Inserting the above expression into $I(a, b)$ in (7.21), we can verify the two sides of (7.20)

$$\text{LHS} = 2z e^{\mu_* z / \sigma^2} I(a, b) = 2z e^{\mu_* z / \sigma^2} \frac{\sqrt{\pi}}{z\sqrt{2}} e^{-z\sqrt{\mu_*^2 + 2r\sigma^2}/\sigma^2} = \text{RHS},$$

which completes the proof. □

Now we return to the original problem of finding the distribution function of the running supremum. In view of (7.10), we obtain that $\mathbb{P}[\overline{B}_T \leq m | \mathcal{F}_t] = f(t, B_t, \overline{B}_t)$ where for $x \leq y$ and $y \leq m$

$$f(t, x, y) = \Phi \left(\frac{m - x - \mu_*(T - t)}{\sigma\sqrt{T - t}} \right) - e^{2\mu_*(m-x)/\sigma^2} \Phi \left(\frac{-(m - x) - \mu_*(T - t)}{\sigma\sqrt{T - t}} \right).$$

Since $\mathbb{P}(\overline{B}_T \leq m) = f(0, 0, 0)$, then we must have

$$\mathbb{P}(\overline{B}_T \leq m) = \Phi \left(\frac{m - \mu_* T}{\sigma\sqrt{T}} \right) - e^{2\mu_* m/\sigma^2} \Phi \left(\frac{-m - \mu_* T}{\sigma\sqrt{T}} \right). \qquad (7.24)$$

7.1.3 Finite difference method

While we have the luxury of an explicit solution in the illustrative example, it is often the case that exact solution is either not available or too technical to be useful in applications. Numerical methods typically have wide applicability and are more suitable for practical applications such as pricing and risk management of equity-linked insurance.

7.1.3.1 General methodology

Here we provide a brief introduction of a simple numerical method known as the (fully discrete) *finite difference method*[*]. Its essential idea can be summarized as follows.

1. Transform the domain of the PDE to a mesh grid;
2. Approximate partial derivatives by difference quotients;
3. Turn a differential equation into a difference equation;
4. Solve the resulting equation by a recursive formula.

Consider a function f with necessary differentiability. According to Taylor's theorem, the function f may be represented as

$$f(x + \Delta x) = f(x) + \Delta x f'(x) + \frac{1}{2}\Delta x^2 f''(x) + \frac{1}{6}\Delta x^3 f'''(x) + \cdots, \quad (7.25)$$

for any arbitrary Δx. In later applications, we typically set Δx to be a very small number and Δx is often referred to as *step size*. Therefore, the derivative of f can be approximated by a difference quotient according to

$$f'(x) = \frac{f(x + \Delta x) - f(x)}{\Delta x} + O(\Delta x). \quad (7.26)$$

As Δx tends to be small, we expect the term $O(\Delta x)$ to be very small as well. With $O(\Delta x)$ dropped in (7.26), the expression is known as a *forward approximation*. We can also think of $O(\Delta x)$ as the error term of the approximation.

Similarly, we can also rewrite (7.25) as

$$f(x - \Delta x) = f(x) - \Delta x f'(x) + \frac{1}{2}\Delta x^2 f''(x) - \frac{1}{6}\Delta x^3 f'''(x) + \cdots \quad (7.27)$$

This shows that the derivative of f can be approximated by another difference quotient,

$$f'(x) = \frac{f(x) - f(x - \Delta x)}{\Delta x} + O(\Delta x). \quad (7.28)$$

Without $O(\Delta x)$ in (7.28), the expression is known as a *backward approximation*.

Subtracting (7.27) from (7.25) yields

$$f'(x) = \frac{f(x + \Delta x) - f(x - \Delta x)}{2\Delta x} + O(\Delta x^2). \quad (7.29)$$

Dropping the remaining term $O(\Delta x^2)$ in (7.29), we obtain the *central approximation*

---

[*]There are other finite difference methods for the discretization of derivatives. The word *fully discrete* is used in contrast to *semidiscrete* methods. A typical fully discrete method is based on the finite difference approximation of derivatives in all variables, whereas semidiscrete methods utilize only finite difference approximations of derivatives in some variables while relying on explicit solution of the differential equation in other variables. Detailed accounts of finite difference methods can be found in Heath [63].

of a derivative. Since the term $O(\Delta x^2)$ in (7.29) would be much smaller than $O(\Delta x)$ in (7.26) and (7.28) when Δx is small, the central approximation is more accurate than forward and backward approximations.

Adding up (7.25) and (7.27) leads to

$$f''(x) = \frac{f(x + \Delta x) + f(x - \Delta x) - 2f(x)}{\Delta x^2} + O(\Delta x^2), \qquad (7.30)$$

which suggests an approximation of the second derivative. This approximation can be viewed as the composition of central approximations.

$$f''(x) \approx \frac{f'(x + \Delta x/2) - f'(x - \Delta x/2)}{\Delta x}$$

$$\approx \frac{\frac{f(x+\Delta x)-f(x)}{\Delta x} - \frac{f(x)-f(x-\Delta x)}{\Delta x}}{\Delta x} \qquad (7.31)$$

$$= \frac{f(x + \Delta x) + f(x - \Delta x) - 2f(x)}{\Delta x^2}. \qquad (7.32)$$

Example 7.3. Let us test the approximation methods on a few simple functions. All results are rounded to nearest fifth decimals. As shown in Tables (7.1) and (7.2), central approximation is always more accurate than other approximation methods. This is consistent with the observation on the order of error terms in (7.26), (7.28) and (7.29). In the case of linear function, the approximation is in fact exact.

$(\Delta x = 0.1)$	$f(x) = x$	$f(x) = x^2$	$f(x) = e^x$
$f'(0)$	1	0	1
Forward approximation	1	0.1	1.05171
Backward approximation	1	−0.1	0.95163
Central approximation	1	0	1.00167

TABLE 7.1: Finite difference approximation of $f'(0)$ with step size of 0.1

Comparing the results from Tables (7.1) and (7.2), one can tell that the errors from all methods tend to diminish as the step size Δx decreases. When Δx is reduced by a factor of 10, the errors from forward and backward approximations decrease roughly by a factor of 10 and those from the central approximation is reduced by a factor of 100.

$(\Delta x = 0.01)$	$f(x) = x^2$	$f(x) = e^x$
$f'(0)$	0	1
Forward approximation	0.01	1.00502
Backward approximation	−0.01	0.99502
Central approximation	0	1.00002

TABLE 7.2: Finite difference approximation of $f'(0)$ with step size of 0.01

Similarly, we test the accuracy of the approximation formula (7.32) for second derivatives of various functions, as shown in Table 7.3. As expected, when Δx is reduced by a factor of 10, approximation error decreases by a factor of 100. The error is zero for any quadratic function.

($\Delta x = 0.01$)	$f(x) = x^2$	$f(x) = e^x$
$f''(0)$	2	1
Approximation ($\Delta x = 0.1$)	2	1.00083
Approximation ($\Delta x = 0.01$)	2	1.00001

TABLE 7.3: Finite difference approximation of $f''(0)$

7.1.3.2 Application

With regard to the application to the model problem, we are interested in finding the numerical value of the solution to (7.11) h for any given combination of s and z. In this section, we provide a simple finite difference scheme.

While the solution h is defined for $(s, z) \in [0, T] \times [0, \infty)$, we restrict the domain of the function h to be $[0, T] \times [0, b]$ for some large enough b. As illustrated earlier with various approximation methods, derivatives are approximated by differences of function values at neighboring discrete points. Thus the first step is to create a grid to position the approximate solution. Define a uniform grid on $[0, T] \times [0, b]$ to be the collection of points (s_i, z_j) where

$$s_i = i\Delta s, \qquad \text{for } i = 1, \cdots, N_s + 1, \qquad \Delta s = T/(N_s + 1);$$
$$z_j = j\Delta z, \qquad \text{for } j = 1, \cdots, N_z + 1, \qquad \Delta z = b/(N_z + 1);$$

The points (s_i, z_j) are often referred to as *mesh points*. We seek approximations of the true solution h to the PDE on these mesh points. Let h_i^j denote the approximate solution at the mesh point (s_i, z_j), i.e.

$$h_i^j \approx h(s_i, z_j).$$

The next step is to convert the original partial differential equation into a difference equation. In this application, the scheme based at the mesh point (s_j, z_i) uses backward differences for all first-order derivatives, i.e.

$$\frac{h(s_i, z_j) - h(s_{i-1}, z_j)}{\Delta s} \approx \frac{\partial}{\partial s} h(s_i, z_j),$$
$$\frac{h(s_i, z_j) - h(s_i, z_{j-1})}{\Delta z} \approx \frac{\partial}{\partial z} h(s_i, z_j).$$

The scheme uses a centered second difference for the second order derivative, i.e.

$$\frac{h(s_i, z_{j+1}) - 2h(s_i, z_j) + h(s_i, z_{j-1})}{(\Delta z)^2} \approx \frac{\partial^2}{\partial z^2} h(s_i, z_j).$$

Replacing the derivatives in (7.11) by finite difference approximations on all mesh points (s_i, z_j) with $1 \leq i \leq N_s, 1 \leq j \leq N_z + 1$ generates the recursive relation

$$\frac{h_i^j - h_{i-1}^j}{\Delta s} + \mu \frac{h_i^j - h_i^{j-1}}{\Delta z} = \frac{1}{2} \cdot \frac{h_i^{j+1} - 2h_i^j + h_i^{j-1}}{\Delta z^2}. \qquad (7.33)$$

This recursive relation encodes a system of $N_s(N_z - 1)$ equations. We also translate initial and boundary conditions (7.12), (7.13), (7.14) as

$$\begin{aligned}
h_{i=1}^j &= 1, && \text{for } 1 \leq j \leq N_z + 1, \\
h_i^{j=N_z+1} &= 1, && \text{for } 1 \leq i \leq N_s + 1, \\
h_i^{j=1} &= 0, && \text{for } 1 \leq i \leq N_s + 1.
\end{aligned}$$

Note that the there are two points, $h_{i=1}^{j=1}$ and $h_{i=1}^{j=N_z+1}$, which are constrained by the above boundary conditions twice. In practice, we can pick either condition if there is a conflict. These further conditions add up to $(N_z + 1 - 2) + (N_s + 1) + (N_s + 1) = 2N_s + N_z + 1$ constraints. In total, we have $N_z N_s + N_z + N_s + 1$ independent equations. Recall our fully discrete grid, we have $(N_z + 1)(N_s + 1) = N_z N_s + N_z + N_s + 1$ mesh points. Hence, the system uniquely determines the approximate solution on all mesh points.

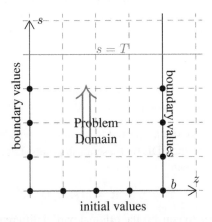

FIGURE 7.1: Pattern of mesh points in a finite difference scheme

We rewrite the recursive relation in (7.33) in a more explicit form

$$h_{i-1}^j = \alpha h_i^{j-1} + \beta h_i^j + \gamma h_i^{j+1},$$

where

$$\alpha = -\left(\frac{\Delta s}{2\Delta z^2} + \mu \frac{\Delta s}{\Delta z}\right), \qquad \beta = \frac{\Delta s}{\Delta z^2} + \mu \frac{\Delta s}{\Delta z} + 1, \qquad \gamma = -\frac{\Delta s}{2\Delta z^2}.$$

In matrix notation, we can write

$$\mathbf{h}_{i-1} = \mathbf{A}\mathbf{h}_i + \mathbf{b}, \qquad i = 2, 3, \cdots, N_s + 1$$

where $\mathbf{h}^i = \left(h_i^1, h_i^2, \cdots, h_i^{N_z}\right)$, $\mathbf{b} = (0, \cdots, 0, \gamma)^\top$, and $\mathbf{A}$ is an $N_z \times N_z$ matrix given by

$$\mathbf{A} = \begin{pmatrix} \beta & \gamma & 0 & \dots & 0 & 0 & 0 \\ \alpha & \beta & \gamma & \dots & 0 & 0 & 0 \\ & & & \cdots\cdots & & & \\ 0 & 0 & 0 & \dots & \alpha & \beta & \gamma \\ 0 & 0 & 0 & \dots & 0 & \alpha & \beta \end{pmatrix}.$$

The recursive update formula is given by

$$\mathbf{h}_{i+1} = \mathbf{A}^{-1}(\mathbf{h}_i - \mathbf{b}), \tag{7.34}$$

with the initial value $\mathbf{h}_{i=1} = 1$. As illustrated in Figure 7.1, funciton values are known on the solid dots and the matrix formula (7.34) allows us to find the approximate solution on the rest of mesh points by marching through the time s axis.

Returning to the original model problem, we can obtain the approximation of the desired value $\mathbb{P}(\overline{B}_T \leq m) = f(0,0,0) = h(T, m)$ given by

$$h(T, m) \approx h(s_{N_s+1}, z_{\lceil m/\Delta z \rceil}) = h_{N_s+1}^{\lceil m/\Delta z \rceil}.$$

When designing the grid, one could choose an appropriate step size Δz such that m is divisable. Even if m cannot be divided by Δz, one may use other approximations such as a linear interpolation of $h_{N_s+1}^{\lfloor m/\Delta z \rfloor}$ and $h_{N_s+1}^{\lceil m/\Delta z \rceil}$.

7.1.4 Risk measures: guaranteed minimum withdrawal benefit

Let us recapitulate the formulation of individual net liability of the GMWB rider in the continuous-time setup. As shown in Section 2.12.2, if the underlying equity index/fund of the policyholder's choosing can be modeled by a geometric Brownian motion as in (2.44), then the dynamics of a policyholder's account value is given by

$$dF_t = \mu^* F_t \, dt - w \, dt + \sigma F_t \, dB_t, \qquad F_0 > 0, \tag{7.35}$$

where $\mu^* = \mu - m$. Note that the withdrawal rate is typically a fixed percentage of the benefit base G. In the case of a full guarantee refund, the benefit base G is set equal to F_0. The amount of time needed for the policyholder to recoup the original premium payment $G = F_0$ by withdrawing w per time unit is $T = G/w$. Clearly, there is no financial obligation to the insurer until the time at which the account value hits zero, i.e.

$$\tau = \inf\{t : F_t \leq 0\}. \tag{7.36}$$

It is only when the account value is depleted prior to the maturity T that the maximum withdrawal rate w is paid at the cost of the insurer. Therefore, the present value of the cost to an insurer of the GMWB rider (gross liability) is thus given by

$$\int_{\tau \wedge T}^{T} e^{-rs} w \, ds, \tag{7.37}$$

where r is the yield rate on the assets backing up the liability. To compensate for undertaking the risk with the GMWB rider, the insurer receives fees as fixed percentages of the policyholder's account until the account value hits zero. The accumulated present value of the fee income is given by

$$\int_0^{\tau \wedge T} m_w e^{-rs} F_s \, ds, \tag{7.38}$$

where m_w is the portion of the fee rate which is allocated to fund the GMWB rider. Thus, the individual net liability for the GMWB rider is given by

$$L = \int_{\tau \wedge T}^T e^{-rs} w \, ds - m_w \int_0^{\tau \wedge T} e^{-rs} F_s \, ds. \tag{7.39}$$

7.1.4.1 Value-at-risk

We can show how to determine the value-at-risk of the GMWB net liability

$$\text{VaR}_\alpha := \inf\{y : \mathbb{P}[L \le y] \ge \alpha\}. \tag{7.40}$$

Since L is modeled by continuous random variables in this model, we seek a number V such that

$$\mathbb{P}[L > V] = 1 - \alpha. \tag{7.41}$$

Such number can be found through a root search algorithm such as the bisection method introduced in Section 3.2.1.

Observe that the net liability L depends on two random processes, the value of the equity index/fund F_t and the present value of the accumulated capital

$$A_t := \int_0^t e^{-rs} F_s ds.$$

It is known from Exercise 2.12.2 that the bivariate process $\{(F_t, A_t), 0 \le t \le T\}$ is a Markov process.

Let us define function $v(t, x, y)$ for a fixed number K as

$$\begin{aligned} v(t, x, y) &= \mathbb{E}[I(L \le K)|F_t = x, A_t = y] \\ &= \mathbb{P}(L \le K|F_t = x, A_t = y). \end{aligned} \tag{7.42}$$

We denote the partial derivatives of v with respect to t, x, y by v_t, v_x, v_y respectively and the second partial derivative of v with respect to x by v_{xx}. In particular, the loss distribution at time $t = 0$ corresponds to $v(0, G, 0) = \mathbb{P}(L \le K)$.

Theorem 7.4 (Computation of $\mathbb{P}(L < K)$). *The function v is a solution of the following partial differential equation for $t \in (0, T), x \in (0, \infty), y \in (0, \infty)$*

$$v_t + (\mu^* x - w)v_x + e^{-rt} x v_y + \tfrac{1}{2}\sigma^2 x^2 v_{xx} = 0 \tag{7.43}$$

with terminal condition

$$v(T, x, y) = 1, \tag{7.44}$$

and boundary conditions

$$v(t, 0, y) = I\left(f(t, K) \leq y\right), \tag{7.45}$$

$$\lim_{x \to \infty} v_x(t, x, y) = 0, \tag{7.46}$$

$$\lim_{y \to \infty} v(t, x, y) = 1, \tag{7.47}$$

where

$$f(t, K) := \frac{w}{rm_w}(e^{-rt} - e^{-rT}) - \frac{K}{m_w}.$$

Proof. The process $v(t, F_t, A_t)$ is a martingale with stochastic dynamics

$$\begin{aligned} dv(t, F_t, A_t) &= v_t \, dt + v_x \, dF_t + v_y \, dA_t + \tfrac{1}{2} v_{xx} \, d[F, F]_t \\ &= v_t \, dt + (\mu^* F_t - w) v_x \, dt + \sigma F_t v_x \, dW_t \\ &\quad + v_y e^{-rt} F_t \, dt + \tfrac{1}{2}\sigma^2 F_t^2 v_{xx} \, dt. \end{aligned}$$

The dt terms must vanish, so the function v must satisfy the partial differential equation (7.43). The partial differential equation applies in the case when none of the boundaries is hit, more specifically when $F_T > 0$ so the fund is not depleted until the end of the contract. When the contract reaches maturity, the insurer in this case makes a profit which corresponds to the accumulated present value of the fee income (the loss is negative):

$$L = -m_w A_T.$$

Should v represent the probability $\mathbb{P}_t(L < K)$, we need $I(L \leq K)$ as the terminal condition which translates to

$$I(L \leq K) = I(-m_w A_T \leq K) = I(A_T \geq -\tfrac{K}{m_w}).$$

This gives the terminal condition (7.44) given that $A_T = y > 0$. Since only the first derivative is involved in the y-dimension, we treat y as a time-like variable, which requires only one trivial boundary condition (7.47). A more challenging boundary is when $x = 0$. This corresponds to the absorbing boundary $F_t = 0$. Given the value of A_t, the process $\{F_s, t < s < T\}$ becomes deterministic, i.e.

$$\begin{aligned} I(L \leq K) &= I\left(\int_t^T e^{-rs} w \, ds - m_w A_t \leq K\right) \\ &= I\left(\frac{w}{m_w \cdot r}(e^{-rt} - e^{-rT}) - \frac{K}{m_w} \leq A_t\right), \end{aligned}$$

which leads to the boundary condition (7.45). The boundary for $x \to \infty$ can be taken anything consistent with other boundaries since $\mathbb{P}(F_t \to \infty) = 0$. In particular, we can impose the Neumann boundary condition (7.46). $\qquad\square$

Remark 7.5. The finite domain approximation of the Neuman boundary condition (7.46) has a probabilistic interpretation. As we shall see in a numerical example, an approximation of the boundary condition is given by

$$v_x(t, b, y) = 0, \qquad \text{for some large } b.$$

This condition corresponds to the case where the underlying Brownian motion is instantaneously reflecting at the boundary $x = b$, i.e. the Brownian motion bounces back immediately after it hits the boundary. Although this is not the intended problem of (7.42), we can choose b sufficiently large that the probability of the Brownian motion reaching b is so negligible that the resulting solution provides a good approximation to the original problem.

7.1.4.2 Conditional tail expectation

For the computation of conditional tail expectation, we observe that

$$\mathrm{CTE}_\alpha = \frac{1}{1-\alpha} \mathbb{E}[LI(L > \mathrm{VaR}_\alpha)].$$

Therefore, we introduce for any fixed $K > 0$,

$$u(t, x, y) = \mathbb{E}[LI(L > K)|F_t = x, A_t = y].$$

In particular, the conditional tail expectation is determined by $\mathrm{CTE}_\alpha = u(0, G, 0)/(1 - \alpha)$ with $K = \mathrm{VaR}_\alpha$, which is determined by the PDE method described in the previous section.

Theorem 7.6 (Computation of $\mathbb{E}[LI(L > K)]$). *The function u is a solution of the following partial differential equation for $t \in (0, T), x \in (0, \infty), y \in (0, \infty)$*

$$u_t + (\mu^* x - w)u_x + e^{-rt}xu_y + \tfrac{1}{2}\sigma^2 x^2 u_{xx} = 0 \qquad (7.48)$$

with terminal condition

$$u(T, x, y) = 0, \qquad (7.49)$$

and boundary conditions

$$u(t, 0, y) = \left[\frac{w}{r}(e^{-rt} - e^{-rT}) - m_w y\right] I\left(f(t, K) > y\right) \quad (7.50)$$

$$\lim_{x \to \infty} u_x(t, x, y) = 0, \qquad (7.51)$$

$$\lim_{y \to \infty} u(t, x, y) = 0. \qquad (7.52)$$

Proof. The derivation of (7.48) is very similar to that of (7.43). Given that $A_T = y > 0$, we note that

$$u(T, x, y) = LI(L > K) = LI(y < -\tfrac{K}{m_w}) = 0,$$

which produces the terminal condition (7.49). When the process F_t hits the absorbing boundary 0, we know that

$$LI(L > K) = \left(\int_t^T e^{-rs}w\,\mathrm{d}s - m_w A_t\right) I\left(\int_t^T e^{-rs}w\,\mathrm{d}s - m_w A_t > K\right),$$

which leads to the boundary condition (7.50). The other two boundary conditions (7.51) and (7.52) follow trivially from the definition of u.   □

7.1.4.3 Numerical example

In this section, we illustrate how the finite difference method is implemented to determine the value-at-risk of the GMWB net liability.

In a manner similar to that in Section 7.1.3.2, we look for numeric approximation to the solution of (7.43). The PDE (7.43) is re-defined on a finite domain $[0, T] \times [0, b] \times [0, c]$ where $b \geq G$ and c are sufficiently large. Boundary and terminal conditions are defined by

$$
\begin{aligned}
v(T, x, y) &= 1, & x \in (0, b), y \in (0, c), \\
v(t, x, c) &= 1, & x \in (0, b), t \in (0, T), \\
v(t, 0, y) &= I(f(t, K) \leq y), & t \in (0, T), y \in (0, c), \\
v_x(t, b, y) &= 0, & t \in (0, T), y \in (0, c),
\end{aligned}
$$

where

$$
f(t, K) := \frac{w}{rm_w}(e^{-rt} - e^{-rT}) - \frac{K}{m_w}.
$$

We apply a change of variable by letting $s(t, x, y) = v(T - t, x, c - y)$ and transform (7.43) to

$$
s_t + e^{-r(T-t)}x s_y = (\mu^* x - w)s_x + \frac{1}{2}\sigma^2 x^2 s_{xx}, \tag{7.53}
$$

subject to conditions

$$
\begin{aligned}
s(0, x, y) &= 1, & x \in (0, b), y \in (0, c); & \tag{7.54} \\
s(t, x, 0) &= 1, & x \in (0, b), t \in (0, T); & \tag{7.55} \\
s(t, 0, y) &= I(f(T - t, K) \leq c - y), & t \in (0, T), y \in (0, c); & \tag{7.56} \\
s_x(t, b, y) &= 0, & t \in (0, T), y \in (0, c). & \tag{7.57}
\end{aligned}
$$

We set up the grid with mesh points (x_i, y_j, t_k) and denote the approximate solution of $s(x_i, y_j, t_k)$ by $s_i^{j,k}$ where

$$
\begin{aligned}
x_i &= i\Delta x, & \text{for } i = 0, \cdots, N_x, & \quad Nx = b/\Delta x; \\
y_j &= (j - 1)\Delta y, & \text{for } j = 1, \cdots, N_y + 1, & \quad Ny = c/\Delta y; \\
t_k &= (k - 1)\Delta t, & \text{for } k = 1, \cdots, N_t + 1, & \quad Nt = T/\Delta t.
\end{aligned}
$$

Indices for y and t variables are shifted by 1 so that they are consistent with indices for matrix representation in the sample MATLAB code in Appendix F.2. On the left-hand-side of the (7.53), we adopt a scheme which uses backward difference in the space variable y, i.e.

$$
\frac{s(x_i, y_{j+1}, t_{k+1}) - s(x_i, y_{j+1}, t_k)}{\Delta t} \approx s_t(x_i, y_{j+1}, t_{k+1}),
$$

and which uses backward difference in the time variable t, i.e.

$$
\frac{s(x_i, y_{j+1}, t_{k+1}) - s(x_i, y_j, t_{k+1})}{\Delta y} \approx s_y(x_i, y_{j+1}, t_{k+1}).
$$

On the right-hand-side of the (7.53), we use central differences to approximate the derivatives in the space variable x, i.e.

$$\frac{s(x_{i+1}, y_{j+1}, t_{k+1}) - s(x_{i-1}, y_{j+1}, t_{k+1})}{2\Delta x} \approx s_x(x_i, y_{j+1}, t_{k+1});$$

$$\frac{s(x_{i+1}, y_{j+1}, t_{k+1}) - s(x_{i-1}, y_{j+1}, t_{k+1}) + 2s(x_i, y_{j+1}, t_{k+1})}{(\Delta x)^2}$$

$$\approx s_{xx}(x_i, y_{j+1}, t_{k+1}).$$

Therefore, the approximate solution generated by substituting derivatives with finite differences in (7.53) must satisfy

$$\frac{s_i^{j+1,k+1} - s_i^{j+1,k}}{\Delta t} + e^{-r(T-k\Delta t)} i \Delta x \frac{s_i^{j+1,k+1} - s_i^{j,k+1}}{\Delta y}$$

$$= (\mu^* i \Delta x - w) \frac{s_{i+1}^{j+1,k+1} - s_{i-1}^{j+1,k+1}}{2\Delta x} + \frac{\sigma^2}{2} (i\Delta x)^2 \frac{s_{i+1}^{j+1,k+1} + s_{i-1}^{j+1,k+1} - 2s_i^{j+1,k+1}}{(\Delta x)^2},$$

which can be rewritten as the recursive relation

$$-\frac{1}{2} \left(\sigma^2 i^2 + i\mu^* + \gamma \right) s_{i+1}^{j+1,k+1} + \left(\sigma^2 i^2 + \beta g^k i + \alpha \right) s_i^{j+1,k+1}$$

$$-\frac{1}{2} \left(\sigma^2 i^2 + \mu^* i - \gamma \right) s_{i+1}^{j+1,k+1} = \alpha s_i^{j+1,k} + \beta g^k i s_i^{j,k+1}, \quad (7.58)$$

where

$$\alpha := \frac{1}{\Delta t}, \beta := \frac{\Delta x}{\Delta y}, \gamma := \frac{w}{\Delta x}, g^k := e^{-r(T-k\Delta t)}.$$

It follows from (7.54) that the approximate solution starts at the initial time with the value of 1 across the whole x-y plane.

$$s_i^{j,1} = 1, \qquad \text{for all } i, j. \tag{7.59}$$

Similarly, it follows from (7.55) that the solution is set to 1 on x-t plane at the boundary $y = 0$, i.e.

$$s_i^{1,k} = 1 \qquad \text{for all } i, k. \tag{7.60}$$

Other boundary conditions can be determined as follows. The Dirichlet condition (7.56) requires that for all j, k

$$s_0^{j,k} = \mathbb{I}\left((j-1)\Delta y \le c + \frac{K}{m_w} - \frac{w}{rm_w} e^{-rT} \left(e^{r(k-1)\Delta t} - 1 \right) \right).$$

The Neumann condition (7.57) can be approximated by setting a central difference to zero, i.e.

$$\frac{s(t_k, x_{N_x+1}, y_j) - s(t_k, x_{N_x-1}, y_j)}{2\Delta x} \approx s_x(t_k, b, y_j) = 0,$$

which implies that for all j, k

$$s^{j,k}_{N_x+1} = s^{j,k}_{N_x-1}. \tag{7.61}$$

Setting $i = N_x$ in (7.58) and using the identity in (7.61) gives the relation

$$\left(\sigma^2 N_x^2 + \beta g^k N_x + \alpha\right) s^{j+1,k+1}_{N_x} - \sigma^2 N_x^2 s^{j+1,k+1}_{N_x-1} = \alpha s^{j+1,k}_{N_x} + \beta g^k N_x s^{j,k+1}_{N_x}. \tag{7.62}$$

For notational brevity, we shall represent the recursive relation in matrix form. Since t represents time and y is a time-like variable, we can start with "initial values" of the solution at $t = 0$ and $y = 0$ and utilize the recursive relation (7.58) in x-variable to determine vectors of the form

$$\mathbf{s}^{j,k} := \left(s^{j,k}_1, s^{j,k}_2, s^{j,k}_3, \cdots, s^{j,k}_{N_x}\right)^\top.$$

We can combine (7.58) and (7.62) in the following form

$$\mathbf{B}^k \mathbf{s}^{j+1,k+1} = \alpha \mathbf{s}^{j+1,k} + \mathbf{C}^k \mathbf{s}^{j,k+1} + \mathbf{d}^{j,k},$$

where $\mathbf{d}^{j,k}$ is an N_x-dimensional vector

$$\mathbf{d}^{j,k} = \left(\frac{1}{2}(\sigma^2 - \mu + m + \gamma)s^{j+1,k+1}_0, 0, \cdots, 0\right)^\top,$$

and $\mathbf{C}^k$ and $\mathbf{B}^k$ are $N_x \times N_x$ matrices

$$\mathbf{C}^k = \begin{pmatrix} \beta g^k & 0 & 0 & \cdots & 0 & 0 \\ 0 & 2\beta g^k & 0 & \cdots & 0 & 0 \\ \vdots & \vdots & \vdots & & \vdots & \vdots \\ 0 & 0 & 0 & \cdots & 0 & N_x \beta g^k \end{pmatrix},$$

$$\mathbf{B}^k = \begin{pmatrix} \sigma^2 + \beta g^k + \alpha & -\frac{1}{2}(\sigma^2 + \mu^* - \gamma) & 0 & \cdots & 0 & 0 \\ -\frac{1}{2}(4\sigma^2 - 2\mu^* + \gamma) & 4\sigma^2 + 2\beta g^k + \alpha & -\frac{1}{2}(4\sigma^2 + 2\mu^* - r) & \cdots & 0 & 0 \\ \vdots & \vdots & \vdots & & \vdots & \vdots \\ 0 & 0 & 0 & \cdots & -\sigma^2 N_x^2 & \sigma^2 N_x^2 + N_x \beta g^k + \alpha \end{pmatrix}.$$

Therefore, we can determine $\mathbf{s}^{j+1,k+1}$ by

$$\mathbf{s}^{j+1,k+1} = (\mathbf{B}^k)^{-1}\left(\alpha \mathbf{s}^{j+1,k} + \mathbf{C}^k \mathbf{s}^{j,k+1} + \mathbf{d}^{j,k}\right)$$

marching alternatively in the i and j directions, starting from $i = 1$ and $j = 1$, where it follows from (7.59) and (7.60) that

$$\mathbf{s}^{j,1} = \mathbf{1}, \qquad \mathbf{s}^{1,k} = \mathbf{1}.$$

Returning to the original problem of value-at-risk, we realize that

$$\mathbb{P}(L \leq K) = v(0, G, 0) = s(T, G, c) = s\left(t_{N_t+1}, x_{G/\Delta x}, y_{N_y+1}\right),$$

which can be approximated by the numerical solution on the mesh point $(N_t + 1, G/\Delta x, N_y + 1)$, i.e. $s_{G/\Delta x}^{N_y+1,N_t+1}$.

Here we illustrate the computation of the probability distribution function using the PDE method described above. We also use Monte Carlo simulation as the benchmark to test the accuracy of the PDE method. In this numerical example, we set the valuation assumptions as follows. All parameters are provided on per annum basis.

- Drift parameter $\mu = 0.09$ and volatility parameter $\sigma = 0.3$;

- M&E fee rate $m = 0.01$ and the GMWB fee $m_w = 0.0035$;

- Rate of return on insurer's assets backing up the GMWB liability, $r = 0.05$;

- Fixed rate of withdrawals per annum, $w = 0.07G$.

The guarantee base is chosen to be $G = F_0 = 1$ so that the resulting risk measures are represented as percentages of the guarantee base amount. For the PDE algorithm, we set mesh size $\Delta t = \Delta x = \Delta y = 0.01$, maximum cutoff point for $x \in (0, b = 6)$, and cutoff for $y \in (0, c = 12)$. Table 7.4 shows that the PDE algorithm can reach an accuracy up to three to four decimals. (Standard deviation of Monte Carlo estimates are printed in parentheses in the table.) However, in general, the PDE method is much more time-efficient than Monte Carlo simulations with comparable accuracy. A comparison of time consumption can be seen in Feng and Vecer [47].

K	0.00	0.05	0.10	0.15	0.20
MC ($\Delta t = 0.1$)	0.640570	0.697059	0.756167	0.815808	0.872781
	(0.000250)	(0.000228)	(0.000220)	(0.000193)	(0.000176)
MC ($\Delta t = 0.01$)	0.635529	0.691627	0.750476	0.810114	0.867442
	(0.000257)	(0.000241)	(0.000221)	(0.000190)	(0.000184)
MC ($\Delta t = 0.001$)	0.634963	0.691042	0.749874	0.809524	0.866930
	(0.000265)	(0.000278)	(0.000278)	(0.000257)	(0.000206)
PDE	0.635076	0.691099	0.749851	0.809359	0.866573

TABLE 7.4: Loss distribution of GMWB net liability

7.2 Comonotonic approximation

7.2.1 Tail value-at-risk of conditional expectation

For insurance applications, we often encounter problems of computing risk measures of random variables arising from complex product designs or diverse portfolios. When it is difficult to directly determine the distribution of a random variable, X, we may consider an approximation based on the convex order relation

$$X^l = \mathbb{E}(X|\Lambda) \leq_{cx} X,$$

which implies by Theorem 5.39 that for all $p \in (0, 1)$,

$$\mathrm{TVaR}_p[X^l] \leq \mathrm{TVaR}_p[X].$$

The TVaR of the comonotonic approximation X^l is sometimes much easier to compute than that of the original variable X and serves as a lower bound. This is in particular the case where X is the sum of the components of a multivariate lognormal random vector. We want to know the magnitude of the error with the lower bound.

Theorem 7.7. *For all $p \in [0, 1)$,*

$$\boxed{\mathrm{TVaR}_p[X] - \mathrm{TVaR}_p[X^l] \leq \frac{1}{2(1-p)} \mathbb{E}(|X - X^l|).} \tag{7.63}$$

Proof. It is easy to prove that for two real-valued functions f and g bounded from below with the same domain,

$$\inf f + \inf g \leq \inf\{f + g\},$$

which implies

$$\inf f - \inf g \leq -\inf\{g - f\}.$$

Furthermore, if $g - f$ is bounded, then

$$\inf f - \inf g \leq \sup\{f - g\}.$$

Recall from (5.8) that

$$\mathrm{TVaR}_p(X) = \inf_{a \in \mathbb{R}} \left\{ a + \frac{1}{1-p} \mathbb{E}(X - a)_+ \right\}.$$

Denote the expression inside the brackets by $f_X(a)$. Then it is clear that

$$f_X'(a) = 1 - \frac{1}{1-p} \mathbb{P}(X > a).$$

Therefore, there exists some number a_0 such that f is non-increasing on (∞, a_0) and non-decreasing on (a_0, ∞). Since

$$\lim_{a \to -\infty} a + \frac{1}{1-p} \mathbb{E}(X - a)_+ \geq \frac{1}{1-p} \lim_{a \to -\infty} a + \mathbb{E}(X - a)_+ = \frac{1}{1-p} \mathbb{E}(X) > -\infty,$$

we find that f_X is indeed bounded from below. Note that by Jensen's inequality,

$$f_X(a) - f_{X^l}(a) = \frac{1}{1-p} \{\mathbb{E}(X - a)_+ - \mathbb{E}(X^l - a)_+\} \geq 0, \qquad \forall a \in \mathbb{R}.$$

Moreover, $f_X - f_{X^l}$ is differentiable and

$$\lim_{a \to +\infty} f_X(a) - f_{X^l}(a) = 0.$$

Thus $f_X - f_{X^l}$ is bounded. Therefore,

$$\text{TVaR}_p[X] - \text{TVaR}_p[X^l] \le \frac{1}{1-p} \sup_{a \in \mathbb{R}} \left\{ \mathbb{E}(X-a)_+ - \mathbb{E}(X^l-a)_+ \right\}.$$

It follows from Exercise 7.2.1 that for any pair of random variables (Y, Λ)

$$\mathbb{E}(Y_+) - \mathbb{E}(\mathbb{E}(Y|\Lambda)_+) \le \frac{1}{2}\mathbb{E}(|Y - \mathbb{E}(Y|\Lambda)|).$$

Let $Y = X - a$. Therefore, we find the error bound (7.63).   □

Hereafter we provide some examples to demonstrate that (7.63) is a tight upper bound of the difference in the sense that the upper bound can be reached for a particular choice of $p \in (0,1)$.

Example 7.8. Let Λ be independent of X, then (7.63) is reduced to the special form

$$\text{TVaR}_p[X] - \mathbb{E}[X] \le \frac{1}{2(1-p)}\mathbb{E}|X - \mathbb{E}[X]|.$$

(a) Consider X to be a standard normal random variable with the distribution function Φ. It follows immediately that

$$\text{VaR}_p[X] = \Phi^{-1}(p) \quad \text{and} \quad \text{TVaR}_p[X] = \frac{1}{(1-p)\sqrt{2\pi}}e^{-\frac{1}{2}(\Phi^{-1}(p))^2}.$$

Since $\mathbb{E}[X] = 0$ and $\mathbb{E}|X| = \sqrt{2/\pi}$, the upper bound is attainable if and only if $p = \frac{1}{2}$.

(b) Consider X to be an exponential random variable with mean $1/\lambda$. Then

$$\text{VaR}_p[X] = -\frac{1}{\lambda}\ln(1-p) \quad \text{and} \quad \text{TVaR}_p[X] = \frac{1 - \ln(1-p)}{\lambda}.$$

It turns out that the upper bound is attainable at the constant $p = (e-1)/e \approx 0.6321205588$.

(c) Let X be a gamma random variable with mean α/β and variance α^2/β. Then $\text{VaR}_p[X]$ is the inverse function of $F(x) = \frac{1}{\Gamma(\alpha)}\gamma(\alpha, \beta x)$ and γ is the lower incomplete gamma function. And

$$\text{TVaR}_p[X] = \frac{1}{(1-p)\beta\Gamma(\alpha)}\Gamma(\alpha+1, \beta\text{VaR}_p[X]),$$

$$\mathbb{E}|X - \mathbb{E}[X]| = \frac{2\alpha^\alpha e^{-\alpha}}{\beta\Gamma(\alpha)},$$

where $\Gamma(\cdot)$ and $\Gamma(\cdot, \cdot)$ are the gamma function and the upper incomplete gamma function respectively. It can be shown that the upper bound is attainable at the constant $p = \gamma(\alpha, \alpha)/\Gamma(\alpha)$, which is independent of β.

Remark 7.9. In applications, it is often difficult to determine a closed-form expression for $\mathbb{E}(|X - X^l|)$. Therefore, using the fact that $\mathbb{E}|X - X^l| \leq \mathbb{V}(X|\Lambda)$, we find the following weaker upper bound:

$$\mathrm{TVaR}_p[X] - \mathrm{TVaR}_p[X^l] \leq \frac{1}{2(1-p)} \mathbb{E}(\mathbb{V}[X|\Lambda]^{1/2}), \qquad \text{for } p \in [0, 1). \quad (7.64)$$

Note, however, the upper bound in (7.64) may not be attained for any p in $[0, 1)$.

Although the error bounds in (7.63) and (7.64) are tight in the examples above, they are generally very conservative for large p. In many applications, actual errors from comonotonic approximation can be orders of magnitude smaller than the error bounds.

7.2.2 Comonotonic bounds for sums of random variables

We are often interested in the aggregate sum of random variables such as $S = X_1 + X_2 + \cdots + X_n$, where the marginal distributions of random variables $X_1, X_2, \cdots, X_n$ are known but their joint distribution is either unknown or too complex to be useful for computations. In such cases, one can exploit the theory of comonotonic bounds to find closed-form approximations that can be implemented efficiently.

Recall that the random vector $(X_1, X_2, \cdots, X_n)$ is comonotonic if

$$(X_1, X_2, \cdots, X_n) \sim \left(F_1^{-1}(U), F_2^{-1}(U), \cdots, F_n^{-1}(U)\right),$$

where $\sim$ means equality in distribution and F_k^{-1} is the value-at-risk/quantile function of X_k for $k = 1, \cdots, n$. For any random vector $(X_1, X_2, \cdots, X_n)$ and any random variable Λ,

$$S^l := \sum_{i=1}^n \mathbb{E}[X_i|\Lambda] \leqslant_{cx} S := \sum_{i=1}^n X_i \leqslant_{cx} \sum_{i=1}^n F_{X_i}^{-1}(U)$$

where the random variable U is uniformly distributed on $[0, 1]$. The random variable S^l is known as the *comonotonic lower bound* of S based on Λ. The right-hand side of the second inequality is called the *comonotonic upper bound*.

It is known in the literature that in a multivariate lognormal setup with appropriate choices of Λ, the comonotonic lower bound S^l provides a better approximation of S than the comonotonic upper bound. By Theorem 5.39, we know that for $p \in (0, 1)$,

$$\mathrm{TVaR}_p(S^l) \leq \mathrm{TVaR}_p(S). \quad (7.65)$$

Then we can try to obtain the maximum value of the lower bound $\mathrm{TVaR}_p(S^l)$,

$$\max_{\Lambda \in \Theta} \mathrm{TVaR}_p(S^l), \quad (7.66)$$

as an approximation of $\mathrm{TVaR}(S)$, where Λ is taken from a family Θ of normal random variables.

7.2.3 Guaranteed minimum maturity benefit

Comonotonic approximation techniques have natural applications in risk management problems of variable annuity guaranteed benefits. Consider the GMMB net liability in the aggregate model (5.38) with the assumption that the equity fund is driven by a geometric Brownian motion (2.48). To discretize the integral in the GMDB net liability, we assume that both T and n are integers and each year is divided into n periods. Given that $L > 0$, a discrete-time version of the GMMB net liability is given by

$$L = e^{-rT} \, {}_T p_x G - \left(\frac{1}{n} m_e F_0 + S \right), \tag{7.67}$$

where

$$S = \sum_{i=1}^{nT} \alpha_i e^{Z_i}, \qquad Z_i = (\mu - r - m)\frac{i}{n} + \sigma W_{i/n},$$

and the α_i's are positive constants defined by

$$\alpha_i = \begin{cases} \dfrac{1}{n} \, {}_{i/n} p_x m_e F_0, & i = 1, \cdots, nT - 1, \\ {}_T p_x F_0, & i = nT. \end{cases}$$

Consider the comonotonic lower bound of S given by

$$S^l = \mathbb{E}[S|\Lambda] = \sum_{i=1}^{nT} \alpha_i \mathbb{E}[e^{Z_i}|\Lambda],$$

where the conditioning random variable Λ is a linear combination of M appropriately chosen normal random variables, $\{N_1, \cdots, N_M\}$, i.e.

$$\Lambda = \sum_{k=1}^{M} \lambda_k N_k. \tag{7.68}$$

There are many ways to choose such normal random variables. For example, we could simply set $N_k = Z_k$. Then a total of $M = nT$ normal random variables are used in the construction of Λ. However, one can achieve roughly the same results with fewer random variables, which require less computational efforts. For example, we sample the random variables by taking one in every η periods, i.e. $N_k = Z_{\eta k}$, $M = nT/\eta$, provided that η divides n.

Using properties of conditional distributions (Exercise 7.2.2), we obtain

$$S^l = \sum_{i=1}^{nT} \alpha_i e^{\mathbb{E}[Z_i] + \frac{1}{2}(1 - r_i^2)\sigma_{Z_i}^2 + r_i \sigma_{Z_i} (\Lambda - \mathbb{E}[\Lambda])/\sigma_\Lambda}, \tag{7.69}$$

where $\mathbb{E}[Z_i]$ and $\sigma_{Z_i}^2$ are the expectation and variance of Z_i, i.e.

$$\mathbb{E}[Z_i] = (\mu - r - m)\frac{i}{n}, \qquad \sigma_{Z_i} = \sigma\sqrt{\frac{i}{n}},$$

while r_i is the correlation coefficient of Z_i and Λ,

$$r_i = \frac{\mathbb{C}[Z_i, \Lambda]}{\sigma_{Z_i} \sigma_\Lambda} = \frac{1}{\sigma_{Z_i} \sigma_\Lambda} \sum_{k=1}^{M} \lambda_k \mathbb{C}[Z_i, N_k],$$

with the variance of Λ given by

$$\sigma_\Lambda^2 = \mathbb{V}\left[\sum_{k=1}^{M} \lambda_k N_k\right].$$

Here we choose $\{N_k = Z_{\eta k}, k = 1, \cdots, M\}$. Let $\Delta W_k = W_{k\eta} - W_{(k-1)\eta}$. It follows that

$$
\begin{aligned}
\mathbb{V}[\Lambda] &= \mathbb{V}\left[\sum_{k=1}^{M} \lambda_k Z_{k\eta}\right] = \mathbb{V}\left[\sum_{k=1}^{M} \lambda_k \left(\sigma \sum_{i=1}^{k} \Delta W_i\right)\right] \\
&= \frac{\eta\sigma^2}{n} \sum_{i=1}^{M} \sum_{k=i}^{M} \lambda_k^2 = \frac{\eta\sigma^2}{n} \sum_{k=1}^{M} k\lambda_k^2.
\end{aligned}
$$

The covariance of Z_i and Λ can be written as

$$\mathbb{C}[Z_i, \Lambda] = \mathbb{C}\left[Z_i, \sum_{k=1}^{M} \lambda_k Z_{\eta k}\right] = \frac{\sigma^2}{n} \sum_{k=1}^{M} \lambda_k \min(\eta k, i).$$

Assume that all r_i's are nonnegative numbers. Owing to the structure of the sum S^l, we can find explicit expressions for the risk measures (Exercise 7.2.2) such as the value-at-risk

$$\mathrm{VaR}_p[S^l] = \sum_{i=1}^{nT} \alpha_i e^{\mathbb{E}[Z_i] + \frac{1}{2}(1-r_i^2)\sigma_{Z_i}^2 + r_i\sigma_{Z_i}\Phi^{-1}(p)} \tag{7.70}$$

and the left tail-value-at-risk

$$
\begin{aligned}
\mathrm{LTVaR}_p(S^l) &= \frac{1}{p} \int_0^p \mathrm{VaR}_q(S^l)\,\mathrm{d}q \\
&= \frac{1}{p} \sum_{i=1}^{nT-1} \alpha_i \mathbb{E}[e^{Z_i}](1 - \Phi(r_i\sigma_{Z_i} - \Phi^{-1}(p))). \tag{7.71}
\end{aligned}
$$

Observe from (7.67) that any information with regard to the right tail of L can be extracted from the left tail of S.

Theorem 7.10. *The value-at-risk and the conditional tail expectation of the comonotonic lower bound* $L^l = E[L|\Lambda]$ *of the GMMB net liability* L *in (7.67) are given by*

$$\mathrm{VaR}_p(L^l) = e^{-rT}\, {}_Tp_x G - \left(\frac{1}{n}m_e F_0 + \mathrm{VaR}_{1-p}(S^l)\right) \tag{7.72}$$

and

$$\text{TVaR}_p(L^l) = e^{-rT} {}_T p_x G - \frac{1}{n} m_e F_0 - \text{LTVaR}_{1-p}(S^l) \tag{7.73}$$

where $\text{VaR}_p(S^l)$ *and* $\text{LTVaR}_p(S^l)$ *are given by* (7.70) *and* (7.71).

The next step is to look for appropriate choices of coefficients $\{\lambda_1, \cdots, \lambda_M\}$ in (7.68) so that the TVaR of the comonotonic lower bound S^l is as large as possible. There are many approaches proposed in the literature, some of which are briefly introduced here. The first two approaches are developed under the condition that $M = nT$.

1. (Approximate) global optimization

   It is known that $\mathbb{V}[S^l] \leq \mathbb{V}[S]$ since $S^l \leq_{cx} S$. It is shown in Exercise 7.2.3 that the linear approximation of the variance of S^l is given by

   $$\mathbb{V}[S^l] \approx \rho \left[\sum_{j=1}^{nT} \alpha_j \mathbb{E}[e^{Z_j}] Z_j, \Lambda \right]^2 \mathbb{V} \left[\sum_{j=1}^{nT} \alpha_j E(e^{Z_j}) Z_j \right],$$

   where ρ is the correlation coefficient. Note that the approximated value is maximized when the correlation coefficient is 1. Hence, the optimal choice of the conditioning normal random variable must be given by

   $$\Lambda^{MV} = \sum_{j=1}^{nT} \alpha_j \mathbb{E}[e^{Z_j}] Z_j,$$

   and consequently

   $$r_k^{MV} = \frac{1}{\sigma_{Z_k} \sigma_\Lambda} \sum_{j=1}^{nT} \alpha_j \mathbb{E}[e^{Z_j}] \mathbb{C}[Z_k, Z_j]. \tag{7.74}$$

   The covariances of the Z_i's and the variance of Λ can be calculated from the basic properties of Brownian motion:

   $$\mathbb{C}[Z_k, Z_j] = \frac{\sigma^2}{n} \min\{k, j\} \qquad \sigma_\Lambda^2 = \frac{\sigma^2}{n} \sum_{i=1}^{nT} \left(\sum_{j=i}^{nT} \lambda_j \right)^2.$$

2. (Approximate) local optimization

   Observe that $\text{LTVaR}_p(S^l)$ only depends on the unspecified vector $(\lambda_1, \cdots, \lambda_M)$ through the vector $(r_1, \cdots, r_M)$. It is shown in Exercise Exercise 7.2.4 that a linear approximation of TVaR_p given by

   $$\text{TVaR}_p[S^l] \approx \frac{1}{1-p} \sum_{j=1}^{nT} \alpha_j \mathbb{E}[e^{Z_j}] \phi[r_j^{MV} \sigma_{Z_j} - \Phi^{-1}(p)] r_j \sigma_{Z_j} + \text{constant},$$

where the remaining term is constant with respect to $(r_1, r_2, \cdots, r_{nT})$. It is also shown in the same exercise that the first term is maximized when the conditioning normal random variable is chosen to be

$$\Lambda^{(p)} = \sum_{j=1}^{nT} \alpha_j \mathbb{E}[e^{Z_j}]\phi[r_j^{MV}\sigma_{Z_j} - \Phi^{-1}(p)]Z_j,$$

and consequently

$$r_k^{(p)} = \frac{1}{\sigma_{Z_k}\sigma_\Lambda} \sum_{j=1}^{n} \alpha_j \mathbb{E}[e^{Z_j}]\phi[r_j^{MV}\sigma_{Z_j} - \Phi^{-1}(p)]\mathbb{C}[Z_k, Z_j]. \quad (7.75)$$

3. Numerical optimization

There are many numerical algorithms that can be used to search for local maximizers/minimizers for a nonlinear function. For example, MATLAB has a built-in function `fminsearch` that minimizes functions of several variables. Since the expression of $\text{TVaR}_p(L^l)$ is explicitly known, one can utilize those numerical algorithms to look for best choices of $\lambda_1, \cdots, \lambda_M$ that maximize $\text{TVaR}_p(L^l)$.

7.2.4 Guaranteed minimum death benefit

We can also use the comonotonic approximation to calculate risk measures of the GMDB net liability (5.53) in an aggregate model. Suppose that the maturity T is an integer and each year is divided into integer n periods. A discrete-time version of the GMDB net liability (5.53) is given by

$$L = \sum_{i=1}^{nT} u_i(Ge^{\delta i/n} - F_{i/n})_+ - \sum_{i=0}^{nT-1} v_i F_{i/n}, \quad (7.76)$$

where

$$u_i := e^{-ri/n} {}_{(i-1)/n}p_x {}_{1/n}q_{x+(i-1)/n}, \qquad v_i := \frac{1}{n}e^{-ri/n}m_d {}_{i/n}p_x.$$

We use normal random variables N_k's with mean zero,

$$\Lambda = \sum_{k=1}^{M} \lambda_k N_k.$$

Since $F_{i/n} = \exp(Z_i)$ where $Z_i = \mu^*\frac{i}{n} + \sigma W_{i/n}$, we must have

$$Z_i|\Lambda = \lambda \sim \text{Norm}\left(\mu_i\left(\frac{\lambda}{\sigma_\Lambda}\right), \sigma_i^2\right),$$

where

$$\mu_i(y) := \mu^* \frac{i}{n} + r_i \sigma \sqrt{\frac{i}{n}} y, \qquad \sigma_i^2 := \sigma^2 \frac{i}{n}(1 - r_i^2).$$

It is shown in Exercise 7.2.5 that the conditional expectation

$$\mathbb{E}[L|\Lambda = \lambda] = \sum_{i=1}^{nT} u_i \left[Ge^{\delta i/n} \Phi\left(\frac{\ln(G/F_0) - \mu_i^*\left(\frac{\lambda}{\sigma_\Lambda}\right)}{\sigma_i} \right) \right.$$

$$\left. - F_0 e^{\mu_i\left(\frac{\lambda}{\sigma_\Lambda}\right)+\sigma_i^2/2} \Phi\left(\frac{\ln(G/F_0) - \sigma_i^2 - \mu_i^*\left(\frac{\lambda}{\sigma_\Lambda}\right)}{\sigma_i} \right) \right]$$

$$- \sum_{i=0}^{nT-1} v_i F_0 \exp\left\{ \mu_i\left(\frac{\lambda}{\sigma_\Lambda}\right) + \sigma_i^2/2 \right\},$$

where $\mu_i^*(y) = \mu_i(y) - \delta i/n$, and that $\mathbb{E}[L|\Lambda = \lambda]$ is a decreasing function of λ. Therefore, we could obtain closed-form formulas for both risk measures of $L^l := \mathbb{E}[L|\Lambda]$.

Theorem 7.11. *Consider the GMDB net liability in the aggregate model (7.76). The value-at-risk and the conditional tail expectation of the comonotonic lower bound L^l are given by*

$$\mathrm{VaR}_p(L^l) = \sum_{i=1}^{nT} u_i \left[Ge^{\delta i/n} \Phi\left(b_i\left(\Phi^{-1}(1-p)\right)\right) \right.$$

$$\left. - F_0 e^{\mu_i\left(\Phi^{-1}(1-p)\right)+\sigma_i^2/2} \Phi\left(b_i\left(\Phi^{-1}(1-p)\right) - \sigma_i \right) \right]$$

$$- \sum_{i=0}^{nT-1} v_i F_0 \exp\left\{ \mu_i\left(\Phi^{-1}(1-p)\right) + \sigma_i^2/2 \right\} - \frac{1}{n} m_d F_0, \qquad (7.77)$$

and

$$\mathrm{CTE}_p(L^l) = \frac{1}{1-p} \sum_{i=1}^{nT} u_i \left[Ge^{\delta i/n} H\left(\Phi^{-1}(1-p); a_i, b_i(0)\right) \right.$$

$$\left. - F_0 \exp\left\{ \mu_i(0) + \frac{1}{2}\sigma^2 \frac{i}{n} \right\} H\left(\Phi^{-1}(1-p) - r_i\sigma\sqrt{\frac{i}{n}}; a_i, b_i(0) - \frac{i\sigma^2}{n\sigma_i} \right) \right]$$

$$- \frac{1}{1-p} \sum_{i=0}^{nT-1} v_i F_0 \exp\left\{ \mu_i(0) + \frac{\sigma^2}{2n} \right\} \Phi\left(\Phi^{-1}(1-p) - r_i\sigma\sqrt{\frac{i}{n}} \right) - \frac{1}{n} m_d F_0,$$

$$(7.78)$$

where

$$a_i = \frac{r_i}{\sqrt{1 - r_i^2}}, \qquad b_i(y) = \frac{\ln(G/F_0) - \mu_i^*(y)}{\sigma_i}.$$

and H is a special function whose definition and computation are discussed in the Appendix D.3.

It should be pointed out that it is in general difficult to find explicit formulas for optimal choices of r_i because of the complex structure of H functions. Nevertheless, numerical methods for nonlinear optimization problems are readily available in computational software packages such as MATLAB.

Example 7.12. We illustrate the computation of risk measures for variable annuity guaranteed benefits by two examples, which are based on the following assumptions. The policyholder is 65-year-old at policy issue, and the term of the variable annuity is 10 years, i.e. $T = 10$. The mean and standard deviation of log-returns per annum in the geometric Brownian motion model (2.48) are given by $\mu = 0.09$ and $\sigma = 0.3$ or 0.4. The yield rate per annum of the assets backing up the guarantee liabilities is $r = 0.04$. The M&E fee per annum is $m = 0.01$, and rider charge m_e or m_d is assumed to be 35 basis points per annum of the separate account. The initial guarantee amount is set to be the initial purchase payment $G = F_0$. The survivorship model is based on the illustrative life table in Appendix A.3. All computations in this example are carried out on a personal computer with Intel Core i7-4700MQ CPU at 2.40GHz and an RAM of 8.00 GB.

Guaranteed minimum maturity benefit

The purpose of the first example is to test the accuracy and efficiency of the comonotonic approximations proposed in Theorem 7.10. As we shall demonstrate, the comonotonic approximations appear to be very efficient with only small compromise of accuracy, which is likely negligible for practical purposes. Hence, the comonotonic approximation is arguably superior to the PDE method for this example.

We first run Monte Carlo simulations for the discrete-time GMMB net liability (7.67) with fees collected on a quarterly basis. The probability of the policyholder surviving a non-integer period is calculated under the assumption of constant force of mortality in each year. For each scenario of investment accounts generated by the geometric Brownian motion, we calculate the net liability based on the formulation (7.67). After repeating the simulation 1 million or 100 million times, the net liability values form an empirical distribution, from which we use order statistics to obtain one estimate of the value-at-risk and conditional tail expectation. Then we repeat the whole procedure 20 times to obtain a sample of risk measure estimates. In Table 7.5, we show the mean and standard deviation (in brackets) of the estimated risk measures.

We test the comonotonic approximations (7.72) and (7.73) with various choices of Λ. In the first case, we set $N_k = Z_k$ for $k = 1, \cdots, nT$ and use the *globally optimal choice* of Λ, which is the optimization of the linear approximation of $\mathbb{V}(S^l)$ as a function of the vector $(r_1, \cdots, r_M)$. The exact expressions for r_i's are given in (7.74). In the second case, we use the *locally optimal choice* of Λ, proposed in the same paper, which is the optimization of the linear approximation of $\mathrm{TVaR}_p(S^l)$

as a function of the vector $(r_1, \cdots, r_M)$. The exact expressions for r_i's are given in (7.75). In the third case, we treat the risk measures as nonlinear functions of the vector $(\lambda_1, \cdots, \lambda_M)$ and use MATLAB's `fminsearch` to find the optimal value of the vector that minimizes $-\text{TVaR}_p(S^l)$. This algorithm uses a version of the Nelder-Mead simplex search method to obtain a local minimum value of the function. Based on empirical data, we observe that $\text{TVaR}_p(S^l)$ is in fact unimodal and hence the numerical algorithm is very stable and efficient. To verify its accuracy, we also use the Quasi-Newton method, which produces very similar results to those from the Nelder-Mead method. After finding the optimal choice of λ_i's that maximizes $\text{TVaR}_p(S^l)$, we verify that all resulting r_i's are positive and insert them in (7.72), producing an estimate of $\text{VaR}_p(S^l)$.

It is not surprising that the approximations based on the global and local optimal choices of r_i's are more efficient than the nonlinear optimization, as the former pins down the values of r_i's by closed-form formulas whereas the latter invokes a search algorithm for λ_i's. It is also worth noting that the nonlinear optimization brings $\text{TVaR}_p(S^l)$ closer to the true value of $\text{TVaR}(S)$.

To further test if the aforementioned methods work well for other situations, we increase the value of the volatility parameter σ. As expected, risk measures increase with the volatility coefficient, as high volatility increases the likelihood and severity of large losses. Comparing the first part and the second part of Table 7.5, one observes the same level of accuracy and efficiency with various methods.

	Method	$\text{VaR}_{0.9}$	$\text{CTE}_{0.9}$	Time (secs)
	Global optimization Λ^{MV}	0.14900	0.25944	0.04
	Local optimization $\Lambda^{(p)}$	0.14901	0.25948	0.04
$\sigma = 0.3$	Nonlinear optimization	0.14902	0.25948	33.95
	Monte Carlo	0.14914	0.25966	179.84
	(20 repetitions of 1 million)	(0.00043)	(0.00034)	
	Monte Carlo	0.14902	0.25949	18042.09
	(20 repetitions of 100 millions)	(0.00007)	(0.00004)	
	Global optimization Λ^{MV}	0.26283	0.35307	0.03
	Local optimization $\Lambda^{(p)}$	0.26287	0.35307	0.04
$\sigma = 0.4$	Nonlinear optimization	0.26287	0.35317	31.16
	Monte Carlo	0.26315	0.35334	181.26
	(20 repetitions of 1 million)	(0.00043)	(0.00028)	
	Monte Carlo	0.26288	0.35319	18079.13
	(20 repetitions of 100 millions)	(0.00005)	(0.00003)	

TABLE 7.5: Risk measures for the GMMB net liability

Guaranteed minimum death benefit

Consider the discrete-time GMDB net liability in (7.76). For simplicity, the net liabilities are evaluated under the same valuation basis as in the GMMB case. Keep in mind that we no longer have closed-form solutions to $(\lambda_1, \cdots, \lambda_M)$. In the case of $N_k = Z_k$ for $k = 1, \cdots, 4T$ (quarterly valuation), a 10-year contract with quarterly fee payments requires 40-dimensional optimization (the first row in Table 7.6). Therefore, we intend to reduce computational efforts by restricting the space of normal random variables Θ in (7.66). We use the results from Monte Carlo simulations as the bench mark for accuracy and efficiency. In the second row of Table 7.6, the normal random variables are sampled every half-year, i.e. $N_k = Z_{2k}$ for $k = 1, \cdots 2T$. (The number of random variables is reduced by half from the quarterly case.) In the third row of Table 7.6, the normal random variables are chosen on yearly basis, i.e. $N_k = Z_{4k}$ for $k = 1, \cdots, T$. (The number of random variables is reduced by 75% from the quarterly case.) Note that comonotonic approximations in this paper are all lower bounds of the actual quantities of interest as shown in (7.65), the maximums attained with a reduced number of variables are smaller than the maximum attained with the whole set of variables. However, it appears that the running time can be reduced significantly with only a small compromise of accuracy. We run the numerical example for both $\sigma = 0.3$ and $\sigma = 0.4$ to show that the algorithm works consistently for various situations.

	Method	VaR$_{0.9}$	CTE$_{0.9}$	Time (secs)
$\sigma = 0.3$	Nonlinear optimization	0.03037	0.06126	69.97
	(50% reduced)	0.03035	0.06123	46.45
	(75% reduced)	0.03026	0.06110	17.15
	Monte Carlo	0.03059	0.06137	226.16
	(20 repetitions of 1 million)	(0.00013)	(0.00010)	
	Monte Carlo	0.03035	0.06128	22602.80
	(20 repetitions of 100 millions)	(0.00002)	(0.00002)	
$\sigma = 0.4$	Nonlinear optimization	0.05911	0.09043	65.80
	(50% reduced)	0.05908	0.09039	39.95
	(75% reduced)	0.05896	0.09024	15.84
	Monte Carlo	0.05901	0.09057	227.65
	(20 repetitions of 1 million)	(0.00013)	(0.00011)	
	Monte Carlo	0.05899	0.09054	22726.37
	(20 repetitions of 100 millions)	(0.00001)	(0.00001)	

TABLE 7.6: Risk measures for the GMDB net liability with $\delta = 0$

In the next example, we intend to consider the impact of offering a roll-up bonus on the GMDB net liability. In this case, the guarantee base accumulates interest at the rate of $\delta = 0.06$ per annum. In comparison with the tail behavior in Table 7.6 with no roll-up, the 90% risk measures show that the tail of the net liability is heavier owing to the richer benefit payments. We have also experimented with the reduction of normal random variables in Λ as was done in the previous case (see Table 7.7).

Method	$\text{VaR}_{0.9}$	$\text{CTE}_{0.9}$	Time (secs)
Nonlinear optimization	0.10330	0.13681	63.75
(50% reduced)	0.10327	0.13677	45.67
(75% reduced)	0.10311	0.13660	22.24
Monte Carlo	0.10346	0.13710	223.51
(20 repetitions of 1 million)	(0.00016)	(0.00009)	
Monte Carlo	0.10335	0.13706	21955.19
(20 repetitions of 100 millions)	(0.00001)	(0.00002)	

TABLE 7.7: Risk measures for the GMDB net liability with $\delta = 0.06, \sigma = 0.3$

7.3   Nested stochastic modeling

As shown with many examples in Chapter 3, *stochastic modeling* is commonly used when financial reporting procedures, such as reserving and capital requirement calculation, are performed under various economic scenarios, which are stochastically determined. *Nested stochastic modeling* is required whenever modeling components under each economic scenario are themselves determined by stochastic scenarios in the future. An example might be the stochastic reserving of equity-linked insurance for which a dynamic hedging strategy is employed and the Greeks are stochastically determined. As financial and insurance industries move toward more detailed and sophisticated financial reporting standards and practices, it is expected that the computational burden and technical difficulty will rise with the increasing use of nested stochastic modeling.

To appreciate the technical challenges of nested stochastics, let us first understand its common structural properties. When stochastic modeling is nested, there are typically two levels of simulation procedures, as shown in Figure 7.2. Here we introduce some common terminology for nested stochastics.

- Outer loop: the simulation in the first stage of projection. For example, in the case of stochastic reserving for equity-linked insurance, an outer loop may refer to the projection of cash flows in the separate account in a year, which fluctuate with risk factors such as equity values, equity volatility, interest rates, etc. We shall call sample paths of risk factors or resulting cash flows **outer loop scenarios**. These scenarios are typically projected under a real-world measure. We often denote the set of n scenarios by $\omega_1, \cdots, \omega_n$. Figure 7.2 provides a visualization of outer loop scenarios and inner loop paths emanating from nodes on the outer loop scenarios. Each trajectory that begins at time 0 represents a particular sample path of some risk factor, whereas each node represents a realization of the risk factor at a time point.

- Outer loop estimator: the quantity to be determined as the ultimate objective of the nested simulation. A risk measure of an insurer's accumulated surplus or deficiency

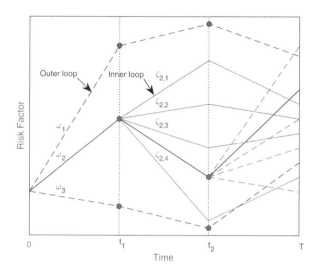

FIGURE 7.2: An illustration of nested simulations. Copyright © 2016 by the Society of Actuaries, Schaumburg, Illinois. Reprinted with permission.

from a particular product line or overall product portfolio could be considered an outer loop estimator.

- Inner loop: the simulation in the second stage of projection, under each scenario in the outer loop. For example, in the case of stochastic reserving, the inner loop may refer to the projection needed to determine the Greeks for a hedging portfolio starting from the valuation date to the end of projection horizon, say twenty years. Note that each greek value at every single rebalancing date is calculated by projections of future cash flows under the risk-neutral measure. We shall call sample paths of cash flows in this stage of simulation **inner loop paths**. For each scenario in the outer loop, say, ω_k, we denote the subsequent m inner loop paths by $\zeta_{k1}, \cdots, \zeta_{km}$, respectively. For simplicity, only two sets of inner loop paths are shown in Figure 7.2 by trajectories emanating from nodes in outer loop scenarios.

- Inner loop estimator: the quantity to be determined by the inner loop simulation. To project the insurer's cash flows for the purpose of reserving, we need to assess the impact of a hedging program and the greeks at each time point under each outer loop scenario would be inner loop estimators.

- Time step: Most financial reporting exercises involve recursive evaluation of surplus/earnings over accounting periods. The time step refers to the length of each period for recursive calculation. For example, if all cash flows are projected with time step of a quarter, then samples of risk factors are drawn and resulting cash flows are evaluated for every quarter throughout the projection horizon. Note that one may use different time steps for outer loops and inner loops.

For consistency, we shall denote the number of outer loop scenarios by n and the number of inner loop paths by m for each scenario. In other words, we only consider Monte Carlo simulation with a uniform sampling scheme in this introductory book. Readers are referred to Feng et al. [40] and references therein for simulations with non-uniform sampling schemes.

It is widely known in the insurance industry that the current market practice of stochastic modeling relies primarily on intensive and brute-force Monte Carlo simulations. With the increasing sophistication of nested stochastics, many companies simply cope with it by investing on more computing facilities, trying to make brute force methods faster and more palatable. However, the reliance on heavy hardware investment is not sustainable. Calculation runtimes are often too long for insurance companies to get results and take actions in a timely manner. Here is an example provided in Reynolds & Man [87], illustrating the computational burden of a typical nested stochastic model based on 30-year projection with quarterly reporting cycles. They estimate the total number of liability cell projections to be

$$(30 \text{ years}) \times (4 \text{ quarters}) \times (1 \text{ millions cells}) \times (100 \text{ paths}) \times (1+2\times 10 \text{ shocks}) \times$$
$$(1{,}000 \text{ scenarios}) = 252 \text{ trillion cell-path projects}$$

They conclude that, even if there is an extraordinarily fast system available that can project $10{,}000$ cell paths per second, it is impractical to run such a model in real time.

$$252 \text{ trillion cell-paths}/10{,}000 \text{ cell paths per second}$$
$$=25.2 \text{ billion seconds} \approx \mathbf{799 \text{ years}}.$$

Many technical methods have been developed in the literature to address the apparent lack of efficiency with raw Monte Carlo simulations. Here we introduce a number of common techniques to speed up calculations.

7.3.1 Preprocessed inner loops

The essence of this method is to preprocess inner-loop calculations under a small set of outer-loop scenarios and then use interpolation to infer values for other outer-loop scenarios outside the preprocessed set. This approach is also referred to as a factor-based approach in Hardy [61, p. 189].

Preprocessing inner loops

Suppose there are two quantifiable risk factors at a fixed time point $X^{(1)}$ and $X^{(2)}$ to be considered in an outer-loop simulation. There are many ways in which we can set up a grid of possible values of $(X^{(1)}, X^{(2)})$ to be preprocessed. For example, we could consider the set

$$\left\{ (x_k^{(1)}, x_k^{(2)}) : x_k^{(1)} = \text{VaR}_{k/n}[X^{(1)}], x_k^{(2)} = a + \frac{(b-a)(k-1)}{n-1}, k = 1, \cdots, n \right\},$$

where both $X^{(1)}$ and $X^{(2)}$ are assumed to have finite domains and $X^{(2)} \in [a, b]$. Similarly, we can create a set of partition points for $X^{(2)}$. These pairs are then tabulated to form a grid system as shown in Table 7.8. At each grid point, an inner-loop calculation is carried out to determine the corresponding inner loop estimator, which is denoted by $\hat{L}_{ij}$ corresponding to the i-th scenario of the risk factor $X^{(1)}$ and j-th scenario of the risk factor $X^{(2)}$.

		equity returns			
		$x_1^{(2)}$	$x_2^{(2)}$	$\cdots$	$x_n^{(2)}$
interest rate	$x_1^{(1)}$	$\hat{L}_{11}$	$\hat{L}_{12}$	$\cdots$	$\hat{L}_{1n}$
	$x_2^{(1)}$	$\hat{L}_{21}$	$\hat{L}_{22}$	$\cdots$	$\hat{L}_{2n}$
	$\vdots$	$\vdots$	$\vdots$	$\vdots$	$\vdots$
	$x_{n'}^{(1)}$	$\hat{L}_{n'1}$	$\hat{L}_{n'2}$	$\cdots$	$\hat{L}_{n'n}$

TABLE 7.8: Preprocessed inner loop estimators. Copyright © 2016 by the Society of Actuaries, Schaumburg, Illinois. Reprinted with permission.

Note that the number of preprocesses points $n \times n'$ are determined by an insurer's preference of granularity, which is often a compromise between accuracy and efficiency. High density the grid, more accurate are the end results. However, as the main purpose of such an exercise is to reduce run time, the size of the grid is not expected to be very large.

Interpolation for outer loops

In the outer-loop simulation, a wide range of outer-loop scenarios are generated to reflect the insurer's anticipation of market conditions. When an outer loop requires the liability evaluated with various levels of risk factors, $(x^{(1)}, x^{(2)})$, which are typically not on the grid $\{(x_i^{(1)}, x_j^{(2)}), i = 1, \cdots, n, j = 1, \cdots, n'\}$, approximations are made by interpolating liability values at neighboring points on the table. While there are many multivariate interpolation methods available, the most common one appears to be the bilinear interpolation. Suppose $x_i^{(1)} < x^{(1)} < x_{i+1}^{(1)}$ and $x_j^{(2)} < x^{(2)} < x_{j+1}^{(2)}$. Then a first linear interpolation is done in one direction:

$$\hat{L}(x^{(1)}, x_j^{(2)}) = \frac{x_{i+1}^{(1)} - x^{(1)}}{x_{i+1}^{(1)} - x_i^{(1)}} \hat{L}_{ij} + \frac{x^{(1)} - x_i^{(1)}}{x_{i+1}^{(1)} - x_i^{(1)}} \hat{L}_{(i+1)j},$$

$$\hat{L}(x^{(1)}, x_{j+1}^{(2)}) = \frac{x_{i+1}^{(1)} - x^{(1)}}{x_{i+1}^{(1)} - x_i^{(1)}} \hat{L}_{i(j+1)} + \frac{x^{(1)} - x_i^{(1)}}{x_{i+1}^{(1)} - x_i^{(1)}} \hat{L}_{(i+1)(j+1)}.$$

Then the desired estimate follows from a second linear interpolation:

$$\hat{L}(x^{(1)}, x^{(2)}) = \frac{x_{j+1}^{(2)} - x^{(2)}}{x_{j+1}^{(2)} - x_j^{(2)}} \hat{L}(x^{(1)}, x_j^{(2)}) + \frac{x^{(2)} - x_j^{(2)}}{x_{j+1}^{(2)} - x_j^{(2)}} \hat{L}(x^{(1)}, x_{j+1}^{(2)}). \quad (7.79)$$

Example 7.13. In this section, we show the accuracy of inner loop valuation based on the preprocessed inner loop method. The inner loop estimator under consideration is the risk-neutral value of the GMMB gross liability defined in (4.50). We consider two risk factors in the outer loop simulation – equity value F_0 and equity volatility σ. It is clear from (4.50) that $B_e(t, F)$ is a non-linear function of F and σ. However, in practice, the risk-neutral value of insurer's liability is often not known explicitly. Therefore, each value under a combination of parameters (σ, F_0) requires evaluation under thousands of inner loop sample paths, which can be very time consuming. The preprocessed inner loop method allows us to estimate a range of liability values based on inner loop estimates from a selected set of combinations.

σ \\ F_0	600.00	800.00	1000.00	1200.00	1400.00
0.2100	272.3934	201.6840	149.8638	112.1732	84.7051
0.2550	293.0028	230.0998	182.6420	146.5504	118.8044
0.3000	314.3290	257.9828	214.5057	180.4075	153.2561
0.0310	335.7530	285.1014	245.3194	213.4103	187.3648
0.0320	356.8849	311.2894	274.9650	245.3275	220.6890

TABLE 7.9: Exact values of GMMB no-arbitrage cost for different parameters.

Suppose that all necessary combinations of (σ, F_0) for outer loop calculation are identified in Table 7.9. Actuarial assumptions and model parameters are given in Appendix A.1. Owing to the explicit formulation in (4.50), we obtain their exact values in Table 7.9, which shall be used to benchmark against results from the linear interpolation method. Cells highlighted in gray are used as inputs for linear interpolation.

σ \\ F_0	600.00	800.00	1000.00	1200.00	1400.00
0.2100	272.3934	211.1286	149.8638	117.2844	84.7051
	(0.00 %)	(+4.68 %)	(0.00 %)	(+4.56 %)	(0.00 %)
0.2550	293.3612	237.7730	182.1847	150.5827	118.9806
	(+0.12 %)	(+3.33 %)	(-0.25 %)	(+2.75 %)	(+0.15 %)
0.3000	314.3290	264.4173	214.5057	183.8809	153.2561
	(0.00 %)	(+2.49 %)	(0.00 %)	(+1.93 %)	(0.00 %)
0.3450	335.6069	290.1711	244.7354	215.8539	186.9725
	(-0.04 %)	(+1.78 %)	(-0.24 %)	(+1.15 %)	(-0.21 %)
0.3900	356.8849	315.9250	274.9650	247.8270	220.6890
	(0.00 %)	(+1.49 %)	(0.00 %)	(+1.02 %)	(0.00 %)

TABLE 7.10: Estimation of GMMB no-arbitrage cost using preprocessed inner loop method.

Based on the interpolation formula (7.79), we obtain inner loop estimates in Table

7.10 where relative errors are shown in brackets. Despite the non-linear functional relationship, the estimation of inner-loop risk-neutral values performs reasonable well with all errors contained within 5%.

The total amount of inner-loop calculations can be reduced tremendously due to fewer inner-loop calculations. Most computing software packages provide built-in interpolation functions. It is relatively easy to implement an interpolation procedure. However, a challenge with the implementation of this technique is that combination of risk factor values are stochastically determined in the outer loops and hence one has to prepare a large enough grid so that required items can be interpolated from the table of preprocessed inner loops. When risk drivers reside on a very large domain, choosing appropriate boundaries can be tricky, especially in high dimensions. We shall demonstrate in Section 7.3.4 that the method is no longer sufficiently accurate when dealing with four variables.

7.3.2 Least-squares Monte Carlo

The idea of LSMC is to establish a functional relationship between the underlying risk factors and the desired inner loop estimator and to replace inner-loop calculations by statistical inferences based on the functional relationship. This method is the most popular among all curve-fitting techniques used in the industry. Suppose that an inner loop estimator L depends on a number of risk factors/drivers $\mathbf{F} = (F_1, F_2, \cdots, F_d)$, such as equity returns, equity volatility and interest rates. In other words, there exists an unknown function g such that for any scenario ω:

$$L(\omega) = g(F_1(\omega), F_2(\omega), \cdots, F_d(\omega)).$$

As shown in Figure 5.8, the dependence of inner loop estimators on risk factors can be highly complex and hence the function g is usually not known explicitly. Because the graph of g can be viewed as a curve on the $\mathbb{R}^d$ space, there are many curve fitting techniques that can be used to approximate the unknown g by a mixture of known functions, often called *basis functions*. The LSMC method is based on the approximation of this data-driven relationship by a set of s real-valued basis functions $\phi_1(\cdot), ..., \phi_s(\cdot)$, which can be written as a row vector

$$\Phi(\cdot) = (\phi_1(\cdot), ..., \phi_s(\cdot)) \in \mathbb{R}^s.$$

Some typical examples of basis functions are polynomials. For examples, in a model with two risk factors, one might use $\phi_1(x_1, x_2) = x_1, \phi_2(x_1, x_2) = x_2, \phi_3(x_1, x_2) = x_1 x_2$. Then the inner loop estimator L is to be approximated by a linear combination of these basis functions, for some vector $\boldsymbol{\beta} = (\beta_1, \cdots, \beta_s)^\top$ to be determined,

$$L(\omega) = g(\mathbf{F}(\omega)) \approx \Phi(\mathbf{F}(\omega))\boldsymbol{\beta} = \sum_{l=1}^{s} \beta_l \phi_l(\mathbf{F}(\omega)),$$

where $\top$ denotes the transpose of a vector. Ideally, basis functions should be easy to evaluate and capture main features of the functional relationship g. However, it is common that only empirical data on the functional relationship is available and practitioners resort to lower term polynomials.

The unknown vector β is typically determined by minimizing mean-squared error

$$\beta^* \in \operatorname*{argmin}_{\beta \in \mathbb{R}^s} \mathbb{E}[(L - \Phi(\mathbf{F})\beta)^2]. \tag{7.80}$$

As it is not possible to directly compute β without the exact distribution of L, which is unknown in the context of LSMC, we often consider the statistical analog of the optimization problem (7.80),

$$\hat{\beta} \in \operatorname*{argmin}_{\beta \in \mathbb{R}^s} \frac{1}{n} \sum_{k=1}^{n} (\hat{L}_k - \Phi(\mathbf{F}(\omega_k))\beta)^2, \tag{7.81}$$

which is a standard ordinary least-squares problem. Recall that we write $\hat{L}_k = \hat{L}(\omega_k)$ for short and each $\hat{L}(\omega_k)$ is estimated by inner loop simulations. If we let $\mathbf{Y} = (\hat{L}_1, \cdots, \hat{L}_n)$ and $\mathbf{X} = (\Phi(\mathbf{F}(\omega_1))^\top, \cdots, \Phi(\mathbf{F}(\omega_n))^\top)^\top$, then

$$\hat{\beta} = (\mathbf{X}^\top \mathbf{X})^{-1} \mathbf{X}^\top \mathbf{Y}.$$

Once the vector $\hat{\beta}$ is determined, then inner-loop calculation for the nested simulation can be replaced by evaluation of the analytical approximation function. For example, if the outer loop estimator is the probability distribution of the inner loop estimator, i.e. $\alpha := \mathbb{P}(L < V)$ for any real value V, we may generate a large set of outer loop scenarios $\{\omega_1, \omega_2, \cdots, \omega_n\}$ and approximate the inner loop estimator by $\Phi(\mathbf{F}(\omega_k))\beta$ under each scenario ω_k. Consequently, the outer loop estimator is determined approximately by

$$\hat{\alpha} := \frac{1}{n} \sum_{k=1}^{n} I(\Phi(\mathbf{F}(\omega_k))\beta < V).$$

As such evaluation does not involve generating additional scenarios on the fly or estimating liabilities by complex accounting rules, the approximate inner loop estimates can be determined very efficiently.

Example 7.14. We continue with the same model as in Example 7.13. In place of the linear interpolation, we employ the LSMC method with the same set of inputs (shaded cells in Table 7.9). Stated explicitly, the functional relationship is to be viewed as the polynomial regression model

$$B_e(t, F) = \beta_0 + \beta_1 \sigma + \beta_2 \sigma^2 + \beta_3 F + \beta_4 F^2 + \beta_5 \sigma F + \epsilon,$$

where ϵ is the error term. There are six parameters to be estimated – one intercept

(β_0), fives coefficients ($\beta_1, \beta_2, \beta_3, \beta_4, \beta_5$), and the variance of the model error ($\widehat{\mathbb{V}}[\epsilon]$). Hence we need at least seven data points to determine all these quantities. In this case, nine points are available as shown in Figure 7.9.

As most computational software packages have build-in algorithm for least square estimation, this method can be easily implemented. Table 7.11 shows estimated coefficients and sample variance of errors.

Parameter	Estimated Value	Standard Error
$\hat{\beta}_0$	451.0562	47.7585
$\hat{\beta}_1$	340.1534	272.9982
$\hat{\beta}_2$	-96.3036	438.2651
$\hat{\beta}_3$	-0.5668	0.0493
$\hat{\beta}_4$	0.0001	0.0000
$\hat{\beta}_5$	0.3576	0.0697
$\widehat{\mathbb{V}}[\epsilon]$	9.4516	NA

TABLE 7.11: Least-squares parameter estimation.

Once we determine the coefficients for the polynomial regression model, we can carry out approximation of inner loop estimator with different combinations of parameters (σ, F_0), i.e.

$$\hat{B}_e(t, F) = \hat{\beta}_0 + \hat{\beta}_1\sigma + \hat{\beta}_2\sigma^2 + \hat{\beta}_3 F + \hat{\beta}_4 F^2 + \hat{\beta}_5 \cdot \sigma F.$$

The resulting inner loop estimates are shown in Table 7.12. Shaded cells indicate that exact values of $B_e(t, F)$ for these combinations of (σ, F_0) are used in the polynomial regression to determine the coefficients. However, unlike the highlighted cells in Table 7.10, the numbers in Table 7.12 are all estimates from the fitted polynomial. Numbers in brackets indicate relative errors of the inner loop estimates.

F_0 / σ	600.00	800.00	1000.00	1200.00	1400.00
0.2100	**269.5527** (**-1.04 %**)	207.2545 (+2.76 %)	**155.2554** (**+3.60 %**)	113.5553 (+1.23 %)	**82.1542** (**-3.01 %**)
0.2550	292.4993 (-0.17 %)	233.4193 (+1.44 %)	184.6385 (+1.09 %)	146.1566 (-0.27 %)	117.9738 (-0.70 %)
0.3000	**315.0558** (**+0.23 %**)	259.1941 (+0.47 %)	**213.6315** (**-0.41 %**)	178.3680 (-1.13 %)	**153.4034** (**+0.10 %**)
0.3450	337.2223 (+0.44 %)	284.5789 (-0.18 %)	242.2346 (-1.26 %)	210.1893 (-1.51 %)	188.4430 (+0.58 %)
0.3900	**358.9988** (**+0.59 %**)	309.5737 (-0.55 %)	**270.4476** (**-1.64 %**)	241.6205 (-1.51 %)	**223.0925** (**+1.09 %**)

TABLE 7.12: Estimation of GMMB no-arbitrage cost using LSMC.

We can compare two estimation methods and comment on their pros and cons. Note that estimates from both methods are reasonably close to exact values. Relative errors are generally smaller on interior points than boundary points, as more information is available on neighboring points in the interior. Also, note that the linear interpolation method keeps the input data intact while the least squares method may not (because it fits a hyperplane rather than simply connecting dots). When a limited number of inner loop estimates are available and combination of risk factors are generated at random as opposed to on a predetermined grid, the least squares method is in general more accurate than the linear interpolation method. This is because least squares method fits a hyperplane on all input data but linear interpolation only looks at (no more than) four nearest sampled data locally. However, one should keep in mind that local behavior of the functional relationship to be estimated can vary greatly. For a given degree of polynomial, the basis functions may only be capable of capturing changes within a certain local region. Therefore, in practice, one needs fine tune the degree of polynomial to determine the best model.

LSMC is also known to be efficient to reduce computational time. In the nested setting of a crude Monte Carlo with n outer loops and m inner loops, the total number computation units is $n(\gamma_0 + m\gamma_1)$ where γ_0 is the computation cost of an outer loop and γ_1 is that of an inner loop. LSMC finds an approximation of inner-loop calculation in a procedure separate from outer-loop simulation. If we use m inner loops to find the approximation and n outer loops to generate an empirical distribution of approximated inner-loop values, then the computation cost would be $n\gamma_0 + m\gamma_1$ plus the cost of least-squares estimation, which is typically significantly less than that of crude Monte Carlo. However, an apparent shortcoming of the approach is often the lack of guidance on the choice of basis functions. The choices of basis functions such as polynomials, particularly those used in practitioners' publications, appear to be arbitrary. Exercise 7.3.2 provides some theoretical justification by Taylor's expansion. In practice, one may use some statistical procedures for variable selection such as stepwise regression to identify the appropriate polynomial to use.

7.3.3 Other methods

In many applications, if the inner loop estimator has some stochastic representation, it is possible to use differential equation methods to replace Monte Carlo simulations. We have already seen such an example in Section 7.1.4. Another example will be shown in Section 7.3.4.

Another technique that uses a different philosophy from interpolation and curving fitting techniques discussed previously is the *sampling recycling method*. One criticism of the (brute-force) Monte Carlo simulation is that managing scenario data tends to be expensive and nested stochastic modeling often requires generating scenarios on the fly, as inner loop simulations are invoked in the process of outer loop simulations. Sample recycling method provides a remedy to this problem as it relies only on the exclusive use of pre-generated scenarios. When starting at different combined values of risk factors, the inner loop estimator is evaluated by stored values based on pre-generated scenarios under a changed probability measure. Technical details of a sampling recycling method can be found in Li and Feng [73].

7.3.4 Application to guaranteed lifetime withdrawal benefit

7.3.4.1 Overview of nested structure

Following the discussion in Section 5.7, we shall perform an AG-43 stochastic scenario amount calculation for a line of business with a "clearly defined hedging strategy."* Recall that the stochastic scenario amount is calculated in three key steps. The projection begins with starting assets consisting of hedging portfolio, general account assets and separate account assets.

1. (Projection of scenarios) Use either AAA's prepackaged scenarios or internal scenario generators to project cash flows of a line of business (on both the liability and asset sides).

2. (Pathwise accounting procedure) Calculate the accumulated surplus/deficiency at the end of each projection period and determine the greatest present value of accumulated deficiencies (GPVAD) for each scenario. The *scenario amount* is determined by the sum of starting assets and the GPVAD.

3. (Application of risk measures) Collect scenario amounts for all scenarios and apply the 70% conditional tail expectation risk measure to the sample of scenario amounts to determine the *stochastic scenario amount*.

Hedging programs are implemented and should be included in cash flows if the reporting company has a "clearly defined hedging strategy" (CDHS). The stochastic scenario amount is determined by

$$\text{CTE (best efforts)} \times E + \text{CTE (excluding CDHS)} \times (1 - E).$$

The CTE (best efforts) is calculated from the above-mentioned steps where cash flows reflect the implementation of the hedging program, whereas the CTE (excluding CDHS) is calculated from the same steps except that all existing assets are assumed to be held to maturity and no further actions of hedging are taken. The "effectiveness factor" E is determined based on the sophistication of its hedging projections and must be capped at 70%. As we shall see below, nested simulations appear only in the AG-43 procedure with the consideration of a hedging program, where most computational burden rises from the calculation of the CTE (best efforts). Therefore, we shall focus on the efficiency of computation with CTE (best efforts).

---

*The designation of "clearly defined hedging strategy" applies to strategies undertaken by an insurer to manage risks through the purchase or sale of hedging instruments which meet the principles outlined in the AAA guidelines. A precise definition of the CDHS can be found in Gorski and Brown [58].

Here we perform CTE calculations for variable annuity contracts with a guaranteed lifetime withdrawal benefit (GLWB) rider. All policyholders in the cohort under consideration are 61 years old at the time of issue, and the projection is performed at the end of four years after issue. All policyholders invest their purchase payments (premiums) into a single fund, which will be linked to an equity index, such as the S&P 500. Each policyholder is provided with a *nominal account* to keep track of their investments and equity returns as well as a *guarantee base* to be used as the basis of calculating free withdrawal amounts. Starting from the valuation date, policyholders take withdrawals up to the maximum allowable amount of its guarantee base per year. Withdrawals are taken out of policyholders' nominal accounts and do not reduce the guarantee base. Upon the death of a policyholder, his/her beneficiary will receive the remaining balance of the policyholder's nominal account. The GLWB rider also offers a combination of a roll-up option, under which the guarantee base accrues interest, and step-up (ratchet) options, under which the guarantee base would be always matched to the account value, should the latter exceeds the former. For simplicity, we shall consider a flat deterministic yield curve for interest rate. From an insurer's standpoint, the investments from the cohort are aggregated and considered as a single fund under stochastic scenarios. The product features and model assumptions can be found in Appendix A.2.

The computation of the CTE (best efforts) will be carried out in a nested setting as follows.

1. Outer loop (stochastic reserving: CTE (best efforts))

    We use a geometric Brownian motion (independent lognormal model) to project equity returns over the next 30 or 50 years. Under each scenario of equity returns, we determine cash flows from separate accounts (withdrawal payments, interest on surplus, rider charges, management fees) and the cash flows from the hedging portfolio (buy and sell of index futures and bonds). The change in surplus is determined by the following recursive relation over each period:

    Change in surplus

    =   Fee income + Surrender charge − GLWB withdrawals − Expenses

        + Investment income on cash flows − Change in asset values

        + Investment income on surplus.   (7.82)

    Asset values are determined by starting assets, which are assumed to be long-term bonds, and the value of a hedging portfolio. An inner-loop calculation is invoked every time a dynamic hedging portfolio is rebalanced.

    In the example, we also consider dynamic lapse rates, which vary with the account value and guarantee base. The stochastically determined lapse rates are included to capture policyholder behaviors where persistence is high when the guarantee is much higher than account value.

2. Inner loop (Hedging program)

For simplicity, the hedging program under consideration is based on a delta neutral strategy, which only utilizes index futures and bonds. In the ensuing numerical example, we consider both biweekly and quarterly hedging, with the former aimed at illustrating accuracy of hedging and the latter aimed at reducing computational efforts. The initial net value of the hedging portfolio is assumed to be zero. Keep in mind that the risk-neutral value of the GLWB rider at any given point in time depends on four factors: account value, guarantee base, time to maturity and (dynamic) survivorship. At each point in time, we project the future evolution of account value, guarantee base conditional on the then-current account value and guarantee base. We record two components of benefit payments to policyholders:

(a) Quarterly withdrawals: This amount is always assumed to be 4% of the then-current guarantee base.

(b) Return of account values upon death and return of cash values upon surrender.

The delta, Δ, of the GLWB rider, which determines how many units of index futures to hold in the hedging portfolio, is calculated as follows: (1) Evaluate the risk-neutral value of the GLWB rider with the then-current account value and the then-current guarantee base. (2) Shock the then-current account value by 1% and evaluate the risk-neutral value of the GLWB rider. (3) Determine the delta by the difference quotient of risk-neutral values.

In the corresponding outer loop, the hedging portfolio always consists of Δ shares of index futures and a certain amount of bonds. Over each period, we shall short-sell or buy just enough one-month bonds in order to finance Δ shares of the futures.

3. Final result

In each outer-loop calculation, we observe the evolution of the present value of the accumulated deficiency over the projection period of 50 years. Record the largest value over time for each outer loop, which is the scenario amount. The CTE(best efforts) is determined by the average of 30% of the largest scenario amounts.

The guaranteed lifetime withdrawal benefit (GLWB) guarantees a policyholder the ability to withdraw up to a maximum percentage of the guarantee base for the whole life, regardless of the balance in his/her nominal account.

To formulate this problem, we introduce the following notation.

- F_t, the market value of a policyholder's sub-account at $t \geq 0$. F_0 is considered to be the initial purchase payment (premium) invested at the start of the contract. For simplicity, we consider the single-premium variable annuity where no additional purchase payment is made into the account.

- G_t, the guarantee base at time $t \geq 0$. The guarantee base may also accrue compound interest at the so-called roll-up rate.

- ρ, the annualized roll-up rate for the guarantee base.

- Y_t, the in-the-moneyness ratio. While there are many ways to define the moneyness, we use the ratio $Y_t = F_t/G_t \in [0,1]$.

- S_t, the market value of the underlying equity index or fund at t. If more than one fund is involved, this is considered to be the portfolio value of all funds.

- B_t, the market value of risk-free bonds at time t.

- p, the percentage of the investment account invested in equities. For example, a "conservative" allocation portfolio with 40% stocks and 60% bonds would have $p = 40\%$.

- m, the annualized rate at which account-value-based fees are deducted from the separate account. As the fees are used to compensate for costs of covering mortality risks and expenses, they are often referred as the mortality and expenses (M&E) fees. Except for purchase-payments-based withdrawal charges, all contract fees and expenses are typically calculated and accrued on daily basis.

- m_w, the annualized rate of the guarantee-based-rider-charge, allocated to fund the GLWB rider.

- r, the continuously compounding annual risk-free interest rate.

- σ, annualized volatility per annum of the underlying equity index.

- $_tp_x$, the survival probability after t years of a policyholder of age x at issue. However, as we shall consider dynamic policyholder behavior later, it would be more appropriate to view $_tp_x$ as the proportion of in-force policies in the initial population.

- μ_t^d, the instantaneous death rate at time t.

- μ_t^l, the instantaneous lapse rate at time t.

- h, the free partial withdrawal rate per annum.

- c_t, the account-value-based surrender charge rate at time t.

- V_t, the risk-neutral value of the GLWB.

One should keep in mind that all annualized rates, such as ρ, r, m, are all nominal rates with compounding frequency according to their uses. For example, if the fees are taken on a daily basis, then m is the corresponding annual nominal fee rate compounded daily. Regardless of different frequencies in examples, all rates should be equivalent to their corresponding annual effective rates.

7.3.4.2 Outer loop: surplus calculation

Before we introduce the continuous-time model, let us consider how the model is formulated with a typical discrete-time model. Note that in practice a discrete-time model can be implemented with a spreadsheet or computer algorithm. To make a connection between the discrete-time model (recursive calculation) and the continuous-time model, we shall divide each year into n periods. For example, if the projection is done on a quarterly basis, then we are assuming $n = 4$.

Section 1: Fund values before decrements

Discrete-time model (recursive calculation)

Under the GLWB, the amount of systematic withdrawals per period is typically determined by a pre-specified percentage of a guarantee base. It is typical that the starting value of the guarantee base matches with the initial premium $G_0 = F_0$, and the evolution of the guarantee base over each period is based on the combination of roll-up and step-up options in (1.18). Keep in mind, however, that the guarantee base is a nominal account that serves only as a base for determining withdrawal amounts. The actual withdrawals, which are typically a fixed percentage, denoted by h, of the then-current guarantee base, are taken out of the policyholder's own investment account (not the guarantee base).

In a recursive calculation, we would observe that the incremental change per period for the account value is given by

$$
\begin{aligned}
F_{(k+1)/n} - F_{k/n} &= p\frac{S_{(k+1)/n} - S_{k/n}}{S_{k/n}}F_{k/n} + (1-p)\frac{B_{(k+1)/n} - B_{k/n}}{B_{k/n}}F_{k/n} \\
&\quad - \frac{m_w + h}{n}G_{k/n} - \frac{m}{n}F_{k/n}.
\end{aligned}
\tag{7.83}
$$

Immediately after the policyholder's account hits zero, the recursive relation is no longer valid as there is no money left to invest. Therefore, we would write for $k = 0, 1, \cdots$

$$
\begin{aligned}
F_{(k+1)/n} = \max\bigg\{ &\left[p\frac{S_{(k+1)/n}}{S_{k/n}} + (1-p)\frac{B_{(k+1)/n}}{B_{k/n}} \right] F_{k/n} \\
&- \frac{m_w + h}{n}G_{k/n} - \frac{m}{n}F_{k/n}, 0 \bigg\}.
\end{aligned}
$$

Continuous-time model

Although the above formulation works for all model assumptions of equity indices, we shall consider a specific model for the equity index to facilitate continued discussion of continuous-time models. For simplicity, we assume that the equity index is driven by a geometric Brownian motion, also known as the independent lognormal model in the industry. Under the risk-neutral measure,

$$
\mathrm{d}S_t = rS_t\,\mathrm{d}t + \sigma S_t\,\mathrm{d}W_t,
$$

where $\{W_t : t \geq 0\}$ is a Brownian motion. The money market account accrues interest, $B_t = B(0)e^{rt}$, or equivalently

$$dB_t = rB_t \, dt.$$

Keep in mind, however, that the rest of the analysis can be extended to more general models.

If we write the time increment $\Delta t = 1/n$ and $t = k/n$ in (7.83), then

$$F_{t+\Delta t} - F_t$$
$$= p\frac{S_{t+\Delta t} - S_t}{S_t}F_t + (1-p)\frac{B_{t+\Delta t} - B_t}{B_t}F_t - (m_w + h)G_t\Delta t - mF_t\Delta t.$$

When we shrink the time period Δt to zero, the continuous-time version of the recursive relation in (7.83) becomes the stochastic differential equation

$$\begin{aligned} dF_t &= p\frac{F_t}{S_t}\,dS_t + (1-p)\frac{F_t}{B_t}\,dB_t - (m_w + h)G_t\,dt - mF_t\,dt \\ &= [(r-m)F_t - (m_w+h)G_t]\,dt + p\sigma F_t\,dW_t. \end{aligned} \qquad (7.84)$$

Note that the product offers a combination of step-up option and roll-up option. It is known from Section 1.2.2 that, as the projection period shrinks to zero, the growth of guarantee base is driven by a continuous-time stochastic process

$$G_t = e^{\rho t} \sup_{0 \leq s \leq t} \left\{e^{-\rho t}F_t\right\}.$$

Section 2: Fund values after decrements

Discrete-time model (recursive calculation)

As we consider withdrawals to in-force policies, the following notation is to be used for modeling decrements.

- $_tq_x^d$, the probability that a policyholder at age x dies within t periods.

- $_sq_t^l$, the probability that a policy still in force at time t lapses within s periods.

- $_sq_t^b$, the probability that a policy still in force at time t lapses within s periods without the consideration of dynamic policyholder behavior

- $_tp_x$, the probability that the policy from a policyholder at age x is still in force after t periods.

The values of $_tq_x^d$ are typically provided in a life table for integer values x and t. We may use fractional year assumptions to infer their values at non-integer values.

We consider $_tq^b$ to be base lapse rates, which are estimates of lapse rates in the absence of dynamic policyholder behavior. As the in-the-moneyness ratio increases and is close to 1, we expect policyholders to feel confident of their own investment and more likely to surrender their contracts. As the in-the-moneyness ratio decreases, policyholders are more likely to rely on guarantee benefits from the GLWB rider and hold on to their policies. Therefore, the dynamic lapse rate at time t is the product of the base lapse rate and the dynamic factor, which is a function f of the in-the-moneyness ratio Y_t,

$$_{\Delta t}q_t^l = {}_{\Delta t}q_t^b\, f(Y_t). \tag{7.85}$$

Note that survival probabilities are usually calculated from the recursive relation

$$_{(k+1)/n}p_x = {}_{k/n}p_x(1 - {}_{1/n}q_{x+k/n}^d)(1 - {}_{1/n}q_{k/n}^l), \qquad k = 1, 2, \cdots. \tag{7.86}$$

Readers should be reminded that the survivorship model $\{{}_tp_x, t \geq 0\}$ is path dependent on equity returns through the in-the-moneyness ratio process $\{Y_t, t \geq 0\}$.

Continuous-time model

In the continuous-time model, we consider the instantaneous rate of mortality

$$\mu_{x+t}^d = \frac{\partial({}_tq_x^d)/\partial t}{{}_tp_x}.$$

We can infer the instantaneous death rates $\{\mu_s^d, s \geq 0\}$ from a life table with fractional age assumptions. For example, the constant force of mortality assumption implies that

$$\mu_{x+s}^d = -\ln(1 - q_x^d), \qquad \text{for all integer } x \text{ and } 0 \leq s \leq 1.$$

In other words, for integer x and $t \geq 0$,

$$_tq_x^d = 1 - e^{-\int_0^t \mu_{x+s}^d\, ds}.$$

Similarly, we can define the instantaneous lapse rates $\{\mu_s^l, s \geq 0\}$ and the instantaneous base lapse rates $\{\mu_s^b, s \geq 0\}$:

$$\mu_t^l = \left.\frac{\partial({}_sq_t^l)}{\partial s}\right|_{s=0}, \qquad \mu_t^b = \left.\frac{\partial({}_sq_t^b)}{\partial s}\right|_{s=0}.$$

Observe that (7.85) can be rewritten as

$$\frac{_{\Delta t}q_t^l}{\Delta t} = \frac{_{\Delta t}q_t^b}{\Delta t}\, f(Y_t),$$

which implies by taking the limit $\Delta t \to 0$ that

$$\mu_t^l = \mu_t^b f(Y_t).$$

To see the analogue of (7.86) in the continuous time model, we set $t = x + k/n$ and $\Delta t = 1/n$ in (7.86) and then let $\Delta t \to 0$. It follows that

$$d_t p_x = -{}_tp_x(\mu_t^l + \mu_{x+t}^d)\, dt.$$

Section 3: Income statement

The accumulated surplus/deficiency is calculated under each projection of account values in this last section. Let us use the following notation to capture the cash flows in each period:

- R_t, the accumulated surplus at time t

- c_t, the surrender charge at time t

- E_t, the expense per time unit at time t, which may include percentage of AV unit maintenance/overhead expense and per policy unit maintenance

Discrete time model (recursive calculation)

Before consideration of hedging, the incremental changes in surplus are determined by the recursive relation (7.82), which can be translated as follows:

$$R_{t+\Delta t} - R_t = rR_t\Delta t + (1+r\Delta t)\Big[\, {}_tp_x(mF_t + m_wG_t)\Delta t I(F_t > 0)$$

$$+ \, {}_tp_x\,{}_{\Delta t}q^l_{x+t}c_tF_tI(F_t > 0) - {}_tp_xhG_t\Delta tI(F_t \le 0) - {}_tp_xE_t\Delta tI(F_t > 0)\Big].$$
$$(7.87)$$

Continuous-time model

Taking Δt to zero, we obtain immediately a pathwise-defined ordinary differential equation,

$$\mathrm{d}R_t \;=\; \Big[rR_t - {}_tp_xhG_tI(F_t \le 0) + {}_tp_x(m_wG_t + mF_t)I(F_t > 0)$$

$$+ \mu^l_t f(Y_t)\,{}_tp_xc_tF_tI(F_t > 0) - {}_tp_xE_tI(F_t > 0)\Big]\,\mathrm{d}t,$$

together with the initial condition $R_0 = 0$, which yields the solution

$$R_t \;=\; e^{rt}\Big[\int_0^t e^{-rs}\,{}_sp_x(m_wG_s + mF_s)I(F_s > 0)\,\mathrm{d}s$$

$$+ \int_0^t e^{-rs}\mu^l_s f(Y_s)\,{}_sp_xc_sF_sI(F_s > 0)\,\mathrm{d}s$$

$$- \int_0^t e^{-rs}\,{}_sp_x\,hG_sI(F_s \le 0)\,\mathrm{d}s - \int_0^t e^{-rs}\,{}_sp_xE_sI(F_s > 0)\,\mathrm{d}s\Big].$$

7.3.4.3   Inner loop: risk-neutral valuation

Let us now consider the risk-neutral value of the insurer's net liability from a GLWB rider. Recall that the GLWB guarantees systematic withdrawals until the policyholder's death regardless of whether or not his/her investment account is depleted. There are four components of cash flows from the insurer's point of view:

1. Withdrawal benefits

   Observe that the GLWB rider incurs cost when the policyholder continues to withdraw after the account is depleted. Hence, the present value of all GLWB benefit payments is given by

   $$\sum_{k=n\tau}^{\infty} e^{-r(k+1)/n} {}_{k/n}p_x \frac{h}{n} G_{k/n},$$

   where the first time when the account is exhausted, called the *ruin time*, is given by

   $$\tau := \min\left\{\frac{k}{n} > 0 : F_{k/n} = 0\right\}.$$

   In the discrete-time case, there is the possibility that the last withdrawal payment before the account is depleted comes partly from the policyholder's account and partly from the insurer's general account. We ignore the small payment from the insurer here, because this payment appears in the continuous-time model to be introduced next.

2. Fee incomes

   On the revenue side, the GLWB is funded by the collection of rider charges, which include account-value-based fees and guarantee-based fees. The present value of total rider charges is given by

   $$\sum_{k=0}^{n\tau} e^{-r(k+1)/n} {}_{k/n}p_x \left(F_{k/n} \frac{m}{n} + G_{k/n} \frac{m_w}{n}\right).$$

3. Surrender charges

   If a policyholder voluntarily surrenders a contract, then the remaining balance of the investment account is subject to a surrender charge, which is determined by the surrender charge rate:

   $$\sum_{k=0}^{n\tau} e^{-r(k+1)/n} {}_{k/n}p_x {}_{1/n}q^l_{x+k/n} c_{(k+1)/n} F_{(k+1)/n}.$$

4. Expenses

   The present value of all expenses is given by

   $$\sum_{k=0}^{n\tau} e^{-r(k+1)/n} {}_{k/n}p_x \frac{E_{(k+1)/n}}{n}.$$

Note, however, although not written explicitly, the survival rate ${}_{k/n}p_x$ in all four components is path dependent as shown in (7.86).

It follows from the definition of Riemann integral that as the projection period shrinks to zero, i.e., $n \to \infty$, the limit of the withdrawal benefits can be written as

$$\lim_{n \to \infty} \sum_{k=0}^{\infty} e^{-r(k+1)/n} \, _{k/n}p_x \, h \, G_{k/n}\left(\frac{1}{n}\right) I(F_{k/n} > 0)$$

$$= \int_0^{\infty} e^{-rt} \, _t p_x \, h \, G_t I(F_t \le 0)\, \mathrm{d}t.$$

The fee incomes can be written as

$$\lim_{n \to \infty} \sum_{k=0}^{\infty} e^{-r(k+1)/n} \, _{k/n}p_x \left(F_{k/n}\frac{m}{n} + G_{k/n}\frac{m_w}{n} \right) I(F_{k/n} > 0)$$

$$= \int_0^{\infty} e^{-rt} \, _t p_x (mF_t + m_w G_t) I(F_t > 0)\, \mathrm{d}t.$$

Similarly, the surrender charges can be written as

$$\lim_{n \to \infty} \sum_{k=0}^{\infty} e^{-r(k+1)/n} \, _{k/n}p_x \, \frac{1/n \, q^l_{x+k/n}}{1/n} \, c_{(k+1)/n} F_{(k+1)/n}\frac{1}{n} I(F_{k/n} > 0)$$

$$= \int_0^{\infty} e^{-rt} \mu^l_t f(Y_t) \, _t p_x c_t F_t I(F_t > 0)\, \mathrm{d}t,$$

and the expenses can be written as

$$\lim_{n \to \infty} \sum_{k=0}^{\infty} e^{-r(k+1)/n} \, _{k/n}p_x \, E_{(k+1)/n}\frac{1}{n} I(F_{k/n} > 0) = \int_0^{\infty} e^{-rt} \, _t p_x \, E_t I(F_t > 0)\, \mathrm{d}t.$$

Net liability hedging

If we consider all cash flows from an insurer's perspective, then the risk-neutral value of the insurer's net liability in the continuous time model is given by

$$V_0 = \mathbb{E}\Bigg[\int_0^{\infty} e_t^{-rt} p_x h G_t I(F_s \le 0)\, \mathrm{d}t - \int_0^{\infty} e^{-rt} \, _t p_x (m_w G_s + mF_t) I(F_t > 0)\, \mathrm{d}t$$

$$- \int_0^{\infty} e^{-rt} \mu^l_t f(Y_t) \, _t p_x c_t F_t I(F_s > 0)\, \mathrm{d}t$$

$$- \int_0^{\infty} e^{-rt} \, _t p_x E_t I(F_t > 0)\, \mathrm{d}t \Bigg].$$

In this formulation, we included only the cash flows in and out of the insurer's general account (not a separate account). This is not to be confused with the benefits from a policyholder's perspective.

From now on, we shall ignore the expenses for simplicity. Note, however, that the expenses term can be easily incorporated in the following calculations. It is known from Chapter 6 that the risk-neutral value of the insurer's net liability at time t is given by the conditional expectation of future cash flows,

$$
\begin{aligned}
V_t \;:=\; \mathbb{E}\Bigg[&\int_t^\infty e^{-r(s-t)} \, {}_sp_x \, h \, G_s I(F_s < 0) \, ds \\
&- \int_t^\infty e^{-r(s-t)} \, {}_sp_x (m_w G_s + m F_s) I(F_s > 0) \, ds \\
&- \int_t^\infty e^{-r(s-t)} \mu_s^l f(Y_s) \, {}_sp_x c_s F_s I(F_s > 0) \, ds \Bigg| \mathcal{F}_t \Bigg], \quad (7.88)
\end{aligned}
$$

where $\{\mathcal{F}_t, t \geq 0\}$ is the natural filtration of the Brownian motion driving the dynamics of the equity index process. It is not difficult to show that $\{(F_t, G_t, {}_tp_x) : 0 \leq t \leq T\}$ is a Markov process and hence there exists a smooth function $v(t, x, y, z)$ that

$$
V_t = v(t, F_t, G_t, {}_tp_x). \tag{7.89}
$$

Delta-hedging program

We now discuss how to construct a hedging portfolio in order to hedge against the GLWB liability. To make a clear presentation, we consider the hedging program in the continuous-time model. Since the hedging is done in theory at every instant of time and the underlying equity process has constant volatility and a constant risk-free interest rate, it is sufficient to conduct delta hedging alone to eliminate equity risk. Recall that delta measures the sensitivity of the GLWB liability to changes in equity index values assuming all other variables remain the same. We have shown that the GLWB liability is given by $V_t = v(t, F_t, G_t, {}_tp_x)$, and hence the delta should be defined as

$$
\Delta_t = v_x(t, F_t, G_t, {}_tp_x). \tag{7.90}
$$

In practice, the derivative is often approximated by the difference quotient

$$
\Delta_t \approx \frac{v(t, F_t, G_t, {}_tp_x) - v(t, F_t - \Delta F, G_t, {}_tp_x)}{\Delta F}. \tag{7.91}
$$

For example, an approximation of the delta can be obtained from the percentage change of the GLWB liability when the current account value F_t is shocked by 1%. Since we cannot trade policyholders' accounts, we can buy and sell equity index futures instead. In practice, hedging (rebalancing) is performed at discrete-time intervals generally ranging from daily to quarterly, in accordance with market circumstances and company philosophy.

Dynamics of mixed surplus and hedging portfolio

The idea is to keep track of deltas needed to create a hedging portfolio, and the cost of changes in delta is entirely financed by the accumulated surplus. In other words, the insurer's entire portfolio consists of two components at any point of time:

the hedging instruments on the asset side and the accumulation of surplus from the liability side. We denote the value of the entire portfolio by H_t and the value of accumulated surplus/deficiency by R_t. For a better presentation of the results, we write $h_t = (F_t/S_t)v_x(t, F_t, G_t, {}_tp_x)$ for the number of units of equity index futures at time t. Then it is clear that

$$H_t = h_t S_t + R_t.$$

Although this formulation is not usually stated explicitly in practice, we will show next that it is indeed consistent with the recursive relation (7.82), which is used in practitioners' discrete-time models.

It follows immediately from (6.11) that the dynamics of the self-financing port-folio $\{H_t : 0 \leq t \leq T\}$ with exogenous cash flows $\{C_t : 0 \leq t \leq T\}$ is given by

$$\mathrm{d}H_t \quad = \quad h_t\,\mathrm{d}S_t + r(H_t - h_t S_t)\,\mathrm{d}t + C_t\,\mathrm{d}t. \qquad (7.92)$$

where

$$
\begin{aligned}
C_t \quad = \quad & {}_tp_x(m_w G_t + mF_t)I(F_t > 0) + \mu_t^l f(Y_t)\,{}_tp_x\,c_t F_t I(F_t > 0) \\
& - {}_tp_x hG_t I(F_t \leq 0).
\end{aligned}
\qquad (7.93)
$$

It can be shown with martingale arguments (Exercise 7.3.1) that

$$
\begin{aligned}
\mathrm{d}v(t, F_t, G_t, {}_tp_x) \quad = \quad & rv(t, F_t, G_t, {}_tp_x)\,\mathrm{d}t + C_t\,\mathrm{d}t + p\sigma F_t v_x(t, F_t, G_t, {}_tp_x)\,\mathrm{d}B_t \\
= \quad & r[v(t, F_t, G_t, {}_tp_x) - v_x(t, F_t, G_t, {}_tp_x)F_t]\,\mathrm{d}t + C_t\,\mathrm{d}t \\
& + \frac{F_t}{S_t}v_x(t, F_t, G_t, {}_tp_x)\,\mathrm{d}S_t.
\end{aligned}
\qquad (7.94)
$$

If we set the number of shares invested in the underlying stock to be

$$\Delta_t = \frac{F_t}{S_t}v_x(t, F_t, G_t, {}_tp_x),$$

It follows from (7.94) that

$$\mathrm{d}v(t, F_t, G_t, {}_tp_x) = r[v(t, F_t, G_t, {}_tp_x) - \Delta_t S_t]\,\mathrm{d}t + C_t\,\mathrm{d}t + \Delta_t\,\mathrm{d}S_t. \quad (7.95)$$

Note that the GLWB liability $V_t = v(t, F_t, G_t, {}_tp_x)$ and $h_t = \Delta_t$. Subtracting (7.94) from (7.95) yields

$$\mathrm{d}(V_t - H_t) = r(V_t - H_t)\,\mathrm{d}t,$$

which implies that for some constant C and all $t \geq 0$

$$e^{-rt}(V_t - H_t) = C.$$

Since $H_0 = 0$, then it shows that $C = V_0$.

$$H_t = V_t - e^{rt}V_0.$$

Furthermore, if the fee rates are set in such a way that the no-arbitrage value of the GLWB net liability is zero, i.e. $V_0 = 0$, then it is clear that $H_t = V_t$ for all $0 \leq t \leq T$.

7.3.4.4 Implementation

(1) Crude Monte Carlo

For inner loop simulations, we estimate the GLWB liability by its sample mean with a sample of size 20,

$$\hat{V}_t = \frac{1}{20} \sum_{i=1}^{20} \hat{V}_i,$$

where each V_i is a realization of the discrete time version of (7.88):

$$
\begin{aligned}
\hat{V}_i =\ & \frac{1}{N} \sum_{j=1}^{N} \Bigg[\sum_{k=\lfloor n(t \vee \tau^{(j)}) \rfloor}^{nT} e^{-r[(k+1)/n-t]}\, _{k/n}p_x^{(j)} \frac{h}{n} G_{k/n}^{(j)} \\
& - \sum_{k=\lfloor n(t \wedge \tau^{(j)}) \rfloor}^{\lfloor n(\tau^{(j)} \wedge T) \rfloor} e^{-r[(k+1)/n-t]}\, _{k/n}p_x^{(j)} \left(F_{k/n}^{(j)} \frac{m}{n} + G_{k/n}^{(j)} \frac{m_w}{n} \right. \\
& \left. + F_{(k+1)/n}^{(j)} \frac{\left(1/n\, q_{x+k/n}^l\right)^{(j)}}{1/n} \frac{c_{(k+1)/n}}{n} \right) \Bigg].
\end{aligned}
$$

The superscript (j) indicates the j-th repetition of simulations. Sample paths of the equity index $\{S_t : 0 \le t \le T\}$ are generated using the simulation technique in Example 3.7. Subsequently, we generate sample paths of a policyholder' subaccount and guarantee base according to (7.83), (1.17) with dynamic lapse rates determined by (7.85) and (7.86).

(2) Preprocessed inner loops

Since there are four determining factors in this model, we have to construct a four-dimensional grid for preprocessed scenarios. For each point on the grid, we run an inner-loop calculation to determine risk-neutral valuation of GLWB liability and use difference quotient to approximate delta. The interpolation formula is the four-dimensional extension of the two-dimensional formula (7.79).

(3) Least-Squares Monte Carlo

We intend to estimate the functional relationship between the deltas of GLWB liability and four determining factors: time t, account value F_t, guarantee base G_t and survivorship $_tp_x$. Following the discussion in Section 7.3.2, we approximate the functional relationship by a linear combination of basis functions.

$$\bar{\Delta}_t = v_x(t, F_t, G_t, {}_tp_x) \approx \sum_{l=1}^{s} \beta_l \phi_l(t, F_t, G_t, {}_tp_x),$$

where ϕ_l's are basis functions: Ideally basis functions should incorporate features of the time-space surface v_x which determines the deltas. However, without any insight about the curve, we follow the standard practice as shown in Koursaris[71] to choose lower term polynomials.

The first and most naive approach of least-squares estimates is to regress the four variables $(t, F_t, G_t, {}_tp_x)$ against the response variable Δ_t. Keep in mind, however, that we do not know exact values of v_x, which should be estimated from inner-loop calculations according to the formula (7.91). The second approach, which requires understanding the structural property of the four-variable function, is to make use of the fact that v is determined by a function u of only two variables in (7.96). Therefore, deltas can be determined by the function u in the following way:

$$\bar{\Delta}_t = v_x(t, F_t, G_t, {}_tp_x) = {}_tp_x G_t u_s(t, Y_t).$$

Then we can approximate the functional relationship

$$u_s(t, Y_t) \approx \sum_{l=1}^{s} \beta_l^* \phi_l^*(t, Y_t),$$

where ϕ_l^*'s are basis functions and β_l^*'s are to be determined by the least-squares method. Again exact values of u_s are not known in advance but can be estimated from the formula (7.99). Note that it is in fact impossible to find the stochastic representation of $u(t, s)$ in Exercise 7.3.3, which can be used for inner-loop simulations.

(4) Numerical PDE method

As shown in Exercise 7.3.1, the function v can be determined by

$$v(t, x, y, z) = zyu(t, x/y), \tag{7.96}$$

where the function u satisfies a relatively simple PDE

$$\frac{1}{2}p^2\sigma^2 s^2 u_{ss} + [(r - m - \rho)s - (m_w + h)]u_s + u_t$$
$$- [\mu_{x+t}^d + \mu_t^l f(s) + r - \rho]u - (m_w + ms) - \mu_t^l f(s)c_t s = 0, \tag{7.97}$$

where u_{ss}, u_s, u_t are second derivatives with respect to s and first derivatives with respect to s, t respectively. The PDE is subject to the boundary conditions

$$u(t, 1) = u_s(t, 1), \tag{7.98a}$$
$$u(t, 0) = h\bar{a}_{x+t}, \tag{7.98b}$$
$$\lim_{t \to \infty} u(t, s) = 0, \tag{7.98c}$$

where the annuity symbol refers to

$$\bar{a}_{x+t} := \int_0^\infty e^{-(r-\rho)s} \, {}_sp_{x+t} \, ds.$$

It follows from the reduction of dimensions in (7.96) that $v_x(t, x, y, z) = zu_s(t, x/y)$. Hence, we obtain an alternative approach to approximate the delta:

$$\Delta_t \approx {}_tp_x \frac{u(t, F_t/G_t + \Delta s) - u(t, F_t/G_t - \Delta s)}{2\Delta s}. \tag{7.99}$$

Example 7.15. Model assumptions and parameters for the AG-43 CTE calculation and risk-neutral valuation of the GLWB liability are provided in Appendix A.2. The majority of product features and model parameters in this example are taken from an actual example illustrated through a sample spreadsheet donated by an actuarial software vendor. Keep in mind that instantaneous rates (interest, withdrawal, roll-up, fee etc.) are used in the continuous-time model for PDEs, while the Monte Carlo methods are based on the discrete-time model, which utilizes periodic rates (annual, quarterly, monthly, daily etc.). For consistency, we shall always use equivalent rates for different frequencies. For example, the roll-up rate is assumed to be 5% effective per annum. If we run projections on a monthly basis, $n = 12$, then ρ in discrete-time formulas such as (1.18) should be interpreted as the nominal rate compounded monthly $\rho = \rho^{(n)} = n[(1+5\%)^{1/n}-1] = 4.889\%$. The corresponding instantaneous rate for the PDE method would be $\rho = \ln(1 + 5\%) = 4.879\%$. The acquisition cost is not actually used in this calculation, because the valuation date is four years after issue and the acquisition cost has already occurred prior to the start of projection. The survivorship is assumed to follow the Illustrative Life Table in Appendix A.3 with a fractional age assumption (constant force of mortality). The modeling of dynamic policyholder behavior is described in Appendix A.4.

There are two steps of computation to determine the conditional tail expectation risk measure of the greatest present value of the accumulated deficiency:

> 1. Outer loops: Generate the cash flows including fee incomes, surrender charges, expenses, GLWB benefits and change in hedging instruments under each scenario of equity returns.

> 2. Inner loops: Every step of rebalancing with the hedging instruments requires the computation of deltas. Deltas are approximated by difference quotients, which rely on risk-neutral valuation of the GLWB liability.

The most time-consuming component of the nested simulations is the computation of deltas. Let us first compare the delta calculation using the Monte Carlo (MC) method and the PDE method.

Monte Carlo and PDE methods

Consider the risk-neutral valuation of GLWB liability in five years:

$$t = 5, F_t = 5,755,800, G_t = 7,674,000, S_t = 1,268, {}_tp_x = 0.72.$$

The equity index is always projected for $T = 50$ years at which ${}_Tp_x$ is zero for practical purposes. In Tables 7.13 and 7.15, we report the results on deltas for both Monte Carlo simulations with different numbers of repetitions, $N = 100, 1,000, 10,000$, and those from the PDE method with grid sizes $\Delta t = 0.01$ and $\Delta s = 0.001$. The first column represents the values of v_x in (7.90). Sample standard deviations are quoted in brackets under each estimate from a Monte Carlo simulation. The deltas obtained from the PDE approach are determined by (7.99).

There are two reasons why results from Monte Carlo simulations tend to differ from those from PDE methods:

1. Continuous-time versus discrete-time models: The PDE method is based on the assumptions of continuous cash flows, whereas MC simulations are performed on a discrete-time basis.

2. Sampling errors from the MC method: As a statistical procedure, MC methods inevitably introduce sampling errors that can be reduced only with very large sample sizes.

	$v_x(t, F_t, G_t, {}_tp_x)$	Net liability $(F_t = 5,755,800)$	After 1% shock	Time (secs)
Monte Carlo (100, 0.01)	-0.197038	$-57,163$ (79,768)	$-68,503$ (80,056)	15
Monte Carlo (1,000, 0.01)	-0.193887	$-42,407$ (21,165)	$-53,568$ (21,169)	141
MC (Antithetic) (1,000, 0.001)	-0.189232	$-29,361$ (13,834)	$-40,253$ (13,981)	1,689
MC (Antithetic) (1,000, 0.0001)	-0.188277	$-28,730$ (11,886)	$39,451$ (11,952)	16,389
PDE ($\Delta s = 0.001$)	-0.187765	-27,688	-38,496	307

TABLE 7.13: Delta calculation based on formula (7.91) with parameters $t = 5$ and $\sigma = 0.3$. Copyright © 2016 by the Society of Actuaries, Schaumburg, Illinois. Reprinted with permission.

$\Delta s = 0.001$	${}_tp_x u_s(t, F_t/G_t)$	$u(t, F_t/G_t - \Delta s)$	$u(t, F_t/G_t + \Delta s)$	Time
MC (Antithetic) (1,000,0.01)	-0.197212	-0.005704 (0.001822)	-0.006099 (0.001825)	196
MC (Antithetic) (1,000,0.001)	-0.191669	-0.003701 (0.001380)	-0.004085 (0.001388)	1,934
MC (Antithetic) (1,000,0.0001)	-0.189705	-0.003593 (0.001629)	-0.003972 (0.001631)	19,285
PDE ($\Delta s = 0.001$)	-0.189218	-0.003426	-0.003804	307

TABLE 7.14: Delta calculation based on formula (7.99) with parameters $t = 5$ and $\sigma = 0.3$. Copyright © 2016 by the Society of Actuaries, Schaumburg, Illinois. Reprinted with permission.

(Accuracy) In Tables 7.13 and 7.15, delta values at $t = 5$ and $t = 10$ are estimated from the approximation formula (7.91). In contrast, delta values at $t = 5$ and $t = 10$ are estimated from the approximation formula (7.99) in Tables 7.14 and 7.16.

Table 7.13 shows the case with a relatively high volatility $\sigma = 0.3$, under which we observe a gradual convergence of results from MC methods to those from the

PDE method as the time step $1/n$ decreases. To reduce sampling errors, we implement the method of antithetic variates, which employs the sampling strategy that, for every sample path of cash flows based on randomly generated random variables $\{x_1, x_2, \cdots, x_{nT}\}$, we produce another path determined by opposite values $\{-x_1, -x_2, \cdots, -x_{nT}\}$. Note that in this case there are only 500 randomly generated sample paths even though it is stated that $N = 1,000$. The simulation results for deltas are relatively close to the value from the PDE. We should point out that standard deviations from Monte Carlo simulations with $N = 100$ and $N = 1,000$ are so high that the confidence intervals for the GLWB liability value would be rather wide. For example, the approximate 95% confidence interval for the GLWB liability using the MC with $N = 1,000$ and $1/n = 0.0001$ would be $[-52,026.56, -5,433.44]$ based on asymptotic normality. Delta estimates appear to be close to that from the PDE method.

	$v_x(t, F_t, G_t, {}_tp_x)$	Net liability ($F_t = 5,755,800$)	After 1% shock	Time (secs)
MC (100, 0.01)	-0.322120	$-442,592$ (38,443)	$-461,132$ (38,458)	16
MC (1,000, 0.01)	-0.323383	$-453,226$ (11,534)	$-471,839$ (11,522)	155
MC (10,000, 0.01)	-0.322815	$-452,679$ (2,198)	$-471,260$ (2,201)	1,610
PDE ($\Delta s = 0.001$)	-0.322656	-451,532	-470,104	309

TABLE 7.15: Delta calculation based on formula (7.91) with parameters $t = 5$ and $\sigma = 0.1$. Copyright © 2016 by the Society of Actuaries, Schaumburg, Illinois. Reprinted with permission.

$\Delta s = 0.001$	${}_tp_x u_s(t, F_t/G_t)$	$u(t, F_t/G_t - \Delta s)$	$u(t, F_t/G_t + \Delta s)$	Time
Monte Carlo (1,000,0.01)	-0.324662	-0.058078 (0.001098)	-0.058727 (0.001097)	180
PDE	-0.324676	-0.058514	-0.059164	309

TABLE 7.16: Delta calculation based on formula (7.99) with parameters $t = 5$ and $\sigma = 0.1$. Copyright © 2016 by the Society of Actuaries, Schaumburg, Illinois. Reprinted with permission.

In the case of $\sigma = 0.1$, pilot experiments show that discrete-time versus continuous-time models do not cause a very significant difference. Hence we focus on the demonstration of the fact that sampling errors of Monte Carlo simulations tend to decrease as sample sizes increase in Tables 7.15 and 7.16. As with the previous case, we also observe that computations with the formula (7.99) achieves a higher level of accuracy than those with the formula (7.91).

(Efficiency) Based on the results from Tables 7.13 and 7.15, it is tempting to say that Monte Carlo estimates with $N = 100$ are modestly accurate but highly efficient, and there does not appear to any advantage for the PDE method. However, one should keep in mind that the delta calculation is required for every point of time for rebalancing. Here is a rough estimate of how much time is needed to calculate the CTE risk measures with the Monte Carlo simulations with $N = 1,000$ scenarios, ignoring additional time consumption for generating outer-loop scenarios.

(Monte Carlo $N = 100$) 14 (secs) $\times$ 50 (times of rebalancing each year) $\times$ 50 (years) $\times$ 1000 (outer loops) = 7×10^7 (secs) ≈ 3.82 (months).

(Monte Carlo $N = 1000$) 140 (secs) $\times$ 50 (times of rebalancing each year) $\times$ 50 (years) $\times$ 1000 (outer loops) = 7×10^8 (secs) ≈ 11.25 (years).

In contrast, the PDE method does not require inner-loop simulations. The CTE risk measure calculation with the PDE method **requires only about five minutes** plus additional time for generating outer-loop scenarios.

The drastic reduction of run time for the PDE method is owing to the fact that the algorithm marches through all time-space grid points, moving backwards from the terminal time $T = 50$ to time 0. A by-product of such an algorithm is that the risk-neutral values at all grid points are produced all at once, which can be viewed as a table of risk-neutral values for all combinations of $(t, F_t, G_t, {}_tp_x)$. The deltas can be easily estimated from risk-neutral values at neighboring grid points for all periods.

(t,s)	PDE	Monte Carlo	RE	LSMC	RE
(0,1)	-0.128920	-0.159537	23.75%	-0.245038	90.06%
(1,0.9)	-0.358906	-0.355374	0.98%	-0.401345	11.82%
(2,0.8)	-0.436890	-0.431742	1.18%	-0.497740	13.93%
(3,0.7)	-0.498723	-0.495406	0.67%	-0.551028	10.49%
(4,0.6)	-0.587266	-0.581283	1.02%	-0.578014	1.58%
(5,0.5)	-0.659056	-0.651280	1.18%	-0.595504	9.64%
(6,0.4)	-0.720308	-0.715813	0.62%	-0.620304	13.89%
(7,0.3)	-0.783270	-0.777856	0.69%	-0.669220	14.56%
(8,0.2)	-0.848309	-0.843980	0.51%	-0.759058	10.52%
(9,0.1)	-0.918761	-0.907156	1.26%	-0.906622	1.32%
(10,0)	-0.999415	-1.044595	4.52%	-1.128720	12.94%

TABLE 7.17: Accuracy of $u_s(t, s)$ on the grid using PDE and LSMC. Copyright © 2016 by the Society of Actuaries, Schaumburg, Illinois. Reprinted with permission.

Least-squares Monte Carlo

Here we take advantage of the reduction of dimensions shown in (7.96). Although this would be an unusual approach to apply the LSMC method, we can show significant improvement due to employing the analytical structure of the underlying stochastic model as opposed to brute force Monte Carlo simulations. In this case, we choose the following basis functions to approximate $u_s(t, s)$:

$$1, t, t^2, t^3, s, s^2, s^3, ts, ts^2, t^2 s$$

Applying the method of least squares and ignoring terms with negligible coefficients, we obtain the following approximating function:

$u_s(t, s) = -1.260962 + 0.012849t + 0.000054t^2 - 0.0000016t^3 + 2.334049s - 3.711706s^2 + 2.393581s^3 + 0.048018ts - 0.0003019t^2 s - 0.043594ts^2.$

We use an equidistant grid of (t_i, s_j) given by

$$t_i = (i - 1)\Delta t, \qquad \Delta t = 1, i = 1, \cdots, 51,$$
$$s_j = (j - 1)\Delta s, \qquad \Delta s = 0.1, j = 1, \cdots, 11.$$

A clear advantage of applying the LSMC to the two-dimensional functional relationship is that both t and s have bounded domains. However, as we shall see later, these results may still not be accurate enough to produce a highly effective hedging program. Table 7.17 shows the comparison of accuracy on grid points (t_i, s_j), whereas Table 7.18 reports the accuracy of results on points off the grid.

(t,s)	PDE	Monte Carlo	RE	LSMC	RE
(4.88,0.971)	-0.233102	-0.239505	2.75%	-0.219808	5.70%
(6.35,0.959)	-0.241904	-0.243275	0.56%	-0.214860	11.17%
(13.93,0.957)	-0.160784	-0.159947	0.52%	-0.115662	28.06%
(17.34,0.916)	-0.126440	-0.125833	0.48%	-0.122065	3.46%
(21.62,0.800)	-0.089758	-0.089423	0.42%	-0.142661	58.94%
(24.74,0.792)	-0.068372	-0.068551	0.26%	-0.107248	56.86%
(35.29,0.485)	-0.037405	-0.037354	0.13%	-0.002076	94.45%
(36.67,0.422)	-0.036653	-0.036583	0.19%	-0.006615	81.95%
(41.88,0.158)	-0.110142	-0.104925	4.73%	-0.274434	149.16%
(48.24,0.142)	-0.018514	-0.018683	0.90%	-0.247936	1239.16 %

TABLE 7.18: Accuracy of $u_s(t, s)$ off the grid using PDE and LSMC. Copyright © 2016 by the Society of Actuaries, Schaumburg, Illinois. Reprinted with permission.

Preprocessed inner loops

We apply the preprocessed method to approximate the function $u_s(t, s)$ in Table 7.19. Overall the preprocessed inner loops provide reasonably accurate estimates of neighoring points.

There is an "outlier" in Table 7.19 for the approximate delta value at $(48.24, 0.142)$, which appears to have an error of 150.79%. We look up the neighboring grid points and the corresponding delta values from inner loops in Table 7.20. At first glance, it might be surprising that off-grid points by linear interpolation would be much less accurate than the neighboring four grid points. A careful examination of the delta values would reveal that the surface of $u_s(t, s)$ has more curvature in this

(t,s)	PDE	Monte Carlo	RE	Preprocessed	RE
(4.88,0.971)	-0.233102	-0.239505	2.75%	-0.227417	2.44%
(6.35,0.959)	-0.241904	-0.243275	0.56%	-0.233378	3.52%
(13.93,0.957)	-0.160784	-0.159947	0.52%	-0.160633	0.09%
(17.34,0.916)	-0.126440	-0.125833	0.48%	-0.127042	0.47%
(21.62,0.800)	-0.089758	-0.89423	0.42%	-0.0895989	0.18%
(24.74,0.792)	-0.068372	-0.068551	0.26%	-0.068434	0.09%
(35.29,0.485)	-0.037405	-0.037354	0.13%	-0.037711	0.82%
(36.67,0.422)	-0.036653	-0.036583	0.19%	-0.037003	0.95%
(41.88,0.158)	-0.110142	-0.104925	4.73%	-0.131462	19.35%
(48.24,0.142)	-0.018514	-0.018683	0.90%	-0.046432	150.79 %

TABLE 7.19: Accuracy of $u_s(t, s)$ off the grid using the preprocessed inner loop method. Copyright © 2016 by the Society of Actuaries, Schaumburg, Illinois. Reprinted with permission.

particular neighborhood than other places. If points for interpolation are drawn from regions with deep curvature, then the results would be quite inaccurate unless one uses a very dense grid.

Nested simulations

We employ a biweekly dynamic hedging portfolio in order to better illustrate the visual effect of outcomes from hedging, i.e., $n = 100$. To demonstrate the effect of hedging, we use the same rate of return $r = 0.0576$ per annum and assume that the expected rate of return for the equity index $\mu = r = 0.0577$ per annum in the outer-loop calculations.

We are now ready to present the end results of the AG-43 stochastic scenario amount calculation. Recall that cash flows in outer loops are calculated from the GLWB model with parameters listed in Appendix A.2. The model incorporates dynamic policyholder behavior and all expenses. In Table 7.21, we present CTE stochastic scenario amounts under various volatility assumptions. The formulas for computing deltas in each section of the table are identified in the first column. It is clear that the method of preprocessed inner loops produces results close to those from the PDE methods in the case where $\sigma = 0.3$, and the inner loops are replaced by approximations based on two variable functional relationship v. In contrast, the results

(t,s)	PDE	Monte Carlo	RE
(48,0.1)	-0.128013	-0.083933	34.43%
(48,0.2)	-0.019462	-0.019669	1.06%
(49,0.1)	-0.013582	-0.013738	1.15%
(49,0.2)	-0.013533	-0.013692	1.17%

TABLE 7.20: Errors in the neighborhood of a point of large error. Copyright © 2016 by the Society of Actuaries, Schaumburg, Illinois. Reprinted with permission.

for preprocessed inner loops are not accurate at all when $\sigma = 0.3$, and inner loops are replaced by approximations based on the four variable functional relationship u. In general, all methods produce reasonably close results under the low-volatility assumption $\sigma = 0.1$.

$\sigma = 0.3$	excluding CDHS	LSMC	PDE	Preprocessed
70% CTE	-3,725,724	-2,204,752	-1,471,402	-1,319,600
(7.99)	(1,135,173)	(741,975)	(495,620)	(432,776)
time (secs)	67.89	2692.27	544.135	4632.42
$\sigma = 0.3$	excluding CDHS	LSMC	PDE	Preprocessed
70% CTE	-3,666,006	-11,685,363	-1,551,701	-3,818,887,705
(7.91)	(1,107,968)	(41,661,646)	(484,667)	(6,188,486,393)
time (secs)	68.482	2973.548	473.845	3938.779
$\sigma = 0.1$	excluding CDHS	LSMC	PDE	Preprocessed
70% CTE	-40,255	461,599	665,981	581,240
(7.91)	(169,037)	(31,096)	(67,409)	(187,028)
time (secs)	64.854	2,871.289	489.255	3,921.446

TABLE 7.21: Comparison of CTE (best efforts) with various techniques. Copyright © 2016 by the Society of Actuaries, Schaumburg, Illinois. Reprinted with permission.

Another intuitive way to check the accuracy of inner loop calculations is to examine the histogram of terminal surpluses with a hedging program. The insurer's portfolio with a hedging program should become more or less a risk-free asset according to the no-arbitrage theory. The effectiveness of a hedging program in this model largely relies on the accuracy of delta calculation. In Figure 7.3, we can tell that the hedging program developed from the PDE method is highly effective as terminal surpluses are concentrated around values close to zero. The LSMC method fails to produce any visible effect of hedging against equity risk, as the variation of portfolio values is as big as the surplus prior to hedging. This lack of hedging effect is likely due to the fact that deltas are far from accurate. The method of processed inner loops produces even worse results, as the scale of terminal surpluses can no longer match those from LSMC and PDE methods. In Figure 7.4, we implement similar procedures except that the LSMC and the method of processed inner loops are applied to approximate the two-variable functional relationship, which significantly improves their accuracy. The comparison between Figure 7.3 and 7.4 clearly shows that the accuracy of delta calculation is critical to the success of a hedging program. The method of processed inner loops only shows minor improvement over the LSMC method. More numerical results can be seen in Feng et a. [40].

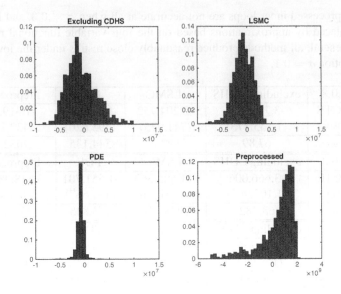

FIGURE 7.3: Effectiveness of hedging with deltas calculated from (7.91) ($\sigma = 0.3$)
Copyright © 2016 by the Society of Actuaries. Reprinted with permission.

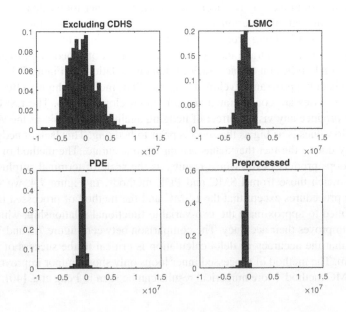

FIGURE 7.4: Effectiveness of hedging with deltas calculated from (7.99) ($\sigma = 0.3$)
Copyright © 2016 by the Society of Actuaries. Reprinted with permission.

7.4 Bibliographic notes

This chapter is mainly intended to offer a glimpse of computational techniques available for computing various risk metrics for equity-linked insurance. Nearly all methods introduced in this chapter can be extended to other types of investment guarantees and in more general setting.

A comprehensive book on applied numerical analysis including topics on differential equation methods is Heath [63]. The application of differential equation method in this chapter on guaranteed minimum withdrawal benefit is based on Feng and Vecer [47]. Interested readers can find other applications of the differential equation method to variable annuity guaranteed benefits, including guaranteed minimum maturity benefit in an aggregate model in Feng [39], guaranteed minimum death benefit in an aggregate model in Feng and Huang [41], optimal initiation of guaranteed lifetime withdrawal benefit in Huang, Milevsky and Salisbury [64], optimal withdrawal strategy for guaranteed minimum withdrawal benefit in Dai, Kwok and Zong [21], flexible premium variable annuities in Chi and Lin [19], etc.

Applications of comonotonic bounds and approximations to finance and insurance have been popularized in many papers, including Roger and Shi [89], Vanmaele et al. [103], Albrecher, Mayer and Schoutens [2], Denuit, Haberman and Renshaw [28], etc. The particular application to the computation of risk measures for variable annuity guaranteed benefits is based on Feng, Jing and Dhaene [43]. Another technique, known as conditional moment matching, has been shown with high efficiency for the computation of risk measures in Privault and Wei [84].

The use of nested stochastic modeling has been on the rise due to increasingly sophisticated regulatory requirements. The discussion of its wide use in the area of financial reporting can be seen in Reynolds and Man [87], Remes [85], Cathcart and Morrison [18], Cramer, Matson and Rubin [20], etc. An overview of nested simulations is in Feng, Cui and Li [40]. Interested readers may learn more about other techniques for nested simulations, such as nested sequential simulation in Broadie, Du and Moallemi [16], optimal allocation of computational resources between inner loops and outer loops in Gordy and Juneja [57], etc.

7.5 Exercises

Section 7.1

1. One can use the same PDE method as in Section 7.1 to determine the joint

distribution of $(B_t, \bar{B}_t)$ at any given time $t \in [0, T]$, where $B_t := \mu_* t + \sigma W_t$, $\bar{B}_t := \sup_{0 \le s \le t}\{B_s\}$. We can start by considering the conditional expectation $\mathbb{E}[I(\bar{B}_T \le a, \bar{B}_T \le b)|\mathcal{F}_t]$, which can be represented in the following way due to the Markov property of the bivariate process $\{(B_t, \bar{B}_t), 0 \le t \le T\}$,

$$g(t, B_t, \bar{B}_t) = \mathbb{E}[I(B_T \le a, \bar{B}_T \le b)|\mathcal{F}_t],$$

where

$$g(t, x, y) = \mathbb{E}[I(B_T \le a, \bar{B}_T \le b)|B_t = x, \bar{B}_t = y].$$

(a) Show that g satisfies the PDE

$$\frac{\partial}{\partial t}g(t, x, y) + \mu_* \frac{\partial}{\partial x}g(t, x, y) + \frac{\sigma^2}{2}\frac{\partial^2}{\partial x^2}g(t, x, y) = 0, \qquad t \ge 0, y \ge x,$$

subject to the terminal and boundary conditions

$$\frac{\partial}{\partial y}g(t, x, y)\Big|_{x=y} = 0$$

$$\lim_{x \downarrow a} g(t, x, y) = 0, \qquad b \le y, 0 \le t \le T$$

$$\lim_{y \downarrow b} g(t, x, y) = 0, \qquad x \le b, 0 \le t \le T$$

$$\lim_{x \to -\infty} g(t, x, y) = 1, \qquad y < b, 0 \le t \le T$$

$$\lim_{t \uparrow T} g(t, x, y) = I(x \le a, y \le b), \qquad x < y$$

(b) Use the PDE method to prove that the joint distribution of $(B_T, \bar{B}_T)$ is given by

$$\mathbb{P}(B_T \le x, \bar{B}_T \le y) = \Phi\left(\frac{x - \mu_* T}{\sigma\sqrt{T}}\right) - e^{\frac{2\mu_* y}{\sigma^2}}\Phi\left(\frac{x - 2y - \mu_* T}{\sigma\sqrt{T}}\right).$$

Section 7.2

1. Show that, for any random variable U,

$$\mathbb{E}[U_+] - (\mathbb{E}[U])_+ = \frac{1}{2}\left(\mathbb{E}|U| - |\mathbb{E}[U]|\right) \le \frac{1}{2}\mathbb{E}\left(|U - \mathbb{E}[U]|\right).$$

2. (a) Derive the expression for the comonotonic lower bound $S^l = \mathbb{E}[S|\Lambda]$ in (7.69) for any arbitrary normal random variable Λ.

   (b) Prove the identities in (7.70) and (7.71) for its VaR and TVaR.

3. Consider the linear approximation of the variance of the comonotonic lower bound S^l defined in (7.69).

(a) Prove that

$$\mathbb{V}[S^l] \approx \sum_{i=1}^{nT}\sum_{j=1}^{n} \alpha_i\alpha_j e^{\mathbb{E}[Z_i]+\mathbb{E}[Z_j]+\frac{1}{2}(\sigma_{Z_i}^2+\sigma_{Z_j}^2)}\left(r_i r_j \sigma_{Z_i}\sigma_{Z_j}\right)$$

$$= \left(\rho\left[\sum_{j=1}^{nT}\alpha_j\mathbb{E}[e^{Z_j}]Z_j, \Lambda\right]\right)^2 \mathbb{V}\left[\sum_{j=1}^{nT}\alpha_j\mathbb{E}[e^{Z_j}]Z_j\right].$$

(b) The approximation of variance as shown above attains its maximum value when the conditioning random variable is taken with the coefficients $\lambda_k^{MV} = \alpha_k\mathbb{E}[e^{Z_k}]$ for $k = 1, 2, \cdots, nT$ and hence,

$$r_k^{MV} = \frac{1}{\sigma_{Z_k}\sigma_\Lambda} \sum_{j=1}^{nT}\alpha_j\mathbb{E}[e^{Z_j}]\mathbb{C}[Z_k, Z_j].$$

4. Consider the linear approximation of the TVaR of the comonotonic lower bound S^l defined in (7.69).

(a) Prove that

$$\mathrm{TVaR}_p[S^l] \approx \frac{1}{1-p}\sum_{j=1}^{nT}\alpha_j\mathbb{E}[e^{Z_j}]\phi[r_j^{MV}\sigma_{Z_j} - \Phi^{-1}(p)]$$

$$+ \frac{1}{1-p}\sum_{j=1}^{nT}\alpha_j\mathbb{E}[e^{Z_j}]\phi[r_j^{MV}\sigma_{Z_j} - \Phi^{-1}(p)](r_i - r_i^{MV})\sigma_{Z_i}.$$

$$(7.100)$$

(b) Show that

$$\sum_{j=1}^{nT}\alpha_j\mathbb{E}[e^{Z_j}]\phi[r_j^{MV}\sigma_{Z_j} - \Phi^{-1}(p)]r_i\sigma_{Z_i}$$

$$= \rho\left[\sum_{j=1}^{nT}\alpha_j\mathbb{E}[e^{Z_j}]\phi[r_j^{MV}\sigma_{Z_j} - \Phi^{-1}(p)]Z_j, \Lambda\right]$$

$$\times \left(\sum_{j=1}^{nT}\alpha_j\mathbb{E}[e^{Z_j}]\phi[r_j^{MV}\sigma_{Z_j} - \Phi^{-1}(p)]Z_j\right)^{1/2}.$$

Observe that the right-hand side of (7.100) is maximized with respect to $(r_1, r_2, \cdots, r_{nT})$ when the above expression is maximized and its maximum value is attained when the conditioning random variable is taken with the coefficients

$$\lambda_k^{(p)} = \alpha_k\mathbb{E}[e^{Z_k}]\phi[r_k^{MV}\sigma_{Z_k} - \Phi^{-1}(p)]$$

for $k = 1, 2, \cdots, nT$ and consequently

$$r_k^{(p)} = \frac{1}{\sigma_{Z_k}\sigma_\Lambda} \sum_{j=1}^{n} \alpha_j \mathbb{E}[e^{Z_j}]\phi[r_j^{MV}\sigma_{Z_j} - \Phi^{-1}(p)]\mathbb{C}[Z_k, Z_j].$$

5. (a) Suppose that U is a uniform random variable on $[0, 1]$. Show that

$$\mathbb{E}\left[(G - F_0 e^{\mu+\sigma\Phi^{-1}(U)})_+\right]$$
$$=G\Phi\left(\frac{\ln(G/F_0) - \mu}{\sigma}\right) - F_0 e^{\mu+\sigma^2/2}\Phi\left(\frac{\ln(G/F_0) - \sigma^2 - \mu}{\sigma}\right).$$
$$(7.101)$$

(b) Use (7.101) to show that the conditional expectation

$$\mathbb{E}[L|\Lambda = \lambda] = \sum_{i=1}^{nT} u_i \left[Ge^{\delta i/n}\Phi\left(\frac{\ln(G/F_0) - \mu_i^*\left(\frac{\lambda}{\sigma_\Lambda}\right)}{\sigma_i}\right)\right.$$
$$\left. -F_0 e^{\mu_i\left(\frac{\lambda}{\sigma_\Lambda}\right)+\sigma_i^2/2}\Phi\left(\frac{\ln(G/F_0) - \sigma_i^2 - \mu_i^*\left(\frac{\lambda}{\sigma_\Lambda}\right)}{\sigma_i}\right)\right]$$
$$- \sum_{i=0}^{nT-1} v_i\, F_0 \exp\left\{\mu_i\left(\frac{\lambda}{\sigma_\Lambda}\right) + \sigma_i^2/2\right\}.$$

where $\mu_i^*(y) = \mu_i(y) - \delta i/n$.

(c) Show that $\mathbb{E}\left[(G - F_0 e^{\mu+\sigma\Phi^{-1}(U)})_+\right]$ is a decreasing function of μ and hence $\mathbb{E}[L|\Lambda = \lambda]$ is a decreasing function of λ.

Section 7.3

1. Consider the function v defined in (7.89) with necessary differentiability.

(a) Show that v satisfies the PDE for $t > 0$ and $x, y > 0, 0 < z < 1$:

$$v_t(t, x, y, z) + v_x(t, x, y, z)[(r - m)x - (m_w + h)y]$$
$$+ \frac{1}{2}v_{xx}(t, x, y, z)p^2\sigma^2 x^2 - v_z(t, x, y, z)[\mu_{x+t}^d + f(x/y)\mu_t^l]z$$
$$+ v_y(t, x, y, z)\rho y = rv(t, x, y, z) + z(m_w y + mx) + \mu_t^l f(x/y)c_t xz$$
$$(7.102)$$

subject to

$$v_y(t, x, y, z)|_{x=y} = 0,$$
$$v(t, 0, y, z) = hyz\bar{a}_{x+t},$$
$$\lim_{t\to\infty} v(t, x, y, z) = 0.$$

(b) Reduce the dimension of the PDE (7.102) by setting

$$v(t, x, y.z) = zyu(t, x/y).$$

Show that u satisfies the PDE (7.97) subject to conditions (7.98a), (7.98b) and (7.98c).

(c) Use Itô formula and the PDE (7.102) to show that

$$
\begin{aligned}
dv(t, F_t, G_t, {}_tp_x) &= rv(t, F_t, G_t, {}_tp_x)\, dt + C_t\, dt \\
&\quad + p\sigma F_t v_x(t, F_t, G_t, {}_tp_x)\, dB_t,
\end{aligned}
$$

where the exogenous cash flow C_t is given by (7.93).

2. We can estimate the errors of linear interpolation method and polynomial approximation in the least squares method in the following way. Recall that Taylor's expansion at (x_0, y_0) of any function f of two independent variables (x, y) with necessary differentiability is given by

$$f(x_0 + \Delta x, y_0 + \Delta y) = \sum_{n=0}^{N} \frac{1}{n!} \left(\Delta x \frac{\partial}{\partial x} + \Delta y \frac{\partial}{\partial y} \right)^n f(x_0, y_0) + R_N$$

where R_N is called Lagrange remainder,

$$R_N = \frac{1}{(N+1)!} \left(\Delta x \frac{\partial}{\partial x} + \Delta y \frac{\partial}{\partial y} \right)^{N+1} f(x_0 + \theta \Delta x, y_0 + \theta \Delta x)$$

with some $\theta \in [0, 1]$. Let M denotes the supremum of f around a neighborhood of (x_0, y_0), and $\rho = \sqrt{(\Delta x)^2 + (\Delta y)^2}$, with Stirling's approximation for factorials, we can obtain

$$|R_N| \le \frac{M}{\sqrt{2\pi(N+1)}} \left(\frac{\sqrt{2}\rho e}{N} \right)^{N+1}.$$

(a) Show that the linear interpolation method is in fact the approximation by Taylor's expansion up to the first order terms. Find an error bound.

(b) Show that the polynomial approximation is in fact also based on the Taylor's expansion. Show that

$$f(x, y) = Ax^2 + Bxy + Cy^2 + Dx + Ey + F + R_2,$$

where A, B, C, D, E, F are constants depending on x_0 and y_0, and the Lagrange remainder R_2 is given by

$$R_2(x, y) = \frac{1}{3!} \left((x - x_0) \frac{\partial}{\partial x} + (y - y_0) \frac{\partial}{\partial y} \right)^3 f(\tilde{x}, \tilde{y})$$

where $\tilde{x}$ and $\tilde{y}$ are some values between x and x_0, y and y_0, respectively.

(c) Show that the remainder is bounded by

$$|R_2(x, y)| \leq \frac{M(x_0, y_0)\Big(e \cdot D(x_0, y_0)\Big)^3}{4\sqrt{3}\pi},$$

where $M(x_0, y_0)$ is the local supremum of f around (x_0, y_0) and $D(x_0, y_0) := \sqrt{\sup_x\{(x - x_0)^2 + (y - y_0)^2\}}$ is the "radius" of the estimation region centered around (x_0, y_0).

3. Show that the no-arbitrage value of the GLWB net liability V_t defined in can be written as

$$V_t = {}_tp_x G_t u(t, Y_t),$$

where the function u has the stochastic representation

$$u(t, s) = \mathbb{E}\Bigg[\int_0^\infty e^{-rv} {}_vp_{x+t}\, h\, \tilde{G}_v I(\tilde{F}_v < 0)\, \mathrm{d}v$$

$$- \int_0^\infty e^{-rv} {}_vp_{x+t}(m_w\tilde{G}_v + m\tilde{F}_v)I(\tilde{F}_v > 0)\, \mathrm{d}v$$

$$- \int_0^\infty e^{-rv} \mu^l_{t+v} f(Y_v)\, {}_vp_{x+t}c_{t+v}\tilde{F}_v I(\tilde{F}_v > 0)\, \mathrm{d}v \Bigg| Y_0 = s, \tilde{G}_0 = 1 \Bigg],$$

and

$$\mathrm{d}\tilde{F}_t = [(r - m)\tilde{F}_t - (m_w + h)\tilde{G}_t]\, \mathrm{d}t + p\sigma\tilde{F}_t\, \mathrm{d}B_t,$$

with $\tilde{F}_0 = s$ and

$$\tilde{G}_t = e^{\rho t} \max\Big\{1,\ \sup_{0 \leq u \leq t}\{e^{-\rho u}\tilde{F}_u\}\Big\}.$$

Appendix A

Illustrative Model Assumptions

A.1 GMMB product features

Item	symbol	value
Guarantee Level	G	$\$1,000$
Initial purchase payment	F_0	$\$1,000$
Initial equity value	S_0	100
Annualized rate of total fee	m	2.63372%
Annualized risk-free interest rate	r	3%
Annualized equity volatility rate	σ	30%
GMMB maturity date	T	10 years
Age of policyholder at issue	x	60

The fee rate m in the table is determined by the equivalence principle (4.56) under the risk-neutral measure based on the no-arbitrage theory. However, readers should be reminded that fee rates are typically determined in practice by the actuarial pricing method in Section 4.8 to allow for certain profit margin.

A.2   GLWB product features

Parameters	Assumptions
Age at issue	61
Age on valuation date	65
Initial account value on valuation date	5,850,000
GLWB ratchet	Yes
GLWB roll-up	5% per annum
Free partial withdrawal percentage	4% per annum
GLWB initial in-the-moneyness ratio as of valuation date (guarantee base/ account value)	100%
Management fees	0.56% per annum
Kick back rate (percentage of management fees distributed to insurer)	40%
GLWB base charge	1% per annum
Mortality and expense charge	1.40% per annum
Number of policies at the start of projection	117.18
Acquisition cost (percentage of initial premium)	3% per annum
Per policy unit maintenance overhead expense	21.25
Percentage of AV unit maintenance overhead expense	0.064% per annum
Inflation rate applied to per policy expense	3% per annum
Investment income earned rate on cash flows	5.76% per annum
Investment income earned rate on accumulated surplus	5.76% per annum
Discount rate on accumulated surplus or guaranteed benefit cash flows	3.76% per annum

A.3 Life table

x	$1000q_x$	$_xp_0$	x	$1000q_x$	$_xp_0$	x	$1000q_x$	$_xp_0$
1	0.587	0.99941	40	1.317	0.97381	79	69.595	0.47012
2	0.433	0.99898	41	1.424	0.97242	80	77.114	0.43387
3	0.350	0.99863	42	1.540	0.97093	81	85.075	0.39696
4	0.293	0.99834	43	1.662	0.96931	82	93.273	0.35993
5	0.274	0.99806	44	1.796	0.96757	83	101.578	0.32337
6	0.263	0.99780	45	1.952	0.96568	84	110.252	0.28772
7	0.248	0.99755	46	2.141	0.96362	85	119.764	0.25326
8	0.234	0.99732	47	2.366	0.96134	86	130.583	0.22019
9	0.231	0.99709	48	2.618	0.95882	87	143.012	0.18870
10	0.239	0.99685	49	2.900	0.95604	88	156.969	0.15908
11	0.256	0.99660	50	3.223	0.95296	89	172.199	0.13169
12	0.284	0.99631	51	3.598	0.94953	90	188.517	0.10686
13	0.327	0.99599	52	4.019	0.94571	91	205.742	0.08488
14	0.380	0.99561	53	4.472	0.94148	92	223.978	0.06587
15	0.435	0.99518	54	4.969	0.93681	93	243.533	0.04982
16	0.486	0.99469	55	5.543	0.93161	94	264.171	0.03666
17	0.526	0.99417	56	6.226	0.92581	95	285.199	0.02621
18	0.558	0.99362	57	7.025	0.91931	96	305.931	0.01819
19	0.586	0.99303	58	7.916	0.91203	97	325.849	0.01226
20	0.613	0.99242	59	8.907	0.90391	98	344.977	0.00803
21	0.642	0.99179	60	10.029	0.89484	99	363.757	0.00511
22	0.677	0.99112	61	11.312	0.88472	100	382.606	0.00316
23	0.717	0.99041	62	12.781	0.87341	101	401.942	0.00189
24	0.760	0.98965	63	14.431	0.86081	102	422.569	0.00109
25	0.803	0.98886	64	16.241	0.84683	103	445.282	0.00060
26	0.842	0.98802	65	18.191	0.83142	104	469.115	0.00032
27	0.876	0.98716	66	20.259	0.81458	105	491.923	0.00016
28	0.907	0.98626	67	22.398	0.79633	106	511.560	0.00008
29	0.935	0.98534	68	24.581	0.77676	107	526.441	0.00004
30	0.959	0.98440	69	26.869	0.75589	108	536.732	0.00002
31	0.981	0.98343	70	29.363	0.73369	109	543.602	0.00001
32	0.997	0.98245	71	32.169	0.71009	110	547.664	0.00000
33	1.003	0.98147	72	35.268	0.68505	111	549.540	0.00000
34	1.005	0.98048	73	38.558	0.65863	112	550.000	0.00000
35	1.013	0.97949	74	42.106	0.63090	113	550.000	0.00000
36	1.037	0.97847	75	46.121	0.60180	114	550.000	0.00000
37	1.082	0.97741	76	50.813	0.57122	115	1000.000	0.00000
38	1.146	0.97629	77	56.327	0.53905			
39	1.225	0.97510	78	62.629	0.50529			

A.4   Lapsation rates

A.4.1   Base lapse rates

Policy year	Base lapse rates	Surrender charge rate
1	0.8%	7.0%
2	2.0%	6.0%
3	2.0%	5.0%
4	2.0%	4.0%
5	3.0%	3.0%
6	4.0%	2.0%
7	5.0%	1.0%
8	10.0%	0.0%
9	6.0%	0.0%
≥ 10	2.0%	0.0%

A.4.2   Dynamic lapse rates

Dynamic policyholder behavior is considered based on the observation from market data that contracts tend to persist when the perceived value of embedded option is high and contracts tend to lapse when the perceived is low. While each company may have its own way of modeling dynamic policyholder behavior, the following offers an example of how it is done in practice.

In a factor-based model, base lapse rates are stated in the previous section and dynamic lapse rates are determined by

$$\text{dynamic lapse rate} = \text{base lapse rate} \times \text{dynamic factor}$$

and the dynamic factor function

$$\text{dynamic factor} = (3 - 2x)x^2, \tag{A.1}$$

where x is known as the *in-the-moneyness* ratio defined by

$$x = \frac{\text{then-current account value}}{\text{then-current guarantee base}}.$$

The dynamic factor function (A.1) is often referred to one sided function, as the factor stays between 0 and 1. All computations in Section 7.3 are based on this particular assumption.

There are other known examples of the in-the-moneyness ratio, such as

$$x = \max\left\{ \frac{\text{then-current account value}}{\text{present value of future withdrawals}}, 1 \right\}.$$

In such a case, the dynamic factor becomes a function of account value only, and all methods in Chapter 7 can be adapted to address this type of dynamic lapse rates as well. There are also other dynamic factor functions which can be two-sided, meaning that the factor can be greater than one. More examples of modeling dynamic policyholder behavior can be found in the book by the International Actuarial Association [66, II.B.2].

Appendix B

Big-O and Little-o

The relation $f(x) = O(g(x))$ as $x \to 0+$ is read as "$f(x)$ is big-o of $g(x)$". It is used to describe the limiting behavior of f as the argument x goes to 0. By definition, it means that there exist a constant $M > 0$ and a real number x_0 such that

$$|f(x)| \leq M|g(x)|, \qquad \text{for all } 0 < x \leq x_0.$$

Example B.1. Note that $x^n \leq x^2$ for $n = 3, 4, \cdots$ and $0 < x \leq 1$. Therefore, by Taylor expansion, as $x \to 0+$,

$$e^x = 1 + x + \frac{x^2}{2!} + \frac{x^3}{3!} + \cdots = 1 + x + O(x^2).$$

The relation $f(x) = o(g(x))$ as $x \to 0$ is read as "$f(x)$ is little-o of $g(x)$". Intuitively, it means that $f(x)$ decays faster than $g(x)$ near zero. In the limit notation, it means

$$\lim_{x \to 0} \frac{f(x)}{g(x)} = 0.$$

For example, we can write $x^n = o(x)$ for $n > 1$ because

$$\lim_{x \to 0} \frac{x^n}{x} = \lim_{x \to 0} x^{n-1} = 0.$$

Here are some properties that we use frequently in our calculations and which can be proven very easily by the definition.

1. $o(x) + o(x) = o(x)$;
2. $o(x) \cdot o(x) = o(x)$.

Example B.2. Show that for any integer $k \geq 0$

$$\left(\frac{1}{2} e^{\frac{u}{\sqrt{n}}} + \frac{1}{2} e^{-\frac{u}{\sqrt{n}}} \right)^k = \left(1 + \frac{u^2}{2n} \right)^k + o\left(\frac{1}{n} \right).$$

355

Proof. It follows from the Taylor expansion of the exponential function that

$$e^x = 1 + x + \frac{x^2}{2} + o(x).$$

Using Property 1, we obtain that

$$\frac{1}{2}e^{\frac{u}{\sqrt{n}}} + \frac{1}{2}e^{-\frac{u}{\sqrt{n}}} = 1 + \frac{u^2}{2n} + o\left(\frac{1}{n}\right).$$

Applying the binomial theorem, we see that

$$\left(1 + \frac{u^2}{2n} + o\left(\frac{1}{n}\right)\right)^k = \sum_{j=0}^{k} \binom{k}{j}\left(1 + \frac{u^2}{2n}\right)^{k-j}\left(o\left(\frac{1}{n}\right)\right)^j$$

$$= \left(1 + \frac{u^2}{2n}\right)^k + o\left(\frac{1}{n}\right),$$

where the last equality follows from Properties 1 and 2. □

Appendix C

Elementary Set Theory

In this chapter, we introduce elementary concepts from set theory for readers not familiar with the subject matter.

C.1 Sets

> **Definition C.1.** A *set* is a collection of objects. The objects that make up a set are known as *elements*.

There are two common ways of defining a set. One approach is to list its elements. For example, $\Omega = \{\text{red, green, yellow}\}$, where Ω represents the set of three colors and the double brackets "$\{\ \}$" are used to indicate a set and to embrace all elements. If there are infinitely many elements, we often use the ellipsis "$\cdots$" to suggest that a pattern continues indefinitely. For example, $\mathbb{N} = \{1, 2, 3, \cdots\}$ is the set of all natural numbers. The other approach is to not list all elements but rather state the properties that a candidate should have in order to be considered as an element. Take $\Omega = \{t : t > 5\}$ as example. The statement following the colon "$:$" sets the criterion for a membership of the set. In other words, Ω includes all t's which are greater than 5. A special type of set is an interval, for which special notation has been developed. For example, the closed set $[a, b] := \{\omega : a \leq \omega \leq b\}$, where $b \geq a$ and a, b are both real numbers, is the set of all numbers between a and b with a, b included. The symbol "$:=$" means "is defined by". The open set $(a, b) := \{\omega : a < \omega < b\}$ is the set of numbers between a and b excluding a and b. Half open and half closed sets are similarly defined. We often write $\mathbb{R} := (-\infty, \infty)$. If ω is an element of a set Ω, then we often say ω is in Ω, or symbolically, $\omega \in \Omega$. Consider two sets Ω_1 and Ω_2. If every element in Ω_1 is also in Ω_2, then we say Ω_1 is a subset of Ω_2, or write $\Omega_1 \subset \Omega_2$. If ω is an element in Ω_2 but not in Ω_1, then we write $\omega \in \Omega_2 \backslash \Omega_1$.

C.2   Infimum and supremum

Now let us consider sets of real numbers. We are often interested in the minimum and the maximum of an ordered set, which are defined as the smallest and the largest element of the set respectively. However, they do not always exist for a given set. For example, the set of all real numbers $\mathbb{R}$ does not have a maximum. (Infinity is not a real number!) Therefore, we often need generalizations of minimum and maximum that always exist and play similar roles.

> **Definition C.2.** The *infimum* of a set of real numbers A, denoted by inf A, is the largest real number smaller than or equal to all numbers in the set A; The *supremum* of the set A, denoted by sup A, is the smallest real number greater than or equal to all numbers in the set A.

Note that the difference between the minimum and the infimum of a set is that the former needs to be an element of the set whereas the latter may not be. Therefore, the infimum of a set of real numbers always exists but the minimum may not. The same can be said about the maximum and the supremum. For example, the interval $(0, 1)$ has neither a minimum nor a maximum. But it does have an infimum of 0 and a supremum of 1. Another example would be the set $\{1/n : n$ is a positive integer$\}$, which has no minimum but an infimum of 0 and whose maximum and supremum are both given by 1.

C.3   Convex function

> **Definition C.3.** A function $f : \mathbb{R} \mapsto \mathbb{R}$ is convex if, for any $\lambda \in [0, 1]$,
>
> $$f(\lambda x + (1 - \lambda)y) \leq \lambda f(x) + (1 - \lambda)f(y).$$

Geometrically it is easy to see that any tangent line of the graph of a convex function always lies below the graph. Since the tangent line that passes through any point is the only straight line that touches the curve of the convex function exactly once, then we know that it represents the maximum of all linear functions that lie below.

Theorem C.4. *If ϕ is a convex function, then for every $x \in \mathbb{R}$,*

$$\phi(x) = \sup\{l(x) : l(y) = a + by, l(y) \leq \phi(y) \text{ for all } y \in \mathbb{R}\}.$$

Appendix D

List of Special Functions

D.1 Gamma functions

The upper incomplete gamma function is defined for any complex number z with positive real part by

$$\Gamma(a, x) = \int_x^\infty t^{a-1} e^{-t} \, dt.$$

The gamma function is given by $\Gamma(a) = \Gamma(a, 0)$.

D.2 Confluent hypergeometric functions

Whittaker functions M and W are defined for 2μ not equal to negative integers by

$$M_{\kappa,\mu}(z) = e^{-z/2} z^{1/2+\mu} \sum_{s=0}^\infty \frac{(1/2 + \mu - \kappa)_s}{(1 + 2\mu)_s s!} z^s,$$

and when 2μ is not an integer,

$$W_{\kappa,\mu}(z) = \frac{\Gamma(-2\mu)}{\Gamma(1/2 - \mu - \kappa)} M_{\kappa,\mu}(z) + \frac{\Gamma(2\mu)}{\Gamma(1/2 + \mu - \kappa)} M_{\kappa,-\mu}(z).$$

Kummer's function M is defined by

$$M(a, b, z) = \sum_{s=0}^\infty \frac{(a)_s}{(b)_s s!} z^s,$$

except that $M(a, b, z)$ does not exist when b is a non-positive integer.

When b is not an integer, Kummer's function U is connected with M through the identity

$$U(a, b, z) = \frac{\Gamma(1 - b)}{\Gamma(a - b + 1)} M(a, b, z) + \frac{\Gamma(b - 1)}{\Gamma(a)} z^{1-b} M(a - b + 1, 2 - b, z).$$

An asymptotic property of the function M is used in this book, that is, as $z \to \infty$,

$$M(a, b, z) \sim \frac{\Gamma(b)}{\Gamma(a)} z^{a-b} e^z. \tag{D.1}$$

D.3   Owen's T and related functions

A key element in the computation of the conditional tail expectation is the double integral

$$H(z) = \int_{-\infty}^{z} \int_{-\infty}^{b-ay} \frac{1}{2\pi} e^{-(x^2+y^2)/2} \, dx \, dy.$$

This function was not previously studied in the literature. Although the integral can be evaluated numerically, our application requires efficient computation as the integrals appear repeatedly for multiple time points. Hence, we take advantage of the Owen's T-function, for which fast and accurate algorithms have been developed in the statistics literature. Owen's T function was introduced in Owen (1956). For $a, h \in \mathbb{R} \cup \pm\infty$, $T(h, a)$ is defined by

$$T(h, a) = \frac{1}{2\pi} \int_{0}^{a} \frac{\exp\left\{-\frac{1}{2}h^2(1 + x^2)\right\}}{1 + x^2} \, dx.$$

This special function was implemented in Mathematica and can be computed very efficiently. The probabilistic interpretation of the function is as follows: $T(h, a)$ stands for the probability mass of two independent standard normal random variables falling in the domain on a plane between $y = 0$ and $y = ax$ and to the right of $x = h$, which is referred to as a polygon in Owen (1956).

Theorem D.1. *For $a, b > 0$ and $z \neq 0$, one has that*

$$\begin{aligned}
H(z; a, b) &= \frac{1}{2}\text{sgn}(z)\Phi(|z|) + T\left(z, \frac{az - b}{z}\right) \\
&\quad + \frac{1}{2}\Phi\left(\frac{b}{\sqrt{1 + a^2}}\right) - T\left(\frac{b}{\sqrt{1 + a^2}}, \frac{(1 + a^2)z - ab}{b}\right).
\end{aligned}$$

For $a > 0, b < 0$ and $z \neq 0$, one has that

$$\begin{aligned}
H(z; a, b) &= -\frac{1}{2}\text{sgn}(z)\Phi(-|z|) + T\left(z, \frac{az - b}{z}\right) \\
&\quad + \frac{1}{2}\Phi\left(\frac{b}{\sqrt{1 + a^2}}\right) - T\left(\frac{b}{\sqrt{1 + a^2}}, \frac{(1 + a^2)z - ab}{b}\right).
\end{aligned}$$

When $z = 0$, the expressions are given by their limits:

$$H(0; a, b) = \frac{1}{2}\Phi\left(\frac{b}{\sqrt{1 + a^2}}\right) + T\left(\frac{b}{\sqrt{1 + a^2}}, a\right).$$

Similarly, when $b = 0$, then one finds

$$H(z; a, 0) = \frac{1}{2}\Phi(z) + T(z, a).$$

Proof of Theorem D.1 and its applications can be found in Feng and Jing [42].

Appendix E

Approximation of Function by an Exponential Sum

The approximation of a probability density function by an exponential sum has many applications in pricing and hedging of insurance product designs, such as stochastic life annuities in Dufresne [35], equity-linked death benefits in Gerber, Shiu and Yang [55], mortality-linked derivatives in Shang, Goovaerts and Dhaene [93], guaranteed life withdrawal benefit in Feng and Jing [42], etc. Dufresne [34] provides a collection of approximation methods based on orthogonal polynomials. The technique to be introduced in this section allows both exponents and coefficients in the exponential sum to be complex-valued. As a result, for a given level of accuracy the approximation uses significantly fewer terms of exponential functions than many other approximation methods. To make this section self-contained, we briefly outline the main idea behind such a numerical method. Readers are referred to Beylkin and Monzon [9] for technical details.

We are interested in identifying an exponential sum to be as close as possible to the desired probability density function q in the sense that for a given $\epsilon > 0$ we can always find a sequence of pairs $\{(a_i, s_i), i = 1, \cdots, M\}$ such that

$$\left| q(t) - \sum_{i=1}^{M} a_i e^{-s_i t} \right| \leq \epsilon, \qquad \text{for all } 0 < t < \infty. \tag{E.1}$$

We can recast this problem as a slightly different one. Given $2N + 1$ values of a function $q(x)$ on a uniform grid in $[0, 1]$ and a target level of error $\epsilon > 0$, the goal is to find a sequence of complex weights and nodes $\{(w_i, \gamma_i) : i = 1, 2, \cdots, M\}$ such that

$$\left| q\left(\frac{k}{2N}\right) - \sum_{i=1}^{M} w_i \gamma_i^k \right| \leq \epsilon, \qquad \text{for all } 0 \leq k \leq 2N. \tag{E.2}$$

Then we use the same set of complex weights and complex nodes to construct a linear combination of exponential functions as a smooth approximation

$$q(x) \approx \sum_{m=1}^{M} w_m e^{t_m x}, \qquad \text{for all } x \in [0, 1], \qquad t_m = 2N \ln \gamma_m. \tag{E.3}$$

In our application, the mortality density can be defined theoretically on $[0, \infty)$. Nevertheless, the probability mass should be negligible beyond a certain advanced age for any reasonable mortality model. For any continuous function q, we can find large enough N such that

$$\left| q(t) - q\left(\frac{\lfloor 2Nt \rfloor b}{2N} \right) \right| \leq \frac{1}{2N} \max_{t \in [0,b]} |q'(t)| \leq \frac{\epsilon}{3}, \qquad \text{for all } t \in [0,b],$$

where $\lfloor x \rfloor$ is the integer part of x. Hence, for any given level of error $\epsilon > 0$, we can set a large enough upper limit $b > 0$ such that $q(b) < \epsilon/3$ and apply the approximation in (E.2) so that

$$\left| h_k - \sum_{m=1}^{M} w_m \gamma_m^k \right| \leq \epsilon/3, \qquad \text{for all } 0 \leq k \leq 2N, \qquad h_k := q\left(\frac{kb}{2N} \right). \quad \text{(E.4)}$$

If q is continuous and has a non-increasing tail for $[b, \infty)$, then the above procedure would produce a solution to the continuous problem in (E.1).

We now sketch the idea of the Hankel matrix approximation for identifying the complex weights $\{w_m, m = 1, \cdots, M\}$ and the complex nodes $\{\gamma_m, m = 1, \cdots, M\}$. Consider the $(N+1) \times (N+1)$ Hankel matrix H defined as follows.

$$\mathbf{H} = \begin{bmatrix} h_0 & h_1 & \cdots & h_{N-1} & h_N \\ h_1 & h_2 & \cdots & h_N & h_{N+1} \\ \vdots & & & & \vdots \\ h_{N-1} & h_N & \cdots & h_{2N-2} & h_{2N-1} \\ h_N & h_{N+1} & \cdots & h_{2N-1} & h_{2N} \end{bmatrix}.$$

To the practical purpose of this application, we shall only consider the case where the Hankel matrix is real-valued. Then we can solve for the eigenvalue problem

$$\mathbf{H}\mathbf{u} = \sigma \mathbf{u}, \tag{E.5}$$

where, by the property of real-valued Hankel matrix, σ is a real and nonnegative eigenvalue and $\mathbf{u} = (u_0, \cdots, u_N)$ is the corresponding eigenvector. By the definition of Hankel matrix, it is easy to show that $\{h_n, n = 0, \cdots, 2N\}$ satisfied the following recursive relation.

$$\sum_{n=0}^{N} h_{k+n} u_n = \sigma u_k, \qquad k = 0, \cdots, N.$$

If we extend the eigenvector $\mathbf{u}$ to a periodic sequence of period $L(L > N)$ and where $u_k = 0$ for $N < k < L$, then we can define an inhomogeneous recurrence relation

$$\sum_{n=0}^{N} x_{k+n} u_n = \sigma u_k, \qquad k \geq 0, \tag{E.6}$$

given the initial conditions $x_k = h_k$ for $k = 0, 1, \cdots, N - 1$. The solution to the recurrence relation is unique and can be solved by

$$x_{N+k} = - \sum_{n=0}^{N-1} \frac{u_n}{u_N} x_{k+n} + \sigma \frac{u_k}{u_N}, \qquad k \geq 0,$$

provided that $u_N \neq 0$. It is well-known that the solution to (E.6) can be written as the sum of a general solution to the corresponding homogeneous recurrence relation and a particular solution, denoted by $\{x_k^{(p)}, k \geq 0\}$.

$$x_k = \sum_{n=1}^{N} w_n \gamma_n^k + x_k^{(p)}, \qquad k \geq 0,$$

where $\{\gamma_1, \cdots, \gamma_N\}$ is the set of N roots to the eigenpolynomial $P_{\mathbf{u}}(z) = \sum_{k=1}^{N} u_k z^k$. A particular solution is given by

$$x_k^{(p)} = \frac{\sigma}{L} \sum_{l=0}^{L-1} \alpha^{lk} \frac{P_{\mathbf{u}}(\alpha^{-l})}{P_{\mathbf{u}}(\alpha^l)}, \qquad \alpha := \exp\left\{\frac{2\pi i}{L}\right\},$$

because for all $k = 0, 1, \cdots, N$,

$$\sum_{n=0}^{N} x_{k+n}^{(p)} u_n = \frac{\sigma}{L} \sum_{l=0}^{L-1} \alpha^{lk} \frac{P_{\mathbf{u}}(\alpha^{-l})}{P_{\mathbf{u}}(\alpha^l)} \sum_{n=0}^{N} u_n \alpha^{nl} = \frac{\sigma}{L} \sum_{l=0}^{L-1} \alpha^{lk} P_{\mathbf{u}}(\alpha^{-l})$$

$$= \frac{\sigma}{L} \sum_{n=0}^{N} \left(\sum_{l=0}^{L-1} \alpha^{(n-k)l}\right) u_k = \sigma u_k.$$

Note that $|x_k^{(p)}| \leq \sigma$ for all $k \geq 0$. Therefore, it follows immediately that

$$\left| h_k - \sum_{n=1}^{N} w_n \gamma_n^k \right| \leq \sigma, \qquad k = 0, 1, \cdots, 2N.$$

To find the approximation, we rank all the eigenvalues of $\mathbf{H}$ in a decreasing order

$$\sigma_0 \geq \sigma_1 \geq \cdots \geq \sigma_N. \tag{E.7}$$

The idea of [9] is to choose an eigenvalue σ_M ($0 \leq M \leq N$) smaller than the level of error tolerance in (E.4), say $\epsilon/3$. Then we can obtain the expected approximation with absolute error of at most σ. Beylkin and Monzon [9] made the observation that only first M weights $\{w_1, \cdots, w_M\}$ are larger than σ_M and hence made the claim that $\sum_{m=1}^{M} w_m \gamma_m^k$ has the "nearly optimal" representation of the Hankel matrix. Observe one can obtain the unknown weights $(w_1, \cdots, w_N)$ by finding the unique solution to the Vandermonde system

$$h_k - \sigma x_k^{(p)} = \sum_{n=1}^{N} w_n \gamma_n^k, \qquad 0 \leq k < N.$$

The equation is also valid for $N \leq k \leq 2N$. Thus, the authors recommended using the least squares solution $(\rho_1, \cdots, \rho_N)$ to the overdetermined problem

$$h_k = \sum_{n=1}^{N} \rho_n \gamma_n^k, \qquad 0 \leq k \leq 2N.$$

To summarize the method, we shall carry out the computation in the following steps.

1. (Identify eigenvalue and eigenvector) Construct an $(N + 1) \times (N + 1)$ Hankel matrix with elements $h_k = q(kb/(2N))$ where $k = 0, 1, \cdots, 2N$. Find all eigenvalues of the eigenvalue problem (E.5), which are ranked from the largest to the smallest as in (E.7). Choose the largest σ_M smaller than the level of error tolerance. Find the corresponding eigenvector $\mathbf{u}$.

2. (Determine complex nodes) Construct the eigenpolynomial $P_{\mathbf{u}}(z) = \sum_{k=0}^{N} u_k z^k$ and find all of its roots. Find the M roots with smallest absolute values $\{\gamma_1, \cdots, \gamma_M\}$.

3. (Determine complex weights) Use the method of least squares to determined all the unknowns $\{\rho_1, \cdots, \rho_M\}$ in the equation $h_k = \sum_{n=1}^{N} \rho_n \gamma_n^k$, for $0 \le k \le 2N$.

    The end product of the above-mentioned algorithm will produce the desired approximation (E.3), or written in terms of the mortality density,

$$q(x) \approx \sum_{m=1}^{M} \rho_m e^{t_m x}, \qquad x \in (0, \infty),$$

where $t_m = (2N/b) \ln \gamma_m$.

Example E.1. Suppose that a variable annuity contract is issued to a 65-year-old, whose survival model is determined by the Gompertz-Makeham law of mortality with the probability density

$$q(t) = (A + Bc^{x+t}) \exp \left\{ -At - \frac{Bc^x(c^t - 1)}{\ln c} \right\}.$$

where

$$x = 65, A = 0.0007, B = 0.00005, c = 10^{0.04}.$$

A plot of the density function q can be seen in Figure E.1a. We sample function values on $N = 128$ equidistant sample points in the interval $[0, 100]$. Following the algorithm described above, we obtain all eigenvalues of the Hankel matrix in (E.5). Figure E.1d shows the magnitudes of 30 largest eigenvalues whereas their locations on a complex plane are shown in Figure E.1b. It is clear from Figure E.1d that the magnitudes decline sharply for the first few eigenvalues and level off after the fifth largest eigenvalue. Suppose that we approximate the mortality density by a combination of $M = 15$ terms of exponential functions. The weights of the 15 terms are shown on a complex plane in Figure E.1c. The error from the 15-term approximating exponential sum is shown in Figure E.1e. It is clear that the maximum error is controlled,

$$\sup_{t \in [0,100]} \left| q(t) - \sum_{i=1}^{M} w_i e^{-s_i t} \right| < 10^{-6}.$$

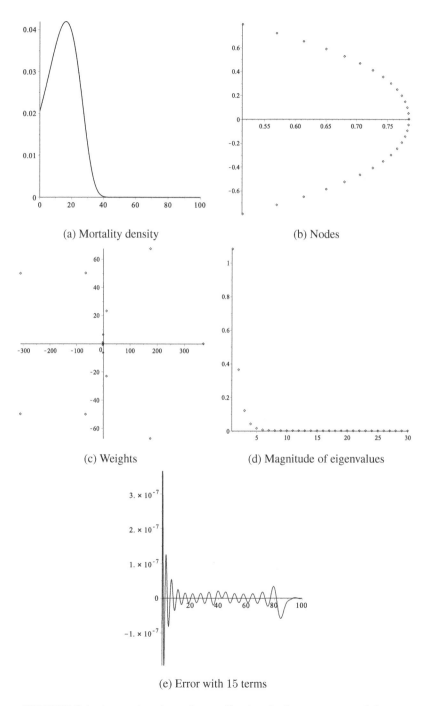

(a) Mortality density

(b) Nodes

(c) Weights

(d) Magnitude of eigenvalues

(e) Error with 15 terms

FIGURE E.1: Approximation of mortality density by an exponential sum

Appendix F

Sample Code for Differential Equation Methods

F.1 Distribution function of the running supremum of Brownian motion

```
% return approximate solution matrix h
function h = sol(ds,dz,T,b,mu)

% set up a uniform grid
Ns = round(T/ds);      % time variable indexed by i
Nz = round(b/dz);      % space variable indexed by j
h = zeros(Nz+1,Ns+1);  % set up grid

% boundary condition
for i = 1:Ns+1
    h(Nz+1,i) = 1;
    h(1,i) = 0;
end

% initial condition
for j = 1:Nz+1
    h(j,1) = 1;
end

% define constants
alpha = ds\(dz^2);
beta = ds\dz;
B1 = diag((1+alpha+mu*beta)*ones(Nz-1,1));
B2 = diag((-alpha/2)*ones(Nz-2,1),1);
B3 = diag(-(mu*beta+alpha/2)*ones(Nz-2,1),-1);
B = B1+B2+B3;
rem = zeros((Nz-1),1);
rem(Nz-1,1) = -alpha/2;

% update solution matrix recursively
for i = 1:Ns
    h(2:Nz,i+1) = B \ (h(2:Nz,i)-rem);
```

```
end

end
```

F.2   Probability of loss for guaranteed minimum withdrawal benefit

```
% return approximate solution matrix s
function s = val(dt, dx, dy, T, b, c, K, w, r, mw, sig, mu, m)

% set up a uniform grid
Nt = round(T / dt);
Nx = round(b / dx);
Ny = round(c / dy);

% initialize solution matrix
s = zeros(Nx + 1, Ny + 1, Nt + 1);

% set up initial condition
for i = 1:(Nx + 1)
    for j = 1:(Ny + 1)
        s(i, j, 1) = 1;
    end
end

% set up boundary condition for ``time-like" variable
for i = 1:(Nx + 1)
    for k = 1:(Nt + 1)
        s(i, 1, k) = 1;
    end
end

% define constants
alpha = 1 / dt;
beta = dx / dy;
gamma = w / dx;

% update matrix solution recursively
for k = 1:Nt
    C = diag(((1:Nx) * beta * exp(- r * (T - (k - 1) * dt))));
    B1 = diag((((1:Nx) .^ 2) * (sig ^ 2) + (1:Nx) * beta * ...
        (exp(- r * (T - (k - 1) * dt))) + alpha, 0);
    B2 = diag(- ((((1:(Nx - 1)) .^ 2) * (sig ^ 2) + ...
        (1:(Nx - 1)) * (mu - m) - gamma) / 2, 1);
    B3 = diag(- (((2:Nx) .^ 2) * (sig ^ 2) - (2:Nx) * ...
        (mu - m) + gamma) / 2, - 1);
    B = B1 + B2 + B3;
```

```
B(Nx, Nx - 1) = - (sig ^ 2) * (Nx ^ 2);
[L, U] = lu(B);
for j = 1:(Ny)
    rhs3 = zeros(Nx, 1);
    rhs3(1, 1) = ((sig ^ 2) - mu + m + gamma) * ((j - 1) ...
        * dy <= (c + K / mw - w * exp(- r * T) * ...
        (exp(r * (k - 1) * dt) - 1) / (r * mw))) / 2;
    rhs = alpha * s(2:(Nx + 1), j + 1, k) + C * ...
        s(2:(Nx + 1), j, k + 1) + rhs3;
    s(2:(Nx + 1), j + 1, k + 1) = U \ (L \ rhs);
end
end

end
```

Bibliography

[1] Carlo Acerbi and Dirk Tasche. On the coherence of expected shortfall. *Journal of Banking and Finance*, 26(7):1487–1503, 2002.

[2] Hansjoerg Albrecher, Philipp A. Mayer, and Wim Schoutens. General lower bounds for arithmetic Asian option prices. *Appl. Math. Finance*, 15(1-2):123–149, 2008.

[3] Philippe Artzner, Freddy Delbaen, Jean-Marc Eber, and David Heath. Coherent measures of risk. *Math. Finance*, 9(3):203–228, 1999.

[4] Anna Rita Bacinello, Pietro Millossovich, Annamaria Olivieri, and Ermanno Pitacco. Variable annuities: a unifying valuation approach. *Insurance Math. Econom.*, 49(3):285–297, 2011.

[5] Mathieu Bargès, Hélène Cossette, and Étienne Marceau. TVaR-based capital allocation with copulas. *Insurance Math. Econom.*, 45(3):348–361, 2009.

[6] Richard F. Bass. The basics of financial mathematics. Technical report, University of Connecticut, 2003.

[7] Daniel Bauer, Alexander Kling, and Jochen Russ. A universal pricing framework for guaranteed minimum benefits in variable annuities. *Astin Bull.*, 38(2):621–651, 2008.

[8] Daniel Bauer and George Zanjani. The marginal cost of risk in a multi-period risk model. Technical report, Casualty Actuarial Society, 2013.

[9] Gregory Beylkin and Lucas Monzon. On approximation of functions by exponential sums. *Applied and Computational Harmonic Analysis*, 19:17–48, 2005.

[10] Tomas Björk. *Arbitrage Theory in Continuous Time*. Oxford Finance. Oxford University Press, 2009.

[11] Newton L. Bowers, Hans U. Gerber, James C. Hickman, Donald A. Jones, and Cecil J. Nesbitt. *Actuarial Mathematics*. Society of Actuaries, 1997.

[12] Phelim Boyle and Weidong Tian. The design of equity-indexed annuities. *Insurance Math. Econom.*, 43(3):303–315, 2008.

[13] Phelim P. Boyle and Eduardo S. Schwartz. Equilibrium prices of guarantees under equity-linked contracts. *The Journal of Risk and Insurance*, 44(4):639–660, 1977.

[14] Paul Bratley, Bennett L. Fox, and Linus E. Schrage. *A Guide to Simulation*. Springer, New York, second edition, 1987.

[15] Michael J. Brennan and Eduardo S. Schwartz. The pricing of equity-linked life insurance policies with an asset value guarantee. *Journal of Financial Economics*, 3(3):195–213, 1976.

[16] Mark Broadie, Yiping Du, and Ciamac C Moallemi. Risk estimation via regression. *Operations Research*, 63(5):1077–1097, 2015.

[17] Marc Busse, Michel Dacorogna, and Marie Kratz. The impact of systematic risk on the diversification benefits of a risk portfolio. *Risks*, 2:260–276, 2014.

[18] Mark Cathcart and Steven Morrison. Variable annuity economic capital: the least-squares monte carlo approach. *Life & Pensions*, pages 36–40, 2009.

[19] Yichun Chi and Sheldon X. Lin. Are flexible premium variable annuities under-priced? *Astin Bull.*, 42(2):559–574, 2012.

[20] Errol Cramer, Patricia Matson, Leonard Reback, and Larry Rubin. Common practices relating to fasb statement 133, accounting for derivative instruments and hedging activities as it relates to variable annuities with guaranteed benefits. *Practice Note, American Academy of Actuaries*, 148:151–159, 2007.

[21] Min Dai, Yue Kuen Kwok, and Jianping Zong. Guaranteed minimum withdrawal benefit in variable annuities. *Math. Finance*, 18(4):595–611, 2008.

[22] John P. D'Angelo and Douglas B. West. *Mathematical Thinking: Problem-Solving and Proofs*. Pearson, second edition, 1999.

[23] Griselda Deelstra, Jan Dhaene, and Michèle Vanmaele. An overview of comonotonicity and its applications in finance and insurance. In *Advanced mathematical methods for finance*, pages 155–179. Springer, Heidelberg, 2011.

[24] Jeffrey K. Dellinger. *The Handbook of Variable Income Annuities*. John Wiley & Sons, Inc, 2006.

[25] Łukasz Delong. Pricing and hedging of variable annuities with state-dependent fees. *Insurance Math. Econom.*, 58:24–33, 2014.

[26] Michel Denault. Coherent allocation of risk capital. *J. Risk*, 4:1–34, 2001.

[27] Michel Denuit, Jan Dhaene, Marc Goovaerts, and Robert Kaas. *Actuarial Theory for Dependent Risks: Measures, Orders and Models*. John Wiley and Sons, 2005.

[28] Michel Denuit, Steven Haberman, and Arthur Renshaw. Longevity-indexed life annuities. *N. Am. Actuar. J.*, 15(1):97–111, 2011.

[29] Jan Dhaene, Michel Denuit, Marc J. Goovaerts, Robert Kaas, and David Vyncke. The concept of comonotonicity in actuarial science and finance: applications. *Insurance Math. Econom.*, 31(2):133–161, 2002.

[30] Jan Dhaene, Michel Denuit, Marc J. Goovaerts, Robert Kaas, and David Vyncke. The concept of comonotonicity in actuarial science and finance: theory. *Insurance Math. Econom.*, 31(1):3–33, 2002. 5th IME Conference (University Park, PA, 2001).

[31] Jan Dhaene, Andreas Tsanakas, Emiliano A. Valdez, and Steven Vanduffel. Optimal capital allocation principles. *The Journal of Risk and Insurance*, 79(1):1–28, 2012.

[32] Jan Dhaene, Steven Vanduffel, Marc J. Goovaerts, Robert Kaas, Qihe Tang, and David Vyncke. Risk measures and comonotonicity: a review. *Stoch. Models*, 22(4):573–606, 2006.

[33] David C. M. Dickson, Mary R. Hardy, and Howard R. Waters. *Actuarial mathematics for life contingent risks*. International Series on Actuarial Science. Cambridge University Press, Cambridge, 2009.

[34] Daniel Dufresne. Fitting combinations of exponentials to probability distributions. *Appl. Stoch. Models Bus. Ind.*, 23(1):23–48, 2007.

[35] Daniel Dufresne. Stochastic life annuities. *N. Am. Actuar. J.*, 11(1):136–157, 2007.

[36] Paul Embrechts, Giovanni Puccetti, and Rüschendorf. Model uncertainty and VaR aggregation. *Journal of Banking & Finance*, 37(8):2750–2764, 2013.

[37] Ian Farr, Adam Koursaris, and Mark Mennemeyer. Economic capital for life insurance companies. Technical report, Society of Actuaries, 2016.

[38] Ian Farr, Hubert Mueller, Mark Scanlon, and Simon Stronkhorst. *Economic Capital for Life Insurance Companies*. SOA Monograph, 2008.

[39] Runhuan Feng. A comparative study of risk measures for guaranteed minimum maturity benefits by a PDE method. *North American Actuarial Journal*, 18(4):445–461, 2014.

[40] Runhuan Feng, Zhenyu Cui, and Peng Li. Nested stochastic modeling for insurance companies. Technical report, Society of Actuaries, 2016.

[41] Runhuan Feng and Huaxiong Huang. Statutory financial reporting for variable annuity guaranteed death benefits: market practice, mathematical modeling and computation. *Insurance Math. Econom.*, 67:54–64, 2016.

[42] Runhuan Feng and Xiaochen Jing. Analytical valuation and hedging of variable annuity guaranteed lifetime withdrawal benefits. *Insurance Math. Econom.*, 72:36–48, 2017.

[43] Runhuan Feng, Xiaochen Jing, and Jan Dhaene. Comonotonic approximations of risk measures for variable annuity guaranteed benefits with dynamic policyholder behavior. *J. Comput. Appl. Math.*, 311:272–292, 2017.

[44] Runhuan Feng, Alexey Kuznetsov, and Fenghao Yang. Exponential functionals of Lévy processes and variable annuity guaranteed benefits. *Stochastic Processes and Their Applications*, to appear.

[45] Runhuan Feng and Yasutaka Shimizu. On a generalization from ruin to default in a Lévy insurance risk model. *Methodol. Comput. Appl. Probab.*, 15(4):773–802, 2013.

[46] Runhuan Feng and Yasutaka Shimizu. Applications of central limit theorems on equity-linking insurance. *Insurance: Mathematics and Economics*, 69:138–148, 2016.

[47] Runhuan Feng and Jan Vecer. Risk based capital for guaranteed minimum withdrawal benefit. *Quant. Finance*, 17(3):471–478, 2017.

[48] Runhuan Feng and Hans W. Volkmer. Spectral methods for the calculation of risk measures for variable annuity guaranteed benefits. *Astin Bull.*, 44(3):653–681, 2014.

[49] Runhuan Feng and Hans W. Volkmer. An identity of hitting times and its application to the valuation of guaranteed minimum withdrawal benefit. *Mathematics and Financial Economics*, 10(2):127–149, 2016.

[50] Grant Fredricks, Erin Ingalls, and Angela McAlister. Analysis of fund mapping techniques for variable annuities. Technical report, Worcester Polytechnic Institute, 2010.

[51] Man Chung Fung, Katja Ignatieva, and Michael Sherris. Systematic mortality risk: an analysis of guaranteed lifetime withdrawal benefits in variable annuities. *Insurance: Mathematics and Economics*, 58:103–115, September 2014.

[52] Patrice Gaillardetz and Joe Y. Lakhmiri. A new premium principle for equity-indexed annuities. *The Journal of Risk and Insurance*, 78(1):245–265, 2011.

[53] Guojun Gan and X. Sheldon Lin. Valuation of large variable annuity portfolios under nested simulation: a functional data approach. *Insurance Math. Econom.*, 62:138–150, 2015.

[54] Hans U. Gerber and Elias S. W. Shiu. From ruin theory to pricing reset guarantees and perpetual put options. *Insurance Math. Econom.*, 24(1-2):3–14, 1999. 1st IME Conference (Amsterdam, 1997).

[55] Hans U. Gerber, Elias S. W. Shiu, and Hailiang Yang. Valuing equity-linked death benefits and other contingent options: a discounted density approach. *Insurance Math. Econom.*, 51(1):73–92, 2012.

[56] Paul Glasserman. *Monte Carlo methods in financial engineering*, volume 53 of *Applications of Mathematics (New York)*. Springer-Verlag, New York, 2004. Stochastic Modelling and Applied Probability.

[57] Michael B Gordy and Sandeep Juneja. Nested simulation in portfolio risk measurement. *Management Science*, 56(10):1833–1848, 2010.

[58] Larry M. Gorski and Robert A. Brown. Recommended approach for setting regulatory risk-based capital requirements for variable annuities and similar products. Technical report, American Academy of Actuaries Life Capital Adequacy Subcommittee, Boston, June 2005.

[59] Larry M. Gorski and Robert A. Brown. C3 phase II risk-based capital for variable annuities: Pre-packaged scenarios. Technical report, American Academy of Actuaries, March 2005.

[60] Daniel Haefeli, editor. *Variable Annuities – An Analysis of Financial Stability*. The Geneva Association, 1997.

[61] Mary R. Hardy. *Investment Guarantees: Modeling and Risk Management for Equity-linked Life Insurance*. John Wiley & Sons, Inc., New Jersey, 2003.

[62] J. Michael Harrison. *Brownian motion and stochastic flow systems*. Robert E. Krieger Publishing Co., Inc., Malabar, FL, 1990. Reprint of the 1985 original.

[63] Michael T. Heath. *Scientific Computing: An Introductory Survey*. McGraw-Hill, second edition, 1997.

[64] Huaxiong Huang, Moshe A. Milevsky, and Thomas S. Salisbury. Optimal initiation of a glwb in a variable annuity: no arbitrage approach. *Insurance Math. Econom.*, 56:102–111, May 2014.

[65] John C. Hull. *Options, Futures and Other Derivatives*. Pearson, Boston, ninth edition, 2015.

[66] IAA. *Stochastic Modeling: Theory and Reality from an Actuarial Perspective*. International Actuarial Association, 2010.

[67] Monique Jeanblanc, Marc Yor, and Marc Chesney. *Mathematical methods for financial markets*. Springer Finance. Springer-Verlag London Ltd., London, 2009.

[68] Michael Kalkbrener. An axiomatic approach to capital allocation. *Math. Finance*, 15(3):425–437, 2005.

[69] Ioannis Karatzas and Steven E. Shreve. *Brownian motion and stochastic calculus*, volume 113 of *Graduate Texts in Mathematics*. Springer-Verlag, New York, second edition, 1991.

[70] Stephen Kellison. *The Theory of Interest*. Irwin McGraw-Hill, second edition, 1991.

[71] Adam Koursaris. A least squares monte carlo approach to liability proxy modelling and capital calculation. Technical report, Barrie & Hibbert, 2011.

[72] Andreas E. Kyprianou. *Introductory lectures on fluctuations of Lévy processes with applications*. Universitext. Springer-Verlag, Berlin, 2006.

[73] Peng Li and Runhuan Feng. A new approach for efficient nested simulation – sample recycling method. Technical report, University of Illinois at Urbana-Champaign, 2018.

[74] Life Practice Note Steering Committee. The application of C3 phase II and actuarial guideline XLIII. A public policy practice note, American Academy of Actuaries, 2009.

[75] X. Sheldon Lin and Ken Seng Tan. Valuation of equity-indexed annuities under stochastic interest rates. *N. Am. Actuar. J.*, 7(4):72–91, 2003.

[76] Henry P. Jr. McKean. *Stochastic Integrals*. Academic Press, New York, 1969.

[77] Alexander J. McNeil, Rüdiger Frey, and Paul Embrechts. *Quantitative risk management*. Princeton Series in Finance. Princeton University Press, Princeton, NJ, 2005. Concepts, techniques and tools.

[78] Alexander Melnikov and Amir Nosrati. *Equity-Linked Life Insurance: Partial Hedging Methods*. Chapman & Hall/CRC, 2017.

[79] Moshe A. Milevsky and Steven P. Posner. The Titanic option: valuation of the guaranteed minimum death benefit in variable annuities and mutual funds. *The Journal of Risk and Insurance*, 68(1):93–128, 2001.

[80] Moshe A. Milevsky and Thomas S. Salisbury. Financial valuation of guaranteed minimum withdrawal benefits. *Insurance Math. Econom.*, 38(1):21–38, 2006.

[81] National Association of Insurance Commissioners, Washington, DC. *Accounting Practices and Procedures Manual*, March 2015.

[82] Hal Pedersen, Mary Pat Campbell, Samuel H. Cox, Daniel Finn, Ken Griffin, Nigel Hooker, Matthew Lightwood, Stephen Sonlin, and Chris Suchar. Economic scenario generators – a practical guide. Technical report, Society of Actuaries, 2016.

[83] Jingjiang Peng, Kwai Sun Leung, and Yue Kuen Kwok. Pricing guaranteed minimum withdrawal benefits under stochastic interest rates. *Quantitative Finance*, 12(6):933–941, 2012.

[84] Nicolas Privault and Xiao Wei. Fast computation of risk measures for variable annuities with additional earnings by conditional moment matching. *Astin Bull.*, 48(1):171–196, 2018.

[85] Heather Remes. GAAP and statutory valuation of variable annuities. In *Equity-Based Insurance Guarantees Conference, Atlanta*, 2013.

[86] Andrea Resti and Andrea Sironi. *Risk Management and Shareholders' Value in Banking: From Risk Measurement Models to Capital Allocation Policies.* John Wiley and Sons, 2007.

[87] Craig Reynold and Sai Man. Nested stochastic pricing: the time has come. *Product Matters*, 71:16–20, 2008.

[88] R. Tyrrell Rockafellar and Stanislav Uryasev. Optimization of conditional value at risk. *Journal of Risk*, 2:21–42, 2000.

[89] L. C. G. Rogers and Z. Shi. The value of an Asian option. *J. Appl. Probab.*, 32(4):1077–1088, 1995.

[90] Tomasz Rolski, Hanspeter Schmidli, Volker Schmidt, and Jozef Teugels. *Stochastic processes for insurance and finance.* Wiley Series in Probability and Statistics. John Wiley & Sons Ltd., Chichester, 1999.

[91] Sheldon M. Ross. *Introduction to probability models.* Elsevier/Academic Press, Amsterdam, eleventh edition, 2014.

[92] Ludger Rüschendorf. *Mathematical risk analysis.* Springer Series in Operations Research and Financial Engineering. Springer, Heidelberg, 2013. Dependence, risk bounds, optimal allocations and portfolios.

[93] Zhaoning Shang, Marc Goovaerts, and Jan Dhaene. A recursive approach to mortality-linked derivative pricing. *Insurance Math. Econom.*, 49(2):240–248, 2011.

[94] Keith P. Sharp. CARVM and NAIC actuarial guidelines 33 & 34. *Journal of Actuarial Practice*, 7:125–146, 1999.

[95] Keith P. Sharp. Commissioner annuity reserve valuation method (CARVM). *Journal of Actuarial Practice*, 7:107–124, 1999.

[96] Steven E. Shreve. *Stochastic calculus for finance. I.* Springer Finance. Springer-Verlag, New York, 2004. The binomial asset pricing model.

[97] Steven E. Shreve. *Stochastic calculus for finance. II.* Springer Finance. Springer-Verlag, New York, 2004. Continuous-time models.

[98] Feng Sun. Pricing and risk management of variable annuities with multiple guaranteed minimum benefits. *The Actuarial Practice Forum*, October, 2006.

[99] Serena Tiong. Valuing equity-indexed annuities. *N. Am. Actuar. J.*, 4(4):149–170, 2000. With discussion by G. Thomas Mitchell and Hans U. Gerber and Elias S. W. Shiu.

[100] Andreas Tsanakas and Christopher Barnett. Risk capital allocation and cooperative pricing of insurance liabilities. *Insurance Math. Econom.*, 33(2):239–254, 2003. Papers presented at the 6th IME Conference (Lisbon, 2002).

[101] Eric R. Ulm. Analytic solution for return of premium and rollup guaranteed minimum death benefit options under some simple mortality laws. *Astin Bull.*, 38(2):543–563, 2008.

[102] Eric R. Ulm. Analytic solution for ratchet guaranteed minimum death benefit options under a variety of mortality laws. *Insurance Math. Econom.*, 58:14–23, 2014.

[103] Michèle Vanmaele, Griselda Deelstra, Jan Liinev, Jan Dhaene, and Marc J. Goovaerts. Bounds for the price of discrete arithmetic asian options. *Journal of Computational and Applied Mathematics*, 185(1):51–90, 2006.

[104] Jan Vecer. *Stochastic finance*. Chapman & Hall/CRC Financial Mathematics Series. CRC Press, Boca Raton, FL, 2011. A numeraire approach.

[105] Shaun Wang. Premium calculation by transforming the layer premium density. *Astin Bull.*, 26(1):71–92, 1996.

[106] Shaun Wang and Jan Dhaene. Comonotonicity, correlation order and premium principles. *Insurance Math. Econom.*, 22(3):235–242, 1998.

Index

For Product Safety Concerns and Information please contact our EU
representative GPSR@taylorandfrancis.com Taylor & Francis Verlag GmbH,
Kaufingerstraße 24, 80331 München, Germany

Printed and bound by CPI Group (UK) Ltd, Croydon, CR0 4YY

08/05/2025

01864357-0004